Social Work Law in Scotland

5th Edition

Social Work Law in Scotland

5th Edition

Andrew Farrer
Lecturer in Mental Health Law
University of Edinburgh

Bloomsbury Professional

LONDON • DUBLIN • EDINBURGH • NEW YORK • NEW DELHI • SYDNEY

Bloomsbury Publishing Plc
50 Bedford Square, London, WC1B 3DP, UK
1385 Broadway, New York, 10018, USA

Bloomsbury Publishing Ireland Ltd
29 Earlsfort Terrace, Dublin 2, D02 AY28, Ireland

BLOOMSBURY and the Diana logo are trademarks of Bloomsbury Publishing Plc

First published in Great Britain 2026

1

British Library Cataloguing-in-Publication Data

A catalogue record for this book is available from the British Library.

ISBN:	PB:	978-1-52652-910-7
	Epdf:	978-1-52652-912-1
	Epub:	978-1-52652-911-4

Typeset by Evolution Design and Digital Ltd (Kent)
Printed and bound by TJ Books, Padstow

MIX
Paper | Supporting responsible forestry
FSC www.fsc.org FSC® C013056

For product safety related questions contact productsafety@bloomsbury.com

To find out more about our authors and books visit www.bloomsburyprofessional.com. Here you will find extracts, author information, details of forthcoming events and the option to sign up for our newsletters

Preface

I was honoured to be asked to update this book, and concerned to ensure that the new edition live up to Tom Guthrie's meticulous work. A glance at the table of contents will tell the reader how broad a range of legal issues are encompassed by social work practice. The book is intended for use by social work students but also by social work practitioners. A working knowledge of the law in many areas of social work practice is ever more necessary as the legislative framework expands. The expansion of legislation after the establishment of the Scottish Parliament in 1999 has slowed a little, but in the eight years since the fourth edition of this book there have been significant developments. Legislation passed since the fourth edition includes, The Children (S) Act 2020, Age of Criminal Responsibility (S) Act 2019, Management of Offenders (S) Act 2019 and Domestic Abuse (S) Act 2018. These measures have, among others, changed the law in significant ways and impacted on the legal context of social work practice. In other respects, the pace of change has been slower than might be desirable. There is a need to reform the Mental Health (Care & Treatment) (Scotland) Act 2003 and, although the Scottish Government commissioned the Scott Review (SMHLR) and has consulted on suggested reforms, the pace of change has been slower than many had hoped .

I would like to thank a number of people without whom I could not have completed the work on this new edition. I wish to thank my colleague Katy Macfarlane, whose suggestion it was that I might take on the task of updating Tom Guthrie's work, and whose expertise in Family Law and much else has been invaluable. Katy may at times have regretted the fact that our offices are adjacent and it is all too easy for me to knock on her door and ask yet another question. I wish to extend my fulsome thanks to my research assistants: Kirstin Mackay, Isla Graham and Melanie Dickin, without whose work the book would not have been possible.

Thank you to Paula O'Connell at Bloomsbury Professional for patiently waiting for me to complete the work on the new edition.

Andrew Farrer

April 2026

To my parents.

Contents

Table of Cases

References are to paragraph number.

B

C

D

F

G

H

M

Q

R

S

Table of Statutes

References are to paragraph number.

V

Table of Statutory Instruments

References are to paragraph number

V

Table of Guidance, Circulars etc

References are to paragraph number

Table of International Materials

References are to paragraph number

Abbreviations

Case Reports

AC	Appeal Cases
All ER	All England Law Reports
BMLR	Butterworths Medico-Legal Reports
EHRR	European Human Rights Reports
Fam	Family Law Division
FCR	Family Court Reporter
FLR	Family Law Reports
IRLR	Industrial Relations Law Reports
JC	Justiciary Cases
LGR	Local Government Reports
QB	Queen's Bench Division
SC	Session Cases
SCCR	Scottish Criminal Case Reports
SCLR	Scottish Civil Law Reports
SLT	Scots Law Times
SLT (Sh Ct)	Scots Law Times (Sheriff Court)

Legislation

GDPR	General Data Protection Regulation
1968 Act	Social Work (Scotland) Act 1968
1970 Act	Chronically Sick and Disabled Persons Act 1970
1981 Act	Matrimonial Homes (Family Protection) (Scotland) Act 1981
1985 Act	Family Law (Scotland) Act 1985
1986 Act	Disabled Persons (Services, Consultation and Representation) Act 1986

1987 Act	Housing (Scotland) Act 1987
1990 Act	National Health Service and Community Care Act 1990
1991 Act	Age of Legal Capacity (Scotland) Act 1991
1995 Act	Children (Scotland) Act 1995
2000 Act	Adults with Incapacity (Scotland) Act 2000
2003 Act	Mental Health (Care and Treatment) (Scotland) Act 2003
2007 Act	Adult Support and Protection (Scotland) Act 2007
2011 Act	Children's Hearings (Scotland) Act 2011
2013 Act	Social Care (Self-directed Support) (Scotland) Act 2013
2014 Act	Children and Young People (Scotland) Act 2014
LAC Regs	Looked After Children (Scotland) Regulations 2009, SI 2009/120

Guidance

2016 Act Guidance	Scottish Government, *Carers (Scotland) Act 2016 Statutory Guidance* (2018)
ASP Code of Practice	Scottish Government, *Adult Support and Protection (Scotland) Act 2007: Code of Practice For Local Authorities and Practitioners Exercising Functions Under Part 1 of the Act* (revised 2014)
Code of Guidance	Scottish Executive, *Code of Guidance on Homelessness* (2005)
CPO Guidance	Scottish Government, *National Outcomes and Standards for Social Work Services in the Criminal Justice System: Community Payback Orders Practice Guidance* (2010)
Guidance	*The Children (Scotland) Act 1995 Regulations and Guidance* (1997)
LAC Guidance	Scottish Government, *Guidance on Looked After Children (Scotland) Regulations 2009 and the Adoption and Children (Scotland) Act 2007* (2010)

Other

ASBO	Antisocial Behaviour Order
BASW	British Association of Social Workers
CA	Court of Appeal
CAO	Child Assessment Order
CFREU	Charter of Fundamental Rights of the European Union
CICA	Criminal Injuries Compensation Authority
CPAG	Child Poverty Action Group
CPO	Depending on context, can refer to Child Protection Order (particularly in chapter 5) or Community Payback Order (particularly in chapter 10)
CSO	Compulsory Supervision Order
CTO	Compulsory Treatment Order
DAS	Debt Arrangement Scheme
DCSF	Department for Children, Schools and Families
DMP	Designated Medical Practitioner
ECHR	European Convention on Human Rights
ECtHR	European Court of Human Rights
EDC	Emergency Detention Certificate
EHRC	Equality and Human Rights Commission
EU	European Union
GIRFEC	Getting it Right for Every Child
HC	House of Commons Papers
HDC	Home Detention Curfew
HL	House of Lords
ICSO	Interim compulsory supervision order
IH	Inner House
JP	Justice of the Peace
MAPPP	Multi Agency Public Protection Partnership
MAPPA	Multi Agency Public Protection Arrangements

MHO	Mental Health Officer
MHT	Mental Health Tribunal for Scotland
MWC	Mental Welfare Commission
OH	Outer House
PSED	Public Sector Equality Duty
PVG	Protection of Vulnerable Groups
RMO	Responsible Medical Officer
SCR	Social Circumstances Report
SCRA	Scottish Children's Reporter Administration
SCSWIS	Social Care and Social Work Improvement Scotland (also known as the Care Inspectorate)
SHANARRI	Safe, Healthy, Achieving, Nurtured, Active, Respected, Responsible, Included
SMHLR	Scottish Mental Health Law Review
SSSC	Scottish Social Services Council
STDC	Short-Term Detention Certificate
UNCRPD	United Nations Convention on the Rights of Persons with Disabilities

Chapter 1

The Scottish legal context of social work

INTRODUCTION

1.1 The principal context for social work practice in Scotland are the social work departments, sometimes social services departments, established by local authorities. Recent integration of health and social care functions has introduced some changes and these will be discussed later in this chapter. This text will, for simplicity's sake, refer to social work departments, except where special reference is made to the voluntary or private sector.

There is a legal dimension to all of the work undertaken by social workers employed by the local authority. Social workers are **obliged** to perform some functions and **permitted** to perform others by the laws passed by Parliament (either the UK or the Scottish Parliament). The scope and interpretation of these powers and duties is further elaborated by decisions in court cases, which can also generate further duties. Social workers also have specified **powers** and **duties** which are defined by the law and derive much of their authority from the law. People who come into contact with social workers employed by the local authority have specified **rights** and **responsibilities** which are based in law. The contact between these people and the social worker is therefore driven by the law. Without a knowledge of law, the social worker cannot function competently and the service user may also forfeit various legal entitlements.

Social workers need to be able to recognise and make use of the legal dimension in social work practice. Social workers occupy a privileged and unique position in relation to people who have legal needs. Social workers are uniquely placed to assist in enhancing quality of life by sharing their understanding of the law and the legislative framework with service users. Those service users may be in crisis and so temporarily unable to make sense of their circumstances, or may be unfamiliar with the legal system, and without the necessary social skills to navigate in legal waters.

Further opportunities arise for social workers through direct involvement with those who have offended. The retention of the probation service functions under the auspices of social work departments has provided the continuing recognition that social work values, knowledge, and skills are most appropriate in dealing with this service user population.

Social work law has not, in general, proved an attractive area of specialisation for solicitors.[1] There exists therefore an additional incentive and requirement for social workers to share their awareness and understanding of the legal dimension of their work both with service users and with other professionals. It is not suggested that social workers become second-rate lawyers, but rather that they use their knowledge of law to inform their practice and contribute to the facilitating of shared social work goals. A study of the law relating to social work also contributes to an understanding of the variety of acceptable roles which are appropriate for social workers. In view of society's ambiguous relationship with social workers, these roles are often contradictory and ambivalent. They include investigator, assessor, supervisor, witness, conciliator, reporter, facilitator, liaison, advisor, guide, support, broker, enabler, teacher, mediator and advocate.[2] Social workers may be in a position to help to identify and enforce the rights of vulnerable service users and/or they may be in the position of enforcing service users' compliance with the law. These roles will be explored in more depth subsequently.

The importance of a thorough grounding in the law relevant to social work practice cannot be sufficiently emphasised. This point is made in several places in the *Standards in Social Work Education* which set out the knowledge, skills and competences to be demonstrated by newly graduated social workers.[3] In addition to requirements which imply an underpinning understanding of the law these set out more specific requirements. These requirements include: the requirement to understand 'social worker roles as statutory agents with duties and

1 See, for example, Scottish Government, *Limited Review of the Mental Health (Care and Treatment) (Scotland) Act 2003* (2009), noting (at p 57) that 'Mental health law is not currently an area of law which attracts a broad interest from within the profession'.

2 These last four interventive roles are discussed in B Compton and B Galaway *Social Work Processes* (7th edn, 2005), pp 230–33.

3 These are set out in Scottish Executive, *The Framework for Social Work Education in Scotland* (2003) and form the basis of approval of programmes leading to a social work degree by the Scottish Social Services Council (SSSC) (see SSSC, Rules for Social Work Training 2003, r 6(d)(ii)). See also, Scottish Social Services Council (SSSC) *Standards in Social Work Education* (August 2019). Available at: https://learn.sssc.uk.com/siswe/uploads/files/SiSWE-and-Ethical-Principles.pdf. (Accessed April 2026).

responsibilities to protect the public and uphold the law';[4] the 'nature of legal authority; the application of legislation in practice; statutory responsibility and conflicts between statute policy and practice'.[5] Graduating social workers also need to be able to 'assess and evaluate needs, strengths, risks and options taking account of legal … duties',[6] 'revise and regularly update their own knowledge of relevant legislation…',[7] and 'assess human situations taking account of a number of factors including … legislation'.[8]

Three things should be made clear at the start about the operation of law. The first is that the law does not necessarily specify a precise course of action to be followed in given circumstances. In most cases there is room for considerable discretion in applying the law, though once it is applied there may be precise procedures to be followed (a good example of this is the law relating to child protection orders).[9] The way in which discretion is to be exercised in these areas may be the subject of guidance from various sources or may be the subject of departmental policies. In such areas knowledge of the guidance and policies is essential, but the underlying legal framework must not be ignored.

Secondly, there are areas of social work which are not covered specifically or in detail by legislation (for example, much work with elderly people) and which are simply covered by the general (and very vague) obligation to promote social welfare and assist those in need contained in the Social Work (Scotland) Act 1968 (see **1.10** below) and the power to advance well-being.[10]

Third, legal rules are not self-applying. In other words, legal rules must be put into action by individuals and organisations. This has the consequence that these individuals and organisations have to interpret the law and that they also have to interpret the world to decide whether the circumstances they see are circumstances to which a particular legal rule applies. For example, are the circumstances of a child's life such as to qualify them as a 'child in need' in terms of the Children (Scotland) Act 1995?

This means that there is discretion in applying the legal rules. Individuals and organisations can decide both how to apply the law and when to apply it.

4 *Framework for Social Work Education in Scotland* (2003), p 34.
5 *Framework for Social Work Education in Scotland*, p 37.
6 *Framework for Social Work Education in Scotland*, p 28.
7 *Framework for Social Work Education in Scotland*, p 36.
8 *Framework for Social Work Education in Scotland*, p 28.
9 See chapter 5, **5.6** onwards.
10 Local Government in Scotland Act 2003, s 20.

One final general comment needs to be made about the language of the law and the language of social work. The occasional incompatibility of these two is characteristic of the nature and value base of each. Legal language can seem obscure, arcane and even offensive with its insistence on false generics (such as the use of the pronoun 'he' to represent both sexes). Social work language can seem overly concerned with sensitivity and shaped by social trends.

THE FUNCTIONS OF LAW IN SOCIETY

1.2 Although there has been some dispute about the need for law to regulate society, much of that debate is, in fact, about the precise form of law or about its appropriateness as a means of resolving social problems. There is, in reality, broad agreement about the need for some system of universal rules to regulate the operation of society.[11] Since social workers' interventions are so inextricably entwined with the functions of law, it is useful that they understand and appreciate these functions. The principal functions of law can be said to be:[12]

(1) Social control

1.3 It does this through the enforcement of criminal law and the provision of mechanisms to allow private individuals to resolve their disputes (principally the civil courts). The former of these is sometimes seen, simplistically and erroneously, as the sole or main function of law.

(2) Constitution of law-making and law-enforcing bodies

1.4 The law also provides for the composition and procedure of the UK and Scottish Parliaments and the court system. As part of this process, individuals may be given certain rights and protections, such as the right of access to legal representation for court appearances.

11 The Russian anarchist Kropotkin, for example, noted that 'No society is possible without certain principles of morality generally recognised': *Revolutionary Pamphlets* (1970), p 73.

12 These functions can be formulated in various ways. For an alternative, see Braye, S and Preston-Shoot, M, *Practising Social Work Law* (4th edn, 2016), pp 27–37.

(3) Enabling function

1.5 At a very basic level, it is sometimes argued that law, by guaranteeing a (reasonably) peaceful society, enables people to carry on with their lives. However, it also makes much more specific provision to allow people to make arrangements which will be legally recognised and enforced, such as adoption, contracts and appointment of attorneys.

(4) Promotion of social welfare

1.6 Law is used as a tool for the promotion of social welfare (or at least the policies of various governments which are said to be directed towards this end). With the goal of promoting social welfare, law provides the framework of organisations, such as local authority social work departments. Law confers upon these organisations powers and duties designed to promote social welfare, and confers upon individuals personal rights, such as to benefits.

LAW AND SOCIAL PROBLEMS

1.7 Social problems are not necessarily amenable to purely legal solutions. However, when the legal solution facilitates the potential resolution of a social problem then the use of such means can be justified and the failure to use such means would be inexcusable.

On a broader level there are difficulties in successfully using purely legal means to resolve social problems. One illustration is the failure of anti-discrimination legislation to secure equal pay[13] and employment prospects for women. Legal intervention can bring about benefits and improvements and may, perhaps, perform a function in changing attitudes or raising awareness of issues, but it is often not on its own able to provide a complete resolution of the problem it seeks to address.

In approaching the resolution of either collective or individual problems in society there may be a conflict between the values of law and those of social work.[14] This apparent conflict cannot, however, obscure the

13 See Office for National Statistics, Annual survey of hours and earnings (ASHE) gender pay gap tables.

14 See, for example, Preston-Shoot, M *et al*, 'Working Together in Social Work Law', (1998) *Journal of Social Welfare and Family Law*, 137; Braye, S and Preston-Shoot, M, 'The Role of Law in Welfare Reform: Critical Perspectives on the Relationship between Law and Social Work Practice', (2006) 15 *International Journal of Social Welfare* 19.

reality that practice takes place in a framework of law nor that the discretion inherent in the application of the law permits its application to be mediated by social work values.

THE DISTINCTIVE CHARACTER OF SCOTS LAW

1.8 The Scottish legal system had, at least until 1707, a different history from the legal system in the rest of the UK. One of the consequences of this is that the structure of the court system in Scotland is quite different from that in England, Wales and Northern Ireland. There were also significant differences in substantive law, and these continued after 1707. Despite the existence of a single parliament within the UK, separate and different provision continued to be made for Scotland in many areas. For our purposes a key example of different provision is the Social Work (Scotland) Act 1968. The 1968 Act, in contradistinction to the position in England and Wales, incorporated probation services within generic social work departments and introduced a distinctive means of dealing with the cases of children through the system of children's hearings. Despite the distinctiveness of much legal provision in Scotland, not all the law which applies in Scotland differs from that which applies in other parts of the UK. There are areas of law where the law is the same throughout the UK, examples are, the benefits system,[15] the law relating to rights in employment, the law regarding discrimination and the rules about driving. There is, finally, a third category of law. In this category there are similarities, but also differences, between the law in Scotland and the law in the rest of the UK. These differences may be in the substance of the law, in other words what the law says might be slightly different, or the law might be the same, but the source of the law is different. The creation of the (new) Scottish Parliament in 1999 has not really changed this pattern. The period since 1999 has seen a large number of Acts of the Scottish Parliament (asps) concerned with the services provided by social work departments. Most have made specific Scottish provision, but there are also provisions which mirror developments in England and Wales, for example in relation to the protection of vulnerable groups. Table 1.1 below sets out some of the areas of law relevant to social work practice where there are similarities and differences between Scotland and England and Wales. There are also more general areas of difference, for

15 At least to some extent. The Scottish Parliament now has power to create new benefits and top up benefits available throughout the UK: Scotland Act 2016, Pt 3, amending the Scotland Act 1998.

example large parts of criminal law[16] are different as between Scotland and the rest of the UK.

Table 1.1

Area	Scottish Provision	E & W provision	Similarities/ differences
Mental health	Mental Health (Care and Treatment) (Scotland) Act 2003	Mental Health Act 1983	Significant differences in content, processes and terminology. For example, there is no set of principles set out in the 1983 Act, instead these are in a Code of Practice, and nearest relatives can still make applications for detention.
Adults with Incapacity	Adults with Incapacity (Scotland) Act 2000	Mental Capacity Act 2005	Significant differences in content, processes and terminology. For example, the 2005 Act contains safeguards relating to deprivation of liberty not found in the 2000 Act and the appointees able to take decisions on behalf of adults are described in the 2005 Act as 'deputies'.
Looked after children	Children (Scotland) Act 1995, ss 16 and 17	Children Act 1989, ss 22–23	Some similarities, but also some differences.

16 E.g., there is no crime of manslaughter in Scotland (it is culpable homicide) neither is there breaking and entering in Scotland – this is theft by housebreaking.

Emergency protection of children	Children's Hearings (Scotland) Act 2011, ss 35 (Child Assessment Order (CAO)) and 37 (Child Protection Order)	Children Act 1989, ss 43 (CAO) and 44 (Emergency Protection Order)	Similarities in grounds for action and making of orders, but differences in procedure in obtaining order and subsequent to granting of order.
Children in need of compulsory measures	Children's Hearings (Scotland) Act 2011	Children Act 1989	Procedures entirely different, in E & W application made to court for care order or supervision order, limited court involvement in Scotland (aside from determining existence of grounds of referral & appeals) – dealt with by children's hearings.
Children in need	Children (Scotland) Act 1995, s 22	Children Act 1989, s 17	Very similar, though powers in E & W set out more fully in schedule 2 to 1989 Act.
Aftercare	Children (Scotland) Act 1995, ss 29–30 (and regulations)	Children Act 1989, ss 23A–24D	Similar, but not identical.
Free personal care	Community Care and Health (Scotland) Act 2002	No equivalent	

Community care assessments & services	Social Work (Scotland) Act 1968, Chronically Sick and Disabled Persons Act 1970 and Social Care (Self-Directed Support) (Scotland) Act 2013	Care Act 2014	Initially, provisions virtually identical except that statutory basis in Scotland was slightly different. Divergence after implementation of Care Act 2014 in 2016.
Adult protection	Adult Support and Protection (Scotland) Act 2007	Care Act s 2014, ss 42–46	Some similarities, but definitions and processes different.
Vulnerable groups	Protection of Vulnerable Groups (Scotland) Act 2007	Safeguarding Vulnerable Groups Act 2006	Following from Bichard Report[1] these provide for vetting and barring of people working with children and other vulnerable groups – procedures and administrative bodies differ between Scotland and E & W.

1 The Bichard Inquiry Report (2004), 2003–4 HC 653.

FORMAL SOURCES OF LAW

1.9 Formal sources of law are the actual statements of the law, as opposed to textbooks or commentaries on the law. The main formal sources of law as it affects social workers are Acts of Parliament (either the UK or the Scottish Parliament) (statutes), such as the Children (Scotland) Act 1995 and the Mental Health (Care and Treatment) (Scotland) Act 2003. Statutes are supplemented by delegated legislation (usually in the form of statutory instruments or Scottish statutory instruments), such as the regulations governing the care and placement of looked after children.[17] Finally, case law is the law derived from decisions made by courts.

17 See **chapter 4**.

As we noted in a previous section, one of the functions of law is the promotion of social welfare, and this has resulted in a substantial volume of legislation. This growth in legislation was given further impetus by the creation of the Scottish Parliament in 1999. The Scottish Parliament has power to legislate in any area not reserved to the UK Parliament. The areas reserved to the UK Parliament include:[18] data protection, nationality and immigration, consumer protection, some aspects of social security (excluding support provided under the Social Work (Scotland) Act 1968, the Chronically Sick and Disabled Persons Act 1970 and the Children (Scotland) Act 1995), employment, and equal opportunities (including anti-discrimination legislation). From this list it should be clear that the Scottish Parliament has the power to legislate in most areas related to social work practice. A further feature of legislation passed by the Scottish Parliament is that it must be compliant with the European Convention on Human Rights. The precise mechanism for the passing of an Act of Parliament need not concern us here,[19] but Acts are often preceded by consultation documents[20] produced by the government setting out its intentions as to legislation which allow for comment from interested parties on the proposals before they are finalised.

Most of the law we will be discussing in the remainder of this book is derived from statute.

For a variety of reasons statutes often omit detailed regulations. The power to make these is usually delegated to a government minister or, in the Scottish context, to the Scottish Ministers. Even though the power to legislate is delegated, any delegated legislation made has the same legal effect as an Act of Parliament. Examples of delegated legislation are the rules regulating the conduct of children's hearings[21] and those regulating procedure at the Mental Health Tribunal.[22] These rules can be changed more rapidly than Acts in response to increased awareness of their potential implications. The power to make more detailed rules may be delegated to other bodies. Thus, the power to make procedural rules for civil court cases such as adoption cases has been delegated to the Court of Session.

18 The powers of the Scottish Parliament are set out in Scotland Act 1998, ss 29 and 30 and Schs 4 and 5.

19 And differs as between the UK and Scottish Parliaments.

20 For example the *Consultation on Children's Hearings Redesign* (2024) consulting on potential changes to improve the operation of the children's hearings system.

21 Children's Hearings (Scotland) Act 2011 (Rules of Procedure in Children's Hearings) Rules 2013, SSI 2013/194.

22 Mental Health Tribunal for Scotland (Practice and Procedure) (No 2) Rules 2005, SSI 2005/519.

Statutes may also provide for the Scottish Ministers to issue guidance, such as the guidance issued on the Children (Scotland) Act 1995 and the Children and Young People (Scotland) Act 2014[23] and the general power to issue guidance conferred by the Social Work (Scotland) Act 1968.[24] Although guidance does not have the force of law, the courts expect that local authorities will follow it unless there is a good reason not to. Failure to follow guidance may form the basis for a successful challenge to a decision taken by a local authority.[25] Most guidance is directed at particular practice areas, but some is overarching, like the Health and Social Care Standards.[26]

Acts of Parliament do not necessarily or usually become part of the law as soon as they are passed. Instead, an Act will usually provide that it is to be brought into force (that is, become part of the law) by orders made by the appropriate Minister. Different sections of the Act may be brought into force at different times. One example of this is the Children (Scotland) Act 1995. Part of this came into force in November 1995, other provisions came into force in November 1996 and virtually all the remainder in April 1997. Acts are also subject to amendment and (total or partial) repeal, for example the Social Work (Scotland) Act 1968 in its current form is very different from the Act passed in 1968.

Case law may offer a definitive interpretation of the provisions of an Act of Parliament, such as, for example, the grounds for compulsory supervision orders. It is also the source of legal rules in some areas, for example the law relating to liability for negligence.[27]

RIGHTS, POWERS AND DUTIES

1.10 As indicated at the beginning of this chapter, most social workers work for social work departments. It is particularly important for social workers to understand the statutory basis for most of their work. Local authorities, social work departments and individual social workers, are subject to law; their powers and duties are based on Acts of Parliament. Were it not for the Local Government (Scotland) Acts, local authorities would not exist and would have no powers. Were it not for

23 Extensive guidance has been issued on a range of topics and in a variety of forms. It will be discussed in the text as appropriate.

24 Social Work (Scotland) Act 1968, s 5.

25 See, for example, *R v Islington Borough Council, ex parte Rixon* (1998) 1 CCLR 119.

26 Scottish Government, *Health and Social Care Standards: My support, my life* (2017).

27 Usually seen as being based on *Donoghue v Stevenson* 1932 SC (HL) 31, apocryphally credited with giving rise to the phrase 'gie's a slug of your ginger'.

the Social Work (Scotland) Act 1968 there would be no duty to provide reports for courts.

The notions of rights, powers and duties merit some further discussion. Duties[28] are obligations imposed on authorities and workers to act. There are different types of duty imposed on social workers. They may be subject to ethical, moral or professional duties,[29] but they, and their employers, also have legal duties. Legal duties are requirements to act (they might be seen as orders to do something). Some of these duties are very general and impose rather vague obligations on local authorities and workers. The classic example of this is section 12 of the 1968 Act, which begins by stating that 'it shall be the duty of every local authority to promote social welfare by making available advice, guidance and assistance on such a scale as may be appropriate for their area'.[30] This is arguably so broad that it confers a general power on local authorities to provide services rather than imposing a duty.

Other duties are much more specific and will confer rights on specific individuals enabling them to enforce these duties. For example, the local authority has a duty to assess the needs of a person with possible need for community care services. If the authority failed, or refused to carry out an assessment, that person could take court action to obtain an order forcing it to do so. The more general duties imposed on local authorities are more difficult to enforce because it is more difficult to argue that they impose specific duties towards (and confer specific rights on) specific individuals. In many cases a duty will arise only where certain prior conditions have been fulfilled. For example, a specific duty to provide support may arise only following an assessment and the making of a judgement about need. Not all duties imposed on social workers are imposed by statute or by a statute specific to local authorities, for example duties to exercise reasonable care in the performance of their work derive from case law. Duties imposed by law can sometimes conflict with other types of duty to a service user and with service users' expectations.[31]

Powers are authorisations to act. They may give the authority or worker the ability or capacity to do something, but do not require that it is done. An example is the power to apply for a child protection order. This

28 Duties are sometimes referred to as responsibilities or obligations.

29 For example, those set out in Scottish Social Services Council, *Code of Practice for Social Service Workers* (2016) and BASW, *Code of Ethics for Social Work* (2012).

30 Social Work (Scotland) Act 1968, s 12(1).

31 See, for example, Shardlow, S, 'Confidentiality, Accountability and the Boundaries of Client-worker Relationships' in Hugman and Smith (eds) *Ethical Issues in Social Work* (1985).

discretionary nature of powers means that their use is not determined by the law, but is, rather, informed by the professional judgment of those entitled to exercise them. One consequence of the statutory basis of social work is that local authorities and social workers only have the powers conferred on them by statute or implied by duties imposed on them and any attempt to exercise powers beyond these would be unlawful. The law would describe such an attempt as acting *ultra vires,* that is, beyond the powers conferred by statute.[32]

Legal rights usually refer to entitlements conferred on individuals which they can enforce through the legal system. In many cases the rights exist because of a duty imposed on someone else. Most rights in the context of social work involve service users' rights. Some of these are seen in the duties noted above, such as the right to an assessment, but there are others, for example the right of access to social work records.

As we have seen, use of powers depends on the exercise of judgment by workers. In some cases duties may arise only after the exercise of judgment: for example, a duty to provide services to a disabled person arises only after judgments have been made about the needs of that person and what services should be provided to meet these needs.[33] Decisions involving judgment are described in law as discretionary and the discretion enjoyed by workers is not unrestrained: their decisions can be challenged in a variety of ways, including by judicial review (see **1.59** below and **chapter 11**). Workers may also have to take account of guidance issued by government or by their employers in exercising their discretion.

LEGAL PERSONNEL

(1) Solicitors and advocates

1.11 The basic division within the legal profession is between solicitors and advocates (the latter are sometimes referred to as counsel). Solicitors are the most numerous. They have direct contact with their clients and may practice in all areas of the law, such 'general' practices are common in smaller towns or specialise in a particular area of law. The Law Society of Scotland, the solicitors' professional body, publishes an online directory of firms indicating the areas of work in which they specialise. Often social workers develop a local knowledge of solicitors who have a particular interest in social welfare, mental

32 Though the powers conferred on local authorities are very wide.

33 See **chapter 6**.

health law, family law, and/or criminal law which can prove useful to service users.

Advocates specialise in court appearance and in giving advice on complex matters of law. Advocates cannot be engaged directly by individual clients; instead, in most cases, the relationship is managed by the client's solicitors. Historically, advocates had an exclusive right to appear in the higher courts (that is the High Court, the Court of Session and the Supreme Court) but there are now provisions to allow solicitors to appear in these courts. Solicitor-advocates, as these are described, are solicitors who have passed a test of competence and fulfilled certain other requirements to allow them to represent people in the High Court or in the Court of Session. Complaints about members of the legal profession in Scotland are dealt with through the Scottish Legal Complaints Commission.

(2) Procurators fiscal and the system of public prosecution

1.12 Prosecutions for crimes and offences in Scotland are carried out by the Crown Office and Procurator Fiscal Service. The system is headed by the Lord Advocate who advises the Scottish Government on matters of law generally, as well as being the head of the system of prosecution. The Lord Advocate is assisted by the Solicitor General. Together they are known as 'the Law Officers'. Below these two are a number of Advocates Depute, also referred to as Crown Counsel, though this term also includes the Law Officers. Advocates Depute are advocates who are appointed to the position usually for a relatively short period of time. Solicitor-advocates and senior members of the fiscal service may now also be appointed to act as Crown Counsel. In practice, most of the work in the prosecution system is done by procurators fiscal and procurators fiscal depute who are the local representatives of the public prosecution service. These are full-time permanent civil servants and there will be a procurator fiscal in each sheriff court.[34] The administration of the system of prosecution is the responsibility of the Crown Office and Procurator Fiscal Service.

Where someone has been apprehended on suspicion of having committed a crime, or where a serious crime has been committed, the matter will be reported to the procurator fiscal. The fiscal is, legally, in charge of the investigation of the crime and directs the police investigation. In most

34 Though, because there is now a system of regional offices covering, usually, a number of sheriff courts, the same person may be procurator fiscal for a number of courts.

cases, however, little or no further investigation will be necessary, and the fiscal simply has to decide whether to prosecute.

In cases where prosecution will take place in a summary court (for an explanation of this see **1.26** below), the decision is entirely one for the fiscal, operating under the guidance of a book of regulations issued by the Lord Advocate. It is the fiscal's decision whether to prosecute or not and in which court. If the fiscal decides against prosecution they must decide whether to let the matter drop or to take some other action which falls broadly into the category of diversion.

In more serious cases, where the crime/offence might be prosecuted before a solemn court (for an explanation of this see **1.26** below), the fiscal must report the case to the Crown Office. A decision on how to proceed will be made by a senior advocate depute in cases which will be prosecuted in the High Court. For cases which will be tried in the sheriff solemn court the decision will be taken by a member of staff in the Crown Office.[35]

In deciding whether to prosecute a fiscal will take account of two main factors – whether there is sufficient admissible evidence and the public interest. The latter involves consideration of a variety of matters including the nature and gravity of the offence, the impact of the offence on the victim, the ages of the accused and the victim, mitigating circumstances, the risk of further offending, and public concern.[36]

Despite the history of public prosecution in Scotland, it is still technically possible for an individual to pursue a private prosecution. Such private prosecutions require the consent of either the Lord Advocate or of the High Court. There were only two cases in the twentieth century in which a private prosecution was allowed to proceed.[37]

Prosecutions in the sheriff and district courts will normally be undertaken by the fiscal or a depute. In the High Court the prosecutor will be one of the Law Officers or an Advocate Depute.

In cases where there is sufficient evidence to proceed to prosecution the fiscal may, instead of prosecuting, administer a warning. Before this can be done, there must be sufficient evidence to justify proceedings and the case must not be so trivial as to merit no action. Fiscals also have the power in certain types of cases to offer an individual the option of paying a fixed penalty or the option of paying compensation to the victim as an alternative to prosecution. Finally, there are a number of

35 See *Renton & Brown's Criminal Procedure* (6th edn), 3–03.

36 Crown Office and Procurator Fiscal Service, Prosecution Code (2001).

37 The more famous being *H v Sweeney* 1983 SLT 48.

diversion schemes in operation where individuals are diverted to social work assistance in place of prosecution.[38]

As well as being a prosecutor the fiscal is also responsible for investigating all sudden and suspicious deaths and suicides.

(3) Judges

1.13 Justice of the Peace (JP) courts are most often presided over by one or more lay justices of the peace. These are people who have no legal training but have been appointed to act as justices. They will be guided as to the law by the clerk to the court. The practice as to the number of justices sitting to hear a case may be one or three, and this varies between different areas. Alternatively, a summary sheriff may sit in the JP court. They are legally qualified and sit alone to hear cases. They have greater sentencing powers than lay justices. Sheriff courts are staffed by sheriffs and summary sheriffs who are legally qualified. Summary sheriffs can preside over summary criminal trials (see below) and have limited powers to deal with civil cases, though they can hear applications relating to children's hearings, adoption applications and other family law applications. Finally, there are the judges who preside both in the Court of Session and in the High Court. They are all legally qualified and are variously described as Lords of Session, Lord Commissioners of Justiciary and Senators of the College of Justice. How they are described depends on which role they are fulfilling.

(4) Clerks of court

1.14 Sheriff clerks are responsible for the running of sheriff courts. Their role comprises the recording of proceedings (though not shorthand note-taking), arranging for reports, arranging (in consultation with the procurator fiscal) the court timetable, maintenance of records, collection of fines, and the organisation and distribution of Criminal Justice Social Work Reports. This last task will involve co-operation with the social worker(s) attached to the court, who will make arrangements with the appropriate social work area office for the report to be provided. Each sheriff court will have a sheriff clerk who will be assisted by deputes. The JP and High Courts have clerks who broadly perform the same function for them as sheriff clerks do for the sheriff court.

38 These options are considered in **10.43–10.47**.

(5) Sheriff officers and messengers-at-arms[39]

1.15 Sheriff officers are officers of court who must fulfil certain requirements (for example having completed a period of training and passed specified examinations) and hold a warrant from the sheriff principal to act. They are not directly employed by the court system but rather are court officers in the sense that they are authorised to do certain things by virtue of their warrant and are accountable to court for their actions. Sheriff officers are used to serve summonses and citations in civil cases, to carry out the enforcement of civil judgments, such as evictions, and to serve witness citations for the defence in criminal cases. Messengers-at-arms perform similar functions in relation to actions in the Court of Session.

(6) Miscellaneous

1.16 As well as those noted above, there are a variety of other people involved in the operation of the court system. These include ushers and bar officers who assist in the actual functioning of the courts, directing people to the right court and maintaining order in court.

CIVIL COURT SYSTEM AND PROCEDURES

1.17 The civil court system deals with all cases which do not involve the commission of a crime or offence and which are not dealt with by a special body, such as an employment tribunal, mental health tribunal or children's hearing. Examples of the sorts of case it deals with are given below. Before going on to look at the various courts in the civil court system some explanation of the distinction between courts of first instance and courts of appeal is necessary. Courts of first instance are the courts at which trials take place and in which civil cases are initially disposed of. Appeal courts deal only or mainly with appeals from the decisions of courts of first instance.

(1) Sheriff court

1.18 Scotland is divided up into six sheriffdoms, five of which (the exception being Glasgow and Strathkelvin) are then subdivided into sheriff court districts, each of which has a sheriff court building. Each sheriffdom is staffed by a sheriff principal and a number of sheriffs and,

39 Act of Sederunt (Messengers-at-Arms and Sheriff Officers) Rules 1991, SI 1991/1397.

in some cases, summary sheriffs. The precise organisation of the court will depend on the level of business: in rural areas, for example, the court may sit only on one day a week or as necessary to deal with the business. There is also a sheriff court which deals with personal injury cases and has the power to deal with cases from all over Scotland.

The sheriff civil court involves a sheriff (or summary sheriff) sitting alone to deal with cases at first instance. There are matters it cannot hear, the main exclusion being judicial review (see **1.59** below). On the other hand, there are certain matters that can be dealt with only in the sheriff court, for example eviction and actions for sums of money less than £100,000.[40]

The sheriff civil court deals with such matters as adoption, proofs on reference from children's hearings, divorce, applications under the Adults with Incapacity (Scotland) Act 2000 and (accounting for most of its business) small debt actions.

Decisions of the sheriff can be appealed to the Sheriff Appeal Court – Civil and then to the Inner House of the Court of Session or direct to the Inner House. The ability to appeal to the Inner House is subject to some restrictions.

The Sheriff Appeal Court consists of sheriffs who have been appointed to be Appeal Sheriffs. Three sheriffs sit to hear appeals in civil cases.

(2) Court of Session

1.19 The Court of Session sits only in Edinburgh. It is divided into an Outer House, which consists of judges sitting alone to deal with cases at first instance, and an Inner House. The Inner House is divided into two divisions (usually three judges sit in a case) and deals primarily with appeals from the Outer House and from the Sheriff Appeal Court – Civil. The Inner House is also a court of first instance for a variety of applications under companies legislation and other specialised forms of procedure. Appeals arising from the children's hearing system may end up in the Inner House.

(3) Supreme Court

1.20 The UK Supreme Court is located in London and operates as a court of appeal in Scottish civil cases. Criminal appeals in Scotland are heard in the High Court of Justiciary, see **1.30** below. In cases originating

40 Courts Reform (Scotland) Act 2014, s 39.

in the sheriff court the appeal must be concerned with a question of law rather than a factual dispute. The Supreme Court replaced the Judicial Committee of the House of Lords as the final appeal court in October 2009.[41]

(4) Procedures

(a) Simple procedure

1.21 This procedure is designed to provide a simple and inexpensive form of action which can be easily used by members of the public. It can be used to recover money up to £5,000 or for the recovery of property up to that value. Most cases in practice are likely to be of the former type and may be actions to recover debts (most commonly) or actions to recover damages.

There is no provision for legal aid in this process (see **1.61** onwards below) as the intention is that private individuals will be able to conduct cases themselves. There is, however, provision allowing for an individual to be represented by a lay representative[42] at any stage of the process and for a courtroom supporter to provide support at any hearing.

(b) Summary cause procedure

1.22 Summary cause procedure, again a simplified form of procedure, is similar to simple procedure, it is used for actions for eviction[43] and recovery of damages for personal injury up to £5,000.

(c) Ordinary procedure

1.23 This form of procedure is used in the sheriff court. It is appropriate for claims in excess of £5,000 and for other types of case, including divorces not covered by the 'do-it-yourself procedure.[44] Procedure in the Court of Session is similar to ordinary procedure. Unlike simple and summary cause procedure, this type of procedure is based on extensive written pleadings (essentially the claims and counterclaims made by the parties to the court action).

41 Constitutional Reform Act 2005, Part 3, s 23(1).

42 Who can be stopped from acting as a representative if the sheriff considers them unsuitable.

43 See also **2.4**.

44 See **3.12**.

(d) Special procedures

1.24 A variety of types of case of interest to social workers have their own special forms of procedure. These include proof of grounds of referral to a children's hearing, appeals from hearing decisions, adoption and applications for appointment of a guardian. The procedures will be explained in more detail when we look at these areas.

(5) Standard of proof

1.25 The standard of proof in civil cases is proof on the balance of probabilities. This means that the person initiating the case must satisfy the court that their version of events is more probable than that put forward by the other party. The nature of the evidence used to establish this standard is considered in paras 1.39 to 1.45 below.

CRIMINAL COURT SYSTEM AND PROCEDURES

1.26 Within the criminal court system there is a distinction between solemn and summary courts. The essential distinction between these is that in summary courts the judge(s) takes the decision on guilt or innocence, whereas in solemn courts this is done by a jury of 15. There are also some differences in the procedure followed in the different types of court. These will be considered more fully below.

(1) JP courts

1.27 As noted above, the JP court will normally be presided over by one or more JPs with legal advice from the clerk of court.

The sorts of cases the JP court can deal with are restricted. It cannot deal with housebreaking cases, serious assaults, forgery, theft and fraud cases where the amount involved is more than £2,500, and cases involving the prosecution of children under the age of 16.

The sentencing powers of the court are limited to a fine of up to level 4 on the standard scale (currently £2,500) and up to 60 days' imprisonment. Where the court is presided over by a summary sheriff it has the same sentencing powers as the sheriff summary court. As always in this chapter, references to sentencing powers are to the maximum sentence that can be imposed in the absence of a specific statutory provision restricting or enhancing the power in respect of particular crimes or offences.

Appeals go to the Sheriff Appeal Court – Criminal and then, potentially, to the High Court sitting as a court of appeal.

(2) Sheriff summary court

1.28 The sheriff summary court is held in the same buildings and staffed by the same personnel as the sheriff civil court.

The sentencing powers of this court are, currently, a fine of £10,000 and custodial sentence of up to 12 months. The sheriff summary court deals with over half of all criminal cases.[45] Appeals go to the Sheriff Appeal Court – Criminal and then, potentially, to the High Court sitting as a court of appeal.

(3) Sheriff solemn court

1.29 The sheriff solemn court deals with slightly more serious cases and this is reflected in its sentencing power. The sheriff sitting in this court can impose an unlimited fine and a custodial sentence of up to five years. In cases where the sheriff considers that these sentencing powers are inadequate the case can be remitted to the High Court for sentence. This happens very rarely in practice. The sheriff solemn court deals with about 5% of criminal cases.

(4) High Court of Justiciary

1.30 The High Court of Justiciary is the only court which can deal with certain serious crimes, the most notable being murder and rape. Although this court has the same personnel as the Court of Session, it sits not only in Edinburgh but also at locations throughout Scotland, and is in permanent session in Glasgow. The High Court deals with around 1% of criminal cases.[46]

(5) High Court as court of appeal

1.31 The High Court sits as a court of appeal from solemn courts and, potentially, from the Sheriff Appeal Court – Criminal. For this

45 At least judged by convictions, see *Criminal Proceedings in Scotland 2022–23*, Table 3. Available at: www.gov.scot/publications/criminal-proceedings-scotland-2022-23/. (Accessed April 2026).

46 This figure has been stable over the years. The remaining cases are dealt with by the JP court.

purpose, it sits in Edinburgh and is presided over by three judges or, if the appeal is only about sentence, two judges. It is possible to make a further reference to the Supreme Court in cases involving devolution issues.[47]

(6) Procedures

(a) Summary procedure

1.32 Summary procedure is initiated by the service of a document known as a 'complaint' on the accused. The complaint will contain brief details of the alleged offence, including the time and date. This narration of events is known as 'the libel'. Attached to the complaint will be a notice of previous convictions, if relevant. Where the offence is a statutory offence there will be a notice of penalties setting out the possible penalties on conviction; and where it is one of a list of sexual offences (including rape and indecent assault), a notice covering certain matters, including that the defence may only be conducted by a lawyer.

On the first appearance of the accused person, either from custody or on the date specified for the hearing on the citation accompanying the complaint, they will be asked to enter a plea. Proceedings in criminal cases are known as 'diets', and this diet is sometimes referred to as 'the pleading diet'. If the accused person pleads guilty the court may proceed to sentence or may defer sentence for reports or for the person to be of good behaviour. If the accused person pleads not guilty a date will be set for trial.

If the accused person pleads not guilty there will be an intermediate diet called before the trial diet. The purpose of this diet is to assess the state of preparation on both sides. Factors to be considered at the diet include: the number of witnesses required for trial by the prosecution and defence; establishing whether the accused person intends to maintain the plea of not guilty; and supervising the extent to which the prosecution and defence have fulfilled their duty to identify and agree uncontroversial evidence. This intermediate diet was introduced in an attempt to reduce the number of people pleading not guilty at the first diet and changing the plea to guilty at the trial. Procedure at the trial is considered below.

47 Devolution issues relate to whether an official or the Scottish Government or Parliament has acted competently, for example whether their actions contravene the European Convention on Human Rights. One example is *Dyer v Watson* 2002 SC(PC) 89 where a delay in prosecution was held to infringe the rights of the accused under Article 6(1) of the Convention.

(b) Solemn procedure

1.33 The accused person's first appearance will be on petition. The petition will specify the preliminary form of the charge against them. This first hearing will take the form of a judicial examination in front of the sheriff in the sheriff's chambers. The fiscal may ask questions at this stage and a transcript of the questions and any answers may be read out at any subsequent trial. After examination the accused person may be committed for further examination, in which case they will appear before the sheriff again, or may be committed for trial (sometimes described as being 'fully committed'), and may be released on bail or kept in custody.

Once the accused person has been committed for trial an indictment will be served on them (assuming that the case is proceeding). The indictment will contain the final version of the charge against the accused. The indictment will specify a date for the trial and will have attached to it, as appropriate, a notice of previous convictions. In addition, there will be included a list of the prosecution witnesses and a list of any productions (that is, any physical evidence such as photographs or weapons) the prosecution intend to present at the trial. The indictment will also, where the offence is one of a list of sexual offences (including rape and indecent assault), have attached a notice covering certain matters, including that the defence may only be conducted by a lawyer.

If the accused is kept in custody the indictment must be served within 80 days. If they are to be tried in the High Court the preliminary hearing must start within 110 days, and the trial within 140 days. Where trial is to be in the sheriff court the trial must start within 110 days. In all cases these periods start with the date of full committal but it is possible to apply to have them extended. If there is no extension, the accused person is released on bail.[48] If the accused person is at liberty the trial must start within 12 months of the first appearance on petition. Where the trial is to be in the High Court, the preliminary hearing must take place within 11 months. In cases tried at the sheriff court there will a first diet at least ten days before the trial diet. The function of this is similar to that of the intermediate diet in summary proceedings. If the case is to be tried in the High Court, there will be a preliminary diet covering similar ground.

48 Criminal Procedure (Scotland) Act 1995, s 65.

(c) Procedure at trial

1.34 A large majority of criminal cases do not go to trial. The accused person pleads guilty and is sentenced. Although the accused has a right to defend themselves,[49] in those cases that go to trial, legal representation can greatly assist the accused's case and make sure it is properly presented.

Procedure at trial is similar in solemn and summary procedure, the chief differences being due to the presence of the jury in solemn procedure. The main stages are:

(a) Presentation of the prosecution evidence. There are no opening statements in Scottish trials of the sort which might be familiar from American films or television. The prosecution simply calls its first witness and the trial proceeds from there. Each witness will be examined by the prosecution (this initial questioning is known as the examination-in-chief); they will then be cross-examined by the defence and then, if necessary, be re-examined by the prosecution.

(b) At the end of the prosecution case the defence may move that the charges be dropped on the ground that there is no case to answer, in other words that the prosecution has not produced sufficient evidence to find the accused guilty.

(c) If this motion is rejected the defence will then present their evidence in the same way as the prosecution. There is, of course, no need for the defence to give evidence, or, more particularly, for the accused to give evidence, though failure to give evidence may be commented on by the prosecution and the judge. It is up to the prosecution to prove their case beyond reasonable doubt.

(d) Following the defence case both sides, prosecution first, will make their concluding speeches. In summary cases these are addressed to the judge(s), in solemn cases to the jury.

(e) In solemn cases the judge will then address the jury explaining their function, the standard of proof which the prosecution must meet and any relevant legal points. The judge will usually also highlight some of the significant points of evidence, although the jurors must decide on their own recollection of the evidence. After this the jury will retire to consider its verdict, a process which is widely recognised to be far from scientific.

(f) The judge or jury will then reach a verdict. The verdict may be guilty, or not guilty, decided by a two-thirds majority of the fifteen-person jury; this a change to the previous simple

49 Except in respect of trials for certain sexual offences.

majority requirement.[50] A third possible verdict, 'not proven', unique to Scots law, was abolished on 1 January 2026 when new legislation came into force.[51] The long campaign to abolish the not proven verdict was in part based on the notion that criminal proceedings are concerned with establishing guilt or innocence in some objective sense corresponding to the truth of what actually happened. This, however, is not the case:

> It is sometimes maintained that the object of leading evidence in a criminal trial is, or should be, the elucidation of the truth. That statement, however, requires considerable qualification. First, the matter to be elucidated is not the whole truth about all the circumstances of the events narrated in the libel, but only the question of whether the Crown has proved beyond reasonable doubt that the accused committed the crime charged against him. While a verdict of 'guilty' answers that question in the affirmative, a verdict of 'not guilty' or 'not proven' only means that the question has not been so answered: it is not a determination of the accused's innocence. And whatever the verdict, it may not reflect the truth.[52]

(g) Following a guilty verdict the court will move on to sentence. Sentence may be deferred either for reports or for other reasons. Examples of reasons for deferral might be for the accused person to show that they can be of good behaviour, or for repayment of a sum of money dishonestly obtained. In some cases, the judge must obtain a criminal justice social work report before sentencing, for example, when considering a custodial sentence for a person who has offended and not previously been sentenced to custody, or for a person who has offended and is under 21. Before sentence, the accused person's solicitor or counsel will normally make a plea in mitigation, the purpose of which is to attempt to influence the sentencer to be lenient.

(d) Standard of proof

1.35 As we have noted, the standard of proof in criminal cases is proof beyond reasonable doubt. This is more exacting than the standard in civil cases and requires the prosecution to produce evidence which does not leave any reasonable doubt in the mind of the judge (in summary cases) or the jury (in solemn cases) as to the guilt of the accused person.

50 Victims, Witnesses, and Justice Reform (Scotland) Act 2025, ss 65 and 66 amending the Criminal Procedure (Scotland) Act 1995.

51 Victims, Witnesses, and Justice Reform (Scotland) Act 2025.

52 Scottish Law Commission *Evidence: Report on Hearsay in Civil Proceedings* HC 177 1994–95, para 2.14.

This standard of proof is also relevant in hearings before the sheriff to establish a referral to a children's hearing on offence grounds.[53] The nature of the evidence which can be used to establish this standard is considered in **1.39** to **1.45** below.

(e) Bail[54]

1.36 Bail may be applied for on any appearance in court. Refusal of bail can be the subject of an application for review on the grounds of changed circumstances or new evidence or can be appealed against. It is also possible to seek review of any conditions attached to the grant of bail. There are no non-bailable offences. Bail is to be granted, except where there is a good reason to refuse bail having regard to the public interest and to other, specified, factors. These factors, which can be the grounds for refusing bail, include substantial risk of absconding, substantial risk of further offending and substantial risk of interference with witnesses. The two exceptions, where bail is only to be granted where there are exceptional circumstances justifying bail, are cases where the accused person is facing charges:

(a) of violent or sexual offences and has a previous conviction on indictment for such an offence; or
(b) of drug trafficking and has a previous conviction on indictment for such an offence.

An individual may be released on bail both before conviction and after conviction but before sentence; they may also be released pending the outcome of an appeal against a custodial sentence.

If bail is granted the person released on bail will be subject to a number of standard conditions.[55] The main conditions are:

(a) a requirement to appear at all court diets;
(b) a requirement not to commit further offences;
(c) a requirement not to interfere with witnesses; and
(d) a requirement to be available for the purposes of enabling enquiries or reports to be made to assist the court's disposition of the case. This would include, for example, a criminal justice social work report requested by a court prior to sentencing.

The court may attach other conditions to the granting of bail as appropriate, these can include a requirement for remote monitoring.

53 See **chapter 5, 5.29**.
54 Most people who are not kept in custody after a court hearing will not be on bail. They will be released simply on agreeing to attend the next hearing.
55 Set out in Part III of the Criminal Procedure (Scotland) Act 1995.

Generally speaking, lodging of a sum of money in court by way of guaranteeing future appearances is not required unless there are special circumstances.

It is important to note that breach of any of the bail conditions, except committing another offence while on bail, is itself a criminal offence. So, for example, if a person on bail refused to make themselves available to a social worker in connection with the compilation of a report, that would be breaching one of the conditions of bail and committing a further offence. Where an offence is committed while on bail, that breach of bail conditions is to be reflected in the sentence imposed for that offence.

(f) Appeals

1.37 Appeals can be made against both conviction and sentence. The prosecution in a solemn case has a right of appeal against sentence either on a point of law or if the sentence, or a condition attached to it,[56] is considered to be too lenient. In a summary case the prosecution can appeal against acquittal or sentence. A person who has offended and wishes to appeal must obtain leave to appeal from the Sheriff Appeal Court – Criminal if appealing from a summary court, or from the High Court if appealing from a solemn court. If the appeal is against sentence, the sentence must be shown to be unreasonable. The court can increase as well as decrease the sentence on appeal. The Scottish Criminal Cases Review Commission has the power to review cases and to refer cases back to the High Court where this is in the interests of justice, or where there has been a miscarriage of justice.

(g) Accelerated diets

1.38 There is provision for accelerated diets to take place. This would happen when an accused who has pled not guilty changes their plea to guilty, sometimes after some negotiation of the charges with the prosecution, and wishes the matter dealt with before the date set for the trial diet.

56 Such as a condition attached to a community payback order.

EVIDENCE

1.39 In normal circumstances, individuals make use of a wide range of information to arrive at conclusions. For example, physical evidence, things which can be directly perceived, information from other people, and information about the reported comments of other people. When it comes to taking decisions in court, however, the range of evidence which can be used is restricted. More specifically, if evidence is to be accepted by a court it must be:
(1) relevant; and
(2) admissible.

(1) Relevant evidence

1.40 Relevant evidence is simply evidence which is relevant to proving the matter before the court. Evidence of other matters, such as the past history of the parties or of the accused in a criminal case, are not generally relevant and will not be allowed to be led in evidence. In other words, there must be some logical link between the evidence and the matter before the court.

(2) Admissible evidence

1.41 This is evidence not excluded by some rule of law, that is evidence which will be admissible provided it is not subject to one of the exclusions provided for by the law. Some of these exclusions are:

(a) Hearsay evidence

1.42 This is considered more fully below.

(b) Evidence obtained improperly

1.43 One example of this is evidence that the police have obtained illegally in a criminal case, for example by carrying out a search without a necessary warrant or procuring a confession through violence or the threat of violence. The exclusion also applies in civil cases and, of course, those involving children. One area where this has been an issue is in cases where the courts have taken the view that social workers and police have not acted properly in obtaining evidence of child abuse. The courts may then take the view that such evidence cannot be relied on (though this may be a question of credibility rather than admissibility) and the referral to a children's hearing based on that evidence being discharged.[57]

(c) Evidence protected by privilege

1.44 In certain circumstances the relationship between two parties may be privileged, with the result that information passing between them is privileged and disclosure of this information cannot be required by the court. The main example of this is the solicitor/client relationship. This, indeed, seems to be the only clearly established case and it is apparent that privilege does not apply to communications between a social worker and service user. English courts have recognised a 'public interest privilege'. In one case it was held that this allowed the NSPCC to refuse to disclose the identity of someone who had made an allegation of child abuse.[58] The view of courts in Scotland is that there is no such concept as 'public interest privilege': instead, information will be protected by confidentiality. This was certainly the view expressed in a case where an adoptive parent sought access to social work records concerning the adopted child. It was said that:

> '... [I]f a case arose in Scotland in which a party sought to recover from the RSSPCC [now Children 1st] the name of an informer, it would only be in exceptional circumstances that such a motion would be granted. This would not be because public interest privilege is extended to the RSSPCC, but because the nature of the work of that body is such that their claim to confidentiality would be awarded a high degree of protection.'[59]

Such information is not required to be revealed under the Data Protection Act 2018 or the General Data Protection Regulation.[60]

(d) Opinion evidence

1.45 In general, witnesses are not allowed to express opinions in giving evidence. The main exception to this rule is in respect of expert witnesses, who are permitted to make statements of their opinions about facts which they may or may not have observed for themselves. Social

57 This is essentially what seems to have happened in *L v Kennedy* (6 March 1995, unreported), IH.

58 *D v NSPCC* [1978] AC 171.

59 *P v Tayside Regional Council* 1989 SCLR 165 at 168. See also *Davers v Butler* 1994 SCLR 717; *A v G* 1996 SCLR 787.

60 See **chapter 2, 2.46**.

workers may be called upon to act as expert witnesses in their areas of competence and expertise. Such expert evidence, it should be noted, does not supplant the court: the court has to take its decision based on the whole evidence presented to it, which frequently involves competing opinions expressed by experts. Of course, it is often not possible to question a non-expert witness without seeking expressions of opinion, for example as to whether a car was being driven fast, or whether someone appeared to be upset and it has been argued that identification evidence is, in fact, opinion evidence.[61] There seems to be no clear rule of law explaining to what extent non-experts can state opinions.

(3) A competent witness

1.46 Previously a witness had to be competent, i.e., legally permitted to give evidence, in the sense that they understood the notion of giving evidence and could clearly understand and explain what they had seen or heard. In practice, the assumption was that everyone was a competent witness unless they were excluded by a rule of law. There was no exclusion of children from giving evidence, and the evidence of children as young as three-and-a-half and four has been heard in criminal cases. This requirement for witnesses to be competent has now been removed and the evidence of anyone called as a witness is not inadmissible solely because they do not understand their duty to give truthful evidence or the difference between truth or lies.[62] Because of this, courts are prohibited from taking steps to establish understanding of either of these matters.

(4) Hearsay evidence

1.47 The hearsay rule has been defined as providing that:

> Any assertion other than one made by a person while giving oral evidence in the proceedings is inadmissible as evidence of any fact or opinion asserted.[63]

In other words, any statement made by a third party and reported to court by a witness is not admissible as evidence that what is claimed

61 See, for example, F Raitt Evidence: Principles, Policy and Practice (2008), 4–01 to 4–03.

62 Vulnerable Witnesses (Scotland) Act 2004, s 24.

63 Cross on *Evidence* (7th edn, London, 1990, by the late Sir Rupert Cross and C Tapper) at p 509, quoted in Scottish Law Commission, *Evidence: Report on Hearsay Evidence in Criminal Proceedings* (Scot Law Com No 149), para 3.2.

in the statement actually happened. It is only admissible as evidence of the fact that the statement was made. Assume, for example, that X said to Y 'I saw Ramon Mercador killing Trotsky'. If Y was subsequently called as a witness in the trial of Mercador and repeated the statement made by X, that would only be evidence that the statement was made: it would not be evidence, admissible by the court, that Mercador killed Trotsky. There are, however, some exceptions to the general rule where hearsay evidence is treated as admissible evidence of the facts contained in the second-hand statement. The main exceptions are:

(a) Civil cases

1.48 As a result of the Civil Evidence (Scotland) Act 1988, the hearsay rule was abolished for all civil proceedings in Scotland. This includes all proof hearings on grounds of referral to a children's hearing except where the ground of referral is that the child has committed an offence. The case of *F v Kennedy (No 2)*[64] illustrates the effect of this provision. At a proof hearing, a child witness, J, was called to give evidence. In addition, evidence was given of statements which J had made on previous occasions. These statements were not put to J when he was giving evidence and he was not asked about them. They were reported by other witnesses as hearsay evidence. The child's father challenged the decision to admit J's hearsay evidence, arguing that proceeding in this way was at odds with the best evidence rule which would require J to give all his evidence in court. The challenge was rejected. The Inner House of the Court of Session took the view that 'the fact that the maker of the statement has given oral evidence does not prevent hearsay evidence being given of what he has said upon another occasion'. They then continued: '… there may well be occasions where it will be difficult to take the whole of a child's evidence in court. It may therefore be important for the sheriff to be able to rely to some extent at least on hearsay evidence of what the child has said on other occasions'.[65] In one case, hearsay evidence in the form of a statement made to the police was accepted by the sheriff even though the statement was retracted by the witness when she appeared before him.[66]

64 1993 SLT 1284.
65 1993 SLT 1284 at 1287F–H.
66 *K v Kennedy* 1993 SLT 1281.

(b) Res gestae

1.49 Where statements are made as part of the events which are claimed to constitute an offence, they will be admissible, even though the identity of the maker of the statement is unknown. One of the standard texts on evidence suggests that two obvious examples of statements forming part of the *res gestae* would be the screams and protests of a rape victim and the use of nicknames in an unguarded moment by members of a team of hooded armed robbers.[67]

(c) Confessions

1.50 Confessions made by an accused either to the police or to someone else are admissible evidence.

(d) Previous inconsistent statements

1.51 Where a witness departs from a previous statement, for example if a footballer originally told police that he had been head butted but, in the witness box, suggests that the head contact was accidental, the previous statement is admissible to attack the credibility of the witness and the evidence being given.

(e) Statements made by someone who can no longer give evidence

1.52 One example of this is a statement by someone who has died since the statement was made.

(f) Criminal cases

1.53 Hearsay evidence can be admitted in criminal trials as evidence of any matter stated in that evidence in a number of circumstances including cases where the person making the statement cannot be found, is dead or unfit or unable to give evidence, has been authorised not to give evidence on the grounds that in doing so they might incriminate themselves, or refuses to give evidence.[68]

67 F Raitt *Evidence: Principles, Policy and Practice* 3rd edn (2018), para 11.20.
68 Criminal Procedure (Scotland) Act 1995, s 259.

(5) Corroboration

1.54 Corroboration requires that each fact essential to proving a case is supported by two pieces of evidence. The two pieces of evidence need not be statements by eye witnesses, but may be physical evidence, for example fingerprints, or medical evidence, or circumstantial evidence. The requirement for corroboration no longer applies in civil cases, though the existence of corroboration will strengthen a case. Corroboration is still required in criminal cases (and in proof hearings on referrals from a children's hearings where the grounds of referral involve commission of an offence). In such cases there are two things which must be established by corroborated evidence: that the crime was committed, and that the accused person (or the child) committed it.

(6) Deciding on the evidence

1.55 Once all the relevant admissible evidence has been led, the court (or, in solemn cases, the jury) must arrive at a decision on the case. In order to do this it will have to decide whether the evidence led discharges the burden of proof imposed on the parties involved in the case. In criminal cases it will have to decide whether the prosecution have proved their case beyond a reasonable doubt; in civil cases whether the pursuer has established their case on the balance of probabilities. In arriving at its decision, the court will have to weigh up the evidence. Doing this involves the court looking at whether the evidence was direct or circumstantial, the sufficiency of any corroboration, the coherence of the evidence and, perhaps most importantly, assessing the credibility of the evidence. This last matter is often of crucial importance because there will often be directly contradictory evidence before the court. In such cases the decision as to who is a credible witness will have an important bearing on the outcome of the case.

(7) Children and vulnerable adults giving evidence

1.56 There are special provisions for protecting vulnerable witnesses. In respect of criminal cases a person will be a vulnerable witness if:[69]

(i) They are aged under 18.

69 Criminal Procedure (Scotland) Act 1995, s 271.

(ii) There is a significant risk that the quality of the evidence they will give will be diminished by reason of mental disorder or fear or distress in connection with giving evidence at the trial.
(iii) They are the victim of one of a number of types of offence, including stalking and domestic abuse.
(iv) It is considered that the fact of giving evidence could lead to a significant risk of harm to the witness.

In criminal cases, there are five ways in which the giving of evidence by a vulnerable witness who is called to give evidence can be made less stressful and they can be given some degree of protection.[70] Where the witness falls into category (i) or (iii) above they will, subject to procedural formalities being complied with, be entitled to the benefit of (a), (b) or (d) below:
(a) Giving evidence via a live television link.
(b) A screen can be placed so as to conceal the accused from the witness giving evidence.
(c) Allowing the evidence of the witness to be taken on commission, with the proceedings being videotaped.
(d) Use of a supporter.
(e) Giving evidence in chief in the form of a prior statement.
(f) Exclusion of the public during the time when the witness is giving evidence.

For civil cases, a vulnerable witness will be one who falls into category i or ii above. In addition, in civil cases, including most referrals from a children's hearing, the provisions discussed above regarding hearsay in civil cases mean that the child need not be present at all; instead, their evidence may be given in the form of hearsay either by a witness or in the form of a videotaped interview.[71] In addition, special arrangements can be made for vulnerable witnesses in the form of one of the special measures available that are those listed at (a)–(d) above. These provisions apply, for example, in respect of court proceedings related to children's hearings (e.g. proof hearings in the sheriff court).

CHILDREN'S HEARINGS

1.57 The system of children's hearings was introduced by the Social Work (Scotland) Act 1968 to deal with a whole range of cases relating to children which were formerly dealt with in a variety of different courts. These include offences committed by children, children beyond parental

70 Act of Adjournal (Criminal Procedure Rules) 1996, SI 1996/513, ch 22.
71 As happened in *Ferguson v S*, 1993 SCLR 712.

control, children against whom offences may have been committed and children who do not attend school. The relevant provisions of the 1968 Act were repealed and replaced by provisions in Part II of the Children (Scotland) Act 1995 and these, in turn, have been replaced by the provisions of the Children's Hearings (Scotland) Act 2011. Children's hearings are considered in greater detail in chapter 5.

TRIBUNALS[72]

1.58 Tribunals have been set up to adjudicate in a wide variety of areas affected by state intervention. Examples are Social Security and Child Support Tribunals, mental health tribunals and employment tribunals. Procedure and the rules of representation before tribunals are generally much more relaxed than those before courts. This opens up greater possibilities for representation by non-lawyers, for example, of claimants before social security tribunals. This is particularly important as there is evidence to suggest that claimants who are represented have a greater chance of success than those who are not.

CHALLENGING LOCAL AUTHORITY DECISIONS

(1) Judicial review

1.59 Judicial review is a procedure by which decisions of many public bodies may be challenged. It differs from appeal in that the right to seek review exists without the express statutory provision which is needed to create a right of appeal; indeed, the courts have sometimes reviewed decisions in spite of specific statutory provisions excluding their jurisdiction. This makes review particularly useful in cases where there is no provision for appeal against a decision.

There are, however, three major drawbacks to using judicial review to challenge decisions. The first of these is that actions for judicial review can be dealt with only by the Court of Session in Edinburgh. This is not as much of a problem as it used to be, following the introduction of a simpler and quicker form of procedure, though it makes the process more expensive than it would otherwise be. The second drawback is that review can be sought only on restricted grounds. To succeed, the applicant must be able to show that the person or body taking the decision acted beyond their powers (that is, *ultra vires*), acted unreasonably, or

72 See **chapter 12, 12.12** for the structure of tribunals in Scotland.

did not comply with the requirements of natural justice. In taking its decision the court can also consider human rights issues.[73] Finally, there can be a delay in the availability of judicial review as a remedy in cases involving social work services. The view was taken in one case that judicial review was not available until the claimant had exhausted the local authority's social work complaints procedure.[74] (For examples and further discussion, see chapter 11.)

Despite these drawbacks, judicial review has been a valuable remedy in certain areas. One such area has been its use by people who have been refused accommodation under the homelessness legislation. Judicial review is made necessary in such circumstances because there is no statutory provision for appeal against a local authority decision to refuse housing. In *Kelly v Monklands District Council*[75] a 16-year-old girl left home because of violence inflicted by her father. She had nowhere to stay and had attempted suicide. She applied for housing as a homeless person. One of the cases in which an authority was bound to provide housing was if the applicant was vulnerable. The local authority decided that Ms Kelly was not vulnerable despite a report from the social work department to the contrary. The court decided that the authority had acted unreasonably in arriving at its conclusion on vulnerability and in not taking proper account of the report from the social work department. The council was ordered to house Ms Kelly.[76]

Another use, though not pursued as commonly in Scotland, is to challenge community care assessments and decisions about service provision.[77]

(2) Complaints procedure

1.60 Following a review of complaints procedures, a new complaints procedure was introduced for social work complaints made after 1 April 2017.[78] This covers complaints about action or lack of action in terms

73 See **1.65** below.

74 *McCue v Glasgow City Council* [2014] CSOH 124. Though see *Smart's Guardian v Fife Council* [2015] CSOH 183, where the court allowed an application for judicial review to go ahead on the basis, it seems, that inadequate information had been provided about the complaints procedure and that, as a result, it did not provide an effective alternative remedy.

75 1986 SLT 169.

76 *Kelly v Monklands District Council* 1986 SLT 169. See also **2.5–2.13**. There have been some changes to law and guidance since this case was decided.

77 See, for example, *MacGregor v South Lanarkshire District Council* 2001 SC 502.

78 Public Services Reform (Social Work Complaints Procedure) (Scotland) Order 2016 (SSI 2016/157).

of the local authority's obligations under the 1968 Act and various other pieces of legislation, such as the Chronically Sick and Disabled Persons Act 1970, the Mental Health (Care and Treatment) (Scotland) Act 2003, the Social Care (Self-Directed Support) (Scotland) Act 2013 and the Children and Young People (Scotland) Act 2014. The complaints procedure also covers services commissioned by the local authority from other providers. It involves a three-stage process. Initially, an attempt is made to resolve the complaint informally without proceeding to the formal investigation. If this fails, an investigation is carried out by an officer of the local authority. If the service user is dissatisfied with the outcome of this, there is a right to make a complaint to the Scottish Public Services Ombudsman.[79]

In addition to the local authority complaints procedure, all service providers whose services are registered[80] with the Care Inspectorate must, as a condition of such registration, have a complaints procedure. Complaints about such services can also be made to the Inspectorate through its complaints procedure. This means that an individual whose services are commissioned by the local authority but provided by a body external to the authority may have a choice of three different complaints procedures.

LEGAL AID

1.61 Legal aid in Scotland is administered by the Scottish Legal Aid Board. There are three types of legal aid: advice and assistance; civil legal aid; and criminal legal aid.

(1) Advice and assistance

1.62 This is a means tested scheme which provides free advice and assistance to applicants who qualify based on a means test. Above the qualifying level for free assistance there is a sliding scale for contribution up to the point where full payment must be made. People in receipt of Universal Credit, income support, income-based jobseeker's allowance, income-related employment and support allowance, qualify automatically on income grounds, but may be ineligible through their ownership of capital above the permitted limit. The decision as to entitlement is made by the solicitor who is approached for advice.

79 Scottish Public Services Ombudsman. Available at: www.spso.org.uk/. (Accessed April 2026)..

80 The process of registration is considered in **chapter 11**.

Advice and assistance covers advice about any matter of Scots law, civil or criminal. With very limited exceptions, it only covers assistance short of representation before a court or tribunal, one such exception is representation before the Mental Health Tribunal where assistance by way of representation is available.

(2) Civil legal aid

1.63 Civil legal aid is available to raise or defend actions in the civil courts. Once again, it is means tested, and again those in receipt of the benefits set out above will qualify. As with legal advice and assistance there is a sliding scale of contributions above the level of free entitlement, up to the point where the applicant is not entitled to any assistance.

In urgent cases a solicitor may be able to act before a decision is made by the Scottish Legal Aid Board on the application for legal aid.[81] This might be necessary, for example, to allow a person to obtain an interim exclusion order excluding a violent spouse from the family home.

Children are entitled to apply for legal aid in their own right; their eligibility is determined based on their resources rather than that of other members of their family.

There is a separate form of legal aid, Children's Legal Aid, which provides assistance for both children's hearings, in the form of assistance by way of representation,[82] and for court hearings under the Children's Hearings (Scotland) Act 2011, e.g., proof hearings.

(3) Criminal legal aid

1.64 Applications for legal aid in criminal cases are also decided by the Board. The only ground for refusal of legal aid in solemn cases is that the accused could pay for their defence without undue hardship. In summary cases, as well as applying this hardship test, it must be in the interests of justice to grant legal aid. Where an accused appears in court from custody, that person is entitled to be represented by the duty solicitor assigned to that court.

81 Civil Legal Aid (Scotland) Regulations 2002, SSI 2002/494, reg 18.
82 Considered more fully in **chapter 5**.

HUMAN RIGHTS

1.65 The European Convention on Human Rights was signed in Rome in 1950.[83] The Convention requires signatory states to desist from some activities and to take positive action in other areas to uphold defined human rights principles. The ECHR may require positive action by the state and/or local authorities, and grants individuals certain rights, for example the right to respect for family life.[84] Until 2000, complaints that rights under the Convention had been violated in the UK involved taking a case to the European Court of Human Rights (ECtHR) in Strasbourg, a process which could be time consuming.[85] However, the Human Rights Act 1998 which came into effect in 2000, provided the possibility of direct action being taken against local authorities (and other public authorities) for failing to act consistently with the rights which the Convention provides for. More specifically, section 6 provides: 'It is unlawful for a public authority to act in a way which is incompatible with a Convention right' and section 7 allows individuals to take proceedings against public authorities[86] and also to rely on their Convention Rights in any proceedings brought against them. The right conferred by these sections would allow an individual to seek damages from a local authority or to seek an interdict ordering them to stop any action which is incompatible with a Convention right. In addition to the direct rights conferred by the 1998 Act, and in a related development, convention rights are now considered in judicial review actions.

The rights conferred by the European Convention will be considered more fully later in this text, but there are some general points which set the context for consideration of individual rights. Rights conferred by the Convention may be absolute or relative. An example of an absolute provision is the prohibition on torture contained in Article 3 of the

83 The United Kingdom was one of the original signatories in November 1950. The ECHR came into force in the UK in September 1953.

84 ECHR, Article 8.

85 One example is *McMichael v United Kingdom* (1995) 20 EHRR 205 which concerned procedures in children's hearings. The complaint was made in 1989 and a decision made by the court in 1995.

86 A public authority includes, as well as courts and tribunals, 'any person certain of whose functions are functions of a public nature': Human Rights Act 1998, s 6(3)(b). The definition has been extended to include private sector providers of accommodation, together with nursing, personal care or personal support, as a care home service where this accommodation is provided by arrangement with a local authority: Health and Social Care Act 2008, s 145. This extension was to avoid perceived unfairness in that decisions of local authorities about care homes (for example closure) could be challenged under the Human Rights Act, but those of private providers could not, see *L v Birmingham City Council* [2007] UKHL 27.

Convention. In contrast, other provisions envisage a balancing of rights. For example, Article 8 provides that everyone has the right to 'respect for his private and family life, his home and his correspondence'.[87] The Convention goes on to add a qualification, stating that these rights may be interfered with provided that this interference is in accordance with the law and is necessary in a democratic society to achieve one of a number of objectives, for example the protection of the rights and freedoms of others. A second general point is that some of the rights are expressed in such a way as to prohibit certain types of behaviour. For example, Article 3 mentioned above provides that: '[n]o one shall be subjected to torture or to inhuman or degrading treatment or punishment.'[88] This would, *prima facie,* appear to impose only a negative obligation on public bodies not to subject people to such forms of treatment. However, the ECtHR has taken the view that such obligations go beyond this and impose a positive obligation on public bodies. That obligation is to act when they are (or should be) aware that people are being subjected by others to the treatment described, with the objective of such intervention being to bring the treatment to an end.[89]

Finally, the main convention rights which are likely to be relevant to social work practice are those set out in Articles 2, 3, 5, 6 and 8. Article 2 provides for a right to life; this may at least be a relevant consideration in considering whether to warn relevant authorities of knowledge of a risk to another.[90] Article 3 has been discussed above and may have some application in, for example, cases of suspected child abuse. Article 5 provides that no one is to be deprived of his or her liberty except in a limited number of cases (for example, convicted criminals and detention of those who are of 'unsound mind') and in accordance with procedures established by law. This article may be relevant in considering whether processes involving detention of mentally ill patients or placement of adults with incapacity is compliant with their convention rights. Article 6 provides that civil rights and obligations are to be determined by an independent and impartial body and provides a number of other safeguards. Finally, Article 8 has been mentioned above and might come into play, for example in relation to the removal of a child from their family, or the closure of residential accommodation. These rights, whether they are qualified or not, and examples of cases concerning alleged breaches, are set out in Table 1.2 below.

87 ECHR, Article 8.
88 ECHR, Article 3.
89 See, for example, Z *v United Kingdom* (2002) 34 EHRR 3.
90 See, for example, *Osman v UK* (2000) 29 EHRR 245.

Table 1.2

Article	Text of Article	Qualified right?	Examples
2	Everyone's right to life shall be protected by law. No one shall be deprived of his life intentionally save in the execution of a sentence of a court following his conviction of a crime for which this penalty is provided by law.	Yes	*Osman*:[1] '…article 2 of the Convention may also imply in certain well-defined circumstances a positive obligation on the authorities to take preventive operational measures to protect an individual whose life is at risk from the criminal acts of another individual.' *Savage*:[2] Duty to take steps to avoid risk of harm to suicidal detained patient because of knowledge of immediate risk to her life.
3	No one shall be subjected to torture or to inhuman or degrading treatment or punishment.	No	*Z*:[3] Duty to take action where local authority knew or should have known that treatment of children amounted to inhuman and degrading treatment.

Article	Text of Article	Qualified right?	Examples
5	Everyone has the right to liberty and security of person. No one shall be deprived of his liberty save in the following cases and in accordance with a procedure prescribed by law— (a) the lawful detention of a person after conviction by a competent court; (b) the detention of a minor by lawful order for the purpose of educational supervision or his lawful detention for the purpose of bringing him before the competent legal authority; (c) the lawful detention of persons for the prevention of the spreading of infectious diseases, of persons of unsound mind, alcoholics or drug addicts or vagrants.	No	*P v Cheshire West and Chester Council*:[4] Placement of incapable adult in circumstances which amounted to deprivation of liberty. *Koniarska*:[5] Placement of child in secure accommodation where she received (some) education fell within paragraph (d) as being for the 'purpose of educational supervision', this purpose was not restricted to school attendance.

Article	Text of Article	Qualified right?	Examples
6	In the determination of his civil rights and obligations or of any criminal charge against him, everyone is entitled to a fair and public hearing within a reasonable time by an independent and impartial tribunal established by law.	Yes[6]	*S*:[7] Lack of provision of legal aid for children's hearings breached Art. 6. *McMichael*:[8] Failure to provide parents with social background reports for children's hearing breached Art. 6.
8	Everyone has the right to respect for his private and family life, his home and his correspondence.	Yes	*Bernard*:[9] Failure to provide suitable accommodation which meant that mobility impaired woman could not access toilet or leave room in which she slept breached Art. 8 rights.

1 *Osman v UK* (2000) 29 EHRR 245.
2 *Savage v South Essex Partnership NHS Foundation Trust & Anor* [2007] EWCA Civ 1375.
3 *Z v United Kingdom* (2002) 34 EHRR 3.
4 [2014] UKSC 19.
5 *Koniarska v United Kingdom*, Application no 33670/96, decision 12 October 2000.
6 In relation to publicity of hearing.
7 *S v Miller* 2001 SLT 485.
8 *McMichael v United Kingdom* (1995) 20 EHRR 205.
9 *Bernard v Enfield London Borough Council* [2002] EWHC 2282 (Admin).

THE SOCIAL WORK (SCOTLAND) ACT 1968

(1) Introduction

1.66 The Social Work (Scotland) Act 1968 (the 1968 Act) grew out of two developments. The first was a trend towards generic social work based on the view that social work with all types of people has a common base of values and skills. The second was the recommendation of the Kilbrandon Report[91] for the setting up of a social education department to provide support for the children's hearings which the report proposed. These two developments were brought together in the White Paper *Social Work and the Community*[92] which formed the basis for the 1968 Act.

The 1968 Act is a core piece of legislation, providing much of the framework for the activities of social workers employed by local authorities, as well as setting down specific duties and specific procedures that must be followed in particular circumstances. Although most of the provisions relating to children have been replaced by the Children's Hearings (Scotland) Act 2011, the basic provisions of the 1968 Act regarding the overall duties and powers of social workers remain in place and it is worth undertaking a brief survey of the Act at this point. It must be remembered, of course, that the 1968 Act is only one of a large number of statutes conferring duties and powers on social workers.

The major contribution of the 1968 Act, as far as provision of social work services is concerned, was to draw all the disparate services provided by local authorities into one department under one overall director and with a council committee responsible for its oversight. Although councils must still appoint a chief social work officer, there is no longer any requirement to have a separate social work committee.[93]

(2) Persons in need and assessments

1.67 In keeping with the interventionist tenor of the times, section 12 of the 1968 Act imposes an overall duty to 'promote social welfare' by making available advice, guidance and assistance and securing the provision of facilities, including residential accommodation.

This section also allows the provision of assistance in cash or kind in certain circumstances. This type of assistance can be provided in an emergency to a 'person in need' (see below) aged 18 or over. Such assistance may be provided where doing so would avoid greater cost to the local authority either in the provision of some other service, such as the direct provision of accommodation, or at some future date

91 *Children and Young Persons* Cmnd 2306 (1964).
92 Cmnd 3065 (1966).
93 Social Work (Scotland) Act 1968 as amended by Local Government etc (Scotland) Act 1994, ss 45, 180 and Sch 14.

because of aggravation of the person's need. Social work departments have their own policies and practices in relation to the giving of section 12 assistance. It should be noted that it is not intended to operate as an alternative to the benefits system: indeed, consideration must be given to the person's eligibility for assistance from any other statutory body and the availability of that assistance before a payment is made. Section 12 payments can be made conditional on repayment.[94]

Various interpretations in different authorities and within authorities have led to enormous variation in the use of section 12. The bureaucratic hierarchical structures of social work departments have also been reflected in the policies of departments regarding the amounts of section 12 money which can be dispensed to the public by various grades of staff. For example, many basic grade social workers can dispense only limited sums without authorisation from a higher-grade member of staff.

Section 14 deals with the provision of domiciliary services for households including a person in need or an expectant mother, and also the provision of laundry services in such cases.[95]

As we have seen, these provisions refer to 'persons in need', defined in the 1968 Act as being persons who:

(a) are in need of care and attention arising out of infirmity, youth or age; or
(b) suffer from illness or mental disorder or are substantially handicapped by any deformity or disability; or
(c) being persons prescribed by the Scottish Ministers who have asked for assistance, are, in the opinion of a local authority, persons to whom the local authority may appropriately make available the services and facilities provided by them under the 1968 Act.[96]

In addition, for the purposes of section 12 only, the definition is extended to include those in need as a result of drug or alcohol dependence and release from prison or other form of detention.[97]

Section 12A of the Act, added by the National Health Service and Community Care Act 1990, requires the authority to carry out an assessment of need before providing community care services. This provision is considered more fully in chapter 6.

94 Social Work (Scotland) Act 1968, s 12(4).
95 Social Work (Scotland) Act 1968, s 14.
96 Social Work (Scotland) Act 1968, s 94(1). This power has only been used once: Prescription as 'Persons in Need' (Persons subject to Immigration Control) (Scotland) Order 1997, SI 1997/2452.
97 Social Work (Scotland) Act 1968, s 12(6).

(3) Reports and supervision of offenders

1.68 Section 27 deals with the responsibilities of the social work department in relation to the provision of reports to criminal courts and the provision of supervision to those made subject to a Community Payback Order and those released from custody on licence. Chapter 10 looks at this area in more detail.

(4) Residential establishments

1.69 Part IV of the Act deals with the provision of residential establishments by local authorities. The system of registration with the local authority of other residential establishments, for example private residential homes for persons who are elderly which was created by the 1968 Act has now been replaced by a system of registration for services (including those provided by a local authority) with the Care Inspectorate.[98]

FURTHER STATUTORY CHANGES

(1) Children

1.70 The years between the passing of the Children Act 1989, which made major changes to childcare law in England and Wales, and the Children (Scotland) Act 1995 were relatively tumultuous ones for childcare in Scotland. Initially, the view had been that unlike the position in England and Wales, Scotland did not require a major overhaul of childcare law. Many events, including ones in Orkney,[99] Fife[100] and Ayrshire, provided the impetus to thoroughly take stock, adapt some initiatives from south of the border, and move beyond those innovations to others designed to take childcare law in Scotland into the next millennium. Additionally, a paradigm shift occurred which is seen in the move from parental rights to parental responsibilities and children's rights, these now occupying a central position reflecting the significance of the United Nations *Convention on the Rights of the Child.* The importance of this Convention was reinforced in the Children and Young People (Scotland) Act 2014 which places an obligation on public authorities to report on steps taken to secure better

98 See **chapter 11**.

99 See the Clyde Report, The Report of the Inquiry into the Removal of Children from Orkney in February 1991 (1992).

100 Kearney, B, The Report of the Inquiry into Child Care Policies in Fife (1992).

or further effect of the Convention requirements.[101] The 2014 Act also legislated for aspects of the Scottish Government's Getting it Right for Every Child (GIRFEC),[102] initiative, which introduced provisions about corporate parenting and a new child's plan, and made further provision for aftercare of looked after children.

Other relevant post-1968 legislation includes the Adoption and Children (Scotland) Act 2007 which, as well as amending the law of adoption in Scotland, paved the way for a change in the regulatory regime for looked after children.

(2) Other areas

1.71 Since the establishment of the Scottish parliament a large amount of legislation has come into force which affects social work practice. Some of this applies to both adults and children, for example the Mental Health (Care and Treatment) (Scotland) Act 2003, which deals with provision of services for, and compulsory treatment of, individuals with a mental disorder. Others are more specifically directed at services for adults, for example the Adults with Incapacity (Scotland) Act 2000, which provides a framework for taking decisions on behalf of adults who cannot do this for themselves. The Adult Support and Protection (Scotland) Act 2007, imposes a duty to investigate cases where vulnerable adults may be suffering abuse. The Community Care and Health (Scotland) Act 2002, provides for (limited) free personal care for the elderly and the Social Care (Self-directed Support) (Scotland) Act 2013 (on how adult care services are to be provided to service users). Related to this is the Carers (Scotland) Act 2016 providing a new set of rules about support for carers. Still other legislation has been concerned with offenders (the Management of Offenders (Scotland) Act 2005 and the Criminal Justice and Licensing (Scotland) Act 2010, introducing Community Payback Orders), with regulation of services (Public Services Reform (Scotland) Act 2010) and the profession (Regulation of Care (Scotland) Act 2001) and with the integration of health and social work functions (Public Bodies (Joint Working) (Scotland) Act 2014).

EXCLUSIONS FROM SOCIAL WORK SERVICES

1.72 Following the introduction of a system of asylum support in legislation in 1999, a number of groups of people were excluded

101 Section 2.

102 See **chapter 4**.

from entitlement to the provision of certain social work services. For those who have made a claim for asylum support is instead provided through the National Asylum Support Service. Three main groups are affected by these rules and the scope of the exclusions differs as between these groups. The first group[103] largely comprises people who have been given leave to enter the UK subject to a condition that they will not have recourse to public funds and those who are subject to immigration control, for example those who require leave (permission) to enter and remain in the UK.[104] For this group the exclusion extends to services under section 12 of the Social Work (Scotland) Act 1968 (including community care) where need for these arises solely because of destitution or the physical effects of destitution,[105] but the exclusion does not extend to other services which the authority might provide.

The second group[106] includes:

(a) former asylum seekers who have been refused permission to stay in the UK and who have not co-operated with their removal from the UK;
(b) those who are recognised as refugees in other EEA state (and who can therefore reside there); and
(c) those, other than asylum seekers, who are in the UK in breach of immigration controls (for example by overstaying the period for which they were allowed to enter the UK).

For this group most services provided by a local authority are excluded, except that in appropriate cases powers and/or duties under the Mental Health (Care and Treatment) (Scotland) Act 2003 will have to be exercised and/or performed and services may have to be provided to avoid breach of Article 3 of the European Convention on Human Rights.[107]

The final group[108] excluded from service provision are the dependent children of asylum seekers who are excluded from services provided under section 22 of the Children (Scotland) Act 1995.[109] However, children travelling independently are entitled to services in the same way as any other child, and in contrast to the restricted provision for adults.

103 Immigration and Asylum Act 1999, ss 115(9) and 120. The exclusions are given effect to in Social Work (Scotland) Act 1968, ss 12(2A), 13A and 13B.
104 Those without permission or leave will be caught by the exclusion of those illegally in the UK, discussed below.
105 See, for example, *M v Slough* [2013] UKSC 27.
106 Nationality, Immigration and Asylum Act 2002, s 54 and Sch 3.
107 See *R (on the application of GS) v Camden LBC* [2016] EWHC 1762 (Admin).
108 Immigration and Asylum Act 1999, s 122(5).
109 See paras **4.4–4.9** and **4.13**.

This has led to local authorities having, in some cases, to determine the age of an individual to establish whether they are under 18 and therefore entitled to children's services.[110]

PROVISION OF SOCIAL WORK SERVICES

1.73 As indicated earlier in this chapter, social work services were traditionally provided by social work departments, though there were some examples of joint working in certain areas between social work and the health service. Particularly in areas like community care, the split between social work services and health services was seen as an obstacle to the most effective provision of services, with the solution being greater integration between them. This led to the Public Bodies (Joint Working) (Scotland) Act 2014, and the Policy Memorandum presented to the Scottish Parliament on the introduction of this legislation noted that:

> Separate – and sometimes disjointed – systems of health and social care can no longer adequately meet the needs and expectations of increasing numbers of people who are living into older age, often with multiple, complex, long-term conditions, and who need joined-up, integrated services.[111]

The 2014 Act required local authorities and Health Boards to work together to produce an integration scheme which would provide for the integrated delivery of certain services.[112] The Act also set out the services which had to be included in the integration scheme; these include services for those aged 18 or over such as social work services for adults and older people, mental health services, care home services and adult primary and community health functions, which include palliative care and mental health services. A second set of services may be delivered through the integration scheme, and these include children's services

110 For the guidelines to be used in doing this, see *R (on the application of Z) v Croydon LBC* [2011] EWCA Civ 59, Glasgow City Council/Scottish Refugee Council, *Age Assessment Practice Guidance: An Age Assessment Pathway for Social Workers in Scotland* (2012) and Home Office, *Assessing Age* (2018). Challenges to age assessments should be by way of judicial review: *AU v Glasgow City Council* [2017] CSOH 122.

111 At para 4.

112 Public Bodies (Joint Working) (Scotland) Act 2014, ss 1 and 2. For the services which must, can or may not be provided under the integration scheme, see also the Schedule to the 2014 Act, the Public Bodies (Joint Working) (Prescribed Heath Board Functions) (Scotland) Regulations 2014, SSI 2014/344, and the Public Bodies (Joint Working) (Prescribed Local Authority Functions, etc) (Scotland) Regulations 2014, SSI 2014/345.

and some criminal justice services. Finally, some services cannot be provided through the integration scheme.

Two delivery models are possible.[113] First, an Integration Joint Board can be established and the performance of services is then delegated to this board by the Health Board and local authority. Second, the lead authority model, where one of the two agencies takes the lead in planning and delivering services.

In carrying out the functions covered by the integration scheme (and at other stages, for example strategic planning) the person carrying out the function must have regard to the national health and wellbeing outcomes[114] and the integration delivery principles. These principles include:[115]

(a) The main purpose of provision of the service is to improve the wellbeing of service users.

(b) Services should be provided:

  (i) In an integrated way.

  (ii) Taking account of the particular needs of individual service users.

  (iii) Respecting the rights of and taking account of the dignity of service users.

113 Public Bodies (Joint Working) (Scotland) Act 2014, s 1(4).

114 Public Bodies (Joint Working) (Scotland) Act 2014, s 40. The outcomes are set out in the Public Bodies (Joint Working) (National Health and Wellbeing Outcomes) (Scotland) Regulations 2014, SSI 2014/343; see also Scottish Government, *National Health and Wellbeing Outcomes* (2015).

115 Public Bodies (Joint Working) (Scotland) Act 2014, s 31.

Chapter 2

General law relevant to social work

INTRODUCTION

2.1 As well as a knowledge of what has been described as professional law, namely, that law which is central to the professional activities of a social worker, social workers also need to have some knowledge of other areas of law to be able to assist service users. This chapter is intended to give a brief outline of the law in the areas of housing, discrimination, debt, information sharing and education. The coverage is not exhaustive so we have attempted to give further references where more detail may be found. It may also be the case that where a service user has in these areas counsel to seek qualified legal advice, perhaps under the legal advice and assistance scheme, would be warranted. An earlier edition of this text contained a section on welfare benefits, a section omitted from subsequent editions. This omission is because of the frequent changes in benefits; in the space available it was not possible to give proper coverage of the topic. References to various benefits will still be found at various stages in the text as appropriate. This omission is not to deny or undervalue the link between material deprivation and a range of other factors which bring people to social workers and one which cannot be ignored. It therefore follows that a basic understanding of the benefits system is a crucial component in a social worker's repertoire.[1] Social workers have no legal mandate to become involved in benefits matters other than in pursuing the general obligation to promote social welfare, but notions of good practice suggest that until material needs are addressed, other needs are less accessible. In some social work departments, there is an expectation that benefits checks will be carried out for new service users.

HOUSING

2.2 Housing problems experienced by social work service users are not always limited to the bricks and mortar. The typology of

1 See, for example, UK Government benefit calculator: Available at: www.gov.uk/benefits-calculators.

problems identified by Gill Stewart and John Stewart[2] provides an excellent framework for making sense of and exploring these. The links between housing problems and other problems which seriously detract from service users' quality of life, such as health and parenting, are undeniable. These links provide the rationale and urgency for social workers to 'think housing'[3] when assessing.

(1) Housing condition

2.3 Owner-occupiers are responsible for maintaining the condition of their housing though they can access advice from local authorities and may, in limited circumstances, have access to assistance in the form of a grant, particularly in cases where the work to the house involves adapting it in light of disability.[4]

Obligations are imposed on all landlords, whether in the private, voluntary or public sector, to repair rented houses.[5] In this context the public sector consists mainly of houses let by local authorities and, in the voluntary sector, by housing associations.

There is a general common law duty imposed on landlords to keep premises wind and watertight and in a proper tenantable condition. An example of breach of this duty is *McArdle v City of Glasgow District Council*,[6] where a tenant successfully sued the landlord for damages for loss arising as a result of chronic dampness in the flat.

There are also a number of statutory obligations relating to repairs imposed on landlords, the precise content of which depends on whether the tenancy is in the private or public sector. As will be seen the obligations are similar, but not identical.

For most private sector tenancies, the landlord is responsible for ensuring that premises reach a standard described as the 'repairing standard.' This duty has two components:[7]

(a) The premises must meet this standard at the start of the tenancy and the landlord has an obligation to inspect the premises before the start of the tenancy to identify any work which needs to be

2 G and J Stewart, *Social Work and Housing* (Macmillan, 1993), p 22.
3 *Social Work and Housing*, p 21.
4 There may also be an entitlement to assistance if adaptation of the home is required under the terms of the Chronically Sick and Disabled Persons Act 1970, see **6.5**.
5 Housing (Scotland) Act 2006, Ch 4, The Repairing Standard (2006 Act).
6 *McArdle v City of Glasgow* 1989 SCLR 19.
7 2006 Act, s 14(1).

done.[8] The scope of this first component is not entirely clear, under previous legislation the view was taken that the landlord's duty could be breached by the presence of latent defects, that is, defects which would not necessarily be discovered by inspection.[9] It remains to be seen whether the same view will be taken under the current legislation.

(b) The premises must continue to meet the repairing standard during the currency of the tenancy. The landlord's duty to carry out work to ensure that this is the case is only triggered by notification to the landlord of the need for work (or the landlord becoming aware of this need). Any work must be carried out within a reasonable time of the landlord being notified (or becoming aware). The landlord's obligation to repair does not extend to damage caused by improper use of the premises or to destruction or damage caused by fire, storm or flood.[10]

The 'repairing standard' has a number of components:[11]

(a) The house must be wind and watertight and suitable for human habitation. 'If the state of repair of a house is such that by ordinary use [i.e. occupation] damage may naturally be caused to the occupier, either in respect of personal injury to life or limb or injury to health, then the house is not in all respects reasonably fit for human habitation.'[12] A defect in any part of the house which could cause injury or injury to health in normal use will be enough to render the whole house unfit for human habitation.[13]

(b) The structure and exterior of the house, including any drains and external pipes, must be in a reasonable state of repair (taking into account the age of the house and the locality) and in proper working order.[14]

(c) The water, gas and electricity supply, heating system, sanitation and water heater must be in proper working order and in a reasonable state of repair.[15]

8 2006 Act, s 19.

9 *Todd v Clapperton* 2009 SLT 837.

10 2006 Act, s 14(1).

11 2006 Act, s 13.

12 *Summers v Salford Corporation* [1943] AC 283, per Lord Atkin at 289.

13 For example, in *Morrison v Stirling District Council* 1996 Hous LR 5, even though some rooms in the house, including the kitchen, living room and a bedroom, were not affected by severe dampness, the severe dampness in other rooms rendered the whole house unfit for human habitation.

14 2006 Act, s 13(1)(b).

15 2006 Act, s 13(1)(c).

(d) Any furnishings provided by the landlord must be capable of being used safely for the purpose for which they are designed.[16]

(e) There must be satisfactory smoke detectors, fire alarms and carbon monoxide detectors in the house.[17]

The landlord must also ensure that there are regular electrical safety inspections.[18]

The landlord's obligations cannot be contracted out of by the terms of the lease without the agreement of landlord, tenant and the sheriff,[19] and tenants must be provided with information about the landlord's obligations.

If the landlord does not fulfil their obligations to maintain and repair the house the tenant can apply to the First-tier Tribunal for Scotland (Housing and Property Chamber)[20] which may make a repairing standard enforcement order requiring the landlord to carry out work so that the obligations are met.[21] In addition, the Tribunal may make a rent relief order reducing the amount of rent payable during the period that the landlord was in breach of their obligations.[22]

In the public sector the landlord's repairing obligation is similar,[23] though less detailed (in part reflecting the fact that most public sector tenancies are unfurnished). The landlord must inspect the house prior to the start of the tenancy and must ensure that:

(a) the house is wind and watertight and in all respects fit for human habitation at the start of the tenancy; and

(b) the house in such a condition throughout the tenancy, this duty to carry out work during the tenancy being triggered by notice to the landlord.

Public sector tenants also have limited powers to have repairs carried out themselves. [24] Tenants may have repairs carried out if their landlord fails to do them and may recover the costs and a small compensation payment from the landlord. This power arises only in respect of a limited list of repairs, including blocked drains, loss of electrical power

16 2006 Act, s 13(1)(e).

17 CMOX-Housing Scotland Act 2014, s 22. Fire safety: The Building Scotland (Amendment) Regulations 2022, SSI/136, strengthened existing provisions in response to the Grenfell Tower fire of June 2017.

18 2006 Act, s 19A.

19 2006 Act, ss 17 and 18.

20 2006 Act, s 22; as amended by Housing (Scotland) Act 2014, s 25.

21 2006 Act, s 24(1).

22 2006 Act, s 27. The maximum reduction is 90%.

23 Housing (Scotland) Act 2001, s 27 and Sch 4.

24 Scottish Secure Tenants (Right to Repair) Regulations 2002, SSI 2002/316, reg 3.

and insecure doors and windows, and then only if the landlord fails to carry out repairs within a specified time after being notified (usually one day).[25]

In both public and private sector tenancies, where the landlord is responsible for the maintenance and repair of the premises they must take reasonable care in carrying out repairs to prevent danger to people coming into the premises. *Hughes' Tutrix v Glasgow District Council*[26] is an example where a mother successfully sued for damages for her daughter who was injured on a defective toilet bowl. Tenants may also be able to take action against a landlord if the state of the property amounts to a statutory nuisance, essentially where it is no longer tolerable to live there because of the condition of the property.[27]

In addition to the statutory and common law responsibilities other obligations may be imposed on the landlord in the lease of the property. If the landlord fails in carrying out any of their repairing obligations the tenant has several remedies. In addition to the rights set out above, the tenant may, unless this is excluded by the lease, withhold their rent. They may take legal action against the landlord for damages or for an order requiring the landlord to meet their obligations. Where the tenant withholds rent, all arrears must be repaid when the landlord fixes the defect.[28]

Councils have power to take action against properties which are in disrepair or which are dangerous to health. They may, of course, be reluctant to use these powers where they own the property.

In addition to these specific statutory provisions about housing condition, the condition of a house may be such that the rights of the occupier under Article 8 of the European Convention on Human Rights and the Human Rights Act 1998, s 6, are being infringed.[29] Where the authority does not provide the housing itself, the duty will only arise where it is, or ought to be, aware of the conditions in which the occupier is living.[30]

Accommodation may become unsuitable for the tenant due to personal changes. Should a tenant become disabled or experience deterioration in their mobility, and no longer be able to access the property, the property

25 Scottish Secure Tenants (Right to Repair) Regulations 2002, reg 10 and Sch 1.

26 *Hughes' Tutrix v Glasgow District Council* 1982 SLT (Sh Ct) 70.

27 Environmental Protection Act 1990, s 82. Litigants may meet with limited success: *Quinn v Monklands DC* 1995 SCLR 393.

28 Subject to what is said about reduction of rent at n 21 above.

29 See, for example, *Lee v Leeds City Council* [2002] EWCA Civ 6, *Bernard v London Borough of Enfield* [2002] EWHC 2282 (Admin).

30 2006 Act, s 35.

may no longer be suitable. In such cases the tenant will have the right to apply to the landlord for permission to carry out alterations to the house to make it more suitable.[31] Any refusal of consent by the landlord must be reasonable and will have to take account of the prohibition on discriminating on the grounds of disability. In public sector tenancies any work can be carried out with the landlord's consent and the tenant may be entitled to compensation for improvements to the house.[32]

In the private sector the tenant may carry out works which the tenant considers necessary for the accommodation, welfare, or employment of any disabled person who occupies or intends to occupy the house as their sole or main residence.[33] The scope of these provisions means that the alterations need not be restricted to, for example, making the accommodation accessible to someone with a mobility impairment, but also extending or adapting the accommodation to enable a carer to live there. Some assistance may be available to the tenant in carrying out any work under the Scottish Government's Care and Repair initiative, and this may include access to grants.[34] Assistance may also be available under the Chronically Sick and Disabled Persons Act 1970. Section 2 of the 1970 Act provides that the local authority must, providing other requirements are met,[35] provide assistance in arranging for the carrying out of adaptations to a person's home or the provision of any additional facilities 'designed to secure his greater safety, comfort or security'.[36]

Social workers have limited mandatory duties in relation to people whose assessed needs relate to the condition of their accommodation other than under the general umbrella of the duty to promote social welfare contained in section 12 of the Social Work (Scotland) Act 1968. However, a social worker may be well placed to advise the service user what legal obligations fall to the landlord and what remedies fall to the tenant.

Using the legal knowledge available to inform social work practice can contribute to the empowerment of the service user in arranging, for example, for repairs to be completed. It may well be agreed that the social worker becomes actively involved taking on the role of liaison or advocate with the housing authority, while continuing to support the

31 2006 Act,, s 52.
32 Housing (Scotland) Act 2001, s 30.
33 2006 Act, s 52(2)(a), factors which may be considered by the landlord in deciding whether to give consent are set out in s 53.
34 2006 Act, ss 71–73; Housing (Scotland) Act 2006 (Scheme of Assistance) Regulations 2008, SSI 2008/406.
35 Chronically Sick and Disabled Persons Act 1970. See also **6.5**.
36 Chronically Sick and Disabled Persons Act 1970, s 2(1)(e).

service user through what may well be experienced as a very stressful situation.[37]

(2) Eviction

2.4 Most tenants enjoy some statutory protection against eviction. This takes two forms: first the landlord cannot remove the tenant without first obtaining an order either from the sheriff court, for public sector tenancies, or, in the case of all private sector tenancies, from the First-tier Tribunal for Scotland (Housing and Property Chamber).[38] In either case the tenant will need to be given some form of notice that an application for such an order is to be made. These requirements are discussed more fully below. The other form of protection is a restriction on the grounds on which an order can be made to remove a tenant from rented property. The nature of this last form of protection will depend on the nature of the tenancy. In the private sector, tenants may have an assured tenancy, a short-assured tenancy,[39] a private residential tenancy (all new tenancies after 1 December 2017 are of this type), or may be common law tenants. This last group includes tenants of resident landlords or of educational establishments, and they enjoy very limited protection, the landlord does not have to establish any particular grounds to remove such tenants.

Short assured tenants also enjoy limited protection, it is sufficient to evict such tenants that the period of the lease has expired (provided the landlord has satisfied certain procedural requirements). A further group which enjoys very limited protection against removal (either in the private or public sectors) are those who live in hostel accommodation.[40]

From 1 December 2017 all new tenancies have been private residential tenancies.[41] Assured and short assured tenancies in existence at that date have continued, though there is provision for the landlord and the tenant to agree to convert the tenancy to a private residential tenancy.[42] This new type of tenancy, as well as providing some security of tenure (and

37 Local authorities as corporate bodies are also expected to provide housing advice as appropriate, see COSLA/Scottish Government, *Housing Options Guidance* (2016).

38 Private Housing (Tenancies) (Scotland) Act 2016, s 51.

39 A short-assured tenancy is a tenancy for a fixed period of six months or more and the tenant must be served a notice that the tenancy is a short-assured tenancy before the start of the tenancy.

40 *Conway v Glasgow City Council* 1999 SCLR 248.

41 See Private Housing (Tenancies) (Scotland) Act 2016.

42 Housing (Scotland) Act 1988, s 46A.

being unlimited in duration), reintroduces an element of rent control[43] into the private sector. The landlord can only increase the rent once a year,[44] and a rent-increase notice can be referred to a rent officer. The rent officer has the power to set a rent different from that specified in the notice, though their decision can be appealed against.[45] Provision is also made for the Scottish Government to designate rent pressure zones, and in such zones there will be a limit on the level of permitted rent increases.[46]

Public sector tenants will normally have a Scottish secure tenancy.[47] Some tenants may have a short Scottish secure tenancy.[48] The latter type of tenancy enjoys less protection (the tenant can be evicted simply on the basis that the period of the let has expired) and can only be used in limited circumstances. Examples are temporary lets to intentionally homeless people, and cases where the tenant, or somebody living with them, is subject to an Antisocial Behaviour Order (ASBO).[49] It is possible for the short tenancy to be converted into an ordinary secure tenancy.[50] A secure tenancy can be converted into a short secure tenancy if the tenant or anyone living with them is made subject to an ASBO.[51]

Where a tenant has an assured tenancy, a secure tenancy, or a private residential tenancy, the effect is that an order for possession will only be granted on certain restricted grounds, such as non-payment of rent or causing a nuisance to neighbours.[52] In the private sector, some of these

43 Though tenants under a short-assured tenancy and a statutory assured tenancy (after the contract for an assured tenancy has come to an end) can refer any proposed rent increase to the First-tier Tribunal.

44 Private Housing (Tenancies) (Scotland) Act 2016, Part 4, s 19, as amended by the Cost of Living (Tenant Protection) (Scotland) Act 2022, Sch. 1

45 Private Housing (Tenancies) (Scotland) Act 2016, Part 4, s 28, as amended by the Cost of Living (Tenant Protection) (Scotland) Act 2022, Sch. 1

46 Private Housing (Tenancies) (Scotland) Act 2016, ch 3. See www.mygov.scot/rent-pressure-zone-checker/.

47 Housing (Scotland) Act 2014, ss 12–15.

48 Housing (Scotland) Act 2014, ss 7–11.

49 Housing (Scotland) Act 2014, s 7.

50 Housing (Scotland) Act 2014, s 10, amending Housing (Scotland) Act 2001, s 35.

51 Housing (Scotland) Act 2001, s 35. Note: The Domestic Abuse (Protection) (Scotland) Act 2021, s 22 amended the 2001 Act, providing for the removal of a tenancy from an individual who engaged in abusive behaviour directed at their partner. The Act intended that the abusive partner be removed from the tenancy allowing the landlord to reach a new tenancy agreement with the person who had suffered the abuse and who remained living in the property. At the date of writing these provisions of the Domestic Abuse (Protection) (Scotland) Act 2021 await a date for commencement and are not yet in force.

52 Housing (Scotland) Act 2001, Prt 2, Ch 1.

grounds are mandatory, that is, the Tribunal must grant an order for eviction if the ground is established.[53]

Before a landlord can start proceedings to remove a tenant it will be necessary to serve certain notices on the tenant. There are statutory forms for such notices which require, for example, that they contain advice on possible sources of advice and assistance for the tenant, there are also certain required periods of notice, the minimum period of notice which can be given is 28 days and, in many cases, it must be longer than this. If the notices served do not comply with these requirements, then they cannot be relied on in proceedings for eviction.[54] The forms are:

(a) Common law tenants must be served with a notice to quit.
(b) Assured and short assured tenants must always be served with a notice of intention to raise an action for possession, and in most cases will also have to be served with a notice to quit.
(c) Private residential tenants must be served with a notice to leave.[55]
(d) In the public sector a notice of intention to start proceedings must be served not only on the tenant, but also on any 'qualifying occupier.'[56] Qualifying occupiers include any member of the tenant's family aged 16 or over and any lodger living in the accommodation with the consent of the landlord. It is not clear what effect failure to serve a notice on a qualifying occupier is once an order for removal has been granted.[57]
(e) In all cases the landlord (other than a local authority landlord) must notify the local authority of the raising of proceedings against the tenant.[58]

In many cases a sheriff (in the case of public sector tenants) or the Tribunal (private sector tenants) has the power to adjourn the hearing. This power might be used, for example, to allow payment of arrears of rent or to allow a 'bad neighbour' to mend their ways. It is an offence for a private sector landlord to evict someone with an assured or short assured tenancy without following the correct legal procedure or to harass a tenant into leaving accommodation.[59] In both cases the tenant has a right to damages assessed on the difference in value between the house without the tenant and its value with a sitting tenant.[60] This can

53 Private Housing (Tenancies) (Scotland) Act 2016, s 51.
54 Housing (Scotland) Act 2001, ss 18 and 36.
55 Private Housing (Tenancies) (Scotland) Act 2016, s 50.
56 Housing (Scotland) Act 2001, s 14.
57 Housing (Scotland) Act 2001, s 14(6).
58 Homelessness etc (Scotland) Act 2003, s 11, Notice to Local Authorities (Scotland) Regulations 2008, SSI 2008/324.
59 Rent (Scotland) Act 1984, ss 22 and 23.
60 Housing (Scotland) Act 1988, ss 36 and 37.

amount to a substantial sum.[61] Where the correct procedure is not used in a private residential tenancy, the tenant can apply for a wrongful termination order which involves a payment to the tenant of up to six months' rent.[62]

If possible, the social worker should help the service user identify the type of tenancy or facilitate the service user getting this information from a specialist agency or solicitor. This will, of course, influence which set of statutory procedures and protections apply. The process of possible eviction is potentially extremely stressful and if a social worker is involved with the person/family threatened with eviction there are a number of things which may prove helpful in diminishing unnecessary stress. For example, it may help the person/family to learn that the notice means that there are at least 28 days before the council (or other landlord) can apply for eviction and that they cannot be removed until such an order has been made. If the notice given to the service user is not in the statutory form designed for this purpose it will be invalid.

The social worker should advise the service user not to leave their home unless alternative accommodation is already available and they want to leave. They should further advise their client to seek legal advice under the legal advice and assistance scheme.[63] The social worker should also advise their client to attend the hearing, where, in the case of private sector tenants, they can be assisted by a supporter. Tenants who attend the hearing or are represented at the hearing are less likely to be evicted.

Local authorities have a general obligation to provide housing advice and, as mentioned below, prevent homelessness. This advice may be provided under the banner of Housing Options.[64]

(3) Homelessness

2.5 The law on homelessness and local authority duties is in Part II of the Housing (Scotland) Act 1987 (the 1987 Act) and the Homelessness etc. (Scotland) Act 2003 which operate in conjunction

61 In *Tagro v Cafane* [1991] 2 All ER 235, damages were assessed at £31,000.

62 Private Housing (Tenancies) (Scotland) Act 2016, ss 57–59.

63 See **1.62**. Social workers may become involved with those who are threatened with eviction as a result of the obligation placed on landlords to notify the local authority of possession proceedings.

64 COSLA/Scottish Government, *Housing Options Guidance* (2016).

with a Code of Guidance (the Code) issued to local authorities by the Scottish Government.[65]

The Code is not binding on authorities or on the courts, but it may be taken into account in any proceedings for judicial review of a decision taken by a local authority in this area. The Code emphasises the importance of considering the individual circumstances of each case.

When someone who claims to be homeless approaches a housing authority for assistance the first obligation on the authority is to carry out initial inquiries. These may involve a request for information from the social work department. The code suggests that these inquiries should be completed in 28 days. The inquiries are directed towards answering three questions:

(a) Is the applicant homeless or threatened with homelessness?
(b) Is the applicant in this position intentionally?
(c) Does the applicant have a local connection with the authority dealing with the application?

If the authority has reason to believe that the applicant is homeless, the authority must provide temporary accommodation while these inquiries are being carried out. Where the person being provided with such accommodation is pregnant, a member of their household is pregnant, or the applicant has dependent children, this accommodation must be suitable.[66] Examples of features which would make accommodation unsuitable are: it is outwith the local authority area; inadequate toilet or washing facilities; no adequate cooking facilities; there is not 24-hour access to the accommodation; no ready access to health or educational provision; the accommodation is not suitable for occupation by children.[67] However, where accommodation is suitable for children an applicant can be placed in accommodation which is otherwise unsuitable if:

65 Scottish Government, *Homelessness: Code of Guidance, 2019,* supplemented by: Scottish Government and COSLA, *Prevention of Homelessness Guidance* (2009), Scottish Government, *Guidance for Local Authorities on Regulation 5 of the Homeless Persons (Provision of Non-permanent Accommodation) (Scotland) Regulations 2010* (2010) Scottish Government, *Meeting the Best Interests of Children Facing Homelessness* (2011) and Scottish Government, *Guidance for Local Authorities Published June 2013 Housing Support Duty to Those Found to be Homeless or Threatened With Homelessness – Amendment to Housing (Scotland) Act 1987 (inserted by Housing (Scotland) Act 2010)* (2013).

66 Homeless Persons (Unsuitable Accommodation) (Scotland) Order 2014, SSI 2014/243, reg 3.

67 Homeless Persons (Unsuitable Accommodation) (Scotland) Order 2014, regs 4 and 5.

(a) they express a wish to go there (e.g., for family reasons) despite the availability of suitable accommodation, or

(b) the local authority believes that the applicant may be homeless or threatened with homelessness as a result of an emergency, such as flood, fire or other disaster.[68]

(a) Is the applicant homeless or threatened with homelessness?

2.6 A person is homeless for the purpose of the 1987 Act if one of the following three conditions is satisfied:

(a) *If there is no accommodation in Great Britain that he/she is legally entitled to occupy together with his/her family or any other person it is reasonable for him/her to live with.*[69] This means, for example, that if a family unit has no accommodation that they can occupy together then they will be homeless. The reference to another person with whom it is reasonable for an applicant to live could extend to a carer, and the applicant would be regarded as homeless if there was no accommodation which could be occupied together with the carer.

(b) *If accommodation is available, but it is not reasonable for him/her to continue living there.*[70] Local housing conditions will be relevant in considering whether it is reasonable for an applicant to continue to live in the accommodation. The Code gives examples of accommodation in which it would not be reasonable for a person to remain, these include; housing which is below the tolerable standard (for example, it is badly affected by damp, or has no bath/shower, is structurally unstable, or has an outside toilet), though reasonableness might depend on why the accommodation is below the tolerable standard; bed and breakfast accommodation; short-stay hostel accommodation; accommodation where there is external violence, including racial or other harassment; where continued occupation would pose a substantial risk to health (including mental health); or accommodation which is impracticable for the applicant to occupy because of their impairment(s). The Code also makes the point that possession of an order under the Matrimonial Homes (Family Protection) (Scotland) Act 1981 guaranteeing occupation

68 Homeless Persons (Unsuitable Accommodation) (Scotland) Order 2014, regs 5 and 6.

69 Housing (Scotland) Act 1987, s 24, as amended by Housing (Scotland) Act 2001.

70 Housing (Scotland) Act 1987, s 24, as amended by Housing (Scotland) Act 2001.

or an interdict against abuse or harassment is not, by itself, enough to make continued occupation reasonable.[71]

(c) *If accommodation is available to the person but* one of the following conditions also applies: [72]
   (i) they cannot gain entry to the property; or
   (ii) occupying the property would probably lead to abuse,[73] or threats of abuse whether or not from someone who has previously shared accommodation with the applicant, wherever that sharing may have taken place; or
   (iii) the accommodation is a houseboat or mobile home but there is no mooring or pitching place available, or
   (iv) it is overcrowded as defined in the Housing (Scotland) Act 1987[74] and may endanger the health of the occupants; or
   (v) the accommodation is temporary accommodation and before the applicant moved into it the local authority had a duty under the homelessness legislation to provide them with permanent accommodation.

A person is threatened with homelessness if they are likely to become homeless within the next two months.

(b) Is the applicant in this position intentionally?

2.7 For an applicant to be intentionally homeless the following conditions must be satisfied:[75]

(a) The applicant must deliberately have done or failed to do something as a result of which occupation of available accommodation ceased. An example is deliberate failure to pay rent or a mortgage resulting in eviction.[76] There must be a clear causal connection between the act or omission on the part of the applicant and the homelessness. It must be the applicant who is responsible for the deliberate act or omission. The actions of one member of a family

71 See **3.30** onwards.
72 Housing (Scotland) Act 1987, s 24(3).
73 'Abuse' in this context includes violence, harassment, threatening conduct, and any other conduct giving rise, or likely to give rise, to physical or mental injury, fear, alarm or distress, Housing (Scotland) Act 1987, s 24(3)(b), (bb), Protection from Abuse (Scotland) Act 2001, s 7.
74 Sections 135–137. This consists of a room standard which is contravened if two people of opposite sex over the age of ten who are not married have to share accommodation and a space standard which provides, for example, that a three-room house is overcrowded if more than five people over the age of ten live there.
75 Housing (Scotland) Act 1987, s 26.
76 Though the Code indicates that, where failure is due to real personal or financial difficulties, this should not result in a finding of intentional homelessness.

which might lead to that person being regarded as intentionally homeless do not necessarily mean that if another member of the family applies for housing that other family member will be so regarded, particularly if the applicant had not been aware of or had not acquiesced in the other person's actions, for example non-payment of rent.

(b) It must be reasonable to have expected the applicant to remain in the accommodation. The considerations as to reasonableness discussed above apply also here.

(c) The applicant must have been aware of the consequences of their action, so an act done in ignorance of a relevant fact will not be significant. *Wincentzen v Monklands District Council*[77] illustrates this. In this case a young woman left home temporarily despite her father's warning, which she did not believe, that she would not be allowed to return. When she returned her father refused her access to the house. The Court of Session decided that she was not intentionally homeless as, when she left home, she had acted in good faith and in ignorance of the relevant fact that her father meant what he said.[78]

2.8 The Code suggests that a victim of domestic violence should never be regarded as intentionally homeless, nor should failure to exercise occupancy rights under the Matrimonial Homes (Family Protection) (Scotland) Act 1981 on its own be taken to indicate intentional homelessness. The Code also notes that in considering applications by young people the local authority should consider the position sensitively. Failed tenancies are common when young people first leave home, and the local authority should not automatically consider a young person who has left home because of a clash of lifestyle with their parents as intentionally homeless.[79] Finally, the Code notes that: 'Whether or not someone is found to be intentionally homeless the local authority should seek to find solutions to the person's homelessness and offer support to address any difficulties that they face.'[80]

The same considerations are relevant in deciding whether someone threatened with homelessness is in that position intentionally. The status of intentionally homeless is not immutable: it can be reviewed as circumstances change and time passes

77 1988 SC 329.
78 *Wincentzen v Monklands District Council* 1988 SC 329.
79 Scottish Government, *Homelessness: Code of Guidance*, paras 6.19–6.20.
80 *Code of Guidance*, para 6.3

The concept of intentional homelessness was one of the compromises accepted during the passing of the 1987 Act.[81] It was designed to reduce the demands for housing on local authorities by giving them a ground for refusing permanent accommodation. The Homelessness etc. (Scotland) Act 2003 section 4 made inquiries into intentionality optional rather than mandatory, as in the 1987 Act.[82]

(c) Does the applicant have a local connection with the authority dealing with the application?

2.9 A local connection is a connection arising from voluntary residence,[83] from employment, from family connections or from other special circumstances.[84] The issue of local connection is relevant only if the applicant is not intentionally homeless. The question the local authority must answer is: does the applicant have a local connection with the authority processing their application?[85] If the answer is yes, then that authority must comply with the housing duty set out below. If the answer is no, a further question arises: does the applicant have a local connection with another area in Great Britain? If the answer to this is yes, the applicant's case can be notified to the authority for that area. The exception to this arises where there is evidence that the applicant might be at risk of domestic abuse if housed by this second authority.[86] Should no local connection exist with another area, the duties outlined below fall on the council receiving the application.

If the notified authority accepts that there is a local connection and no risk of domestic abuse, the obligation to secure housing rest with that authority. If this obligation is not accepted, the duty remains with the notifying authority, which, in any event, has a duty to provide temporary housing while this decision is made. Note that the legislation refers to a

81 Housing (Scotland) Act 1987.

82 Homelessness etc. (Scotland) Act 2003, s 4, amending Housing (Scotland) Act 1987, s 28(2).

83 An asylum seeker placed by the National Asylum Support Service would not be considered to be living in the area where they are placed as a result of their own choice: Housing (Scotland) Act 1987, s 27(2)(iii), see *Al-Ameri v Kensington and Chelsea Royal London Borough Council* [2004] UKHL 159. The ability to modify the power to notify another authority exists in an amendment to the Housing (Scotland) Act 1987 contained in the Homelessness etc. (Scotland) Act 2003, s 8.

84 The Code suggests (paras 7.11–7.18.) that this might include the need to continue education or medical treatment in the area.

85 Scottish Government, Homelessness *Code of Guidance*, Chapter 7.

86 *Code of Guidance*, para 7.10

local connection in Great Britain: a local connection with somewhere in Northern Ireland would therefore be irrelevant.[87]

(d) Local authority duties following determination of an application

2.10 Once the authority has carried out its investigation and answered these questions it must notify the applicant of its decision and the reasons for it. The notification must be clear and contain a full explanation of the reasons for the decision and of what happens next.[88] Regardless of the decision the authority will have a duty to provide some form of assistance to the applicant. The nature of that assistance will depend on how the questions have been answered:

(a) The authority has a duty to take reasonable steps to ensure that accommodation does not cease to become available to the applicant where they are threatened with homelessness but this is not intentional. For other categories of those threatened with homelessness the authority has a duty to provide advice and assistance.[89]

(b) It has a duty to secure that permanent accommodation[90] becomes available to an applicant who is not intentionally homeless. This obligation is only to secure the provision of accommodation: the actual provision may be done by someone other than the housing authority.[91] Any accommodation provided must not be overcrowded, must not pose a threat to the health of the occupants. It must meet any special needs of the applicant or a person who might reasonably be expected to live with the applicant, and must be reasonable for the applicant to occupy. The Code notes that, technically, the local authority's obligation could be met by

87 *Code of Guidance*, para 7.20.

88 *Code of Guidance*, Chapter 10.

89 *Code of Guidance*, Chapter 9.

90 Usually a Scottish secure tenancy or private tenancy, though in some cases the duty can be fulfilled by providing a short-assured tenancy. In other cases, the level of housing support required by the applicant may make permanent accommodation inappropriate. See Homeless Persons (Provision of Non-Permanent Accommodation) (Scotland) Regulations 2010, SSI 2010/2; Scottish Government, *Guidance for Local Authorities on Regulation 5 of the Homeless Persons (Provision of Non-Permanent Accommodation) (Scotland) Regulations 2010* (2010). Where an applicant is determined to be homeless because of the condition and/or size of their current accommodation the local authority can leave the applicant in that accommodation for a short (but not indefinite) period while alternative accommodation is secured, *Birmingham City Council v Ali* [2009] UKHL 36.

91 In some cases, the housing authority will control no housing stock of its own.

making a single offer of accommodation which satisfied these requirements but advises that a homeless applicant should be treated in the same way as any other applicant for local authority housing in terms of entitlement to offers.[92]

(c) Where the duty under (b) above arises or where an authority has the duty described under (a) to take reasonable steps to ensure that accommodation does not cease to be available, the authority may also have a duty to assess the applicant (and anyone living with them) with a view to deciding whether they have a need for housing support services.[93] In this context, housing support services include:[94] assistance with or advice about personal budgeting or welfare benefit claims; assisting with engagement with others with an interest in the person's welfare; advice and assistance in understanding and managing tenancy rights; and advice and assistance to settle in to a new tenancy. The duty to assess will only arise where the authority has reason to believe that the applicant may be in need of these services.[95] Triggers for having such a reason to believe that this is the case include age, history of repeat homelessness, substance misuse and health issues.[96]

(d) In cases not covered by (b) the local authority has a duty to secure the provision of accommodation for the applicant for such a period as will give the applicant a reasonable opportunity to secure permanent accommodation.[97] The local authority must also provide the applicant with advice[98] and assistance in attempting to secure accommodation. The Code indicates that what a 'reasonable opportunity' means will depend, at least to some extent, on the characteristics of the applicant. It also indicates that where advice and assistance have been offered but it has not been possible to identify a housing option for the applicant, then the

92 *Code of Guidance,* para 8. 58.

93 Housing (Scotland) Act 1987, s 32B, Housing Support Services (Homelessness) (Scotland) Regulations 2012, SSI 2012/331. See also Scottish Government, *Guidance for Local Authorities Published June 2013 Housing Support Duty to Those Found to be Homeless or Threatened with Homelessness – Amendment to Housing (Scotland) Act 1987 (inserted by Housing (Scotland) Act 2010)* (2013).

94 Housing Support Services (Homelessness) (Scotland) Regulations 2012, SSI 2012/331, reg 2(1).

95 *Code of Guidance*, Chapter 8.

96 See also Scottish Government, *Guidance for Local Authorities Published June 2013 Housing Support Duty to Those Found to be Homeless or Threatened with Homelessness – Amendment to Housing (Scotland) Act 1987 (inserted by Housing (Scotland) Act 2010)* (2013), para 31.

97 *Code of Guidance*, 8.40.

98 See also COSLA/Scottish Government, *Housing Options Guidance* (2016).

applicant cannot be deemed to have had a reasonable opportunity to secure accommodation.[99]

(e) Challenging decisions

2.11 There is no statutory provision for appeal against any of the decisions a local authority may take in processing an application by someone who is homeless or threatened with homelessness. Instead, there is a right to have the decision reviewed within the local authority.[100] This right to review also extends to decisions about housing support assessments or services. The only way of challenging these decisions is by seeking judicial review of them in the Court of Session.[101]

(f) The social work role

2.12 The Morris Committee emphasised that homelessness was an area in which 'there is an overwhelming need for effective co-operation between the two services [social work and housing]'.[102] The importance of co-operation is further stressed in the code of guidance which identifies a role for social work in, for example, the initial inquiries, in preventing arrears and evictions, and in providing support for rehoused families.[103]

There is considerable pressure on housing resources and the housing application and allocation process can be highly bureaucratic. It may well be that the social worker, with the agreement of the service user, takes an active role in assisting the service user with an application and in being supportive throughout the process. Prevention of homelessness is clearly preferable to dealing with the trauma associated with having already lost one's home, and a thorough assessment while co-operating with housing authorities is clearly the key in this respect. There is specific guidance on preventing homelessness, though there is little direct mention of the social work role in this.[104] In addition, social

99 *Code of Guidance*, para 8.35.
100 *Code of Guidance*, para 10.13.
101 *Code of Guidance*, para 10.26.
102 *Housing and Social Work: A Joint Approach* (1995, SDD), para 8.2.
103 *Code of Guidance*, Chapter 9.
104 Scottish Government, *Statutory Guidance for Local Authorities on Preventing Homelessness* (2009). Though a report in 2005 (Communities Scotland, *Thematic Study: Evictions in Practice*) said little about social work involvement and concluded that: 'In many cases, joint working between housing management and arrears staff and services such as housing benefit, homelessness, support and social work services happened too infrequently and too late to prevent eviction.' (p 4).

workers may become involved at the stage where a client is threatened with eviction.

Accommodation provided, particularly temporary accommodation, can prove to be an additional source of anxiety and stress for people and so further warrant the involvement of a social worker. Particular difficulties for families centre on 'first, acccss to mainstream services particularly education, health services and social security benefits; and secondly, personal health and safety'.[105]

Through the provision of a comprehensive initial inquiry report, the social worker may provide relevant information highlighting the factors which are significant in determining the service user's eligibility. Some of these include availability of suitable accommodation, reasons for threatened homelessness or homelessness, responsibility for dependent persons, presence of persons vulnerable through various risks, emergency conditions, pregnancy, and local connection. In light of the decision in *Kelly v Monklands District Council*[106] that housing authorities must take social work reports and information into account in deciding on an application, social workers clearly can play an important part in the process by providing information about and advocating for a service user.

(g) Conclusion

2.13 It should be noted that the statutory framework guiding housing authorities is just that, a framework. It is therefore clearly the case that local authorities retain considerable discretion. Some authorities will simply provide the bare minimum; others will go beyond their strict statutory obligations and provide a more generous service for homeless people. For this reason, knowledge of how the policy is operated by particular authorities is of as much practical importance as an understanding of the legal framework.

DEBT RECOVERY

(1) Court actions

2.14 Generally speaking, the process of debt recovery must be initiated by court action. In the vast majority of cases the action will

105 G and J Stewart, *Social Work and Housing* (1993), p 87.
106 1986 SLT 165. See also *Wilson v Nithsdale District Council* 1992 SLT 1131.

be raised in the sheriff court and will use the simple procedure which is available for claims up to £5,000. This procedure is intended to be much more informal and an individual can be represented by someone other than a solicitor at all stages of the process and can have the assistance of a courtroom supporter to, as the rules describe it, 'provide quiet support, encouragement and advice during a hearing'.[107]

Once someone who is owed money (the creditor) has initiated action by serving a claim form, there are four courses of action open to the person who, it is claimed, owes the money (the debtor). The person can:

(a) dispute the claim or part of it. This would be appropriate if there was a dispute about the amount owed or the quality of goods or services supplied. In order to dispute the claim, the appropriate option in the response form which accompanies the claim form should be chosen.[108] Additional information about the reasons for disputing the claim also has to be provided. Failure to return this form, indicating an intention to dispute the claim, will allow the creditor to apply to the sheriff for an order in their favour;

(b) apply for time to pay, permitting payment by instalments or as a lump sum at some future date. Again, the relevant form must be returned to court with details of the proposal for repayment.[109] If the creditor objects to the repayment proposals they will have to be considered by a court hearing;

(c) do nothing. The result of this is that the creditor will be able to apply for a decision in their favour which will require payment of the whole amount, though even at this stage, after a decision against them, the debtor can still seek time to pay;

(d) pay the debt.

Following the granting of a decision in their favour, the creditor may still decide to write off the debt if there is no realistic hope of payment. Once a decision for the payment of money has been granted in favour of a creditor and they decide to pursue repayment, there are a number of courses of action (collectively known as 'diligence') open to the creditor if payment is still not forthcoming. The main forms of diligence are: attachment; arrestment; and arrestment of earnings. Even after the creditor has embarked on one of these, it is still possible to return to court and seek a time to pay order; such an application can be made after a charge has been served (as a precursor to attachment) or after an arrestment has been executed.[110]

107 Act of Sederunt (Simple Procedure) 2016, SSI 2016/200, Sch 1, Part 2, para 2.5.
108 Act of Sederunt (Simple Procedure) 2016, Sch 1, Part 4.
109 Act of Sederunt (Simple Procedure) 2016, Sch 1, Part 5.
110 Debtors (Scotland) Act 1987, s 5.

(2) Attachment[111]

2.15 There are two types of attachment, depending on whether the goods to be attached are found in a dwellinghouse. If they are not in a dwellinghouse the process involves three stages.[112] First, a charge (or demand for payment) will be served on the debtor, before the creditor does this the debtor must be provided with a debt advice and information package.[113] Second, if payment of the debt is still not made, an attachment will take place.[114] This involves the listing and valuation of the debtor's possessions. There is a short list of items excluded from attachment (which therefore cannot be sold by a creditor) which consists mainly of tools of the trade and money.[115] The debtor can seek to have individual items removed from the attachment. The debtor can also redeem items which have been attached by paying the value given to them. The final stage is sale of the possessions by auction.[116] Any goods not sold are passed to the creditor and the debtor is credited with the value given to them when they were listed plus the sum raised by the sale.[117]

Where the debtor's property is located in a dwellinghouse a different procedure must be followed. An attachment can only take place if an order (an exceptional attachment order) has been granted by the sheriff.[118] Before granting such an order, the sheriff must be satisfied that there are exceptional circumstances (relevant factors include failed attempts to negotiate a settlement and prior use of an arrestment) and must consider whether money advice has been given to the debtor. Thereafter the procedure is similar to that outlined above, except that there is a longer list of excluded items including: clothing, books required for education, medical aids or equipment, toys, and certain items of furniture.[119] The sale must take place away from the house and after an attachment has taken place an application can be made to stop the auction of goods on the grounds that it would be unduly harsh in the circumstances.

111 Debt Arrangement and Attachment (Scotland) Act 2002 (the 2002 Act).
112 2002 Act.
113 2002 Act, Part 1.
114 2002 Act, s 10.
115 2002 Act, s 11. There is separate provision for the attachment of money, Bankruptcy and Diligence (Scotland) Act 2007, Pt 8.
116 2002 Act, s 27.
117 2002 Act, s 31.
118 2002 Act, s 47.
119 2002 Act, Sch 2.

(3) Arrestment[120]

2.16 Arrestment involves the freezing of assets belonging to or owed to the debtor, but which for the time being are in the hands of a third party. A common example would be money in a bank account.[121] The effect of an arrestment is to prevent the third party dealing in any way with the property. For the debtor to have it released, they must raise a separate action known as an action of forthcoming. The effect of this is to order the third party to hand over to the creditor assets to the value owed by the debtor.

(4) Arrestment of earnings[122]

2.17 Arrestment of earnings involves an order to the debtor's employer to pay a part of the debtor's pay to the creditor. The order lasts until the debt is paid. There are statutory restrictions on the amount which can be deducted. There are two forms of arrestment of earnings: the earnings arrestment which covers ordinary debts and arrears of maintenance (that is, payments of periodical allowance or aliment); and current maintenance arrestment to enforce current maintenance payments.

(5) Debt arrangement scheme[123]

2.18 A debt payment programme in effect consolidates all the debts owed by a debtor and prevents diligence being carried out against the debtor whilst it is in force and whilst the debtor complies with its terms. The first stage is that the debtor consults a money adviser. The adviser then seeks to negotiate a debt payment programme with the creditors. This can then be presented to the Debt Arrangement Scheme (DAS) Administrator for approval. Normally the scheme will need the agreement of all of the creditors (though creditors who do not respond will be treated as having agreed), though the Administrator (who is a civil servant) has the power to approve a debt payment without the agreement of all the creditors provided that it is fair and reasonable. In deciding whether it is fair and reasonable the following factors will

120 Debtors (Scotland) Act 1987, Part III.

121 This can include any welfare benefits paid into an account, *North Lanarkshire Council v Crossan* 2007 SLT (Sh Ct) 169.

122 Debtors (Scotland) Act 1987, s 47.

123 Available at: www.aib.gov.uk/debt-arrangement-scheme 23/06/2025 (Accessed April 2026).

be relevant: the total debt, the period of repayment, the comments of the money adviser, the extent of creditors' consent, and the availability of an asset (for example, a house or car) which could be sold to repay the debt.

Once the programme is approved the debtor (or the debtor's employer) will make payments to a payment distributor, who will then distribute the money to creditors as provided for by the programme. Once the programme is approved creditors cannot carry out any diligence against the debtor, nor, in general must they offer the debtor more credit. The debtor also is subject to certain restrictions, they must:

(a) make all payments under a programme as they fall due;
(b) pay a continuing liability when due for payment; continuing liabilities include rent/mortgage payments, utilities bills and hire purchase instalments;
(c) except for a continuing liability, make no payment to a creditor taking part in a programme other than a payment under the programme;
(d) not, except under limited circumstances, apply for or obtain credit;
(e) notify the money adviser for a programme of a change of address or material change of circumstances; and
(f) within 10 days after receipt by the debtor of a written request from the money adviser for the programme, supply the adviser with such information or evidence as the adviser may request in respect of the income, assets or liabilities of the debtor.

It is possible to apply for the programme to be amended. Once the programme is completed, the money adviser must be informed of this by the payment distributor and must in turn inform the DAS Administrator.

(6) Social work contribution

2.19 It is useful to distinguish between debt which is the result of inability to keep up with and pay for essentials like rent and fuel, and debt which is associated with non-essential purchases and commitments. Sometimes the usual coping mechanisms fail. Some people panic and find themselves in a state of crisis. Many go to citizens' advice bureaux and some go to the social work department. Under section 12 of the Social Work (Scotland) Act 1968, social workers are enabled, through the duty to promote social welfare and power, to provide small amounts of money, to become involved with people in debt.[124]

124 The duties to children and families under Children (Scotland) Act 1995, s 17 may also be relevant here. See chapter 4.

Social workers are ideally placed to advise service users about the process of debt recovery. Social workers should remind service users of the following:

(a) that they may be eligible for legal aid;
(b) that they must return the response form to the court if they intend to defend the debt action;
(c) that they may apply for time to make payment toward the debt;
(d) that they may be subject to diligence (attachment and sale of their property or arrestment of assets or earnings);
(e) that only certain items of property are liable to be attached; and
(f) that any surplus money raised in a sale belongs to them; and that only a limited amount of money may be arrested from their earnings.

Social workers may well provide support for families suffering from the stress of these procedures. If the debtor is eligible,[125] it may be possible for the social work department to provide material assistance as well. Families who have defaulted on the payment of rent or mortgages may need advice and guidance about alternative accommodation.[126] Debtors may also be entitled to benefit, about which a social worker might advise them.

DISCRIMINATION

(1) Introduction

2.20 Legislation on discrimination started with the Race Relations Act 1968. This depended on both parties agreeing to the resolution of any dispute and was widely seen as being ineffective. Chronologically, legislation was then passed dealing with equal pay, sex discrimination, race discrimination (repealing the 1968 Act), disability discrimination, discrimination on the grounds of race and ethnic or national origin, discrimination on the grounds of gender reassignment, discrimination on the grounds of religious or other belief, discrimination on the grounds of sexual orientation and discrimination in employment on the grounds of age. All this legislation was replaced by the Equality Act 2010 which provides a single framework covering discrimination on any ground and, in the case of disability, imposes a duty to make reasonable adjustments. Local authorities have both general and specific duties under this legislation and these are considered more fully below.

125 See **1.67**.

126 The requirement to notify the local authority of actions for repossession of rented and mortgaged properties should be noted, see **2.4** above.

The body charged with overseeing the implementation of this legislation is the Equality and Human Rights Commission (EHRC).

(2) Protected characteristics

2.21 The Equality Act 2010 makes it illegal to discriminate against individuals based on one of nine 'protected characteristics'. These protected characteristics are:[127]

(a) Age.

(b) Disability. A disability is any physical or mental impairment having a substantial and long-lasting effect on the ability of a person to carry out normal day-to-day activities.[128] Day-to-day activities are activities which fall into that category for a particular individual rather than being an abstract set of day-to-day activities undertaken by a notional 'normal' person. Therefore, for example, the day-to-day activities undertaken by a deep-sea diver will be very different from those of a social work student. The definition given above is supplemented by others, mainly contained in the first Schedule to the Act. 'Long-term' generally means lasting 12 months or more and an impairment is regarded as affecting the ability to carry out 'day-to-day' activities if it affects, for example, mobility, manual dexterity, speech or perception of physical danger. Regulations provide an additional definition of 'disabled', for example, excluding most drug addictions, disfigurement caused by tattoos and hay fever, but providing that in a case of a child under six the impairment is to be assessed in the context of activities that a child over six would undertake.[129] This means that a very young child is not to be prejudiced just because the child is too young to participate in most of the activities which are used in judging whether a person is disabled. People with progressive

127 The Equality Act 2010, ss 4–12 (the 2010 Act).

128 2010 Act, s 6(1). This definition of 'disability' has been criticised for being medicalised and inconsistent with an individual's perception of themselves as disabled, see Pearson, C & Watson, N, 'Tackling Disability in the United Kingdom: The United Kingdom Disability Discrimination Act' (2007) 25 *Journal of Law & Policy* 25. For a broader discussion of disability, see Thomas, C 'How is Disability Understood? An Examination of Sociological Approaches' (2004) 19 *Disability and Society* 569 and Oliver, M, *Understanding Disability, From Theory to Practice* (2nd edn, 2009).

129 Equality Act 2010 (Disability) Regulations 2010, SI 2010/2128. See also EHRC, *Equality Act 2010: Guidance on matters to be taken into account in determining questions relating to the definition of disability* (2011).

diseases, such as multiple sclerosis or HIV infection are to be treated as disabled for the purposes of the Act.[130]

(c) Gender reassignment.

(d) Marriage and civil partnership.

(e) Pregnancy and maternity.

(f) Race. This includes not only discrimination on the ground of race, but also on the grounds of colour, nationality or ethnic or national origin.[131]

(g) Religion and belief. This includes not only religion and religious belief, but also any similar philosophical belief and any lack of religion. It is not entirely clear what will qualify as a 'philosophical belief', but it has been suggested that:[132]

  (i) The belief must be genuinely held.

  (ii) It must be a belief and not an opinion or viewpoint based on the present state of information available.

  (iii) It must be a belief as to a weighty and substantial aspect of human life and behaviour.

  (iv) It must attain a certain level of cogency, seriousness, cohesion and importance.

  (v) It must be worthy of respect in a democratic society, be not incompatible with human dignity and not conflict with the fundamental rights of others.

A belief in man-made climate change was considered to be a philosophical belief in the case in which these guidelines were suggested; it was also suggested that Pacifism and vegetarianism might also qualify and that: 'belief in the political philosophies of Socialism, Marxism, Communism or free-market Capitalism might qualify'.'[133]

(h) Sex.

(i) Sexual orientation. This is defined as orientation towards: persons of the same sex, persons of the opposite sex and towards people of both the same sex and the opposite sex.

(3) What does discrimination involve?

2.22 The legislation prohibits both direct and indirect discrimination. Direct discrimination simply involves treating persons less favourably

130 2010 Act, Sch 1.

131 National origin is not connected with citizenship, it is possible to make a claim that you were discriminated against on the grounds that you were not Scottish under this provision, *BBC Scotland v Souster* 2001 SC 458.

132 *Grainger v Nicholson* [2010] 2 All ER 253.

133 *Grainger v Nicholson*, [2010] 2 All ER 253, at para 28.

because of a protected characteristic,[134] eg, because they are black or because they are female. This definition is wide enough to provide protection to people who are discriminated against because of their association with a person who has the protected characteristic,[135] or because a person is wrongly thought to have the protected characteristic. Indirect discrimination exists where the same provision, criterion or practice is applied to everyone; in practice, this has the effect of discriminating against someone who has a protected characteristic (excluding pregnancy and maternity). For example, a requirement that all social workers are over two metres in height could apply equally to all aspiring social workers but would discriminate (at least) against female applicants since a smaller proportion of females than males are likely to meet the requirement. The statutory definition of indirect discrimination provides that a person (A) discriminates against another (B) if A applies to B a provision, criterion or practice which is discriminatory in relation to a relevant protected characteristic of B's.[136] It then provides that:[137]

> a provision, criterion or practice is discriminatory in relation to a relevant protected characteristic of B's if—
>
> (a) A applies, or would apply, it to persons with whom B does not share the characteristic,
>
> (b) it puts, or would put, persons with whom B shares the characteristic at a particular disadvantage when compared with persons with whom B does not share it,
>
> (c) it puts, or would put, B at that disadvantage, and
>
> (d) A cannot show it to be a proportionate means of achieving a legitimate aim.

An example of indirect discrimination is a case where employers agreed with a trade union that part-time workers would be made redundant first. This was found to amount to indirect discrimination.[138] The reason for this was that the proportion of women who could meet the requirement for avoiding redundancy, namely full-time employment, was considerably less than the proportion of men who could comply.[139]

The discrimination which is prohibited is discrimination in any aspect of employment as well as discrimination in the provision of goods and

134 2010 Act, s 13.

135 An example would be where a carer who does not have a protected characteristic is discriminated against because they are associated with a person who does, for example, they are caring for someone with a disability.

136 2010 Act, s 19(1).

137 2010 Act, s 19(2)

138 *Clarke and Powell v Eley (IMI) Kynoch Ltd* [1982] IRLR 482.

139 *Clarke and Powell v Eley (IMI) Kynoch Ltd* [1982] IRLR 482.

services, including services provided by local authorities, provision of premises (either by sale or by renting) and provision of education. Separate provision based on race also amounts to discrimination.

(4) The duty to make reasonable adjustments

2.23 In respect of disability the law provides additional protection in that it imposes on employers, as well as the providers of services (considered below), a duty to make reasonable adjustments.

Where a disabled employee would be put at a substantial disadvantage as compared to someone without a disability by an employer's provision, criterion or practice (for example, as to timing of the working day or methods of working), a physical feature of the employer's premises or failure to provide an auxiliary aid, the employer is obliged to make adjustments to the provision, criterion or practice or premises or to provide the auxiliary aid.[140] The duty is to take such steps as are reasonable to avoid the disadvantage.[141]

There is no specific guidance in the Equality Act 2010 on what factors are relevant in determining whether it is reasonable to take certain steps.[142] The EHRC suggests, in the context of employment, the following factors:[143]

(a) how effective the change will be in avoiding the disadvantage;
(b) the practicability of the adjustment;
(c) the costs and disruption to the employer;
(d) the extent of the employer's financial and other resources;
(e) the availability of financial or other assistance to the employer; and
(f) the size of the employer's undertaking.

Examples of steps which might be taken are adjustments to premises, providing a reader or interpreter, or altering the hours worked by the employee. Finally, this duty to make adjustments applies in respect of job applicants whom the prospective employer knows to be disabled.[144]

140 2010 Act, s 20.
141 2010 Act, s 20(4)
142 There is provision for regulations to be made covering this, 2010 Act, s 22, none have been made to date.
143 EHRC, 'What do we mean by reasonable?', 2019. Available at: www.equalityhumanrights.com/guidance/business/employing-people-workplace-adjustments/what-do-we-mean-reasonable. (Accessed April 2026).
144 2010 Act, s 39.

(5) Provision of services

2.24 As far as providers of services are concerned (and this includes local authorities), several duties are imposed:[145]

(a) Not to discriminate by not providing a service.

(b) Not to discriminate either on the terms on which a service is provided, by terminating the services or by subjecting a person to any other detriment in the provision of the service.

(c) Not to harass[146] or victimise a person requiring a service by not providing it or by acting in any of the ways set out in (b).

(d) To make reasonable adjustments. Similar considerations apply here as in the case of employment; for example, the effectiveness of the adjustment, its cost and the resources of the organisation will all be relevant.

Finally, it is unlawful for local authorities (and other public bodies) to do anything that constitutes discrimination, harassment or victimisation in carrying out their public functions even where these do not involve provision of a service to the public or a section of the public.[147] Local authorities and other public bodies also have a duty to make reasonable adjustments.[148] This duty applies to all 'persons' exercising a public function. Private companies may, therefore, also be covered when their functions are of a public nature, for example, a private company running a prison.

(6) When can discrimination be justified?

2.25 In some cases, discrimination on the basis of one of the protected characteristics considered above may be permissible. Both direct and indirect discrimination can be justified if it can be shown that it is a proportionate means of achieving a legitimate aim.[149] In the case of employment discrimination this would be justified if having a particular characteristic is an occupational requirement in the sense that it is necessary for the performance of the job.[150]

Examples where discrimination may be justified may include: special treatment of women in connection with pregnancy or childbirth;

145 2010 Act, s 29.

146 For the purposes of harassment, sexual orientation, religion or belief are not protected characteristics.

147 2010 Act, s 29(6).

148 2010 Act, s 29(7).

149 2010 Act, ss 13(2), 19(2)(d).

150 2010 Act, Sch 3, para 1.

entertainment (where particular characteristics are required to play a role); and provision of personal social or welfare services where this can best be done by a member of a particular sex or racial group.[151] This would allow the appointment of someone of a particular racial group and sex to provide social work services to a particular group. In addition, discrimination on the grounds of religious belief may be justified where the person or organisation discriminating is doing so on the basis of their own religious belief.

Finally, more favourable treatment for disabled people is permitted.[152]

(7) Enforcement of rights

2.26 The EHRC can give advice and/or assistance to people bringing cases alleging discrimination. In addition, it can carry out inquiries into areas of provision[153] and formal investigations into particular organisations or areas of provision. If, as a result of an investigation, it finds discrimination it can serve a non-discrimination notice requiring an end to discrimination, if the notice is not complied with it can ultimately be enforced through the court system. Finally, it has the sole right to enforce provisions concerning discrimination in advertising, pressure to discriminate and instructions/inducements to discriminate.

In general, individuals can enforce their rights relating to employment through the Employment Tribunal system and other rights are enforced through the court system, in Scotland this means initially in the sheriff court.

(8) Local authority duties

2.27 Aside from the general application of the 2010 Act to their activities, local authorities are subject to two duties under the 2010 Act. They are first subject to a general public sector equality duty, and they are also subject to a number of specific duties. The public sector equality

151 These are derived from previous legislation but would still seem to be applicable.
152 2010 Act, s 13(3).
153 For example, EHRC, *Housing and disabled people: Scotland's hidden crisis* (2018). Available at: www.equalityhumanrights.com/sites/default/files/housing-and-disabled-people-scotland-hidden-crisis-long-summary.pdf. (Accessed April 2026).

duty (PSED) requires local authorities, when they are exercising their functions, to have due regard to the need to:[154]

(a) Eliminate discrimination, harassment, victimisation and any other conduct that is prohibited by or under the Act.
(b) Advance equality of opportunity between persons who share a relevant protected characteristic and persons who do not share it. This includes, more specifically, having regard to the need to:
    (i) remove or minimise disadvantage deriving from a protected characteristic;
    (ii) take steps to meet the specific needs of people with a protected characteristic;
    (iii) encourage people with a protected characteristic to participate in public life.
(c) Foster good relations between persons who share a relevant protected characteristic and persons who do not share it.

The PSED also applies to organisations which exercise public functions even though the organisation is not a public authority.

What does having due regard entail? Guidance issued by the EHRC suggests that:[155]

> To 'have due regard' means that in making decisions and in its other day-to-day activities a body subject to the duty must consciously consider the need to do the things set out in the general equality duty: eliminate discrimination, advance equality of opportunity and foster good relations.

Courts have produced a number of lists seeking to explain the requirement, one of which includes the following:[156]

(a) 'due regard' means specific regard by way of conscious approach to the specified needs;
(b) due regard requires analysis of the relevant material with the specific statutory considerations in mind;
(c) general awareness of the duty does not amount to the necessary due regard, being a 'substantial rigorous and open-minded approach';

154 2010 Act, s 149, see also EHRC, *Essential guide to the Public Sector Equality Duty: Scotland* (2016), EHRC. Available at: www.equalityhumanrights.com/guidance/public-sector-equality-duty/essential-guide-public-sector-equality-duty-scotland (accessed 25 June 2025).

155 EHRC, *Technical guidance on the public sector equality duty: Scotland* (2016), para 2.19, see generally paras 2.19–2.23.

156 *R (on the application of W) v Birmingham City Council* [2011] EWHC 1147 (Admin). This approach is approved of in Scotland, see *Watt v Lothian Health Board* [2015] CSOH 117.

(d) in a case where the decision may affect large numbers of vulnerable people, many of whom fall within one or more of the protected groups, the due regard necessary is very high;
(e) the duty … may require positive steps to be taken if the circumstances require it to address disadvantage to disabled people;
(f) thus, if changing a function or proposed policy would lead to significant benefits to disabled people, the need for such a change will carry added weight when balanced against other considerations;
(g) similarly, if a risk of adverse impact is identified, consideration must be given to measures to avoid that impact before fixing on a particular solution;
(h) impact assessments and must contain sufficient information to enable a public authority to show it has paid due regard to the duty and identify methods for mitigating or avoiding adverse impact.

A number of specific duties are also imposed on public bodies.[157] These include a duty to report on progress with mainstreaming, a duty to provide gender pay-gap information, and, perhaps most relevant here, a duty to assess policies and practices.[158] This last requires local authorities to assess[159] the impact of new or revised policies or practices against the list of factors to which they need to have regard set out in the PSED. Relevant evidence about impact on people who share a relevant protected characteristic must be considered before a new or revised policy is approved, and there is also an obligation on the authority to make arrangements which it considers reasonable to review existing policies.

Finally, an authority must, when making decisions of a strategic nature about how to exercise its functions, have due regard to the desirability of exercising them in a way that is designed to reduce the inequalities of outcome which result from socio-economic disadvantage.[160]

157 Equality Act 2010 (Specific Duties) (Scotland) Regulations 2012, SSI 2012/162.
158 This last is in regulation 5, see also EHRC, *Technical guidance on the public sector equality duty: Scotland* (2016), section 6.4 and EHRC, *Assessing impact and the public sector equality duty: A guide for public authorities in Scotland* (2016).
159 Though no specific form of assessment is prescribed.
160 2010 Act, s 1. This duty is sometimes referred to as the Fairer Scotland duty. See also Scottish Government, *Fairer Scotland Action Plan* (2016).

INFORMATION SHARING: INTRODUCTION

2.28 This section is concerned with the circumstances in which it is permissible to share information about an individual, either within an organisation or across organisations. It starts with a general consideration of what confidentiality might mean and the extent to which, in general, it is true that confidentiality does not permit any sharing of information, mentioning also the other side of the coin, the right that individuals must access information about themselves.

Following this introduction, we will consider the legal position on when information can be shared. This legal basis has recently changed, with a new European Union Regulation on data protection, the General Data Protection Regulation (GDPR), which came into effect on 25 May 2018 and the Data Protection Act 2018, part of which implements the GDPR in the UK prior to Brexit, which, as far as the material covered here is concerned, came into effect on the same date. The restrictions on sharing (and the rights of access) are intended to be consistent with the Charter of Fundamental Rights of the European Union (CFREU),[161] which in turn is intended to reflect the individual rights set out in the European Convention on Human Rights (ECHR).[162] The consideration below will refer to the GDPR and to the Act. Finally, on information sharing we will conclude by trying to set out a more systematic account of when information can, or must, be shared. We will then consider rights of access to information, which are also affected by the GDPR and here reference will also be made to the GDPR and the Act, as far as it is clear what changes this will produce.[163]

2.29 One of the requirements of the Code of Practice for social workers in Scotland is that confidential information is respected.[164] Confidentiality is an important factor in enabling clients to engage confidently,[165] but what, exactly, is involved in 'confidentiality'? One interpretation is that confidentiality means information shared by a

161 See CFREU, particularly Article 8.

162 See CFREU Preamble, even though the CFREU will not apply to the UK after Brexit (European Union (Withdrawal) Act 2018, s 5(4)), the ECHR, which has nothing to do with the EU, will still apply by virtue of the Human Rights Act 1998.

163 In fact, the restrictions on the right to access information are largely the same as those existing under the Data Protection Act 1998 and regulations made under it.

164 Scottish Social Services Council, *Codes of Practice for Social Service Workers* (2024), para 2.3, which states that '[I will:] Respect confidential information and clearly explaining my employer's policies about confidentiality to people who use services and carers'.

165 Scottish Government, *Getting It Right For Every Child (GIRFEC) Practice Guidance 4 – Information Sharing* (2022) para 14.

client with their social worker, or information about a client, must never be disclosed to anyone else without the informed consent of the client. This might certainly be the expectation of the service user when the information is disclosed. However, it is unlikely that confidentiality can imply this absolute protection of information.[166] At the most basic level information may have to be shared with others to ensure that a client receives a service. Clark notes that:

> The client's information is often widely distributed without his full understanding, and including content that he supposed was to remain private. What is happening therefore is that the professional and the agency are transmitting information that the client naively imagines is to remain private, not out of negligence or malice, but in order to serve the client's interests: the infringement of confidentiality is thus justified by the professional's legitimate purposes.[167]

There may in some cases be a positive expectation that information will be shared, both without the client's consent and in cases where it would be difficult to argue in any sense that the information sharing is in their interests.

At issue is access to the confidential information; it might be suggested that, with regard to that information, the relationship is between the agency and the client and therefore that information can be shared within the agency, but not, subject to what is said below, outwith it.[168]

The need to share information is recognised indirectly in the Code of Practice in its reference to 'employer's policies' about confidentiality, but more fully in the *BASW Code of Ethics* and in the updated Scottish Government Guidance on the confidentiality of social work records.[169] This last recognises that information will need, as a matter of course, to be shared with others in the social work department. In addition to these codes and guidance which largely *permit* disclosure in certain

166 And it has certainly never been the case that the law takes this view.

167 Clark, C, 'Confidentiality, trust and truthfulness in professional relationships', in Clark, C & McGhee, J, *Private and Confidential? Handling Personal Information in the Social and Health Services* (Policy Press, 2008), at 39. It may be, in fact, that such sharing does not amount to infringement of confidentiality if confidentiality is seen as permitting some sharing rather than as imposing a complete ban on any sharing of information.

168 Scottish Government, *Records Management Code of Practice for Health and Social Care* (2024). In addition, the Information Commissioner notes that 'even in the case of sharing between different local authority departments the Data Protection Principles (discussed below) will apply', *Data Sharing Code of Practice* (2011), p 10.

169 BASW, Code of Ethics (2021); Scottish Government, *Records Management Code Of Practice For Health and Social Care* (2024).

circumstances, there are some cases where disclosure and information sharing is expected or required, some of these are considered below.

Confidentiality extends beyond clients to third parties who provide information to the social work department.[170] Where this information is, at least in part, about the third party, or might serve to identify them, then they will have a right to have the information and their identity treated as confidential. This does not mean that it may not be disclosed, in some cases it may be, and there are statutory provisions to the effect that certain types of informant do not enjoy protection from disclosure of information.

A final aspect of information about a client is the right of the client to see information held about them by the social work department. There is specific statutory provision regarding this, which is discussed below. In addition to this provision, there will also, in certain cases, be a right to access information which flows from Article 8 of the ECHR.[171] This is illustrated in *Gaskin v United Kingdom*.[172] Mr Gaskin had, as a child, been taken into care by Liverpool City Council. He remained in its care between 1960 and 1977, during which time he was in a variety of placements. He subsequently sought access to the case records held by the Council covering his period in care. A combination of government guidance and legal action prevented release of most of this material and Mr Gaskin eventually took his case to the European Court of Human Rights, claiming a breach of Article 8 of the ECHR.[173] The court accepted the view of the European Commission on Human Rights[174] that 'respect for private life requires that everyone should be able to establish details of their identity as individual human beings and that in principle they should not be obstructed by the authorities from obtaining such very basic information without specific justification'.[175] In conclusion it indicated that people in Mr Gaskin's position have 'a vital interest ... protected by the Convention, in receiving the information necessary to know and to understand their childhood and early development', though this had to be balanced against the importance of confidentiality 'for receiving

170 For example, someone providing information about suspected child abuse, see *Parks v Tayside Regional Council* 1989 SC 38 at 42.

171 As we will see below, this can also form the basis for protecting private information about an individual.

172 (1990) 12 EHRR 36.

173 Although Article 8 is phrased negatively to prevent infringement of rights, it has been interpreted as creating positive obligations on the part of government and local government.

174 Under the procedure which existed at this time, cases were first considered by the Commission.

175 At para 39.

objective and reliable information, and that such confidentiality can also be necessary for the protection of third persons'.[176]

A final element of the current context is the expectation, driven by the data protection legislation discussed below, that organisations will put in place data sharing agreements[177] which set out both the procedures for data sharing with other organisations and the circumstances in which personal data will be shared.

THE LEGAL CONTEXT FOR INFORMATION SHARING

(1) Introduction

2.30 As indicated above, there is substantial legislation in this area. The legislation, in particular at European level, is intended to be consistent with the ECHR, and is overlaid on an older common law of confidentiality or breach of confidence, though breach of confidence has, itself, developed in accordance with the ECHR. This section will first consider the ECHR and, briefly, breach of confidence, before considering the relevant United Kingdom legislation.

(2) The ECHR

2.31 Article 8 of the ECHR provides that:

1. Everyone has the right to respect for his private and family life, his home and his correspondence.
2. There shall be no interference by a public authority with the exercise of this right except such as is in accordance with the law and is necessary in a democratic society in the interests of national security, public safety or the economic well-being of the country, for the prevention of disorder or crime, for the protection of health or morals, or for the protection of the rights and freedoms of others.

It is important to note that the right set out in the first paragraph is qualified and can be overridden if this is necessary for the protection of other rights. Both the collection and the sharing of personal information

176 At para 49. One of the difficulties was that, at the time when Mr Gaskin sought access to the records, there was no independent body which could adjudicate on these competing interests if the local authority refused access to information.

177 See Scottish Government, *Public Sector Personal Data Sharing: Framework and Principles* (2023).

engages Article 8,[178] and therefore any information sharing must be justified under that Article. Before sharing will be permitted it must be possible to show that the sharing satisfies three tests:[179]

(a) it must be in accordance with law;
(b) it must pursue a legitimate aim; and
(c) it must be necessary in a democratic society.

To satisfy the first of these it must be possible to show some basis in national law for the information sharing. For example, it might be justified under the GDPR or the Data Protection Act 2018 to protect the vital interests of an individual. It is, however, not sufficient that there is a law which justifies the infringement of Article 8 rights; it is also necessary that the law is compatible with the rule of law. This has been expressed as the requirement that:

> The law must thus be adequately accessible and foreseeable, that is, formulated with sufficient precision to enable the individual – if need be with appropriate advice – to regulate his conduct. For domestic law to meet these requirements, it must afford adequate legal protection against arbitrariness and accordingly indicate with sufficient clarity the scope of discretion conferred on the competent authorities and the manner of its exercise …[180]

This second aspect has been seen to incorporate both a requirement that there are safeguards in place to enable the proportionality of the interference to be examined, and a need to indicate with sufficient clarity the scope of the discretion conferred on a public official.[181]

The final requirement does not require that the infringing measure is indispensable, but that it is more than simply 'useful' or 'desirable'. Measures must respond to a pressing social need and must be a proportionate means of achieving the legitimate aim. In other words, the rights of the individual must be interfered with only to the extent necessary to achieve this aim and no further. Courts in the UK have applied a proportionality test (explained below) which incorporates this. In all of this, states enjoy a certain margin of appreciation or discretion in

178 *MM v United Kingdom* (Application 24029/07), para 195.

179 *MM v United Kingdom*, para 191.

180 *MM v United Kingdom*, para 193.

181 See *The Christian Institute and others v The Lord Advocate* [2016] UKSC 51 at paras 79–80, citing *Gillan and Quinton v United Kingdom* (2010) 50 EHRR 1105, para 77, and *Peruzzo and Martens v Germany* (2013) 57 EHRR SE 17, para 35. Paragraph 42 of *Peruzzo*, not cited, stresses the need for appropriate safeguards to prevent uses of data inconsistent with the guarantees offered by Article 8. See the discussion of proportionality below.

taking measures to achieve a legitimate aim,[182] though the more intimate the area of family life affected, the more limited this margin will be.

(3) Breach of confidence

2.32 In its origins, breach of confidence protected information disclosed in a confidential relationship, and it was the context of disclosure which generated the protection, rather than the nature of the information itself. The protected relationships included doctor and patient, and employer and employee, though it is likely that it would extend to any disclosure to a professional.[183] Beyond this the courts have protected information disclosed in the course of conversation between friends.[184] In this form, the obligation not to disclose information was never absolute, disclosure could be compelled in court proceedings, and it was also recognised that in some cases the public interest in maintaining confidence could be overridden by a public interest in disclosure. For example, in *W v Edgell*[185] it was held that it was justifiable for a doctor commissioned to prepare a medical report by a patient in a high security hospital to share that report with the Home Office.

The concern of the courts to protect the privacy of relationships meant that confidential information which came to light outwith such relationships was not necessarily protected. The courts eventually changed focus in such cases to the nature of the information rather than the context in which it was discovered.[186] The final stage in the development of breach of confidence took place under the influence of Article 8 of the ECHR after the implementation of the Human Rights Act 1998 in 2000. One of the consequences of this has been an increased focus on whether release of private information is justified in terms of Article 8, and the other has been the development of a right to prevent disclosure of private information[187] which is distinct from breach of confidence.[188]

These further developments also envisage that there will be circumstances in which private information can be disclosed. The possible recipients of such disclosure can be quite wide-ranging, including not only

182 See, generally, *Silver v United Kingdom* (1983) 5 EHRR 347 at para 97; *Kennedy v United Kingdom* (2011) 52 EHRR 4 at para 154.
183 This is reflected in various professional codes of practice.
184 See for example, *Stephens v Avery* [1988] 1 Ch 449; *McKennit v Ash* [2005] EWHC 3003 (QB).
185 [1990] Ch 359.
186 *Attorney General v Guardian Newspapers Ltd (No 2)* [1988] UKHL 6; *Lord Advocate v The Scotsman Newspapers* 1989 SC (HL) 122.
187 See, for example, *Mosley v News Group Newspapers Ltd* [2008] EWHC 687 (QB).
188 Though the distinction is not always clearly observed by the courts.

professionals but also, for example, in child protection, members of the public where it is concluded that sharing the information is necessary to protect the child from risk. Case law has established that information may be disclosed where there is a clear risk, either to an identified individual or to a specific class of people, such as children. One example of this is *R v Chief Constable of North Wales Police, ex parte AB*.[189] After their release from custodial sentences for sexual offences involving children, a husband and wife were staying on a caravan park. Shortly before Easter, and after discussions with the offenders who had undertaken to move but did not, the police disclosed to the owner of the caravan park the couple's background (by way of showing the owner press coverage regarding them). A concern about risk to children who were likely to arrive at the caravan park for the holidays prompted the disclosure, which the couple then sought to challenge. The Court of Appeal took the view that there was a pressing need for disclosure in this case.[190]

The idea that there must be a pressing need for disclosure has been replaced, under the influence of the ECHR, by the requirement for proportionality.[191] Proportionality requires that:

(a) the disclosure is undertaken to achieve a legitimate aim which is sufficiently important to justify interfering with an individual's right to privacy and confidentiality;
(b) there must be a rational connection between the disclosure and the aim;
(c) the disclosure must be no more than is required to achieve this aim;[192] and
(d) a fair balance must be struck between the rights of the individual and the interests of the community. This will require a careful assessment of the severity and consequences of the interference.[193]

(4) Data protection law

2.33 Data protection law is overlaid onto and coexists with breach of confidence and, as mentioned above, is to be consistent with Article 8

189 [1999] QB 396.

190 *R v Chief Constable of North Wales Police, ex parte AB* [1999] QB 396.

191 *H and L v A Local Authority* [2011] EWCA Civ 403, where it was noted that: 'There is no difference between the [pressing need] test and the approach mandated by Article 8' at para 37.

192 In, *H and L v A Local Authority* [2011] EWCA Civ 403 the disclosure of a conviction to *all* the organisations with which individuals were involved was considered to be too broad.

193 *H and L v A Local Authority* [2011] EWCA Civ 403 at para 38.

of the ECHR. This means that sharing under this law must respect Article 8 and, although the circumstances in which information can be shared under data protection law reflect the need for sharing to be proportional, the general requirement for proportionality will still need to be considered before information is shared.

(a) Personal data

2.34 The GDPR covers the processing of personal data and is applied to processing in the UK by the Data Protection Act 2018.[194] Processing has a wide scope and includes the collection, storage and disclosure of 'personal data'.[195] It would therefore include, for example, sharing of information about someone where there are child or adult protection concerns. The personal data which is processed can be in any form, physical or digital. Personal data is any information relating to an identified *or* identifiable natural person (described as the 'data subject'). A person will be a data subject if they can be identified directly or indirectly from information held about factors specific to their physical, genetic or social identity.[196]

Any processing by the person who controls the data (referred to as the data controller), must comply with six data protection principles.[197] These are that personal data shall:

(a) be processed fairly, lawfully and in a transparent manner;
(b) be obtained only for one or more specific, explicit and legitimate purposes and not be further processed in a manner incompatible with these purposes;
(c) be adequate, relevant and not excessive in relation to the purposes for which they are processed;
(d) be accurate and kept up to date;
(e) not be kept for longer than is necessary for the purposes for which they are processed; and
(f) be processed in a manner which ensures appropriate security against, for example, unauthorised processing or loss.

(b) When can information be shared under the GDPR?

2.35 To some extent, this depends on the nature of the information being shared. There is one set of requirements that must be satisfied

194 Section 22.
195 GDPR, Art 4(2), 2018 Act, s 3(4).
196 GDPR, Art 4(1).
197 GDPR, Art 5(1), 2018 Act, ch 2.

before any personal data can be shared,[198] and more stringent requirements which have to be satisfied before 'special categories' of personal data can be shared.[199] 'Special categories' include information about racial or ethnic origin, political opinions and, more relevantly here, data concerning health[200] or a natural person's sex life.

For personal data, the most relevant conditions for sharing to be lawful are:[201]

(a) consent of the data subject;[202]

(b) the processing is necessary for compliance with any legal obligation to which the data controller is subject; the legal obligation need not be set out in statute;[203]

(c) the processing is necessary to protect the vital interests of the data subject or of another natural person;[204]

(d) the processing is necessary for the purposes of a task carried out in the public interest or in the exercise of official authority vested in the controller of the data;[205]

(e) processing is necessary for the purposes of the legitimate interests pursued by the controller or by a third party; this condition will not be considered in detail as it cannot be relied on by public authorities in the performance of their public duties; condition (d) above would be relevant here.

In addition, it must also be possible to point to a basis for processing under either EU law or UK law for conditions (b) and (d) above.[206] Any

198 GDPR, Art 6.
199 GDPR, Art 9.
200 'Data concerning health' is defined as 'personal data relating to the physical or mental health of an individual, including the provision of health care services, which reveals information about his or her health status': GDPR, Art 4(15); 2018 Act, s 205(1). GDPR, Recital (35) notes that: 'Personal data concerning health should include all data pertaining to the health status of a data subject which reveal information relating to the past, current or future physical or mental health status of the data subject. This includes information about the natural person collected in the course of the registration for, or the provision of, health care services …; information derived from the testing or examination of a body part or bodily substance, including from genetic data and biological samples; and any information on, for example, a disease, disability, disease risk, medical history, clinical treatment or the physiological or biomedical state of the data subject independent of its source, for example from a physician or other health professional, a hospital, a medical device or an in vitro diagnostic test'.
201 GDPR, Art 6.
202 See **2.37** below.
203 See **2.38** below.
204 See **2.40** below.
205 See **2.41** below.
206 GDPR, Art 6(3).

such law must be a necessary and proportionate measure in a democratic society to safeguard one of a number of interests, most relevantly here, for the protection of the data subject or of others.[207]

2.36 In the case of special categories of personal information, sharing can only take place if at least one of a number of conditions is met; these include:[208]

(a) the data subject has given explicit consent to the processing;[209]

(b) processing is necessary in order to protect the vital interests[210] of the data subject or another person, though this condition is only available in a case where the data subject is physically or legally incapable of giving consent;[211]

(c) the processing is necessary for reasons of substantial public interest and must be in accordance with law and respect the essence of data protection, providing specific measures to safeguard the fundamental rights and interests of the data subject;[212] and

(d) processing is necessary for the purposes of the provision of health care or treatment or social care or the management of health or social care systems and services on the basis of European or domestic law and the processing is carried out by or under the responsibility of a professional who is subject to an obligation of professional secrecy.[213]

These criteria set the bar higher than the conditions discussed above in connection with the sharing of personal information.

(c) Consent[214]

2.37 Where consent is relied on, it must be possible to demonstrate that consent has been given, requiring some evidence to support a claim

207 GDPR, Arts 4 and 23(1)(i).

208 GDPR, Art 9(2), 2018 Act, ss 10 and 11 and Sch 1.

209 Note that this requires explicit consent, where sharing of personal data requires only consent. The Regulation provides that EU or domestic law may set out cases in which consent may not be given, but this has not been done, GDPR Art 9(2)(a). Explicit consent is discussed in Article 29 Data Protection Working Party, *Guidelines on Consent under Regulation 2016/679* (wp259rev.01) (2018), section 4. See also para 2.37 below.

210 See **2.40** below.

211 GDPR, Art 9(2)(c).

212 GDPR, Art 9(2)(g), 2018 Act, s 10(1)(b) and Sch 1, Pt 2. See **2.41** below.

213 GDPR, Art 9(2)(h), 2018 Act, s 10(1)(c) and Sch 1, Pt 1. See **2.42** below.

214 See European Commission, Article 29 Data Protection Working Party, *Guidelines on Consent under Regulation 2016/679* (wp259rev.01) (2018).

that the subject of the information has consented to it being shared. Consent can be withdrawn at any time.[215]

Where there is more than one data subject, consent from all of them will be required or there would need to be a justification for sharing without consent.

In addition:

(a) consent must be freely given; it is noted in the GDPR that consent should not provide a basis for processing where there is a clear imbalance between the individual and the data controller 'in particular where the controller is a public authority and it is therefore unlikely that consent was freely given, in all the circumstances of the situation';[216]

(b) specific consent is required covering the information sharing which is contemplated; in other words, the consent will only be effective if the data subject is aware of the specific type of sharing which is being considered and has consented to that;

(c) sufficient explanation must be given so that the agreement of the data subject meets the requirement that consent is informed; and

(d) any agreement must be clear and unqualified.

(d) When will sharing be necessary?

2.38 For the conditions mentioned above which justify sharing of information without consent to apply, it has to be shown that the information sharing is 'necessary'. Processing will only be regarded as being necessary where the purpose cannot be achieved by some other reasonable means. This is the view which was taken by the Supreme Court, which noted that an interference with the rights protected by the GDPR 'must be the least restrictive for the achievement of the legitimate aim'.[217]

The question that has to be asked in determining whether disclosure is necessary is, therefore, whether the disclosure is the least intrusive (in respect of the rights of the data subject) means to achieve a specific

215 GDPR, Art 7.

216 GDPR, Recital (43). See European Commission Article 29 Data Protection Working Party, *Guidelines on Consent under Regulation 2016/679* (wp259rev.01) (2018), section 3.1.1. In these cases, one of the alternative bases for sharing would need to be established.

217 *South Lanarkshire Council v Scottish Information Commissioner* [2013] UKSC 55, per Lady Hale at para 27.

objective.[218] The Supreme Court contrasted, on the one hand, the sharing of information because it was necessary to achieve an objective with, on the other, sharing because information is relevant:[219]

> Where the disclosure of information constitutes an interference with rights protected by article 8 of the ECHR, as in the present context … , the requirement that disclosure is 'necessary' forms part of a proportionality test: the disclosure must involve the least interference with the right to respect for private and family life which is required for the achievement of the legitimate aim pursued. Disclosure where the data processor considers that the information is likely to be relevant cannot be regarded as necessary if the legitimate aim could be achieved by something less. It cannot be 'necessary', in that sense, to disclose information merely on the ground that it is objectively relevant, let alone on the ground that a particular body considers that it is likely to be relevant. Relevance is a relatively low threshold: information may be relevant but of little significance. A test of potential relevance fails to recognise the need to weigh the importance of the disclosure in achieving a legitimate aim against the importance of the interference with the individual's right to respect for her private and family life. That deficiency is not made good by the requirement that the data controller considers that the information ought to be provided.

(e) Sharing to comply with any legal obligation[220]

2.39 There are a number of instances where there is an obligation to share information. For example:

1 Local authorities have an obligation to carry out investigations and pass information on to the reporter where they consider that a child is in need of protection, guidance or control and that a compulsory supervision order might be necessary.[221] A similar obligation applies to the police,[222] and others may provide information to the reporter in these circumstances.[223] Local authorities may also be required by the reporter to prepare a report on a child who

218 See also *The Christian Institute and others v The Lord Advocate* [2016] UKSC 51 at para 56.
219 *The Christian Institute and others v The Lord Advocate* [2016] UKSC 51 at para 56.
220 Ground (b) in **2.35** above.
221 Children's Hearings (Scotland) Act 2011, s 60.
222 Children's Hearings (Scotland) Act 2011, s 61.
223 Children's Hearings (Scotland) Act 2011, s 65.

has been referred to them, which may include a requirement to provide specific information.[224]

2 In carrying out various types of assessment, for example a single shared assessment or an assessment in preparation of a child's or young person's plan.

3 The Adult Support and Protection (Scotland) Act 2007[225] empowers council officers to require production of records relating to vulnerable adults and requires cooperation with investigations being carried out by the local authority, which by implication will include sharing information.[226]

4 The Protection of Vulnerable Groups (Scotland) Act 2007 requires the passing on of information about an individual if he or she has been dismissed or transferred for one of a specified number of reasons.

5 The duty to cooperate in the management of certain offenders (through Multi-Agency Public Protection Arrangements) includes a duty to share information.[227]

6 Information will have to be disclosed where this is required for court or other legal proceedings. This requirement includes not only criminal cases, where information may be required in the form of a criminal justice social work report,[228] but also various tribunals, for example Children's Hearings and Mental Health Tribunals. The requirement also applies to civil cases, for example the reports prepared in connection with adoption hearings. There may also be other cases where a court may order production of information as part of court proceedings.

In addition, other local authorities and health boards have an obligation to provide information to a local authority in two cases. The first is where that local authority requests help in carrying out its functions in relation, for example, to children in need and children affected by disability.[229] Unless it would be incompatible with its statutory or other duties and obligations, and provided that it would not unduly prejudice

224 Children's Hearings (Scotland) Act 2011, s 66(4). For the sort of information required in such reports see SCRA. Available at: www.scra.gov.uk/wp-content/uploads/2024/08/A-Guide-to-Referral-to-the-Childrens-Reporter.pdf. (Accessed April 2026).

225 Section 10.

226 Adult Support and Protection (Scotland) Act 2007, s 5. See also Scottish Government, *Adult Support and Protection (Scotland) Act 2007 – Code of Practice* (2022), ch 10.

227 Management of Offenders (Scotland) Act 2005, ss 1(2)(a) and 10.

228 The status of information contained in Social Enquiry Reports (now Criminal Justice Social Work Reports, CJSWR) is considered in *X v BBC* [2005] CSOH 80, see also **10.4** for ways in which circulation of information can be restricted.

229 Children (Scotland) Act 1995, s 21.

the delivery of its functions, the organisation to which the request is made must comply with that request.[230] A similar obligation exists where a local authority makes a request whilst carrying out an investigation of a child because of its duty to investigate the cases of children who may be in need of compulsory supervision, or if it is carrying out functions in relation to children's hearings, for example, implementing a compulsory supervision order.[231]

There may also, in very particular circumstances, be a more general duty to take preventative action, which might include passing on information, which derives from Article 2 of the ECHR, the right to life. This possibility was mentioned in *Osman v United Kingdom*.[232] Here it was suggested that public authorities might have a positive obligation to protect a person's right to life where they:

> … knew or ought to have known at the time of the existence of a real and immediate risk to the life of an identified individual or individuals from the criminal acts of a third party and that they failed to take measures within the scope of their powers which, judged reasonably, might have been expected to avoid that risk.[233]

In subsequent cases it has proved very difficult to establish that this test has been satisfied.

(f) Sharing to protect the vital interests of the data subject or of another natural person[234]

2.40 Recital 46 of the GDPR refers to processing which is 'necessary to protect an interest which is essential for the life of the data subject or that of another natural person'. This recital also indicates that this ground for processing should only be used where processing cannot manifestly be based on any other legal basis. In addition, recital 112 describes vital interests as including physical integrity and life.

Finally, the opinion of the Article 29 Working Party on the Directive that formed the basis for the Data Protection Act 1998 suggested that:

> [t]he phrase 'vital interest' appears to limit the application of this ground to questions of life or death, or at the very least, threats that

230 Children (Scotland) Act 1995, s 21(2).
231 Children's Hearings (Scotland) Act 2011, s 18.
232 (2000) 29 EHRR 245.
233 At para 116.
234 See the conditions set out at (c) in **2.35** above and (b) in **2.36** above.

pose a risk of injury or other damage to the health of the data subject ...[235]

The only case in which the notion of vital interests has been considered made limited comment on when these might be engaged. It did note, in line with the explanations already considered, that it was 'a test which requires more than that it is likely to benefit well-being'.[236]

Where the high threshold for vital interests is not reached, information sharing may be justified by the provisions set out in **2.41** below.

(g) Performance of a task in the public interest[237]

2.41 In relation to sharing of personal data, the Data Protection Act 2018 contains a non-exhaustive list of the sort of processing which will be covered by the condition that processing is necessary for the purposes of a task carried out in the public interest or in the exercise of official authority vested in the controller of the data. This includes processing necessary for the administration of justice and, more generally, the exercise of a function conferred by an enactment or rule of law.[238]

The Data Protection Act 2018 also provides further guidance on when there will be a substantial public interest in sharing, as required for the sharing of special categories of information.[239] This requires that the data controller sharing the information has an appropriate policy document which explains the procedures in place for ensuring compliance with the data protection principles. A record must be made which includes details of the condition relied on for processing, and how the processing satisfies the fairness principle. Specific provision is made for sharing information without consent where this is necessary to safeguard children (aged under 18) or adults (aged 18 or over) at risk.[240] For sharing to be justified in such cases:

(a) it must be necessary to protect an individual from neglect or physical, mental or emotional harm or to protect their physical, mental or emotional well-being;

235 Opinion 06/2014 on the notion of legitimate interests of the data controller under Article 7 of Directive 95/46/EC, p 20.

236 *The Christian Institute and others v The Lord Advocate* [2016] UKSC 51 at para 48.

237 See condition (d) in **2.35** above.

238 Data Protection Act 2018, s 8, as amended (the 2018 Act).

239 2018 Act, s 10 and Sch 1, Pts 2 and 4. See condition (c) in **2.36** above.

240 Defined as in the Adult Support and Protection (Scotland) Act 2007, see **9.3**. 2018 Act, Sch 1, Pt 2, paras 5 and 18.

(b) it must be necessary for reasons of substantial public interest;[241] and

(c) it must take place without consent either:
  (i) because consent cannot, in the circumstances, be given by the data subject; or
  (ii) the data controller cannot reasonably be expected to obtain consent; or
  (iii) obtaining consent would prejudice the objective of protecting a person from neglect or physical, mental or emotional harm.

(h) Provision of social care[242]

2.42 Sharing of special categories of information will be justified simply, as suggested in the GDPR, where this is necessary to provide social care, which will include the sort of provision considered in chapter 6. Where information is shared for this purpose, the requirements as to having a policy document in place and recording set out in **2.41** above will apply.[243]

SHARING IN PRACTICE

2.43 It has been said in this area that there is 'a lack of practical advice in guidance … and, ironically, [a large] volume of complex guidance'.[244] Indeed, some of the practice guidance appears rather inconsistent and it is not always clear that it states the law accurately or in a manner that is straightforward to understand.[245]

It is important to be clear that judgements about whether to disclose or share information are not exclusively determined by reference to legal rules or to flow charts or procedures. Fundamental to decisions to share information are professional judgements which give rise to the question as to whether information should be shared or not. These include

241 There is no further definition of when this will arise and it seems rather circular to impose this as a requirement in a criterion which is, itself, supposed to give guidance on when there is a substantial public interest.

242 See condition (d) in **2.36** above.

243 Data Protection Act 2018, s 10 and Sch 1, Pt 1, para 2 and Pt 4.

244 ChildLine Scotland/CLCP, *Roundtable Report, Finding the balance: Children's right to confidentiality in an age of information sharing* (2011).

245 For example, Grampian Strategic GIRFEC Group *A Practitioner's Guide to Information Sharing, Confidentiality and Consent to Support Children and Young People's Wellbeing* (2019).

judgement about what information means (or, indeed, the creation of information based on the application of professional knowledge and understanding), assessment of the risk if information is not shared and no action is taken, and assessment of the implications of disclosure, for example, how far will an unwilling individual's rights be damaged by disclosure? None of these are straightforward, there are difficulties in identifying and assessing risk and identifying the relevance of information. As is pointed out in various pieces of guidance and reports, an individual may be in possession of only a small piece of information which makes sense only when put together with other information. There are also difficulties in sharing information – for example, does the recipient of the information trust/have a good relationship with the provider, will they both give the information the same meaning?[246]

The basic principle is that information can be shared, subject to what is said below, if the person who has provided the information or the person who is the subject of the information agrees to that sharing. As we have discussed above, the consent should be:

(a) informed – the person giving consent should have a clear understanding of the purposes for which the information is to be shared;
(b) voluntarily given – in other words, the person must not give consent because they fear that failure to consent will lead to adverse consequences, for example refusal of future service or, in the case of a parent, removal of a child;
(c) given by someone who has the legal capacity to consent – in some cases, parents can consent on behalf of children, and children may be able to give their own consent, depending on their understanding; and
(d) explicit, in the case of specific categories of information (defined above) – both good practice and the GDPR suggest that there should be evidence that consent has been granted which could be used to establish the existence of consent if that was challenged.

If there is no consent, sharing must be justified by at least one of the other conditions considered in **2.35** and **2.42** above and it must, in all cases, must be proportional, as set out at **2.32** above. The consequence of the application of proportionality under Article 8 of the ECHR is that the competing interests have to be balanced, for example, is the risk of

246 These issues are discussed at length in White, S *et al*, 'Improving practice in safeguarding at the interface between hospital services and children's social care: a mixed-methods case study', *Health Serv Deliv Res* 2015, 3(4), chapters 4 and 5, and Thompson, K, *Strengthening Child Protection* (Bristol, Policy Press, 2016).

harm such that interfering with the right of privacy of another individual is justified?

There is no clear bright line legal test which can be offered to say when sharing will be proportionate and when it will not, it will depend on a professional assessment of risk and a situated assessment of the risks of disclosure. This makes it important that there is a clear decision-making process within organisations and highlights the desirability of recording that process and indicating the factors which were considered to be critical in arriving at the final decision. The requirement for proportionality is linked to the requirement, noted earlier, that there must be adequate safeguards to ensure that sharing is proportionate.

It follows from the proportionality requirement and the data protection principles discussed earlier in this chapter that the information shared must be accurate,[247] it must be up-to-date and it must be relevant to the purpose of sharing. This means that steps will have to be taken to confirm the accuracy of the information where there is any doubt about it. The context of sharing might be relevant as well. In *W v Westminster City Council*[248] a social worker preparing a report for a Child Protection Case Conference (CPC) included in that report information about an individual, W, to the effect that professionals had raised concerns that he might be grooming for prostitution the child who was the subject of the case conference. W was at the CPC and the first time he was aware of these suspicions was when he saw the report. He claimed that his Article 8 rights had been infringed. The court agreed:

> … the disclosure at the CPC on 1st April of the concerns about the Claimant [W] was an interference with the Claimant's right under Art 8. This was highly sensitive and potentially very damaging information. There was no need, whether pressing or at all, to make the disclosure there and then in the way that it was made. [The social workers] had not properly addressed their minds to the question. Focussing on the need to protect [the child], they had omitted to test the balance of the Claimant's rights against those of [the child]. In particular, there was no need or duty to disclose the information at that stage to the mother, and no need to disclose it to the professionals and the mother in the presence of W without having raised any questions with him as to the facts of his relationship with [the child], and without giving him any warning.[249]

247 *W v Westminster City Council* [2005] EWHC 102 (QB); *R(B) v Chief Constable of Hampshire Constabulary* [2015] EWHC 1238 (Admin).

248 *W v Westminster City Council* [2005] EWHC 102 (QB).

249 *W v Westminster City Council*, para 239.

This highlights the need for a proper assessment of the respective interests of the parties involved and also of context, because the judgment goes on to note that: 'Nothing in this judgment is a decision as to what the position would have been if the disclosure had been made only to professionals in the absence of W'.[250]

Even in cases where there is no consent, Article 8 of the ECHR will usually require that a data subject is informed of the decision to share, either before or after the event. Again, there is no directly relevant case law but, in cases involving the decision as to whether a parent should be advised of the intention to remove a child, the level of risk to the child which justifies non-disclosure has been set at a high threshold.[251]

ACCESS TO INFORMATION

2.44 As well as regulating the use of personal data the GDPR also confers rights on data subjects.[252] These rights can be exercised by a child, provided that he or she has a general understanding of what it means to exercise the right.[253] The rights include:

(a) A right to information, i.e., a right for someone to be informed either when information is collected directly from them or where it has been acquired from a third party.[254] The detail of the information to be provided varies between these two cases but always includes information about the purposes of processing the data, the legal basis for processing and the period of time for which the data will be stored.

(b) A right of access, considered more fully below.

(c) A right to rectification of inaccurate information.[255]

(d) A right to be forgotten,[256] that is, a right to erasure of information where, for example, the personal data is no longer necessary in relation to the purpose for which it was collected or where the data subject withdraws consent and there is no other legal basis for processing the data.

250 *W v Westminster City Council*, para 239.

251 See *Bury Metropolitan Council v D* [2009] EWHC 446 (Fam); *X County Council v M, F, C* [2014] EWHC 2262 (Fam).

252 GDPR, Arts 13–18; 2018 Act, ch 3. There are also special rules about access to adoption records, see Adoption and Children (Scotland) Act 2007, s 38, Adoption (Disclosure of Information and Medical Information about Natural Parents) (Scotland) Regulations 2009, SSI 2009/268.

253 2018 Act, s 204, see also **3.3**.

254 GDPR, Arts 13 and 14, 2018 Act, s 93.

255 GDPR, Art 16; 2018 Act, s 100.

256 GDPR, Art 17; 2018 Act, s 100.

(1) The access right[257]

2.45 The access right involves a number of different rights. These first of all give the data subject the right to ask a data controller whether or not personal data concerning them is being processed. If it is, then, as set out in the GDPR, the data subject has a right of access to the data being processed and to the following information:

(a) the purposes of the processing;
(b) the categories of personal data concerned;
(c) the recipients or categories of recipient to whom the personal data have been or will be disclosed, in particular recipients in third countries or international organisations;
(d) where possible, the envisaged period for which the personal data will be stored, or, if not possible, the criteria used to determine that period;
(e) the existence of the right to request from the controller rectification or erasure of personal data or restriction of processing of personal data concerning the data subject, or to object to such processing;
(f) the right to lodge a complaint with a supervisory authority (in the case of the UK, this is the Information Commissioner's Office); and
(g) where the personal data is not collected from the data subject, any available information as to its source.

(2) Restrictions on rights

2.46 The access right is subject to some restrictions which effectively mean that certain types of information may not be disclosed by the organisation holding the data. Some of these restrictions are specific to certain types of information, and we will consider the limitations applying to social work records below. In respect of all types of data, however, there is a restriction on disclosure where the data affects third parties. This provides that, where an access request cannot be complied with without disclosing information about another individual who can be identified from the information,[258] the request need not be complied with unless either the third party has consented to disclosure of the information or it would be reasonable in all the circumstances to disclose the information without such consent.[259] A number of factors

257 GDPR, Art 15, 2018 Act, ss 94–95.

258 This includes identifying the individual as the source of information, 2018 Act, s 15 and Sch 2, Pt 3, para 16(4).

259 2018 Act, s 15 and Sch 2, Pt 3, para 16(1)–(2).

are to be taken into account in deciding whether it is reasonable to disclose information without consent, and these are:

(i) the type of information which would be disclosed;
(ii) any duty of confidentiality owed to the third party by the organisation holding the data;
(iii) any steps taken to seek consent; the capacity of the third party to give consent;
(iv) and any express refusal of consent.[260]

This exception is limited. It only prevents disclosure of information regarding the third party. If the third party does not consent (and the decision is taken that it would not be reasonable to disclose without consent), the organisation must still disclose any other information held about the person making the access request that does not identify the third party and which is not subject to any other restrictions on disclosure. A further limitation is that it does not apply in the case of social work records where the third party is a social work employee.[261]

Specific restrictions affecting social work records provide that:

(a) There is no right of access where providing access would be likely to prejudice the carrying out of social work by reason of the fact that serious harm would be likely to be caused to the physical or mental health or condition of the applicant for access or any other person.[262]
(b) Information provided to the social work department by the reporter can only be disclosed if the reporter certifies that the exception set out in (a) above does not apply to the information.[263]

In addition, none of the rights listed in **2.44** above will apply in the following situations:

(a) Where information is supplied to the court by a social work department, the court may be entitled to withhold the information in whole or in part. The effect of this is that the decision of a court to withhold information cannot be bypassed by seeking direct access to the social work record. This restriction will apply, for example, in relation to reports provided and evidence given in adoption proceedings and proceedings relating to children's hearings.[264]
(b) Where someone having the legal power to do so in relation to a data subject applies to see that person's record, there are restrictions on

260 2018 Act, s 15 and Sch 2, Pt 3, para 16(3).
261 2018 Act, s 15 and Sch 2, Pt 3, para 17.
262 2018 Act, s 15 and Sch 3, Pt 3, paras 7(2) and 11.
263 2018 Act, s 15 and Sch 2, Pt 3, para 12.
264 2018 Act, s 15 and Sch 3, Pt 3, paras 1 and 9.

the information that can be disclosed to them. These apply where the data subject is either under the age of 16 or is incapable of managing their own affairs. Information is not to be disclosed:[265]

(i) where it was provided by the data subject in the expectation that it would not be disclosed to the person making the request;

(ii) where it resulted from an examination or investigation of the data subject, and they consented to this examination or investigation in the expectation that the information would not be disclosed to the person making the request; and

(iii) where the data subject has specifically indicated that the information should not be disclosed.

These restrictions would apply, for example, where a parent with parental responsibilities and rights made an application for access in respect of information about their child or where an application was made by a guardian in respect of an adult with incapacity.

(c) Where disclosure is prohibited by statute, for example in relation to adoption proceedings and disclosure by a children's hearing of information where disclosure would be likely to cause significant harm to the child concerned.[266]

EDUCATION

2.47 This section is intended to deal briefly with the rights and duties of parents and discipline in schools. The principal right that parents have in relation to education is the right, subject to availability of places, to choose the school where their child will be educated.[267] The principal duty of parents is to ensure that their child receives a suitable education while of school age.[268] This may be done at home, or by sending the child to an independent school or, most commonly, to a local authority school. Failure to meet this responsibility can result in an attendance order being served requiring the child to attend a specific school, or in prosecution of the parents. Successful prosecution may result in the parents being fined. The child may be referred to the reporter for the children's hearing as being in need of compulsory measures of supervision if they fails to attend school regularly without a reasonable excuse.[269]

265 2018 Act, s 15 and Sch 3, Pt 3, paras 1 and 10.
266 2018 Act, s 15 and Sch 4, paras 5(3) and 6.
267 Education (Scotland) Act 1980, s 28 onwards.
268 Education (Scotland) Act 1980, s 30.
269 See chapter 5, **5.8**.

A child may no longer be subjected to corporal punishment in school, but may be disciplined in other ways, for example, by being given additional homework or a verbal reprimand. In serious cases the child may be excluded from school. If this happens the parents must be notified immediately and there is a right of appeal against the exclusion and against any conditions imposed on the child's re-attendance at school.[270]

Provision for children who require additional support is discussed in **4.19**.

270 Schools General (Scotland) Regulations 1975, SI 1975/1135, regs 4 and 4A. See also, Scottish Government *Included, Engaged and Involved Part 2: Preventing and Managing School Exclusions* (2017)

Chapter 3

Children and their families

THE RESPONSIBILITIES, RIGHTS AND POWERS OF PARENTS AND CHILDREN

(1) Introduction

3.1 This section starts with an attempt to explain the powers and rights that a child has at different stages of their life. Powers are concerned with the ability or capacity of children to enter into legal transactions, for example contracts, and to give legally effective agreement, such as the giving of consent to medical treatment.[1] Rights are concerned with the child's rights to make choices about their life, for example choices about friends, about religious beliefs and about where to stay. The extent of a child's rights is closely connected with the extent of the responsibilities and rights enjoyed by their parent(s): the child's power to control their own life grows with the decline of the parents' role. For this reason, we will also consider the responsibilities and rights of parents and the major changes brought about by the Children (Scotland) Act 1995 (the 1995 Act).

The age of majority, the age at which, technically, one is fully an adult, is 18 in Scotland. There are other age limits relevant for other purposes.[2] For example, at the age of 16 one can marry[3] and enter into other legal transactions (see below).[4] Sixteen is also the age at which compulsory education finishes and below which children can be referred to a children's hearing and be the subject of actions seeking parental responsibilities or rights (see below). A child under the age of 12 cannot commit an offence or be referred to a children's hearing on the ground that they have committed an offence, and children under the age of 12 cannot be prosecuted in a criminal court.[5]

1 Age of Legal Capacity (Scotland) Act 1991, s 2.
2 See Table 3.1 below.
3 Marriage (Scotland) Act 1977, s 1(1)(1) – No person domiciled in Scotland may marry before he (*sic*) attains the age of 16.
4 Age of Legal Capacity (Scotland) Act 1991, s 1(1)(b).
5 Age of Criminal Responsibility (Scotland) Act 2019, s 1.

Below the age of 18 the historically important division was between pupils and minors. Pupils are boys under 14 and girls under 12, minors are those between those ages and 18. Pupils had very restricted powers and were subject to the control and guidance of their tutor, normally their parent. Minors had slightly greater powers, for example to enter contracts and to consent to some types of medical treatment, and acted with the agreement of a curator, again usually the parent. Where a child had two parents in the legal sense (see below), both were tutor/curator of the child.

The Age of Legal Capacity (Scotland) Act 1991 made some changes to this position. In particular, it made changes which affect the capacity of children and it abolished tutors and curators, creating instead the position of guardian who, in relation to children under the age of 16, was to have the powers of a tutor. The first of these developments is discussed in more detail below, but it should be noted that although the distinction between pupils and minors is generally no longer relevant as far as the powers or capacity of children is concerned it is still relevant as far as children's rights are concerned.

Knowledge and an understanding of the law in this area should prove invaluable to social workers and young persons in such situations as leaving care and planning for independent living. Young people leaving care and entering into contractual arrangements, for example with mobile telephone providers, need to know the legalities of the contract and what rights and responsibilities are relevant.

(2) Legal capacity of children

3.2 The Age of Legal Capacity (Scotland) Act 1991 (the 1991 Act) sets out the rules about the capacity of children. In terms of this Act the important age is 16.[6] Below this age, subject to the exceptions noted below, children have no capacity to enter into what the 1991 Act calls 'transactions'. The term 'transactions' includes contractual agreements, the giving of any consent having legal effect (for example, consent to medical treatment), and the bringing or defending of any legal action in a civil court. It describes, in other words, actions which will have legal consequences for the child. The main exceptions are:[7]

6 The implications of other ages are set out in Table 3.1.
7 Age of Legal Capacity (Scotland) Act 1991, s 2.

(a) Children under 16 may enter into transactions of a kind normally entered into by children of the child in question's age and circumstances,[8] provided the terms of the transaction are reasonable. Note that the comparison here is with other children of the same age and circumstances, and the focus is not on the capacity of the individual child.
(b) Children over the age of 12 have the power to make wills.
(c) A child under 16 may consent to any surgical, medical or dental procedure or treatment[9] where, in the opinion of the medical practitioner attending him or her, the child is capable of understanding the nature and possible consequences of the procedure or treatment. Here the focus is on the specific capacity of the individual child.
(d) Children over 12 have the power to consent (or to withhold consent) to adoption and freeing for adoption.
(e) A child under 16 has the capacity to instruct a solicitor in respect of a civil law matter, provided that the child has a general understanding of what it means to instruct a solicitor. Such children also have capacity to sue and defend in civil court actions.

Children over the age of 16 have full legal capacity in respect of the matters covered by the Act. Sixteen- and 17-year-olds enjoy some additional protection in that before their twenty-first birthday they can challenge any transactions entered into at those ages on the grounds that the transaction was prejudicial.

As we have noted, a child can now give effective consent to medical treatment if capable of understanding the nature and possible consequences of the treatment, with the judgment as to ability to understand being made by the doctor or dentist treating the child. This capacity is also regarded as extending to refusing medical treatment,[10] though in England the view has been taken that the parents of a child can overrule their refusal of treatment.[11]

A problem might arise where the child is unable to consent and the parents refuse to consent to therapeutic treatment. In such cases treatment may be authorised by the general welfare principle extending

8 For example, purchase of small items, payment for leisure facilities.

9 This would include consenting to the prescribing of contraceptives.

10 See Norrie, K, *The Law Relating to Parent and Child in Scotland* (3rd edn) para 3.1; see also *Houston, Applicant* 1996 SCLR 943 and annotation.

11 *Re W (a minor) (medical treatment)* [1992] 4 All ER 627 at 639j–640a. See also *V v F* 1991 SCLR 225 and comment thereon.

to children. There is also the possibility of applying to court for permission for treatment under section 11 of the 1995 Act. Failure on the part of the parent to consent to therapeutic treatment may also give rise to a referral to a children's hearing on the ground of lack of parental care.[12] In emergency cases, treatment can be given without consent.

Table 3.1

Age	Consequences
12 or over	can be responsible for criminal offence, Age of Criminal Responsibility (Scotland) Act 2019, s 1.
12 or over	can be prosecuted for criminal offence, Age of Criminal Responsibility (Scotland) Act 2019, s 1.
	can make a will, Age of Capacity (Scotland) Act 1991 s 2(2).
	deemed to understand what is involved in instructing a solicitor, 1991 Act, s 2(4A).
	must consent to adoption, Adoption and Children (Scotland) Act 2007, s 32.
Under 16	can be prosecuted for a crime (if 12 or over), Criminal Procedure (Scotland) Act 1995, s 42; will be referred to a children's hearing if they have committed an offence, Children's Hearings (Scotland) Act 2011, s 67(2)(j).
	can only enter into transactions of type which children of that age and circumstances would commonly enter into, provided that transaction reasonable, Age of Capacity (Scotland) Act 1991, s 2.
	can only consent to medical treatment if practitioner giving treatment considers them capable of understanding the nature and possible consequences of the treatment, 1991 Act, s 2(4).
	can instruct solicitor in relation to civil matter if has general understanding of what it means to do so – can also raise civil action,1991 Act, ss 2(4A) and 2(4B).
	parent has duty to ensure that child attends school or is otherwise provided with efficient education, Education (Scotland) Act 1980, ss 30 and 31.

12 *Finlayson, Applicant* 1989 SCLR 601. See **5.22(a)**.

Age	Consequences
16 or over	can marry or enter into civil partnership, Marriage (Scotland) Act 1977, s 1; Civil Partnership Act 2004, s 86(1)(c).
	parental responsibilities and rights, aside from responsibility to provide guidance, cease, 1995 Act, ss 1 and 2.
	can only be referred to a children's hearing if already subject to supervision requirement, Children's Hearings (Scotland) Act 2011, s 199(9).
	capacity to enter into any transaction (i.e. contracts and consent to medical treatment), though transactions at age 16 and 17 may, subject to limitations, be set aside if prejudicial – application to set aside can be made up to 21,1991 Act, ss 1 and 3.
	Can vote in local government and Scottish Parliament elections, Representation of the People Act 1983, s 2.
Under 18	subject to parental responsibility to provide advice, Children (Scotland) Act 1995, s 1(2)(b).
	covered by child welfare provisions of Children (Scotland) Act 1995, e.g., provision of accommodation, provision of services to children, s 93(2)(a).
	can be referred to children's hearing if subject to existing supervision requirement, Children's Hearings (Scotland) Act 2011, s 199(6), (7).
	can be subject of adoption order, Adoption and Children (Scotland) Act 2007, s 119(1).
	right to financial support from parent, Family Law (Scotland) Act 1985, s 1.
18 or over	no parental responsibilities/rights (though, if in education/training, can claim support), Children (Scotland) Act 1995, s 1(2)(b); Family Law (Scotland) Act 1985, s 1(5)(b).
	able to vote and stand for UK parliament and stand for election to local government, Local Government (Scotland) Act 1973, s 29; Representation of the People Act 1983, s 1; Electoral Administration Act 2006, s 17.

(3) Children's rights

3.3 As children grow older the responsibilities and rights of their parents diminish, and the rights of the child to manage their affairs and take decisions about their lives increase. Where the exercise of rights involves doing things which have legal consequences for the child the rules in the Age of Legal Capacity (Scotland) Act 1991 explained above apply. In the absence of a coherent list, rights conferred on children at various ages are found scattered through other law and legislation, examples are:

(a) the right to a share of a parent's moveable estate on death of the parent;
(b) the right to be supported by a parent up to the age of 18 (or up to 25 if in education or training[13]), this right extends to give a claim against the biological father even if he has no parental responsibilities or rights, and a claim can also be made against anyone who has accepted a child into their family;[14]
(c) a right of access to personal information kept about them, provided that they 'have a general understanding of what it means to exercise' the access right,[15] children aged 12 or over are deemed to have such an understanding;
(d) the right to have their views taken into account when a major decision is being taken about their life;[16]
(e) the right to have their views taken into account in a variety of court and other proceedings;[17]
(f) the right to attend a children's hearing concerning them;[18] and
(g) the right of children who have been looked after to be provided with certain aftercare services.[19]

In addition, children may be able to rely on the rights protected under various articles of the European Convention on Human Rights and exercise the right given to sue local authorities under the Human Rights Act 1998.[20]

(4) Parental responsibilities

3.4 Parents have responsibilities to their children, and the legal emphasis is on these responsibilities rather than the rights that parents have. The responsibilities of a parent to a child under the age of 16 are:[21]

13 Family Law (Scotland) Act 1985, s 1(5).
14 Family Law (Scotland) Act 1985, s 1.
15 Data Protection Act 2018, s 208.
16 Children (Scotland) 1995 Act, s 6.
17 For example, 1995 Act, s 16.
18 Children's Hearings (Scotland) Act 2011, s 73. This is expressed as a duty, but the child will still have a right to attend a hearing even if they have been excused attendance.
19 1995 Act, ss 29 and 30.
20 Human Rights Act 1998, ss 6 and 7.
21 1995 Act, s 1.

(a) to safeguard and promote the health, development and welfare of the child;[22]

(b) to provide direction to the child appropriate to their age (which implies that as the child grows older the responsibility to direct lessens);[23]

(c) in cases where the child is not living with the parent (for example, because the parents are separated or divorced) the parent has to maintain regular contact and 'personal relations' with the child;[24]

(d) to act as the child's legal representative, for example, in relation to entering contracts and managing property.[25] As we have seen above, when the child grows older, they acquire the capacity to do these things.

For children aged 16 and 17, the parent has a responsibility to provide guidance appropriate to the child's age, though the right to give such guidance expires on the child's sixteenth birthday.[26] In all cases, the responsibilities are to be fulfilled only where this is practicable and in the interests of the child. Fulfilment will also be subject to any court orders about parental responsibilities and any limitations imposed by compulsory supervision orders.

These responsibilities replace any analogous duties imposed by common law. The duties of a parent are as described in the 1995 Act and in other statutory provisions. These duties include, for example, aliment and ensuring that children are provided with education, as well as any duties imposed by common law which are not analogous to those listed above.

There is one further provision of the 1995 Act to be considered under this heading. This is the duty to 'have regard to' the views of the child in taking any major decision involving the exercise of parental responsibilities and rights.[27] The age of the child is relevant to this process and children aged 12 and over are deemed to be capable of forming a view. It is not clear what decisions will be major decisions, though presumably an objective standard will be invoked; nor is it clear how a child could enforce this provision and prevent an action in respect of which their views had not been sought. Perhaps the only remedy would be for the child to seek an order in relation to parental responsibilities or rights. Finally, the requirement is only to have regard

22 1995 Act, s 1(1)(a).
23 1995 Act, s 1(1)(b).
24 1995 Act, s 1(1)(c).
25 1995 Act, s 1(1)(d).
26 1995 Act, s 1(2)(b).
27 1995 Act, s 6(1).

to what the child wants and does not mean that the child's wishes must be followed.[28]

(5) Parental rights

3.5 Parents have certain legal rights, but these are conferred on them for the express purpose of enabling them to fulfil their parental responsibilities. This reflects some views expressed in relation to parental rights before the 1995 Act was passed. For example, Lord Scarman in the case of *Gillick v West Norfolk and Wisbech Area Health Authority* said: 'The principle is that parental right or power of control of the person and property of the child exists primarily to enable the parent to discharge his duty of maintenance, protection and education until [the child] reaches such an age as to be able to look after himself and make his own decisions.'[29]

Parents have the right:[30]

(a) to have their children living with them or to regulate their residence;[31]

(b) to control, direct or guide their children's upbringing in a manner appropriate to the age of the child;[32]

(c) to maintain direct contact on a regular basis with any child who is not living with them and to maintain personal relations with the child;[33]

(d) to act as their children's legal representative.[34]

These rights supersede any analogous common law rights held by parents. One of the rights encompassed in (d) above is the right to manage any property belonging to a child. In doing this a parent must act as a reasonable and prudent person acting on their own behalf would act. Parents still have other rights conferred by statute, such as the right

28 1995 Act, s 6. Note: Children (Scotland) Act 2020, s 1(6) amends s 6(1) of the 1995 Act, but at the time of writing no date of appointment has been made and the amendments are not yet in force.

29 [1985] 3 All ER 402 at 421d.

30 1995 Act, s 2. It is not within the scope of parental rights and responsibilities for a parent to consent to the living arrangements for a 16–17-year-old child who lacked capacity if those arrangements would otherwise amount to a deprivation of liberty within the meaning of ECHR Article 5, see *Re D (A Child)* [2019] UKSC 42; *Re A-F (Children)* [2018] EWHC 138 (Fam). It is not clear that older children could consent to this either; such 'detention' is not likely to be a transaction of a kind normally entered into by a child. See also chapter 7.

31 1995 Act, s 2(1)(a).

32 1995 Act, s 2(1)(b).

33 1995 Act, s 2(1)(c).

34 1995 Act, s 2(1)(d).

to attend a children's hearing involving their child.[35] The rights listed above apply until the child reaches the age of 16.

Where more than one person has parental rights in respect of a child they may exercise their rights independently of each other. For example, if the parents are separated, the mother can take any decision about the child without consulting the father.

(6) Who holds parental responsibilities and rights?

3.6 The mother of a child holds parental responsibilities and rights automatically, as does the father of the child, provided that he was married to the mother either at the time of conception of the child or subsequently.

Aside from this, the biological father does not automatically have responsibilities and rights but can acquire these in one of three ways. He can enter into an agreement with the mother of the child (providing she has not been deprived of any responsibilities or rights). To be effective, this agreement must be in a prescribed form and be registered in the Books of Council and Session.[36] Alternatively, he could apply to court for an order in respect of parental responsibilities and rights under section 11 of the 1995 Act.[37] Other people may come to hold responsibilities and rights as a result of such an order, or as a result of another type of court order, for example, a permanence order. Finally, in the case of a child whose birth is registered after 4 May 2006, a biological father will have parental responsibilities and rights if he is registered as the father on the child's birth certificate.[38]

A second female parent of a child will have parental responsibilities and rights if she is married to, or in a civil partnership with, the mother at the date of fertility or donor insemination treatment (unless she did not consent to this treatment). Otherwise, these responsibilities and rights can be acquired in the same way that an unmarried father would obtain them though, in the case of registration on the child's birth certificate, this only applies after 1 September 2009.[39]

35 Children's Hearing (Scotland) Act 2011, s 74.

36 Parental Responsibilities and Parental Rights Agreement (Scotland) Regulations 1996, SI 1996/2549, as amended by the Parental Responsibilities and Parental Rights Agreement (Scotland) Amendment Regulations 2006, SSI 2006/255. Similar provisions apply to the acquisition of responsibilities and rights by a female parent other than the birth mother, Children (Scotland) Act 1995, s 4A.

37 1995 Act, s 11.

38 1995 Act, s 3(1)(b)(ii).

39 1995 Act, s 3(1)(c) and (d).

Parents holding parental responsibilities and rights can appoint a guardian to take over those rights and responsibilities after their death.[40]

Where someone without responsibilities and rights has care or control of a child, that person has the responsibility of doing what is reasonable in the circumstances to safeguard the child's health, development and welfare.[41] Included within this is the power to consent to medical treatment where the child is unable to and the person does not know that the parent would refuse consent to treatment. These powers are not conferred on teachers but would apply where a child is under the care and control of a foster parent or, possibly, a social worker.[42]

(7) Court orders and parental responsibilities[43]

3.7 Under section 11 of the 1995 Act, anyone claiming an interest can apply to court for an order relating to parental responsibilities and rights.[44] This includes the child concerned, but local authorities are specifically excluded.[45] An application for an order can also be made by anyone holding parental responsibilities and rights. Someone who previously held these but has lost them can also apply, providing they were not lost in a number of specified ways, for example, by being extinguished by the making of an adoption order, though in such a case it is still possible to apply for an order granting contact.[46] An order can be made in other proceedings without application by any of the parties if the court considers that the order should be made.[47] Once a permanence order has been made in respect of a child, none of the orders listed as (a) to (e) below can be applied for.[48] It also appears that a child can make an application for an order regulating contact with a sibling.[49]

40 1995 Act, s 7. The term 'guardian' is not defined in the 1995 Act but essentially describes a parent substitute. It has been said that, where an order is made conferring full parental responsibilities and rights on someone other than a parent, this order is more appropriately a guardianship order rather than an order for parental responsibilities and rights, with the person acquiring the responsibilities and rights becoming a guardian. See *S v S* 2011 Fam LR 86 at [8].

41 1995 Act, s 7(5).

42 1995 Act, s 5.

43 1995 Act, s 11.

44 The right to attend a children's hearing relating to a child is not a parental responsibility/right and therefore cannot be conferred by a court order, *Principal Reporter v K* [2010] CSIH 5.

45 1995 Act, s 11(5).

46 1995 Act, s 11(3), (4).

47 1995 Act, s 11(3), (4).

48 1995 Act, s 11A.

49 *E v E* 2004 Fam LR 115, though see *D v H* 2004 Fam LR 41.

The 1995 Act provides a non-exclusive list of the types of order that may be sought:

(a) an order depriving someone of some or all rights or responsibilities;[50]
(b) an order imposing responsibilities and conferring rights;[51]
(c) a residence order specifying where a child is to live;[52]
(d) a contact order, regulating personal relations and direct contact with someone with whom the child is not living;[53]
(e) a specific issue order which is designed to regulate any specific issue which has arisen with respect to parental responsibilities, for example, a question about medical treatment;[54]
(f) an interdict preventing some action in exercise of parental responsibilities and rights.[55]

The application for such an order can be made in a legal action intended to resolve that particular issue or it can form an incidental part of any other proceedings, such as a divorce action.

In making any of these orders:

(a) The court must regard the welfare of the child as its paramount consideration.[56]
(b) The court must not make any order about parental responsibilities or rights unless it considers that making the order would be better for the child than making no order at all.[57] This emphasises a policy of minimum intervention.
(c) The child involved must be given an opportunity to indicate if they wish to express a view about any order. If the child does wish to express a view they must be given an opportunity to do so and the court must have regard to any views expressed before making an order. In order to allow this to happen, a child must be notified of applications for orders dealing with responsibilities and rights. On the notification there is a form which the child can return indicating whether they wish to express a view. If the child does so wish, the form allows them to nominate someone to communicate their views to the court or to write to the judge

50 1995 Act, s 11(2)(a).
51 1995 Act, s11(2)(b).
52 1995 Act, s 11(2)(c).
53 1995 Act, s11(2)(d).
54 1995 Act, s 11(2)(e).
55 1995 Act, s 11(2)(f). Note: it may be that the same effect can be achieved through a specific issue order. In *M v C* 2002 SLT (Sh Ct) 82 a specific issue order was granted to prevent the child's mother from changing the child's surname.
56 1995 Act, s 11(7)(a).
57 1995 Act, s 11(7)(a).

expressing their views. The procedural rules also envisage the judge either speaking to the child directly or sending someone to speak to the child on their behalf.

(d) Consideration must be given to the need to protect the child from any abuse or risk of abuse which might affect them.[58] 'Abuse' is defined widely and includes violence, harassment, threatening conduct and any other conduct giving rise to, or likely to give rise to, physical or mental injury, fear alarm or distress, as well as domestic abuse and abuse of a person other than the child.[59]

(e) The court will need to consider whether two people would have to co-operate with one another as respects matters affecting the child.[60] The underlying consideration is whether the two (or more) people who have to co-operate would be able to do so.[61]

If, during the course of a hearing on an application for an order under section 11, the judge considers that any of the non-offence grounds of referral to a children's hearing exist, the judge may refer the case of the child to the reporter.[62] The effect of an order conferring parental rights on one person is not, automatically, to remove them from another person having parental rights. For example, if the court were to make a residence order in favour of a wife, that would not automatically deprive the husband of the right to have the child living with him. Deprivation of rights occurs only where the court expressly takes them away from someone who previously enjoyed them.[63]

(8) Support where there is a kinship care order[64]

3.8 Local authorities have an obligation to provide support and assistance to children and carers where a specific type of kinship care is being provided.[65] This will arise where a kinship care order has been made.[66] These obligations arise where there is:

(i) an order giving the carer the right to have a child living with them or to control the child's residence;

58 1995 Act, s (7A).
59 1995 Act, s 11(7B), (7C).
60 1995 Act, s 11(7D).
61 See *Treasure v McGrath* 2006 Fam LR 100.
62 1995 Act, s 12 and Children's Hearings (Scotland) Act 2011, s 62.
63 1995 Act, s 11(11).
64 Children and Young People (Scotland) Act 2014, Part 13, see also Scottish Government, *National Guidance on Part 13 of the Children and Young People (Scotland) Act 2014: Support for Kinship Care* (2016).
65 Children and Young People (Scotland) Act 2014, s 71(1).
66 Though assistance is also available to those who are applying for a kinship care order.

(ii) a residence order requiring that a child lives predominantly with the carer;

(iii) an order appointing the carer as guardian of the child; or an order appointing the carer as guardian of the child.[67]

In addition, the child subject to the order must be 'eligible' and must either be under 16, be aged 16 and have been subject to a kinship care order before reaching that age, or be aged under 16 and have had a guardian appointed without a court order.[68] A child will be eligible if they have previously been looked after, or the local authority takes the view that they are at risk of becoming looked after.[69]

Finally, to be eligible for this type of assistance, the carer must be either related to the child (provided that they are not the child's parent) or a friend or acquaintance of a person related to the child.[70]

If these qualifying criteria are met, assistance can be provided in the form of information and support and, in most cases, in the form of financial support either for making an application for a kinship care order or as an allowance to the carer and/or the child.[71] Financial support can only be granted following an application made to the local authority.[72]

LEGALLY RECOGNISED RELATIONSHIPS

(1) Marriage[73]

3.9 When same-sex marriage became possible there were in existing legislation a large number of references to 'husband and wife' and 'married couple'. These have not been comprehensively amended. In practice, references to a married couple, or to someone who is married, are to be read as including a reference to a same-sex marriage. References to a couple living together as a married couple are to include

67 Children and Young People (Scotland) Act 2014, s 72(1). See fn 24 above for the meaning of 'guardian'.

68 Under 1995 Act, s 7, e.g., by a deceased parent.

69 Children and Young People (Scotland) Act 2014, s 71(5); Kinship Care Assistance (Scotland) Order 2016, SSI 2016/153, art 5. The guidance suggests (at para 44) that 'a child at risk of being looked after is generally one who cannot live with their parents'.

70 Children and Young People (Scotland) Act 2014, s 72(2), there is provision for the Scottish Ministers to add other qualifying categories.

71 Kinship Care Assistance (Scotland) Order 2016, SSI 2016/153, art 4. The guidance identifies the types of information which may potentially be relevant (paras 52, 54 and 58).

72 Kinship Care Assistance (Scotland) Order 2016, art 7.

73 Marriage (Scotland) Act 1977.

a reference to living together with another person of the same sex as a married couple. In addition, a reference to 'husband and wife' or to 'living together as husband and wife' are to be read as including same-sex couples.[74]

Before two people can get married, certain requirements must be fulfilled. Both parties must be over 16, must be of sound mind, must be single, and must not be within the forbidden degrees of relationship.[75] If these requirements are met, the parties will generally go through a regular marriage, that is, a religious ceremony or civil wedding. In the past it was possible to have a legally recognised marriage without such a ceremony, but this is no longer possible. Reference is sometimes made to 'common law' marriages. These situations, where, for example, a man is referred to as being a woman's common law husband, usually amount simply to cohabitation and do not give rise to the legal consequences which follow from a legally formalised marriage. The father of a child who is actually married to the mother will have parental responsibilities and rights in respect of that child, whereas the 'common law' husband who fathers a child will not automatically have parental responsibilities and rights and will have to acquire these in one of the ways set out above.

After marriage the parties have a mutual obligation of financial support and an obligation to live together as a married couple. Marriage also provides rights of inheritance or succession to the other party to the marriage and children. Marriage does not require any change of surname, so both parties can retain their pre-marriage surnames or make whatever other decisions regarding this which they wish. Even while married and living together, a husband may be charged and convicted of raping his wife. In the case deciding this, the earlier view – that, in agreeing to the marriage, a wife was giving blanket consent to sexual intercourse with her husband – was rejected.[76]

(a) Separation

3.10 It is possible to obtain a formal judicial separation requiring the parties to a marriage to live apart but not releasing them from the other obligations of marriage. So, for example, the couple will still be required to support one another financially and the commission

74 Marriage and Civil Partnership (Scotland) Act 2014 and Civil Partnership Act 2004 (Consequential Provisions and Modifications) Order 2014, SI 2014/3229, Sch 1, para 2.

75 As defined in the Marriage (Scotland) Act 1977, Sch. 1.

76 *S v HM Advocate* 1989 SLT 469.

of adultery while separated will still be acceptable as a ground for evidencing the irretrievable breakdown of the marriage. In general, any separation will be informal, as will any arrangements for aliment or for residence and contact regarding any children. If such informal arrangements are impossible it may be necessary to take action in the sheriff court to regulate these matters.

(b) Divorce

3.11 The Divorce (Scotland) Act 1976 introduced a single ground for divorce in Scotland: 'irretrievable breakdown of the marriage'.[77] In some ways this simply amounted to a restatement of the previously existing grounds of divorce, since they, together with two new grounds based on non-cohabitation, were to be considered as evidence of breakdown.

The four grounds evidencing an irretrievable breakdown are–

(a) adultery;[78]
(b) behaviour – where the defender 'has behaved … in such a way that the pursuer cannot reasonably be expected to cohabit with the defender'.[79] This ground would cover violence by the defender, drunkenness or unnatural, excessive or insufficient sexual demands;
(c) one year's non-cohabitation and the defender consents to the divorce;[80]
(d) two years' non-cohabitation – here the defender's consent is not required.[81]

In addition, a divorce can be obtained on the ground that one of the parties has been issued with an interim gender recognition certificate. This ground will not be available where a full gender recognition certificate is granted by the Gender Recognition Panel, as this requires the consent of both parties to the continuation of the marriage.[82]

77 Divorce (Scotland) Act 1976, s 1.
78 Divorce (Scotland) Act 1976, s 1(2)(a).
79 Divorce (Scotland) Act 1976, s 1(2)(b).
80 Divorce (Scotland) Act 1976, s 1(2)(d).
81 Divorce (Scotland) Act 1976, s 1(2)(e).
82 Divorce (Scotland) Act 1976, s 1(1)(b); Gender Recognition Act 2004, s 4C.

(c) Divorce procedure

3.12 Provided that one of these grounds can be established, a spouse may seek a divorce at any time following the marriage ceremony. Most cases are now dealt with in the sheriff court. There are two types of procedure by which a divorce can be obtained: ordinary and simplified. The ordinary procedure is similar to that involved in an ordinary court action, for example, in a claim for compensation following a road accident. If, during a divorce action, it appears to the court that there is a reasonable prospect of reconciliation between the parties, the court has to continue[83] the action to enable attempts to be made to effect a reconciliation.[84]

The simplified procedure amounts essentially to a do-it-yourself divorce. It is available only where the divorce is based on non-cohabitation, there are no children of the marriage under 16, and no financial provisions are being sought. An application is completed and returned to the clerk of the court (either the sheriff court or Court of Session) who notifies the other party. If there is no dispute, a decree of divorce will arrive through the post.

(d) Financial provision on divorce

3.13 There are two types of financial provision to be considered on divorce – provision for children and provision for the other spouse. The first of these generally takes the form of a continuing payment of aliment. In the second case, the statutory guidelines which now exist encourage 'clean break' settlements, i.e., settlements where there is no continuing payment to an ex-spouse, rather payment is a lump sum at the time of divorce.[85] In most cases these financial provisions will be agreed between the parties, if not, there are statutory rules governing the settlement.[86] As between spouses these essentially involve equal sharing of resources. In arriving at its decision, the court must consider a number of factors including, for example, any economic advantage obtained by one spouse from the contributions of the other or any economic disadvantage suffered by one in the interests of the other. This would, for example, allow the courts to compensate a wife for giving up her career to allow the husband to pursue his.

83 Rather counterintuitively, continuation in law effectively means to stop any further procedure.
84 Divorce (Scotland) Act 1976, s 2.
85 Family Law (Scotland) Act 1985.
86 Family Law (Scotland) Act 1985.

(e) Arrangements for children

3.14 There are children involved in a significant proportion of divorces and normally the arrangements for bringing up the children will be agreed between the parties. Even if they are, the court is obliged to consider whether to exercise its power to make an order about parental responsibilities. The court may also exercise its power to refer the case to the reporter because it appears to it that one of the grounds of referral is satisfied in respect of a child of the marriage who is under the age of 16. If it concludes that it should exercise one of these powers the judgment in the divorce action can be postponed if it is necessary to obtain more information before exercising the power.[87] This can include obtaining a report from the social work department.[88] Where an order in relation to parental responsibilities and rights is in issue the case may, at any stage, be referred for mediation.[89]

If required, social workers will need to complete exhaustive inquiries about the backgrounds and parenting capacities of parents and produce a matrimonial proceedings report.[90] This will be used by the judge, in conjunction with other information, to make decisions about the arrangements for children. In situations where the court deems it necessary, social workers will be required to supervise the contact visits for children. Some of the most stressful experiences for parents and children arise over contact arrangements and visits. The verdict of research is clear: children who continue to have close, loving relationships with both parents are least likely to exhibit the worst effects of the divorce and a social worker's attention to alleviating barriers to parental contact may contribute enormously to minimising these effects.

(2) Civil partnerships[91]

3.15 Since 2021 it has been possible for different-sex couples in Scotland to enter into Civil Partnership.[92] Prior to the 2020 Act, Civil Partnership was permitted only for same-sex couples.[93] Before a civil partnership can be entered into the parties must meet certain criteria: they

87 1995 Act, s 12(2).

88 Matrimonial Proceedings (Children) Act 1958, s 11; see *Hardie v Hardie* 1993 SCLR 60, *O'Neill v Gilhooley* 2007 Fam LR 15.

89 Act of Sederunt (Sheriff Court Ordinary Cause Rules) 1993, SI 1993/1956, rr 33.22 and 33A.22; Rules of the Court of Session 1994, r 49.23.

90 Matrimonial Proceedings (Children) Act 1958, s 11.

91 Civil Partnership (Scotland) Act 2020, amending the Civil Partnership Act 2004.

92 Civil Partnership (Scotland) Act 2020, s 1(1).

93 Civil Partnership Act 2004, s 1(1).

must be aged 16 or over; they must not be within the forbidden degrees of relationship; and they must be legally free to enter the partnership, e.g. they must not still be married or in another civil partnership.[94] The ceremony must be preceded, as in the case of marriage, by notice given to the Registrar, which is then published.[95]

The effect of a civil partnership is to put the couple legally in the same position as a married couple, for example:

(a) A partner (including a non-entitled partner) can take advantage of the provisions of the Matrimonial Homes (Family Protection) (Scotland) Act 1981.
(b) Partners have legal rights in succession.
(c) There are rights to financial provision on dissolution of the partnership.
(d) A partner will have the same benefits and pension entitlements as a spouse would have.
(e) Discrimination on the grounds that someone has entered a civil partnership is illegal in the same way that discrimination against people on the grounds that they are married is illegal.

The partnership can be dissolved on the same grounds, aside from adultery, as apply in the case of divorce.[96] Where dissolution proceedings are started, as with divorce proceedings, the court must, in cases where it appears that there are real prospects of reconciliation, continue the case to allow efforts to be made to effect a reconciliation.

(3) Cohabitation

3.16 Historically, simple cohabitation created no legal relationship between the parties[97] and had few legal consequences. The position was changed by the Family Law (Scotland) Act 2006 which conferred certain rights on cohabitants. These rights are, however, limited and it seems clear that the limitations resulted from a desire on the part of the Scottish Parliament to avoid putting cohabitants in the same legal position as a married couple (or civil partners), no matter the length and nature of the relationship.[98] In order to enjoy these rights the cohabitants must

94 Civil Partnership Act 2004, s 86. Schedule 10 provides details of the prohibited degrees of relationship.
95 Civil Partnership Act 2004, Chapter 2.
96 Civil Partnership Act 2004, s 117.
97 Though it could, if other conditions were fulfilled, result in legal recognition by the courts that the cohabitants were married, this possibility no longer exists.
98 See T Guthrie & H Hiram, 'Property and cohabitation: understanding the Family Law (Scotland) Act 2006', 2007 *Edinburgh Law Review* 208.

be living together as husband and wife or as civil partners. The court to which application is made (for the exercise of the rights) will determine whether there is such cohabitation, taking into account factors such as its length, the nature of the relationship and financial arrangements.[99] The main rights granted to cohabitants are, first, a right to apply to the court for financial provision on termination of the cohabitation based on economic advantage obtained or economic disadvantage suffered during the cohabitation.[100] The second right is a right to apply to the court for financial provision on the death of a cohabitant, though this is only available where some or all of the cohabitant's estate has not been disposed of by a will.[101] Other consequences of cohabitation may be possible effects on any benefit claimed, and the entitlement of cohabitants to apply for occupancy rights under the Matrimonial Homes (Family Protection) (Scotland) Act 1981.

(4) Child support

3.17 In addition to the arrangements covered above, there are likely to be situations where a child's parents have separated and the non-residential parent is not paying aliment for the child. The residential parent or a child aged over 12 can apply to the Child Maintenance Service[102] for a maintenance assessment, and any payment may be made direct to the parent seeking support or may be made via the agency which will collect and enforce if so required. Decisions of the Child Maintenance Service may be appealed and are reviewed by the Social Security and Child Support Tribunal.

ADOPTION

(1) Introduction

3.18 Adoption is a process by which a new legal relationship of parent and child is created. Where the application is made by one partner in a couple and the other partner is the parent of the child adopted, the order will not affect any parental responsibilities and rights held by that parent. In other cases, the effect of an adoption order is to extinguish any

99 Family Law (Scotland) Act 2006, s 25.

100 Family Law (Scotland) Act 2006, s 28, for a successful application see *Lindsay v Murphy* 2010 GWD 29–604.

101 Family Law (Scotland) Act 2006, s 29, see, for example, *Windram, Applicant* 2009 Fam LR 157.

102 The Child Maintenance Service replaced the Child Support Agency in 2012.

pre-existing parental responsibilities and rights.[103] Any parent who loses rights as a result of the making of an adoption order can, however, still apply for contact, and it is possible for an adoption order to specifically provide for continued contact between the child and their birth parents.[104] In law, the relationship between the child and adoptive parent(s) is the same as that with their original or birth parent(s). Adoption law is now contained in the Adoption and Children (Scotland) Act 2007 (the 2007 Act), supplemented by a variety of regulations and by guidance.[105] The 2007 Act was passed after a review of adoption law in Scotland which recommended substantial changes.[106]

Around one-third of all adoptions involve someone who is related to the child, mainly involving step-parent adoptions. The remaining adoptions are arranged by adoption agencies. All local authorities are adoption agencies, and there are also a number of independent adoption societies approved by the Scottish Ministers.[107] Local authorities must provide an adoption service[108] which will include provision of arrangements for assessing children for adoption, assessing prospective adopters, placing children for adoption, providing information about adoption and providing adoption support services. This last includes the provision of counselling, guidance and other appropriate assistance. Specific groups are identified as intended beneficiaries of the adoption service, including adopted children, adopters, and the birth parents and siblings of adopted children.[109] In providing the adoption service the local authority can ask for assistance from other agencies, including other local authorities and Health Boards.[110] Planning for adoption services will be part of the children's services plan to be prepared by local authorities.

Slightly different rules apply to related adoptions and to those arranged by an adoption agency. These differences will be considered as appropriate. One of the differences is that adoption agencies must appoint an adoption panel.[111] The functions of this panel[112] are extensive

103 Adoption and Children (Scotland) Act 2007, s 35.

104 See Scottish Government, *Guidance on Looked after Children (Scotland) Regulations 2009 and the Adoption and Children (Scotland) Act 2007* (2011) (LAC Guidance), pp 153–156.

105 The LAC Guidance.

106 Adoption Policy Review Group, *Adoption: Better choices for our children* (2005).

107 All must be registered as adoption services with the Care Inspectorate, see chapter 11.

108 Adoption and Children (Scotland) Act 2007, ss 1–3.

109 Adoption and Children (Scotland) Act 2007, s 1(3).

110 Adoption and Children (Scotland) Act 2007, s 6. In general, such requests can only be refused if agreeing would be incompatible with the functions of the body to which the request is made or would prejudice the body's performance of its functions.

111 Adoption Agencies (Scotland) Regulations 2009, regs 3–6.

112 Adoption Agencies (Scotland) Regulations 2009, reg 6.

and begin with recommendations to the agency about the suitability of prospective adopters. The panel also considers the suitability of a particular placement for adoption and whether adoption is in the child's best interests. Further considerations include whether application should be made for a permanence order including authority for the child to be adopted, and whether there should be continued contact between the child and their birth parents. The agency must take a decision on any recommendation made by the panel within 14 days of the recommendation. Although it must take the panel's recommendation into account, the agency is not bound by it, but if the recommendation is not followed the reasons for this must be recorded in writing. The panel must have at least six members, including a medical adviser and a legal adviser, with the quorum for any meeting of the panel being at least three, excluding these advisers. In some cases, the panel must include, or have received advice from, the legal adviser, these cases include recommendations as to whether adoption is in the best interests of the child or a recommendation that application is made for a permanence order. In addition to its specified functions in relation to adoption, the agency can also refer other matters to the panel (e.g., adoption support plans) for advice, and the guidance suggests that:[113]

> It would be in the spirit of the 2007 Act that the majority of cases where children cannot return home and need a secure family placement should be treated similarly and be referred to the adoption panel for consideration of the plan for permanence.

Special rules apply to inter-country adoptions and these are not considered here. Adoption agencies may be involved in assessing the suitability of prospective adopters who intend to adopt from abroad, and once a child is in Scotland with prospective adopters, they and the child will be monitored by the local authority until the adoption order is granted.[114]

(2) The welfare of the child

3.19 The paramount consideration in all decisions relating to the adoption of a child, whether the decision is taken by an adoption agency or a court, is the need to safeguard and promote the welfare of the child throughout their life.[115] Those involved in decision making must also

113 LAC Guidance, p 155.

114 Adoption and Children (Scotland) Act 2007, ch 6, Adoptions with a Foreign Element (Scotland) Regulations 2009, SSI 2009/182; see also www.mygov.scot/adopting-child-from-abroad/ (accessed April 2026).

115 Adoption and Children (Scotland) Act 2007, s 14(3), LAC Guidance, p 152ff.

take into account the views of the child (children over the age of 12 are deemed mature enough to form a view), the child's religious persuasion, racial origin and cultural and linguistic background, the value of a stable family unit[116] in the development of the child and the likely effect on the child throughout their life of making an adoption order.[117] Before making any arrangement for adoption, agencies must also consider whether adoption is the option which is likely to best meet the needs of the child or whether there is some practicable alternative which would be better.[118] This last will include ensuring that 'all possibilities of retaining the child with their family network have been checked'.[119] Adoption panels, as part of their advisory function, must, if they are recommending that adoption is in the best interests of the child, produce a written report on their consideration of alternatives to adoption.[120] Before making an adoption order the court must also consider the alternatives[121] and analyse the arguments for and against each option.[122]

(3) Who can adopt?

3.20 There are certain restrictions affecting the ability to adopt. A single individual wishing to adopt must be aged 21 or over and is subject to the further condition that they are either:[123]

(a) single; or
(b) married to, or in a civil partnership with, the natural parent (provided they are aged 18 or over) of the child (and provided that they have parental responsibilities and rights); or
(c) married or in a civil partnership but either separated from their partner or the other partner either cannot be found or is incapable of making an application for health reasons; or
(d) living with someone in an enduring family relationship as husband and wife or as civil partners and the other partner is incapable of applying because of ill-health.

116 This implies, of course, that the adopters can provide such a stable unit, see LAC Guidance, pp 152–3.

117 Adoption and Children (Scotland) Act 2007, s 14(1), (4)(a)–(d).

118 Adoption and Children (Scotland) Act 2007, s 14(6), (7). *Edinburgh City Council v RO and RD* [2016] SAC Civ 15 suggests that social workers in their day-to-day work should ask themselves 'what else could we do to avoid a more drastic form of order such as adoption?' (para 3).

119 LAC Guidance, p 156.

120 Adoption Agencies (Scotland) Regulations 2009, reg 6(3).

121 *AV and SV v ASF and IDF* [2017] CSOH 103, paras 78–80.

122 *Fife Council v M and F* [2015] CSIH 79, para 63.

123 Adoption and Children (Scotland) Act 2007, s 30.

An application by a single applicant who is the mother or father of the child is only possible if the other parent (in the sense of a parent having parental responsibilities or rights) is dead or has disappeared, or there must be some other reason justifying their exclusion, or there must be no other parent in terms of the legislation governing fertility treatment.[124]

Couples can adopt if they are either married or in a civil partnership or, alternatively, if they are living together as if they were married or in a civil partnership in 'an enduring family relationship'.[125] In addition, neither of the couple must be a parent of the child and both must be aged 21 or over.

In all cases the adopter(s) must be domiciled in the United Kingdom and have lived in the United Kingdom for at least a year before the application for adoption is made.

Aside from the above there are no **legal** restrictions on ability to adopt. Agencies are obliged to prepare and make available the criteria to be used in deciding whether to assess someone as a prospective adopter[126] and may impose restrictions as a matter of policy, but these will need to be clearly expressed and legally justifiable.[127] They may, for example, refuse to consider smokers as adopters of children under the age of five.

Adoptive parents for children placed by an adoption agency must be approved by the adoption agency. The process of approval involves a detailed investigation of the prospective adopters, their family circumstances and their motives for wishing to adopt, which is likely to be protracted over a period of months. The information required is set out in the Adoption Agencies (Scotland) Regulations 2009,[128] though the guidance notes that good practice goes beyond these requirements, informed by reports into cases where good care has not been provided by adopters.[129] The assessment should be completed within six months of the date of the application to be considered as adopters.[130] On completion of the investigation a report is prepared, a copy of which is provided to

124 Adoption and Children (Scotland) Act 2007, s 30(1), (7).

125 Adoption and Children (Scotland) Act 2007, s 29. The LAC Guidance notes that 'Finding ways of testing and articulating this will be helpful in considering **any** relationships – simply stating that people have been married for a number of years can no longer be taken as a guarantee of this', p 167, emphasis added. The reference to 'living together as if they were married' includes same-sex couples, Marriage and Civil Partnership (Scotland) Act 2014 and Civil Partnership Act 2004 (Consequential Provisions and Modifications) Order 2014, SSI 2014/3229, Sch 1.

126 Adoption Agencies (Scotland) Regulations 2009, reg 7(1).

127 LAC Guidance, p 163.

128 Adoption Agencies (Scotland) Regulations 2009, Sch 1, Pt 1.

129 LAC Guidance, p 166.

130 Adoption Agencies (Scotland) Regulations 2009, reg 7; LAC Guidance, pp 161–165.

the prospective adopters, and is then considered by the adoption panel, which will advise on suitability.[131] The prospective adopters must be allowed to meet the adoption panel before a recommendation is made.[132] A decision maker in the local authority then has to make a decision based on that recommendation within 28 days.[133] If the decision is that the applicant is not suitable then that person can seek a review of the decision, which will be undertaken by a differently constituted adoption panel from that making the original recommendation.[134] The decision on any recommendation following review should be taken by a different decision maker. Once adopters have been approved there are two possible circumstances prompting review; first, if there has been no placement of a child with them within two years; second, where a child has been placed for adoption but no application for adoption has been made and the authority considers that a review is needed.[135] After the initial review there is no provision for further review of approval if no placement is made, though the guidance suggests that this should take place every two years (noting that it will be extremely unusual for no placement to be made with an adopter).

(4) Who can be adopted?

3.21 Anyone under the age of 18 who is not, and has never been, married or been in a civil partnership can be adopted. An adoption order can also be made in respect of someone aged 18 if the adoption application was made before their eighteenth birthday.[136] There are, however, certain requirements as to residence with the proposed adopters before an adoption order can be granted. These are:[137]

(a) Where the prospective adopter is the child's parent, step-parent or a relative or where the placement has been made by an adoption agency, the child must have had a home with the adopters for at least 13 weeks prior to the adoption and be at least 19 weeks old.

(b) In other cases, the child must have had a home with the adopters for 12 months.

131 Adoption Agencies (Scotland) Regulations 2009, reg 8. The LAC Guidance (pp 169–171) suggests that the recommendation made by the panel should also comment on the range and number of children for whom the adopters might be suitable and on possible support needs.

132 Adoption Agencies (Scotland) Regulations 2009, reg 6(5).

133 Adoption Agencies (Scotland) Regulations 2009, reg 8(6).

134 Adoption Agencies (Scotland) Regulations 2009, regs 8(6)(c) and 9.

135 Adoption Agencies (Scotland) Regulations 2009, reg 10; LAC Guidance, pp 167–170.

136 Adoption and Children (Scotland) Act 2007, s 28(4).

137 Adoption and Children (Scotland) Act 2007, s 15.

Before making the order the court must also be satisfied that the local authority (where the placement is not by an adoption agency) or the adoption agency has had sufficient opportunity to see the child with the adopters in their home environment. This requirement may prolong the periods set out above.[138]

Children aged 12 or over must consent to adoption and their consent can be dispensed with only if they are incapable of giving it.[139] In addition, the court must have regard to the views of the child regarding the adoption (taking account of their age and maturity), so the views of children under 12 are also relevant to the adoption decision.[140]

(5) Rights of the child's parents

3.22 Once a decision has been made by an adoption agency that adoption is in the best interests of the child, the parents of the child must be notified. Once the agency proposes to make arrangements for adoption of the child, the parent(s) must be provided with certain information and asked if they agree with the decision.[141] If they do not reply within 28 days, or they indicate that they disagree with the decision, the agency must apply for a permanence order.[142] Where parental agreement is initially given and then withdrawn, the case is to be treated from the date of withdrawal as one where consent is unlikely to be forthcoming.

The parents of the child usually must consent to the adoption, unless a permanence order giving authority for adoption has previously been made. The consent of the child's mother to adoption (or to freeing for adoption) is ineffective if it is given within six weeks of the birth of the child.[143]

There is provision for parental consent to be dispensed with in the following cases:

(a) if the parent is dead;[144]

(b) if the parent cannot be found or is incapable of giving consent;[145]

(c) if the parent is unable to discharge parental responsibilities and rights satisfactorily and this is likely to continue; this involves an

138 Adoption and Children (Scotland) Act 2007, s 16.

139 Adoption and Children (Scotland) Act 2007, s 32.

140 Adoption and Children (Scotland) Act 2007, s 14.

141 Adoption Agencies (Scotland) Regulations 2009, reg 16.

142 Adoption Agencies (Scotland) Regulations 2009, reg 20.

143 Adoption and Children (Scotland) Act 2007, s 31(11).

144 Adoption and Children (Scotland) Act 2007, s 31(3)(a).

145 Adoption and Children (Scotland) Act 2007, s 31(3)(b).

assessment of the parent's abilities, and general considerations as to the welfare of the child are irrelevant to this assessment;[146]

(d) if the parent has no parental responsibilities and rights because a permanence order has been made and is unlikely to have these imposed or granted;[147]

(e) if the welfare of the child otherwise requires that consent is dispensed with.[148]

This last basis for dispensing with consent was challenged as being incompatible with Article 8 of the European Convention on Human Rights.[149] In rejecting this challenge, the Supreme Court noted that the provision had to be read in the context of the remainder of the 2007 Act so that promotion of the child's welfare was the paramount consideration. The Court would also have to take into account the views of the child, the child's religious persuasion, racial origin and cultural and linguistic background, the value of a stable family unit in the development of the child and the lifelong effect on the child of making an adoption order.[150] Emphasis was also placed on the word 'requires' in the provision. Use of this word meant that:[151]

> There must … be an overriding requirement that the adoption proceed for the sake of the child's welfare, which remains the paramount consideration. The court must be satisfied that the interference with the rights of the parents is proportionate: in other words that nothing less than adoption will suffice.

(6) Children subject to supervision requirements

3.23 Where an agency intends to place a child who is subject to a supervision requirement for adoption it must refer this to the reporter who will then organise a hearing to consider the matter. The hearing will then prepare a report to be considered by the court which will take the decision on the application for an adoption order.[152]

146 Adoption and Children (Scotland) Act 2007, s 31(3)(c), see also *LO v NC* [2017] CSIH 14.
147 Adoption and Children (Scotland) Act 2007, s 31(3)(c)
148 Adoption and Children (Scotland) Act 2007, s 31(3)(d).
149 *ANS v ML* [2012] UKSC 30, see also *YC v UK* (2012) 55 EHRR 33.
150 *ANS v ML* at [31]–[32].
151 *ANS v ML* at [34].
152 Children's Hearings (Scotland) Act 2011, ss 137 and 141; Adoption and Children (Scotland) Act 2007, s 106; Adoption Agencies (Scotland) Regulations 2009, reg 22.

(7) Permanence orders

3.24 Paragraph 3.25 below sets out some cases in which the local authority is required to apply for a permanence order as part of the process of placing a child for adoption. The order may also be used in other circumstances to give permanency to arrangements made for looked after children, for example in a long-term fostering placement. Where the authority decides to apply for a permanence order, similar requirements for notification of parents and obtaining their consent, and for action if consent is refused or the parents do not reply, apply as in the case of notifications of an intention to make arrangements for adoption.[153]

Application for the order is made to the sheriff court. The process will involve the appointment of a curator *ad litem* and, where the application includes seeking authority for the child to be adopted or where the child is aged 12 or above, a reporting officer. These have functions similar to the equivalents appointed as part of the adoption application process.[154] The order can only be granted if any child aged 12 or over consents (unless they are incapable of consenting) and:[155]

(a) the court considers that making the order is better for the child than not making it;
(b) the court has had regard to the paramount consideration of safeguarding and promoting the welfare of the child throughout their childhood;
(c) the court has had regard to the views of the child, the likely effect of making the order and the child's religious persuasion, racial origin and cultural and linguistic background; and
(d) the court is satisfied that there is no one with the parental right to regulate the child's residence or, if there is such a person, that residence with that person is, or is likely to be, seriously detrimental to the welfare of the child.

This last requirement has been described as setting a threshold, factual test,[156] so that, where there is a parent with a right to regulate a child's residence, it must be established that residing with this parent is likely to be severely detrimental to the interests of the child. Only once this test is met will there be consideration of the other requirements set

153 Adoption Agencies (Scotland) Regulations 2009, regs 17, 20, 21 and 23. See **3.25** below and *TW and JW v Aberdeenshire Council* [2012] CSIH 37.

154 See **3.26** below.

155 Adoption and Children (Scotland) Act 2007, s 84.

156 *In the matter of EV (A Child) (Scotland)* [2017] UKSC 15. See also *Perth and Kinross Council for Permanence Order* [2017] CSIH 101.

out in (a) to (d) above. A factual basis must be established from which likelihood of detriment can be predicted; in other words, 'a prediction of future harm has to be based on facts that have been proved on the balance of probabilities'.[157] On the basis of the evidence, the court must be clear about the nature of the detriment, that this is likely and that it is serious.[158] As is the case with an adoption order, it is not enough that a child would simply benefit from being brought up elsewhere.[159]

Any permanence order must contain certain mandatory provisions, these are:[160]

(a) A transfer to the local authority of the responsibility to provide guidance to the child.

(b) A transfer to the local authority of the right to regulate the residence of the child.

The order may also contain ancillary provisions which can include extinguishing parental responsibilities or rights held by anyone or vesting in the local authority or in someone else (e.g., a foster carer) any or all of the other parental responsibilities and rights.[161]

Finally, the order may also grant authority for the child to be adopted. Before authority can be granted the court must be satisfied on two counts. First, that the child has been placed, or is likely to be placed, for adoption, and that it would be better to grant the order than not to grant it.[162] Second, that the child's parents have either consented or their consent can be dispensed with on grounds similar to those which apply in the case of consent to adoption.[163]

Special provisions apply where the local authority intends to apply for a permanence order in respect of the child who is subject to a compulsory supervision order. The case must be referred to the Reporter and an advice hearing held. The view of the hearing that an application should not be made does not, however, prevent the local authority from going ahead with it. If the court making a permanence order considers that supervision of the child is no longer required, it can terminate the compulsory supervision order.[164]

157 *In re J (Children) (Care Proceedings: Threshold Criteria)* [2013] UKSC 9, per Lord Hope at [84], cited in *In the matter of EV (A Child) (Scotland)* at [23].

158 *In the matter of EV (A Child) (Scotland)* [2017] UKSC 15 at [29].

159 *In the matter of EV (A Child) (Scotland)* [2017] UKSC 15 at [27].

160 Adoption and Children (Scotland) Act 2007, s 81.

161 Adoption and Children (Scotland) Act 2007, s 82.

162 Which will include an assessment of the other options, *R v Stirling Council* [2016] CSIH 36.

163 Adoption and Children (Scotland) Act 2007, s 83, see **3.22** above.

164 Adoption and Children (Scotland) Act 2007, s 89.

Once a permanence order has been made it can be varied or revoked and will be revoked if an adoption order is made. Variation can involve adding authority for a child to be adopted to an existing order.

(8) Placement with proposed adopters

3.25 Placement of children for adoption by an adoption agency will be the culmination of a number of decisions. Where the child is looked after there will have been a decision that the best way of securing permanency for the child is by pursuing adoption. A decision will have been made that adoption is in the best interests of the child, following consideration of this matter and a recommendation by the adoption panel. Consideration of whether adoption is in the child's best interests may reach the conclusion that it is not, in which case steps will need to be taken to pursue alternatives which are considered to be in their best interests. These alternatives may have to be secured by a permanence order. Finally, there will need to be a decision to make arrangements for adoption and placement of the child with an adopter, again following consideration and recommendation by the adoption panel.

If a decision is taken that adoption is in the best interests of a child, notification must be given to the child's parents.[165] Others to be notified, include the child (if it is considered that they will understand the effect of the decision), and, if considered to be in the child's best interests, parents not holding parental responsibilities and/or rights.[166]

When a decision that adoption is in the interests of the child has been made and an agency proposes to make arrangements for the adoption of the child, the child's parents (or guardians) must be provided with specific information about this in the form of a memorandum.[167] The agency must then take reasonable steps to ensure that anyone provided with this information signs and returns a certificate confirming that they have read and understood the memorandum[168] and a form indicating whether or not they consent to the arrangements being made.[169] If the agency is aware that there are parents who do not have parental rights and/or responsibilities it must seek to obtain information about such parents and if possible find out if they intend to seek parental

165 For these purposes, anyone who holds *any* parental responsibilities and/or rights or has had these removed by a permanence order. The requirement also extends to guardians.

166 Adoption Agencies (Scotland) Regulations 2009, reg 14(1).

167 Adoption Agencies (Scotland) Regulations 2009, reg 16.

168 In the form set out in Sch 2 to the Adoption Agencies (Scotland) Regulations 2009.

169 In the form set out in Sch 3 to the Adoption Agencies (Scotland) Regulations 2009.

responsibilities or rights or to enter into a parental responsibility and rights agreement.

If the parent does not consent to the making of arrangements for adoption, or if they do not respond to the notification, the procedure that follows depends on whether the adoption agency is the local authority or an independent adoption service. If it is the latter, it must refer the case to the local authority for the area in which the child lives. If it is a local authority, or if a case is so referred to the local authority, the authority must then make an application for a permanence order with authority for the child to be adopted and which also vests certain parental responsibilities and rights in the local authority.[170] The requirement to apply for a permanence order does not apply where an application has been made for an adoption order.

Placement with a specific adopter cannot be made unless the agency is satisfied that the specific placement is in the child's best interests and has complied with a number of further requirements, including obtaining reports on the health of the child and adopter(s), interviewing the adopter(s) and passing a report to an adoption panel which must then make a recommendation which will be followed by a decision made by the agency.[171] The consent of the child's parent(s) to the placement should also be sought.

Placements must be notified to the child's parents and to a variety of others, for example, the education authority and health board for the area where the prospective adopter stays.[172] The child must also be visited within one week of the placement and thereafter whenever necessary to supervise the child's welfare. Written reports of the meetings must be prepared.[173] A child who has been placed for adoption cannot be removed from that placement, by a parent or anyone else, in any of the following circumstances:[174]

(a) Where the parent has consented to adoption as noted above.
(b) Where the child is looked after by the local authority.

170 Adoption Agencies (Scotland) Regulations 2009, reg 21. These are the responsibilities to safeguard and promote the child's health, development and welfare, to provide guidance to the child and to act as the child's legal representative, and the rights to control, direct or guide, in a manner appropriate to the stage of development of the child, the child's upbringing and to act as their legal representative.

171 Adoption Agencies (Scotland) Regulations 2009, reg 18.

172 Adoption Agencies (Scotland) Regulations 2009, reg 24(3), (5).

173 Adoption Agencies (Scotland) Regulations 2009, reg 25.

174 Adoption and Children (Scotland) Act 2007, ss 20–23.

(c) Where the child has had a home for five years with prospective adopters who give notice of an intention to adopt or apply to adopt.

(9) Adoption procedure

3.26 The main feature of the adoption process in court is the emphasis on confidentiality. There are strict limits on those allowed to see the court papers which must be sealed at the end of the case. Any court hearings must be held in private unless the court directs otherwise and this is unlikely.

If the child has not been placed for adoption by an adoption agency, the local authority must be informed of the intention to adopt.[175] Before an adoption order can be granted in such cases a report must be produced by the local authority.[176] The report will cover such matters as the suitability of the applicant and any matters relevant to the effect of the adoption on the safeguarding and promotion of the child's welfare; relevant matters would include the occupations of the adopters and their ability to look after the child. In addition, the report must comment on the feelings and wishes of the child. Finally, the report must confirm that the placement has not been made contrary to section 75 of the Adoption and Children (Scotland) Act 2007, which permits placements to be made only by an adoption agency, unless the proposed adopter is a relative of the child. Where the placement has been made by an adoption agency it must provide a report covering all of these matters.

Once the relevant reports have been obtained, the petition for adoption can be lodged in court and in virtually all cases the court will be the sheriff court.[177] Along with the petition the report mentioned above will be lodged, together with evidence as to the health of the proposed adopters.

Once the petition is lodged a curator *ad litem* and reporting officer will be appointed. In sheriff court cases these two posts can be combined if the sheriff considers this to be appropriate. The individual appointed may be drawn from a panel maintained by the local authority, and if this is done and the adoption order is granted the authority will pay their fees.

175 Adoption and Children (Scotland) Act 2007, s 18.
176 Adoption and Children (Scotland) Act 2007, s 19.
177 The rules for this are set out in the Act of Sederunt (Sheriff Court Rules Amendment) (Adoption and Children (Scotland) Act 2007) 2009, SSI 2009/284, as amended.

The duty of the curator *ad litem* is to protect the interests of the child in the proceedings and to produce a report to the court. The functions of the curator are dealt with at length in the court rules. Briefly, they are to protect the child's interests; to ascertain whether the facts stated in the petition are correct; to establish whether the adoption is likely to safeguard and promote the welfare of the child; and to establish the reasons for adoption.

Reporting officers' duties are principally to witness the parents' consent to the adoption and to ensure that they understand the effects of adoption.

Following receipt of the reports a pre-proof hearing will be held, to establish whether the proof can proceed on the date set for it. The child's parent may appear at the proof hearing and object to the granting of the order;[178] in such a case it will be necessary to ascertain whether the consent of the parent can be dispensed with.[179]

At the end of the proceedings a number of options are open to the court. The court must not make an adoption order unless it considers that it would be better for the child that the order be made than not, and the decision is subject to the considerations discussed above.[180] The options are:

(a) to refuse the order;
(b) to grant the order as sought;
(c) to exercise its general powers under section 11 of the 1995 Act to make an order in respect of parental responsibilities or rights;
(d) if it considers that any of the grounds of referral, except commission of an offence by the child, is satisfied in respect of the child, to refer the case to the reporter who must then investigate and decide whether the child is in need of supervision. If the reporter decides that this is the case a hearing must be arranged.[181]

The court has the power to terminate a compulsory supervision order if it considers that, as a result of its order, compulsory supervision is no longer necessary.[182] Once an adoption order is made it will be recorded in the Adopted Children's Register kept in the General Register Office for Scotland in Edinburgh.

178 Though, if they have previously consented to the adoption, they may need leave from the court to do this, Adoption and Children (Scotland) Act 2007, s 31(12), (14).
179 See **3.18** above; Adoption and Children (Scotland) Act 2007, s 14.
180 See Adoption and Children (Scotland) Act 2007, ss 14 and 28, and **3.19** above.
181 Children's Hearings (Scotland) Act 2011, s 137.
182 Adoption and Children (Scotland) Act 2007, s 36.

(10) Adoption allowances[183]

3.27 Adoption agencies are enabled to pay adoption allowances. These are paid, for example:

(a) where payment is necessary to ensure that the adopter(s) can look after the child;

(b) where it is desirable to place a child with siblings or with a child who has previously shared their home;

(c) where the child needs special care requiring additional spending because of disability or emotional or behavioural difficulties or the consequences of past abuse or neglect.

The amount of the allowance is determined after considering the resources available to the adopters, the financial needs of the adopters (excluding the costs incurred in respect of the child) and the financial needs of the child. Where an adopter had previously looked after the child as a foster or kinship carer and had received a fee element in addition to any allowance, this can be paid for a period of two years after the adoption.

(11) Access to adoption records

3.28 As we have noted, the making of an adoption order is recorded in the Adopted Children Register. In addition, the Registrar General must keep other registers and information linking the Adopted Children Register with a child's original birth certificate. Once an adopted child reaches the age of 16 they are entitled to access to these records. On application the Registrar General must advise the child of the availability of counselling. Counselling is optional but if it is requested it will be provided by an adoption agency, if it made the original placement; otherwise, it will be provided by the local authority for the area where the child resides. The adopted person is also entitled to access their local authority records (and may be given access to these if under 16 and the authority thinks it appropriate to give access) and the court adoption records.[184]

183 Adoption and Children (Scotland) Act 2007, s 71; Adoption Support Services and Allowances (Scotland) Regulations 2009, SSI 2009/152, regs 10–17, LAC Guidance, pp 214–218.

184 Adoption (Disclosure of Information and Medical Information about Natural Parents) (Scotland) Regulations 2009, SSI 2009/268; Act of Sederunt (Sheriff Court Rules Amendment) (Adoption and Children (Scotland) Act 2007) 2009, SSI 2009/284, r 25.

(12) Adoption support services[185]

3.29 Local authorities have a duty to provide adoption support services to a range of individuals, including children who may be adopted, children and older people who have been adopted, adopters and prospective adopters, and the birth parents of adopted children. These services are wide-ranging and include the provision of counselling, provision of guidance about adoption and the provision of any other assistance which is considered appropriate in the circumstances.[186] Although, as discussed below, the process of providing support will be triggered by a request, the guidance makes it clear that at certain key points in the process the local authority will have to consider the need for an adoption support plan.

In most cases the authority must, on request, carry out an assessment of the need for support services, and, normally, services are only to be provided following an assessment. Services can be provided without assessment in cases where support is required as a matter of urgency,[187] and a limited range of services, for example assessment of prospective adopters, can be provided simply on request.

The assessment for services must consider the needs of the person who is being assessed, the needs of any adopted child and a variety of other environmental and family factors.[188] Those being assessed must be given notice of the proposed decision following assessment and have the opportunity to make representations before a final decision is made. The form of provision will depend on whether it is intended to provide services for a member of a relevant family. A relevant family is one which includes a child who has been placed for adoption or adopted, the person who has adopted the child or with whom they have been placed, and any other children in the household. Where the person being assessed is in a relevant family then an adoption support plan will need to be prepared setting out services to be provided and a draft of this plan will have to be sent to those concerned for comment before a final decision is made. A support plan is, by default, required for each member of the relevant family, but it is possible for the members of the family (aged 12 or over) to agree that a single plan should be prepared covering the whole family. Once made, anyone being provided with services can seek a review of the plan and the local authority must, in any case, review it from time to

185 Adoption Support Services and Allowances (Scotland) Regulations 2009; *LAC Guidance*, pp 200–213.

186 Adoption and Children (Scotland) Act 2007, s 10

187 Adoption and Children (Scotland) Act 2007, s 11.

188 Adoption Support and Allowances (Scotland) Regulations 2009, reg 6.

time. The guidance indicates that local authority procedures should set out both the frequency of, and the procedures for, such reviews.

OCCUPANCY RIGHTS

(1) Introduction

3.30 Under older law the only person with a legal right to occupy a home was the person who was the owner or tenant of the property, or who enjoyed some other permission from the owner to occupy it. The difficulty in this was that, historically, the ownership or tenancy of the family home was usually taken in the name of the husband alone. This almost universal practice had the consequence that the wife had no legally recognised right of occupation. In the event of family breakdown, a woman could be ejected from the family home by her husband and had no legal power to prevent this or to resume occupation after it had happened.

The Matrimonial Homes (Family Protection) (Scotland) Act 1981 provides a partial remedy for this. It does this by defining the spouse who is the owner or tenant of the family home (referred to in the Act as the matrimonial home) as an 'entitled spouse' and the other spouse as a 'non-entitled spouse', and by granting all non-entitled spouses what is referred to as an 'occupancy right' in the family home.[189]

The precise content of this occupancy right depends on whether the non-entitled spouse is in occupation of the matrimonial home. If they are in occupation, the right is to remain in occupation and to have free access to the home: if not the right is to be allowed to enter and occupy the matrimonial home. Should access be refused or should the non-entitled spouse be excluded from the home, the occupancy right can only be enforced by application to court.

The situation noted above, where the title to the matrimonial home was in the name of only one of the spouses, is now rarer, and it is usual for the title to be taken in the names of both spouses. Where this is the case both have property rights, including occupancy rights, in the home regardless of the 1981 Act.

189 Matrimonial Homes (Family Protection) (Scotland) Act 1981, s 1. Similar rights apply in the case of civil partnerships, see the Civil Partnership Act 2004, s 101. Where an entitled spouse ceases to be entitled, for example because he is ejected from a tenancy, then the non-entitled spouse will lose her occupancy right since this is dependent on the existence of an entitled spouse, *Morgan v Morgan & Kyle & Carrick DC* 2000 Hous LR 90.

Wherever occupancy rights exist, either spouse can apply to court for an order enforcing the rights, restricting the occupancy rights of the other spouse, regulating the exercise of the other spouses occupancy rights, or protecting the occupancy rights of the spouse applying for the order. Either spouse may also apply for an exclusion order excluding the other spouse from the matrimonial home.

The non-entitled spouse will lose the benefit of the occupancy right if they have ceased cohabitation for two years and during that period did not occupy the matrimonial home.

(2) Transfer of tenancy

3.31 Where one spouse is the legal tenant of the matrimonial home, and therefore the entitled spouse, the non-entitled spouse may apply to court for the tenancy to be transferred to them. Before granting such an order the court must consider all the circumstances[190] of the case and in particular: the conduct of the spouses; the respective needs and resources of the spouses; the needs of any children;[191] the extent of any business use of the home by one of the spouses; and any offer by the entitled spouse to provide accommodation for the non-entitled spouse.

(3) Cohabiting couples

3.32 In the case of a couple living together as if married, or a same-sex couple living together as if they were civil partners, there is also the possibility that one has a title to the shared home and the other does not. In such cases the non-entitled partner may apply to court for the grant of occupancy rights. This grant may be made for up to six months but is renewable for further six-month periods. Where such an order is in force, the provisions set out above in relation to occupancy rights, exclusion orders and transfer of tenancy apply to the non-entitled partner.[192] It is also possible that both partners here are 'entitled', in which case the provisions about occupancy rights and exclusion orders will apply to both.

190 For example, which of the parties would be the less troublesome neighbour, *Soutar v McAuley*, Dundee Sh Ct, 31 March 2010.

191 See *Guyan v Guyan* 2001 Hous LR 99, noting that in balancing the interests of adults and children, children have to come first. In this case the spouse with care of children obtained the tenancy.

192 See *Soutar v McAuley*, 2010 SLT (Sh Ct) 21 for a case involving parties living together as if civil partners.

MEASURES DIRECTED AT DOMESTIC ABUSE

(1) Introduction

3.33 As well as providing some protection for non-entitled partners, the 1981 Act also contained a number of measures directed at providing protection against domestic abuse. These protections were originally extended only to spouses and to cohabitants living as if husband and wife, but similar provision is now made in the Civil Partnership Act 2004 for civil partners and for those living as if they were civil partners. The 1981 Act measures are now supplemented by the provisions of the Domestic Abuse (Scotland) Act 2018. The 2018 Act broadened the definition of domestic abuse beyond physical violence and provides protection from behaviour intended to intimidate and threaten and which constitutes a campaign of psychological abuse against the subject.[193] The 2018 Act recognised the need to provide protection from abuse which, without the use of physical violence, was intended to cause the subject to be subordinate, socially isolated, controlled, restricted in their freedom of action and to feel humiliated, degraded and punished.[194] Domestic abuse will impact on any children present and the 2018 Act recognises this, the presence of a child witnessing the abuse will aggravate the offence.[195]

(2) Exclusion orders

3.34 A spouse, civil partner or a cohabitant holding an order conferring occupancy rights,[196] can apply to court for an exclusion order suspending the occupancy rights of the other partner. This can be done both where there is an entitled and non-entitled partner and where the title to the property is held in common and both partners are effectively entitled partners. It is now clear that the partner applying for the exclusion order need not be in occupation of the matrimonial home when the application is made.

There are two requirements to be fulfilled before the court can grant the order. Firstly, the order must be necessary to protect the applicant or any child of the family from actual or threatened conduct of the other partner which would be detrimental to their physical or mental health. Secondly, the court must not make an order if it would be unjustified or unreasonable to do so.

193 Domestic Abuse (Scotland) Act 2018, s 1.
194 Domestic Abuse (Scotland) Act 2018, s 2.
195 Domestic Abuse(Scotland) Act 2018, s 5.
196 For ease of explanation these will be collectively referred to as 'partners'.

(a) Need for protection

3.35 In the first place, making the order must be necessary. The implication is that there must be no other remedy, for example an interdict,[197] which will provide the necessary protection. However, it does not mean that an applicant must proceed in stages, first seeking interdict and then, if that is unsuccessful, applying for an exclusion order.

The threat must come from some conduct on the part of the other partner; the provision will therefore not cover a case where the upset arises simply from the desire of the other partner to remain in the home despite the break-up of the relationship. Finally, it should be noted that actual physical injury need not have occurred for an order to be granted. There is no need for the behaviour to be violent or notably offensive, behaviour termed coercive and controlling will amount to abuse.[198] In one case the conduct was characterised as involving imposition of the husband's aspirations for reconciliation in such a way as to continuously upset and distress his wife.[199]

The courts have formulated four relevant questions to be considered in deciding on this type of application. They are:

(a) What is the nature and quality of the alleged conduct?
(b) Is the court satisfied that the conduct is likely to be repeated if co-habitation continues?
(c) Has the conduct been, or, if repeated would it be, injurious to the physical or mental health of the applicant spouse or any child of the family?
(d) If so, is the order sought necessary for the future protection of the physical or mental health of the applicant or child?[200]

(b) Unjustified or unreasonable

3.36 In deciding on whether granting the order would be unjustified or unreasonable the Act directs the court to consider several factors. These include the conduct of the parties, the respective needs and resources of the parties, the needs of any children, and the offer by an entitled partner to make accommodation available to the non-entitled partner. In the specific case of tied housing where there is a requirement

197 The behaviour involved may be such that it is difficult to frame an interdict to prevent it, *Roberton v Roberton* 1999 SLT 38.
198 Domestic Abuse (Scotland) Act s 2.
199 *Roberton v Roberton* 1999 SLT 38.
200 *McCafferty v McCafferty* 1986 SLT 650.

that the non-applicant partner reside there the courts must consider that requirement and the possible consequences of making an exclusion order in deciding whether it is unjustified or unreasonable to make the order.

When the court makes an exclusion order it must also, if requested to do so by the applicant, grant a warrant for the ejection of the other partner from the home and/or an interdict preventing the other partner from entering the matrimonial home without the permission of the partner applying for the order. The court may also grant an interdict prohibiting the other partner from entering or remaining in a specified area in the vicinity of the matrimonial home.

Pending the grant of a full exclusion order the court may make an interim (temporary) order, this may only be done if the non-applicant partner has been afforded an opportunity of being heard or represented before the court prior to the order being made.

(3) Interdicts

3.37 In general terms an interdict is a court order ordering an individual to desist from a course of conduct which is causing or is likely to cause injury (whether physical, mental or financial) or detriment to another. Normally, at common law, breach of the terms of an interdict will only be punished if the person who has obtained the interdict takes proceedings to bring the offender before the court. If this is done the offender can be punished since they are effectively guilty of contempt of court. Specific provision for other remedies is made in relation to interdicts in cases involving domestic violence. The terminology for these interdicts varies depending on the nature of the relationship. The ability to apply for an interdict exists even where parties are living together and, in such cases, does not depend on having or exercising an occupancy right.

The first category are matrimonial interdicts.[201] A matrimonial interdict is one which either:

(a) restrains or prohibits any conduct of one spouse towards the other spouse or a child of the family; or
(b) prohibits a spouse from entering or remaining in:
    (i) a matrimonial home (an interdict to prevent this can only be granted if the person against whom it is sought is the subject of an exclusion order excluding them from the matrimonial

201 Matrimonial Homes (Family Protection) (Scotland) Act 1981, s 14(2).

home or where the court has refused leave to exercise occupancy rights);

(ii) any other residence occupied by the applicant spouse;

(iii) any place of work of the applicant spouse;

(iv) any school attended by a child in the permanent or temporary care of the applicant spouse.

The court can attach a power of arrest to the interdict which gives the police the power to arrest the person subject to the interdict if there is reasonable cause to suspect that a breach of the interdict has taken place. There are two circumstances in which the power of arrest must be attached to a matrimonial interdict:[202]

(a) where the interdict is ancillary to an exclusion order or interim exclusion order;

(b) where the non-applicant spouse has had the opportunity of being heard or represented before the court, and attaching the power of arrest is necessary to protect the applicant from a risk of abuse in breach of the interdict.

A matrimonial interdict with a power of arrest attached must be notified to the non-applicant spouse and the Chief Constable.

The power of arrest[203] is to the effect that a constable *may* arrest if breach of the interdict is suspected and it is considered that there would be a risk of abuse or further abuse if the person breaching the interdict were not arrested. Once the spouse has been arrested, they must be detained until charged with an offence arising from the circumstances of the arrest. If they are not so charged they must be brought before the sheriff. If the sheriff is satisfied that there is a *prima facie* breach of interdict, and that there will, if detention is not ordered, be a substantial risk of abuse or further abuse in breach of the interdict, they may order further detention for up to two days.

Similar provisions to those set out in relation to married couples exist for civil partners.[204] Where partners are living together as husband and wife or as civil partners it is still possible to obtain an interdict, referred to as a domestic interdict.[205] This is available on the same terms as a matrimonial interdict except that an interdict prohibiting entry to the family home may only be granted if it is ancillary to an exclusion order or if an order granting or extending occupancy rights is recalled.

202 Protection from Abuse (Scotland) Act 2001, s 1.

203 Protection from Abuse (Scotland) Act 2001, ss 4 and 5.

204 See Civil Partnership Act 2004, Chs 3 and 4.

205 Matrimonial Homes (Family Protection) (Scotland) Act 1981, s 18A.

(4) Protection from Harassment Act 1997

3.38 This allows a victim of harassment to claim damages for any injury suffered because of the harassment or to seek either an interdict or a non-harassment order to prevent future harassment. Breach of a non-harassment order will be a criminal offence.

(5) Protection from Abuse (Scotland) Act 2001

3.39 A person who is applying for, or who has obtained, an interdict for the purpose of protection against abuse may apply to the court for a power of arrest to be attached to the interdict under this Act. The court must attach a power of arrest to the interdict if satisfied that:

(a) the interdicted person has been given an opportunity to be heard by, or represented before, the court; and
(b) attaching the power of arrest is necessary to protect the applicant from a risk of abuse in breach of the interdict.

Abuse includes violence, harassment, threatening conduct, and any other conduct giving rise, or likely to give rise, to physical or mental injury, fear, alarm or distress and conduct includes speech and presence in a specified place or area.

The court must specify a date of expiry for the power of arrest which must be not later than three years after the date when the power is attached. Procedures on breach of an interdict containing a power of arrest are as set out above in relation to matrimonial interdicts.

Chapter 4

Local authority services to children

INTRODUCTION

4.1 Three major developments have shaped the interaction of local authorities with children: the Children (Scotland) Act 1995 (the 1995 Act); the development of the approach known as Getting it Right for Every Child (GIRFEC); and, related to GIRFEC and in part providing a statutory basis for it, the Children and Young People (Scotland) Act 2014 (the 2014 Act).

One of the major changes in emphasis introduced in the 1995 Act was the importance placed on providing services to promote the welfare of children and their families and to ensure that children are brought up by their families. The Act emphasised that provision of services should not be seen negatively, concerned only with preventing care being taken over by the local authority.[1] Instead, the Act should be seen in a positive light, enabling children to achieve and maintain a reasonable standard of development and was expressed in a duty to provide services to promote welfare.[2]

The focus of service provision in the 1995 Act is not on children generally, but on children in need, many of whom may also potentially be in need of protection or at risk. There is no explicit link between the categories of children at risk and children in need, though the guidance issued under the 1995 Act does say:

> … the Act introduces various powers enabling authorities to provide a range of different types of support for children and their families. The effective use of those powers will help to avoid situations which

1 Children (Scotland) Act 1995 (the 1995 Act), s 22.
2 1995 Act, s 22.

could lead to children being subjected to abuse and may thus avert the need for child protection intervention.[3]

There is some evidence that priority is given to children who are at risk rather than simply being in need. Research published in 2007, for example, concluded that being in need could sometimes be used to justify provision of services to children and their families, but that it was more common for this to be justified on the basis that the child was at risk.[4]

Other changes introduced by the 1995 Act included a changed view of the role of accommodation for children provided by a local authority. Such accommodation is seen as part of promoting the welfare of children and a resource to support the upbringing of a child by their family.[5] The 1995 Act adopted a change in terminology so that children were no longer 'in care', but are being 'looked after' by the local authority.[6] This second change was made as an attempt to remove the stigma attached to being labelled as 'in care'. The change was also intended to signal the notion of partnership with parents, and was accompanied by a clarification of which groups of children are to be regarded as looked after.[7]

In considering these provisions below, three definitions should be noted. The first is that for the purpose of these provisions a child is a person under 18;[8] the second is that the term 'family' extends not only to someone with parental responsibility, but also to any person with whom the child has been living;[9] and the third is that a 'relevant person' is anyone holding parental responsibilities or parental rights, and any parent of a child as long as they have not had parental responsibilities and rights removed by a court.[10]

3 *The Children (Scotland) Act 1995 Regulations and Guidance: Volume I, Support and Protection for Children and their Families* (1997), ch 7, para 2. The other two volumes, both published by the Stationery Office in 1997, are volume 2 on Children Looked After by Local Authorities and volume 3 on Adoption and Parental Responsibilities Orders. Volume 2 was replaced in 2010 by Scottish Government, *Guidance on Looked After Children (Scotland) Regulations 2009 and the Adoption and Children (Scotland) Act 2007* (2010) (LAC Guidance). In future the two remaining volumes will be referred to as *'Guidance'* with the relevant volume number.

4 Tisdall, K & Plows, V, *Children in Need; Examining its use in practice and reflecting on its currency for proposed policy changes* (University of Edinburgh, 2007), pp 61–62 and 70.

5 1995 Act, ss 25 and 26.

6 1995 Act, s 17(6).

7 1995Act, ss 25 and 26

8 1995 Act, s 93(2)(a).

9 1995 Act, s 93(1).

10 Children's Hearings (Scotland) Act 2011, s 200; Children's Hearings (Scotland) Act 2011 (Review of Contact Directions and Definition of Relevant Person) Order 2013, SSI 2013/193, art 3.

A number of innovations are introduced by the 2014 Act.[11] The Act replaced the provisions about local authority planning for children which had been set out in the 1995 Act and made changes to a number of other provisions of this Act, particularly in relation to the aftercare duties of local authorities.[12]

The main innovations were:

(a) a duty to report on steps taken by the local authority to secure better or further effect of the requirements set out in the United Nations Convention on the Rights of the Child;[13]

(b) a duty to prepare a children's services plan; setting out a set of obligations for a wide range of 'corporate parents'; [14]

(c) introducing a new duty to provide services to children at risk of being looked after; and providing further support for kinship care in cases where a child is not looked after.[15]

Further provisions in the 2014 Act involved the requirement to provide a Named Person for every child, and the obligation to prepare a Child's Plan for an individual child in certain circumstances. These provisions were challenged through the courts and, following a decision of the Supreme Court,[16] repealed.[17]

Finally, statutory provision in this area is supplemented by regulations and directions from central government and by local procedures.

Planning children's services

4.2 A local authority, working with the health board which includes the area of the local authority, must prepare a children's services plan[18] every three years (though it must be reviewed annually and can be amended during that period).[19] The scope of the plan is wide ranging as children's services are defined as including not only services provided wholly or mainly to children. Also included are services provided for

11 Children and Young People (Scotland) Act 2014 (the 2014 Act).

12 2014 Act, Part 10, s 66.

13 See Scottish Government, Guidance on Part 1, Section 2 (Duties of Public Authorities in relation to the UNCRC) of the Children and Young People (Scotland) Act 2014 (2016).

14 2014 Act, s 9.

15 2014 Act, Part 13.

16 *The Christian Institute and others v The Lord Advocate* [2016] UKSC 51.

17 Repealed by Children (Care and Justice) (Scotland) Act 2024, Part 5, s 32(a) & (b).

18 Scottish Government, Children and Young People (Scotland) Act 2014: *Statutory Guidance on Part 3: Children's Services Planning – Second Edition (2020).*

19 2014 Act, s 11.

the benefit of children[20] and the plan must further include what are described as 'related services'.[21] These are services which are capable of having a significant effect on the well-being of children.[22] During the planning (and subsequent review) process a wide range of organisations must be given the opportunity to participate or must be consulted.[23]

The aims of the plan are:[24]

(a) that children's services in the area concerned are provided in the way which:
   (i) best safeguards, supports and promotes the well-being of children in the area concerned,
   (ii) ensures that any action to meet needs is taken at the earliest appropriate time and that, where appropriate, action is taken to prevent needs arising,
   (iii) is most integrated from the point of view of recipients, and
   (iv) constitutes the best use of available resources,

(b) that related services in the area concerned are provided in the way which, so far as consistent with the objects and proper delivery of the service concerned, safeguards, supports and promotes the well-being of children in the area concerned.[25]

GETTING IT RIGHT FOR EVERY CHILD

4.3 Getting it Right for Every Child (GIRFEC) had its genesis in a review of the children's hearing system,[26] but developed into an approach concerned with all children. As its name suggests, GIRFEC applies to *every* child, not just those who are in need or at risk, and there are no thresholds for access to support. There are a number of core components of the GIRFEC approach, set out in Box 4.1 below. The approach identifies a number of objectives for children, for them to be successful learners, confident individuals, effective contributors and

20 2014 Act, s 7(1).

21 2014 Act, ss 7(1) and (2).

22 2014 Act, s 7(1). Examples given in Scottish Government, *Statutory Guidance on Part 3 (Children's Services Planning) of the Children and Young People (Scotland) Act 2014* (2016) are leisure services, housing and drug and alcohol services.

23 Children and Young People (Scotland) Act 2014, s 10. See also, Scottish Government, *Children and Young People (Scotland) Act 2014*: *Statutory Guidance on Part 3: Children's Services Planning – Second Edition* (2020), pp 25–35.

24 2014 Act, s 9. See also, Scottish Government, *Children and Young People (Scotland) Act 2014: Statutory Guidance on Part 3*, pp 16–24.

25 2014 Act, s 9(2)(b).

26 Scottish Executive, Getting it Right for Every Child: Consultation Pack on Review of the Children's Hearings System (2004).

responsible citizens. Achievement of these objectives can be measured against the so-called SHANARRI indicators of well-being which consider the extent to which a child is safe, healthy, achieving, nurtured, active, respected, responsible and included.[27]

Box 4.1

The Core Components of GIRFEC[28]

- A focus on improving outcomes for children, young people and their families based on a shared understanding of well-being.
- A common approach to gaining consent and to sharing information where appropriate.
- An integral role for children, young people and families in assessment, planning and intervention.
- A co-ordinated and unified approach to identifying concerns, assessing needs, agreeing actions and outcomes, based on the Well-being Indicators.[29]
- Streamlined planning, assessment and decision-making processes that lead to the right help at the right time.
- Consistent high standards of co-operation, joint working and communication where more than one agency needs to be involved, locally and across Scotland.
- Maximising the skilled workforce within universal services to address needs and risks at the earliest possible time.
- A confident and competent workforce across all services for children, young people and their families.
- The capacity to share demographic, assessment, and planning information electronically within and across agency boundaries.

The GIRFEC approach involves progressive support for children and families based on an assessment of their needs against the above objectives, with a focus, where appropriate, on inter-agency working. This starts with the support provided by universal services such as education and health. Support may then increase, compulsorily if necessary, directed at supporting the achievement by the child of the objectives above. This is represented in the material prepared as part of

27 See, Scottish Government, GIRFEC, Wellbeing (SHANARRI). Available at: www.gov.scot/policies/girfec/wellbeing-indicators-shanarri/ (accessed 20 May 2025).

28 Scottish Government, *A Guide to Getting it Right for Every Child* (2012), p 7.

29 See **4.2** below.

GIRFEC in the graphic reproduced as Figure 4.1[30] below, starting in the centre with 'normal' support and moving out to more intensive support.

Figure 4.1

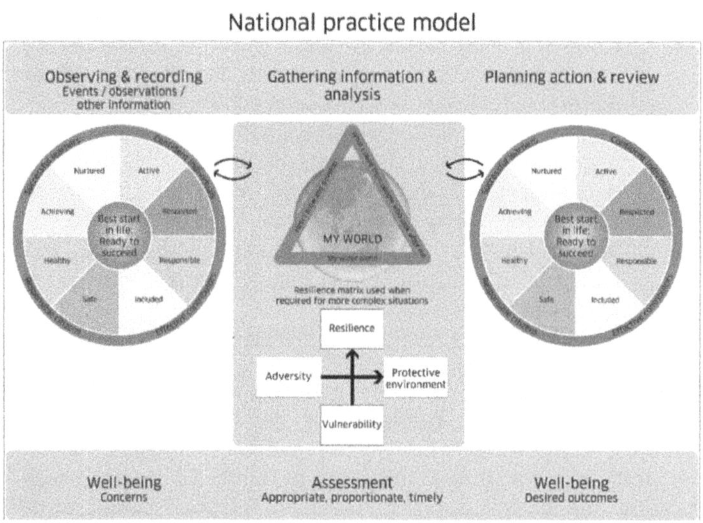

Figure 4.2

Assessment under GIRFEC makes use of the National Practice Model (see Figure 4.2 above).[31] This incorporates a number of tools, including

30 See Scottish Government, *A Guide to Getting it Right for Every Child* (2012), p 12.
31 *A Guide to Getting it Right for Every Child*, pp 14–16.

the well-being indicators. These indicators include, the extent to which the child is safe, healthy, achieving, nurtured, active, respected, responsible and included (set out here in the form of a well-being wheel). A tool to measure these indicators is the My World Triangle, which focuses on the information required about the child and their environment, and a resilience matrix.[32] Once the needs of the child have been identified they can be organised using the well-being wheel. The 2014 Act gives well-being a statutory basis by legislating for the SHANARRI indicators[33] and by requiring that local authorities give specific consideration to the child's well-being in exercising certain of their functions.[34] Well-being is not defined, rather it is to be assessed by reference to the extent to which the SHANARRI indicators are met in respect of the child.[35]

SERVICES FOR CHILDREN IN NEED

(1) Promoting welfare

4.4 Two main duties are imposed by the 1995 Act on local authorities.[36] First, they must safeguard and promote the welfare of children in need living in their area.[37] Second, they must promote the upbringing of such children by their families, provided that this is consistent with safeguarding and promoting the children's welfare.[38] Both of these duties are to be fulfilled by providing a range and level of services which are appropriate to the children's needs.[39] In carrying out these duties, as noted above, the local authority must give specific consideration to the child's well-being.[40]

In addition, where a child has a mental disorder, whether or not they have been in hospital for treatment, the local authority has certain obligations.[41] These include:

32 *A Guide to Getting it Right for Every Child*, pp 14–24.
33 Children and Young People (Scotland) Act 2014, s 96.
34 1995 Act, s 23A. These are the duties under s 22 of the 1995 Act (considered immediately below), the duties towards looked after children in section 17 of the 1995 Act (see **4.15** below) and continuing care (see **4.17** below).
35 Children and Young People (Scotland) Act, 2014, s 96.
36 1995 Act, s 22(1).
37 1995 Act, s 22(1)(a).
38 1995 Act, s 22(1)(b).
39 1995 Act, s 22.
40 1995 Act, s 23A(2). See **4.3** above.
41 Mental Health (Care and Treatment) (Scotland) Act 2003, ss 25(1) and 26(1).

(a) Provision of care and support services designed to minimise the effect of the disorder and allow the opportunity to lead as normal a life as possible.[42]

(b) Provision of social, cultural and recreational activities, training and assistance in obtaining employment for people over school age.[43]

(2) Children in need

4.5 A child will be considered in need if they are in need of care and attention for one of the following reasons:[44]

(a) The child is unlikely to achieve or maintain, or have the opportunity to achieve or maintain, a reasonable standard of health or development unless services are provided.

(b) The child's health or development is likely to be significantly impaired or further impaired unless services are provided.

(c) The child is disabled. In this context 'disabled' means chronically sick or disabled or suffering from a mental disorder.[45]

(d) The child is adversely affected by the disability of another member of their family. This could be a sibling or a parent.

This definition of a child in need is almost identical to that contained in the Children Act 1989, in which context it has been described as 'rather broad and indeterminate, except in so far as it is clear that we are dealing with a restricted category of children'.[46] No further definition is offered either in the 1995 Act or in the guidance issued on it. This means that a great deal of discretion is left to local authorities to define their own terms for implementation of these provisions. For example, when is a child 'in need of care and attention'? What amounts to significant impairment, and what is a reasonable standard? It is clear that, in practice, there is considerable variation amongst practitioners in their working definition of 'a child in need' as well as variation in the extent

42 Mental Health (Care and Treatment) (Scotland) Act 2003, s 25(2).

43 Mental Health (Care and Treatment) (Scotland) Act 2003, s 26(2).

44 1995 Act, s 93(4)(a).

45 Defined in Mental Health (Care and Treatment) (Scotland) Act 2003, s 328, see **8.9**.

46 A Bainham, *Children – The Modern Law* (3rd edn, 2005, Family Law), p 422.

to which the term 'in need' is used in practice.[47] It is clear, however, that the definition looks not only to past and present disadvantage, but also to possible future disadvantage. There is some judicial guidance about when a child will be in need, for example, a child will be in need if their parents are homeless,[48] or where the child is at risk of radicalisation.[49]

(3) Assessment

4.6 It is clear from the guidance which accompanied the original implementation of the 1995 Act that children who may be in need must be assessed. The assessment should establish what needs they might have and whether it is necessary for the local authority to provide services to the child and/or the child's family.[50] The assessment will use the GIRFEC approach and the National Practice Model referred to above. In carrying out the assessment the authority must exercise its functions in a way that is designed to safeguard, support and promote the child's well-being[51] and it must have regard to the principles set out in the Social Care (Self-directed Support) (Scotland) Act 2013.[52]

The local authority has considerable discretion in the assessment process and it is clear that the resources available to the authority are a relevant factor both in the assessment of needs and in the decision as to provision of services.[53]

There is, in general, no right to have an assessment carried out, nor is there any statutory trigger for such an assessment. Where a child's parent requests an assessment or where a problem requiring assessment

47 Tisdall, K & Plows, V, *Children in Need; Examining its use in practice and reflecting on its currency for proposed policy changes* (University of Edinburgh, 2007), pp 61–62 and 70. The Report, *For Scotland's Children: Better Indicated Children's Services* (Scottish Executive, 2001) noted (at p 33) that: 'There is a general problem in that, although local authorities have a statutory responsibility in relation to Children in Need, no one has defined exactly which groups fall within the category of "Children in Need". There is certainly no common understanding of which groups we are actually talking about.'

48 *R(O) v London Borough of Lambeth* [2016] EWHC 937 (Admin).

49 *A v London Borough of Enfield* [2016] EWHC 567 (Admin).

50 *The Children (Scotland) Act 1995, Regulations and Guidance: Vol 1, Support and Protection for Children and their Families (1997).*

51 1995 Act, s 23A(2).

52 Social Care (Self-directed Support) (Scotland) Act 2013, s 1; see **6.4**. See also Scottish Government, *Social Care (Self-Directed Support) (Scotland) Act 2013, Statutory Guidance* (2022) pp 10 and 36–38.

53 See *Crossan v South Lanarkshire Council* [2006] CSOH 28.

has been identified, either by a social worker or by others, then an assessment should be carried out.[54]

Different cases will call for assessments of differing complexity involving varying groups of professionals. Where a number of different professionals is involved, one will need to be designated as Lead Professional. In some cases, a simple, brief assessment carried out by the social work department will be all that is required. In other cases, those involved with the child's health and education will also need to participate and the process of assessment will be more complex.[55]

Where different types of assessments need to be carried out, they should, as far as possible, be conducted at the same time. Regardless of the form of the assessment, it should include an assessment of risk to the child as well as the needs of the child and family. Children in need may also be at risk and an assessment, and the initial referral triggering the assessment, may indicate the need to take some appropriate child protection measures.

There is an expectation that children and their families will be fully involved in the process of assessment and planning and will agree any final plan. In some cases, such involvement and agreement may not be appropriate; for example, when there are child protection concerns, or where compulsory measures are in place.[56] Any planning process and final plan should be outcome driven. The focus should be on the desired outcome for the child or young person, rather than concentrating on inputs in the form of services or support to be provided.[57]

Although the National Practice Model provides a framework for assessment it does not provide a detailed algorithm into which data and information can be added to produce a clear definitive outcome. Rather it is what Aldgate and Rose describe as a structured professional judgement approach:[58]

> It is neither appropriate nor possible to provide simple answers for practitioners about how to do analysis as this is determined by

54 Scottish Government, *Scotland's Children – The Children (Scotland) Act 1995 Regulations and Guidance: Volume 1, ch 1, para 16.*

55 Scottish Government, *Getting It Right for Every Child, Practice Statement, GIRFEC Child's Plan* (2023), pp 5–6.

56 Scottish Government, *GIRFEC Child's Plan* (2023), p 3. It should be noted that parents have a right to be involved in meetings where decisions are taken about their children by virtue of Art 8 of the European Convention on Human Rights, subject to protecting the rights and welfare of the child.

57 *GIRFEC Child's Plan (2023),* p 3.

58 Aldgate, J & Rose, W, *Assessing and Managing Risk in Getting it Right for Every Child* (2011).

individual case circumstances and the available practitioner skills, ability and knowledge as well as the service responses to these.[59]

Finally, local authorities will be expected to follow guidance in carrying out assessments, particularly statutory guidance, and to adopt an approach to assessment and to reaching decisions that is reasonable.

Once needs have been identified it may be that these can be met by a single agency or it may be that a multi-agency plan is required. In the national guidance there is no real distinction, except in terms of the complexity of the process and of management of the plan, between single-agency plans and other plans, though some local authorities do distinguish between them as different types of plan.[60] However, even in the case of single-agency plans the expectation is that the National Practice Model will be used to develop the plan.[61] Any plan should include and record:[62]

(a) The reasons for the plan.
(b) Partners to the plan.
(c) The views of the child or young person and their family or carers.
(d) A summary of the child's or young person's needs.
(e) What is to be done to improve the child's or young person's wellbeing.
(f) Details of the action to be taken.
(g) Resources to be provided.
(h) Timescales for action and for change.
(i) Contingency plans.
(j) Arrangements for reviews of the plan.
(k) Lead Professional arrangements when these are appropriate (this is likely to be the case where the plan includes more than one agency).
(l) Details of any compulsory measures required.

As with all decisions about support, the question arises whether there is a clear right or entitlement to support once needs have been identified. The vagueness of the definition of 'in need', referred to above, and the reference to providing 'appropriate' services leaves considerable

59 Scottish Government, *National Risk Framework to Support the Assessment of Children and Young People* (2012), pp 24–25, this also notes that a key assessment principle is to 'balance informed reasoned analysis and practitioner intuition'.

60 See, for example, Glasgow City Council, *Guidance on a common approach for professionals in Glasgow to assessment, planning and care management for children and young people* (2017).

61 Scottish Government, *A Guide to Getting it Right for Every Child* (2012), pp 14–15; Scottish Government, *Getting It Right For Every Child, Practice Guidance 1, Using the National Practice Model* (2022).

62 *Getting it Right for Every Child, Practice Guidance 1.*

discretion to the local authority. The second edition of this text explained that:[63]

More specifically, the guidance says:

> 'Once a need has been identified, the local authority should consider whether assistance is appropriate, and if so should plan with the family how best to meet this need *within the resources and services available*.'[64]
>
> This seems to indicate that resources are a relevant consideration in deciding whether to meet needs,[65] though it should be borne in mind that in some cases the need will be so great and clear that a refusal to provide services will be regarded by the courts as unreasonable and so be open to challenge.

Since the publication of the above, some guidance has been offered by the Scottish courts on the nature of the duty owed towards children in need. In *Crossan*, the court interpreted the duty towards children in need to be a general duty owed towards the class of 'children in need', rather than as conferring rights on, or imposing a duty towards, an individual child.[66] The consequence of this is that a child who has been assessed as needing the provision of particular support will, subject to what is said below, have no right to that support, nor will the local authority have a legally enforceable duty to provide it. Support for the court's conclusion came from English case law[67] and from the terms of the 1995 Act, particularly the provision in section 22(3) which confers a *discretion* to provide services to an individual child.[68]

There will be cases in which a child's need will be so substantial that a refusal to provide services would be open to challenge as unreasonable. A further limit is that in some cases the circumstances of a child's life might be such that their rights under Article 8 of the European Convention on Human Rights (or, in an extreme case, Article 3) are being infringed. In such cases the local authority will have a duty to take action to prevent continued infringement.

Any refusal to provide services under the 1995 Act can be challenged on the grounds that the decision was unreasonable or did not pay proper

63 *Getting It Right for Every Child, Practice Guidance 1*, p 112.

64 *Scottish Government, Scotland's Children – The Children (Scotland) Act 1995 Regulations and Guidance: Volume 1* Ch 1, para 29.

65 See also *R v Kingston-upon-Thames Royal Borough Council, ex parte T* [1994] 1 FLR 798.

66 *Crossan v South Lanarkshire Council* [2006] SLT 441.

67 *R (on the application of G) v Barnet London Borough Council* [2003] UKHL 57.

68 1995 Act, s 22(3).

attention to the need for the local authority to act proportionately.[69] It has been suggested that if a local authority decides both that a child is in need of support and that that support should not be provided, then that second decision will be subjected to strict scrutiny.[70] Such scrutiny may be sceptical of the decision not to provide support, particularly if there is no available argument based on lack of resources.[71]

(4) Children and disability

4.7 Special provision is made for children affected by disability.[72] A child may be affected by disability either because the child is disabled or because they are affected by the disability of another family member. Support services provided to such children under the local authority's obligation to promote welfare are to be designed to give the child the opportunity to lead as normal a life as possible and to minimise the effect of the disability.

As well as the obligation to provide services the local authority has specific assessment duties in respect of children affected by disability.[73] The parent or guardian of such a child can request an assessment of the child or of the disabled family member.[74] Although only the parent or guardian has the statutory right to request an assessment, the guidance makes it clear that it is good practice to carry out an assessment if requested to do so by a child affected by disability.[75] A request for assessment can also be made by a Mental Health Officer who is involved with the child.[76]

The purpose of the assessment is to identify the needs of the child. Having identified a child's needs, the local authority can carry out its duties as regards provision of services. Such services should be designed both to minimise the effect of the disability and to give the child the chance to lead as normal a life as possible. More generally, support services should promote the welfare of the child. The 1995 Act restricts assessments to identifying needs flowing from disability, but

69 See eg, *R (Jalal) v Greenwich RLBC* [2016] EWHC 1848 (Admin), para 11, referring to *R (G) v London Borough of Barnet (& others)* [2003] UKHL 57.

70 *R (VC) v Newcastle City Council* [2011] EWHC 2673 (Admin), para 26.

71 *R (VC) v Newcastle City Council* [2011] EWHC 2673 (Admin), para 26.

72 1995 Act, s 23; *Scottish Government, Scotland's Children – The Children (Scotland) Act 1995 Regulations and Guidance: Volume 1*, ch 6.

73 1995 Act, s 23.

74 1995 Act, s 23(3).

75 *Scottish Government, Scotland's Children – The Children (Scotland) Act 1995 Regulations and Guidance: Volume 1* ch 6, para 5.

76 1995 Act, s 23(3)(b).

the guidance goes further. The guidance suggests that the assessment should 'consider whether services available for children in need … should be provided to meet the child's wider needs, in addition to those attributable to his or her disability'.[77]

A final element of the assessment process is that, where a disabled child is being assessed, the child's carer may also be assessed.[78] In this context a parent or other person looking after a child will not be regarded as a carer if they are only providing care appropriate to the age of the child.[79] The care provided by the carer must be taken into account, as must the views of the parent or guardian of the child, and the views of the child as far as reasonable and practicable, in deciding on the needs of the child and in taking decisions about provision of support.[80]

In addition to the statutory rights of assessment and involvement, the GIRFEC approach makes it clear that carers and parents must be fully involved in any assessment of a child.

Once the assessments have been carried out a decision will need to be made about the provision of services for the child and their family. If the local authority decides that the child has a specific need for a service, then, subject to what is said below about the Chronically Sick and Disabled Persons Act 1970, the 1995 Act does not require the local authority to provide that service or give the child an enforceable right to it.[81]

Duties to disabled children under the 1995 Act are superimposed on other duties owed to people with disabilities, but the relationship between these provisions is unclear. Other duties owed by local authorities are considered in chapter 6, but there is one specific statutory provision which should be briefly examined here. Section 2(1) of the Chronically Sick and Disabled Persons Act 1970 imposes a duty on the local authority to provide certain services (which are listed in the subsection) to certain classes of disabled people if it is satisfied that this is necessary to meet their needs.[82] Important consequences follow

77 *Scottish Government, Scotland's Children – The Children (Scotland) Act 1995 Regulations and Guidance: Volume 1* ch 6, para 5.

78 See the discussion of assessment of carers and provision of services to them at **6.7**.

79 Carers (Scotland) Act 2016, s 1(2)(a).

80 1995 Act, s 23(4)(b)(i).

81 *Crossan v South Lanarkshire Council* [2006] SLT 441, following *R (G) v London Borough of Barnet (& others)* [2003] UKHL 57 decided on the equivalent provision of the Children Act 1989. It has been suggested that the England and Wales equivalent of s 22 'creates a discretion in a local authority to make a decision to meet an individual child's assessed needs', *R (C & Ors) v Southwark LBC* [2016] EWCA Civ 707, para 12.

82 Chronically Sick and Disabled Persons Act 1970, s 2(1).

from this. The first is that disabled children to whom a duty arises under the 1995 Act are one of the classes to which this section applies. The second is that once a decision has been made that the child's needs call for the provision of such a service, then that service must be provided. This contrasts with the position under the 1995 Act. Third, even though a specific request for assessment for services under the 1970 Act is not made by the child or their parent/guardian, the local authority must be alive to the possibility of duties arising under it. If the local authority fails to consider it and carry out an appropriate assessment considering services under the 1970 Act, any decision on provision of services could be illegal.[83] Where a child is affected by the disability of an adult in their family, the local authority's duties to adults affected by disability must also be considered.[84]

(5) Assistance from other bodies

4.8 In carrying out its duties a local authority may request assistance from another local authority, a health board or an NHS trust.[85] These bodies must comply with this request unless doing so would either be incompatible with their own statutory or other duties, or would prejudice the discharge of any of their functions.[86] The inclusion of this section is significant in recognising the pivotal nature of collaboration and co-operation amongst agencies which has so evidently been at the root of difficulties in service provision in the past. Getting it Right for Every Child in particular stresses the need for joint working and the involvement, where appropriate, of different services in providing support for a child.

(6) Provision of services

4.9 The local authority is under an obligation to offer the four options for support set out in the Social Care (Self-directed Support) (Scotland) Act 2013.[87]

If services are to be provided, then the outcome of the assessment process will be a care plan agreed with the family, which should be

83 *R v Bexley LBC, ex parte B (Care Hours Provision)* [1995] 7 WLUK 389.
84 See chapter 6.
85 1995 Act, s 21.
86 1995 Act, s 21(2).
87 Social Care (Self-directed Support) (Scotland) Act 2013 (SC(SDS)(S) Act 2013) Statutory Guidance (2-22), p 11.

in the form of a child or young person's plan.[88] This plan should be a written document and its implementation will have to be monitored and reviewed.[89] Service provision under the plan may include the provision of services by the local authority, provision by other agencies, or provision of self-directed support.[90]

In providing services the local authority must take account of a number of factors. First it must act in partnership with families and pursue the duty to promote the upbringing of the child in their own family. Secondly, the local authority must listen to the child and take into account their views. Thirdly, it must 'have regard so far as practicable to each child's religious persuasion, racial origin and cultural and linguistic background'.[91] Finally, for a child away from home, the local authority must promote the child's contact with their family.

If support is to be provided, it can be provided directly to the child, to their family, or to any other member of the family.[92] In the latter two cases the support must be provided with a view to safeguarding or promoting the welfare of the child.[93]

Specific provisions apply to the choice of options for the provision of support to children.[94] As is the case with adult social care, a choice of options has to be offered.[95] Where support is being provided to a child aged at least 16, they will make the selection from the options available.[96] For children who have not yet reached their sixteenth birthday the decision will be made by an 'appropriate person', being someone having parental responsibilities and/or parental rights.[97] The relevant parental responsibilities/rights can arise for a number of reasons, e.g., as birth parents (subject to what is said at chapter 3, para 3.6), because of an order under section 11 of the 1995 Act, or where parental responsibilities and rights vest as a result of a permanence order.[98] Where support is being provided to a member of the child's family over the age of 16 then that person will make the choice.[99] Information and support will need to be provided to ensure that the choice is properly

88 See also the specific plan requirements where a child is looked after (see **4.17** below).
89 Scottish Executive, *Guidance on the Child's or Young Person's Plan*, 2007.
90 See **6.11**.
91 1995 Act, s 22(2).
92 1995 Act, s 22(3).
93 1995 Act, s 22(3).
94 SC(SDS)(S) Act 2013, s 8.
95 SC(SDS)(S) Act 2013, s 8.
96 SC(SDS)(S) Act 2013, s 8(9).
97 SC(SDS)(S) Act 2013, s 8(9).
98 SC(SDS)(S) Act 2013, s 8(9).
99 SC(SDS)(S) Act 2013, s 8(9).

informed[100] and, in the cases where the child is under 16, they must be provided with an explanation of, and information about, the nature and effect of the options.[101]

Finally, where the decision about options is being taken by an appropriate person the child must, (as far as practicable, and taking account of the child's maturity), be given an opportunity to:

(a) indicate whether he or she wishes to express a view about the choice; and

(b) express that view. The appropriate person must have regard to these views in making the choice.[102]

It is important to remember that not only does the social work department have a duty to promote welfare, but also that the same duty is owed by the council as a whole. Because of this, all the services of the local authority as a whole should be considered. When it comes to identifying and meeting needs, the services provided by the housing and education departments will be particularly relevant.

The relationship between services for children and families and other services provided by the local authority is not entirely clear. When a local authority requests help from an outside body, that body is entitled to refuse if complying with the request would be inconsistent with its statutory duties or detrimental to the performance of these duties. Does this apply within the same local authority? One area where this may arise is in respect of housing and families who are intentionally homeless. If a family with children approaches the housing department of a local authority to ask for housing as homeless persons, they will usually need to be given temporary accommodation.[103] The housing department will then have to decide if it has an obligation to secure the provision of permanent accommodation for the family. This obligation will arise only if the applicant is not intentionally homeless. If the family were evicted because of non-payment of rent or anti-social behaviour, they may be regarded as intentionally homeless. An approach might then be made to the social work department for assistance, which might then approach the housing department seeking the provision of accommodation. It now seems to be clear that the services provided to children under section 22 of the 1995 Act can include providing housing for children and

100 SC(SDS)(S) Act 2013, s 9.
101 SC(SDS)(S) Act 2013, s 10.
102 SC(SDS)(S) Act 2013, s 8(5), (6).
103 *R (on the application of W) v Lambeth London Borough Council* [2002] EWCA Civ 613.

their families.[104] Can the housing department, though part of the same authority, refuse? Given what has been said above about the nature of the duty to provide services the answer would appear to be that there is no automatic duty owed to a particular child and their family to provide housing.

A final point on the relationship between housing and social work services is that it has been suggested that before a local authority takes a decision which may have the result that duties will be owed to children and families it must consider the potential obligations to provide housing under the 1995 Act, and that failure to do this will leave the decision open to legal challenge.[105] This suggests that, before taking a decision to implement or enforce eviction, a local authority will have to take into consideration the possibility that it will have a duty to accommodate the family under the 1995 Act.

(7) Daycare and after-school services

4.10 Appropriate daycare services must be provided for children in need who are under five and have not started school, and after school/school holiday services must be provided for children in need who are at school.[106] Authorities are empowered to provide these services to other children.

(8) Provision of accommodation to children

4.11 A local authority has a duty to provide accommodation to any child who appears to require it for one of the following reasons:[107]

(a) no one has parental responsibility for the child;
(b) the child is lost or abandoned; or
(c) the person caring for the child is prevented temporarily or permanently from providing suitable accommodation and care.

104 *R (on the application of W) v Lambeth London Borough Council* [2002] EWCA Civ 613.

105 *R v Avon County Council, ex parte Hills* (1995) 27 HLR 411.

106 1995 Act, s 27.

107 1995 Act, s 25. In considering what a child requires, reference should be made to future as well as current needs: *Re T (Accommodation by Local Authority)* [1995] 1 FLR 159. Unlike some other duties imposed under the 1995 Act, the duty to accommodate is enforceable by individual children, *R (on the application of A) v London Borough of Croydon* [2008] EWCA Civ 1445.

This last criterion has been interpreted widely by the courts in England and Wales, taking the view that the carer will be unable to provide suitable accommodation in the following circumstances:

(a) the child's carer is seriously ill or unable to control the child;
(b) the child has assaulted their carer;
(c) the child is not prepared to be accommodated by the carer;[108]
(d) the parents cannot provide accommodation for the child because of violence by the child towards a sibling;[109]
(e) because of the condition of the accommodation where the child is staying.[110]

Before providing accommodation, the authority must have regard to the views of the child, (if they wish to express a view) taking into account the child's age and maturity,[111] as far as is practicable. There is no requirement to comply with or follow the views expressed by the child. In the English courts there has been some discussion about whether a child aged 16 or over can be forced to accept accommodation, the prevailing view appears to be that they cannot.[112]

Local authorities also have the power under section 25 of the 1995 Act to provide accommodation to any other child and to anyone aged between 18 and 21.[113]

A child can be accommodated in a variety of settings:[114]

(a) with a family, relative or other suitable person, but a family consisting of the people who have parental responsibilities for the child or people with whom the child has been living are excluded, so the child cannot be accommodated with them;
(b) in a residential establishment;[115] or
(c) by the authority making other arrangements that appear to be appropriate.[116]

A child cannot be cared for by their parents while being accommodated by the local authority.[117] The consequence of this would appear to be that the local authority cannot fulfil its obligation to accommodate a

108 See, eg, *R (L) v Nottinghamshire CC* [2007] EWHC 2364 (Admin).
109 *JG v Kent County Council* [2016] EWHC 1102 (Admin).
110 *London Borough of Hackney v Williams* [2017] EWCA Civ 26 at para 67; [2018] UKSC 37 at para 54.
111 Children aged 12 or over are deemed to have sufficient maturity to express a view.
112 *R(G) v London Borough of Southwark* [2009] UKHL 26.
113 1995 Act, s 25(3).
114 1995 Act, s 26. Placements need not be in Scotland.
115 1995 Act, s 26(1)(b).
116 1995 Act, s 26(1)(c).
117 Looked After Children (Scotland) Regulations 2009 (the 'LAC Regs'), SI 2009/210, reg 8(2).

child by providing accommodation for the child and their family. There is, of course, no reason why this accommodation cannot be provided under the authority's duties and powers towards children in need.

The provision of accommodation for a child by the local authority is likely to be one of the most stressful events in the lives of all concerned. The social worker's role in these situations can often be contradictory. At its crudest and simplest, there are often conflicts of interest amongst the child, the family and the local authority at the point of accommodation being provided. When a child is removed from the family and is being looked after by the local authority, the resulting tensions must be carefully managed. Social workers will be hard pressed to make assessments, negotiate decision-making, and marshal appropriate resources, while remaining open to the feelings of all those involved in the process, including themselves.

(9) Rights to object to provision of accommodation

4.12 Good practice is to obtain the consent of the child's parent or another person with parental rights and responsibilities, but this is not necessary in order for the local authority to be able to continue to provide accommodation to a child. All that is required is that there is no objection to the continued provision of accommodation.[118] A child cannot be accommodated against the objection of a person who both:[119]

(a) holds parental responsibilities and the parental rights to have the child living with them and to control, direct or guide the child; and
(b) is willing to provide or arrange the provision of accommodation for the child.

Such a person can remove the child from accommodation provided by the local authority at any time. This power to object to the provision of accommodation and to remove the child is subject to two limitations. First, it will not arise where accommodation is being provided to a child of 16 or over who agrees to be provided with accommodation,[120] or where a person holding a residence order in respect of the child agrees to the provision of accommodation. Second, 14 days' notice must be given

118 *London Borough of Hackney v Williams* [2017] EWCA Civ 26.

119 1995 Act, s 25(6).

120 It might be argued that the provision that children over the age of 16 cannot be removed against their will is redundant, since there can be no one with the parental rights needed to remove the child once the child is 16: see 1995 Act, s 2(7).

of the intended removal once the child has been being accommodated for six months.[121]

Where a child is being provided with accommodation, their plan, which should be agreed with the child's parents, should contain an express agreement about the ending of the provision of accommodation. The plan may also say something about the need to give notice before a child is removed. This agreement, of course, does not override the parent's right to remove the child, though some parents may feel, wrongly, that because they have entered into a written agreement, they are bound by it and cannot exercise their rights.

The right of parents to remove children who are being provided with accommodation gives rise to two problems. First, who is to judge whether the parent is qualified to remove the child? It will have to be established that the parent holds responsibilities and the relevant rights, and it should be remembered that unmarried fathers will not always hold these. It will also have to be established that the parent is willing and able to provide accommodation for the child. Does this mean that if, in the judgment of the local authority, the parent is unable to provide accommodation then the parent has no right to take the child? What criteria might be used in arriving at that decision? Is the nature and suitability of the accommodation relevant? It is notable that the 1995 Act refers only to providing 'accommodation' and makes no reference to the suitability of the accommodation.[122] If the local authority was of the opinion that the accommodation was not suitable, then its objection might come under the heading of the second problem, namely what is to be done when the parent demands that children are returned but the local authority does not think that it is in the interests of the child to comply with this?

In *M v Dumfries and Galloway Regional Council*[123] it was decided that if a local authority considered it not to be in the child's best interests to be returned to the parents it could refuse to do this. If the parents objected, they would have to go to court to seek an order for delivery of the child. Such an application was to be treated as an application under section 3 of the Law Reform (Parent and Child) (Scotland) Act 1986 (the 1986 Act), which meant that the court could not grant it unless it was satisfied that it was in the best interests of the child to do so. The authority of this

121 The notice requirement is not part of the Children Act 1989. The reason for this is that the view was taken that retaining the notice requirement blurred the distinction between voluntary and compulsory care.

122 1995 Act, s 25(8).

123 1991 SCLR 481.

decision has been doubted[124] on the grounds that the 1986 Act did not allow local authorities to rely on section 3, being purely a private law provision which could only be relied on by individuals. This seems to have been confirmed by the express provision in section 11(5) of the 1995 Act excluding local authorities from applying for orders relating to parental responsibilities or rights. It is debatable whether the local authority was in fact 'relying' on the 1986 Act and whether the 1995 Act overrules the decision. However, the precedent set is undesirable for the different reason that it appears to allow the local authority to override the safeguards for parents and children, safeguards built into the procedures which allow it to exercise compulsory powers over a child.[125] What options then are open to the local authority in this situation?

(a) The local authority could apply for a child protection order if it considered that the conditions for this were fulfilled, or it could refer the case to the Principal reporter if it considered that the child was in need of compulsory measures of supervision. Indeed, if it thought the child was in need of such measures it would have a duty to make the referral.[126] These powers would not help, however, where instant action was needed as they both take time.

(b) Any foster carer with whom the child had been placed or any individual social worker might be able to rely on section 5 of the 1995 Act. This states that:

> ... it shall be the responsibility of a person who has attained the age of sixteen and who has care or control of a child under that age, but in relation to him either has no parental responsibilities or rights or does not have the parental responsibility [to safeguard or promote the child's health, development or welfare], to do what is reasonable in all the circumstances to safeguard the child's health, development and welfare; and in fulfilling his responsibility ... the person may ... [subject to certain conditions] give consent to any surgical, medical or dental treatment or procedure...[127]

This could be supplemented by the duty of the authority to safeguard and promote the welfare of children whom it is looking after. There is some support for the view that the equivalent English provision would allow the local authority to refuse to hand over a child, at least temporarily, while some other measures

124 See K Norrie, *The Law Relating to Parent and Child in Scotland* (23rd edn, 2013) para 8.39 and *City of Edinburgh Council v M* 1996 SCLR 779.

125 See Professor Thomson's commentary on *M v Dumfries and Galloway Regional Council* 1991 SCLR 481.

126 Children's Hearings (Scotland) Act 2011, s 60(2).

127 1995 Act, s 5(1).

were taken.[128] Indeed, while this provision was going through Parliament, reference was made to the use of the provision to refuse to hand over a child to an inebriated parent.[129] It was also suggested that unless a social worker's decision to refuse to return a child to their parent was 'wholly unreasonable' the social worker would be protected by this provision.[130] No similar debate took place during the passage of section 5 of the 1995 Act; indeed the section was seen as being entirely a private law matter, and the provisions as to medical treatment were described as concerning 'private law' and not dealing with 'public intervention on behalf of the child'.[131] For this reason it might be difficult to argue that section 5 gives powers to social workers and foster carers. The relevant part of the original guidance noted that:

> Carers will need advice on how to handle those occasional cases in which it may be necessary for the social worker to seek an emergency order to prevent an inappropriate and unplanned removal where this would be likely to cause significant harm to the child (for example, a drunk parent coming to 'collect' his or her child in the middle of the night).[132]

The above guidance does not provide a legal basis for retaining a child until an emergency order is obtained. It is therefore suggested, notwithstanding the terms of the debate in Parliament, that section 5 of the 1995 Act does empower social workers and foster carers to refuse to return a child, but only temporarily while other action is taken to protect the child.[133]

Even if we are wrong and no protection is offered by section 5 of the 1995 Act, it would be unlikely that a claim against the worker by the parent(s) for interference with the exercise of their rights would succeed.[134]

(c) The police could be called and asked to exercise their emergency powers to protect children.[135]

128 Children Act 1989, s 3(5), *Williams v London Borough of Hackney* [2018] UKSC 37 at para 44.

129 By David Mellor (HC Standing Committee B, 18 May 1989, col 148) and by the Lord Chancellor (HL, vol 505, cols 370–371).

130 HC Standing Committee B, 18 May 1989, col 152.

131 By Lord James Douglas-Hamilton, HC Special Standing Committee, 23 February 1995, col 279.

132 1995 Act, *Regulations and Guidance: Volume 2,* ch l, para 121. There is no specific coverage of this in the LAC Guidance.

133 1995 Act, s 5

134 See *F v Wirral Metropolitan Borough Council* [1991] Fam 69.

135 Children's Hearings (Scotland) Act 2011, s 56.

(10) Assistance in cash or kind

4.13 The support provided by the local authority to children in need may be in kind or, in exceptional circumstances, in cash.[136] If support is provided in this way it may be unconditional or subject to repayment, in whole or in part, either of the cash sum or of the value of the benefit in kind. No repayment can be required of anyone receiving universal credit, income support, working families' tax credit, child tax credit (subject to some exceptions), income-based jobseeker's allowance or employment and support allowance.[137] Any requirement to repay can be made only after full consideration of the means of the child and their parent(s).

CHILDREN 'LOOKED AFTER' BY THE LOCAL AUTHORITY

(1) Who is looked after?[138]

4.14 Children defined as being looked after by the local authority are:

(a) children being provided with accommodation under section 25 of the 1995 Act;[139]

(b) children subject to a compulsory supervision order or interim compulsory supervision order made by a children's hearing and in respect of which the local authority is the implementation authority;[140] this is the case even if the child is staying at home;

(c) children sentenced to detention by the sheriff summary court;[141]

(d) children in respect of whom a permanence order has been made;[142] or

(e) children subject to an order made elsewhere in the UK under which the local authority has responsibility for them, e.g., a care order made in England or Wales.

136 1995 Act, s 22(3)(b). This would, presumably, not include provision of support through a direct payment under the Social Care (Self-Directed Support) (Scotland) Act 2013, but the 1995 Act has not been amended to reflect this.

137 1995 Act, s 22(4).

138 1995 Act, s 17(6).

139 1995 Act, s 17(6)(a).

140 1995 Act, s 17(6)(b). See **5.30**.

141 Criminal Procedure (Scotland) Act 1995, s 44(3).

142 1995 Act, s 17(6)(e).

In cases where a child has removed to a place of safety under a Child Protection Order the local authority has the same duties to that child as it would have to a looked after child.[143]

Although these children are all being looked after by the local authority, it is important to remember that, with the exception of those children in respect of whom a permanence order extinguishing parental responsibility and rights has been made, the child's parent(s) retain parental responsibilities and rights in respect of the child. In some cases, these rights will be limited, as where a children's hearing, in making a compulsory supervision order, regulates contact between the child and their parent(s), or, by definition, in cases where a permanence order has been made. The extent to which parental responsibilities and rights have been lost by the parents will depend on the precise terms of the order.

(2) Duties to children at risk of being looked after

4.15 If a child is at risk of becoming looked after then, provided the benefit to the child's well-being of doing so outweighs any adverse effect of doing so, the local authority must provide certain services to the child and their family.[144] The range of services which is to be provided is relatively limited, extending to:[145]

(a) Family group decision-making services, designed to facilitate decision-making by a child's family in relation to the services and support required by the child.

(b) Support services in relation to parenting designed to improve parenting skills.

143 Children's Hearings (Scotland) Act 2011, s 44.

144 2014 Act, s 68 and Children and Young People (Scotland) Act 2014 (Relevant Services in relation to Children at Risk of Becoming Looked After etc) Order 2016, SSI 2016/44, art 3. See also Scottish Government, *Children and Young People (Scotland) Act 2014: National Guidance on Part 12: Services in Relation to Children at Risk of Becoming Looked After, etc.* (2016). The duties owed as corporate parents (see **4.23** below) and to give specific consideration to a child's well-being (**4.3** above) will also apply.

145 2014 Act, s 68(3) and Children and Young People (Scotland) Act 2014 (Relevant Services in relation to Children at Risk of Becoming Looked After etc) Order 2016, art 2.

(3) Statutory duties to looked after children[146]

4.16 The Children (Scotland) Act 1995 imposes upon local authorities a number of duties towards children who are being looked after. These duties are supplemented by further obligations contained in regulations which are further explained in guidance. The regulations and guidance will be dealt with below. The duties directly imposed by the 1995 Act are:

(a) To safeguard and promote the welfare of the child.[147] This is to be the paramount concern of the local authority and includes the duty to provide advice and assistance to prepare the child for when they are no longer looked after by the local authority.[148]

(b) To make use of such services for children being looked after by their parents as appear to be reasonable.[149]

(c) To take steps to promote regular direct contact and personal relations between the child and anyone having parental responsibilities in respect of the child. These steps must only be taken so far as the authority considers them to be practicable and appropriate in light of its paramount duty. A duty to take active steps to promote contact and to avoid arrangements which inhibit or prevent contact arises also under Article 8 of the European Convention on Human Rights.[150] This duty, like that under the 1995 Act, may be limited by the need to consider and protect the child's interests.[151]

(d) To seek the views of the child, their parents, any non-parent holding parental rights and anyone else considered to be relevant (e.g., a sibling) before taking any decision with respect to a child that the authority is looking after or proposing to look after. The authority must obtain these views only as far as is reasonably practicable.[152]

146 1995 Act, s 17. See also: Scottish Government, *Guidance on the Looked After Children (Scotland) Regulations 2009 and the Adoption and Children (Scotland) Act 2007 (2011)* (LAC Guidance).

147 1995 Act, s 17(1)(a).

148 1995 Act, s 17(2).

149 1995 Act, s 17(1)(b).

150 See, eg, *Olsson v Sweden (No 2)* (1994) 17 EHRR 134.

151 *Covezzi & Morselli v Italy* (2004) 38 EHRR 28.

152 1995 Act, s 17(3). The views of those mentioned in subs (1A) must also be ascertained. Such individuals are a sibling of the child, and any other person with whom the child has lived and with whom the child has an ongoing relationship with the character of a relationship between siblings, as per the 1995 Act, s 13(2)(c)(ii). Subsection (1B) provides that, 'for the purposes of subsection (1A), two people are siblings if they have at least one parent in common'. 1995 Act, s 13(2)(b).

(e) To take the views of the child into account before making a decision.[153]

(f) To take the views of those others identified in (d) above into account as far as it has been possible to obtain them.[154]

(g) To take the child's religious persuasion, racial origin, culture and language into account before taking a decision.[155]

Authorities may act inconsistently with these duties only where they consider that this is necessary to protect members of the public from serious harm.[156]

(4) Assessment and care plans

4.17 A local authority must obtain certain information about and then carry out an assessment of any child who is about to be or who becomes looked after.[157] The assessment is then to be used as the basis for preparing a care plan (the 'child's plan') for the child.[158] The objective of the assessment is to identify the needs of, and any problems facing, the child and their family, to identify how these might be addressed and to identify any strengths within the family which can be built on.[159]

In preparing the plan the local authority must, as far as reasonably practicable, obtain certain information set out in Box 4.2.[160] This is the minimum information which is required, additional information needed will depend on the circumstances of the child and their family. In addition, the authority must obtain a written assessment of the child's health and of their need for healthcare.[161]

Box 4.2

Information to be obtained by the local authority in respect of a child to be or being looked after by them[162]

1 Name, sex, date and place of birth and present address of the child, their parents and any relevant person.

153 1995 Act, s 17(4)(a). The age and maturity of the child must be taken into account.
154 1995 Act, s 17(4)(b).
155 1995 Act, s 17(4)(c).
156 1995 Act, s 17(5).
157 Looked After Children (Scotland) Regulations 2009 (LAC Regs), SSI 2009/210, regs 3 and 4.
158 LAC Regs, reg 5.
159 LAC Regs, reg 4.
160 LAC Regs, Sch 1.
161 LAC Regs, reg 3(3)(b).
162 LAC Regs, Sch 1, paras 1–12.

2	Nationality, race, religion and language.
3	Physical description.
4	Present legal status of the child, including any statutory responsibility the local authority has for the child.
5	Why consideration is to be given to the child being looked after by the local authority.
6	Previous history of involvement of the child with any local authority or other relevant organisation.
7	Details of any siblings of the child, including their dates of birth, addresses and any details in respect of their being looked after by a local authority.
8	The extent of contact with members of the child's family and any other significant person who does not live in the same household as the child.
9	The child's health history, current state of health and development and existing arrangements for their medical and dental care.
10	The child's education history and current arrangements for provision of education.
11	Personality and social development.
12	Interests and recreational activities.

After the information has been obtained the local authority must carry out an assessment of the child. What the assessment is to cover for all children is set out in Box 4.3 below.[163] In making the assessment the local authority must seek and take account of the views of:

(a) the child, taking into account their age and maturity;[164]
(b) the child's parents;[165]
(c) anyone else with parental responsibilities/rights in relation to the child; any sibling of the child;[166] and
(d) anyone else the local authority considers to be appropriate.[167]

The guidance stresses the need for the active involvement of the child, their parents and any other carer in the process of assessment.[168]

163 LAC Regs, reg 4.
164 LAC Regs, reg 4(2)(a).
165 LAC Regs, reg 4(2)(b).
166 LAC Regs, reg 3(3)(a)(ii) (26 July 2021).
167 LAC Regs, reg 4(2)(d).
168 Scottish Government, *Guidance on the Looked After Children (Scotland) Regulations 2009 and the Adoption and Children (Scotland) Act 2007 (2011)*(LAC Guidance). This involvement is also required by Article 8 of the European Convention on Human Rights, see e.g., *W v United Kingdom* (1987) 10 EHRR 29.

Where the child is to be placed away from home a number of additional matters must form part of the assessment:

(a) there must be an assessment of contact arrangements with the child's family, including any sibling of the child and others, and whether changes need to be made to them;[169] and

(b) where the placement will be in a residential establishment there must be an assessment made as to whether that placement is appropriate.[170]

As indicated above, the assessment will look both at the immediate needs of the child (which will be the initial focus of the assessment) and their longer-term needs. As regards the latter, the guidance indicates that:[171]

> From the outset in every case, there should be active consideration of the purpose of a child becoming looked after and of the possible outcomes. In its broadest interpretation, 'permanence planning', should cover all options, with the aim of a stable living situation for a child and one which meets his or her needs for consistent, sustainable positive relationships, normally within a family setting.[172]

The assessment should be recorded in writing and discussed with the child, parents and any carer.[173]

Box 4.3

Matters to be covered in assessment of child[174]

(a) the child's immediate needs and how those needs can be met;

(b) the child's long-term needs and how those needs can be met;

(c) proposals for safeguarding and promoting the child's welfare;

(d) proposals for making sustainable and long-term arrangements for the care of the child;

169 LAC Regs, reg 4(3).

170 LAC Regs, reg 4(4).

171 LAC Guidance.

172 The local authority's adoption panel may have a role in giving advice on plans for permanence for looked after children not involving adoption: LAC Guidance, p 155.

173 LAC Guidance, p 25.

174 LAC Regs, reg 4.

(e) the nature of the services proposed for the child in the immediate and long term with particular regard to the information specified in Schedule 1;[175]

(f) alternative courses of action including the possibility of making an arrangement in accordance with regulation 8 or approving a person as a kinship carer;

(g) whether the local authority should seek a change in the child's legal status;

(h) the arrangements which require to be made for the time when the child will no longer be looked after by the local authority;

(i) the existing health arrangements for the child and whether there is a need to change such arrangements taking into account the information specified in paragraph 9 of Schedule 1;[176]

(j) having regard to the information specified in paragraph 10 of Schedule 1,[177] the child's educational needs, the proposals for meeting those needs, and the proposals for achieving continuity in the child's education;

(k) the child's religious persuasion and the need for the child to continue to be brought up in accordance with their religious persuasion; and

(l) any other matter relating to the welfare of the child either in the immediate or long term as appears to the local authority to be relevant.

After completing the assessment, the local authority then has to produce a child's plan for the child.[178] In preparing this plan it must consult, so far as reasonably practicable and consistent with the interests of the child with:[179]

(a) the child, taking account of their age and maturity;
(b) the child's parents;
(c) any relevant person in relation to the child;

175 This is the information set out in Box 4.2.
176 This is the information set out at point 9 in Box 4.2.
177 This is the information set out at point 10 in Box 4.2.
178 Used with a specific meaning distinct from the more general child's plan under GIRFEC (see LAC Guidance, p 26) and the Child's Plan proposed by the Children and Young People (Scotland) Act 2014, s 33, a proposal repealed by Children (Care and Justice) (Scotland) Act 2024, Pt 5 s 32(b).
179 LAC Regs, reg 5(2).

(d) any person other than a relevant person who appears to the authority to have (or to recently have had) a significant involvement in the upbringing of the child;
(e) anyone with (or who has had, to the knowledge of the authority) parental responsibilities or rights in respect of the child;
(f) anyone who has, or who the authority is aware has had, charge of or control over the child;
(g) anyone else the authority considers appropriate; and
(h) any sibling of the child.[180]

The plan as finally formulated must include the matters required by the LAC Regulations and set out Box 4.4 below.

Box 4.4

Contents of the child's plan

The child's plan must include:
(a) The assessments made by the local authority under regulation 4.
(b) Arrangements concerning the matters specified in Part I of Schedule 2 of the LAC Regulations,[181] i.e.:
  (i) The local authority's immediate and longer-term plans for the child.[182]
  (ii) Details of any services to be provided to meet the care, education and health needs of the child.[183]
  (iii) The respective responsibilities of:
    (A) the local authority;[184]
    (B) the child;[185]
    (C) any person with parental responsibilities for the child;[186]
    (D) any foster carer or kinship carer of the child;[187]
    (E) the designated manager of that establishment who is responsible for the care of the child whilst in that establishment where the child has

180 LAC Regs, reg 5(2)(ea).
181 LAC Regs, reg 5(3)b.
182 LAC Regs, Sch 2, Part 1, para 1.
183 LAC Regs, Sch 2, Part 1, para 2.
184 LAC Regs, Sch 2, Part 1, para 3(a).
185 LAC Regs, Sch 2, Part 1, para 3(b).
186 LAC Regs, Sch 2, Part 1, para 3(c).
187 LAC Regs, Sch 2, Part 1, para 3(d).

been placed in a residential establishment;[188] and

(F) any other relevant person.[189]

(c) In each case where the local authority is considering placing, or have placed, the child with a kinship carer, with a foster carer, or in a residential establishment, arrangements concerning the matters specified in Part II of Schedule 2 of the LAC Regulations,[190] i.e.:

(i) The type of accommodation to be provided and its address together with the name of any person who will be responsible for the child at that accommodation on behalf of the local authority.[191]

(ii) The contribution the child's parents or any other person will make to the child's day to day care.[192]

(iii) The arrangements for involving those persons and the child in decision making.[193]

(iv) The arrangements for contact between the child and any of the categories of persons mentioned in section 17(3)(b) to (d) of the 1995 Act and, if appropriate, the reasons why contact with such a person would not be reasonably practicable or would be inconsistent with the child's welfare.

(v) The expected duration of arrangements and the steps which should be taken in bringing the arrangements to an end including arrangements for the return of the child to their parents or other suitable person.

(d) The nature of services proposed for any person to ensure the arrangements concerning the matters specified in Part I or II of Schedule 2 are met;

(e) The health assessment of the child referred to above.

Once the plan is agreed a copy must be provided to the child if, having regard to their age and maturity, the authority considers that they are capable of understanding the meaning and effect of the plan. A copy must also be provided to the child's parent(s) and to any person with parental responsibilities or rights in respect of the child. This will not

188 LAC Regs, Sch 2, Part 1, para 3(e).
189 LAC Regs, Sch 2, Part 1, para 3(f).
190 LAC Regs, reg 5(3)(c).
191 LAC Regs, Sch 2, Part 2, para 4.
192 LAC Regs, Sch 2, Part 2, para 5.
193 LAC Regs, Sch 2, Part 2, para 6.

apply if the authority is of the view that, taking into account its duties towards looked after children and the terms of any order or warrant affecting the child, it would not be in the child's best interests for a copy of the child's plan to be given to someone in one of these classes. In practice the plan should, as far as possible, be agreed with the child and their parent(s) and this should be confirmed by signature of the plan. Where there are disagreements about the plan these should be recorded in writing.[194]

The plan should set out clearly what needs to be done in order to meet the objectives set out in the plan.[195] This covers actions by the local authority and other agencies and actions by the child and their family or carer. It should also set out how long it is expected that the child will be looked after. The plan will need to be regularly monitored and reviewed.

(5) Health care

4.18 The local authority must obtain an assessment of the health of a looked after child and of the child's need for healthcare. Following from this the child's plan must set out any services required to meet the child's health needs, which will include ensuring adequate health care for the child. When the child stays at home the parents will retain parental responsibilities and rights which give them control over medical care of a young child. The exception to this would arise where there is a compulsory supervision or other order requiring medical assessment or treatment, in this circumstance the local authority will be responsible for medical care. As children grow older they acquire the ability to consent to treatment themselves, and the authority will have to work with these children.

Where the child is placed away from home the local authority should act as a good parent would in relation to the health of children placed away from home. This does not confer on the authority any powers of consent. Instead, it is suggested that the authority should obtain the consent of the parents to allow it to seek and obtain any immunisations and treatment recommended for the child. This consent should take the form of a general medical consent form.[196] If consent is withheld or no agreement is reached, the authority does not have the power to authorise treatment. It may be possible to seek a child protection or child assessment order, to refer the case to the reporter or to get a doctor or other medical

194 LAC Guidance, p 28.
195 LAC Guidance, p 29.
196 LAC Guidance, p 33.

professional to apply to court for an order relating to parental rights to allow the treatment to be given[197] (since local authorities cannot apply for such orders). In cases where no agreement is reached (but not in cases where there is opposition to the treatment) the provisions of section 5 of the 1995 Act may be useful.[198] This allows someone who has care or control of a child to consent to medical treatment in fulfilment of the obligation to do what is reasonable to safeguard the child's health, development and welfare. This provision would seem to include local authority workers who have care or control of children as part of their job, as well as foster carers (see the discussion above). This consent can be given only if the child is unable to consent and if the person consenting is ignorant of the fact that the child's parents would refuse consent.[199]

(6) Education

4.19 The guidance on looked after children explains that:[200]

> Children who are looked after should have the same opportunities as all other children for education, including further and higher education, and access to other opportunities for development. They should also receive additional help, encouragement and support to address special educational needs or compensate for previous disadvantage and gaps in educational provision.

The reference to additional support is appropriate as local authorities have a duty to provide additional support for children who have additional support needs. A child will have such additional support needs where:

> for whatever reason, the child or young person is, or is likely to be, unable without the provision of additional support to benefit from school education provided or to be provided for the child or young person.[201]

Looked after children are considered to have such additional support needs simply because they are looked after, at least until it is established

197 1995 Act, s 11.
198 1995 Act, s 5.
199 The LAC Guidance suggests, at p 33, that foster carers should be discouraged from consenting to major treatment where this is not urgent.
200 LAC Guidance, p 34.
201 Education (Additional Support for Learning) (Scotland) Act 2004, s 1(1), Scottish Government, *Supporting Children's Learning Code of Practice*, 3rd edition, 2017.

that they do not.[202] If a child has additional support needs then the local authority has a duty to provide the additional support required to meet the identified needs and keep this provision under review.[203] The support may be provided by the school or the wider education department, but it may also involve services from other parts of the council. Support may be provided by other bodies, for example from another local authority providing a specific type of educational provision required by a child. The authority has an obligation to carry out an assessment of a child if requested to do so by a child's parent or by a young person (or, if the young person lacks capacity, by their parent). The authority must also have its own arrangements for identifying children with additional support needs and the specific needs of any child so identified.[204]

The additional support needs can be met through personal learning planning.[205] Where more detailed planning or more substantial alteration is needed to support learning and teaching, an individualised education programme may be developed.[206] In some cases a co-ordinated support plan will be required. A co-ordinated support plan will be needed where a child has additional support needs:[207]

(a) which arise from one or more complex factors or multiple factors: the former are factors which are likely to have a significant adverse effect on the child's education, the latter will arise when multiple factors, taken together, have or are likely to have a significant adverse effect on the school education of the child or young person;
(b) which are likely to continue for more than a year; and
(c) which require significant additional support to be provided both by the education authority and by either another agency or the local authority exercising functions other than education.

In the period leading up to a child with additional support needs leaving school the education authority must seek information from other agencies. The education authority must pass on information to other agencies concerning the date on which the child or young person is expected to cease receiving school education. The authority may also

202 Education (Additional Support for Learning) (Scotland) Act 2004, s 1(1A), (1B); LAC Guidance, p 35; Scottish Government, *Supporting Children's Learning*, ch 1, paras 5–7.
203 Education (Additional Support for Learning) (Scotland) Act 2004, s 4.
204 Education (Additional Support for Learning) (Scotland) Act 2004, s 4.
205 Scottish Government, *Supporting Children's Learning*, ch 3, paras 82–91.
206 *Supporting Children's Learning*, ch 3, paras 82–91.
207 Education (Additional Support for Learning) (Scotland) Act 2004, ss 2 and 9–11; *Supporting Children's Learning*, ch 5.

pass on other information the authority considers appropriate about the child or young person and their additional support needs.[208]

(7) Respite care

4.20 Children who are provided with short periods of care away from home to provide respite for their families will qualify as looked after children as they are being provided with accommodation under section 25 of the 1995 Act during these short periods of respite care.[209] Periods of respite can occur relatively frequently. It would clearly be problematic if each short period of respite was treated as being a new episode of the child coming to be looked after and therefore setting in motion the processes described above. Therefore, a series of planned short-term placements will be treated as a single placement and the regulations will apply as if what was involved was a single placement. There are limits placed on this: the individual placements must not be for longer than four weeks, and the total duration of the series of placements must not exceed 120 days in the course of one year.[210]

There is one modification of the regulations as they apply to such single placements. The first review is to take place within three months of the date of the first placement and reviews should thereafter take place at least every six months.[211]

(8) Contact with the child's family[212]

4.21 In the case of children placed away from home, the local authority must bear in mind its obligation to 'promote, on a regular basis, personal relations and direct contact' between the child and their family.[213] This obligation is limited by the requirement that the contact is practicable and appropriate, as well as by the need to safeguard and promote the welfare of the child. Reasons for any restriction on contact should be clearly recorded. Contact may, of course, be restricted under

208 Education (Additional Support for Learning) (Scotland) Act 2004, ss 12 and 13; Scottish Government, *Supporting Children's Learning*, ch 6, paras 37–48. Where a child is looked after this will overlap with the authority's aftercare duties, see **4.44–4.46** below.

209 1995 Act, s 25.

210 LAC Regs, regs 14 and 30.

211 LAC Regs, reg 45(3)(a).

212 LAC Guidance, pp 38–43.

213 1995 Act, s 17(1)(c), such an obligation is also implied by Article 8 of the European Convention on Human Rights, requiring active steps to be taken to maintain contact unless this is against the interests of the child.

the terms of any court order or supervision requirement in terms of which the child is being looked after. The arrangements made by the social work department must comply with the terms of any such order or requirement. The child's wishes in respect of contact must also be taken into account. Where the child has siblings who are placed in a different setting from the child consideration will need to be given to ensuring contact between the siblings.

Most children looked after by the local authority and placed away from home will be returning to their parent(s) and families to live and so the requirement to encourage and facilitate meaningful contact arrangements works to provide a sound basis for the preparation for a return home.[214]

(9) Records

4.22 Records must be kept in relation to any looked after child.[215] This record should include any child's plan, any reports about the welfare of the child, any documentation associated with review of a child's case and details of any placements.[216] The guidance indicates the importance of these records for children later on in life when they may wish to exercise their right to access these records.[217] It suggests that it is important that records include:[218]

(a) a chronology of significant events in the child's life to which all relevant services contribute;
(b) consistent recording of all staff contacts with children and families, including details of when the child has been seen;
(c) decisions taken and reasons for these;
(d) a distinction made between facts and opinions;
(e) outcomes of interventions; and
(f) details of the child's views.

Where the child has been placed in accommodation by the local authority the records are to be kept for 100 years from the birth of the child, or if the child dies before their eighteenth birthday, for 25 years from the date of death.[219] There is no duration set out for looked after children who have not been placed by the local authority, e.g., those looked after because on home supervision. The guidance however suggests that

214 1995 Act, s 17(1)(c).
215 LAC Guidance, pp 126–128.
216 LAC Regs, reg 42.
217 See also the comments in *Gaskin v UK* (1990) 12 EHRR 36, quoted at **2.29**.
218 LAC Guidance, p 126.
219 LAC Regs, reg 43.

it would be good practice to retain such records for at least 30 years following the child's eighteenth birthday.[220]

(10) Corporate parenting[221]

4.23 A range of obligations is placed on what the 2014 Act defines as 'corporate parents'.[222] This definition[223] is drawn widely and includes not only local authorities, but also health boards, universities and other post-16 education providers, and the police.[224] Corporate parents owe responsibilities to looked after children and to people under the age of 26 who were looked after on their sixteenth birthday (all referred to as 'relevant young people' below).[225] The main responsibilities owed to relevant young people by a corporate parent are:[226]

(a) to be alert to matters which might adversely affect them;
(b) to assess their needs for the services it provides;
(c) to promote their interests;
(d) to seek to provide them with opportunities to participate in activities designed to promote their well-being and take action to help them to access these;
(e) to take action to make use of the services it provides; and
(f) to take any other appropriate action to improve the way it exercises its functions in relation to them.

Corporate parents must prepare (and keep under review) a plan setting out how they propose to exercise their responsibilities.[227] Such responsibilities will include collaborating with other corporate parents where they consider that doing so would safeguard and promote the

220 LAC Guidance, p 128.
221 Children and Young People (Scotland) Act 2014, Pt 9; Scottish Government, *Statutory Guidance on Part 9 (Corporate Parenting) of the Children and Young People (Scotland) Act 2014* (2015). See also the implementation notes here: https://www.celcis-uk.com/application/files/3114/8542/6899/Inform_Briefing_Part_9_2017updated.pdf (accessed April 2026).
222 2014 Act, s 58.
223 2014 Act, s 56(1) and Sch 4.
224 2014 Act, Sch 4.
225 2014 Act, s 57(1).
226 2014 Act, s 58; Scottish Government, *Statutory Guidance on Part 9 (Corporate Parenting) of the Children and Young People (Scotland) Act 2014* (2015), paras 66–106. The precise nature of these will vary as between different corporate parents, e.g., Scottish Government, *Statutory Guidance on Part 9 (Corporate Parenting)*, paras 58–59.
227 2014 Act, s 59.

welfare of relevant young people,[228] and reporting on the exercise of their responsibilities.[229]

PLACEMENT OF LOOKED AFTER CHILDREN

(1) Introduction

4.24 Looked after children can be accommodated in a variety of settings. In some cases, the setting will be regulated by the terms of a compulsory supervision order made by a children's hearing in respect of the child.[230] Where a placement is made by a children's hearing, that placement will not be subject to the arrangements and regulations discussed here. Otherwise, arrangements will have to be made by a local authority for the care of children who are looked after and this can be done by arranging foster care, kinship care and residential care. In some cases, authorities will have to find accommodation in an emergency, for example if a child is removed from home on a child protection order. Below we will consider the specific rules applying to each type of care.

One general restriction is that placements are subject to the terms of any compulsory supervision order made by a children's hearing, any permanence order, any warrant to secure the attendance of a child at a hearing, and any exclusion order.[231] In addition, they are subject to the terms of any child protection order.[232] Where siblings are to be looked after, the local authority has a duty to find placements allowing siblings to remain together; this duty applies to placements in kinship care, foster care or residential establishments.[233] Finally, the authority may not return the child to anyone from whose care they have been removed by virtue of any order, authorisation or warrant.

(2) Care by parents

4.25 A looked after child can be cared for by their parents or by someone having parental rights *and* responsibilities in relation to them.[234] The exception to this arises if the child is being provided with accommodation under section 25 of the 1995 Act, at least as long as

228 2014 Act, s 60.
229 2014 Act, s 67.
230 See **5.30** onwards.
231 LAC Regs, regs 8 and 11.
232 Children's Hearings (Scotland) Act 2011, s 44.
233 LAC Regs, reg 3.
234 LAC Regs, regs 8(1).

the conditions giving rise to the local authority duty to accommodate continue to exist.[235] Children who are looked after because they are subject to a compulsory supervision order which involves them living at home form the largest group of looked after children who are cared for by their parents.[236]

(3) Kinship care[237]

4.26 Kinship care provides a means for a looked after child to be cared for by someone the child knows or by a member of their family. The LAC Regulations only apply where children who are looked after by the local authority are provided with kinship care. They do not apply to informal arrangements made by the child's parent(s), though such arrangements may be subject to regulation as private fostering.[238] Two classes of person can be approved as kinship carers in respect of a child: someone who is related to the child by blood, marriage or civil partnership, or someone who is known to the child and with whom the child has a pre-existing relationship.[239]

In order to approve such an individual as a kinship carer the local authority must first, as far as reasonably practicable, obtain specified information about the individual. The information required, includes full personal details, details of those in their household, their religious persuasion, and ability to care for a child of any particular religious persuasion. Further information may include; the racial origin of the individual, cultural or linguistic background, their capacity to care for their own children, their motivation and references.[240] On the basis of this information the local authority then has to carry out an assessment of the suitability of the individual to care for a child and decide whether to approve them as a kinship carer.[241] There is no formal process for approving kinship carers set out in the LAC Regulations, though the guidance suggests that local authorities[242] should consider using a process similar to that involved in approval of foster carers. Approval will be as a kinship carer for a specific child.

235 LAC Regs, regs 8(2).
236 LAC Guidance, pp 50–56.
237 See **3.8** for a discussion of kinship care where a child is not looked after.
238 See **4.37** below.
239 LAC Regs, reg 10(1), (2).
240 LAC Regs, reg 10(3)(b). The information gathered should be recorded in writing; see LAC Regs, reg 10(3)(b).
241 LAC Regs, reg 10(3)(b).
242 Or registered fostering services.

Before making a placement with an approved kinship carer the local authority must be satisfied that:[243]

(a) the placement is in the best interests of the carer;
(b) the placement of the child with the particular kinship carer is in the best interests of the child;
(c) the kinship carer is a suitable person to care for the child, based on the local authority's assessment of them;
(d) the local authority has taken into account all the information available to it which is relevant to performing its duties towards looked after children;
(e) the kinship carer has entered into a kinship carer agreement with the local authority regulating their relationship with the authority; and
(f) the kinship carer has entered into a kinship placement agreement with the local authority, setting out the responsibilities of the carer and the local authority in respect of the particular placement.

Kinship care is also subject to the regulations as to notification, review, short-term placements, termination and records which are considered below. Kinship carers caring for looked after children should be paid an allowance by the local authority.[244] The intention of the Scottish Government is this will be on the same basis as payment of allowances to foster carers, though normally excluding any fee element.[245] The kinship carer agreement should set out the support and training which the carer is to be given.

(4) Foster care

4.27 Local authorities can provide a fostering service[246] themselves and/or enter into an arrangement with a registered fostering service to provide these services.[247]

243 LAC Regs, reg 11(2).
244 LAC Regs, reg 33.
245 See: Scottish Government, *Scottish Recommended Allowance: Information for carers and professionals (2023).*
246 Which will need to be registered, see chapter 11.
247 LAC Guidance, pp 142–145.

(a) Fostering panels[248]

4.28 Fostering panels carry out various functions in relation to arrangements for children to be cared for by foster carers.[249] A panel must consist of at least six members, with a quorum for any meeting of at least three. Local authorities (or registered fostering services)[250] must appoint medical advisers to provide advice to the panel and may appoint a legal adviser, though in many cases legal advice will be provided by the legal services department of the authority. The functions of the fostering panel include consideration of the case of every foster carer and proposed foster carer referred to it by the local authority.[251] It must also make recommendations on:[252]

(a) whether a prospective foster carer is, or existing foster carers continue to be, suitable to be foster carers;

(b) the suitability of a prospective foster carer for a particular child, any child, or certain categories of child; and

(c) the maximum number of children a particular foster carer may have in their home at any one time.

The panel also has other functions noted in passing below.

(b) Approval and review of foster carers[253]

4.29 There is no longer any legal restriction on who can act as a foster carer. Prospective foster carers will initiate the process of formal approval by completing an application form, though it is likely that there will have been previous contact with the local authority. After the application has been made the local authority must carry out an assessment of the applicant, which must normally be completed within 6 months of the application.[254] On completion of the assessment a report will be prepared containing a recommendation. The report should be shared with the applicants and they should be asked to identify any elements of the report with which they disagree.[255] This report will then go to the fostering panel, and the guidance indicates that the applicants

248 LAC Regs, regs 18–20.
249 LAC Regs, reg 20.
250 In general, the regulations discussed in this section apply equally to local authorities and to registered fostering services unless this is made clear in the text.
251 Prospective foster carers must be given the opportunity to meet the panel.
252 LAC Regs, reg 20.
253 LAC Guidance, pp 83–105.
254 LAC Guidance, p 83.
255 LAC Guidance, p 89.

should be invited to meet the panel.[256] The panel will then make a recommendation to the local authority, though the final decision on the prospective carer is made by the local authority.[257] In making the decision that a prospective foster carer is suitable to be approved as a foster carer the local authority must be satisfied that they have been interviewed by or on behalf of the authority and that they are a suitable person with whom to place a child or children.

Approval may be restricted to a particular child or children, or to certain categories of children (for example those over a certain age), or it may be unrestricted, approving the foster carer for all children.[258] It may also limit the number of children which a foster carer may have in their home at any one time.

Once a foster carer is approved, they must enter into a foster carer agreement with the local authority which will cover the support, including financial support, and training to be given by the local authority.[259] The agreement will also cover complaints procedures, procedures for placement, confidentiality obligations, and the foster carer's obligation not to use corporal punishment on any child.[260]

After approval the regulations require that a foster carer's suitability must be reviewed, initially within 12 months of approval and then at least every three years.[261]

Anyone approved as a foster carer can seek a review of the terms of that approval. Review can also be requested of a decision not to approve a person as a foster carer, to vary the terms of an approval after review, or to terminate approval after review. Where review of a decision is sought the case must be referred to a fostering panel which is constituted differently from the panel involved in the original decision. Once the review panel has made a recommendation the local authority must take a decision, which should be taken by someone other than the person who took the decision under review. There is no further review of this decision provided for in the regulations.

256 LAC Guidance, p 90; there is no statutory requirement for this.

257 LAC Regs, reg 22. The person taking the decision is designated as the Agency Decision Maker, LAC Guidance, p 79.

258 LAC Regs, reg 22. The LAC Guidance indicates that: 'It is unlikely that foster carers will be given completely open approval for any child for any duration' (p 80).

259 Scottish Social Services Council, *The Standards for Foster Care* (2017) set out the 'learning foster carers need to undertake for the foster carer role' (para 1.1). See also: LAC Regs, reg 24.

260 LAC Regs, reg 24 and Sch 6.

261 LAC Regs, reg 25(1), (2).

A foster carer who has already been approved by one local authority can be approved by another authority without going through the whole approval process.[262] This is described as derivative approval.

(c) Foster care: arranging a placement[263]

4.30 A child can only be placed in foster care with an approved foster carer and proposed placements will be considered by the fostering panel.[264] Before making an individual placement the local authority must be satisfied that:[265]

(a) the placement is in the best interests of the child;
(b) the placement of the child with the particular foster carer is in the best interests of the child;
(c) it has taken into account all the information available to it which is relevant to performing its duties towards looked after children;
(d) it has given full consideration to the possibility of arranging for the child to be cared for by their parents or by a kinship carer;
(e) the foster carer has entered into a foster carer agreement with the local authority regulating their relationship with the authority;
(f) the foster carer has entered into a foster placement agreement[266] with the local authority, setting out the responsibilities of the carer and the local authority in respect of the particular placement; and
(g) the terms of the foster carer's approval are consistent with the placement.

A placement with a particular foster carer cannot be made where more than three children would be placed with them. This restriction does not apply where the placement involves a group of more than three siblings or where the placement is either an emergency placement or a short-term placement lasting less than four weeks.[267]

Placements with a foster carer are subject to the provisions about notification, review, short-term placements, termination and records considered below. Foster carers will be paid an allowance by the local authority, and this allowance should ensure that:[268]

262 LAC Regs, reg 23; LAC Guidance, pp 91–93.
263 LAC Guidance, pp 105–109.
264 The exception is an emergency placement, discussed below.
265 LAC Regs, reg 27(2).
266 LAC Regs, reg 27(2)(g), Sch 4. This should set out specific requirements for the child and be discussed with the child and their parents as well as the foster carer(s), LAC Guidance, p 107.
267 LAC Regulations, reg 3(6).
268 LAC Guidance, p 113: 'Foster carers are … charged with providing not just basic care but optimum care for looked after children.'

children are offered high quality physical care and provision, and also that they have the opportunities to fill some of the gaps in experience that are often found in looked after children

The level of the allowance will be set by the local authority. Local authorities may also pay a fee to foster carers over and above any allowances.[269]

(d) Residential care

4.31 A looked after child may be placed in residential care. Such placements are partly regulated by the LAC Regulations, but also by separate regulations, which impose specific duties as regards some aspects of residential care.[270] The managers of the residential establishment must ensure that the child:[271]

(a) receives an efficient and adequate education;
(b) is, as far as possible, able to attend such religious services and religious instruction as might be appropriate;
(c) is able to maintain hygiene; and
(d) receives medical treatment is available.

(e) Emergency placements not involving a residential establishment[272]

4.32 It is preferable for placements to be planned, but this is not always possible and the local authority will sometimes have to find accommodation for a child in an emergency.[273]

An emergency placement can be made initially for up to three working days.[274] This can be with an approved foster carer, someone who is approved as a kinship carer in relation to the child, or any person who is known to and who has a pre-existing relationship with the child.[275] Before making the placement, the authority must be satisfied that it is the

269 LAC Guidance, p 114.
270 Residential Establishments – Child Care (Scotland) Regulations 1996, SSI 1996/3256; 2013 Regulations.
271 Residential Establishments – Child Care (Scotland) Regulations 1996, regs 11–15.
272 LAC Guidance, pp 116–125.
273 The LAC Guidance also suggests (at p 116) that, where a family's situation is deteriorating, efforts should be made to identify people who could assist in an emergency.
274 LAC Regs, reg 36(1).
275 LAC Regs, reg 36(1)(c).

most suitable way of meeting the child's needs.[276] The carer must agree to comply with certain duties, including a duty to care for the child as if they were a member of the carer's own family in a safe and appropriate manner.[277] The carer must agree to allow visiting by the local authority or someone authorised by the authority, and to allow the child to be removed if the placement is terminated.[278] The carer must also agree to keep information obtained in their role as a carer confidential, and to allow contact with any person with parental responsibilities.[279] The carer must be provided with information about the child's background and health and emotional development. Where a child is placed with someone who is not an approved carer, the local authority must carry out certain other tasks, including visiting the address at which the child will stay.[280]

A review of the child's case must be held within three working days of the placement to determine if the placement is still in the best interests of the child.[281] After the review the local authority may conclude that the placement is no longer in the interests of the child, in which case alternative arrangements will need to be made, or it might be the case that the emergency has passed. If however the placement continues to be in the best interests of the child the local authority can allow the placement to continue for a further period of up to 12 weeks from the end of the original three-day period, with a further review within six weeks of that date.[282] If the authority does this it must then, unless this has already been done, carry out a full assessment and prepare a child's plan for the child.

An emergency placement cannot be continued beyond this 12-week period. This remains the case unless the placement becomes, effectively, either a kinship care placement or a foster care placement. The appropriate procedures must be followed in either case. Where the original placement is with someone known to the child and who has a pre-existing relationship with them, but who is not an approved carer, the placement can only continue if that person is approved as a kinship carer for the child and the procedure involved in making arrangements for kinship care is carried out.

276 LAC Regs, reg 36(2)(a).
277 LAC Regs, reg 36(3)(a).
278 LAC Regs, reg 36(3)(c).
279 LAC Regs, reg 36(3)(e)(i).
280 LAC Guidance, p 119.
281 LAC Guidance, pp 121–122.
282 LAC Regs, reg 39.

(f) Emergency placements in residential establishments[283]

4.33 Before placing a child in a residential establishment, the local authority must be satisfied that this is the most suitable way of meeting the child's needs, and it must have given full consideration to the possibility of other forms of emergency placement.[284]

The initial emergency placement will be for up to three days.[285] Within that period the placement must be reviewed.[286] The child can continue in the placement if the review concludes that it continues to be in the child's best interests.[287] If the placement continues, the local authority must, if this has not already been done, carry out a full assessment of the child and prepare a child's plan for them. The authority must, supply the information to the managers of the residential establishment which is required for such placements and enter into the required agreements and make any necessary notifications.[288]

(g) Common provisions: notification

4.34 Once an arrangement has been made for a child to be cared for in foster care, kinship care, a residential establishment or by way of an emergency placement which has been extended, the local authority is responsible for making a number of notifications as soon as this is reasonably practicable. These notifications must be in writing and give particulars of the placement.[289]

(a) In cases where the child is placed in the area of another local authority, that other authority must be notified.
(b) The health board for the area where the child is placed must be notified.
(c) The child's parents and any person having any parental rights or responsibilities in relation to the child must be notified. If the child is subject to a compulsory supervision order or interim compulsory supervision order the reporter and the child's relevant person(s) must also be notified. These notification requirements are subject to three exceptions:

283 LAC Regs, regs 37 and 41; LAC Guidance, pp 116–125.
284 LAC Regs, reg 37(2).
285 LAC Regs, reg 37(1).
286 LAC Regs, reg 38(2).
287 LAC Regs, reg 38(2).
288 LAC Regs, reg 38(4).
289 LAC Regs, regs 13, 29, 34, 40 and 41(4).

(i) where the person to be notified has already received a written copy of the child's plan, though this exception does not apply to notifications of extended emergency placements not involving a residential establishment;
(ii) no notice is to be given where the authority considers, in light of its overall duties to looked after children, that it would not be in the best interests of the child for notification to be made; and
(iii) where the child is subject to a permanence order, an exclusion order, a compulsory supervision order or a warrant requiring attendance at a children's hearing which specifies that the whereabouts of the child should not be disclosed to a particular person.

(h) Common provisions: visits and reviews[290]

4.35 Local authorities have a duty to carry out visits to children for whom *they* have arranged care,[291] subject to the following exceptions:
(a) looked after children cared for by their parents or someone with parental responsibilities and rights;
(b) where children have been placed in foster care on behalf of the local authority by a registered fostering service; and
(c) emergency placements.

The first visit should take place within one week of the placement being made and is a visit to the child and their carer.[292] Further visits must take place at least every three months, and additional visits are to be made where requested by the child or carer. Further visits may take place at any other times where the authority considers that a visit is necessary and appropriate to safeguard and promote the welfare of the child. A visit may also be appropriate on any occasion where the local authority considers it necessary to give support and assistance to a foster carer or kinship carer for the purpose of safeguarding and promoting the welfare of the child.[293] Written reports of these visits must be produced and must be considered at any review.[294]

290 LAC Regs, regs 44–46.
291 These duties do not extend to cases where a placement has been made by a children's hearing, see LAC Guidance, pp 137–139.
292 LAC Regs, reg 46(2)(a).
293 LAC Regs, reg 46(3).
294 LAC Regs, reg 46(4).

Regular reviews of all looked after children must take place.[295] The focus of these reviews[296] is the same regardless of the nature of the child's placement, though there are differences in the frequency of reviews. As part of the review process the views of the child, their carers and anyone with parental responsibilities or rights in relation to the child need to be sought and taken account of.[297] The child's needs, both in the short and in the long term, need to be assessed as does how these are being met. The assessment will also have to consider whether the child's welfare is being safeguarded and promoted, the child's development, whether current accommodation is suitable for the child and, finally, the child's educational needs and whether these are being met.[298] Reports of placement visits must also be considered as part of the review. Reviews should be chaired by someone without direct day-to-day responsibility for the case.[299]

If a child is being cared for by their parent(s) or by someone who has parental rights and responsibilities, the frequency of review is to be agreed with the carer. If agreement cannot be reached then an initial review must take place within six weeks of the placement being made, with further reviews every 12 months, though the guidance indicates that in practice the agreed reviews should be more frequent than this, at least in the initial stages.[300]

Where a placement is with a foster or kinship carer or in a residential establishment the normal position is that the first review will take place within six weeks of the start of the placement. A further review should take place within three months of the first review, and further reviews every six months.[301] Different time limits apply where the placement is not continuous, but involves a number of short placements, typically cases involving respite care. The first review in such cases must take place within three months of the start of the placement, with subsequent reviews every six months.[302] In cases where an emergency placement has been extended the first review under the general provisions for review must take place within three months of the start of the placement, with subsequent reviews every six months.

295 LAC Regs, reg 34 and 45.
296 LAC Guidance, pp 133–134.
297 LAC Regs, reg 44(3)(a) and 45(5)(a).
298 LAC Regs, reg 44(3)(c) and 45(5)(c).
299 LAC Guidance, p 134.
300 LAC Regs, reg 44(6).
301 LAC Regs, reg 45(2).
302 LAC Regs, reg 45(3)(a) & (b).

The time limits set out for reviews are maximal, in practice reviews may be, and may need to be, to be more frequent than this.[303] After a child has been placed away from home by the local authority and has not returned home after six months then any review after this 'should consider whether a plan for permanence away from birth parents is required'.[304]

In addition to these scheduled reviews, further reviews must be carried out before a decision by the local authority to refer the case of a child to the Principal Reporter. This review must be carried out, before the local authority applies for a permanence order in respect of the child and, if practicable in the circumstances, when a children's hearing is convened to consider the case of a looked after child.[305]

(5) Records

4.36 Records must be compiled for approved kinship carers and foster carers with whom a child has been placed as well as for perspective kinship and foster carers.[306] Case records should be retained until the death of the carer or, if later, for a period of 25 years.[307] In the case of kinship carers this will date from the date when the placement was terminated[308] and for foster carers or prospective foster carers the date on which their approval was terminated.[309] The regulations make no provision as to how long the records of prospective kinship carers should be retained, though the guidance suggests that they are treated in the same way as prospective foster carers.[310]

PRIVATE FOSTERING[311]

4.37 It is possible for fostering to be arranged privately and for situations which are legally defined as private fostering to arise without any necessary intention on the part of those involved.

303 LAC Guidance, p 122.
304 LAC Guidance, p 135, see also pp 135–137.
305 LAC Guidance, pp 135–137.
306 LAC Regs, regs 15 and 31; LAC Guidance, pp 71–72 and 110–112. At p 110 the Guidance notes that, although there is no mention of foster carers who have not had a child placed with them, it is good practice to treat them in the same way as carers who have had a child placed with them.
307 LAC Regs, reg 16.
308 LAC Regs, reg 16.
309 LAC Regs, reg 32.
310 LAC Guidance, p 72.
311 See Scottish Government, *Be Safe, Be Sure: Private Fostering in Scotland, Practice Guidance for Local Authority Children's Services* (2013).

Private fostering is regulated by the Foster Children (Scotland) Act 1984 and by the Foster Children (Private Fostering) (Scotland) Regulations 1985.[312] These will apply in general to any situation where a child under the age of 16 is placed by their parents for a period which is intended to or does exceed 27 days 'with someone who is neither a guardian appointed to the child (e.g., in a parent's will) or who is not a relative of the child'.[313] In this context, relative means a grandparent, brother, sister, uncle or aunt and covers relatives both of the full and of the half blood.[314]

Where it is intended to place a child in private fostering, at least two weeks' notice must be given to the local authority,[315] unless in an emergency, where notification must be made with one week of the placement.[316] On receipt of the notification the local authority must carry out certain investigations:

(a) obtaining a statement as to the child's health and that of the foster carer;[317]

(b) to find out as far as possible, bearing in mind the age and understanding of the child, their wishes and feelings in relation to the proposed placement;[318]

(c) to interview the proposed foster parents and satisfy itself as to the suitability of the foster home;[319] and

(d) to ensure that the child and their parent, or any guardian or relative from whom they have received notice, are visited on their behalf.[320]

The purpose of these investigations is to allow the authority to satisfy itself that the placement will not be detrimental to the child's welfare and to decide whether the placement is appropriate to the child's needs.[321]

The decision as to whether the placement is appropriate must be communicated to those involved. The authority may seek to have

312 SI 1985/1798.

313 Foster Children (Scotland) Act 1984, s 1. See also: Scottish Government, *Be Safe, Be Sure* (2013), p 5. There are some exceptions to this covering, for example, children at boarding school, children in hospital, children placed for adoption, placements by a children's hearing and compulsory detention under the Mental Health (Care and Treatment) (Scotland) Act 2003.

314 Foster Children (Scotland) Act 1984, s 21.

315 Foster Children (Private Fostering) (Scotland) Regulations 1995 (the 1995 Regulations) SSI 1985/1798, reg 3(1).

316 Foster Children (Scotland) Act 1984, s 5(2).

317 1995 Regulations, reg 4(2)(b).

318 1995 Regulations, reg 4(2)(c).

319 1995 Regulations, reg 5(b).

320 1995 Regulations, reg 4(2)(a).

321 1995 Regulations, reg 4(2)(d).

changes made, or impose conditions on the foster carer, to make the placement more appropriate or better able to promote the welfare of the child.[322] If necessary, the authority can prohibit the placement if it considers that it would be detrimental to the child.

Certain types of persons cannot act as foster parents.[323] These include: people convicted of Schedule 1 offences;[324] anyone who has previously had a foster child removed from their care; anyone who has had a child removed from their care under a compulsory supervision order; and anyone whose parental responsibilities and rights have been transferred to the local authority by a parental responsibilities order.

Once a placement has been made the authority must visit the child within seven days, then every three months for the first year and subsequently every six months.[325] Other visits may be made as the authority thinks necessary. If, as a result of these visits, the authority considers that the placement is no longer in the child's interests it must notify the foster parents of this.[326]

Where a child is in imminent danger of being kept by any person unfit to care for the child, the local authority may apply to the court for an order removing the child to a place of safety.[327] Such an order may be obtained if the child is in danger of being in the care of a person who falls into one of the categories of person prohibited from being a foster parent, or being in any premises or environment likely to be detrimental to the child.[328]

If a foster carer refuses to allow a visit either to the child or to inspect the premises, this is to be regarded as establishing that there is reasonable cause to suspect that the child is being so treated or neglected that they are suffering, or are likely to suffer, significant harm for the purpose of an application for a child assessment order. The place of safety order will apply until other arrangements can be made for the child, and any child removed from private fostering is to be treated as requiring accommodation under section 25 of the 1995 Act.[329]

322 1995 Regulations, reg 6.
323 Foster Children (Scotland) Act 1984, s 7.
324 I.e., Schedule 1 to the Children and Young Persons Act 1933 and Schedule 1 to the Criminal Procedure (Scotland) Act 1995. See **chapter 5, Box 5.3** and **Appendix**.
325 1995 Regulations, reg 7(1)(a)(i) and (ii).
326 1995 Regulations, reg 7(2).
327 Foster Children (Scotland) Act 1984, s 1. See also: Scottish Government, *Be Safe, Be Sure* (2013), p 10.
328 *Private Fostering in Scotland, Practice Guidance for Local Authority Children's Services* (2013), p 10.
329 1995 Act, s 25.

The number of private fostering arrangements in Scotland is unknown. The most recent Care Inspectorate commentary notes that, in 2022, there were 13 notifications of private fostering.[330]

SECURE ACCOMMODATION

(1) Introduction

4.38 Children may be placed in secure accommodation provided by a local authority in a variety of ways. The placement may be of a child subject to a compulsory supervision order not including a secure accommodation authorisation;[331] it may be a condition of an order made by a hearing or a court;[332] a child being looked after by the local authority may be placed in secure accommodation; or a child detained under an order made by a criminal court may be placed in secure accommodation.

Regardless of the method of placement the managers of the secure accommodation unit must ensure that the welfare of the child is promoted and safeguarded.[333] The period for which a child is kept in secure accommodation must not, subject to two exceptions,[334] exceed a total of 72 hours in any 28-day period unless the secure placement has been authorised by a court or a hearing.[335] The European Convention on Human Rights indicates that a child is to be deprived of their liberty only in two cases.[336] The first of these is for the purpose of bringing them before the competent legal authority, the second is for the purposes of educational supervision. Secure accommodation as described here is likely to be covered by one or other of these, in relation to the latter it has been said that:[337]

> The Court considers that, in the context of the detention of minors, the words 'educational supervision' must not be equated rigidly with notions of classroom teaching. In particular, in the present context

330 Care Inspectorate, *Fostering and Adoption 2022–23: A Statistical Bulletin* (August 2023) pp 13–14.

331 Such authorisations are considered at **5.31**.

332 These are an interim compulsory supervision order made under sections 92, 93, 95, 96, 98–100, 109, 115 or 119 of the Children's Hearings (Scotland) Act 2011 or a medical examination order under ss 92 or 120.

333 Secure Accommodation (Scotland) Regulations 2013 (SSI 2013/205) ('2013 regulations'), reg 4.

334 The first of these is for children placed under the Children Act 1989, the second is referred to below.

335 2013 Regulations, reg 5.

336 ECHR, Article 5(1)(d).

337 *Koniarska v United Kingdom* (2000) 30 EHRR CD 139.

of a young person in local authority care, educational supervision must embrace many aspects of the exercise, by the local authority, of parental rights for the benefit and protection of the person concerned.[338]

(2) Rules applying to all placements [339]

4.39 Certain rules apply to all placements in secure accommodation which are made by the local authority. The chief social work officer of the local authority and the person in charge of the secure accommodation must be satisfied that either:

(a) the child has previously absconded and is likely to abscond unless kept in secure accommodation and if the child absconds their mental, physical or moral welfare will be at risk; **or**

(b) the child is likely to engage in self-harming behaviour; or

(c) the child is likely to cause injury another person.

They must also be satisfied that the placement is in the best interests of the child and the chief social work officer for the authority must be satisfied that the placement is appropriate to the needs of the child.[340]

A record must be kept with details of a child's placement in secure accommodation.[341]

(3) Children subject to compulsory supervision orders[342]

4.40 Children who are subject to a compulsory supervision order which does not contain a secure accommodation authorisation may still be placed in such accommodation.[343] If this is done each relevant person and the reporter must be told about it immediately, including, in writing, the chief social work officer.[344] Within 24 hours, regardless of whether the child is still in secure accommodation, the chief social worker must require a review of the compulsory supervision order[345] or inform the

338 *Koniarska v United Kingdom* (2000) 30 EHRR CD 139, para 143.

339 2013 Regulations, regs 7(3)(a)–(c), 8(3)(a)–(c), 9(4)(a)–(c).

340 2013 regulations, regs 7(2), (3), 8(2), (3) and 9(2), (3).

341 2013 regulations, reg 15.

342 2013 regulations, reg 7.

343 2013 regulations, reg 7(1).

344 2013 regulations, reg 7(4).

345 Children's Hearings (Scotland) Act 2011, s 131. See also the 2013 regulations, reg 7(4)(b)(i).

reporter of the need to initiate a review.[346] In addition, the reporter must be informed of the details of the placement (and whether it continues), the reasons why it was considered that the conditions for placement were met (and whether these are still met) and the views of the chief social work officer and head of the secure accommodation unit as to the need for detention in secure accommodation. [347]A review hearing to consider the supervision requirement must be held within 72 hours of the original placement in secure accommodation.[348]

(4) Children being looked after[349]

4.41 Children who are being looked after in local authority accommodation, or because a permanence order has been made in respect of them, may be placed in secure accommodation. This can only happen if, in addition to the general requirements set out in (a)–(c) of **4.39** above, the chief social work officer is satisfied that the placement is appropriate to the child's needs.[350] Once the child has been placed in secure accommodation the child's parents, each relevant person, anyone else who appears to have a significant involvement in the upbringing of the child, and the reporter must be informed immediately.[351] The case must be referred to the reporter within 24 hours from the time of the placement, and the reporter must be supplied with a range of information including details of the placement and the reasons why the chief social work officer believes that the child may be in need of compulsory measures of supervision.[352]

The reporter then has to decide what to do, and the decision must be taken within 72 hours of placement in secure accommodation.[353] There are two possible decisions. It might be decided that no hearing is necessary, in which case the child would have to be released from secure accommodation.[354] As a complement to this decision the reporter can refer the child's case to the local authority for advice, guidance and assistance provided by virtue of the local authority's duties to children and families.[355] The second option is to refer the case of the child to

346 Children's Hearings (Scotland) Act 2011, s 136.
347 2013 regulations, reg 7(4)(c)(iii).
348 2013 regulations, reg 7(5).
349 2013 regulations, reg 9.
350 2013 regulations, reg 9(3)(b).
351 2013 regulations, reg 9(5)(a).
352 2013 regulations, reg 9.
353 2013 regulations, reg 10(2).
354 2013 regulations, reg 10(4).
355 2013 regulations, reg 10(3)(b).

a hearing, which is possible only if the reporter thinks the child is in need of compulsory measures of supervision.[356] The hearing must take place within 72 hours, though an extra 24 hours is allowed if it is not reasonably practicable for the hearing to take place within 72 hours.[357]

(5) Children subject to an order made by a hearing or a court[358]

4.42 If such a child is placed in secure accommodation each relevant person and the reporter must immediately be informed.[359] In addition, the Principal Reporter must be informed by the chief social work officer.[360] Procedure when the child is subject to an interim compulsory supervision order depends on who made the order. Where the order was made by a children's hearing there must, generally, be a hearing within 72 hours of the child being placed in secure accommodation. The exception to this is where such a hearing would not be able to make a further interim compulsory supervision order, in which case an application must be made to the court for variation of the order. In cases where the order was made by a sheriff, application must be made to the sheriff within 72 hours of the start of the placement. For children subject to a medical examination order made by a children's hearing, a hearing must be arranged within the 72-hour period.[361]

(6) Children detained by order made by a criminal court[362]

4.43 The criminal courts (with the exception of the district court) may remand children to residential accommodation provided by the local authority.[363] For example, a child found guilty in the sheriff summary court may be detained in residential accommodation for up to 12 months.[364] Subject to the exception considered below, such children may be placed in secure accommodation if the general requirements set out in **4.39** above apply; in addition, the child, the relevant person and

356 2013 regulations, reg 10(5).
357 2013 regulations, reg 10(6).
358 2013 regulations, reg 8.
359 2013 regulations, 8(5)(a)
360 2013 regulations, reg 8(5)(b).
361 2013 regulations, reg 8(6).
362 2013 regulations, regs 11–14.
363 2013 regulations, reg 11.
364 Criminal Procedure (Scotland) Act 1995, s 44.

the head of the secure accommodation unit must be consulted.[365] Once a child has been placed in secure accommodation they must not be kept there for longer than the person in charge and the chief social work officer consider necessary.[366] In addition, the cases of such children must be reviewed within seven days of the placement (even if the child is no longer in secure accommodation) and then at least every three months or more often if this is necessary in light of the progress made by the child.[367] As part of this review the views of a Secure Placement Review Panel, including one person independent of the local authority, must be obtained.[368] The secure placement is to continue after review only if the person in charge and the chief social work officer consider that it is in the best interests of the child.[369] The main exception to these requirements is children sentenced for murder or after conviction on indictment. The conditions for the detention of such children are specified by the Scottish Ministers.[370]

AFTER-CARE

(1) Powers and duties

4.44 Local authorities have certain powers and duties to provide assistance to young people who have been looked after by them.[371] In order to qualify, the young person must have been looked after on or after their sixteenth birthday and must no longer be looked after.[372] The duty is to provide guidance and assistance (including financial assistance) to such people aged from 16 to 18 unless the local authority is satisfied that the guidance or assistance is not needed for the welfare of the person involved.[373]

The powers are:

(a) to provide guidance and assistance (including financial assistance) if requested to do so by someone aged between 19 and 26;[374]

(b) to provide financial support to people aged 16–25 to help with education, training or employment costs or with accommodation/

365 2013 regulations, reg 11(3).
366 2013 regulations, reg 11(5).
367 2013 regulations, reg 13.
368 2013 regulations, reg 13(4).
369 2013 regulations, reg 13(2).
370 Criminal Procedure (Scotland) Act 1995, ss 205 and 209.
371 The corporate parenting duties will also be relevant here, see **4.23** above.
372 1995 Act, s 29(1).
373 1995 Act, s 29(1).
374 1995 Act, s 29(2).

maintenance associated with the education/training/ employment.[375]

Where the duty arises, or where a request is made under (a) above, the local authority must carry out an assessment of the person's need (in the form of a pathway assessment, see below). In the case of those who are aged over 18 but below 26[376] and have made a request for assistance, there are three possible outcomes:

(a) no support is provided;
(b) if the person has 'eligible needs'[377] then the local authority must provide advice, guidance and assistance if these needs cannot otherwise be met;[378]
(c) the local authority may at its discretion provide appropriate advice, guidance and assistance, as it considers appropriate having regard to the person's welfare.[379]

Regulations impose more specific duties on local authorities.[380]

(2) To whom are duties owed?

4.45 The regulations identify four categories of young people:[381]

(a) Currently looked after = those still being looked after who are aged 16 or 17.
(b) Compulsorily supported person = those aged 16–18 who were being looked after on their sixteenth birthday or later and those aged 19–25 who are being provided with assistance because they have an eligible need.
(c) Prospective supported persons = those aged 19 and less than 26 who were being looked after on their sixteenth birthday or later and who have applied to the local authority to provide them with services under the power the local authority has to provide assistance to this group.
(d) Discretionarily supported person = those aged 19 and below 26 who were being looked after on their sixteenth birthday or later and who are receiving discretionary services from the local

375 1995 Act, s 30.
376 The authority has discretion to support after the person reaches the age of 26. 1995 Act, s 29(5B).
377 Eligible needs are defined by Aftercare (Eligible Needs) (Scotland) Order 2015 (SSI 2015/156), art 2.
378 1995 Act, s 29(5A)(a).
379 1995 Act, s 29(5A)(b).
380 Support and Assistance of Young People Leaving Care (Scotland) Regulations 2003 (the 2003 Regulations) (SSI 2003/608).
381 2003 Regulations, reg 2(1).

authority or those who are continuing to receive support after reaching age 26.

(3) Pathway assessments

4.46 The pathway assessment must be carried out in respect of the first three groups set out above to assess their need for provision of services.[382] The assessment must include the views of the young person involved (referred to as their pathway views) and should include the following matters:[383]

(a) The young person's emotional state, day-to-day activities, personal safety, influences on the young person and the young person's personal identity.

(b) The young person's family relationships, their children, other caring responsibilities, life story, friends, and other significant people in their life.

(c) The young person's general health (including any mental health needs), contact with health services, medical conditions and disabilities, activities that might affect the young person's health, and emotional and mental well-being.

(d) The young person's future plans for study, training or work, schooling (including support needs), skills and experience, qualifications and certificates, and training and work.

(e) The young person's accommodation arrangements, practical living skills, accommodation options for the future, and support required for living.

(f) The young person's sources of income, outgoings, savings and debts, requirement for financial support, and budgeting skills.

(g) The young person's knowledge of their rights and legal entitlements, involvements in legal proceedings, including criminal proceedings as a victim, witness, or alleged perpetrator.

(4) Pathway plan[384]

4.47 Following the assessment a pathway plan must be completed for compulsorily and discretionarily supported persons and may be produced for currently looked after persons. The plan will set out how

382 2003 Regulations, regs 7–9.
383 2003 Regulations, Sch 2.
384 2003 Regulations, regs 10–12.

the local authority plans to meet the person's identified need and the timescale and who will be responsible for doing this.[385]

In the preparation of the plan the authority has to appoint a pathway co-ordinator who will be involved in the preparation of the assessment and the plan. The co-ordinator should be involved in any review of the plan and will also have the responsibility of providing support to the young person and co-ordinating provision of services.[386] The young person may also appoint someone, the young person's supporter, to assist them through this process.[387]

The identity of the pathway co-ordinator, the timetable for the assessment, and the list of who are to be consulted, all have to be agreed with the young person.[388] All stages of the assessment, obtaining of views and preparation of the plan, need to be documented in writing.[389] The young person has the right to attend at and participate in meetings where the assessment is being considered.[390] Once the plan is complete, the young person has a right of appeal to a nominated local authority officer against decision on the provision or nature of services and support.[391]

The plan must be reviewed at least every six months and a review can be triggered at any time by the young person, the review co-ordinator, or the local authority.[392]

One thing which can be provided under a plan is regular financial assistance.[393] This is relevant because of limited entitlement to social security benefits for 16- and 17-year-olds. The regulations provide that such financial assistance can be provided to 16- and 17-year-olds, at a level no less than the social security payments they would previously have been entitled to, subject to two conditions:

(a) They must have been looked after *and* accommodated by the local authority for at least 13 weeks in total after reaching the age of 14.[394] In calculating this period, short periods of respite care are to be discounted.

(b) They must not be living at home.[395]

385 2003 Regulations, regs 10(4).
386 2003 Regulations, reg 4(5).
387 2003 Regulations, reg 5.
388 2003 Regulations, reg 7.
389 2003 Regulations, regs 8, 3.
390 2003 Regulations, regs 8, 3.
391 2003 Regulations, regs 16, 17.
392 2003 Regulations, reg 12.
393 2003 Regulations, reg 13.
394 2003 Regulations, reg 13(1).
395 2003 Regulations, reg 13(2).

These specific provisions cover regular financial payments, one-off payments can also, of course, be made to any of the young people covered by the regulations.

The local authority must also, if necessary, assist the young person to obtain suitable accommodation or help to stay in such accommodation.[396]

Obligations in relation to plans and assessment are summarised in the table below:

Table 4.1

Category of young person	Pathway assessment[397]	Pathway plan[398]	Pathway co-ordinator[399]
Currently supported	Yes	Possibly	Possibly
Compulsorily supported	Yes	Yes	Yes
Prospective supported	Yes	N/A no decision on support yet	No
Discretionarily supported	N/A decision to support made	Yes	Yes

(5) Continuing care[400]

4.48 Sixteen and 17-year-olds who cease to be looked after have to be provided with continuing care i.e., the same accommodation and assistance as was being provided before they stopped being looked after. This obligation continues until the child's twenty-first birthday.[401] Before the child stops being looked after, the local authority must complete a welfare assessment of the young person and must consider whether continued provision of continuing care would significantly adversely affect the young person.[402] A further assessment must be undertaken at least every 12 months.[403]

396 2003 Regulations, reg 14.
397 2003 Regulations, regs 7, 8 and 9.
398 2003 Regulations, regs 10, 11 and 12.
399 2003 Regulations, reg 4.
400 1995 Act, s 26A; Continuing Care (Scotland) Order 2015 (SSI 2015/158).
401 Continuing Care (Scotland) Amendment Order 2019 (SSI 2019/91), art 2(2).
402 Continuing Care (Scotland) Order 2015, arts 4 and 7.
403 Continuing Care (Scotland) Order 2015, art 5.

CHALLENGING DECISIONS

4.49 Children or their families may be unhappy about decisions made about the provision of services or other decisions taken by the local authority in exercising its powers and duties. Decisions taken can be challenged using the complaints procedure.[404]

It may also be possible to challenge decisions by seeking judicial review of the decision.[405] The challenge will generally be on the grounds that the local authority has exercised the considerable discretion conferred on it in an unreasonable way, though the very extent of the discretion may make challenges difficult. Grounds for a challenge might include a failure to take proper account of procedures laid out in the guidance[406] or a failure to follow a decision or recommendation resulting from pursuing the complaints procedure,[407] unless proper consideration has been given before doing this.[408] In light of the comments made above about the relevance of resources to decisions involving service provision, it will be difficult, but not impossible, to challenge a refusal to provide services on resource grounds.

404 See **1.60**.
405 See **1.59**.
406 *R v North Yorkshire County Council, ex parte Hargreaves* (1997) 5 WLUK 347; *R v London Borough of Islington, ex parte Rixon* (1997) 1 CCLR 119.
407 *R v Avon County Council, ex parte M* [1994] 2 FCR 259.
408 *Re T (Accommodation by Local Authority)* [1995] 1 FLR 159.

Chapter 5

Children in need of supervision or emergency protection

INTRODUCTION

5.1 Child care and child protection are the two areas of social work practice with the highest public profile and subject to the most intense scrutiny. This scrutiny extends to the practitioners in the field. Changing public attitudes and views about what amounts to good enough parenting, the rights and responsibilities of parents, the rights of children, the justification for state intervention into family life, and the need to protect children have each contributed to the ongoing debate about the most appropriate role for social workers. An intricate dynamic is in operation between social work departments and other childcare professionals. The children's hearings system and the courts further complicate an understanding of the duties and responsibilities of social workers.

There are two broad sets of provisions concerned with child protection in Scotland. The first involves a non-statutory system of child protection committees and a child protection register. The second is a statutory system which involves referrals to the children's hearings system. In addition, there is a large amount of guidance on practice.[1]

The child protection register

5.2 The child protection register is a formal list of names of children about whom there are concerns. Concerns may be about either past abuse or the possibility or risk of future abuse causing or likely to cause significant harm,[2] and where a child protection plan has been

1 See www.gov.scot/Topics/People/Young-People/protecting and https://beta.gov.scot/policies/child-protection (accessed April 2026).

2 See Box 5.1.

agreed. Before a child is placed on the register, their safety must be considered to require an inter-agency child protection plan.[3]

In this context, harm involves ill-treatment of the child or impairment of their health and development, and the significance of the harm is to be determined by the responsible professional, taking into account the criteria contained in the guidance.[4]

The guidance sets out a process for dealing with concerns about children summarised in Figure 5.1 below.[5] This process envisages, in appropriate cases, that decision making and investigation will be a joint activity potentially involving a variety of agencies. Decisions, for example to place a child on the child protection register or to refer the case to the children's reporter, would normally be taken at a multi-agency child protection case conference. Where there is a child protection plan in place for the child, this will be implemented and managed by a core group.

3 Scottish Government, *National Guidance for Child Protection in Scotland* (2021 – updated 2023), paras 1.87–1.90.

4 *National Guidance for Child Protection in Scotland*, paras 1.44–1.73.

5 *National Guidance for Child Protection in Scotland*, p 135.

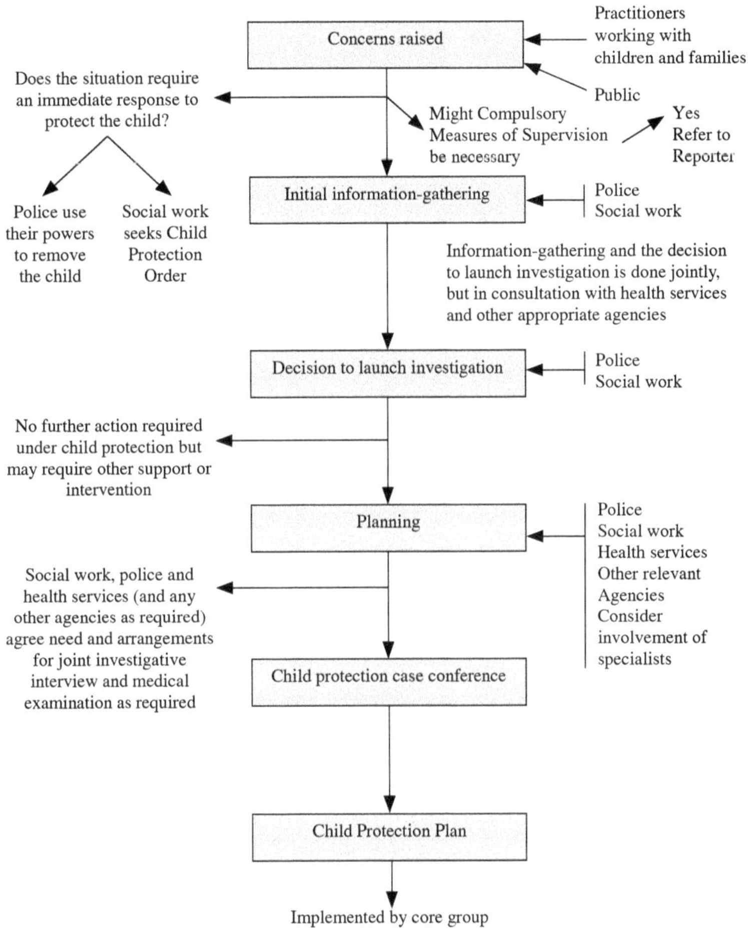

Figure 5.1 Process of responding to child protection concerns

Guidance on the composition and functions of child protection committees is set out in the *National Guidance for Child Protection in Scotland*.[6] These committees incorporate representatives of a variety of agencies and their core membership should include representatives from the following:

(i) local authority social work services;

6 *National Guidance for Child Protection in Scotland*, paras 2.14–2.45.

(ii) local authority education services:
(iii) community services;
(iv) housing services;
(v) health services and services in relation to drugs and alcohol;
(vi) police and procurator fiscal;
(vii) Scottish Children's Reporter Administration;
(viii) the armed services where there is a significant local presence;
(ix) the independent education service where this is a significant local presence; and
(x) the voluntary sector.

Each committee will have a chair, who should be experienced in inter-agency work and child protection and a lead officer responsible for implementing the core functions of the committee. A committee has a variety of functions including:[7]

(a) providing information to the public, including raising awareness of child protection issues;
(b) development and review of inter-agency child protection policies;
(c) encouraging agencies to have up-to-date policies and procedures,
(d) having mechanisms for assuring the quality of practice and procedures;
(e) promoting good practice; and
(f) strategic planning for child protection work.

CHILDREN'S HEARINGS AND CHILD PROTECTION

(1) Introduction

5.3 The Social Work (Scotland) Act 1968 (the 1968 Act), following on from the report of the Kilbrandon Committee, introduced a new way of dealing with what were described as 'children in need of compulsory measures of care'.[8] This category covered all of the groups of children who would previously have come into contact with the court system and whose behaviour the Kilbrandon Committee regarded as being symptomatic of some social or family dysfunction. The Committee concluded that:[9]

7 Scottish Government, Protecting Children and Young People, Child Protection Committee and Chief Officer Responsibilities (2019) Section 3.
8 Social Work (Scotland) Act 1968, Part III.
9 *Report on Children and Young Persons, Scotland* (The Kilbrandon Report) Cmnd 2306 (1964), para 252.

> In terms of the treatment measures to be applied, the children appearing before the courts, whatever the precise circumstances in which they do so, show a basic similarity of underlying situation. The distinguishing factor is their common need for special measures of education and training, the normal upbringing process for whatever reason having failed or fallen short.

These children are now referred to the children's reporter who, after an initial investigation, decides whether the case should go on to a children's hearing. The courts are only involved in cases where there is a dispute about the grounds for taking action in respect of a child, (known as the 'grounds for referral') and as the forum for dealing with appeals against decisions of the children's hearing. Referrals to the children's reporter can be made by local authority workers, the police and the courts. In addition, in law, any person can refer a case to the children's reporter if that person considers that a child is in need of protection, guidance, treatment or control and it might be necessary for a compulsory supervision order to be made. This could mean for example, a concerned neighbour could report suspicions of child abuse.[10] In practice, however, the overwhelming majority of referrals (78.5% in 2023/24) come from the police, followed by social work departments, educational sources, courts and health professionals.[11]

Despite these changes, the children's hearing system and the Kilbrandon philosophy have continued to take centre stage in child care law.[12]

Box 5.1

What is harm and significant harm in a child protection context? (*National Guidance for Child Protection in Scotland*)

40. Child protection is closely linked to the risk of 'significant harm'. 'Significant harm' is a complex matter and subject to professional judgment based on a multi-agency assessment of the circumstances of the child and their family. Where there are concerns about harm, abuse or neglect, these must be shared with the relevant agencies so that they can decide together whether the harm is, or is likely to be, significant.

10 See Children's Hearing Scotland Act 2011, ss 60–64 for the categories of bodies or persons who can make a referral to the children's reporter.

11 Scottish Children's Reporter Administration, Statistical Analysis 2023/24, p 14.

12 For example, the Policy Memorandum for the Children's Hearings (Scotland) Bill (which became the 2011 Act) stated that: 'It is right that the Children's Hearings system evolves to adapt to these changes without losing the vision and philosophy of Kilbrandon', (para 14).

Through early and effective intervention and the sharing of wellbeing concerns it is hoped that crisis can be avoided in many cases.

41. Significant harm can result from a specific incident, a series of incidents or an accumulation of concerns over a period of time. It is essential when considering the presence or likelihood of significant harm that the impact (or potential impact) on the child takes priority and not simply the suspected or reported abusive behaviour. It should be remembered that the threshold for referral to the children's reporter is not the significant harm threshold; the test is whether the child is in need of protection, guidance, treatment or control, and if a compulsory supervision order might be necessary. The following sections illustrate considerations that need to be taken into account when exercising that professional judgment.

42. In order to understand the concept of significant harm, it is helpful to look first at the relevant definitions.

- 'Harm' means the ill treatment or the impairment of the health or development of the child, including, for example, impairment suffered as a result of seeing or hearing the ill treatment of another. In this context, 'development' can mean physical, intellectual, emotional, social or behavioural development and 'health' can mean physical or mental health.[13]
- Whether the harm suffered, or likely to be suffered, by a child or young person is 'significant', is a matter of professional judgment taking into account all the facts and information available.[14]43. There are no absolute criteria for judging what constitutes significant harm. In assessing the severity of ill treatment or the risk of future ill treatment, it may be important to take account of: the degree and extent of physical harm; the duration and frequency of abuse and neglect; the extent of premeditation; and the presence or degree of threat, coercion, sadism and bizarre or unusual elements. Sometimes, a single traumatic event may constitute significant harm, for example, a violent assault, suffocation or poisoning. More often, significant harm results from

13 *National Guidance for Child Protection in Scotland*, para 1.56.
14 *National Guidance for Child Protection in Scotland*, para 1.58.

an accumulation of significant events, both acute and long-standing, that interrupt, change or damage the child's physical and psychological development.[15]

44. To understand and identify significant harm, it is necessary to consider:[16]
    - the nature of harm, either through an act of commission or omission;
    - the impact on the child's health and development, taking into account their age and stage of development;
    - the child's development within the context of their family and wider environment;
    - the context in which a harmful incident or behaviour occurred;
    - any particular needs, such as a medical condition, communication impairment or disability, that may affect the child's development, make them more vulnerable to harm or influence the level and type of care provided by the family;
    - the capacity of parents or carers to meet adequately the child's needs; and
    - the wider and environmental family context.

45. The reactions, perceptions, wishes and feelings of the child must also be considered, with account taken of their age and level of understanding. This will depend on effective communication, including with those children and young people who find communication difficult because of their age, impairment or particular psychological or social situation. It is important to observe what children do as well as what they say, and to bear in mind that children may experience a strong desire to be loyal to their parents/carers (who may also hold some power over the child). Steps should be taken to ensure that any accounts of adverse experiences given by children are accurate and complete, and that they are recorded fully.[17]

15 *National Guidance for Child Protection in Scotland*, para 1.63.
16 *National Guidance for Child Protection in Scotland*, para 1.62.
17 *National Guidance for Child Protection in Scotland*, para 1.64.

ADMINISTRATION OF THE CHILDREN'S HEARINGS SYSTEM

5.4 The Children's Hearings (Scotland) Act 2011 (the 2011 Act) made some major changes to children's hearings, one of which was to change the structures through which the system is managed,[18] creating a new organisation, Children's Hearings Scotland. At the head of this is the National Convenor who is responsible for appointing individuals to a national Children's Panel (replacing the previously existing regional panels). From this panel, three members are appointed to constitute a children's hearing to deal with a referral of a child. Members selected for a hearing should, as far as practicable, live or work in the local authority area where the hearing will take place and, as far as practicable, should include both male and female members of the Panel.[19]

Although Children's Hearings Scotland organises the hearings and deals with their administration, children are referred to the hearings by the local reporters, who form part of the Scottish Children's Reporter Administration (SCRA), headed by the Principal Reporter.

PRINCIPLES GOVERNING DECISIONS BY A COURT OR HEARING

5.5 When a court, pre-hearing panel or children's hearing, is coming to a decision under the 2011 Act, it must pay attention to three overarching principles:

(a) the paramount consideration is the need to safeguard and promote the welfare of the child throughout their childhood. A decision inconsistent with this can be made if necessary to protect members of the public from serious harm, albeit in such cases the need to safeguard and promote the child's welfare is still to be regarded as a primary consideration;[20]

(b) where a sheriff or a children's hearing is taking any decision about a matter relating to a child, the child must be given the opportunity to express their views before a decision is made, and the decision maker must have regard to these views. The main exception to this is where a sheriff is taking a decision about whether to make a child protection order;[21]

18 Children's Hearing Scotland Act 2011 (the 2011 Act), Part 1 and Sch 1.
19 2011 Act, s 6.
20 2011 Act, ss 25 and 26 for cases where a decision inconsistent with this requirement can be made.
21 2011 Act, s 27.

(c) in the cases set out in Box 5.2, the children's hearing or sheriff must not make an order or grant a warrant unless they consider that it would be better for the child to make the order or grant the warrant than to make none, i.e., a principle of minimum intervention applies.[22]

CHILD PROTECTION ORDERS[23]

5.6 In some circumstances, it will be necessary to take action to secure the protection of children in an emergency. The main mechanism for this is the Child Protection Order which is granted by a sheriff, but there is also provision which allows action to be taken where there is no time to apply to a sheriff (though this will be extremely unusual in practice). Research suggests that most children in respect of whom a Child Protection Order (CPO) is made are already known to services and have siblings who are also in that position; in 2023/24, CPOs were granted for 478 children, of that number, 100 were aged under 20 days, 185 aged under one year, and 220 were under two years old.[24]

Box 5.2

Where a children's hearing is considering:
(a) whether to make; vary or a compulsory supervision order;
(b) whether to make an interim compulsory supervision order;
(c) whether to make an interim variation of a compulsory supervision order;
(d) whether to make a medical examination order; or
(e) whether to grant a warrant to secure attendance.

Where a sheriff is considering:
(a) making a child assessment order;
(b) making or varying a child protection order;
(c) varying or continuing a compulsory supervision order;
(d) making or varying an interim compulsory supervision order or an interim variation of a compulsory supervision order;
(e) varying a medical examination order;
(f) granting a warrant to secure attendance; or

22 2011 Act, ss 28 and 29.
23 See also **5.46** below.
24 On CPOs and siblings, see: Scottish Children's Reporter Administration, Child Protection Orders (2015); for recent data on ages of children with CPO, see, Scottish Children's Reporter Administration, Statistical Analysis 2023/24, p 7.

(g) extending or varying an interim compulsory supervision order.

Application for an order is made to the sheriff and will be heard without notification to the child's parent(s). To allow the sheriff to consider the application properly, sufficient evidence must be provided with the application to allow her/him to be satisfied that the grounds set out below are established.[25]

(1) General grounds for application

5.7 There are two sets of grounds on which a CPO can be granted. The first of these applies to an application which can, in principle, be made by anyone, though usually it will be made by the local authority. The sheriff can grant such an application if they are satisfied that:[26]

(a) there are reasonable grounds to believe that the child **either**:
  (i) has been or is being so treated or neglected that they are suffering or are likely to suffer significant harm; **or**
  (ii) is likely to suffer significant harm if not removed to and kept in a place of safety or if they do not remain in the place where they are presently accommodated; and

(b) a CPO is necessary to protect the child from harm or further harm.

There is no further explanation or definition of when harm will be 'significant' – the *Guidance* (to the 1995 Act) has this to say:[27]

> 'It will, therefore, be a matter for the judgement of those concerned with determining the outcome of applications to consider whether the degree of harm to which the child is believed to have been subjected or is suspected of having been subjected (or is likely to be subjected) is significant. Those contemplating an application for an order or authorisation will need to make a judgment based on as much information as can be obtained about the child and his or her family. They must be satisfied that they can demonstrate to a sheriff…that the criteria for granting the particular Order … are met.'

This is consistent with the view expressed in one English case that significant harm was harm which was 'considerable, noteworthy or

25 See *Application for a child protection order* 2015 SLT (Sh Ct) 9.

26 2011 Act, s 39.

27 *Guidance*, Vol 1, chapter 7, para 5. See also paras 1.57 and 1.73 of the national Guidance for Child Protection for Scotland 2021 (updated 2023).

important'.[28] Guidance in Scotland sets out the considerations in Box 5.1 above as relevant to deciding when 'significant harm' exists.

(2) Application by local authority[29]

5.8 The second set of grounds is only available where the application is made by a local authority. The sheriff may grant a CPO if satisfied that:

(a) the local authority has reasonable grounds to suspect that a child is being or will be so treated or neglected that they are suffering, or will suffer, significant harm;

(b) the local authority is making enquiries to allow it to decide whether to take action to safeguard the welfare of the child, or is causing those enquiries to be made;

(c) those enquiries are being frustrated by access to the child being unreasonably denied; and

(d) the local authority has reasonable cause to believe that access to the child is needed as a matter of urgency.

Note that an application under section 39 to a sheriff for a CPO requires the sheriff to be 'satisfied that there are reasonable grounds to believe…', whereas a section 38 application requires the sheriff to be 'satisfied that the local authority has reasonable grounds to suspect …' This suggests that a section 38 application requires more substantive information and evidence to support the suspicion.

(3) Making and content of the CPO

5.9 Where an order is made, the sheriff must consider whether to include:

(a) A direction about non-disclosure of information about the child, for example, the location of any place of safety.[30]

(b) A direction about contact, either prohibiting contact or making it subject to conditions, for example, supervision.[31]

The application for the order may be accompanied by an application for a parental responsibilities and rights direction, which concerns the fulfilment of parental responsibilities or exercise of parental rights.[32]

28 *Humberside County Council v B* [1993] 1 FLR 257.

29 2011 Act, s 38.

30 2011 Act, s 40.

31 2011 Act, s 41.

32 2011 Act, s 42.

Notice of making the order must be given to a number of people including the Principal Reporter, the child and any relevant person in relation to the child.[33]

(4) Effect of the order [34]

5.10 The order can contain one or more of these requirements or authorisations:

(a) a requirement addressed to whomever is in a position to produce the child to do so;
(b) authorisation for removal of the child to a place of safety and to keep the child there;
(c) authorisation to prevent the removal of the child; and
(d) authorisation for assessment of the child.[35]

It should be clear from this that the order can provide either for the removal of a child from a place where they are not safe, or for the child to be kept somewhere to avoid harm,[36] although an order could be made without including one of these provisions.

(5) Implementation[37]

5.11 Before attempting to implement an order, the person doing so must reasonably believe that implementation is necessary to safeguard or promote the child's welfare. An attempt must be made to implement an order which provides for removal of the child to a place of safety within 24 hours of it being granted or it will lapse. If an unsuccessful attempt to implement is made within 24 hours the CPO will lapse unless the child is taken to a place of safety within six days of the making of the order.[38] If the order provides for a child to be kept in a safe place, it will be implemented as soon as the order is granted, provided the child is still in a safe place at the time.

If a child is removed to a place of safety, the local authority will have the same obligations towards them as it has towards a looked after child.[39]

33 2011 Act, s 43.
34 2011 Act, s 37.
35 Though if a child has the capacity to consent to any assessment or medical examination, their consent is needed for the assessment or examination to go ahead, 2011 Act, s 186.
36 For the human rights considerations applying to orders, see **5.46** below.
37 2011 Act, s 52.
38 2011 Act, s 52(2) and (3).
39 2011 Act, s 44.

(6) How long does the CPO last and what happens next?

5.12 Once the order has been implemented, this must be reported to the children's reporter.[40]

(a) *Discharge by the children's reporter.*[41] The order can be discharged by the children's reporter on the grounds that the conditions for making a CPO are no longer satisfied. The children's reporter may also discharge any direction attached to the order if satisfied that the conditions for including the direction are no longer satisfied. Discharge by the children's reporter is no longer possible if the second day hearing (see below) has begun or if the children's reporter is notified that an application has been made seeking termination or variation of the order.

(b) *Arranging an initial hearing.*[42] If the order is not discharged, a children's hearing must be organised to take place on the second working day after implementation; the sole purpose of this hearing is to consider whether the grounds for making the order are met. This requirement only applies where the CPO contains an authorisation either to remove a child or to prevent removal of a child.[43] A children's hearing is not to be organised if the children's reporter is notified that an application has been made seeking termination or variation of the order.

(c) *Application to vary or terminate the order.*[44] An application to have the order varied or terminated can be made by the child or relevant person[45] before the initial hearing starts, and this application must be disposed of within three working days. Once the children's reporter receives notice that such an application is being made, they may arrange a hearing, the purpose of which is to give advice to assist the sheriff in disposing of the application.[46]

(d) *Sheriff's options.* If an application is made to the sheriff to vary or terminate the order, the sheriff may grant an application to terminate if not satisfied that the relevant grounds for making the order existed at the time when it was made. Otherwise, the sheriff

40 Children's Hearings (Scotland) Act 2011 (Child Protection Emergency Measures) Regulations 2012, SSI 2012/334, reg 4.

41 2011 Act, s 53.

42 2011 Act, ss 45 and 46.

43 2011 Act, ss 45(1)(b) and 46(1)(b), though it is highly unlikely that a CPO will not contain one of these.

44 2011 Act, s 48.

45 And some others, including the reporter and the applicant for the CPO, see 2011 Act, s 48(1).

46 2011 Act, s 50.

can confirm or vary the order (including varying, removing or adding directions).

(e) *Other termination of the order.*[47] If not terminated in any of the ways set out above, the order will terminate on the earliest of the following:
   (i) When a children's hearing to consider the case of the child is convened.
   (ii) When a decision is made by the children's reporter not to refer the case of the child to a children's hearing.
   (iii) Where the order contains an authorisation to remove the child to a place of safety at the end of eight working days from the day after the child was taken to the place of safety.
   (iv) In the case of an order not including authorisation for the removal of the child, at the end of the eighth working day beginning on the day after the day on which the order was made.

EMERGENCY PROTECTION WHEN THERE IS NO TIME TO APPLY TO THE SHERIFF

5.13 In emergencies, where a justice of the peace (JP) is satisfied that 'it is not practicable in the circumstances for an application for a child protection order to be made to or considered by the sheriff',[48] the JP can authorise removal of the child to a place of safety or keeping a child in a place of safety on either of the sets of grounds set out above for granting a CPO. The authorisation may require production of the child by whomever is in a position to do this. The authorisation will lapse 12 hours from the time it was made if no arrangements have been made to prevent removal of the child, or if the child has not been or are not being taken to a place of safety. Otherwise, the authorisation will lapse 24 hours after being granted or, if this is earlier, when an application for a CPO is disposed of.[49]

Police constables have the power to take a child to a place of safety if they have reasonable cause to believe that: the conditions for making a CPO on application by the local authority are satisfied; it is not practicable to apply for a CPO or to have the application considered by a sheriff; and it is necessary to remove the child to a place of safety to protect them from significant harm or significant further harm. This power cannot be used if a CPO is in force in respect of the child or if an

47 2011 Act, s 54.
48 2011 Act, s 55(2)(b).
49 2011 Act, s 55.

application for a CPO, or to a JP for authorisation, based on the facts before the constable, has been refused.[50]

Both types of emergency action will terminate if the children's reporter forms the view that the grounds for them no longer exist or that it is no longer in the child's best interests to be kept in the place of safety.[51]

EXCLUSION ORDERS[52]

5.14 The traditional approach to the emergency protection of children involved the removal of children from danger or risk of danger. The 1995 Act introduced the possibility of removing the alleged source of the danger and leaving the child at home. This is done by way of exclusion orders which are, to some extent, based on the exclusion orders provided for in the Matrimonial Homes (Family Protection) (Scotland) Act 1981.[53] One significant difference is that these exclusion orders can be applied for only by the local authority. There are issues about where the excluded person will live;[54] what financial provisions might be made available; and significantly about the principle of excluding a person who is only just alleged to have been the cause of a child suffering. These concerns may be reduced given that the person accused has the opportunity to appear and be represented at court hearings. Many social workers and others have long held the view, based on their experience, research and their value base, that removing a child from their home environment and primary carer at a time of trauma and stress is illogical, significantly damaging, and counterproductive in both the short and long term. Despite what may prove to be insurmountable practical and civil rights problems, exclusion orders provide the possibility to consider an alternative. This alternative may prove to be much better aligned with the three overarching principles; the paramountcy of the child's welfare,

50 2011 Act, s 56.

51 2011 Act, ss 55(6) and 56(5).

52 It has been noted that 'there are so many practical difficulties relating to implementation and protection of the child and also the rights of the … person who is to be excluded, that in practice they have been used on very limited number of cases.' Scottish Government, *The Children's Hearings System in Scotland: Training Resource Manual,* Volume 1, Section 10.

53 See **3.30**.

54 In contrast to the position in Scotland, the Children Act 1989 makes specific provision for assisting someone who has left accommodation to protect a child: Sch 2, para 5. It could be argued that the same sort of assistance could be provided by the local authority in Scotland under the terms of s 22 of the 1995 Act, given that a service can be provided to another member of the child's family if it will safeguard and promote the child's welfare.

the child's right to be heard, and the minimum intervention principle, i.e., not making an order if this would be better for the child.

(1) When can an exclusion order be made?

5.15 Exclusion orders can be made if these three conditions exist:[55]

(a) the child has suffered, is suffering or is likely to suffer significant harm as a result of any conduct or threatened or reasonably apprehended conduct by the person named in the application for the order;

(b) the order is necessary to protect the child regardless of whether they are living in the family home and would better safeguard the child's welfare than removal from the family home; and

(c) the application properly identifies someone who is capable of looking after the child and any other family members left in the family home (the 'appropriate person').

No final exclusion order can be made until the named person has been given an opportunity to be heard by the sheriff, but until this is done an interim order can be made and this order has the same effect as a final one.[56]

Even if the grounds are made out, the sheriff still must take account of the overriding principles set out above before making an order and must also not make an order if doing so would be unreasonable and unjust.[57] This has two aspects. First, the order may be unreasonable and unjust in all the circumstances of the case. The sheriff must, in particular, look at: the conduct of members of the child's family; the needs and resources of members of that family; and the extent to which the family home and anything in it is used in connection with a trade, business or profession. The second aspect to be considered is the possible consequences of making an order if the home involved is an agricultural tenancy or tied accommodation.

If the sheriff dealing with an application for an exclusion order thinks that the conditions for granting a CPO have been established, they may instead of making an exclusion order make a CPO.[58]

55 Children (Scotland) Act 1995, s 76(2).

56 1995 Act, s 76(3).

57 1995 Act, s 76(9), (11). The overriding principles are those set out in **5.5** above, 1995 Act, s 16.

58 1995 Act, s 78(8).

(2) The effect of an order[59]

5.16 The effect of an exclusion order is to exclude the named person from the family home, which they can enter only with the permission of the local authority. Additional orders can be attached to the exclusion order. For example, a warrant to eject the named person; an interdict preventing the named person from entering the home or entering the vicinity of the home; an interdict preventing the named person from taking any step in respect of the child; and an order regulating contact between the child and the named person. A power of arrest can be attached to these orders.[60]

(3) How long does the order last?

5.17 The exclusion order will last for six months.[61]

SHORT-TERM REFUGES

5.18 Local authorities can provide short-term refuges for children (who for this purpose are those under 18) who appear to them to be at risk.[62] The provision of accommodation is triggered by a request from the child and can be either in a residential establishment or with foster carers approved for the purpose. Refuge can be provided for up to seven days, or up to 14 days if the local authority has been unable to find a responsible person in relation to the child and has no suitable accommodation for the child.[63] The main categories of 'responsible person' are the child's parent; a non-parent with parental responsibilities; someone who ordinarily has charge or control of the child; a local authority looking after the child; and anyone providing accommodation for the child under the 1995 Act.

The local authority must inform the 'authorised officer' of the fact that the child is being provided with refuge. The authority must also provide to the 'authorised officer' the child's name, their last permanent address, the address of any responsible person, and a contact telephone number. [64] Notification must be made as soon as reasonably practicable and at the

59 1995 Act, s 77.
60 1995 Act, s 78.
61 1995 Act, s 79(1).
62 1995 Act, s 38(1)(a).
63 Refuges for Children (Scotland) Regulations 1996 SSI 1996/3259, reg 2.
64 Refuges for Children (Scotland) Regulations 1996, reg 8(4).

latest within 24 hours of providing refuge.[65] An 'authorised officer' is a police officer identified by the Chief Constable for the purposes of these provisions.[66] The local authority may approve residential establishments run by others for the purpose of providing refuge. If refuge is provided in one of these establishments, the local authority and the authorised officer must be notified as soon as practicable and, in any event, within 24 hours.[67]

As soon as reasonably practicable after providing refuge or being notified of the provision of refuge by an approved establishment, the local authority must notify the responsible person and the local authority in which the child had their last permanent address.[68]

This provision allows social work departments to listen to children who are saying they are at risk and can no longer stay in the place where they believe themselves to be in danger. It provides the time for the social worker to complete a full assessment of the child and their whole situation, with a view to ensuring as high a quality of life for the child as possible. There may be occasions when children's motivations for claiming to be at risk may be questionable, but the possibility of short-term refuge ensures that children who are genuinely at risk can be accommodated.[69]

CHILDREN IN NEED OF COMPULSORY SUPERVISION

5.19 The 2011 Act contains definitions of the situations in which a child may be referred to a children's hearing, now described as the 'section 67 grounds'.[70] These definitions provide the basis for referrals to the reporter and then, potentially, to a children's hearing.

(1) Obligations of the social work department[71]

5.20 Where the department considers it likely that a child is in need of protection, guidance, treatment or control and that it might

65 Refuges for Children (Scotland) Regulations 1996, reg 8(4).
66 Refuges for Children (Scotland) Regulations 1996, reg 2(1).
67 Refuges for Children (Scotland) Regulations 1996, reg 2(1).
68 Refuges for Children (Scotland) Regulations 1996 SSI 1996/3259, reg 8(4).
69 See also *Guidance,* vol 1, ch 8; Refuges for Children (Scotland) Regulations 1996, SI 1996/3259.
70 See **5.22** below.
71 Children's Hearings (Scotland) Act 2011, s 60.

be necessary for a compulsory supervision order (CSO) to be made in respect of the child, it has an obligation to make all necessary enquiries into the child's circumstances. Once these enquiries are complete, the authority must also give any information it has about the child to the children's reporter if a CSO might be necessary.[72]

(2) Child assessment orders[73]

5.21 The local authority can apply to the sheriff for a child assessment order, though applications for such orders are rare,[74] partly because similar grounds allow the authority to apply for a child protection order.

A sheriff can grant a child assessment order if they are satisfied that:[75]

(a) the local authority has reasonable cause to suspect that the child is being so treated or neglected that they are suffering or are likely to suffer significant harm;

(b) an assessment is needed to establish whether there is reasonable cause to believe that the child is being so treated or neglected; and

(c) an assessment is unlikely to be carried out or carried out successfully without an order being made.

The child assessment order, which must begin within 24 hours of being granted, will specify the period for which it is to have effect, which may be no more than three days. It permits the local authority to carry out an assessment of the health and development of the child or of the treatment or neglect of the child. Where the child has capacity to consent to any aspect of an assessment, the existence of the order will not override their refusal of consent.[76] The order may require anyone in a position to do so to produce the child, or allow the child to be taken to a particular place for assessment though, if it does this, it must include directions about contact.

72 Guidance states that: 'The key question for potential referrers is whether working together with a child and family on a consensual basis is enough to meet the child's needs or is likely to do so. This is often referred to as voluntary support or engagement. It is important to consider likelihood, as it is not necessary for voluntary supports to have been tried and failed before a referral is made.' Children's Hearings Improvement Partnership, A Guide to Referral to the Children's Reporter, (2024) p. 2.

73 2011 Act, ss 35 and 36.

74 One example where a child assessment order was made use of is *R v Grant* 2000 SLT 372.

75 2011 Act, s 36.

76 2011 Act, ss 35 and 186, and the Age of Legal Capacity (Scotland) Act 1991, s 2(4).

ON WHAT GROUNDS CAN A CHILD BE REFERRED TO A CHILDREN'S HEARING?[77]

5.22 A child can be referred to a children's hearing on one or more of the following grounds.

(a) *The child is likely to suffer unnecessarily, or the health or development of the child is likely to be seriously impaired due to lack of parental care.*[78]

The question here is whether the care being provided by the parent(s) is likely to result in harm to a child, regardless of the intention of the parents.[79] There may be a lack of parental care even where the parents act with the best of motives. This may be the case even if the child appears to be well looked after, and regardless of whether blame should be attached to the parents.[80] For example, this ground was held to be established in a case where the parents of a haemophiliac child were unwilling to give consent to treatment using Factor VIII, even though the court accepted that the parents were concerned parents and that their refusal to consent to this treatment arose from a fear that the child might become HIV positive as a result of the treatment.[81] In another case children were described by the sheriff as well-nourished and clean, but on two occasions they had effectively been thrown out of the house and left to fend for themselves; in both instances a long delay ensued before their absence was reported to the police by their father.[82] This ground can apply even where the child has never actually ever been in the care of the parents.[83] It can involve excessive restriction and supervision of the child as well as the opposite.[84]

This ground of a lack of parental care was held to exist where parents were convinced that their children had an autistic spectrum disorder, insisting on them attending a special school and refusing access to the children for assessment.[85] A further example involved failure on the part of a mother to recognise the risk posed to her child by a partner with a history of abusing children. Additional factors here were the partner's

77 2011 Act, s 67.

78 2011 Act, s 67(2)(a).

79 In one case the sheriff took the view that the children's mother had acted 'out of the best of motives', *R v Grant*, 2000 SLT 372 at 376.

80 *D v Kelly* 1995 SLT 1220.

81 *Finlayson, Applicant* 1989 SCLR 601.

82 *Kennedy v S* 1986 SLT 679.

83 *McGregor v L* 1981 SLT 194.

84 *D v Kelly* 1995 SLT 1221, it was considered sufficient that lack of care was likely to occur based on the known habits of the carers.

85 *R v Grant* 2000 SLT 372.

failure to complete a programme to address their behaviour and the mother's lack of honesty about her relationship with the partner.[86]

It has been said that the test for determining whether this ground is satisfied is:[87]

> whether a reasonable person looking to the circumstances of the particular case would consider that this child is likely to be caused unnecessary suffering or serious impairment to her health or development through lack of parental care on the part of this mother?

In the case in which this test was formulated, failure by a mother to visit a child in hospital for five months was not sufficient to establish likely lack of parental care where the mother had serious medical problems and lived a considerable distance from the hospital.[88]

'Likely' in this context is not to be regarded as equivalent in meaning to 'probably' or to 'more likely than not', but indicates that there must be a significant or substantial risk of the harm set out in the definition occurring.[89] An alternative formulation would be 'a real possibility, a possibility that cannot sensibly be ignored having regard to the nature and gravity of the feared harm in the particular case'.[90] Judgment about likelihood must be based either on a risk assessment or on clear current evidence[91] from which an inference about the likelihood of harm could be drawn. There is a need to consider the past and to draw inferences about what is likely in the future based on past events and other information about the character of those involved.

(b) *A Schedule 1 offence has been committed in respect of the child.*[92]

Schedule 1[93] offences are mainly assaults and sexual offences committed against children, they are set out briefly in Box 5.3 below.[94] It is not necessary that the alleged offence is committed against the child in Scotland,[95] nor is it necessary that the person who is alleged to have

86 *M v Scottish Children's Reporter for Renfrewshire* [2009] CSIH 49.
87 *M v McGregor* 1982 SLT 41, at 43.
88 *M v McGregor* 1982 SLT 41.
89 *M v McClafferty* [2007] CSIH 88.
90 *M v Children's Reporter* 2015 SLT (Sh Ct) 215, referring to *In Re J (Children) (Care Proceedings: Threshold Criteria)* [2013] UKSC 9.
91 *M v Children's Reporter* 2015 SLT (Sh Ct) 215, referring to *In Re J (Children) (Care Proceedings: Threshold Criteria)*.
92 2011 Act, s 67(2)(b).
93 Criminal Procedure (Scotland) Act 1995, Sch 1.
94 A fuller explanation of some of these is given in the Appendix to this chapter.
95 *S v Kennedy* 1996 SCLR 34, otherwise, offences committed whilst on holiday overseas would not be relevant, for example.

offended is identified – the point is that the child has been the victim of such an offence.[96]

One example of a Schedule 1 offence is section 12(1) of the Children and Young Persons (Scotland) Act 1937 which creates a number of offences to do with child neglect. One of these offences is neglect likely to cause unnecessary suffering or injury to the child's health.[97] In one case,[98] a nine-month-old baby was left alone in the house for a short period of time by his mother who was very drunk. She was convicted of this offence and appealed. The appeal court held that for this offence to be committed the behaviour had to be wilful, in the sense of being deliberate and intentional; there had to be neglect in the form of failing to do '… what a reasonable parent, in all the circumstances, would regard as necessary to provide proper care and attention to the child';[99] and there must be some evidence that there was a substantial risk to the child. The court was not satisfied that the third requirement was met. Their view, which was also applied in the case of a 15-year-old girl left alone in the house for an evening,[100] was that leaving a child alone in the house did not automatically mean that the offence had been committed.

Parents no longer have the right to use force on their children by way of punishment. The Children (Equal Protection from Assault) (Scotland) Act 2019 repealed section 51 of the Criminal Justice (Scotland) Act 2003. The effect is that parents, or anyone exercising a parental right, can no longer use the defence of 'reasonable chastisement' to mitigate their actions.[101] The 2019 Act extends the same protection from assault to children as is afforded to any other person. The use of physical punishment on a child by a parent will now be treated as an assault.

Box 5.3

SCHEDULE 1 OFFENCES[102]

OFFENCES AGAINST CHILDREN UNDER THE AGE OF 17 YEARS TO WHICH SPECIAL PROVISIONS APPLY

1. Any offence under Part I of the Criminal Law (Consolidation) (Scotland) Act 1995.

96 *McGregor v K* 1982 SLT 293.

97 Children and Young Persons (Scotland) Act 1937, s 12(1).

98 *H v Lees, D v Orr* 1994 SLT 908. See also *McD v Orr* 1994 SCCR 645, dealing with a case of abandonment under the same provision.

99 *H v Lees* 1994 SLT 908 at 913H.

100 *H v Lees, D v Orr* 1994 SLT 908.

101 Children (Equal Protection from Assault) (Scotland) Act 2019, s 1(2).

102 Criminal Procedure (Scotland) Act 1995, Sch 1.

2. Any offence under section 18 (rape of a young child) or 28 (having intercourse with an older child) of the Sexual Offences (Scotland) Act 2009.
3. Any offence under section 19 (sexual assault on a young child by penetration) or 29 (engaging in penetrative sexual activity with or towards an older child) of that Act.
4. Any offence under section 20 (sexual assault on a young child) or 30 (engaging in sexual activity with or towards an older child) of that Act.
5. Any offence under section 42 of that Act (sexual abuse of trust) towards a child under the age of 17 years but only if the condition set out in section 43(6) of that Act is fulfilled.
6. Any offence under sections 12, 15, 22 or 33 of the Children and Young Persons (Scotland) Act 1937.
7. Any offence under the Prohibition of Female Genital Mutilation (Scotland) Act 2005 where the person mutilated or, as the case may be, proposed to be mutilated, is a child under the age of 17 years.
8. Any offence under sections 52 or 52A of the Civic Government (Scotland) Act 1982 in relation to an indecent photograph of a child under the age of 17 years.
9. Any offence under sections 1, 9, 10, 11 or 12 of the Protection of Children and Prevention of Sexual Offences (Scotland) Act 2005 in respect of a child under the age of 17 years.
10. Any other offence involving bodily injury to a child under the age of 17 years.
11. Any offence involving the use of lewd, indecent or libidinous practice or behaviour towards a child under the age of 17 years.
12. Any offence under section 5 (coercing a person into being present during a sexual activity), 6 (coercing a person into looking at a sexual image), 7 (communicating indecently etc), 8 (sexual exposure) or 9 (voyeurism) of the Sexual Offences (Scotland) Act 2009 towards a child under the age of 17 years.
13. Any offence under any of sections 21 to 26 or 31 to 37 of that Act (certain sexual offences relating to children).

(c) *The child has, or is likely to have, a close connection with a person who has committed a Schedule 1 offence.*[103]

103 2011 Act, s 67(2)(c).

A close connection will be taken to exist where the child is a member of the same household as the person (the meaning of 'household' is discussed below) or, if not in the same household, has significant contact with them.[104]

(d) *The child is, or is likely to become, a member of the same household as a child against whom a Schedule 1 offence has been committed.*[105]

The most notable feature of this ground is the broad approach that has been taken by the courts to the interpretation of 'household'. Their general view is that it is not necessary for all the members of the household to be living together or even living at the same place at the same time. In *Kennedy v R's Curator ad litem*[106] it was said that:

> The important question … is whether the ties of affection and regular contact which hold the parties together as a group of persons still continue.

Two cases illustrate the breadth of the interpretation of the term. In the first, the child who had been the victim of the offence was staying with foster parents separated from their family, his sister was regarded as being in the same household as the fostered child.[107] The term 'household' was 'plainly intended to connote a family unit or something akin to a family unit – a group of persons held together by a particular kind of tie who normally live together, even if individual members of the group may be temporarily separated from it'.[108] In the second case,[109] the child who was referred under this ground was born eight-and-a-half years after the death of a previous child as the result of a Schedule 1 offence. The child was still regarded as being a member of the same household as the deceased child. A household was still considered to exist even if one or more members were separated from it permanently where, as here, there was continuity in the form of the parents of the two children and of an elder sister who had been part of the household when the child died.

(e) *The child is being, or is likely to be, exposed to persons whose conduct is (or has been) such that it is likely that*
  (i) *the child will be abused or harmed, or*
  (ii) *the child's health, safety or development will be seriously adversely affected.*[110]

104 See *ZM, AM v Locality Reporter* [2016] SAC Civ 16.
105 2011 Act, s 67(2)(d).
106 1992 SC 300, at 307.
107 *McGregor v H* 1983 SLT 626. See also *Cunningham v M* 2005 SLT (Sh Ct) 73.
108 1983 SLT 626 at 628.
109 *A v Kennedy* 1993 SLT 1188.
110 2011 Act, s 67(2)(e).

The Explanatory Note for this ground states that it:

> is designed to protect the child exposed to significant negative influences. It may include situations of a child in a home frequented by drug addicts or alcoholics, a child who is frequenting a neighbour's house where the child is being involved in harmful activity, and a child who has been groomed by a paedophile, whether within or outwith the home or online.[111]

This ground was considered in a case where a grandmother had failed to protect her daughter from actions of the child's stepfather, including physical assault and controlling behaviour. The grandmother also facilitated the involvement of the stepfather in the life of her daughter and had demonstrated indifference to the welfare of her daughter and granddaughter (who was the subject of the referral) which had caused emotional harm to the daughter. She was considered to be a person covered by this ground.[112]

(f) *The child has, or is likely to have, a close connection with a person who has carried out domestic abuse.*[113]

See above for what is involved in a 'close connection'.

(g) *The child has, or is likely to have, a close connection with a person who has committed an offence under Part 1, 4 or 5 of the Sexual Offences (Scotland) Act 2009.*[114]

There is an overlap between this ground and ground (c), as some of the offences under the 2009 Act are also Schedule 1 offences.

(h) *The child is being provided with accommodation by a local authority under s 25 of the Children (Scotland) Act 1995 and special measures are needed to support the child.*[115]

Section 25 imposes a duty on a local authority to provide accommodation for a child in certain cases. Special measures in this context are measures necessary to support the child over and above being looked after by the local authority, for example, where it is necessary to place the child in secure accommodation.[116]

111 2011 Act, s 67, Explanatory Notes.
112 *H v Children's Reporter* [2016] 3 WLUK 142
113 2011 Act, s 67(2)(f). See also ss 1, 2 and 5 of the Domestic Abuse (Scotland) Act 2018.
114 2011 Act, s 67(2)(g).
115 2011 Act, s 67(2)(h).
116 For the circumstances in which secure accommodation may be used, see **4.38–4.41**.

(i) *A permanence order is in force in respect of the child and special measures are needed to support the child.*[117]

Permanence orders are sometimes a stage towards adoption of a child.[118] For an example of 'special measures', see ground (h) above. Special measures will be support through measures over and above those specified in the permanence order.

(j) *The child has committed an offence.*[119]

This follows from the provision that no child under the age of 16 is to be prosecuted except on the instructions of the Lord Advocate.[120] These instructions may relate to an individual case or may be general regarding the types of case where children should be prosecuted. If a child under 16 is prosecuted, this may be done only in the High Court or in the sheriff court. Generally, children will be prosecuted only in a limited number of cases, for example, if they have been charged with serious crimes or offences, such as murder, rape, robbery (if aged 15 or over), or they have been charged with an offence which can be punished by disqualification and it is in the public interest to obtain this.[121] This ground for referral is available only in respect of children aged 12 and over, which is the age of criminal responsibility in Scots law.[122] For this condition to be established, the higher standard of proof used in criminal law applies, namely 'beyond reasonable doubt'.

As noted above, a child under the age of 12 cannot be brought to a children's hearing on ground for referral (j) – *the child has committed an offence*. Where, *prima facie*, the child's behaviour may amount to a criminal offence, the child would more likely be brought to the children's hearing on, for example, ground (a) – *lack of parental care*.

(k) *The child has misused alcohol.*[123]

(l) *The child has misused a drug (whether or not a controlled drug).*[124]

The term 'drug' is explicitly stated to cover all kinds of drugs, not only those which are controlled under the Misuse of Drugs Act 1971. This

117 2011 Act, s 67(2)(i).

118 See **3.24**.

119 2011 Act, s 67(2)(j)

120 1995 Act, s 42(1).

121 Lord Advocate's Guidelines to the Chief Constable – Reporting to Procurator Fiscal of Offences Alleged to have been Committed by Children (March 2014).

122 Criminal Procedure (Scotland) Act 1995, ss 41 and 42, see *Merrin v S* 1987 SLT 193.

123 2011 Act, s 67(2)(k).

124 Children's Hearings (Scotland) Act 2011, s 67(2)(l).

means that a child could fulfil this condition if, for example, they were addicted to bottled cough medicine.[125]

(m) *The child's conduct has had, or is likely to have, a serious adverse effect on the health, safety or development of the child or another person.*[126]

An example would be where the child participates in risk-taking behaviour.

(n) *The child is beyond the control of a relevant person.*[127]

The term 'relevant person' is used in several places in the 2011 Act and covers: parents enjoying parental responsibilities or parental rights; anyone in whom parental responsibilities or parental rights are vested either under the Children (Scotland) Act 1995 (for example, someone who has had them conferred on them by an order under section 11 of the 1995 Act) or because of a permanence order; and any parent of a child who does not have parental responsibilities and parental rights, as long as these have not been taken from the parent by a court order.[128]

(o) *The child has failed to attend school regularly without a reasonable excuse.*

A child who has been excluded from school cannot be referred under this ground unless, possibly, the exclusion from school was made necessary by their behaviour.[129]

(p) *The child:*
   (i) *has been, is being, or is likely to be, subjected to physical, emotional or other pressure to enter into a marriage or civil partnership, or*
   (ii) *is, or is likely to become, a member of the same household as such a child.*

(q) *The child:*
   (i) *has been, is being or is likely to be forced into a marriage (that expression being construed in accordance with section 1 of the Forced Marriage etc (Protection and Jurisdiction) (Scotland) Act 2011), or*

125 See, for example, M Darboe *et al*, 'The Abuse of Dextromethorphan-based Cough Syrup: A Pilot Study of the Community of Waynesboro, Pennsylvania', *Adolescence* 1996; 31: 633–44.

126 2011 Act, s 67(2)(m).

127 2011 Act, s 67(2)(n).

128 2011 Act, s 200: Children's Hearings (Scotland) Act 2011 (Review of Contact Directions and Definition of Relevant Person) Order 2013, SSI 2013/193.

129 2011 Act, s 67(2)(o): See also, *D v Kennedy* 1988 SLT 55.

(ii) *is, or is likely to become, a member of the same household as such a child.*[130]

INVESTIGATION BY THE REPORTER[131]

5.23 Once the children's reporter receives information about a child they must carry out an initial investigation. Any person can give information to the children's reporter about a child whom they consider may be in need of protection, guidance, treatment or control and that it might be necessary for a compulsory supervision order to be made. The police have particular duties to report offences committed by children to the children's reporter and to report other cases where they have reasonable cause to believe that a child may need intervention. Local authority workers, including school staff, are also under a duty of care to report any similar concerns to the children's reporter. As part of this initial investigation the children's reporter may request information from the local authority.

If it appears that, in light of information received, the child may be in need of protection, guidance, treatment or control, the children's reporter must determine whether a section 67 ground for referral exists and, if so, whether a CSO may be necessary. In doing this, the local authority can be requested to provide a report on the child generally or on any specific matter specified by the children's reporter. The children's reporter can also decide that a referral to a children's hearing should be made even where there has been no referral from an outside source. This can be done where it appears to the children's reporter that a child may be in need of protection, guidance, treatment or control.[132]

Once a case has been referred and investigated, the children's reporter has three main options: to take no further action; to refer the case for the provision of advice, guidance and assistance by the local authority;[133] or to refer the case to a children's hearing. Cases referred to a hearing are in the minority. If a case is referred to a hearing, the reporter must prepare a statement setting out the section 67 grounds which are believed to apply and the supporting facts on which this belief is based.[134] The local authority will also be required to prepare a report to be considered by

130 2011 Act, s 67(2)(p)–(q).

131 2011 Act, s 66. See also SCRA, *Framework for Decision Making by Reporters.*

132 2011 Act, s 66(1)(b). See also *Children's Hearings (Scotland) Act 2011 – An Operational Framework and agreements between Social Work, Children's Hearings and the Reporter*, (2014), paras 9.2 and 9.3.

133 2011 Act, s 68(5).

134 2011 Act, s 89.

the hearing; this may be a report from a health visitor, pre-school or school staff, or social worker.[135]

WHO CAN ATTEND A CHILDREN'S HEARING?

5.24 In general, both the child[136] and the child's relevant person(s)[137] are obliged to and have a right to attend. 'Relevant person' is defined as:[138]

(a) any parent enjoying parental responsibilities or parental rights under Part I of the Children (Scotland) Act 1995;

(b) any person in whom parental responsibilities or rights are vested by a court order;[139]

(c) a person having parental responsibilities and rights because a residence order has been made requiring the child to live with them;

(d) any person in whom parental responsibilities or parental rights are vested by, under or by virtue of a permanence order;

(e) any parent of the child not already covered by (a) to (d) who has not had their parental responsibilities and rights removed by a court.

The child's attendance can be *excused* in the circumstances set out below, but where this is done the child still has a *right* to attend. The hearing can decide to excuse a relevant person where requiring their attendance would be unreasonable or where their attendance is not necessary for the matter before the hearing to be properly considered.[140] If a relevant person is not excused, the hearing can proceed in their absence.[141]

135 2011 Act, s 69. GIRFEC will inform the preparation of the report, which may make recommendations about placement of the child where that is considered to be in the best interests of the child, Looked After Children (Scotland) Regulations 2009, SSI 2009/210, reg 7.

136 2011 Act, s 73.

137 2011 Act, s 74.

138 2011 Act, s 200. Individuals having parental responsibilities and rights under equivalent legislation in England and Wales will also be relevant persons, s 200(1)(d), (e).

139 See **3.4–3.7**.

140 2011 Act, s 74(3).

141 2011 Act, s 75.

(1) Grounds on which child's attendance at hearing can be excused[142]

5.25 The child's attendance at a hearing can be excused on the following grounds:

(a) the hearing is considering a referral on ground (b), (c), (d) or (g) and it considers that the child's presence is not necessary for a fair hearing; **or**

(b) attendance of the child would place their physical, mental or moral welfare at risk; **or**

(c) taking account of the child's age and maturity, they would not be capable of understanding what happens at the hearing.

(2) When can a relevant person be excluded?[143]

5.26 A relevant person can be excluded from a hearing where the hearing is satisfied that the presence of the relevant person:[144]

(a) is preventing the hearing from obtaining the views of the child; or

(b) is causing the child distress or is likely to cause significant distress to the child.

As far as the first of these is concerned, there must be a current effect on the child preventing them from expressing their views and this must be causally connected to the presence of the person being excluded.[145] This causal effect must apply to everyone who is excluded, meaning that a simple blanket clearing of the room is not permissible. Adequate reasons must be given by the hearing for any exclusion.

Where someone is excluded, the chair of the hearing must explain to the person excluded the substance of what has taken place in their absence (subject to certain non-disclosure provisions considered below).

(3) Who else can attend?

5.27 Rights of attendance also extend to representatives of the child and relevant persons, the children's reporter, safeguarder and representatives of newspapers or news agencies (although the attendance

142 2011 Act, s 73(3). Unless (c) applies, the child cannot be excused from the explanation of the grounds of referral which takes place at the beginning of a grounds hearing.

143 2011 Act, s 76.

144 2011 Act, s 76.

145 *G v Children's Reporter* 2016 SLT (Sh Ct) 293, a statement of preference by the child before the start of the hearing did not satisfy this test.

of press or media personnel is very rare).[146] In addition, people whose attendance is considered necessary for the matter before the hearing to be properly considered may attend (this would include the social worker who prepared any report for the hearing), as may any other person granted permission to attend by the chair of the hearing.[147]

In addition, the 2011 Act makes provision for an individual to be deemed to be a relevant person, and such deemed relevant persons have the same rights (in general) as a relevant person.[148] The Act provides for a pre-hearing to decide whether or not to deem an individual to be a relevant person[149] This is not done on the hearing's own initiative, but must follow a request for a determination from that individual, the child, or a relevant person.[150] The background to this provision is that, in the years preceding the 2011 Act, there were a number of cases in which the fathers of children who held only a right to contact with the child sought recognition as a relevant person. The argument was that, since the hearing could regulate contact between the child and anyone else, the Article 8 ECHR right of a father with a contact order could be interfered with were he not permitted to attend. This litigation resulted in an extended reading of the provisions which were contained in the Children (Scotland) Act 1995 to include a father in this position within the definition of 'relevant person' found in that Act.[151]

The pre-hearing panel *must* deem someone to be a relevant person if they have (or have recently had) a significant involvement in the upbringing of the child.[152] Determining this is a question of fact and the best interests of the child are irrelevant. Applying that definition in practice, it has been held to extend to a grandmother who had considerable involvement in the upbringing of her grandson and was given deemed relevant person

146 Though what can be published about hearings is limited, 2011 Act, s 182.
147 2011 Act, s 78(2).
148 2011 Act, s 81.
149 2011 Act, s 81(1).
150 2011 Act, s 80.
151 See *Principal Reporter v K* [2010] UKSC 56.
152 2011 Act, s 81(3). To ensure compliance with Art 8 of the ECHR this definition should be read as if it also included 'persons whose established family life with the child may be interfered with by the hearing and whose rights require the procedural protection of being a relevant person' *ABC v Principal Reporter and Ors* [2018] CSOH 81.

status.[153] Similarly, a father who had significant involvement in caring for a baby but whose involvement ceased when a bail condition was imposed on him.[154] Foster carers do not automatically have relevant person status, and will have to request that the pre-hearing panel, if appropriate to do so, will grant them deemed relevant person status.[155] Simply taking children to school and running occasional errands for the mother will not be sufficient to meet the criterion for 'significant involvement in the upbringing of the child'.[156]

Some cases have considered the fact that a person has ceased to have significant involvement because of state intervention (for example, a ban on contact made by a children's hearing) in deciding whether or not involvement is recent.[157] The question to be asked is; would there have been significant involvement 'but for' the state intervention? However, the Inner House has suggested that 'it is not thought necessary to embark upon any elaborate "but for state intervention" test or hypothesis, something which is likely to be unrealistic and impractical'.[158] Box 5.4 contains guidance to children's pre-hearing panels on taking the decision as to whether someone should be deemed a relevant person.

153 *M, Appellant* 2014 Fam LR 55. A grandchild was placed with the grandmother for just over three weeks. The child had stayed overnight with her at least once a week and she had provided assistance to the child's mother. The hearing which had rejected her claim had asked about involvement in medical, dental and nursery decisions involving the child (aged 3), referring to the Practice and Procedure Manual (see Box 5.4 below); the approach taken there, focusing on treatment and instruction, was considered too narrow.

154 *DH v Scottish Children's Reporter* 2014 Fam LR 63. See the comments below about the relevance of state intervention.

155 *AG & MT v Principal Reporter* [2014] CSIH 108. In this case a distinction was made between significant involvement in upbringing and significant involvement in day-to-day care, considered the basis for not deeming the foster carers to be relevant persons. In *CF v Scottish Reporter* [2017] CSIH 44, it was commented (at [46]) that: 'Perhaps surprisingly, the court appeared to suggest that day-to-day care for the past 18 months was not enough in itself to constitute the foster carers as relevant persons'. *Children's Hearings (Scotland) Act 2011 – An Operational Framework and Agreements Between Social Work, Children's Hearings and the Reporter* notes (at para 2.8) that 'foster carers will likely attend at the discretion of the chair on the basis that they are involved in the child's life and have information to share with the hearing'.

156 *MP v Principal Reporter* [2014] CSIH 66.

157 *DH v Scottish Children's Reporter* 2014 Fam LR 63; *CC v Manns* [2016] SAC (Civ) 13.

158 *CF v Scottish Reporter* [2017] CSIH 44, at [49]. The basis for this conclusion (at [48]) was that: 'Whether the lack of significant involvement for an extended period is to be attributed to the CSO and the refusal of contact, or to the child's directions to the social work department, or a combination of both, are questions which are difficult to answer with confidence.[..] One suspects that a decision [..] would require a detailed scrutiny beyond that likely to be achievable at a pre-hearing panel.'

There is a right of appeal to the sheriff against a determination that a person is or is not deemed a relevant person.[159]

Box 5.4

Extract from Children's Hearings Scotland, *Practice and Procedure Manual* **(2013)**

4.3 This is a factual test. Decisions should therefore be based on the facts and circumstances of each individual child. Making decisions in this area will sometimes involve sensitive issues and some complexity. There are no set rules as each child's relationships must be considered individually. Some suggested factors to consider are given below, along with some case examples, however **these should not be considered as fixed rules to be applied**. Interpretation of the definition will likely develop over time as a result of case law.

4.4 The test is of **significant** involvement in the **upbringing** of the child, rather than any particular care of, or contact with, the child. Other considerations such as the best interests of the child or the character of the individual are not relevant considerations for being deemed a relevant person.

4.5 In general terms the children's hearing might consider the following criteria:

- the nature of the involvement in the child's life, for example is the person fulfilling a parental role in relation to the child – this could be involvement in key decisions in relation to the child, such as education or medical treatment, without necessarily having care of the child;
- the length of time the person has been involved in the child's life;
- living arrangements, for example do the child and the person live in the same house;
- where the person and the child do not live in the same house, the level and quality of contact the person has with the child; and
- the child's view, if they are old enough to provide it, of the significance of their relationship with the person

159 2011 Act, s 160.

> 4.6 This is not a complete list and the hearing should consider any factual information presented to it which appears relevant to deciding if a person has, or has recently had, a significant involvement in the upbringing of a child. What is significant in the upbringing of one child may not necessarily be as significant in the upbringing of another child. No single factor will lead to an automatic decision of relevant person status. It is the strength and combination of factors which requires careful consideration.

SAFEGUARDERS, LEGAL REPRESENTATION[160] AND PROVISION OF INFORMATION

5.28 Pre-hearings and children's hearings must consider whether to appoint a safeguarder from a national safeguarders panel. The main function of the safeguarder is to protect the interests of the child (rather than act as their representative) and they have obligations to provide reports and attend hearings.[161]

It has always been possible for a child or relevant person to bring along a solicitor to a hearing, but there was, until 2002, no right to legal aid for this. Such representation can now be provided under the Assistance by Way of Representation (ABWOR) strand of legal aid in certain limited circumstances.[162] As far as the child is concerned, representation is automatically available, without any assessment of means:

(a) for the second day hearing to consider a child protection order;
(b) in cases where the hearing or a pre-hearing considers that it might be necessary to make a CSO including a secure accommodation authorisation in relation to the child; and
(c) for hearings where the child is appearing from a place of safety after the alleged commission of an offence.

Assistance is also available to a relevant person in these cases, but only where two additional conditions are met:

160 See Scottish Legal Aid Board, *Code of Practice in relation to Children's Legal Assistance Cases*. There are widely different perceptions amongst participants in hearings as to the nature and effect of the involvement of solicitors, see CELCIS, *The Role of the Solicitor in the Children's Hearings System* (2016), noting, for example, a perception that 'the presence of solicitors can detract from the child-centred focus of hearings' (p 21).

161 2011 Act, s 33.

162 Legal Aid (Scotland) Act 1986, s 28C; Advice and Assistance (ABWOR) (Scotland) Regulations 2003, SSI 2003/179, reg 3A.

(i) The relevant person meets the current financial eligibility tests.
(ii) Legal representation is required to allow the relevant person to participate effectively.

Assessment of the second of these involves consideration of a number of factors:[163]

- the complexity of the case, including the points of law in issue;
- the nature of the issues involved;
- the ability of the individual to consider and challenge any document or information before the hearing without the assistance of a solicitor; and
- the ability of the individual to present their views in an effective manner without the assistance of a solicitor.

Legal aid can be provided for other hearings provided that the financial eligibility tests and the test of requirement to participate effectively are met.[164] Unlike the cases above, where the decision on eligibility is taken by the solicitor, in these other cases a decision must be made by the Scottish Legal Aid Board.

The reporter has an obligation to provide full information, including local authority reports, to all participating in a hearing, but a non-disclosure request can be made to a hearing (or pre-hearing) requesting that a document, part of a document or information be withheld from a specific person on the ground that disclosure would be likely to cause significant harm to the child to whom the hearing relates.[165]

PRE-HEARING PANELS[166]

5.29 A pre-hearing panel may be arranged in some cases to decide on certain matters before the grounds hearing takes place. If requested to do so by the individual in question, the child, or a relevant person, the children's reporter must refer to a pre-hearing panel the question of whether that individual should be deemed a relevant person. This issue may be referred to a pre-hearing panel by the children's reporter

163 Scottish Legal Aid Board, *Children's Legal Aid Handbook*, paras 5.20–5.25; see also the considerations noted in *K v Authority Reporter* 2009 SLT 1019.

164 Advice and Assistance (ABWOR) (Scotland) Regulations 2003, SSI 2003/179, reg 3A(1)(b)(ii).

165 2011 Act, s 178; Children's Hearings (Scotland) Act 2011 (Rules of Procedure in Children's Hearings) Rules 2013, SSI 2013/194, reg 84 (Hearings Rules). See also Children's Hearings Improvement Partnership, *Non-Disclosure of Information in the Children's Hearings System – A Good Practice Guide* (2016).

166 2011 Act, s 79.

even where there is no such request . Under s 79(3) of the 2011 Act, the children's reporter may also refer the following matters to a pre-hearing:

(a) whether the child or a relevant person should be excused from attending the children's hearing;
(b) whether a relevant person in relation to the child should be excused from attending the children's hearing;
(c) whether it is likely that the children's hearing will consider including a secure accommodation authorisation in a CSO in relation to the child;
(d) a non-disclosure request;[167]
(e) whether or not legal representation will be needed to enable the child or a relevant person to participate effectively in the proceedings before them.[168]

The three members of the pre-hearing need not be involved in any subsequent grounds hearing.

PROCEDURE AT THE GROUNDS HEARING[169]

5.30

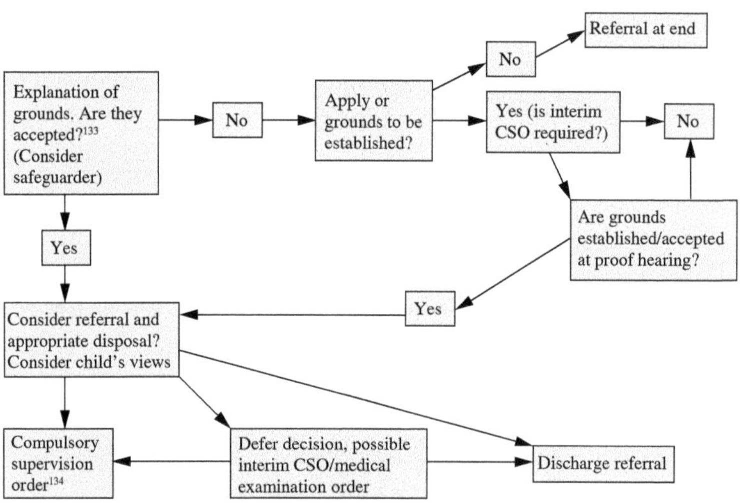

167 See **5.26** above.
168 Hearings Rules, reg 50(7).
169 2011 Act, ss 90–96.

1 Even if the grounds for referral are accepted at the hearing, the person accepting them can still challenge these grounds at a proof hearing, see: *Kennedy v R's Curator ad litem* 1993 SLT 295.
2 A compulsory supervision order is made if the hearing is satisfied that it is necessary for the protection, guidance, treatment or control of the child.

Figure 5.2: Overview of stages of a children's hearing after any pre-hearing

The first children's hearing is known as the grounds hearing and begins with the chair explaining the ground for referral to the child and the relevant person(s). Where the grounds for referral are accepted by the child and the relevant person(s) then the hearing can continue and may be disposed of at the first (grounds) hearing. However, the panel may decide to defer the hearing where, for example, the decision is taken to appoint a safeguarder and so the hearing will be postponed until the safeguarder has had time to write and submit a report.

If the grounds for referral are not accepted by either the child or one or more relevant persons, or, if the child, for whatever reason, is unable to understand the grounds, or if the children's hearing considers it otherwise necessary, then the panel has several options: (i) it may discharge the referral on the basis that the concerns that brought the child to the children's hearing no longer exist or have been addressed; (ii) it may instruct the children's reporter to refer the matter to the sheriff court where the sheriff, will determine if the ground(s) are established; and (iii) even where the case is being referred to the sheriff court, the panel may decide to impose an interim compulsory supervision order (ICSO) on the child. This is a protective measure intended to keep the child safe while the case is dealt with in the sheriff court.[170] In cases where the child referred to a children's hearing is already subject to a compulsory supervision order (CSO), the hearing on the referral will proceed as if it was a review hearing considering a review of the existing CSO.[171]

If the grounds for referral are accepted in part, the children's hearing can either proceed on the basis of those grounds accepted or proceed as if the grounds were not accepted. It is possible for there to be an amendment to the statement of facts if there is a disagreement about these, this will be the case where, after amendment, the statement still provides support

170 2011 Act, s 93
171 2011 Act, s 97.

for the existence of the ground of referral.[172] Where the panel considers it necessary to protect and secure the interests of the child, it will appoint a safeguarder. The reasons for appointing a safeguarder must be stated in writing by the chair of the hearing. If an appointment is made at the beginning of the hearing, it will be necessary to defer the hearing to allow for the preparation of a report by the safeguarder.

If the grounds for referral are accepted, or if they are established after a proof hearing before the sheriff, the hearing moves on to consider the case. This takes the form of a discussion involving all the participants (except those excused attendance or excluded). The discussion is not limited to the grounds for referral. Anything that is relevant to a consideration of the case can be taken into account.[173] The sole possible exception being allegations which have been found not to be established by the sheriff at a proof hearing.[174] The panel has the task of investigating the case as far as is necessary for a complete consideration of what is in the child's best interests. This consideration includes taking account of information which is not included in the grounds for referral which were accepted or established. Indeed, it has been decided that the hearing can consider allegations which were deleted from the grounds for referral and which were then accepted by the child or relevant person(s) at the proof hearing.[175] Also admissible is information which may disclose grounds of referral additional to those established at a proof hearing or accepted by the child or relevant person.[176] There is no need for the hearing to seek to have these additional grounds accepted or established before they can be taken into account. Once consideration of a child's case has been triggered by the acceptance or establishment of any ground of referral, the hearing can consider any relevant information, meaning information relevant to the issue of what should be done in the child's best interests.

At the beginning of the children's hearing at which the grounds for referral are being discussed, the age of the child must be established.[177] During the course of the children's hearing, the views of the child must be considered before reaching a decision.[178] Anyone preparing any document to be given to members of a children's hearing (or pre-hearing panel), has an obligation to include any views expressed by the child

172 Hearings Rules, r 59(4)–(6).
173 *O v Rae* 1993 SLT 570.
174 *M v Kennedy* 1991 SCLR 898.
175 *O v Rae* 1993 SLT 570.
176 *R, Petitioner* 1993 SLT 910.
177 2011 Act, s 122.
178 2011 Act, s 27(1).

which have been given to them.[179] During the hearing the child must be asked whether their views are accurately reflected in the documents provided to the hearing which refer to the child's views.[180] If this is not the case, the chair must clarify the child's views.[181]

The child's views can be conveyed to the hearing by the child in person, by their representative or advocate, by the child in writing by way of a Hearing About Me form, or by an appointed safeguarder. When the child is notified of the hearing, that notification will provide information about how the child can express their views to the hearing.[182] The relatively informal atmosphere of a children's hearing was intended to be an environment in which all participants, including the child and relevant persons or parents, would contribute fully and freely. In practice, the structures may be experienced as intimidating and/or an individual's attitudes towards authority may be such that the inherent power imbalances are insurmountable. Here, the social worker who has established good working relationships with the child and others may work to facilitate their full participation.

After the discussion the hearing reaches a decision. Three decisions are possible:

(a) to discharge the referral;

(b) to make a compulsory supervision order, a precondition for this being that the hearing is satisfied that making the order is necessary for the protection, guidance or treatment or control of the child; or

(c) to defer making a decision on whether to make a compulsory supervision order.[183]

As stated above, where a decision is deferred, the children's hearing may make an interim compulsory supervision order[184] if this is necessary as a matter of urgency for the protection, guidance, treatment or control of the child.[185] A medical examination order may be made, if this is necessary to obtain further information or carry out further investigation,[186] and the children's reporter may be required to obtain further reports.[187]

179 Hearings Rules, reg 8.
180 2011 Act, s 121. The Practice and Procedure Manual indicates that this should be approached indirectly rather than using leading questions to check the child's views (Children's Hearings Scotland, *Practice and Procedure Manual* (2013), para 6.43).
181 Hearings Rules, reg 58.
182 Hearings Rules, reg 23.
183 2011 Act, s 91.
184 See **5.33** below.
185 2011 Act, s 92(2).
186 2011 Act, ss 92(2) and 87.
187 Hearings Rules, reg 61.

A note of the decision and of the reasons for the decision (which must be clear, unambiguous and intelligible to the person receiving it) is sent to the child and the relevant person(s). It may sometimes be appropriate for the social worker to spend time with the child and family following the children's hearing's decision to clarify the meaning of the decision, to discuss the practicalities and to make arrangements for future contact. Children's hearings can be fraught with tension and may even contribute toward the precipitation of a crisis in the family, so the intervention of a social worker may be welcomed and necessary.

PROOF HEARINGS[188]

5.31 Where, for whatever reason, the grounds for referral were not accepted at the grounds hearing, a proof hearing before the sheriff must take place within 28 days of the instruction to the children's reporter to make an application to the sheriff court. The sheriff has to consider whether to appoint a safeguarder to look after the interests of the child in the proceedings. If a safeguarder has already been appointed by the children's hearing, then that safeguarder must make a report to the court if required by the sheriff. The report may contain recommendations.

The proof hearing will take place at the sheriff court for the area where the child lives, unless the ground for referral is commission of an offence, in which case it will take place in the court for the area where the offence was allegedly committed. The fact that the crime alleged is not one which could be tried in a sheriff criminal court is irrelevant, the sheriff can still conduct a proof hearing.[189]

After hearing evidence[190] and considering the terms of any safeguarder's report, the sheriff may find the grounds not established and discharge the referral.[191] Alternatively, the sheriff may find the grounds established in whole or in part and the matter will be referred back to a children's hearing for consideration and disposal. If the ground is that the child has committed an offence, the sheriff must be satisfied beyond reasonable doubt that the child has committed the offence; in other cases the sheriff must simply be satisfied that the ground(s) is established on the balance

188 2011 Act, ss 101–118.

189 *Walker v C (No 2)* 2003 SLT 293, the offence here was rape.

190 There are restrictions on certain types of evidence or questioning at the proof hearing where the grounds of referral involve sexual behaviour, 2011 Act, ss 173–175.

191 2011 Act, s 108(3). Though referral back to the hearing will be appropriate where there were some grounds accepted at the initial grounds hearing even if grounds referred to the sheriff were not established, 2011 Act, s 108(2), (4).

of probabilities.[192] In making a finding, the sheriff may make deletions from the supporting statements in the grounds for referral, but cannot amend the grounds themselves.[193] Where the ground for referral is that a Schedule 1 offence has been committed by a named individual, the court hearing on establishing the ground for referral should not, unless there are exceptional circumstances, be adjourned pending the outcome of any criminal trial.[194] Evidence at the proof hearing should not be restricted because of the possible trial of the alleged perpetrator.[195] An acquittal of a Schedule 1 offence in criminal proceedings does not indicate that a CSO which was made on the basis that the offence was established as a ground of referral should automatically be terminated.[196] Where the evidence establishes that a Schedule 1 offence has been committed, but the sheriff is unable to decide which Schedule 1 offence, the ground of referral should be held to be established.[197]

It is also clear that the sheriff should not, in most cases, rule on any procedural objections without hearing the evidence first. The only exceptions to this are where the objections, if successful, would mean that the grounds for referral could never be established.[198] An example of this would be a case where the referral was of a child under 12 accused of an offence.

If, during the course of the hearing, the child and the relevant person accept the grounds for referral, the sheriff has to stop the hearing and deem the grounds to be established unless satisfied that evidence in relation to the ground(s) should be heard.[199] Where only the relevant person accepts the grounds, the sheriff can determine the application without hearing evidence. There are two exceptions to this; first, there is a request that evidence be heard from the child, a relevant person, a safeguarder or the children's reporter; second, the sheriff considers

192 2011 Act, s 102(3). See *S v Kennedy* 1987 SLT 765; *Harris v F* 1991 SLT 242. The higher standard of proof cannot be avoided by a referral of what is really an offence on one of the other grounds: *Constanda v M* 1997 SC 217.

193 *S v Kennedy* 1996 SCLR 34.

194 *Humphries, Petitioner* 1982 SLT 481; *Ferguson v P* 1989 SCLR 525.

195 *P v Kennedy* 1995 SCLR 1.

196 *Kennedy v B* 1992 SCLR 55. The main reason for this is the difference in standard of proof. The evidence may be such that the sheriff taking the proof hearing is satisfied on the balance of probabilities that the offence was committed. That same evidence may not satisfy a criminal court beyond a reasonable doubt. In *Kennedy v B* it was noted that acquittal in a criminal trial was a factor to be taken into account in determining whether a CSO was still necessary.

197 *M v Kennedy* 1996 SLT 434.

198 *Sloan v B* 1991 SLT 530.

199 2011 Act, s 105.

that it would not be appropriate to determine the application without a hearing.[200]

If grounds for referral are established and the case is referred back to the hearing for disposal, the sheriff may make an interim compulsory supervision order (ICSO)[201] and this may specify that the child is to reside in a place of safety.[202] If this is specified, the hearing to consider the referral must start within three days of the child starting to live in a place of safety.[203]

COMPULSORY SUPERVISION ORDERS[204]

5.32 A decision to make a CSO must be taken in conformity with the principles set out at para 5.5 above. In addition, the hearing must consider whether to include in the order a direction regarding contact between the child and a specified person or class of people.[205] A CSO must specify the local authority responsible for giving effect to the measures contained in the CSO, known as the implementation authority. A local authority can appeal against being specified as the implementation authority on the grounds that it is not the 'relevant authority'.[206] 'Relevant authority' means the authority for the area where the child predominantly lives or, where the child has no predominant residence, the area with which he or she has the closest connection.[207]

The CSO can include a wide variety of conditions, for example, regarding residence, contact, authorising the use of secure accommodation, a movement restriction order, and a requirement that the local authority carry out certain specific duties.

200 2011 Act, s 106.
201 See **5.33** below.
202 2011 Act, s 109.
203 2011 Act, s 109(7).
204 2011 Act, s 83.
205 2011 Act, s 29A. Though this consideration is not a precondition for making a CSO, *Spence v AM* [2017] SAC (Civ) 36.
206 2011 Act, s 166.
207 2011 Act, s 201. See *East Renfrewshire Council* [2016] SAC (Civ) 14.

(1) Secure accommodation authorisation[208]

5.33 A compulsory supervision order requirement can include an authorisation for the use of secure accommodation where **either**:

(a) the child has previously absconded, is likely to abscond again and, if they do, it is likely that there will be a risk to their physical, mental or moral welfare; **or**

(b) they are likely to engage in self-harming conduct; **or**

(c) they are likely to cause injury to someone else.[209]

A secure accommodation authorisation effectively permits the Chief Social Work Officer, in consultation with the person in charge of a residential establishment, to place the child in secure accommodation. Such an authorisation can only be made where one of the conditions noted above is satisfied and in addition:

(i) the CSO also contains a requirement to reside in accommodation which contains secure accommodation, and

(ii) having considered the other options available, including a movement restriction condition, the hearing is satisfied that a secure accommodation authorisation is necessary.[210]

Where a CSO includes an authorisation and it has not ceased to have effect, the CSO must be reviewed within three months.[211] There is a right of appeal against a decision to implement an authorisation.[212]

(2) Movement restriction condition[213]

5.34 This contains provisions restricting the movements of the child. It must specify where the child is to live, the times when they must be there (up to 12 hours a day) and the duration of the condition. Additional provisions include restricting where the child can go, planned respite,

208 2011 Act, ss 83(2), (5), (6), 85 and 151; Children's Hearings (Scotland) Act 2011 (Implementation of Secure Accommodation Authorisation) (Scotland) Regulations 2013, SSI 2013/212. See also Scottish Government, *Good Practice Guidance: The Children's Hearings (Scotland) Act 2011 (Implementation of Secure Accommodation Authorisations) (Scotland) (Regulations) 2013* (2013).

209 2011 Act, s 88(3)

210 2011 Act, s 88(2)

211 2011 Act, s 135.

212 2011 Act, s 162(3).

213 2011 Act, ss 83(2), (6) and 84; Children's Hearings (Scotland) Act 2011 (Movement Restriction Conditions) Regulations 2013, SSI 2013/210 (MRC Regs). See also Scottish Government, *Intensive Support and Monitoring System, Guidance on the use of Movement Restriction Conditions (MRCs) in the Children's Hearings System* (2014).

and a requirement to participate in, and cooperate with, a child's plan.[214] This last provision is relevant because, where a movement restriction condition is made, a child's plan must be prepared which must, as far as practicable, address the immediate and long-term needs of the child with a view to safeguarding and promoting their welfare.[215]

Before a condition can be attached to a CSO the hearing must be satisfied that one of the first set of three conditions explained above in relation to a secure accommodation authorisation applies, and also that including the condition is necessary. Where a movement restriction condition is included in the CSO, the children's hearing must specify a date for review of the CSO or a period within which a review must take place.[216]

(3) Interim Compulsory Supervision Order[217]

5.35 An ICSO is a short-term CSO which can last for up to 22 days. An ICSO can be renewed if necessary. The grounds for making an ICSO are the same as those for a CSO, though making an ICSO must be necessary as a matter of urgency. ICSOs can include any of the measures which could be included in a CSO, and it is also possible to specify that the child stay at a place of safety away from their normal residence.

An ICSO made by a grounds hearing, pending the outcome of an application to the sheriff to establish the grounds for referral, can be renewed by a later hearing as long as this renewal does not mean that the child will have been subject to the order for a continuous period in excess of 66 days.[218] However, the order can be extended, and further extended, by the sheriff, apparently without any limit of time.[219] In the case of other ICSOs, there appears to be no limit on the number of times a hearing can renew the order.

(4) Parenting orders

5.36 A children's hearing, whether considering a referral for the first time or conducting a review of an existing compulsory supervision

214 MRC Regs, reg 6.
215 MRC Regs, reg 3.
216 2011 Act, s 125.
217 2011 Act, s 86.
218 2011 Act, s 96.
219 2011 Act, ss 98–99.

order, can require the reporter to consider whether to apply for a parenting order.[220] Before doing this, the hearing must consider that such an order might be appropriate. The requirement must identify the parent in respect of whom the application is to be made, and the ground on which the application might be made. The ground should state whether the hearing is of the opinion that the behaviour condition, the conduct condition, or the welfare condition for making such an order exists in relation to the child (see Box 5.5). The children's reporter is not obliged to apply for a parenting order and must consider the matter before making a decision as to whether to apply. As part of this consideration the reporter may request a report from the local authority which it is obliged to provide.

Box 5.5

> The *behaviour condition* is satisfied if the child has engaged in antisocial conduct and making the order is desirable in the interests of preventing further such behaviour.
>
> The *conduct condition* is satisfied if the child has engaged in criminal conduct and making the order is desirable in the interests of preventing further such conduct.
>
> The *welfare condition* is that making the order is desirable in the interests of improving the welfare of the child.

The Guidance provided some indication of the reasoning behind the introduction of Parenting Orders.[221]

(5) Local authority duties

5.37 Where a compulsory supervision order is made in respect of a child, a local authority (the 'implementation authority') will be identified as being responsible for giving effect to the measures set out in the order.[222] The local authority has a legal obligation to give effect

220 A parenting order imposes certain requirements on the parents of the child. See, Children's Hearings (Scotland) Act 2011, s 128; Antisocial Behaviour etc (Scotland) Act 2004, Pt 9.

221 Scottish Government, *Guide to the Antisocial Behaviour etc. (Scotland) Act 2004*, p 10.

222 2011 Act, ss 202(1) and 83(1)(b). See *East Renfrewshire Council* [2016] SAC (Civ) 14 for a dispute over which authority is the implementation authority when an order is transferred.

to the order and to comply with any specific requirements in it.[223] This includes checking that the requirements of the order are being complied with where the child who is subject to the order is not living in local authority accommodation.[224]

It is suggested that the minimum requirement to be set out in any CSO is that 'the implementation authority will provide supervision and support to the child'.[225] The implementation authority can request assistance from another local authority or from a health board in carrying out its duties under the 2011 Act. Such a request must be complied with unless it would be incompatible with any function of the organisation to which the request is made or would prejudice the carrying out of its functions.[226] Where the CSO requires the child to reside in a particular place, the implementation authority must check from time to time that the requirement is being complied with and, if not, take appropriate action.[227]

If it appears at a review of a compulsory supervision order that the implementation authority is in breach of a duty imposed on them, the children's hearing can direct the National Convenor to give the local authority notice of an intention to apply to the sheriff principal for an order requiring the authority to perform the duty. The guidance suggests that a requirement should only be made where there is a specific failure that, if left unchecked, would have a serious impact on the child.[228] The notice gives the authority 21 days to respond. After this period has passed the hearing will meet again to consider the response and decide whether to direct the National Convenor to apply for an enforcement order. In taking this decision any lack of resources on the part of the authority must not be taken into account. The application is made direct to the sheriff principal who has the power to order the authority to perform its duty. This order is final.[229]

Where it appears to a children's hearing that a local authority is failing in its duty to provide education to a child who is excluded from school, it can require the National Convenor to refer this to Scottish Ministers.[230]

223 2011 Act, s 144.
224 2011 Act, s 145.
225 Children's Hearings Scotland, *Practice and Procedure Manual* (2022), p 23, para 3.4.
226 Children's Hearings (Scotland) Act 2011, s 183.
227 2011 Act, s 145.
228 Children's Hearings Scotland, *Practice and Procedure Manual* (2022), Ch 3.
229 2011 Act, ss 146–148.
230 2011 Act, s 127.

(6) Duration and review of compulsory supervision orders[231]

5.38 Compulsory supervision orders last for a year and will terminate after this time has passed unless renewed. They will also terminate on the child's eighteenth birthday. Departments supervising CSOs should be aware of the general principle that the CSO should last no longer than is necessary to promote or safeguard the welfare of the child. When the CSO is made, the hearing can also specify a review date.

A requirement to review may arise because of court proceedings related to the child.[232] In addition, reviews of the CSO can be requested as follows:

(a) The local authority can require a review, for example, where it is satisfied that the CSO should be varied or terminated, where the order is not being complied with, or where it intends to place the child for adoption.

(b) The child or relevant person(s) can request a review after three months have passed from the making of the order/last review.

(c) The children's reporter must initiate a hearing if the order has not been reviewed and will lapse on the passing of a year or on the eighteenth birthday of the child or where the child is to be taken out of Scotland.

The review hearing can continue or terminate the CSO can add to or vary the conditions attached to it. One of the grounds for referral which was the foundation for the CSO must continue to exist before a CSO can be continued at a review hearing.[233] The review hearing should consider all issues relating to the CSO reasonably raised by the parties at the hearing.[234]

231 2011 Act, s 83(1), (7).

232 For example, application for an adoption order or for a permanence order, see **3.23** and **3.24**.

233 *GD* 2-014 FamLR 66, noting that in the instant case there had been 'mission creep'.

234 *P v Children's Reporter* 2016 SLT (Sh Ct) 339 – failure to consider mother's request for consideration of a rehabilitation plan and to defer to receive psychoanalyst's report considered to be unreasonable.

RIGHTS OF APPEAL[235]

(1) Appeal to sheriff

5.39 The child, relevant person or safeguarder can appeal certain decisions to the sheriff. Pending the resolution of the appeal, a request can be made for the children's reporter to arrange a hearing to consider suspension of the CSO pending the appeal being decided.[236] The decisions in respect of which there is a right of appeal are:

(a) a decision to make, vary or continue a compulsory supervision order;
(b) a decision to discharge a referral by the Principal Reporter;
(c) a decision to terminate a compulsory supervision order;
(d) a decision to make an interim compulsory supervision order;
(e) a decision to make an interim variation of a compulsory supervision order;
(f) a decision to make a medical examination order; or
(g) a decision to grant a warrant to secure attendance.

The sheriff's options (depending on the decision being appealed) are:

(1) If satisfied that the decision appealed is justified, the sheriff must confirm the decision and may take one or more of the steps mentioned in (3) below if satisfied that the circumstances of the child in relation to whom the decision was made have changed since the decision was made.
(2) In any other case, the sheriff–
    (a) must–
        (i) where the decision is a decision to grant a warrant to secure attendance, recall the warrant,
        (ii) where the decision is a decision to make an interim compulsory supervision order or a medical examination order, terminate the order,
    (b) may take one or more of the steps mentioned in (3).
(3) the steps are–
    (a) require the Principal Reporter to arrange a children's hearing for any purpose for which a hearing can be arranged under this Act;
    (b) continue, vary or terminate any order, interim variation or warrant which is in effect;

235 2011 Act, ss 154–156.
236 2011 Act, ss 154, 156 and 158.

(c) discharge the child from any further hearing or other proceedings in relation to the grounds that gave rise to the decision;
(d) make an interim compulsory supervision order or interim variation of a compulsory supervision order; or
(e) grant a warrant to secure attendance.

At issue is whether the decision of the children's hearing was justified; an appeal should be allowed only where the decision cannot be justified. This decision is taken by looking holistically at the decision, and it has been said that:[237]

> the sheriff should only uphold an appeal on the basis of an error in law, procedural irregularity or the like, if satisfied that the decision cannot nonetheless be supported. In other words, the identified problem must go to the root of the decision – it must vitiate it to a significant extent, and it must be clear that the outcome is unjustified, in the sense that it is wrong on any reasonable appraisal of the known facts.

The appeal is not an opportunity to revisit the merits of the decision of the hearing.

If an appeal is considered to be frivolous or vexatious, the sheriff can make an order which provides that the person concerned must obtain the permission of the sheriff before any further appeal against a decision is made. This lasts for 12 months.[238]

(2) Appeal to Sheriff Appeal Court (Civil) and/or Court of Session

5.40 A further appeal can be made from the sheriff to the Sheriff Appeal Court (Civil) (and then to the Inner House of the Court of Session). This appeal can be made either on a point of law or in respect of any irregularity in the conduct of the case.

237 *CF v Scottish Reporter* [2017] CSIH 44, at [38], referring to *W v Schaffer* 2001 SLT (Sh Ct) 86. See also *Children's Reporter v N* 2016 SLT (Sh Ct) 23 and *P v Children's Reporter* 2016 SLT (Sh Ct) 339.

238 2011 Act, s 159. In *MB v Local Authority Reporter Manager* [2017] SAC (Civ) 10, the appeal was considered to be covered by this provision where the appellant had failed to put forward any arguable point of law or procedural irregularity as a basis for the appeal.

(3) Review of finding that grounds for referral established[239]

5.41 Separately from the provisions as to appeal, it is possible to seek a review of a finding that grounds of referral are established. An application for such review is made to the sheriff who must review the finding where:[240]

(a) there is evidence in relation to the ground which was not considered by the sheriff;
(b) the evidence would have been admissible;
(c) there is a reasonable explanation for the failure to lead this evidence before a grounds determination was made; and
(d) the evidence is significant and relevant to the question of whether the grounds determination should have been made.

(4) Outcomes of review[241]

5.42 If a review takes place, the possible outcomes are:

(a) discharge of the referral and terminate any CSO based on grounds for referral not found to be established;
(b) original grounds do not exist, but others do – remit the case back to the hearing for disposal; and
(c) original ground(s) established – refuse application.

REFERRALS FROM THE COURT SYSTEM

5.43 In August 2024, the Children (Care and Justice) (Scotland) Act 2024 amended the definition of 'child' (for the purposes of children's hearings) from age 16 to age 18. This means that a person under the age of 18 may be referred to a children's hearing. Note that persons aged 16 and 17 will not be referred to a children's hearing on, for example, a ground that relates to lack of parental care, as parental responsibilities and parental rights cease when a person reaches the age of 16. This means that it is likely that the majority of referrals of 16- and 17-year-old persons will be on the offence ground (s 67(2)(j) of the 2011 Act).

NOTE: While the following paragraphs are current law at the time of writing, the reader is directed to pending amendments to s 49 of the Criminal Procedure (Scotland) Act 1995 and s 17 of the Children (Care

239 2011 Act, ss 110–111.
240 2011 Act, s 111.
241 2011 Act, ss 114–117.

and Justice) (Scotland) Act 2024 for the amendments. A child under the age of 16 not subject to a compulsory supervision order or an interim compulsory supervision order who pleads or is found guilty in a criminal court may be referred to a hearing for advice or for disposal. After considering the advice of the hearing the court may refer the case to it for disposal. Where a child under 16 who is subject to a compulsory supervision order or an interim compulsory supervision order pleads or is found guilty the High Court may, and sheriff and JP courts must, ask the reporter to arrange a hearing to consider the case and give advice on the treatment of the child. On receipt of the advice the case can be referred back to the hearing for disposal.[242]

Summary courts can also refer cases of people aged between 16 and 17½ to a hearing for advice if they plead or are found guilty. After receiving the advice, the case can be referred to a hearing for disposal. None of these provisions apply in cases where there is a fixed penalty, for example, murder or for certain minor traffic offences.[243]

If a court convicts someone of a Schedule 1 offence it may refer the child who was the victim of the offence, or a child who is or is likely to become a member of the same household as the offender, to the reporter.[244] Note that the current law refers to a 'person under the age of 17 years'. When the amendments in the 2024 Act come into force, the word 'child' will be substituted for this phrase.

If, during the course of a variety of court hearings, including actions for divorce, actions under section 11 of the 1995 Act in relation to parental responsibilities and rights, adoption proceedings or proceedings relating to permanence orders, it appears to the judge that any of the non-offence grounds of referral to a children's hearing exist in respect of a child involved in the hearing, the judge may refer the case of the child to the children's reporter. When this is done a statement must be provided which sets out which of the grounds for referral that the court considers might apply, the reasons for reaching this conclusion and any other information which appears to the court to be relevant.[245] The children's reporter must then investigate and decide whether a children's hearing is necessary.

242 Criminal Procedure (Scotland) Act 1995, s 49. There are some limited exceptions to the power to refer to a hearing.

243 Criminal Procedure (Scotland) Act 1995, s 49.

244 Criminal Procedure (Scotland) Act 1995, s 48, and Children (Care and Justice) (Scotland) Act 2024, Sch 1(3), para 3(a).

245 Children's Hearings (Scotland) Act, s 62.

COURT ORDERS SENDING CHILDREN TO LOCAL AUTHORITY ACCOMMODATION

5.44 Children remanded in custody by criminal courts are to be remanded to the care of a local authority. It is no longer possible to remand a child aged 14 or 15 to a remand centre or prison or to a young offender institution.[246]

Where a child pleads guilty or is found guilty before a sheriff in summary proceedings (other than, if the child is under the age of 16 years, an offence under section 9(1) of the Antisocial Behaviour etc. (Scotland) Act 2004), the sheriff may order that the child is detained in a residential establishment for a period of no more than one year.[247] A child so sentenced is to be treated as subject to a compulsory supervision order.[248]

Social work involvement includes negotiating for the most appropriate resource for the child. Police involvement and the accompanying proceedings may be experienced as especially traumatic by the child and family. There may be a need for a social worker to become further involved with the family, for example, in supporting them through the criminal processes, in clarifying the meaning and implications of any order made, and in making practical arrangements to ensure contact arrangements, if appropriate, are in place.[249]

HUMAN RIGHTS

5.45 Some human rights issues which affect child protection have already been mentioned and this section will briefly explore some other issues, focusing particularly on Articles 3, 6 and 8 of the European Convention on Human Rights (ECHR) and some of the principles that can be derived from the interpretation of these by the European Court of Human Rights (ECtHR).

(1) Article 3[250]

5.46 Article 3 of the ECHR states that:

246 Criminal Procedure (Scotland) Act 1995, s 51.
247 Criminal Procedure (Scotland) Act 1995, s 44(1).
248 Criminal Procedure (Scotland) Act 1995, s 44(3).
249 Children's Hearings Scotland, Practice and Procedure manual (2022) Ch 3, b.vii.
250 See also United Nations Convention on the Rights of a Child (UNCRC), Article 19.

> No one shall be subjected to torture or to inhuman or degrading treatment or punishment.

This clearly imposes a duty on states not to treat individuals in this way, but it goes beyond this to impose a duty on states and on government organisations, including local authorities, to act to prevent further infringement of an individual's rights when they become aware of such infringement. In a European Court of Human Rights case concerning children, the point was put in this way:

> [States are required] to take measures designed to ensure that individuals within their jurisdiction are not subjected to torture or inhuman or degrading treatment, including such ill-treatment administered by private individuals. These measures should provide effective protection, in particular, of children and other vulnerable persons and include reasonable steps to prevent ill-treatment of which the authorities had or ought to have had knowledge.[251]

What this means for local authorities is that they will have a duty to intervene when a child's treatment appears to meet the threshold of torture or inhuman and degrading treatment, if they were aware, or ought to have been aware, of this. If a local authority is (or ought to be) so aware, then it must take reasonable steps to prevent the continued infringement of the child's rights, but it is not required to guarantee against harm to children. The threshold is high for the duty to arise under Article 3, though it can be met. In the case from which the quotation was taken, the threshold was considered to have been reached and exceeded: the children were poorly fed, lived in extremely poor home conditions and had little supervision. If the treatment of the children does not amount to a breach of Article 3 rights, then it may still amount to a breach of their rights under Article 8 which will also require positive action by a local authority. It is clear, however, that not all neglect or mistreatment of children will involve infringement of their rights under Article 8. While there may be no breach of ECHR articles, social workers must remain vigilant to the conditions under which the child lives that may meet the threshold for referral on the ground for referral pertaining to lack of parental care. [252]

(2) Article 6[253]

5.47 Article 6 of the ECHR provides that:

251 *Z v United Kingdom* (2002) 34 EHRR 3, at para 73.
252 2011 Act, s 67(2)(a).
253 See also United Nations Convention on the Rights of a Child (UNCRC), Art 40.

> In the determination of his civil rights and obligations … everyone is entitled to a fair and public hearing within a reasonable time by an independent and impartial tribunal established by law.

Issues of a fair hearing have arisen in respect to procedure before the children's hearing. This has resulted in the introduction of legal representation in some cases, as well as the decision (under the legislation preceding the 2011 Act) that individuals who hold a contact order permitting contact with a child, but who do not have any parental responsibilities or rights, and do not have day-to-day care of the child, should be permitted to attend a children's hearing. The reason for this is that any compulsory supervision requirement may regulate the contact the child has with any other person and so may suspend the contact provided for by the contact order. As the right to contact is a civil right, the hearing would then be determining the civil rights of the holder of the contact order. If the holder were not permitted to attend, then they would not get a fair trial in the determination of these civil rights.[254] Individuals who hold a contact order can now seek to be deemed to be a relevant person.[255]

A further issue about Article 6 is whether the procedure for obtaining a Child Protection Order is compliant with this Article. This involves application to the sheriff without notice to the child or their parents (though they may, in fact, be aware of the intention to apply for the order). However, Article 6 does not require that a decision is always taken by a process and by a tribunal which allows a party to be present and be represented, as long as such a decision can be reviewed by a body and through a process which does allow this. Since there is a right to seek recall of a CPO before the sheriff with full legal representation, the process, as a whole, complies with Article 6.[256]

(3) Article 8

5.48 Article 8 of the ECHR states that:

1. Everyone has the right to respect for his private and family life, his home and his correspondence.
2. There shall be no interference by a public authority with the exercise of this right except such as is in accordance with the law and is necessary in a democratic society in the interests of national security, public safety or the economic well-being of the country,

254 *Knox v S* [2010] CSIH 45. See also *Principal Reporter v K* [2010] UKSC 56.
255 See **5.25** above.
256 See *K and F, Applicants* 2002 SCLR 769.

> for the prevention of disorder or crime, for the protection of health or morals, or for the protection of the rights and freedoms of others.

The second paragraph of the Article clearly indicates that interference with family life can be justified in certain circumstances, the most relevant exception in the case of children is likely to be 'the protection of the rights and freedoms of others'. There will in many cases be a balance to be struck between the interests of the child and those of the parents and it has been said that in carrying out this balancing:

> [T]he Court will attach particular importance to the best interests of the child, which depending on their nature and seriousness, may override those of the parent. In particular … the parent cannot be entitled under Article 8 of the Convention to have such measures taken as would harm the interests of the child.[257]

Beyond any direct treatment of children, Article 8 was held to be breached when the state failed to take steps to protect a child from the adverse effects of witnessing violence against her mother by her father.[258]

Any removal of a child from their family will involve an interference with family life and this interference will have to be, first of all, in accordance with law, in other words following the procedures prescribed for removal of a child, i.e. by applying for a child protection order or making use of one of the other ways of authorising this.[259]

In addition, the decision to remove must be justified by 'sufficiently weighty considerations in favour of the child'.[260] In light of ECtHR decisions it will be particularly difficult to justify the removal of a newly born child, especially where they are or will be in hospital and under supervision, though there may be cases where this can be justified, for example where there is likely to be a risk to the child from the actions of the mother as soon as the child is born.[261] The conclusion that action to remove a child is necessary must follow on from a proper assessment

257 *Johansen v Norway* (1997) 23 EHRR 33, para 78.

258 *Eremia v Moldova* (2014) 58 EHRR 2.

259 In *R(G) v Nottingham City Council* [2008] EWHC 1152 (Admin) a child was removed without following the correct procedures.

260 *Olsson v Sweden* (1988) 11 EHRR 72.

261 *Bury Metropolitan Council v D* [2009] EWHC 446 (Fam) and *North Somerset Council v W* [2014] EWHC 1670 (Fam). In contrast, where there was no such danger, failure to involve the parents of a child was not justified, *AZ & Ors v Kirklees Council* [2017] EWFC 11.

and consideration of the alternatives,[262] though it is clear that, given the circumstances, this assessment need not be exhaustive.

After a child has been removed (and while a child is being looked after away from home) there will be a duty, so far as this is consistent with the interests of the child, to promote contact between the child and their family, including parents and siblings, though there is a limit to the extent to which children can be forced into such contact. This obligation implies that the placement of children should not make contact practically impossible and is related to the view frequently expressed by the ECtHR that the objective, if possible, should be reunification of the child with their family.[263]

As well as conferring substantive rights on children and their families, Article 8 also confers procedural rights, and, in particular a right to be involved in decision making about the child.[264] This right extends even to the decision-making process involved in emergency removal of children, though this may not always be possible[265] or desirable.[266]

APPENDIX

Offences under Schedule 1 to the Criminal Procedure (Scotland) Act 1995 – some further explanation

NB These offences qualify as Schedule 1 offences only if they are committed against a person under the age of 17.

(a) Any offence under Part 1 of the Criminal Law (Consolidation) (Scotland) Act 1995. These offences include:
   (1) procuring for the purposes of prostitution or unlawful intercourse;
   (2) procuring by the use of threats, intimidation or false pretences, or using drugs to facilitate unlawful intercourse;
   (3) a group of offences related to incest. These offences include sexual intercourse within the forbidden degrees of relationship; intercourse with a step-child under the age of 21 or who has lived in the same household as the step-parent while under the age of 18; and intercourse by a person in a

262 *P, C & S v United Kingdom* (2002) 35 EHRR 31.
263 On these points, see *K & T v Finland* (2003) 36 EHRR 18.
264 *W v United Kingdom* (1987) 10 EHRR 29.
265 *K & T v Finland* (2003) 36 EHRR 18.
266 For example, see *Covezzi and Morselli v Italy* (2004) 38 EHRR 28, where involvement of parents was undesirable because of their close links with alleged abusers. See also *Errico v Italy*, Application number 29768/05, 24 February 2009. See also the cases referred to in footnote 217 above.

position of trust (for example, a foster parent) with someone under the age of 16 living in the same household as him or her;

(4) intercourse with a girl under the age of 13;

(5) unlawful detention in a brothel or for the purposes of having unlawful intercourse;

(6) permitting a girl under the age of 16 to use premises for the purposes of unlawful sexual intercourse;

(7) causing or encouraging the seduction or prostitution of, unlawful intercourse with, or indecent assault on, a girl under the age of 16;

(8) allowing a child between the ages of four and 16 to reside in or frequent a brothel;

(9) the commission or procuring of a homosexual act: (i) otherwise than in private; (ii) without the consent of both parties; and (iii) with a person under the age of 18.

(b) Any offence under ss 12, 15, 22 or 33 of the Children and Young Persons (Scotland) Act 1937.

(1) Section 12 makes it an offence for someone over the age of 16 having parental responsibility for or custody, care or charge of a child to ill-treat, abandon, or expose the child in a manner likely to cause unnecessary suffering or injury to the health (including mental health) of the child. Procuring the commission of any of these acts is also an offence. Aside from any other circumstances where it might be established, neglect is deemed to take place in two cases. First, where the person legally liable to maintain a child has failed to provide or procure the provision of (for example, by obtaining available benefits) adequate food, clothing or medical aid for the child. Secondly, where the death of a child is caused by suffocation (other than that involving a foreign body) and the child at the time of death was sharing a bed with someone over the age of 16 who was under the influence of drink when he or she went to bed.

(2) Section 15 makes it an offence to cause or allow a child to beg or be used for begging.

(3) Section 22 deals with the situation where a child under the age of seven is left in a room with an improperly guarded open grate fire without reasonable precautions being taken against the risk of burning or scalding. An offence is committed if the child is killed or suffers serious injury.

(4) Section 33 makes it an offence to allow a child under the age of 16 to take part in a performance where his or her life or limb is endangered.

Chapter 6

Social care

BACKGROUND

6.1 Social care (then described as 'community care')[1] was introduced by the National Health Service and Community Care Act 1990 and associated guidance, regulations and financial transfers. Its introduction followed a number of reports, particularly *Community Care: Agenda for Action* (the Griffiths Report) and the government White Paper *Caring for People*.[2] A number of factors influenced the development of policy in this area. First, a consensus emerged that provision for people in need was service led rather than needs led; services were being provided on the basis of what was available rather than what the user needed. Secondly, changes in the benefits system allowing payments to be made for private residential care had led to spiralling costs for central government.

According to *Caring for People*, the objectives of the new system were:[3]

(a) to promote the development of domiciliary, day and respite services to enable people to live in their own homes wherever feasible and sensible;

(b) to ensure that service providers made practical support for carers a high priority;

(c) to make proper assessment of need and good case management the cornerstone of high-quality care;

1 The term 'community care' still features in some legislation, eg, in Social Work (Scotland) Act 1968, s 12A (1968 Act). 'Social care' is defined in Public Bodies (Joint Working) (Scotland) Act 2014, s 68(1), largely referring to the definition of 'social services' in Public Service Reform (Scotland) Act 2010, s 46.

2 Cm 849 (1989). For a brief history, see McDonald, A, *Understanding Community Care: A Guide for Social Workers* (2nd edn, 2006), ch 2. A fuller background is given in Means, R *et al*, *Community Care* (4th edn, 2008), esp chs 1 to 3.

3 Paragraph 1.11 of the White Paper.

(d) to promote the development of a flourishing independent sector alongside good-quality public services (ie, encouraging the development of private and third sector providers);[4]
(e) to clarify the responsibilities of agencies and so make it easier to hold them to account for their performance; and
(f) to secure better value for taxpayers' money by introducing a new funding structure for social care.

Following the lead of the Griffiths Report, the White Paper identified local authorities as the lead agency in provision of community care. Local authorities would have the remit to organise and co-ordinate the provision of packages of care for persons in need.[5] The overall system was initially described as 'care management',[6] since after the assessment had taken place and a service package (care plan) had been agreed, the social worker (or other local authority worker) managed that care plan. This could have involved purchasing from and monitoring a range of providers. From a practical point of view the main immediate consequences of community care were:
(a) assessments of need had to be carried out before services were provided;
(b) a split between purchasers of services and providers of services was encouraged;
(c) a mixed economy of care was to be encouraged; and
(d) the responsibility of paying for people in residential care was transferred from central government to local authorities, with an associated transfer of resources.

Since the introduction of community care by the 1990 Act, there have been a number of developments both in the law and in practice and implementation. Legal changes include greater recognition for carers, the introduction of free personal and nursing care in Scotland and specific provision for those suffering from a mental disorder.[7] Changes in practice and implementation include the fulfilment of the planned development of a 'mixed economy' of care, with much direct service provision being undertaken by private or third-sector organisations.

4 See now, Social Care (Self-directed Support) (Scotland) Act 2013, s 19(2) (2013 Act), imposing a duty on local authorities to promote, as far as reasonably practicable, a variety of providers and support, applied also to provision of short breaks for carers, Carers (Scotland) Act 2016, s 25.
5 2013 Act, s 19(2).
6 Though this term later came to have a much more specific meaning, limited to complex cases, see Scottish Executive Circular CCD8/2001, Guidance on Care Management in Community Care.
7 See **chapter 8**.

A final significant change involves both practice and legislation. The introduction of community care was intended to herald a move from the position where individuals were allocated to existing services, to one where provision was tailored to the needs of the individual. This person-centred approach would be based on an assessment of individual needs.[8] Policy makers identified failings in delivering this approach; for example:

> Professional roles too often become focused on managing access to existing services rather than on helping people find solutions to their problems. In this way, people become passive recipients of services rather than active participants in their care.[9]
>
> In the past, people assessed as being eligible for support have sometimes been expected to 'fit' into existing services and care planning tended to be 'resource led'.[10]

The central idea of the new approach was described as the personalisation of services.[11] The personalisation approach enabled individuals to find the right services for themselves, becoming actively involved in selecting and shaping their support. The focus would be on providing individuals with funds to allow them to do this.[12] It led, in Scotland, to the introduction of the Social Care (Self-directed Support) (Scotland) Act 2013, which was prompted by two factors. First, the perceived failings of the existing law and practice, and the slow take-up of the self-directed support that was then available. Second, the variation in availability and effectiveness of services across Scottish local authority areas.[13]

8 See, eg, Audit Commission, Community Care: Managing the Cascade of Change (1992), Scottish Office Circular SWSG 11/91, Community Care in Scotland: Assessment and Care Management, para 3.1.

9 Changing Lives: Report of the 21st Century Social Work Review (2006), p 10.

10 Scottish Government, *Self Directed Support: Practitioner Guidance* (2014), p 22.

11 The definition is taken from Scottish Government, *Personalisation: A Shared Understanding*, (2009). Personalisation, both as a philosophy and as an (implemented) policy, has proved to be controversial, see, eg, Needham, C and Glasby, J (eds), *Debates in Personalisation* (2014); Beresford, P, *Personalisation* (2014).

12 Scottish Government, *Personalisation: A Shared Understanding*, (2009).

13 See the assessment of the impact of the 2013 Act and the extent to which it has delivered change in Pearson, C *et al*, 'Changing the culture of social care in Scotland: Has a shift to personalization brought about transformative change?' (2017) *Soc Policy Admin* 1.

LEGAL FRAMEWORK

6.2 Although community care was introduced by the National Health Service and Community Care Act 1990 this operated in Scotland to amend the Social Work (Scotland) Act 1968, which sets out the general duties of local authorities[14] to assess and decide on the provision of services or support. There are a number of other pieces of legislation which must be read along with, or which amend, the provisions of the 1968 Act. These include the Chronically Sick and Disabled Persons Act 1970,[15] the Disabled Persons (Services, Consultation and Representation) Act 1986, the Community Care and Health (Scotland) Act 2002,[16] the Mental Health (Care and Treatment) (Scotland) Act 2003, and the Carers (Scotland) Act 2016. The most important piece of subsequent legislation is the Social Care (Self-directed Support) (Scotland) Act 2013. The 2013 Act established some general principles on how assessments should be conducted and how decisions on provision of support be taken, as well as identifying options for the provision of that support.

Work carried out to assess a need for community care services may identify concerns about whether an adult has full capacity or whether they are vulnerable or at risk. Where children are involved, either being disabled themselves or being affected by the disability of an adult member of their family, the Children (Scotland) Act 1995 and Children and Young People (Scotland) Act 2014 may also be relevant.

The legislation applying to adult residential care, community care and support for carers is not always consistent and can be difficult to piece together. In England and Wales it was said that the statutory framework was 'inadequate, incomprehensible and outdated'.[17] The same could be said of legislation in Scotland.

As well as these statutory provisions, there has been a constant flow of guidance, sometimes general, sometimes directed at particular groups[18]

14 Although these functions will be delegated, mainly to Integrated Joint Boards under the Public Bodies (Joint Working) (Scotland) Act 2014 (see **1.73**), the text will refer to local authorities.

15 Which gives a list of services which may have to be provided after assessment, these are considered more fully below. The Act was only extended to Scotland in 1972.

16 On the introduction of free personal and nursing care: See, Scottish Office Circular CCD3/2018, Guidance on Free Personal and Nursing Care in Scotland for Adults.

17 Law Commission, *10th Programme of Law Reform*, Law Comm No 311 (2008), p 10.

18 For example, Scottish Government, *National Standard Eligibility Criteria and Waiting Times for the Personal and Nursing Care of Older People – Guidance* (October 2009). (*Guidance* 2009).

or particular types of provision.[19] This guidance, of course, does not have the force of law, but guidance documents may be a point of reference in the event of a challenge. If the decision of a local authority about provision of community care services is challenged the court may look at whether the authority has followed guidance and, if it has not, may set aside the authority's decision on this ground.[20]

WHAT ARE COMMUNITY CARE SERVICES?

6.3 The term 'community care services' covers a wide range of services. Section 12A of the Social Work (Scotland) Act 1968 requires local authorities to assess any adult whom they believe may need community care services.[21] Section 12A(8) defines community services as services other than services for children which the local authority is under a duty or has power to provide, or secure the provision of.[22] These services include the following:

(a) provision of residential accommodation with nursing care for people who appear to be in need of such accommodation by reason of infirmity, age, illness or mental disorder, dependency on drugs or alcohol or being substantially handicapped by any deformity or disability;[23]

(b) arrangements for the prevention of illness, the care of persons suffering from illness and after-care of such persons;[24]

(c) provision of domiciliary services[25] for a person in need,[26] an expectant mother, or someone who is lying-in;

(d) provision of laundry services for households for which domiciliary services are being or can be provided;[27]

(e) local authorities may make payments to any parent, relative or other person connected with:

19 For example, Scottish Government, *Guidance on Short Breaks (Respite)* CCD 4/2008.

20 For example, *R v North Yorkshire Council, ex parte Hargreaves* (1994) 26 BMLR 121 and *R (B) v Cornwall County Council* [2009] EWHC 491 (Admin).

21 1968 Act, s 12A.

22 1968 Act, s 12A (8)

23 1968 Act, s 13A(1)(b). Note: Some of the terminology employed in the 1968 Act is now anachronistic and potentially offensive, but the Act remains in force as written.

24 Excluding medical, dental, nursing care or health visiting. 1968 Act, s 13B(2)

25 The services here are services provided in the service user's home which are designed to enable her/him to maintain an independent existence for as long as possible.

26 A person will be in need if he or she is in need of care and attention arising out of infirmity, youth or age; or suffers from illness or mental disorder or is substantially handicapped by any deformity or disability. 1968 Act, s 94(1).

27 1968 Act, s 14.

(i) a person, other than a child, in the care of the authority or receiving assistance from the authority: or

(ii) a child who is being looked after by the authority in respect of travelling, subsistence or other expenses incurred by the parent, relative or other person in visiting the person, [or child] if it appears to the authority that the parent, relative or other person would not otherwise be able to visit [them] without undue hardship and that the circumstances warrant the making of the payments.[28]

(f) payments to allow for attendance at the funeral of a child who had been looked after or an adult who had been either in the care of the local authority or receiving assistance from them;

(g) certain services provided under the Mental Health (Care and Treatment) (Scotland) Act 2003;[29]

(h) any services provided under section 12(1) of the Social Work (Scotland) Act 1968, this subsection enables provision of a wide range of services, including provision of facilities and accommodation, by imposing a very general duty on the local authority to promote social welfare and enabling it to pursue this objective by providing assistance in cash or in kind.[30]

As noted in (h) above, the scope of 'community care services' is wide, though it is likely to exclude services which are provided by local authorities under, or as a result of, other enactments which make specific provision for these services or their provision. For example, services provided as a result of an assessment under the Chronically Sick and Disabled Persons Act 1970 are provided under the specific umbrella of that Act rather than under section 12. Also excluded from the definition of community care services are any services for children. In addition, local authorities are not permitted to provide community care services to certain categories of adult who are subject to immigration control.[31]

GENERAL PRINCIPLES AND CONTEXT

6.4 As discussed in **1.73**, there are certain general outcomes to which local authorities must have regard in carrying out their

28 1968 Act, s 29. Note that, as of April 2019, s 29 no longer provides for the 'Power of local authority to defray expenses of parent, etc., visiting persons or attending funerals'. These words amended by the Burial and Cremation (Scotland) Act 2016, Sch 1, para 1(a), inserting, 'certain travelling expenses'.

29 See **8.14**.

30 1968 Act, s 12.

31 See **1.72**.

functions.[32] Most relevant here are the outcomes that people are, as far as reasonably practicable, able to live independently at home or in a setting in their community, and that services are centred on maintaining or improving quality of life. Local authorities also have a duty to ensure that unpaid carers are supported.[33] In addition, the Social Care (Self-directed Support) (Scotland) Act 2013 sets out certain principles which should underpin the exercise of social care functions including assessment, decisions about support, provision of support and reviews of provision.[34] These principles are summarised in Table 6.1 below, but in more detail are:

- *Involvement.* The person concerned is to have as much involvement as they wish, both in the process of assessment of needs and outcomes and in the provision of support.[35]
- *Assistance.* Assistance is to be provided to the extent required in order to allow a person to express their views about the options for self-directed support (see below) and to make an informed choice.[36] Assistance can be provided in a number of ways, for example by a circle of support or by an advocacy organisation.[37] Although the statutory provision does not mention assistance in relation to assessment, this might be implied from the overall principles of the Act. The guidance on the Act indicates that all reasonable measures should be taken to ensure full participation in the assessment. These measures should include consideration of the assistance that an individual might need to be able to participate.[38] If the person being assessed has a mental disorder,

32 Public Bodies (Joint Working) (Scotland) Act 2014, s 40. The outcomes are set out in the Public Bodies (Joint Working) (National Health and Wellbeing Outcomes) (Scotland) Regulations 2014, SSI 2014/343; see also Scottish Government, *National Health and Wellbeing Outcomes* (2015).

33 Public Bodies (Joint Working) (National Health and Wellbeing Outcomes) (Scotland) Regulations 2014, Sch.

34 2013 Act (as amended).

35 2013 Act, s 1(2). Ever since the inception of community care, guidance has emphasised the need for involvement, and failure to involve a service user has led to successful challenge to local authority decisions and plans, eg *R v London Borough of Islington, ex parte Rixon* (1997) 1 CCLR 119.

36 2013 Act, s 1(3).

37 Scottish Government, *Social Care (Self-directed Support) (Scotland) Act 2013: Statutory Guidance* (2022), p 11 (*Statutory Guidance* (2022)).

38 Scottish Government, *Self Directed Support: Practitioner Guidance* (2014), p 16, see also *Statutory Guidance* (2022), pp 5–6. These pages relate to SDS definition and statutory principles, including the need for the person being assessed to be "provided with any assistance that is reasonably required to enable the person to express views about the options for SDS available to them and to make an informed choice".

then they will have a right of access to independent advocacy during the whole process of assessment and decision-making.[39]

- *Collaboration.* There should be collaboration both in assessment and in the provision of support.[40] This duty to collaborate supports the idea of an equal partnership in assessment and support between the person being assessed or supported and the professional involved.[41]

Two further principles are set out which local authorities must take reasonable steps to facilitate:

- The right to dignity is to be respected.[42]
- The person's right to participate in the life of the community is to be respected.[43]

Although these principles reflect the terms of the UN Convention on the Rights of Persons with Disabilities,[44] this Convention does not seem to have been considered while the legislation was being discussed and were intended to 'introduce on to the face of the [Act] core principles of independent living'.[45]

One of the consequences of having different pieces of legislation covering this area is that the legislation which pre-dates the 2013 Act does not reflect the underlying principles or philosophy of that Act. The 2013 Act focused on involvement by a supported person (previously referred to as 'service user' – in this chapter, reference will be made to 'supported person', even in contexts where no decision has been made about provision of support)[46] in designing their support. The earlier legislation usually refers to decisions being made about the provision of services

39 Mental Health (Care and Treatment) (Scotland) Act 2003, s 259. This is simply a specific application of the general right of a person with a mental disorder to be able to access an independent advocacy service.

40 2013 Act, s 1(4).

41 *Statutory Guidance* (2022), p 6.

42 2013 Act, s 2.

43 2013 Act, s 2.

44 United Nations Convention on the Rights of Persons with Disabilities, Arts 3(1), 19, 29 and 30.

45 Minister for Public Health (M Matheson), Health and Sport Committee, 30 October 2012, col 2912. It was also noted that the s 1 principles were largely concerned with the process of self-directed support, whilst the s 2 principles defined the end goal of the person's social care assessment and support plan. See also Health and Sport Committee 10th Report 2012 (Session 4), Stage 1 Report on the Social Care (Self-directed Support) (Scotland) Bill.

46 Following the terminology adopted in the *Statutory Guidance* to accompany the Social Care (Self-directed Support) (Scotland) Act 2013 (2014) (*Statutory Guidance* (2014)). The only exceptions will be cases involving quotations which include a reference to 'service user'. See also *Statutory Guidance* (2022).

(rather than support), followed by the provision of these services. The legislation pre-dating 2013 reflects an older model of provision where local authorities decided to provide services to individuals (though, as we will see below, the current law does still envisage that this will happen in some cases). What follows seeks to reflect the 2013 Act terminology and approach and is structured according to what seems the logical sequence of stages:

- assessment;
- deciding whether an individual is eligible for support;
- allocation of a budget;
- selecting one of the four options for support;
- developing a support plan; and
- reviewing that plan.

ASSESSMENT

6.5 Provision of social (community) care services, as well as of services under the Chronically Sick and Disabled Persons Act 1970, will normally follow on from an assessment.[47] This assessment will be triggered 'where it appears to a local authority that any person for whom they are under a duty or have a power to provide, or to secure the provision of, community care services may be in need of any such services'.[48] There is no need for an assessment to be requested before a duty to assess arises, though clearly such a request might alert the authority to the potential need for community care services. There is additional provision for triggering an assessment provided by the Mental Health (Care and Treatment) (Scotland) Act 2003.[49]

There are no specific time limits for the carrying out of an assessment, although it might be argued that a long delay in a case where the need was obvious or urgent might be seen as being unreasonable.[50] In any event, if a delay is seen as being excessive it could be the subject of a complaint to the local authority.

47 1968 Act, s 12A(5) provides that community care services can be provided without a prior assessment in cases of urgency, though normally if this is done an assessment will require to be carried out after provision of services has started (s 12A(6)).

48 1968 Act, s 12A(1).

49 See **8.14**.

50 There is some evidence of extensive delays in the process of assessment and provision of support. See Health and Social Care Alliance, *Personal Experiences of Self-directed Support* (2017), pp 35–36; Audit Commission, *Self-directed Support: 2017 Progress Report* (2017), para 50; Health and Social Care Alliance Scotland, *My Support My Choice: People's Experiences of Self-directed Support and Social Care in Scotland* (National Report) (October 2020), pp 43–46.

In the case of services provided under the Chronically Sick and Disabled Persons Act 1970 the assessment can be triggered by a request for an assessment made by a person with a disability or someone who provides a substantial amount of care to them on a regular basis.[51] The assessment in this case will be limited to assessing the needs of the person with a disability and whether these needs call for the provision of services from a specific menu set out in section 2 of the 1970 Act. [52] These services are:

(a) provision of practical assistance in the home;
(b) provision of, or assistance in obtaining, wireless, television, library or similar recreational facilities;
(c) provision of lectures, games, outings or other recreational facilities outside the home or assistance in taking advantage of available educational facilities;
(d) provision of facilities for, or assistance in, travelling to and from home for the purpose of participating in any services provided under arrangements made by the authority under section 12 of the 1968 Act or, with the approval of the authority, in any other services which are similar to services which could be provided under such arrangements;
(e) provision of assistance in arranging for the carrying out of any works of adaptation to the home or the provision of any additional facilities designed to secure greater safety, comfort or convenience;
(f) facilitating the taking of holidays;
(g) provision of meals;
(h) provision of, or assistance in obtaining, a telephone and any special equipment necessary to enable use of a telephone.

Once the duty to carry out an assessment has been triggered, the local authority cannot refuse to carry out the assessment because it does not have the resources to do so, or because it currently does not provide the sort of services which might be identified as being necessary for the person being assessed.[53]

Any assessment must be carried out in accordance with guidance (and the principles set out in the 2013 Act, see Table 6.1 below) and must be carried out by, or under the final control of, the local authority. It

51 Disabled Persons (Services, Consultation and Representation) Act 1986, s 4.

52 Chronically Sick and Disabled Persons Act 1970, s 2 Note: Section 2 of the Act is partially repealed with amendments pending.

53 *R v Bristol City Council ex p Penfold* (1997–98) 1 CCLR 315; *R v Royal County of Berkshire ex p P* (1997) 33 BMLR 71.

is not possible to rely purely on a self-assessment carried out by the (prospective) supported person.[54]

Table 6.1

The principle	What it means in practice
Participation – a statutory principle and a key aspect of independent living[55]	The supported person should be provided with the help that they need to participate in, and be part of, the life of their community and wider society. Underpinned by section 2 of the 2013 Act.
Dignity – a statutory principle and a key aspect of independent living [56]	The professional should facilitate the supported person's right to dignity. Underpinned by section 2 of the 2013 Act.
Involvement – a statutory principle [57]	The professional should involve the supported person in a genuine and active way in deciding their outcomes and in planning and delivering their support. Underpinned by section 1 of the 2013 Act. Communities should be assisted to play an active role in the commissioning of services.
Informed choice – a statutory principle[58]	The supported person should receive the assistance they need to help them to make an informed choice. Underpinned by section 1 of the 2013 Act.
Collaboration – a statutory principle[59]	The professional and the supported person should work together in the completion of the assessment, the support plan and in the provision of support. Underpinned by section 1 of the 2013 Act.

54 *R (B) v Cornwall County Council* [2009] EWHC 491 (Admin), noting that: 'the authority cannot avoid its obligation to assess needs etc by failing to make an appropriate assessment themselves, in favour of simply requiring the service user himself to provide evidence of his needs' (para [69]). See also Law Commission, Adult Social Care – a Consultation Paper (Law Com 192, 2010), paras 4.38–4.40}. This does not prevent a self-assessment contributing to and forming part of the assessment carried out by the local authority.

55 2013 Act, s 2(b).

56 2013 Act, s 2(a).

57 2013 Act, s 1(2) and s 1(3)(a).

58 2013 Act, s 1(3)(b).

59 2013 Act, s 1(4).

The principle	What it means in practice
Responsibility[60]	The supported person should be able to take as much control over their support as they wish. In return, the supported person should exercise that choice and control in a responsible way.
Risk enablement	The supported person should be assisted to feel safe and secure in all aspects of life, to enjoy safety but not to be over-protected and, in so far as possible, to be free from exploitation and abuse.
Innovation	The professional and the supported person should develop creative solutions to meet the outcomes identified in the support plan.

(Adapted from Scottish Government, *Statutory Guidance to Accompany the Social Care (Self-directed Support) (Scotland) Act 2013* (2014), Table 1.)

The assessment process can involve two separate assessments: an assessment of the (potential) supported person; and an assessment of their carer.

(1) Assessment of the (potential) supported person

6.6 An assessment of the need for services under the Chronically Sick and Disabled Persons Act 1970 will need to consider whether the person being assessed falls within the definition of 'chronically sick and disabled' and whether they have any needs. In social care assessments the local authority can request information from the health board. The authority may also request information from a housing authority outside the authority undertaking the assessment. This request will enquire about what services the housing authority might provide for the supported person.[61] Where the person being assessed appears to the local authority to be disabled then, as part of the community care assessment, it must

60 Scottish Government, *Social Care – Self-directed Support: Framework of Standards* (May 2024), p 17: 'Systems of accountability are designed to promote responsibility, to protect people using services and form the basis of trusted relationships.'

61 This is one of a number of instances where legislation passed before the 2013 Act seems out of step with the ethos of the Act. The emphasis of personalisation and the Act is on outcomes for the individual and supporting these outcomes and needs rather than finding existing services into which they can be slotted (though this ethos may not always be respected, Dalrymple, J et al, *Self-Directed Support: Your Choice, Your Right* (2017)).

also assess need for services under the Chronically Sick and Disabled Persons Act 1970 and inform the person that it is doing so, and of their rights under the act.[62]

Specific guidance on the conduct of this assessment is relatively limited. The requirement for participation and collaboration was discussed above, and the final assessment should show evidence of collaboration in its production.[63] The nature and extent of the assessment may vary between different cases, being proportionate to the needs, circumstances and risks presented in an individual case.[64] Assessment may be very straightforward where needs and risks can be easily identified and support provided, or, conversely, may involve complex needs and require the involvement of a range of practitioners. To avoid multiple assessments and duplication of planning there should where possible be one process of assessment and one plan for an individual.[65] The potentially supported person must be given an opportunity to discuss the assessment outwith the presence of any carer. Guidance emphasises that the assessment must be outcomes-based,[66] that is, looking at the desired outcomes for the person being assessed. The focus should be on the strengths and capacities of the person rather than on deficits.[67] The assessment must nonetheless also consider the needs of the person being assessed. This is because, as the statutory guidance points out:[68]

> The initial purpose of the assessment is to identify the person's needs with a view to determining how the person can best be supported, and whether the authority has an obligation to meet those needs.

Local authority resources are a key factor in assessing and meeting the needs of an individual and the case law on this is not definitive. In one case it almost seemed to be suggested that if the local authority had no resources then there could be no needs, although recognising that there would be some cases of need which were so extreme that they could not be denied.[69] It is likely that this only applies to cases in which

62 1968 Act, s 12A(4).

63 Scottish Government, Self-directed Support: Practitioner Guidance (2014), p 16.

64 Scottish Government, Self-directed Support: Practitioner Guidance, p 16.

65 Scottish Government, Self-directed Support: Practitioner Guidance, p 22.

66 Suggesting use of the 'Talking Points' approach, see Cook, A and Miller, E, *Talking Points Personal Outcomes Approach: A Practical Guide* for Organisations (2012).

67 Scottish Government, *Social Care – Self-directed Support: Framework of Standards* (May 2024) pp 13–14.

68 *Social Care – Self-directed Support: Framework of Standards*, p 31.

69 *R v Gloucestershire County Council, ex parte Barry* [1997] AC 584, though see the comments on this decision in *McDonald v Royal Borough of Kensington and Chelsea* [2011] UKSC 33 at [72]–[74] and *KM v Cambridgeshire County Council* [2012] UKSC 23 at [45]–[48].

an assessment of need for services provided under section 2 of the Chronically Sick and Disabled Persons Act 1970 is being undertaken.[70] In addition, there is clear Scottish authority that resources are not relevant in assessing need.[71]

The final assessment document has been described as 'operational and inevitably judgmental', and it has been said that: 'It is an assessment prepared by a social worker for his or her employers. It is not a final determination of a legal dispute by a lawyer which may be subjected to over-zealous textual analysis.'[72] From the same case came this further comment on assessments, 'Courts must be wary, in my view, of expecting so much of hard pressed social workers that we risk taking them away, unnecessarily, from their front line duties'.[73] It is clear that a minimum requirement is that any assessment should set out the basis for the conclusions reached and show how the views of the carer and the person being assessed were taken into account.[74] It should also take into account all relevant information[75] and, if relevant, give appropriate weight to expert opinion. Such expert opinion might concern, for example, the nature and seriousness of the illness of the person being assessed[76] and, where necessary, human rights issues. Such issues may arise, for example, where proposed action involves moving the person being assessed from their established residence.[77]

(2) Assessment of a carer

6.7 From 1 April 2018, assessment of, and provision of support to, carers is governed by the Carers (Scotland) Act 2016 (the 2016 Act).[78] The 2016 Act introduced a number of innovations. Carers are no longer

70 See some of the comments in *R v Gloucestershire County Council, ex parte Barry* [1997] AC 584 and *R v East Sussex, ex parte Tandy* [1998] AC 714.

71 *MacGregor v South Lanarkshire Council* 2001 SC 502.

72 Quotations from *R (Ireneschild) v Lambeth London Borough Council* [2007] EWCA 234 at [71].

73 *R (Ireneschild) v Lambeth London Borough Council* [2007] EWCA 234 at [57]. The views expressed in *Ireneschild* have been approved of in several later decisions, eg, *PQ v Glasgow City Council* [2016] CSOH 137; [2018] CSIH 5.

74 *R (on the application of JF) v London Borough of Merton* [2017] EWHC 1519 (Admin).

75 *R (on the application of Goldsmith) v London Borough of Wandsworth* [2004] EWCA Civ 1170.

76 *R (on the application of Clarke) v Sutton London Borough Council* [2015] EWHC 1081 (Admin).

77 *R (on the application of Goldsmith) v London Borough of Wandsworth* [2004] EWCA Civ 1170.

78 Though, of course, a carer may also be eligible for a community care assessment in their own right or, if a child, an assessment under the Children (Scotland) Act 1995.

required to provide a substantial amount of care on a regular basis to qualify for assessment or, potentially, support; there is a right to receive support if a carer reaches a threshold set by eligibility criteria, these criteria to be determined locally.[79] A distinction is drawn in the Act between adult carers and young carers, with young carers being those who are aged under 18 or who are aged over 18 and still at school.[80] The 2016 Act also introduces an obligation on local authorities to produce a local carers strategy and on Scottish Government to prepare a national Carers' Charter.[81]

Under the 2016 Act a carer is someone who provides or intends to provide care to another person.[82] This is subject to two limitations. It does not include age-appropriate care provided to someone under 18, nor does it include cases where the care is provided either under a contract of employment or as voluntary work.[83]

There is no definition of care in the 2016 Act, nor is there any threshold of care to be reached before its provisions apply. Rather, the Act focuses on the impact on the carer of providing care.[84] Underlying the 2016 Act is the intention, for adult carers, to maximise opportunities and minimise negative impacts and allow the carer to have a life alongside caring.[85] For young carers the intention is to 'help and empower young carers, provide them with confidence and assist the child or young person to recognise their own needs and identify personal outcomes which are important to them'.[86] Guidance also states that adult carers are to be valued as equal partners in the provision of care[87] and that 'young carers are seen as children and young people first and foremost and are protected from undertaking caring responsibilities and tasks which are inappropriate having regard to their age and maturity'.[88]

79 Carers (Scotland) Act 2016, s 2 (2016 Act).
80 2016 Act, s 2.
81 2016 Act, Part 5 (local carer strategies), s 36 (carer's charter)
82 2016 Act, s 1(1).
83 2016 Act, s 1(2). Care provided under a contract of employment or through voluntary work is excluded only to the extent that the care is provided in this way, see Scottish Government, *Carers (Scotland) Act 2016 Statutory Guidance*, paras 1.1.13–1.1.14. In this context, 'contract' does not include an agreement between a local authority and a kinship carer, Carers (Scotland) Act 2016 (Agreements of a Specified Kind) Regulations 2017, SSI 2017/257, reg 2.
84 Scottish Government, *Carers (Scotland) Act 2016 Statutory Guidance* (updated July 2021), paras 1.1.36–1.1.37 *Statutory Guidance* (2021).
85 *Statutory Guidance* (2021), para 2.1.47.
86 *Statutory Guidance* (2021), para 2.2.3.
87 *Statutory Guidance* (2021), p 13.
88 *Statutory Guidance* (2021), para 2.2.2.

The obligation to assess and to prepare a plan[89] can arise either where the local authority identifies an individual as a carer and the carer accepts an offer to prepare a plan,[90] or where the carer requests that a plan be prepared.[91] The obligation to prepare and maintain a plan applies regardless of the eligibility of the carer for specific support (see below).[92] Responsibility for preparing an adult carer support plan lies with the local authority in which the cared-for person lives and for a young carer responsibility lies with the local authority in which the young person lives.[93] There is no timescale specified for completion of the plan, except in cases where the cared-for person is terminally ill,[94] though the local carer strategy should contain a statement about timescales. Plans should be outcome-based, identifying the carer's personal outcomes and needs for support.[95] These outcomes are to be identified in conversation with the carer and reviewed when the plan is reviewed.[96]

There are statutory requirements about the content of the plan and the assessment will, in part, be directed to ensuring that these requirements are met. Amongst other things, plans must include information about the following:[97]

(a) the carer's personal circumstances, including the nature and extent of the care to be provided, and the impact of this on the carer's well-being and day-to-day life;[98]
(b) the carer's willingness and ability to provide care (in some cases the carer may be willing, but unable in practice, to provide care);[99]
(c) arrangements in place for emergency care (if any);
(d) arrangements for future care;

89 Two types of assessment and planning are contemplated by the Act: an adult carer support plan; and a young carer statement. Except where a distinction needs to be made, the word 'plan' will be used to indicate both.

90 2016 Act ss 6(2), (3)(a) and 12(2), (3)(a).

91 2016 Act, ss 6(4) and 12(4).

92 *Statutory Guidance* (2021), para 3.2.16.

93 2016 Act, s 19. There are two exceptions to this. Where the young person is a pre-school child the responsibility will lie with the health board (s 19(1)(a)), and there are other special cases, for example where a young person has been placed by a local authority outside the area where they would normally live (s 20).

94 2016 Act, ss 7 and 13. The expectation is that plans will be produced within a reasonable timescale, taking account of the urgency of need for support and any fluctuation in this need (2016 Act Guidance, paras 2.1.84 and 2.2.116). Regulations setting time limits when the cared-for person is terminally ill have not yet been made.

95 2016 Act, ss 8 and 14. Personal outcomes are defined as including outcomes which, if achieved, would enable carers to continue to provide care (2016 Act, s 4).

96 Carers (Scotland) Act 2016 (Adult Carers and Young Carers: Identification of Outcomes and Needs for Support) Regulations 2018, SSI 2018/109.

97 2016 Act, ss 9 and 15.

98 2016 Act, ss 9(1)(a)(i) and (ii) and 15(1)(a)(i) and (ii).

99 *Statutory Guidance* (2021), para 2.1.32.

(e) identification of personal outcomes, including the carer's personal outcomes; and
(f) need for support, including, if the adult/young carer has identified needs, those needs, and noting if no needs for support are identified.[100]

In the case of a young carer statement the authority will also have to consider whether the nature and extent of the care being provided by a young carer is appropriate.[101] Consideration will also need to be given to other local authority duties towards children and to the child's well-being.[102]

Once the plan has been prepared, a decision must be made as to whether the local authority has a duty to provide support to the carer. A duty to provide support will arise where the needs of the carer:[103]

- cannot be met by services or assistance provided for the cared-for person (aside from the provision of respite care to the cared-for person);
- cannot be met by services provided generally to all people (or to all carers) living in the local authority area; and
- are eligible needs – needs will be eligible where they satisfy the two previous criteria and the carer meets the local eligibility criteria.[104]

If the carer does have eligible needs the local authority must, in particular, consider whether the support should take the form of a break from caring.[105] The authority which is obliged to consider the need for support and to provide the support will, in all cases, be the authority for the area where the cared-for person lives.[106] This means that the duty to provide support for a young carer may fall on a local authority which is not the one which had responsibility for carrying out the assessment. Where it is decided that the carer does not have eligible needs the

100 2016 Act, s 9(1)(f)(i) and (ii).
101 2016 Act, s 15(1)(c); *Statutory Guidance* (2021), para 2.2.53.
102 See **chapter 4**. The requirement to consider well-being is in the 2016 Act, s 15(3).
103 2016 Act, s 24.
104 2016 Act, ss 21 and 22 impose a duty on local authorities to set, publish and revise eligibility criteria, though there is also power for the Scottish Ministers to specify national eligibility criteria, s 23. Guidance on setting local eligibility criteria is set out in Scottish Government, *Carers (Scotland) Act 2016 – Statutory Guidance: Local Eligibility Criteria* (2017). The eligibility framework uses different indicators from that used for community care services, see Annex A(c) of the guidance referred to here and **6.9** below.
105 2016 Act, s 25. See also *Statutory Guidance: Local Eligibility Criteria* (2017), para 46.
106 2016 Act, s 24(6).

local authority still has the power provide support over and above any universal services to meet the carer's identified needs.[107] Any support provided cannot be charged for.[108]

Plans should contain information about when they will be reviewed. They must be reviewed if:

(a) the cared-for person moves to a different local authority;
(b) into residential care; or
(c) where there is any change in circumstances which has a material impact on the care provided.[109]

Even where there is no formal carer's assessment, the local authority will have to make some sort of assessment of certain carers in deciding whether to provide support to a cared-for person. This is because, where no carer's assessment takes place, the authority must have regard to the ability of the carer to continue to provide care in taking decisions about adult care support.[110] In this case the definition of 'carer' is limited to someone who provides a substantial amount of care on a regular basis.[111]

PROVISION OF SUPPORT

(1) Deciding on eligibility of the (potential) supported person

6.8 Once the assessment has been completed, a decision must be made about provision of support, though the legislation refers to a decision about the provision of services. The precise statutory wording which governs this process depends on the services being provided. In the case of services provided under the Chronically Sick and Disabled Persons Act 1970, the statute requires a decision to be taken as to whether the needs of the person assessed call for the provision of any of the services listed in section 2.[112] In reaching this decision, account

107 2016 Act, s 24(4)(b).
108 Carers (Waiving of Charges for Support) (Scotland) Regulations 2014, SSI 2014/65, reg 2.
109 Carers (Scotland) Act 2016 (Review of Adult Carer Support Plan and Young Carer Statement) (Scotland) Regulations 2018, SSI 2018/33, reg 2.
110 Disabled Persons (Services, Consultation and Representation) Act 1986, s 8.
111 Disabled Persons (Services, Consultation and Representation) Act 1986, s 8(1)(a)
112 Chronically Sick and Disabled Persons Act 1970, s 2.

will need to be taken of any assessment made of a carer[113] or, if no such assessment has been carried out, of the ability of the carer to continue to provide care.

Following the completion of a community care assessment a decision will be made as to whether the needs of the person require the provision of support.[114] In reaching any decision the assessment must be taken into account, and consideration given to:

(a) the views of the supported person;

(b) the outcome of any consultation with a medical practitioner if it is likely that the supported person will require nursing care;[115] and

(c) care provided by a carer as set out in an adult carer support plan or a young carer statement,[116] and even if no assessment of the carer has been carried out their ability to continue to provide care still has to be considered.[117]

The decision will be informed by the eligibility criteria used by the local authority, which are considered more fully below.

(2) Resources and eligibility criteria

6.9 In recent years there have been a number of challenges against local authority decisions on resources for the provision of social care.[118] The issue of local authority budgets and resources can be taken into account in taking the decision as to provision of support. Where the need is acute, it may be unreasonable for the local authority to refuse provision. The question of limited resources is recognised through the use of eligibility criteria; these criteria are applied during the decision-making process for claims for access to support.[119] The Scottish Government Guidance notes that, in setting eligibility criteria, local authorities:

> will have regard to a range of factors including the overall level of resources available to meet need, the cost of service provision and

113 Though this does not appear to be a statutory requirement where only services under s 2 of the 1970 Act are being considered, any failure to do this, would be likely to lead to successful challenge to the decision of the local authority. The statutory position is explained in detail in Note 4 and the associated text in para 203 of the *Stair Memorial Encyclopaedia* title 'Social Work'.

114 1968 Act, s 12A(1).

115 1968 Act, s 12A(2).

116 1968 Act, s 12A(1)(b), (1A). See also **6.7** above.

117 Disabled Persons (Services, Consultation and Representation) Act 1986, s 8.

118 See, eg, *Redcroft Care Homes Ltd v Edinburgh City Council* 2025 S.C. 103.

119 See the criteria set out in *Guidance* (2009).

> ensuring equity in their service decisions. Eligibility criteria are a method for deploying limited resources in a way that ensures that those resources are targeted to those in greatest need, while also recognising the types of low-level intervention that can be made to halt the deterioration of people in less urgent need of services.[120]

The guidance sets out four levels of risk which define the bands of a national eligibility framework.

1. *Critical risk*[121] meaning there are major risks to an individual's independent living or health and well-being likely to call for the immediate* or imminent* provision of social care services (*high priority) Immediate is defined in the Guidance as required now or in 1–2 weeks. Imminent is defined as being required within six weeks.

2. *Substantial risk,*[122] indicates there are significant risks to an individual's independent living or health and well-being likely to call for the immediate* or imminent* provision of social care services* (high priority).

3. *Moderate risk,*[123] indicates there are some risks to an individual's independence or health and well being. These risks may require the provision of some social care services, managed on an ongoing basis, or they may be manageable over the foreseeable future without service being provided, subject to periodic review. 'Forseeable future' is defined in the Guidance as within the next six months.

4. *Low risk.*[124] Indicates there are some quality-of-life issues, but a low risk to a person's independence, health and well being with a very limited requirement for the provision of social care services. There may be some need for alternative support or advice and appropriate arrangements for review over the foreseeable future or longer term. Longer term is defined in the Guidance as within the next 12 months or subsequently.

Although this framework was originally described in the context of older supported persons, it has subsequently been indicated that it should be applied to all community care supported persons.[125] In most cases, eligibility for support will be restricted to those who come within

120 *Guidance* (2009), para 7.1.
121 *Guidance* (2009), p 8.
122 *Guidance* (2009), p 8.
123 *Guidance* (2009), p 8.
124 For example, there will be low risk where someone is able to manage most aspects of basic domestic activities. *Guidance* (2009), p 8.
125 Scottish Government, *Self-directed Support: A National Strategy for* Scotland (2010), para 2.3.

the critical and substantial risk categories, which means that the fact that someone is not eligible for support does not mean that they do not have needs, and they should be given advice and signposted to other available resources.[126]

In effect, a decision as to whether support should be provided to a supported person may take account of resource availability, either indirectly (through the way in which eligibility criteria are set) or directly.

Once a decision is made that support should be provided, a local authority cannot use lack of available resources as a reason to refuse to provide this.[127] In addition, although there has been no specific discussion of this in a reported Scottish case, there must be some doubt as to the extent to which waiting lists can be used in cases where need for support in the form of a particular service has been identified. This must be the case where waiting times extend beyond a reasonable period of time to make arrangements for provision of the service. Such arrangements will often be made with a provider external to the local authority with whom a contract may have to be agreed for provision of the service.[128] Once a need for support has been identified, resources may be relevant in deciding how the support is provided, and the local authority will have some discretion in making this decision.

Another factor relevant to decisions on the provision of support will be any personal resources available to the supported person. Any resources will be considered in determining whether services are to be paid for, and at what rate, but such resources are not in themselves grounds for refusing to provide support. There is judicial authority to the effect that resources should be completely discounted in the decision as to provision of support.[129] Although this view seems to be inconsistent with the views expressed in England and Wales on provisions intended

126 *Statutory Guidance* (2022), section 6: eligibility, assessment and review, *Statutory Guidance* (2014), para 7.5.

127 See: *R v Gloucestershire County Council, ex parte Barry* [1997] AC 584 (referring particularly to Chronically Sick and Disabled Persons Act 1970, s 2), *MacGregor v South Lanarkshire Council* 2001 SC 502 and *Argyll and Bute Council v Scottish Public Services Ombudsman* [2007] CSOH 168. See also *R (Savva) v Royal Borough of Kensington and Chelsea* [2010] EWCA Civ 1209. See also *Scottish Government, Social Care: Eligibility and Waiting Times* (October 2023).

128 See the comments of Lord Hardie in *MacGregor v South Lanarkshire Council* 2001 SC 502 at 507 and Lord Macphail in *Argyll and Bute Council v Scottish Public Services Ombudsman* [2007] CSOH 168 at [90]. For older people assessed as being at critical or substantial risk and whose assessed needs include personal or nursing care, this is to be delivered within six weeks, in *Guidance* (2009), paras 9.4–9.5.

129 *Robertson v Fife Council* [2002] UKHL 35.

to have the same effect, it is binding in Scotland. In Scotland it has also been held that the fact that needs were already being met by a third party was irrelevant to the local authority decision on whether there is a need for support.[130] There seems to be no reason in principle why, if an individual has considerable means, the authority should not consider whether support could be provided or arranged by another individual or organisation. In practice, however, such an approach would have a potential negative consequence for the supported person. As we will see below, a person is only entitled to free personal and nursing care if this is arranged by the local authority. Should the authority refuse to make such an arrangement because of the supported person's resources, the effect of this would be to debar them from receiving free care. In any event, the resources available to supported persons will be relevant to decisions about charging (see **6.14** and **6.15** below).

(3) Identifying a budget

6.10 An assessment will identify needs and desired outcomes. A decision will then be made that a person is eligible for support, either as a carer or as a supported person. Such support will be designed to address the needs and desired outcomes. Finally, a budget will be developed to show the amount which is available to provide the support. There is no statutory provision directing a particular method for determining a budget; in practice there are different ways of arriving at this budget. A resource allocation system may be used. Such a system works by allocating points depending on the replies to questions designed to assess the levels of need and risk for the person being assessed. These points are then totalled and the total mapped on to a defined monetary equivalent to provide an indicative budget. It is likely that the final amount awarded will differ from any initial allocation.[131] Some authorities use an equivalency method for calculating the budget. This equivalency method is based on fixing cash equivalents for services, and these are then added up according to assessed needs to provide a budget.[132] Whatever method is used, it must be:

130 See *Smart's Guardian v Fife Council* [2015] CSOH 183.

131 For a discussion of these variations, see Series, L and Clements, L, 'Putting the Cart Before the horse: resource allocation systems and community care', (2013) 35 *Journal of Social Welfare and Family Law*, 207. See also the difference between the sum generated by the resource allocation system and the sum actually allocated in *PQ v Glasgow City Council* [2018] CSIH 5 at [25]. On resource allocation systems more generally, see Duffy, S, 'Commentary – what is a resource allocation system?' (2015) 20 *Tizard Learning Disability Review*, 207.

132 Though this method has been criticised, see Dalrymple, J *et al*, *Self-Directed Support: Your Choice, Your Right* (2017), p 5.

- 'allocated in a way that is transparent, fair, equitable and sufficient, across all communities and for all individuals'[133] or 'fair and clear to everyone';[134] and
- sufficient to meet the needs identified as eligible in the assessment[135] or, as set out in the 2013 Act, what the authority considers 'a reasonable estimate of the cost of securing support'.[136] Of the latter it has been said that: 'It is an estimate rather than anything more precise, and while it must be reasonable … that is a concept which affords significant leeway to the … decision-maker'.[137]

These two requirements also emerge from judicial consideration of resource allocation, in this case using a resource allocation system.[138] In *KM v Cambridgeshire County Council*[139] the Supreme Court said that:

- Use of a resource allocation system is acceptable to kick-start the process of costing services and to provide an indicative sum.[140]
- There must be a realistic connection between needs and points, and points and cost.[141]
- The use of the allocation system is only the first step. Once, as suggested above, this has identified a starting point the resources needed must be costed with a reasonable amount of detail so that a judgement can be made about whether the initial sum is too high, too low or about right. The process by which the final budget is arrived at should be explained.[142]

The Statutory Guidance notes that systems and tools are no substitute for the skilled judgement of a professional in collaboration with the person being assessed and that the approach taken to allocation of resources must be 'both fair and transparent'; it goes on to say:[143]

> The authority and the relevant professionals acting on its behalf should ensure that the nature and level of support meets the person's eligible needs. The authority should ensure that professional expertise is brought to bear. The approach to defining the budget should be

133 *Statutory Guidance* (2022), p 55.
134 Scottish Government, *Self Directed Support: My support, my choice: your guide to social care* (2014), p 13.
135 *Statutory Guidance* (2014), para 7.10.
136 2013 Act, s 4(2).
137 *PQ v Glasgow City Council* [2018] CSIH 5 at [31].
138 Though the same principles should apply to any methodology used to fix a budget.
139 [2012] UKSC 2. See also the comments in *PQ v Glasgow City Council* [2018] CSIH 5 at [29]–[30].
140 *KM v Cambridgeshire County Council* [2012] UKSC 23 at [24].
141 *KM v Cambridgeshire County Council* [2012] UKSC 23 at [25].
142 *KM v Cambridgeshire County Council* [2012] UKSC 23 at [28].
143 *Statutory Guidance* (2014), para 7.10.

> robust, rational and transparent. The level of resource identified in the final support plan should be sufficient to meet the needs identified as eligible in the assessment.[144]

A final point on available resources is that the amount available for each option may differ.[145]

(4) Choice of options

6.11 Each person to whom support is to be provided, which includes carers, must normally be given the choice of which one of four options they wish to select for the delivery and management of their support. To assist them in making this choice, an explanation must be provided of the nature and effect of these four options. In addition, information about people or organisations who can provide further information and assistance in relation to the options should be provided, including 'where the authority considers it appropriate to do so, information about independent advocacy services'.[146]

Further assistance is to be provided where either:[147]

- the person has a mental disorder and would benefit from further assistance; or
- the person has difficulties in communicating because of a physical disability and would benefit from receiving assistance in relation to communicating decisions about relevant matters.[148]

In these cases, where there is no guardian, attorney or intervention order, the authority must take reasonable steps to enable the making of a choice and to identify someone who can assist the person and, with the agreement of the person, involve them in the decision-making process. There will be cases where a person is unable to make a decision, and the guidance is vague[149] about processes for decision-making where an adult lacks capacity; we will consider this more fully in **6.13** below.

144 This is reflected in the 2013 Act which talks about payment of the 'relevant amount' for services. 'Relevant amount' is defined as a reasonable estimate of the cost of securing provision of support for the supported person (s 4(2)).

145 Scottish Government, *Self-directed Support: Practitioner Guidance* (2014), p 20 refers to 'how much money is available under each of the four options'.

146 2013 Act, s 9(2)(d).

147 2013 Act, s 6.

148 2013 Act, s 6(2)(b).

149 It is also, in one case, inaccurate, suggesting that where an adult may lose capacity the family should be made aware 'of the option to apply for power of attorney'. *Statutory Guidance* (2022) section 4, pp 28–32.

Although it will normally be the case that an offer of all four options has to be made, there are some cases, discussed below, where the offer of Option 1 (a direct payment) cannot be made or does not have to be made. Equally, there may be other cases where there is no requirement to offer the choice of options at all. One example is crisis support, which it may not be possible to deliver through the four options,[150] though a longer list is offered in the practitioner guidance.[151]

In outline, the four options are:[152]

1. *Option 1.* This involves the making of a direct payment to the person, who will then manage the provision of support to meet their needs and outcomes. This option cannot be offered to pay for long-term residential care.[153] Long-term residential care is residential care for a period in excess of four consecutive weeks in any 12-month period. This means that direct payments can still be offered where short periods of residential care will be needed to meet a person's needs and outcomes. In addition, the local authority is not required to offer this option where either:[154]
   (a) a direct payment has previously been terminated in certain circumstances;[155] or
   (b) making the direct payment is likely to put the safety of the recipient at risk, an example of this given in the guidance is where the recipient is an adult at risk,[156] there is a protection order[157] in place and there are specific concerns about the safety of the recipient if a direct payment is made.[158]

150 *Statutory Guidance* (2014), para 8.22.

151 *Statutory Guidance* (2022), pp 16–26.

152 2013 Act, s 4. The first set of statistics after the 2013 Act came into effect showed the distribution of these as: Option 1 – 11%; Option 2 – 9%; Option 3 – 75%; and Option 4 – 5%. There was considerable variation between different local authorities, Scottish Government, *Self-directed Support, Scotland, 2015–16* (2017). See Audit Commission, *Self-directed Support: 2017 Progress Report* (2017) also noting significant differences between authorities both in the options chosen and in what was involved in Option 2 (paras 67–70).

153 Except in two areas (East Renfrewshire and Moray) where pilot projects involving direct payments for long-term residential care were run, concluding in late 2017, Self-directed Support (Direct Payments) (Scotland) Regulations 2014, SSI 2014/25, reg 12.

154 Self-directed Support (Direct Payments) (Scotland) Regulations 2014, reg 11.

155 For example, because a previous direct payment has been used for a purpose not related to the person's needs or outcomes or was impermissibly used to employ a family member.

156 *Statutory Guidance* (2022), p 23.

157 See **chapter 9**.

158 *Statutory Guidance* (2022), p 23.

2. *Option 2.* In this option the choice of support, who is to provide it and how it is to be provided is made by the person being supported, and the local authority then has the responsibility for putting these choices into effect and managing the support.[159]
3. *Option 3.* The local authority both chooses the support and arranges and manages its provision. This is the default option where no choice is made by the supported person.[160]
4. *Option 4.* This involves a combination of the previous three options, so where a number of different types of support are being provided the supported person may choose to manage each in a different way.[161]

The direct payments approach is designed to provide maximum flexibility for the person being supported and the payment can be spent in *any* way[162] which is related to the outcomes set out in the person's support plan. The use of the money must be in line with the person's assessment and support plan. It must contribute to meeting the eligible needs which were the basis for its provision and the spending must otherwise be lawful.[163] Before the decision is made to select this option, the responsibilities which come with a direct payment must be explained, as must sources of support. For example, in cases where a direct payment is used to employ a personal assistant there are support organisations which will deal with the administrative requirements which fall on an employer.[164] Where a direct payment is chosen, the responsibilities of both parties – local authorities and supported person – should be set out in a Supported Person Agreement.

Direct payments must be monitored by the local authority, though this monitoring should be proportionate and will cover both the financial management of the payment and welfare monitoring, to ensure that the money is being used to meet the person's assessed needs and outcomes.[165]

As already suggested, a direct payment can be used to employ a personal assistant, though there are restrictions on employing family members

159 *Statutory Guidance* (2022), p 20.

160 *Statutory Guidance* (2022), p 21.

161 *Statutory Guidance* (2022), p 21.

162 Although local authorities may seek to limit how direct payments are spent, the only legal restrictions are those set out here.

163 *Statutory Guidance* (2022), pp 17–19.

164 *Statutory Guidance* (2022), p 19. See also: Self-Directed Support Scotland website: www.sdsscotland.org.uk/ (accessed 16 April 2025).

165 *Statutory Guidance* (2022), pp 70–71.

in this role.[166] Before a family member can be employed, the family member, the supported person and the local authority must all agree. The family member must be capable of providing the support, and one of a number of further factors must apply.[167] These further actions include:

(i) there being a limited choice of providers;

(ii) other providers not being available at the time that the support is required:

(iii) that either the intimate nature of the support or religious or cultural beliefs of the supported person make provision by a family member preferable;

(iv) and that there are other factors which, in the opinion of the local authority, make provision by a family member appropriate.[168]

Even if employing a family member might otherwise be permitted, it cannot be done:[169]

- if the relevant family member has the power to make decisions about the support to be provided through the direct payment by virtue of being the supported person's guardian or attorney. This exclusion will only apply once the attorney's powers have been triggered.[170] If this were not the case, a close family member could never be paid to provide support because of the existence of a document appointing them as attorney, even though they would only actually have any legal power to make decisions if the supported person lost capacity, and this might never happen; or
- if the local authority determines that either the family member or the supported person is under undue pressure to agree to the arrangement.[171]

Once a direct payment has been put in place, it can be withdrawn if:

- the supported person would prefer to revert to arranged services or an arrangement under Option 2 or Option 3 in the 2013 Act (individual service funds or similar arrangements);
- The supported person is no longer able to manage their direct payment with the available support;

166 The definition of 'family member' includes not only spouses and civil partners (or those living as if they were a spouse or civil partner), parents, children, brothers and sisters, but also more distant relatives such as cousins and nieces/nephews. It also includes the spouse or civil partner of anyone on the list and anyone living with them as if a spouse or civil partner, Self-directed Support (Direct Payments) (Scotland) Regulations 2014, reg 8(4).

167 Self-directed Support (Direct Payments) (Scotland) Regulations 2014, reg 8(2).

168 Self-directed Support (Direct Payments) (Scotland) Regulations 2014, reg 8(3), see also *Statutory Guidance* (2022), pp 65–66.

169 Self-directed Support (Direct Payments) (Scotland) Regulations 2014, reg 9(1).

170 See **7.6**.

171 Self-directed Support (Direct Payments) (Scotland) Regulations 2014, reg 9(1)(a).

- the local authority is not satisfied that the person's needs are being met; or
- the local authority has concerns over misspent funds.[172]

Notice will be given before termination, and account must be taken of any existing contractual arrangements and the time required to put in place alternative arrangements. There is no requirement for any particular period of notice.[173] The period of notice may be short and the local authority may take over management of the support in the meantime.[174]

For Option 2, the guidance suggests that there should be no restrictions on flexibility[175] and creativity in designing packages. The term 'service' should be interpreted broadly to cover anything which makes a positive difference to the supported person's needs and is delivered under the broad concept of social welfare.[176] The authority should use Option 2 to widen the flexibility offered to supported persons to the maximum possible extent. It should make use of Option 2 to provide a route to greater freedom of choice and control for those who want to take greater control over their day-to-day support but prefer not to choose the direct payment option.[177]

The authority, through its approach to commissioning and procurement of services, should seek to ensure that the services provided are as flexible as possible, are appropriately personalised and are ready to adapt to the wishes of the individuals who use them.[178]

If the agreed support includes the provision of long-term residential accommodation, the supported person has some choice of accommodation (directly or indirectly). This is subject to the person's preferred accommodation being suitable and available. The person providing the accommodation must be prepared to provide it on the local authority's normal terms and conditions. The accommodation should cost no more than the authority would normally be expected to pay for accommodation for someone with the supported person's

172 2013 Act, s 6(1); see also *Statutory Guidance* (2022), pp 24–25.
173 2013 Act, s 6(3).
174 *Statutory Guidance* (2022), p 25. Note that the local authority cannot take over a contract with a provider not registered with the Care Inspectorate.
175 Though these do seem to exist in practice, see Audit Commission, *Self-directed Support: 2017 progress report* (2017), paras 67–70 and Exhibit 7.
176 *Statutory Guidance* (2022), p 20.
177 *Statutory Guidance* (2022), p 20.
178 *Statutory Guidance* (2022), p 21.

needs.[179] If the preferred accommodation is not currently available, it is possible to agree that an interim placement will be made pending transfer to the preferred accommodation, though if the supported person does not agree to this, or to be provided with any other accommodation, the local authority cannot provide accommodation.[180]

(5) Development of a support plan

6.12 If it is decided that the person assessed is eligible for support, then a support plan must be developed for them. In developing this, the principles set out in **6.4** should be followed. The focus will be on identifying and agreeing outcomes for the person who is to be supported and putting together a plan to achieve these.[181] Carers should be fully involved in the development of the plan and, once implemented, the plan must be reviewed at least once every 12 months.[182] Changes to support can only take place following a reassessment.[183]

(6) Adults with incapacity[184]

6.13 Where an adult has, in legal terms, limited capacity to take decisions, this may affect their ability to take a decision about the options for support. It may affect their ability to take a decision about which support to accept and, where this is assessed as being required to meet their needs, to move to new accommodation. Capacity can be viewed as a sliding scale, and it will be necessary to establish clearly what level of understanding, and about which matters, the adult has. Of particular importance is an assessment of the ability of the adult to

179 Social Work (Scotland) Act 1968 (Choice of Accommodation) Directions 1993, paras 2–4. See generally the Directions and the accompanying circular, Scottish Office Circular SWSG5/93.

180 There is additional provision relating to choice of accommodation on discharge from hospital, see Scottish Government Circular CEL 32 (2013) *Guidance on choosing a care home on discharge from hospital.* Scottish Government Circular CEL32/2013. Available at: www.publications.scot.nhs.uk/files/cel2013-32.pdf (Accessed 16 April 2025).

181 The contents of an effective support plan are set out in Scottish Government, *Self-Directed Support: Practitioner Guidance* (2014), p 23.

182 *Statutory Guidance* (2022), Section 6, p 53.

183 *R (on the application of McDonald) v Royal Borough of Kensington and Chelsea* [2010] EWCA Civ 1109.

184 See also Scottish Government, *Adults with Incapacity (Scotland) Act 2000: Code of Practice for Local Authorities Exercising Functions under the 2000 Act* (2008), ch 4 and Scottish Government Circular CEL 32 (2013) Guidance on choosing a care home on discharge from hospital, pp 8–9.

make decisions. The principles set out in section 1 of the Adults with Incapacity (Scotland) Act 2000 are also relevant:

(a) no intervention in the affairs of the adult should take place unless the person responsible for authorising or effecting the intervention is satisfied that it will benefit the adult and that the benefit cannot reasonably be achieved without the intervention;[185]

(b) any intervention shall be the least restrictive option in relation to the freedom of the adult, consistent with the purpose of the intervention;[186] and

(c) the present and past wishes and feelings of the adult so far as they can be ascertained must be taken into account.[187]

Issues of involvement in assessment and consent to provision of support arise where the supported person does not have capacity to select an option or to agree to the support plan (or to elements of this). The position of an adult who is placed in residential accommodation where issues of restriction of liberty may arise is considered in **7.20–7.23**, and the concern here is with other types of service.

The requirement to provide assistance to adults with incapacity has already been discussed in **6.4** above. Where there is no one with the power to select between the options, and the adult does not have capacity to make a choice, the choice will default to Option 3.[188]

Where there is no one who can consent on behalf of the adult to the intended service provision under Option 3 (and there is no pending application for guardianship or an intervention order)[189] the local authority is empowered by section 13ZA of the Social Work (Scotland) Act 1968 to take 'any steps which they consider would help the adult to benefit' from the services to be provided under the support plan.[190] In doing this, the authority is bound by the principles set out in the Adults with Incapacity (Scotland) Act 2000 (see above). Use of the section 13ZA power is only appropriate where the adult is incapable of consenting to the services which it is intended should be provided or to the taking of a particular step, for example moving to residential care. In other words, it cannot be used to force services or choices on an adult who has capacity to agree to the particular service being provided or step being taken.

185 Adults with Incapacity (Scotland) Act 2000, s 1(2).
186 Adults with Incapacity (Scotland) Act 2000, s 1(3).
187 Adults with Incapacity (Scotland) Act 2000, s 1(4).
188 2013 Act, s 5(5).
189 See **7.8** and **7.11**.
190 1968 Act, s 13ZA(1)(b)

The process[191] for providing services under section 13ZA starts with a multidisciplinary review. The review should take into account the views of the adult, their relatives and carer(s), the GP, any independent advocate the adult may have and any attorney or guardian whose powers do not extend to taking a decision on the provision of services to the adult. A mental health officer's input may also be sought.[192] This review process will assess whether the adult has capacity in respect of the specific issue of consent to the services which the authority is to provide (or arrange provision of) in terms of the care plan. If it is concluded that capacity is lacking then consideration will need to be given as to whether an intervention under the Adults with Incapacity (Scotland) Act 2000 is required or whether the services can be provided without this.[193] The relevant guidance suggests that intervention under the 1968 Act might be appropriate if all concerned agree with (or at least, in the case of the adult, do not disagree with) the support plan. Intervention under the 2000 Act might be appropriate where the adult is opposed to the care plan or the carer or other relatives disagree with it.[194]

A full record should be kept of this decision-making process. If a decision is made that services are to be provided using the powers conferred under the 1968 Act, or that an order should be sought under the 2000 Act, a letter setting out this decision and the reasons for it should be sent to the adult, their primary carer and relevant professionals. This letter should set out the outcome of the decision-making process, explain the reasons for reaching the decision and set out the arrangements for review of the decision.[195]

191 This is set out in Scottish Executive: Guidance for Local Authorities (March 2007): Provision of Community Care Services to Adults with Incapacity, Circular CCD5/2007, this also forms Annex 1 to Scottish Government, *Adults with Incapacity (Scotland) Act 2000: Code of Practice for Local Authorities Exercising Functions under the 2000 Act* (2008) (Code of Practice 2008).

192 Code of Practice (2008), paras 4.7–4.8.

193 1968 Act, s 13ZA(1)(b): Code of Practice 2008, para 4.8.

194 Scottish Executive: *Guidance for Local Authorities* (March 2007): Provision of community care services to adults with incapacity, Circular CCD5/2007, paras 23–24. This guidance also forms Annex 1 to Code of Practice 2008.

195 Code of Practice 2008, para 4.1.4

CHARGING FOR SUPPORT

(1) The basis of charging for services

6.14 The language of charging does not sit logically with cases where the local authority is not providing services and it has been suggested that:[196]

> The underlying structure of the traditional system of charging is linked to services. However, in a personalised or self-directed system of support, the focus shifts to enabling people to control and adjust their support at the point of delivery in order to meet their needs and achieve their outcomes. As such, the connection between 'the service' and 'the charge' becomes less well defined – and in some cases will disappear altogether. In view of this, a conceptual shift will have to be made in respect of how councils charge for services.

In the context of charging for non-residential care, the old 'charge' has been referred to as a 'care and support charge' but, in some contexts, it may be referred to as a contribution.[197] Below, the reference will be to charging.

One final point is that, once a budget has been identified for self-directed support and this is to be provided by Option 1, a financial assessment of the supported person may indicate that they have to make a contribution to their support.[198] Where this is the case the authority may choose to make the payment either without deducting the contribution or after deduction of the contribution.[199]

With the exception of free personal and nursing care, local authorities are permitted to charge for social (community) care services,[200] and are obliged to recover the costs of providing accommodation.[201] The way in which liability to pay and the amount to be paid are calculated differ as between provision of accommodation and provision of other services.

Where accommodation is provided, there is a statutory scheme. This requires the authority to recover the actual cost to it of providing the accommodation. Where the adult satisfies the local authority that they

196 COSLA, Charges Applying to Non-residential Social Care Services 2017/18, para 6.4.
197 COSLA, Charges Applying to Non-residential Social Care Services 2017/18, para 6.6.
198 *Statutory Guidance* (2022), pp 17–19.
199 *Statutory Guidance* (2014), para 8.6.
200 1968 Act, s 87.
201 National Assistance Act 1948, s 22(1), applied to Scotland by the 1968 Act, s 87(3).

are unable to pay the amount required then an assessment must be carried out. The basic provisions of the scheme for assessing liability and payment are:[202]

(a) Any house which is occupied, at the date when the adult goes into residential accommodation,[203] by the adult's partner or a relative aged 60 or over or 15 and under will generally be excluded from any calculation.

(b) Where the capital owned by the adult exceeds a certain limit then they must pay the full amount.[204] Adults who hold capital below a certain amount will have this ignored in calculating liability to pay.[205] Where the adult's capital falls in between these sums it is deemed to generate a certain amount of income. This income, together with any other income which the adult has, will be taken into account in determining liability to pay. In some circumstances the local authority can treat the adult as still having capital even when he or she has disposed of it, for example by transferring ownership of their house to a relative.[206] The value of the asset disposed of can only be taken into account where it is reasonable for the local authority to conclude that the disposal took place for the purpose of reducing liability to pay for accommodation. This will involve looking at the whole circumstances surrounding the transfer, and it has been suggested that the person disposing of the asset must be aware of the possibility that they might have to pay for accommodation.[207] If the transfer takes place at a time when the transferor is fit and well this will indicate that the transfer was not directed at reducing liability. A transfer taking place some considerable time before the need for accommodation arose would be considered exempt. In certain circumstances a third party may be liable to pay the cost of accommodation because of a transfer of property. This liability will arise where the third party has received a transfer of property from the adult either below

202 Set out in the National Assistance (Assessment of Resources) Regulations 1992, SI 1992/2977. These regulations are regularly amended to change the sums specified in them. Regularly updated guidance is published by the Scottish Government, the current version is *Revised Guidance on Charging for Residential Accommodation* (March 2024), this accompanied Circular CCD1/2024.

203 *R (Walford) v Worcestershire County Council* [2015] EWCA Civ 22.

204 Currently (from 8 April 2024) £35,000, The National Assistance (Assessment of Resources) Amendment (Scotland) Regulations 2024, SSI 2024 No 21, reg 2(2).

205 Currently (from 8 April 2024) £21,500, The National Assistance (Assessment of Resources) Amendment (Scotland) Regulations 2024, reg 2(3)(a).

206 As happened in *Yule v South Lanarkshire Council* 1999 SCLR 985.

207 *R v Dorset County Council, ex parte Beeson* [2001] EWHC Admin 986, this point was not subject to appeal: *R v Dorset County Council, ex parte Beeson* [2002] EWCA Civ 1812.

value or for nothing. Further requirements are that the transfer took place either after the adult was in residential accommodation or in the six months before moving there, and that the transfer was made knowingly and with the intention of avoiding charges for accommodation.[208]

(c) There are no statutory rules linking income to how much is to be paid, it is up to each local authority to determine its own rules on this. In taking decisions on income the authority must take account of the need to leave a specified weekly amount to the supported person.[209]

Charges for other, non-residential, services are calculated in accordance with guidance issued by the Convention of Scottish Local Authorities which is updated annually.[210] In addition, local authorities cannot require a supported person to pay more than it appears practicable for them to pay.[211]

Where residential accommodation is provided on a temporary basis, the local authority can limit the amount payable for the first eight weeks of a stay.[212] The authority may enter an arrangement which allows the supported person to defer payment of any sums due for accommodation. The preferred method of doing this is a deferred payment agreement,[213] which involves the local authority taking a security over the supported person's house. Therefore, payment can only be deferred where the supported person has a property over which a security can be granted. The value of the property must exceed any amount which is likely to be due to the local authority. There are three further conditions applying to deferred payment agreements:

208 Health and Social Services and Social Security Adjudications Act 1983, s 21. See *Argyll and Bute Council v Gordon* [2017] SAC (Civ) 6 for a case where it was alleged that such a transfer had taken place.

209 Currently (from 8 April 2024) £34.50.The National Assistance (Sums for Personal Requirements) (Scotland) Regulations 2024, SSI 2024 No 22, reg 2.

210 The current version is *Charges Applying to Non-residential Social Care Services 2025/2026*. Available on the COSLA website: www.cosla.gov.uk/about-cosla/our-teams/health-and-social-care/social-care-charging-information.

211 1968 Act, s 87(1A). Assessment (and reassessment) of liability to pay should involve the supported person, *R(B) v Cornwall County Council* [2009] EWHC 491 (Admin).

212 National Assistance Act 1948, s 22(5A), the amount can be limited to such an amount as it seems to the local authority to be reasonable to pay.

213 Community Care (Deferred Payment of Accommodation Costs) (Scotland) Regulations 2002, SSI 2002/266; *Deferred Payments and Other Funding Arrangements Which Allow Care Home Residents to Delay Selling Their Homes*, Circular CCD13/2004.

(a) the supported person must be unwilling or unable to sell the property;[214]
(b) excluding the property, the capital held by the supported person must be less than the amount to be ignored as described above, if it exceeds this, payments will have to come from this other capital until it falls below this limit;[215] and
(c) the property must have been taken into account in assessing liability to pay and not excluded from the calculation (eg, a property will be excluded from the calculation if it is occupied by the supported person's spouse, see above).

An alternative method of securing payment is to take out a charging order[216] over the supported person's house, though the guidance makes it clear that deferred payment agreements are the preferred means for doing this.[217]

(2) Free personal care

6.15 Certain types of care do not have to be paid for, at least up to a certain value. The types of care covered are:[218]
(a) Personal care, that is, care relating to the day-to-day physical tasks and needs of the person being provided with care. This includes tasks such as eating or washing and extends to the mental processes associated with these tasks, for example remembering to wash or to eat.[219]
(b) Personal support, in other words counselling and support provided as part of a planned programme of care.[220]
(c) A variety of other types of care[221] including activities related to personal hygiene (such as shaving or cleaning teeth); preparation

214 Community Care (Deferred Payment of Accommodation Costs) (Scotland) Regulations 2002, SSI 2002/266, reg 2(2)(b)
215 Community Care (Deferred Payment of Accommodation Costs) (Scotland) Regulations 2002, reg 2(2)(a)
216 Health and Social Services and Social Security Adjudications Act 1983, s 23; Charging Orders (Residential Accommodation) (Scotland) Order 1993, SI 1993/1516; *Community Care: Health and Social Services and Social Security Adjudications Act 1983 (HASSASSA): Sections 21–24: Orders and Guidance*, Circular SWSG15/93.
217 The National Assistance (Assessment of Resources) Amendment (Scotland) Regulations 2024
218 Community Care and Health (Scotland) Act 2002, s 1 (2002 Act). See also Guidance on Free Personal and Nursing Care in Scotland for Adults, Circular CCD3/2018.
219 2002 Act, s 1(1)(a). For the definition of personal care see: Public services Reform (Scotland) Act 2010, Sch 12, para 20.
220 2002 Act, s 1(1)(b).
221 These are set out in the 2002 Act, Sch 1.

or assistance with the preparation of the supported person's food and fulfilment of special dietary needs;[222] dealing with problems of immobility where the supported person is immobile or substantially immobile; assistance with medication, for example, administration of eye drops; and, assistance related to general well-being, for example, dressing, getting up and going to bed, behaviour management and psychological support.

(d) Nursing care so far as not covered above.[223]

Nursing care is provided free, regardless of age, to people who are receiving care at home or who are not paying for residential accommodation. The care described in (a) to (c) above is free to those aged 65 or over who are receiving care at home or who do not pay for residential accommodation. For those who pay for residential accommodation then, subject to the assessment described in the next paragraph, the authority is to make payments to third parties to cover personal and nursing care. The authority may where appropriate make direct payments to supported persons to cover the costs of personal and nursing care. The maximum amount of these payments is prescribed.[224]

One difficulty in practice with these provisions was their application to so-called 'self-arrangers', those people who make their own arrangements for the provision of services without approaching the local authority and being assessed by it. It was originally assumed that such self-arrangers were covered by these provisions, but it was subsequently held that this was not the case.[225] This conclusion was based on the wording of the legislation which provides that 'a local authority are not to charge for social care provided by them (or the provision of which is secured by them)'.[226] The reference to care provided by a local authority or secured by them was held to exclude self-arrangers. In order to address this the Scottish Government issued Directions and guidance in January 2010[227] which provided for self-arrangers to be assessed by the local authority with a view to having services either provided by or arranged by the local authority. Any assessment of the person's needs for the provision of services, should discount any self-arranged services.

222 This excludes 'meals on wheels' provision.

223 2002 Act, s 1(1)(d)

224 Community Care (Personal Care and Nursing Care) (Scotland) Regulations 2002 (SSI 2002/303), as amended.

225 *Argyll and Bute Council v Scottish Public Services Ombudsman* [2007] CSOH 168.

226 2002 Act, s 1(1).

227 Personal Care and Nursing Care (Self Arrangers) (Scotland) Directions 2009, appended to *Guidance and Directions for Self Arrangers of Free Personal and Nursing Care*, Circular CCD 1/2010.

There is guidance on eligibility criteria for access to personal and nursing care.[228] The eligibility criteria identify four categories of risk or priority: critical, substantial, moderate and low.[229] These are defined by reference to risks relating to neglect or health,[230] risk relating to the home, domestic routines and personal care,[231] risks relating to participation in community life,[232] and risks relating to carers.[233] Linked to these criteria are waiting times.[234] For those assessed with critical or substantial priority the maximum period of time which should pass between confirmation of the need for services and delivery of the service is six weeks, though there is an expectation that in critical cases services will be delivered very quickly. There is, at present, no target time for completing an assessment.

(3) Which local authority pays?

6.16 In general, liability to make payment for community care services provided to an individual lies with the local authority for the area in which that person is ordinarily resident.[235] So, for example, if a resident in Area A was on holiday in Area B and whilst in Area B required to be assessed and provided with community care services, the local authority in Area B would generally be able to recover the costs of this provision from the local authority for Area A. In determining ordinary residence any period of in-patient hospital care is ignored, but otherwise the main factor is the individual's voluntary choice as to where they wish to live. The current guidance refers to a definition

228 *Guidance* (2009).

229 *Guidance* (2009), p 8.

230 For example, critical risk will be present where there are major health problems causing life-threatening harm to the supported person or others.

231 For example, there will be substantial risk where the supported person is unable to manage many aspects of domestic routines causing significant risk to independence.

232 For example, there will be moderate risk if the supported person is unable to manage several aspects of involvement in work, learning or education and this will pose a risk to independence in the future.

233 For example, there will be low risk where the carer is able to manage most aspects of their role, even if some difficulty is experienced with one or two aspects of this as long as these pose a low risk.

234 Though see the comments above about waiting lists.

235 1968 Act, s 86; Recovery of Expenditure for the Provision of Social Care Services (Scotland) Regulations 2010, SSI 2010/72.

of ordinary residence offered by Lord Scarman as giving guidance on applying the term:[236]

> Unless, therefore, it can be shown that the statutory framework or the legal context in which the words are used requires a different meaning, I unhesitatingly subscribe to the view that 'ordinarily resident' refers to a man's abode in a particular place or country which he has adopted voluntarily and for settled purposes as part of the regular order of his life for the time being, whether of short or long duration.

These provisions also extend to cases where local authority A makes arrangements for someone who is ordinarily resident within its area to be provided with accommodation situated in the area covered by local authority B, or where it makes an arrangement for the provision of services and facilities to enable someone to live in accommodation with support in the area of local authority B. In such cases local authority A remains responsible for the costs of the provision of accommodation or placement made. If that placement is in the area of local authority B, it does not change the ordinary residence of the supported person. Disputes between local authorities are to be resolved by the Scottish Ministers.

It is clear from the quotation cited above that a change of residence involves a voluntary decision on the part of an individual deciding to move from one area to another. Such a decision cannot be made by an adult who lacks capacity to take that type of decision. In such cases, a change of ordinary residence will only take place where the decision to move the adult with incapacity is taken by someone who has the legal power to do so, in the Scottish context a welfare attorney or guardian. So, for example, when the daughter of an adult with incapacity, who had no legal power to take decisions about her mother's residence, moved her mother from England to Scotland it was decided that the ordinary residence of the mother remained the English local authority where she had previously lived.[237] One further issue which has arisen in disputes between local authorities is what happens when a guardian is appointed some time after an adult moves from the area of one local authority to that of another. Here the view has been taken that, if the guardian does

236 Scottish Government, Guidance on the Recovery of Expenditure on Accommodation and Services Under Section 86 of the Social Work (Scotland) Act 1968 – Ordinary Residence, Circular CCD3/2015, *citing R v Barnet London Borough Council, ex parte Shah* [1983] 2 AC 309 at 343. On the responsibility of local authorities, see also *R (on application of Worcestershire CC) v Secretary of State for Health and Social Care* [2023] UKSC 31.

237 *Milton Keynes Council v Scottish Ministers* [2015] CSOH 156.

not object to the current residence of the adult, they will have taken a tacit decision to approve it and, therefore, that the ordinary residence of the adult will change from the date on which the guardian was appointed.

CHALLENGING DECISIONS[238]

6.17 Decisions taken as part of the process of providing community care or a related service can be challenged by using the complaints procedure of the local authority. If the person challenging the decision is not satisfied they may potentially seek judicial review of the decision of the authority. A complaint may be made about the assessment process, the outcomes of the process, the decisions about budgets and support, the budget or support itself, changes in the budget or support, decisions about charging for support and decisions to take account of capital which has been disposed of. Where a supported person has a complaint about a service which is not provided directly by the local authority, they will also be able, provided that the service is registered with the Care Inspectorate, to make use of the service provider's own complaints procedure and make a complaint to the Social Work and Social Care Improvement Scotland (the Care Inspectorate).

The reduction in local authority spending as a result of austerity has resulted in reductions in budgets available to individual supported persons and, in some cases, these have been significant. The fact that there has been a significant reduction does not mean that the assessment and decision-making process that led to the reduced budget is flawed and it will not be open to challenge if the correct process has been followed and all relevant factors have been carefully considered.[239] The case of *McDonald*[240] in Box 6.1 below illustrates some of the issues, including those which can arise under the European Convention on Human Rights.

Box 6.1

> Ms McDonald had mobility problems, partly caused by a stroke. There was a danger that she would fall and injure herself if she got up to the toilet unaided during the night. She was assessed by her local authority as needing overnight assistance, which

238 See also **1.59** and **1.60**.

239 See, eg, *Davey v Oxfordshire County Council* [2017] EWCA Civ 1308.

240 Reported, in order, as [2009] EWHC 1582 (Admin), [2010] EWCA Civ 1109, [2011] UKSC 33 and [2012] ECHR 814. See also Clements, L, 'Disability, dignity and the cri de coeur' [2011] EHRLR 675.

involved someone staying with her during the night who would be able to assist her to get to the toilet safely. In November 2008, because of the reduction in funding available to it, the local authority decided that Ms McDonald should be provided with incontinence pads for use overnight instead of being provided with overnight assistance. Her assessed need remained the same. In November 2009 her need was reassessed as being a need for provision of incontinence pads. Ms McDonald was very unhappy about this, she took the very strong view that using incontinence pads was undignified, that it was also inappropriate and that her problem, and the need arising from it, was not one which related to continence, but to mobility.

Ms McDonald unsuccessfully challenged the actions of the council in the courts in England and then took her case to the European Court of Human Rights (ECtHR).

The ECtHR decided that Ms McDonald's rights under Article 8 of the European Convention on Human Rights were engaged:

> insofar as the present applicant believed that the level of care offered by the local authority would have undignified and distressing consequences, she … was faced with the possibility of living in a manner which 'conflicted with [her] strongly held ideas of self and personal identity'. In the Supreme Court, Baroness Hale, in her dissenting opinion, appeared to accept that considerations of human dignity were engaged when someone who could control her bodily functions was obliged to behave as if she could not … . The Court agrees with this general assessment of the applicant's situation and it does not exclude that the particular measure complained of by the applicant in the present case was capable of having an impact on her enjoyment of her right to respect for private life as guaranteed under Article 8 § 1 of the Convention. It therefore finds that the contested measure reducing the level of her healthcare falls within the scope of Article 8 ([2012] ECHR 814, para 47).

As illustrated in the quotation above, the ECtHR took the view that someone's Article 8 rights could be engaged where they were forced to live in a way that conflicted with their strongly held ideas of self and personal identity. The Court clearly took the view that Ms McDonald had a very clear idea about herself and her identity and a very clear belief that it was undignified to expect her to use incontinence pads.

However, the engagement of Article 8 is not the end of the issue, and the engagement of rights does not mean that they have necessarily been infringed. This is because Article 8 is a qualified right, which means that an individual's rights under Article 8 can be overridden by other considerations. In order to succeed in a claim based on Article 8, you need to be able to establish that the action of the government or other state organisation, such as a local authority, was not in accordance with law, did not pursue a legitimate aim and was not necessary in a democratic society.

- '*In accordance with law*'. For our purposes it is enough to note that this requires that decisions are taken in accordance with the domestic law of the state against which the claim is made. In respect of this the ECtHR distinguished between the first decision in November 2008 and the later decision in 2009. They took the view that the first decision to change provision was not in accordance with law because no reassessment had been carried out before the decision to change the service, contrary to the requirement imposed by community care law in the UK for such a reassessment. Because the decision was not in accordance with law, the ECtHR decided that Ms McDonald's Article 8 rights had been infringed. However, the ECtHR decided that provision after November 2009 was in accordance with law as it had been preceded by a reassessment.
- '*Legitimate aim*'. This decision was also considered to pursue a legitimate aim, namely the economic well-being of the state and the interests of the other care-users.
- '*Necessary in a democratic society*'. Finally, it had to be determined whether interfering with her rights was necessary in a democratic society, and whether the action was a proportionate way of achieving its aim. In this context the ECtHR gives states a wide margin of appreciation, in other words it recognises that states must have some range of discretion when it comes to taking decisions, particularly decisions of the sort involved in this case which concern allocation of scarce resources. Looking at Ms McDonald's position, it took the view that the decision was proportionate because, at every stage in the court proceedings in England, the interests of the public and, for example, of other supported persons competing for scarce funds, and those of Ms McDonald, had been carefully balanced.

In relation to the November 2009 decision, therefore, Ms McDonald was unsuccessful, and this illustrates the difficulties that arise in effectively using Article 8 in community care cases where there are always going to be these sorts of decision about resource allocation.

As well as individual decisions about services for individual supported persons, supported persons may want to challenge changes to services affecting groups of people. Where a local authority proposes to make changes to services there must be, particularly where the supported persons are disabled, adequate consultation before a final decision is taken. There will also need to be clear consideration of the impact of the proposed change on disabled supported persons. This consideration takes place in the context of the specific duties imposed on local authorities to take account of the disabilities of disabled people and to promote equality of opportunity.[241] Similar obligations to consult will apply prior to the closure of residential accommodation. Provided that adequate consultation has taken place, there is careful planning of the move, and provision is made for proper assessment of and support of residents who are being moved, it is unlikely that the closure will be open to challenge.[242] Where the residents are disabled there will, in addition, be a requirement to specifically consider the specific duties of the local authority just mentioned.

HOSPITAL-BASED COMPLEX CLINICAL CARE

6.18 Although the emphasis in social care is on supporting people at home or in a homely setting in the community, there will always be some people who need long-term hospital care. In deciding whether this

241 Equality Act 2010, s 149, see, eg, *Boyejo v Barnet London Borough Council* [2009] EWHC 3261 (Admin). See also **2.27**.

242 A number of challenges had previously been made to such closures founded on either Article 2 of the ECHR, the basis here being increased mortality as a result of moving, or Article 8 of the ECHR, based on interference with the resident's home. The initial case law established the requirements set out here. Any challenge based on Article 2 will require evidence of a real and immediate risk to the life of one of the residents being moved (*R (Emily Turner) v Southampton City Council* [2009] EWCA Civ 1290). It has been suggested that current research on the effects of relocation is inconclusive and not sufficient to establish that this threshold is reached (*R (Wilson) v Coventry City Council* [2008] EWHC 2300 (Admin)). See also *Watts v United Kingdom* [2010] ECHR 793.

is the case, the question which has to be asked is: 'Can this individual's care needs be met in any setting other than a hospital?'.[243] If the answer is 'no', then the person will remain in hospital under hospital-based complex clinical care.[244] If the answer is 'yes', then the expectation is that the person will be accommodated in the community with support for medical needs being delivered there.

243 Scottish Government Circular DL (2015) 11, *Hospital Based Complex Clinical Care*.

244 *Hospital Based Complex Clinical Care*. As from 1 June 2015 this replaced NHS Continuing Healthcare, described in Circular CEL 6 (2008).

Chapter 7

Incapacity

BACKGROUND

7.1 This chapter is concerned largely with adults with incapacity. Adults with incapacity are those adults who, to at least some extent, have no legal capacity. The effect of incapacity on these adults is that, in law, there are some decisions they cannot take for themselves:[1]

> A person who is mentally incapable or lacks mental capacity is incapable in the legal sense of entering into a transaction or making a decision. This is because the person, due to his or her mental state, cannot understand the nature of the transaction or decision or comprehend its consequences or effects.[2]

Discussion is limited to adults since, as we have seen, parents are able to take action or decisions on behalf of their children.[3]

The Adults with Incapacity (Scotland) Act 2000 (the 2000 Act) brought about significant change in the law. However, there are some older types of provision for adults with incapacity which continue to exist although some, such as powers of attorney, are now subject to different requirements. The main provisions of the 2000 Act are considered below, but provision not derived from this include:

(a) *Benefits appointees*. It is possible for someone aged 18 or over to be appointed to receive any benefits to which the adult is entitled and to deal with them. Appointment is made following application to the Department of Work and Pensions.[4] No one can be appointed as an appointee where a financial guardian with power to receive benefits has been appointed to the adult.

1 As we will see in **7.3** below, incapacity is not necessarily all or nothing.
2 Scottish Law Commission Discussion Paper No 94 (1991). A similar definition is: 'Capacity is the ability to understand information relevant to a decision or action and to appreciate the reasonably foreseeable consequences of taking or not taking that decision', Scottish Government, *Adults with Incapacity (Scotland) Act 2000: Communication and Assessing Capacity: A Guide for Social Work and Healthcare Staff* (2008), ch 1, para 3.
3 See **3.5**.
4 Social Security (Claims and Payments) Regulations 1987, SI 1987/1968, reg 33, as amended.

(b) *Setting up a trust*. A trust can be set up to manage property or money for the benefit of an adult. One way of using a trust might be the setting up of a trust by parents to benefit a child who will have no, or limited, capacity as an adult. The setting up of a trust involves the transfer of ownership of property and/or money to trustees who will then administer the property/money in line with the purposes set out in the document setting up the trust. Trusts will only have effect in relation to property and trustees will have no power to take decisions about the welfare of the adult.

(c) *Negotiorum gestio*. This is a legal principle which allows someone to act on your behalf when you are incapable of acting for yourself, and where, were you able to, you would have authorised the other person to act on your behalf. The relevance here is that the inability to act may be due to mental disability and this principle may, for example, allow a friend or relative to act on behalf of someone who is unable to do so themselves. It is likely that the power to act under this doctrine is now very limited. The use of *negotiorum gestio* seems inconsistent with fundamental elements of the 2000 Act, in particular, the provision of scrutiny over those acting on behalf of an adult and the principle of maximum involvement considered below.

(d) The *parens patriae* jurisdiction of the Court of Session. This is an inherent jurisdiction held by the Court of Session to do what is for the benefit of an incompetent adult. Its limits are undefined and it appears to be the case that it has not been displaced by the passage of legislation or time. The only relatively recent case where this jurisdiction was invoked involved seeking a decision to turn off the life support being provided to a patient in a Persistent Vegetative State.[5]

Interventions in respect of an adult with incapacity may engage various articles of the European Convention on Human Rights. The main articles involved are: Article 5 which requires certain procedures to be followed before an individual is deprived of their liberty;[6] Article 6 requiring access to due process; and Article 8, the right to respect for private

5 *Law Hospital NHS Trust v Lord Advocate* 1996 SC 301. It has been held in England that the inherent jurisdiction extends beyond adults who are incapable to vulnerable adults who are either '(i) under constraint; or (ii) subject to coercion or undue influence; or (iii) for some other reason deprived of the capacity to make the relevant decision, or disabled from making a free choice, or incapacitated or disabled from giving or expressing a real and genuine consent' per Munby J in *Re SA (Vulnerable Adult with Capacity: Marriage), Re* [2005] EWHC 2942 (Fam) at para 77, see also *DL v A Local Authority* [2012] EWCA Civ 253.

6 Discussed in **7.19–7.23** below.

and family life. Also relevant is the United Nations Convention on the Rights of Persons with Disabilities (UNCRPD) in particular, Article 12. This requires that persons with disabilities enjoy legal capacity on an equal basis with others and that appropriate support is provided to such persons to exercise their legal capacity. This has been interpreted as requiring that any substitute decision-making processes which exist are replaced by supported decision-making.[7] Substitute decision-making involves a process which has at least one of the following characteristics:

(a) Legal capacity is removed for at least one decision.
(b) The appointment of a decision-maker by someone other than the person with disability.[8]
(c) Decisions taken based on 'best interests'[9] rather than 'will & preferences'.

The view has been taken, in line with this definition, that guardianship involves impermissible substitute decision-making.[10]

Partly influenced by deprivation of liberty issues and the UNCRPD, the Scottish Government commissioned a widespread review on changes to the law on adults with incapacity and other aspects of mental health law in Scotland. The resulting review, the Scottish Mental Health Law Review (SMHLR), was chaired by Lord Scott and published in September 2022.[11] Following publication of the Scott Review, the Scottish Government has engaged in consultation on possible changes to the Adults with Incapacity (Scotland) Act 2000.[12]

7 Committee on the Rights of Persons with Disabilities, *General Comment No 1* (2004). This interpretation has been disputed, see Dawson, J, 'A realistic approach to assessing mental health law's compliance with the UNCRPD', (2015) 40 *Intl Jrnl of Law and Psychiatry* 70 and de Bailís, C & Flynn, E, 'Recognising legal capacity: commentary and analysis of Article 12 CRPD' (2017) 13 *Intl Jrnl of Law in Context* 6.

8 See **7.7** onwards below.

9 Consideration of best interests forms no part of the law in Scotland, see **7.4** below.

10 Committee on the Rights of Persons with Disabilities, *Concluding observations on the initial report of the United Kingdom of Great Britain and Northern Ireland* CRPD/C/GBR/CO/1 (2017), paras 30–31. Though see then, S *et al,* 'Reinforcing guardianship regimes through assisted decision-making – a Scottish perspective' (2014) *Juridical Review* 263 and Ward, A, 'Abolition of guardianship? "Best interests" versus "best interpretation"', 2015 SLT 150.

11 The Scottish Mental Health Law Review, Final Report, September 2022. Available at: https://webarchive.nrscotland.gov.uk/20230327160310/https:/cms.mentalhealthlawreview.scot/wp-content/uploads/2022/09/SMHLR-FINAL-Report-.pdf.

12 Scottish Government, *Adults with Incapacity Amendment Act: Consultation* (July 2024) Available at: www.gov.scot/publications/adults-incapacity-amendment-act-consultation/.

LOCAL AUTHORITY FUNCTIONS AND RELEVANT ORGANISATIONS

7.2 Local authorities have a variety of obligations and functions under the 2000 Act, which are closely related to duties and functions under the legislation on mental health, vulnerable adults and community care. The principal duties are:[13]

(a) To investigate complaints about how guardians, welfare attorneys or persons authorised under an intervention order have carried out their functions in relation to the personal welfare of an adult.[14]

(b) To investigate cases where the authority become aware that the personal welfare of an adult appears to be at risk.[15] Following an investigation the authority has the power to take any action it deems necessary to safeguard the welfare of the adult. This might include seeking an order under the 2000 Act or taking steps under other legislation. Although there is a duty to investigate, the 2000 Act does not confer any additional powers on the local authority which might assist it to carry out such an investigation. The authority may, if the circumstances are appropriate, invoke powers set out in the Adult Support and Protection (Scotland) Act 2007.[16]

(c) To supervise welfare guardians[17] and, where this has been ordered by the sheriff, welfare attorneys or someone authorised under an intervention order.[18]

(d) Finally, (to be discussed more fully below) the local authority must apply, in certain circumstances, for an intervention order or the appointment of a guardian.

Local authorities will also provide reports in connection with applications for the appointment of a guardian or for an intervention order and will be notified when someone resigns as a welfare attorney.

13 The first two of these and the duty to supervise welfare guardians arise under s 10 of the 2000 Act and must be delegated in terms of the Public Bodies (Joint Working) (Scotland) Act 2014, see **1.73**.

14 Adults with Incapacity (Scotland) Act 2000, s 10(1)(c) (the 2000 Act).

15 See Scottish Government, *Adults with Incapacity (Scotland) Act 2000: Code of Practice for Local Authorities Exercising Functions under the 2000 Act* (2008), ch 9 (*Code of Practice* 2008).

16 See **chapter 9**.

17 2000 Act, s 10(1)(a).

18 2000 Act, s 10(3). See also *Code of Practice* 2008, ch 8.

Most local authority functions under the 2000 Act will be carried out by a Mental Health Officer (MHO).[19] The Mental Welfare Commission[20] has some powers of investigation related to substitute decision making in the field of personal welfare, as well as investigating complaints about the conduct of investigations carried out by the local authority. A final regulatory body is the Public Guardian.[21] This body deals with all applications to access an adult's funds, supervises guardians and interveners who have powers in respect of an adult's property or financial affairs as well as individuals who have been given power to access an adult's funds. The Public Guardian also investigates complaints about the management of adult's property and financial affairs, maintains a number of registers and provides information and advice.[22]

THE MEANING OF 'INCAPACITY'

7.3 An adult will be incapable if they are incapable of acting, making decisions, communicating decisions, understanding decisions or retaining the memory of decisions.[23] The incapacity must arise either from mental disorder or an inability to communicate because of physical disability.[24] A mental disorder can be either a mental illness, personality disorder or learning disability.[25] A person is not considered to have a mental disorder by reason only of certain attributes, including dependence on, or use of, alcohol or drugs, acting as no prudent person would act, behaviour that causes, or is likely to cause, harassment, alarm or distress to any other person.[26] A person is also not considered mentally disordered by reason of sexual orientation, sexual deviancy, transsexualism or transvestism.[27] Mental disorder may not lead directly to incapacity, but may mean that the adult is susceptible to pressure or influence from others to decide in a particular way, with the consequence that they are effectively unable to take their own decisions.[28] An adult will not be incapable because of physical disability if human (for example, an interpreter) or mechanical (for example a voice synthesiser) aids can

19 See **8.2**.
20 See **8.5**.
21 See www.publicguardian-scotland.gov.uk/.
22 For the general functions of the Public Guardian, see; 2000 Act, s 6.
23 2000 Act, s 1(6).
24 2000 Act, s 1(6).
25 The 2000 Act refers to the definition of 'mental disorder' contained in Mental Health (Care and Treatment) (Scotland) Act 2003, s 328 and 2000 Act,s 87(1). See **8.9**.
26 Mental Health (Care and Treatment) (Scotland) Act 2003, s 328.
27 Mental Health (Care and Treatment) (Scotland) Act 2003, s 328.
28 *A (Capacity: Refusal of Contraception) Re [2010] EWHC 1549 (Fam).*

overcome the difficulty which they have in communicating decisions.[29] The definition of incapable and of incapacity is slightly extended in relation to the appointment of a guardian. Such an appointment can be based either on a number of grounds. First, the adult being incapable of taking or communicating decisions in the sense discussed above. Second, the adult's being incapable of acting to safeguard or promote their interests in property/financial affairs or in respect of personal welfare.[30] Therefore, for the purposes of appointing a guardian only, an adult may have the capacity to take decisions, but be incapable of safeguarding or promoting their own interests.[31] For the purpose of determining this second type of incapacity the Communication and Assessing Capacity guide provides guidance to practitioners.[32]

Regardless of the type of incapacity involved, incapacity is context specific – an adult who is incapable of taking some decisions is likely, unless the incapacity arises from an inability to communicate, to have the capacity to take other decisions:

> ... capacity is not merely issue specific in relation to different types of transaction; capacity is also issue specific in relation to different transactions of the same type. Thus a vulnerable adult may have capacity to consent to a simple medical procedure but lack capacity to consent to a more complex medical procedure.[33]

Capacity will often not be completely lost, and incapacity to take decisions in one area should not be assumed to imply loss of capacity in all areas. Even where an adult is incapable of taking particular decisions, the principles set out below make it clear that, as far as possible, they are to be involved in the decision-making process.

Unlike England and Wales,[34] there is no statutory presumption in Scotland that an adult has capacity. However, in practice, the Scottish position is the same – there will need to be clear evidence that an adult lacks capacity before any court order in respect of the adult will be made or other action requiring authorisation will be permitted. Such evidence will also be required before decisions can be taken on behalf of

29 2000 Act, s 1(6).

30 2000 Act, s 58(1).

31 *Edinburgh City Council v D* 2011 SLT (Sh Ct) 15.

32 Scottish Government, *Adults with Incapacity (Scotland) Act 2000:Communication and Assessing Capacity: A Guide for Social Work and Health Care Staff*, (2008).

33 *Re MM (An Adult); Local Authority X v MM* [2007] EWHC 2003 (Fam) at [65], per Munby J.

34 Mental Capacity Act 2005, s 1(1).

an adult by a welfare attorney. This is captured in Scottish Government Guidance as follows:[35]

> The starting point for assessing someone's capacity to make a particular decision is always the assumption that the individual has capacity. In legal proceedings the burden of proof will fall on the person who asserts that capacity is lacking. A court must be satisfied that on the balance of probabilities, capacity has been shown to be lacking.

PRINCIPLES GOVERNING INTERVENTION IN THE LIVES OF ADULTS WITH INCAPACITY

7.4 Interventions in the lives of adults with incapacity under the 2000 Act must be undertaken in accordance with the principles set out in the Act. These principles govern the courts as they take decisions on applications for orders. The principles also apply to local authorities exercising functions under the Act. For example and authority acting as welfare guardians to adults, and individuals acting as guardians, as attorneys, or who are authorised under intervention orders. The principles as set out in the Act[36] are set out in Box 7.1 below.

Any benefit provided to the adult under Principle 1 need not be financial or physical[37] and can be intangible, for example in the form of a psychological benefit[38] or a benefit in ensuring that the adult's wishes expressed while they had capacity are given effect to.[39] As long as the intervention confers some benefit on the adult it doesn't matter that it also confers a benefit on someone else.[40] In one case for example, an intervention order was sought to discharge the adult's claims on the estate of his recently deceased wife in order to ensure that the couple's children would get the whole of the wife's estate, as had been their intention.[41] The adult benefited by having his previous wishes given

35 Scottish Government, *Adults with Incapacity (Scotland) Act 2000: Communication and Assessing Capacity: A Guide for Social Work and Healthcare Staff* (2008), ch 1, para 4.

36 2000 Act, s 1(2)–(5).

37 Though it can be, eg in *FB, Applicant* [2005] ScotSC 26, an intervention order was sought to allow a compensation payment to the adult to be negotiated.

38 For example, in having her son continue living with the adult, *A's Guardian, Applicant* 2007 SLT (Sh Ct) 24 or 'peace of mind' *Applications by the Guardian of P* [2012] ScotSC 108.

39 *M, Applicant* 2007 SLT (Sh Ct) 24; *G, Applicant* 2009 SLT (Sh Ct) 122.

40 See *Applications by the Guardian of P* [2012] 11 WLUK 722, where the only possible benefits were to others leading to refusal of the relevant applications.

41 *M, Applicant* 2007 SLT (Sh Ct) 24; *G, Applicant* 2009 SLT (Sh Ct) 122.

effect to and the order could be made even though the children of the couple also benefited.

Principle 2 seems to include a number of aspects:

(a) The intervention must be likely to achieve its purpose, if it will not then it cannot be undertaken or authorised by the court. The 2000 Act states that no intervention shall take place in the affairs of an adult unless the person responsible for authorising or effecting the intervention is satisfied that the intervention will benefit the adult and the benefit cannot be obtained without such an intervention.[42]

(b) There is a trade-off between achievement of the purpose and the freedom which is left to the adult. A restriction may be justified if it is the only way to achieve a specific objective which provides benefit to the adult. In reaching the conclusion that the restriction is justified, it may be necessary to weigh up different possible courses of action and decide which is most likely to achieve the purpose of the intervention.[43]

(c) The option selected, if there is a choice, must be the least restrictive way of achieving the purpose and impose the least limitation on the adult compatible with this.[44]

All of these factors will be relevant in deciding whether any intervention is necessary; for example, it may be possible to achieve the purpose without any intervention,[45] and, if an intervention is needed, what form this should take. Matters to consider will be whether the issue may be resolved by way of an intervention order rather than guardianship, and, if there is to be an application for guardianship, what powers should be sought for the guardian under such an application. However, where the alternative to guardianship would be use of a number of different mechanisms, this is not likely to be the least restrictive option.[46]

Box 7.1

The 2000 Act Principles[47]

1 There shall be no intervention in the affairs of an adult unless the person responsible for authorising or effecting the intervention is satisfied that the intervention will

42 2000 Act, s 1(2).

43 See, eg, *Fife Council v X*, Kirkcaldy Sh Ct, 22 December 2005; *City of Edinburgh Council v Z* 2005 SLT (Sh Ct) 7.

44 2000 Act, s 1(3).

45 This point was argued unsuccessfully in *Muldoon, Applicant* 2005 SCLR 611.

46 *CJR in respect of the Adult JMR* [2013] ScotSC 25.

47 2000 Act, ss 1(2)–1(5).

benefit the adult and that such benefit cannot reasonably be achieved without the intervention.

2 Where it is determined that an intervention as mentioned in subsection (1) is to be made, such intervention shall be the least restrictive option in relation to the freedom of the adult, consistent with the purpose of the intervention.

3 In determining if an intervention is to be made and, if so, what intervention is to be made, account shall be taken of:

(a) the present and past wishes and feelings of the adult so far as they can be ascertained by any means of communication, whether human or by mechanical aid (whether of an interpretative nature or otherwise) appropriate to the adult;

(b) the views of the nearest relative, named person and the primary carer of the adult, in so far as it is reasonable and practicable to do so;

(c) the views of:

(i) any guardian, continuing attorney or welfare attorney of the adult who has powers relating to the proposed intervention; and

(ii) any person whom the sheriff has directed to be consulted,

in so far as it is reasonable and practicable to do so; and

(d) the views of any other person appearing to the person responsible for authorising or effecting the intervention to have an interest in the welfare of the adult or in the proposed intervention, where these views have been made known to the person responsible, in so far as it is reasonable and practicable to do so.

4 Any guardian, continuing attorney, welfare attorney or manager of an establishment exercising functions under this Act or under any order of the sheriff in relation to an adult shall, in so far as it is reasonable and practicable to do so, encourage the adult to exercise whatever skills he has concerning his property, financial affairs or personal welfare, as the case may be, and to develop new such skills.

In seeking the views of the adult under Principle 3, 'strenuous efforts must be made to assist and facilitate communication' before it is concluded that the adult cannot communicate their views.[48] There may be a written record of the adult's wishes, for example in one case where the adult had given instructions as to his will which had not been carried out properly.[49] In England and Wales provision is made for an adult to make an advance decision refusing treatment.[50] In Scotland, despite the recommendation of the Scottish Law Commission, there is no such provision.[51] An adult may express their wishes in advance, and if capacity were to be lost such wishes would have to be taken into account. Principle 3 only requires that views are taken into account and not that they are given effect to. In some cases there will be a conflict of views which makes it impossible to give effect to all of them.[52] Views cannot simply be dismissed out of hand, they must be considered, and where there is a conflict, a clear reason will need to be set out for preferring one view over another. The limitation to doing what is reasonable and practicable extends beyond taking account of views, it also covers the process of obtaining views. It will not be necessary to obtain views from anyone with an interest in the adult listed in the Act where this would not be reasonable or practicable.

Principle 4 is of more limited scope than the other principles, applying only to specific types of person. The Principle does not, for example, apply to someone authorised under an intervention order.

Missing from the principles is any reference to decisions being taken in the best interests of the adult, which plays a significant role in England and Wales.[53] In Scotland the emphasis is more on seeking a benefit for the adult and on the use of substitute decision making to reach a decision reflecting what it is considered the adult would have decided based on their own wishes and views. The notion that an adult benefits from the intervention does not mean that any intervention must be entirely risk free:

> The fact is that all life involves risk, and the young, the elderly and the vulnerable, are exposed to additional risks and to risks they are

48 *Code of Practice* 2008, p 8. This guidance refers to (a) in Principle 3 as being Principle 3, with the remaining requirements to consult being Principle 4.

49 *G, Applicant* 2009 SLT (Sh Ct) 122.

50 Mental Capacity Act 2005, ss 24–26. The only exception is the possibility of an advance statement relating to treatment for a mental disorder, see **8.26**.

51 See: *Report on Incapable Adults*, Scot Law Comm No 151 (1995), recommendation 68.

52 For example, *Cooke v Telford* 2005 SCLR 367.

53 Mental Capacity Act 2005, s 1(5), though Stevenson, G *et al* in 'Principles, Patient Welfare and the 2000 Act,', (2009) 32 *International Journal of Law and Psychiatry* 120 argue that some courts in Scotland have effectively applied a best interests test in their decision making, one example is *CJR in respect of the Adult JMR* [2013] ScotSC 25, at [16].

less well equipped than others to cope with. But just as wise parents resist the temptation to keep their children metaphorically wrapped up in cotton wool, so too we must avoid the temptation always to put the physical health and safety of the elderly and the vulnerable before everything else. Often it will be appropriate to do so, but not always. Physical health and safety can sometimes be bought at too high a price in happiness and emotional welfare. The emphasis must be on sensible risk appraisal, not striving to avoid all risk, whatever the price, but instead seeking a proper balance and being willing to tolerate manageable or acceptable risks as the price appropriately to be paid in order to achieve some other good – in particular to achieve the vital good of the elderly or vulnerable person's *happiness*. What good is it making someone safer if it merely makes them miserable?[54]

MECHANISMS FOR TAKING DECISIONS ON BEHALF OF AN ADULT PROVIDED BY THE 2000 ACT

7.5 Many adults who are incapable of taking some decisions will retain capacity in other areas – in such areas there is no need for anyone else to take decisions or make choices on behalf of the adult. Unless a person can take advantage of the doctrine of *negotiorum gestio* there is no legal basis for them taking such decisions or making such choices. Where, however, decisions and choices do have to be made on behalf of an adult the 2000 Act provides, in addition to the powers derived from other sources discussed above, a number of different routes for doing this. These routes are, appointment of an attorney, guardianship, an intervention order, access to funds, management of funds in a residential setting and decisions on medical treatment.

(1) Attorneys[55]

7.6 An attorney is someone who is appointed by the adult to take decisions on their behalf. The appointment must be made while the adult still has the legal capacity to do so. Appointment of an attorney is made by the adult granting a deed appointing the attorney to which must be added a certificate that the adult has capacity at the date of granting

54 *Re MM (an adult); Local Authority X v MM* [2007] EWHC 2003 (Fam) at [120], per Munby J.

55 See *Scottish Government, Adults with Incapacity (Scotland) Act 2000: Code of Practice for Continuing and Welfare Attorneys* (Updated February 2018).

the deed.[56] Two types of attorney may be appointed and it is possible to appoint joint attorneys or for the person granting the power of attorney to appoint a substitute who will take over if the attorney is unable to act.[57] First, an attorney may be appointed to look after the financial affairs or property of the adult. It has always been possible to grant a power of attorney to authorise someone manage your affairs. Prior to the 2000 Act such a power of attorney would continue in effect after the adult lost capacity *unless* the adult specifically stated in the appointment of the attorney that it was not to continue following their incapacity.[58] The 2000 Act now provides for the appointment of continuing attorneys, but for the power of attorney to continue after the adult loses capacity the document appointing the attorney must specifically state that the power granted is to be a continuing one.[59] Any such power of attorney will take effect immediately, ie, while the adult still has capacity, though it may be specifically provided that it is not to take effect until the adult loses capacity. If this is provided for, the deed appointing the attorney must also state that the adult has considered how their capacity is to be determined.[60]

The second type of attorney is a welfare attorney, someone who is entitled to take decisions about the adult's personal welfare.[61] A welfare attorney will not have any power to act on behalf of an adult until the adult has lost capacity, or the welfare attorney reasonably believes that the granter is incapable in relation to decisions about the matters to which the welfare power of attorney relates.[62] The deed appointing the attorney must also state that the adult has considered how their incapacity in respect of decisions covered by the power of attorney is to be determined, and if a particular process has been chosen it should also be set out in the deed.[63] The welfare attorney's power is limited,

56 See also below. Guidance on appointing an attorney and forms for doing this can be found on the Office of the Public Guardian website at: www.publicguardian-scotland.gov.uk.

57 See *Scottish Government, Adults with Incapacity (Scotland) Act 2000: Code of Practice for Continuing and Welfare Attorneys* (Updated March 2018), p 17, paras 2.14–2.15.

58 Law Reform (Miscellaneous Provisions) (Scotland) Act 1990, s 7(1).

59 2000 Act, s 15(3)(b).

60 2000 Act, s 15(3)(ba). It appears that a simple statement that the matter has been considered is sufficient without any need for the means selected for determining incapacity to be set out, *Great Stuart Trustees v Public Guardian* [2014] CSIH 114, rejecting the suggestion in *Application for guardianship in respect of W* 2014 SLT (Sh Ct) 8 that the means had to be set out, though good practice might suggest that this is done.

61 2000 Act, s 16.

62 2000 Act, s 16(5)(b).

63 2000 Act, s 16(3)(ba).

they only have the power to take decisions in respect of which either the adult is incapable or in respect of which the attorney reasonably believes that the adult is incapable.[64] In addition, there are restrictions on the ability of an attorney to consent to certain types of medical procedure or treatment, these are considered below.

Regardless of the type of attorney appointed, the deed granting the power must contain a certificate signed by a solicitor.[65] The certificate must state that the attorney has interviewed the adult and that:

- they are satisfied, either through direct knowledge of the adult or through information from a person with such knowledge, that the adult understands the nature and the extent of the powers being granted;
- that they have no reason to believe that the adult was acting under undue influence or that there was any other factor which would invalidate the deed granting the power of attorney.

It is important that the solicitor carries out adequate enquiries into these matters before signing this certificate. Where it was established that this had not been done, the sheriff authorised the Public Guardian to refuse to register a power of attorney.[66] The consequence of this was that the attorney appointed had no power to act on behalf of the adult, since registration of the power of attorney with the Public Guardian is required as an additional step to give the attorney power to act.[67] The Public Guardian must[68] register any power of attorney provided it has the required certificate and provided that the attorney is prepared to act.[69] When a welfare power of attorney is registered, the Public Guardian must send a copy to the Mental Welfare Commission and to the local authority for the area in which the adult resides.[70]

A power of attorney can be revoked by the adult, provided they still have capacity to do this.[71] Appointment of a guardian will also terminate a power of attorney, to the extent that the powers conferred on the guardian overlap with the powers of the attorney. For example, if a welfare guardian was appointed this would have no effect on the

64 2000 Act, s 16(5)(b).

65 Who must not be the person appointed as attorney.

66 *Application by Public Guardian for Directions* [2010] Scot SC 115.

67 2000 Act, s 19(1).

68 Hence the need for the application to the sheriff for directions in the case cited in footnote 51 above.

69 Though it is possible for the deed granting the power of attorney to contain a term providing that it will not be registered until the happening of a specified event, 2000 Act, s 19(3).

70 2000 Act, s 19(2)(c).

71 2000 Act, s 22A.

powers conferred by a continuing power of attorney. Where the person appointed as attorney is the spouse or civil partner of the adult, the power of attorney may provide that it is to continue even if the marriage or civil partnership comes to an end, otherwise this will bring the power to an end.

A power of attorney can also be brought to an end by resignation of the attorney,[72] and the sheriff may revoke either the appointment of an attorney or any of the powers conferred on an attorney following an application by anyone claiming an interest.[73] The sheriff also has extensive powers to order production of accounts and reports, to require supervision of a continuing attorney by the Public Guardian and a welfare attorney by the local authority,[74] and to make directions regarding the exercise of powers by the attorney.[75]

(2) Guardianship

(a) Background

7.7 Guardians are appointed by the sheriff court and can be given powers to take decisions on behalf of the adult either in relation to the adult's finances and property (a financial guardian) or in relation to the adult's personal welfare (a welfare guardian), or can be given the power to take both sorts of decision.[76] Two guardians may be appointed (who will not be joint guardians) one as a financial guardian and the other as welfare guardian. Joint guardians can also be appointed,[77] though it has been held that this can only be done where the initial application for appointment of a guardian is for appointment of joint guardians, or where there is an existing guardian and an application is made for appointment of an additional, joint, guardian.[78] In general, joint guardians must be related to the adult, either as parents, siblings or children. The sheriff does have power, if it is considered appropriate, to appoint as joint guardians people who are not so related to the adult.[79] Joint guardians can each exercise the powers conferred on them but must normally

72 2000 Act, s 23, though if there is a joint attorney or a substitute attorney, they may continue to exercise the power.
73 2000 Act, s 20(1), (2)(e).
74 2000 Act, s 20(1), (2)(a)–(d).
75 See **7.18** below.
76 2000 Act, ss 57–61.
77 2000 Act, s 62.
78 *Cooke v Telford* 2005 SCLR 367, *M, Applicant* 2009 GWD 24–394. See also **7.9** below.
79 2000 Act, s 62(2).

consult each other before doing this.[80] The other restrictions on who can be a guardian are that the guardian must be an individual (rather than, for example, a company or a charity) and that the chief social work officer cannot be appointed as a financial guardian.[81]

(b) Making the application

7.8 An application for the appointment of a guardian can be made either by the local authority (this happens in around a quarter of cases) or by anyone else who claims to have an interest either in the financial affairs or personal welfare of the adult, or both.[82] Monitoring carried out by the Mental Welfare Commission indicates over 70% of guardianships in 2022–23 were applications by family members.[83] Where an individual intends to apply to be appointed as a welfare guardian, they must notify the local authority (though in practice this is likely to be done by their solicitor). The reason for this is that the application made by the individual must be accompanied by a report from the local authority (a suitability report).[84] This report must be produced within twenty-one days of the local authority being notified of the intention to apply for appointment as guardian.[85] Legal aid is available to assist individuals in making applications for appointment as a guardian.

Unlike individuals, who may decide whether to apply for appointment as a guardian, the local authority has a duty to apply to court for appointment of a guardian if certain conditions are fulfilled:

(a) the adult meets the incapacity threshold for the making of a guardianship order; [86]

(b) a guardianship order is necessary to protect the property, financial affairs or personal welfare of the adult;[87] and

80 2000 Act, s 62(6), consultation is not required if it is impracticable in the circumstances (e.g. if a decision must be taken very quickly), or where the joint guardians agree that it is unnecessary.

81 2000 Act, ss 58(5) and 59(2).

82 2000 Act, s 57(1). See also *Scottish Government, Adults with Incapacity (Scotland) Act 2000: Code of Practice for persons authorised under intervention orders and guardians* (2011), ch 4. An adult's solicitor did not have such an interest purely because of being her solicitor, *J's Application* [2016] SC EDIN 66.

83 Mental Welfare Commission for Scotland, *Adults with Incapacity Act Monitoring Report 2022–2023*, p 9, Fig 2.

84 *Code of Practice* 2008, paras 6.30–6.42 and 7.15–7.42.

85 2000 Act, s 57(4).

86 2000 Act, s 57(2)(c)..

87 2000 Act, s 57(2)(c).

(c) no one else has made or is likely to make an application for an order.[88]

The application made by the local authority may be for appointment of a financial guardian or a welfare guardian or both. In an application by the local authority it is not possible for a local authority officer to be appointed as a financial guardian. It is, however usual (but need not be the case) that where welfare guardianship is applied for, the appointee will be the Chief Social Work Officer for the authority.[89]

The appointment and powers of the guardian must be given some consideration. It will be necessary to consider and apply the principles set out in **7.4** above. In particular consideration must be given to the requirement for the least restrictive option to be taken and the need to seek the views of a variety of people, including the adult.

Applications take the form of a summary application to the sheriff court. The application will, amongst other things, identify the person(s) whose appointment as guardian is sought, and set out both the powers to be conferred on the guardian if appointed and the desired duration of the order. The default duration of a guardianship order is three years, though the sheriff can fix a different period (longer or shorter), including an indefinite period.[90] In 2022–23, 32% of the granted orders were for three years or less, 81.5% were for a period of five years or less (compared to 80% in the previous year). 14.9% were for six years or longer (lower than the previous year's 16%), and 3.6% were indefinite orders. This last figure has declined from 32% in 2013–14.[91]

The application must be accompanied by a number of reports:[92]

(a) Two medical reports. These must be based on an examination and assessment of the adult carried out within 30 days before the application was lodged. The sheriff may can consider an older report if satisfied that the adult's condition has not changed in any relevant respect since the examination and assessment was carried out.[93] If the adult's incapacity is the result of a mental disorder one of the reports must be from a 'relevant medical practitioner', that is, someone who has special experience of the diagnosis and

88 2000 Act, s 57(2)(b). It does not matter that there are others who *could* apply for an order if they are not going to do so.

89 2000 Act, s 59(1)(b).

90 2000 Act, s 58(4).

91 Mental Welfare Commission for Scotland, *Adults with Incapacity Act Monitoring Report 2022–2023*, p10, Table 1.

92 2000 Act, s 57(3).

93 2000 Act, s 57(3B).

treatment of mental disorder and appears on a list of approved practitioners maintained by the Health Board.[94]

(b) A 'suitability report'[95] will be needed where the application is for the appointment of a welfare guardian. The report will normally be prepared by a mental health officer[96] and be based on an interview with and assessment of the adult carried out within 30 days of the application being made. It will give the views of the reporter on whether the order being sought is appropriate and, if the applicant is not the Chief Social Work Officer, an opinion on the suitability of the person(s) seeking appointment. The guidance suggests that the report should be clear about how the writer has reached their conclusions and should also include consideration of possible conflicts of interests, e.g., between the local authority and the adult or between the local authority and the adult's relatives.

(c) Where the application is for appointment of a financial guardian, the 'suitability report' must be produced by someone who has 'sufficient knowledge.' This report will cover both the 'general appropriateness' of the order and the suitability of the proposed guardian and must be based in part on an interview with and assessment of the adult within 30 days before the application is made.[97]

(c) Procedure after making application

7.9 Where the sheriff makes a guardianship order a number of people and bodies must be notified of the application. Those who must be notified are; the adult (though see below), the adult's nearest relative, named person and primary carer, the Public Guardian, any attorney with powers affected by the application along with anyone else whom the sheriff directs to be notified.[98] Where the application is to appoint a welfare guardian, the Mental Welfare Commission and the local authority must be informed. [99] It is possible to apply to the sheriff to dispense with the need to notify the adult. This can only be done if informing the adult would be likely to pose a serious risk to the health

94 2000 Act, s 57(3)(a).

95 *Code of Practice* 2008, paras 6.30–6.42 and 7.15–7.42.

96 Though, in cases where incapacity arises solely because of inability to communicate (ie, the inability to communicate is not the result of a mental disorder), the report may be prepared by a social worker who is not an MHO. The form of report by an MHO is set out in the Adults with Incapacity (Reports in Relation to Guardianship and Intervention Orders) (Scotland) Regulations 2002, SSI 2002/96, Sch 2.

97 *Code of Practice* 2008, para 6.38.

98 2000 Act, s 58.

99 2000 Act, s 58.

of the applicant.[100] The application to dispense with notification to the adult must be supported by two medical certificates which confirm that notification would pose a risk to them. These medical certificates should also explain the basis for reaching that conclusion so that the sheriff has some basis for deciding whether the criterion for dispensing with notification is met.[101]

The application may also seek appointment of an interim guardian pending the final decision on the application.[102] An interim guardian can be appointed for up to six months.[103] The appointment of an interim guardian will come to an end, unless recalled earlier, when a guardian is appointed, or at the end of of the period of appointment, whichever is the earlier.[104]

A hearing will be fixed to take place no more than 28 days after the application, though this hearing will not necessarily decide on the application. Anyone who has been notified of the application can lodge answers opposing the application or challenging some of the statements made in the application. Challenges may be made for example on the need for guardianship or the suitability of the proposed guardian and proposing an alternative guardian. Application may also be made by way of a minute for appointment of a guardian other than the person named in the application. It has been held that joint guardians can only be appointed either where the initial application is for the appointment of joint guardians, or where there is already an existing guardian and a fresh application is made for the appointment of an additional, joint, guardian.[105] This conclusion[106] means, for example, that if an adult's partner applies for appointment as guardian to an adult, the adult's daughter cannot, as part of the same application process, seek appointment as a joint guardian with the partner. There would be two options open to the daughter. First, to oppose the partner's application and seek appointment as sole guardian. Second, to not oppose the partner's application and then, after the partner has been appointed guardian, to make a fresh application to be appointed as joint guardian.

100 2000 Act, s 11.
101 *Application in respect of D* [2010] 10 WLUK 548.
102 2000 Act, s 57(5).
103 2000 Act, s 57(5), (6).
104 2000 Act, s 57(6).
105 *Cooke v Telford* 2005 SCLR 367, *M, Applicant* 2009 GWD 24–394. Though see *JM v Aberdeenshire Council* [2017] CSIH 65.
106 Based on the wording of the statute which refers to '*An* application being made to the sheriff by two or more individuals …', 2000 Act, s 62(1)(a). In cases such as the example, there is no such joint application.

After a hearing, the sheriff must then decide how to dispose of the application.[107] The sheriff can only appoint a guardian to the adult if certain requirements are met:

(a) The sheriff must consider the principles underlying intervention set out above (at **7.4** above) and will need, for example, to be satisfied that appointment will provide a benefit to the adult and be the least restrictive course of action which achieves the desired result.

(b) The adult must be incapable and it must be likely that this incapacity will continue. In this context incapacity covers both the adult being incapable in relation to decision making and being incapable of acting to safeguard or promote their interests and welfare.[108]

(c) No other available measures are sufficient to safeguard and promote the adult's interests.[109] If the sheriff considers that the result could be achieved by the less restrictive option of making an intervention order, then they have the power to make such an order instead of a guardianship order.[110]

(d) The person(s) appointed as guardian(s) must agree to the appointment(s) and must be suitable, though the sheriff doesn't have to be satisfied as to suitability where the Chief Social Work Officer is seeking appointment.[111] At least some of the evidence for taking the decision on suitability will come from the suitability report lodged along with the applications. The factors which the sheriff has to consider in deciding on suitability are:[112]
   (i) how accessible the person is to the adult and the adult's primary carer;
   (ii) the ability of the person to carry out the functions of a guardian;
   (iii) whether the person is likely to have any conflict of interest with the adult, though such a conflict is not to be presumed only because the person is a relative of, or resides with the adult;[113]

107 2000 Act, s 58.
108 2000 Act, s 58(1)(a).
109 2000 Act, s 58(1)(b).
110 2000 Act, s 58(3).
111 2000 Act, s 59(1)(b).
112 2000 Act, s 59(4).
113 2000 Act, s 59(5). In *North Ayrshire Council v JM* 2004 SCLR 956, it was argued that, because there might be financial strain between the local authority and the adult, there could be a conflict of interest between the Chief Social Work Officer and the adult. This, it was argued, made the appointment of someone other than the Chief Social Work Officer appropriate. The relevant guidance indicates that the suitability report should consider potential conflicts of interest, *Code of Practice* 2008, paras 6.33–6.37 and 7.23–7.35.

(iv) if any undue concentration of power over the adult will arise because of the person's appointment as guardian;

(v) any adverse effects which appointment of the person would have on the interests of the adult; and

(vi) any other matters which appear to the sheriff to be appropriate.

(e) the person appointed must be aware of the functions of a guardian as well as of the adult's circumstances and condition and of the needs arising from these.[114]

More than one person may be appointed as guardian; this will be the case where joint guardians are appointed or where one person is appointed as financial guardian and another as welfare guardian.[115] It is also possible for the sheriff to appoint both a guardian (the original guardian) and a substitute guardian who will take over the role of the original guardian if they become unable to act.[116] It is also possible to apply for appointment of a substitute guardian after a guardian has been appointed.[117]

In deciding who to appoint as guardian, the sheriff is not limited to appointing the original applicant; anyone who has entered the process to contest the application may seek appointment of someone other than the original applicant.[118] The sheriff will still, however, need to be satisfied as to the suitability of the person suggested as an alternative to the original applicant, and may order that a report on their suitability be prepared.[119] It has been suggested that it is best practice for this report to be prepared by the same MHO who produced the suitability report lodged with the application.[120]

The sheriff must fix the duration of the appointment. The default duration of a guardianship order is three years, though the sheriff can fix a different or indefinite period, but this can only be done on cause shown, that is, the person seeking the appointment must set out reasons for the longer or shorter duration.[121]

114 2000 Act, s 59(3).
115 2000 Act, s 62.
116 2000 Act, s 63(1).
117 2000 Act, s 63(4).
118 Deriving from the sheriff's power to appoint '*any* individual' considered suitable and who has agreed to act, 2000 Act, s 59(1)(a). *JM v Aberdeenshire Council* [2017] CSIH 65.
119 2000 Act, s 59(1).
120 See *M, Applicant* 2009 GWD 24–394 and *JM v Aberdeenshire Council* [2016] SAC (Civ) 5. No conflict of interest will arise in preparing such a report where the original applicant is the local authority, *JM v Aberdeenshire Council* [2017] CSIH 65.
121 2000 Act, s 58(4). Detail on the length of orders granted is set out in footnote 68 above.

The sheriff will also have to specify the powers to be granted to the guardian, and these will be set out in the application for the appointment of a guardian. The 2000 Act sets out the broad categories of powers which may be granted, though the powers applied for will normally be expressed more specifically:[122]

(a) Power to deal with matters related to the adult's property, financial affairs or welfare specified in the guardianship order. This might include, for example, a specific power to determine where the adult stays.
(b) Power to deal with all aspects of the adult's personal welfare or with those aspects which are set out in the guardianship order.
(c) Power to manage the adult's property and financial affairs, or those parts of them which are set out in the guardianship order.
(d) Power to authorise the adult to carry out either specific transactions or categories of transactions as the guardian may specify, this power should be considered in the context of Principle 4 set out above.
(e) Power to pursue or defend an action of declarator of nullity of marriage, or of divorce or separation in the name of the adult.

In considering which powers to grant, the sheriff will have to consider the Principles set out above (at **7.4** above) and may, for example, refuse to grant some powers because they are considered too restrictive.[123] There are also restrictions on the power of the guardian to consent to certain types of medical treatment or procedure. These restrictions are considered more fully below.

One final matter which must be considered in appointing a financial guardian is whether the guardian should be required to find caution (pronounced 'kayshun'). In practice this takes the form of requiring insurance in case the guardian mismanages the adult's estate. Initially the 2000 Act required caution in every case, though it gave the sheriff discretion in fixing the amount of caution. Because of the difficulty experience by some family member financial guardians in finding caution the amount was in some cases fixed at zero. The 2000 Act has since been amended and the sheriff now has discretion as to whether to require caution.[124] Arrangements have also been made by the Public Guardian which make it easier for guardians who are not solicitors or accountants to get caution.[125]

122 2000 Act, s 64(1)(a)–(e).
123 *Application in respect of EB*, Glasgow Sheriff Court, 1 December 2005.
124 2000 Act, s 58(6).
125 See, Office of The Public Guardian website at: www.publicguardian-scotland.gov.uk (accessed 13 November 2025).

(d) *After the order is granted*[126]

7.10 Once a guardianship order has been granted, the sheriff clerk must notify the Public Guardian, who maintains a register of guardianship orders. The Sheriff Clerk sends to the Public Guardian a copy of the interlocutor containing the order. The Public Guardian will then notify the adult, the local authority for the area in which the adult resides, and, where the incapacity arises from mental disorder, the Mental Welfare Commission.[127] Where the Chief Social Work Office has been appointed as a welfare guardian then they must, within seven days, identify the named individual who will carry out the duties of guardian. The person appointed will normally have been involved with the adult prior to the application being made for a guardianship order. The Code of Practice makes it clear that in considering the appointment of this individual any possible conflict of interest must be considered, for example if the same person would be acting as guardian and also as manager for a support package for the adult.[128]

Welfare guardians must be supervised by the local authority.[129] An initial visit to the adult and the guardian must take place within three months of the making of the order and thereafter at intervals of not more than six months.[130] For longer orders, after the first 12-month visit the local authority can decide that there should be longer periods between visits or to stop visits, though these decisions can be reversed.[131] In the case of an order for less than 12 months, the guardian has to be contacted at least three months before the end of the order to consider renewal of the order and other arrangements for the welfare of the adult. In order to assist with this supervision, the guardian must provide the local authority, on request, with information about the adult's welfare or the guardian's exercise of their power. Where a local authority worker is acting as guardian the required supervision should be carried out by the

126 Scottish Government, *Adults with Incapacity (Scotland) Act 2000: Code of Practice for Persons Authorised under Intervention Orders and Guardians* (2011), chs 5 and 6; *Code of Practice* 2008, paras 6.52–6.66.

127 Adults with Incapacity (Scotland) Act s 58(7)(c) and (d).

128 Scottish Government, *Adults with Incapacity (Scotland) Act 2000: Code of Practice* (2008), para 6.50.

129 Adults with Incapacity (Supervision of Welfare Guardians etc by Local Authorities) (Scotland) Regulations 2002, SSI 2002/95, as amended; see also Scottish Government, *Adults with Incapacity (Scotland) Act 2000: Code of Practice* (2008), ch 8.

130 Scottish Government, *Adults with Incapacity (Scotland) Act 2000: Code of Practice* (2011), para 6.95.

131 Mental Welfare Commission for Scotland, Supervising Welfare Guardians and Powers of Attorney Good Practice Guide (2022), p 7.

worker's line manager. Financial guardians are supervised by the Public Guardian.

During the period of guardianship, it may be felt that it is necessary to change the powers which have been given to the guardian and this can be done by application to the sheriff.[132] If the guardianship is coming to the end of the period fixed as its duration it can be renewed by application to the sheriff.[133] The reports required to renew are slightly different from those required for initial appointment. For example, only one medical report is required and the MHO's report will cover the general appropriateness of continuing the guardianship and, in cases where the Chief Social Work Officer is not the guardian, the suitability of the guardian.[134] If the original guardian is unable or unwilling to continue to act (this, of course, could happen at any time, not just at the end of an order) a substitute or replacement guardian may be appointed. Such appointments (when not involving renewal of the order) don't require a medical or suitability report, though some evidence as to the suitability of the proposed guardian will have to be provided to the sheriff.

If the adult, or someone else, refuses to comply with a welfare guardian's decision it is possible for the guardian to seek a court order requiring compliance.[135] In its original form the 2000 Act provided for a person subject to such an order to be given the opportunity to make representations prior to an order being made.[136] It is now possible for the sheriff to dispense with this requirement, though, as the Code of Practice notes:[137]

> It is anticipated that the section 70 procedure will be used only occasionally by welfare guardians, for example to remove the person from an unsuitable place to one where the guardian has decided he/she should live. It represents a potentially substantial encroachment on the personal autonomy of an individual. Before making an order or granting a warrant, the sheriff would have to be satisfied that the principles in the 2000 Act were being met. There would have to be a positive benefit to the adult and the order or warrant would have to be the only reasonable way of achieving that benefit. In dealing with a habitual absconder a new warrant would be needed for each incident.

132 2000 Act, s 74.
133 2000 Act, s 60(1).
134 2000 Act, s 60(3).
135 2000 Act, s 70.
136 2000 Act, s 70(3).
137 *Code of Practice* 2008, para 6.62.

The sheriff has extensive powers to make directions regarding the exercise of powers by the guardian, and these are explained in **7.18** below.

Aside from the expiry of the period of the guardianship order without the order being renewed, guardianship, or the appointment of an individual guardian, can be terminated in a variety of different ways:

(a) The guardian may resign, though if there is no joint guardian or substitute guardian they cannot resign until a replacement guardian has been appointed.[138]

(b) A financial guardianship may be recalled by the Public Guardian and a welfare guardianship by the Mental Welfare Commission or the local authority. Recall of welfare guardianship may be requested by someone claiming an interest in the welfare of the adult (including the adult) or, for example, the local authority may, following a review, decide to recall a guardianship.[139] Recall can only take place if either, the grounds for appointment of a guardian with such powers are no longer fulfilled, or, there are other means of safeguarding and promoting the interests of the adult.[140]

(c) The guardianship can be recalled by the sheriff, the grounds for this are the same as those set in (b) out above.[141]

(d) A guardian can be removed from their position as guardian by the sheriff provided that there is another guardian prepared to act. Removal can be sought by anyone claiming an interest and might be appropriate if a local authority had significant concerns about a guardian.[142]

(e) Death of the adult or of the guardian.[143]

(3) Intervention orders[144]

7.11 Intervention orders are appropriate where the intervention is likely to be time-limited or where a single action or decision is involved,

138 2000 Act, s 75.

139 2000 Act, s 73(3), (4). In the case of financial guardianship, the decision may be made by the Public Guardian to recall the guardianship or an application may be made by anyone having an interest in the property or financial affairs of the adult, s 73(1), (2).

140 2000 Act, s 73(1).

141 2000 Act, s 71.

142 2000 Act, s 71(1).

143 2000 Act, s 75A.

144 Scottish Government, *Adults with Incapacity (Scotland) Act 2000: Code of Practice for Persons Authorised under Intervention Orders and Guardians* (2011), chs 2 and 3; *Code of Practice* 2008, paras 6.1–6.16.

for example, selling property belonging to the adult[145] or agreeing settlement of a compensation claim.[146] Intervention orders can relate either to the financial or to the personal welfare of the adult, though in practice a very small number of orders is concerned with personal welfare. Where it will be necessary to take decisions on behalf of an adult over a period of time on a continuing basis the appropriate form of intervention is to seek a guardianship order.

As with guardianship orders, anyone claiming an interest may seek an intervention order, and the procedure and reports required are similar, though the reports will refer to an intervention order rather than guardianship.[147] The local authority has duty to apply for an intervention order where it appears that an application is necessary for the protection of the property, financial affairs or personal welfare of an adult who is incapable, and it is apparent that no application has been or is likely to be made by any other party.[148]

As well as these procedural similarities, there are some important differences between guardianship and intervention orders:

(a) Although a local authority cannot apply for appointment as a financial guardian, it can apply for an intervention order in relation to the adult's finances or property.[149]

(b) The sheriff can make an intervention order when guardianship is applied for but cannot do the opposite.

(c) Persons authorised under an intervention order will not automatically be under the supervision of the local authority or the Public Guardian, except that the latter will have to agree to the purchase/sale price where the intervention authorised involves buying or selling a house.[150]

(4) Access to funds[151]

7.12 The access to funds procedure allows an individual or a body to apply to the Public Guardian to be allowed to deal with the adult's money. If the application is granted the Public Guardian will issue a

145 *Code of Practice* 2008, para 2.13.
146 *B, Applicant* 2005 SLT (Sh Ct) 95.
147 2000 Act, s 53.
148 2000 Act, s 53(3).
149 2000 Act, s 53(1).
150 2000 Act, s 53(6).
151 2000 Act, part 3, Scottish Government, *Adults with Incapacity (Scotland) Act 2000 Code of Practice – Access to Funds* (2008).

certificate of authority.[152] One example of use of this provision was the case of a local authority which sought authority to deal with an adult's benefits. The adult spent money freely on their children to the extent that they often did not have enough to pay accommodation, food and utilities costs. The local authority (which was also the adult's welfare guardian) obtained a withdrawal certificate (the form in which authority was granted at the time) from the Public Guardian which allowed it to control as much of the adult's benefits as were required to pay their basic living expenses, leaving an amount for discretionary spending.[153]

The application can be made either by an individual or by a body, for example, the local authority. The purposes for which the authorisation can be granted are limited to; payment of taxes; payment of basic expenses for food, accommodation, clothing and fuel; payment for other services for looking after or caring for the adult; payment of debts owed by the adult; and, payment for other items authorised by the Public Guardian.[154] If an application is made by a body other than the local authority or is made by someone who is both the adult's nearest relative and their primary carer, then it must be notified to the local authority. The local authority must then, if it wishes to oppose the application, be given an opportunity to make representations before a decision is made by the Public Guardian. In all cases, the person authorised must be a fit and proper person or organisation, in the case of organisations approval as fit and proper only needs to be done once.[155]

(5) Management of resident's funds

7.13 One option for the management of the finances of an adult who is staying in a residential establishment is for these to be managed by a manager in that establishment.[156] This is only possible in what are described as 'authorised establishments', and these include hospitals (whether independent or NHS), private psychiatric hospitals, care home services registered with Social Care and Social Work Improvement Scotland (the Care Inspectorate), and a State Hospital.[157] The first step in obtaining an authorisation to manage the funds of a resident is the issue of a medical certificate. The certificate must state that the adult

152 *Code of Practice – Access to Funds* (2008) paras 2.33 and 2.34.

153 *W v Office of the Public Guardian* [2010] 6 WLUK 645.

154 Scottish Government, *Code of Practice – Access to Funds* (2008) paras 3.5 and 3.6.

155 See Office of the Public Guardian, *Access to Funds Scheme Adults with Incapacity (Scotland) Act 2000: Guide for Organisations* (2011); Office of the Public Guardian, *Organisations – Fitness to Access Funds: Notes to Complete Form* (2012).

156 2000 Act, PT part 4.

157 2000 Act, s 35(1).

is unable to manage their finances without assistance.[158] Once such a certificate has been issued, notification must be made to the adult (unless this is likely to pose a serious risk to the health of the adult) and to the supervisory body for the establishment. In the case of NHS hospitals, the supervisory body will be the Health Board, for others it will be the Care Inspectorate.[159] The supervisory body will then inform the nearest relative.[160] The manager must also notify the adult and the supervisory body of the intention to manage the affairs of the adult.[161] Following this the manager must apply to the supervisory body for a Certificate of Authority to withdraw the resident's funds, and only after this Certificate has been issued by the supervisory authority can the manager manage these funds.[162]

Once the Certificate is issued the manager can hold and dispose of moveable property belonging to the adult and can claim, hold and spend a very limited range of benefits, though most benefits are excluded (but could still be managed by a manager if they were appointed as a benefits appointee).[163] One issue is whether this exclusion extends not only to current benefits, but to benefits which have accrued in an account held by the adult. The 2000 Act does not expressly address this issue. Research published in 2009 found differences of approach to this between different supervisory bodies, with some regarding such accrued funds as being excluded from this mechanism and others taking the opposite view.[164] If it is not possible to manage accrued benefits in this way, it is clear that this can be done by seeking appointment of a benefits appointee or by seeking authority to access the adult's funds.

The manager must act for the benefit of the resident and take account of the sentimental value of any item, must keep proper records and must only spend the funds on items which are not provided by the establishment as part of its normal service.[165] There is an upper limit of £10,000 on the amount that can be managed, though agreement can be obtained from the supervisory body to manage larger amounts.

158 2000 Act, s 37(1); Adults with Incapacity (Management of Residents' Finances) (No 2) (Scotland) Regulations 2003, SSI 2003/266; *Adults with Incapacity (Scotland) Act 2000: Code of Practice for Managers of Authorised Establishments under Part 4 of the Act* (SE/2003/177).

159 On supervisory bodies, see: 2000 Act, s 40.

160 2000 Act, s 37(3), (4)(a).

161 2000 Act, s 37 (4)(b).

162 2000 Act, s 42.

163 2000 Act, s 39.

164 Scottish Government Social Research, *Evaluation of the Adults with Incapacity (Scotland) Act 2000, Part 4* (2009).

165 *Adults with Incapacity (Scotland) Act 2000: Code of Practice for Managers of Authorised Establishments under Part 4 of the Act* (SE/2003/177), para 7.66.

It is only possible to manage an adult's funds under an authorisation to the extent that there is no guardian, attorney or other person with powers to do this and there is no intervention order regulating a particular use of or action in relation to the adult's funds.

(6) Medical treatment[166]

7.14 Consent to medical treatment for adults can, subject to certain restrictions described below, be given by a welfare guardian or a welfare attorney. The extent of this consent will be determined by the powers conferred on them . Consent may cover specific treatment or may be the subject of an application for an intervention order.[167] In addition, a decision can only be taken about medical treatment if the adult is incapable of giving or refusing consent and, as with other areas, the capacity of the adult may vary between different types of treatment.[168] Medical practitioners and others also have powers under the 2000 Act to give treatment, both in cases where there is no attorney or guardian and where there is such an appointee.[169]

(a) Treatment by medical practitioners

7.15 Medical practitioners (and certain others)[170] can certify that an adult is incapable in relation to specific medical treatment and, subject to what is said later, medical treatment can be given to the adult on the basis of that certification.[171] The treatment may be provided by someone other than the person issuing the certificate. There is a specific form for the certificate (a Medical Treatment Certificate)[172] and it will need to specify how long the authority to treat will last, though this is normally a maximum of one year.[173] If the adult's condition or circumstances

166 Scottish Government, *Adults with Incapacity (Scotland) Act 2000: Code of Practice (Third Edition) for practitioners authorised to carry out medical treatment or research under Part 5 of the Act* (2010).

167 2000 Act, part 5.

168 2000 Act, s 47(1).

169 2000 Act, s 50(1).

170 Including dentists and registered nurses, 2000 Act, s 47(1A).

171 See Mental Welfare Commission, *Adults with Incapacity, Part* 5 (2013) and Mental Welfare Commission, *Adults with Incapacity Act monitoring report 2015–16*, p 24.

172 Adults with Incapacity (Medical Treatment Certificates) (Scotland) Regulations 2007, SSI 2007/104, reg 2.

173 This is extended to three years where the adult is incapable of consenting because of a severe or profound learning disability, dementia or a severe neurological disorder and is unlikely to improve, Adults with Incapacity (Conditions and Circumstances Applicable to Three Year Medical Treatment Certificates) (Scotland) Regulations 2007, SSI 2007/100.

change the certificate can be revoked and, if that is done, a new certificate may be issued. The authority to treat conferred by a certificate does not extend to:

(a) the use of force or detention, unless this is immediately necessary and then only for as long as necessary;[174]
(b) any action inconsistent with a court decision;[175] or
(c) placing an adult in hospital for treatment of a mental disorder against their will.[176]

In addition, some types of treatment (see Box 7.2) can only be given after permission has been given by the Court of Session or after approval by a medical practitioner appointed by the Mental Welfare Commission.[177]

Box 7.2

Treatments requiring permission of the Court of Session:

- sterilisation in cases where there is no serious malfunction or disease of the reproductive organs;[178] and
- hormonal implants to reduce sex drive.[179]

Treatments requiring approval by MWC appointee:

- drug treatment to reduce sex drive, other than the surgical implantation of hormones;[180]
- ECT (Electro-convulsive Therapy) for mental disorders;[181]
- abortion;[182] or
- treatment which is likely to cause sterilisation.[183]

Treatment cannot be given if the authority to provide treatment is the subject of court proceedings. Treatment is similarly not permitted where

174 2000 Act, s 47(7)(a).
175 2000 Act, s 47(7)(b).
176 2000 Act, s 47(7)(c).
177 2000 Act, s 48, Adults with Incapacity (Specified Medical Treatments) (Scotland) Regulations 2002, SSI 2002/275.
178 Adults with Incapacity (Specified Medical Treatments) (Scotland) Regulations 2002, Sch 1, part 1, para 2.
179 Adults with Incapacity (Specified Medical Treatments) (Scotland) Regulations 2002, Sch 1, part 1, para 3.
180 Adults with Incapacity (Specified Medical Treatments) (Scotland) Regulations 2002, Sch 1, part 2, para 1.
181 Adults with Incapacity (Specified Medical Treatments) (Scotland) Regulations 2002, Sch 1, part 2, para 2.
182 Adults with Incapacity (Specified Medical Treatments) (Scotland) Regulations 2002, Sch 1, part 2, para 3.
183 Adults with Incapacity (Specified Medical Treatments) (Scotland) Regulations 2002, Sch 1, part 1, para 4.

the power to consent to treatment is the subject of an application for a guardianship order or intervention order currently before the court, unless the treatment is otherwise legally authorised to preserve the life of the adult or to prevent serious deterioration in their condition.[184] If there is a proxy[185] who has power in relation to a particular form of treatment, and the person giving that treatment is aware of this, they cannot give treatment unless they have obtained the consent of that proxy, provided that it would be reasonable and practicable to get the proxy's consent. If consent is obtained then the treatment can go ahead, though anyone having an interest (or the person who issued the certificate if they are not providing the treatment) can appeal the decision about treatment to the Court of Session.[186]

(b) Disagreements about medical treatment

7.16 If the person providing treatment and the person with power to take decisions about that treatment on behalf of the adult[187] (the proxy) disagree about medical treatment, a request can be made to the Mental Welfare Commission to nominate someone (a nominated practitioner)[188] to give an opinion on whether or not the treatment should be given. If the opinion of the nominated practitioner is that treatment should be given then it can be provided, though, regardless of the opinion of the nominated practitioner, it is possible to seek a determination from the Court of Session as to whether the treatment should be given or not.[189]

(c) Restriction on powers of proxy to consent to treatment

7.17 There are restrictions on the powers of attorneys,[190] welfare guardians[191] and persons authorised under an intervention order[192] to consent to medical treatment. In particular, leaving aside any restriction deriving from the scope of the powers conferred on them, they cannot:

184 2000 Act, 49(2).
185 A welfare guardian or attorney or a person authorised by an intervention order.
186 2000 Act, 52.
187 Eg, a welfare guardian or attorney or someone authorised under an intervention order.
188 See Mental Welfare Commission, *Adults with Incapacity Act Monitoring Report 2022–2023, p 21.*
189 2000 Act, s 50(5)–(8).
190 2000 Act, s 16(6).
191 2000 Act, s 64(2).
192 2000 Act, s 53(14).

(a) place the adult in hospital against their will for treatment of a mental disorder;[193]
(b) consent to any of the treatments set out in Box 7.2 above;[194]
(c) make a request that the adult's body be used, after death, for anatomical examination;[195]
(d) give authorisation:[196]
    (i) for the removal and use of part of the adult's body after death for transplant, research, education or training or audit;
    (ii) for use of an organ for live transplant;
    (iii) for a post-mortem examination; or
    (iv) for use of a tissue sample or organ for providing information about or confirming the cause of death; investigating the effect and efficacy of any medical or surgical intervention carried out on the person; obtaining information which may be relevant to the health of any other person (including a future person); or audit;
    - withdraw an authorisation, on behalf of the granter, by virtue of section 6A(1) of that Act;
    - make, on behalf of the granter, an opt-out declaration by virtue of section 6B(1) of that Act;
    - withdraw an opt-out declaration, on behalf of the granter, by virtue of section 6C(1) of that Act. [197]
(e) nominate someone who can authorise a post-mortem examination.[198]

(7) Directions

7.18 Under section 3 of the 2000 Act the sheriff has extensive power to make any direction they consider appropriate.[199] In particular, a direction can be made about the exercise by a guardian or attorney of their powers, or about taking any decision or action in relation to the adult.[200] The application can be made by anyone claiming an interest in the personal welfare or financial affairs or property of the adult. Examples of the use of this power are directions being given as to the

193 2000 Act, ss 16(6)(a), 64(2)(a). The effect of which is to suggest that such a placement can be made if the adult is compliant and does not attempt to leave.
194 2000 Act, s 16(6)(b), 64(2)(b).
195 2000 Act, s 16(6)(c), 64(2)(c).
196 2000 Act, s 16(6)(d), 64(2)(d).
197 2000 Act, s 16(6)(da)–(dc), 64(2)(da)–(dc). Provisions added by the Human Tissue (Authorisation) (Scotland) Act 2019 asp 11 (Scottish Act) Pt 4 s 28(2)(a)(ii).
198 2000 Act, s 16(6)(e), 64(2)(e).
199 2000 Act, s 3(1).
200 2000 Act, s 3(3).

use of the adult's property to prevent misuse of it by a relative,[201] and directing a guardian to agree to move the adult from hospital to a care home.[202]

PROVISION OF SERVICES TO ADULTS WITH INCAPACITY

7.19 This has been considered in part in **6.13** which discussed the ability of local authorities to provide services to adults by virtue of section 13ZA of the Social Work (Scotland) Act 1968. As the guidance on section 13ZA notes, it cannot be used to provide services in cases where service provision would result in deprivation of the adult's liberty. This is most obviously likely to arise in cases of placement in residential accommodation and the question will be, 'does the placement of an adult in residential accommodation amount to or involve a deprivation of their liberty?'. This issue will arise even in cases where the adult is compliant with the placement, in that they do not resist it or try to leave, and it also arises where an adult has capacity when the placement is made and agrees to it but subsequently loses capacity.[203] In this latter case the question is whether continuation of the placement involves a deprivation of liberty. However, this issue may also arise where the adult is living in supported accommodation or where they are living at home under close supervision and not permitted to leave.

The 'deprivation of liberty' wording derives from Article 5 of the European Convention on Human Rights, which is in the following terms:

> 1. Everyone has the right to liberty and security of person. No one shall be deprived of his liberty save in the following cases and in accordance with a procedure prescribed by law:
>
> …
>
> (e) the lawful detention of persons for the prevention of the spreading of infectious diseases, of persons of unsound mind, alcoholics or drug addicts or vagrants;
>
> …

201 Application *in respect of D* [2013] 2 WLUK 289, application made by the adult's attorneys.

202 *B, Minuter 2014 S.L.T (Sh Ct) 5*, application made by adult's doctor.

203 See *Anne Docherty*, Glasgow Sheriff Court, 8 February 2005.

> 4. Everyone who is deprived of his liberty by arrest or detention shall be entitled to take proceedings by which the lawfulness of his detention shall be decided speedily by a court and his release ordered if the detention is not lawful.

The current law on these questions is considered below, but most of the discussion in court in recent years has focused on the relatively narrow question of whether a deprivation of liberty exists.[204] In *P v Cheshire West and Chester Council*, the view was expressed, in a dissenting judgment, that domestic settings (eg, cases where the adult is living in their own home) cannot involve deprivation of liberty.[205] A focus on this question (and the rather cumbersome current processes for dealing with deprivation of liberty) obscures the underlying purpose in this context of Article 5.[206] That purpose is to prevent arbitrary detention and to provide protection for the rights and interests of adults with incapacity and to ensure, for example, that there is adequate provision for (independent) review of decisions taken about the lives of such adults.

In the context of adults with incapacity, potential deprivation of liberty raises three questions: when is there a deprivation of liberty; can a proxy consent to deprivation of liberty; and are the processes of review adequate?

(1) Deprivation of liberty[207]

7.20 In *Guzzardi v Italy* it was said that:[208]

> In order to determine whether someone has been 'deprived of his liberty' within the meaning of Article 5 ..., the starting point must be his concrete situation and account must be taken of a whole range of criteria such as the type, duration, effects and manner of implementation of the measure in question ....

204 Reference has been made to courts 'getting tied down in the difficult, time consuming and essentially unnecessary task of deciding whether or not (and, if so, when) the implementation of the care regime constitutes a deprivation of liberty', *A Local Authority v PB* [2011] EWHC 2675 (Fam), para 64(vi)(f).

205 'We are concerned that nobody using ordinary language would describe people living happily in a domestic setting as being deprived of their liberty' *P v Cheshire West and Chester Council* [2014] UKSC 19, at [99].

206 Reinforced by the UN Convention on the Rights of Persons with Disabilities.

207 See also Mental Welfare Commission, *Response to queries related to when to use s 13ZA v Guardianship following the Cheshire West Supreme Court decision* (2014); Mental Welfare Commission, *Deprivation of Liberty: Advice Notes (March 2021).*

208 (1981) 3 EHRR 333, paras 92–93.

> The difference between deprivation of and restriction upon liberty is nonetheless merely one of degree or intensity, and not one of nature or substance. Although the process of classification into one or other of these categories sometimes proves to be no easy task in that some borderline cases are a matter of pure opinion, the Court cannot avoid making the selection upon which the applicability or inapplicability of Article 5 …

In addition to what is described in this quote, which has been referred to as the objective component in deprivation of liberty,[209] ie, the physical conditions in which a person is living, there are two further elements which have to exist before there will be an Article 5 deprivation of liberty:

(a) A subjective element involving a lack of consent. There will be no consent where an adult does not have the capacity to take decisions about where they wish to live, and it is not enough that they acquiesce in a placement. As a consequence (and leaving aside issues about consent by proxies considered below) the subjective element will exist in all cases considered here and will not be further discussed.
(b) The deprivation of liberty must be attributable to the state, and this is considered more fully below.

The quotation above and other case law of the European Court of Human Rights[210] suggest that, in deciding on the objective component of deprivation of liberty, several factors must be considered. There is some authority in Scotland to the effect that any placement of an adult with incapacity in a residential setting will amount to a deprivation of liberty and infringe their rights under Article 5, unless this placement is made by a guardian appointed with powers to make the placement.[211] This is reinforced by the decision of the Supreme Court in *P v Cheshire West and Chester Council*.[212] In that case, an 'acid test' was formulated which involved asking two questions:

(a) is the adult subject to continuous supervision and control in the place where they reside; and
(b) is the adult free to leave (for example, are the premises locked or would they be returned to the place where they are living if they left)?

209 See, e.g, *P v Cheshire West and Chester Council* [2014] UKSC 19 at [37].
210 Discussed in *P v Cheshire West and Chester Council* [2014] UKSC 19.
211 *Muldoon, Applicant* 2005 SCLR 611; *M, Applicant* 2009 SLT (Sh Ct) 185. See below on the powers of attorneys to consent (this was not relevant or considered in these cases).
212 [2014] UKSC 19.

If the adult is not free to leave and is under continuous supervision, the objective element of deprivation of liberty will be established.

Where an adult who lacks the capacity to take the decision about where they wish to live is placed in residential accommodation, they will not realistically have the option of leaving to live elsewhere. It is likely in these circumstances that were they to seek to leave then they would be prevented from doing so. In such cases it is likely that there will be deprivation of liberty.[213]

As well as being found to exist in the context of care homes,[214] the objective element will also exist in supported placements which involve a high degree of supervision and restrictions on leaving.[215] More difficulty has been experienced in cases where the adult is living in their own home but is under supervision and prevented from leaving. The two reported cases on this have reached the conclusion that the objective component does not exist,[216] though on appeal one of these decisions was reversed and the appeal court was clear that there was a deprivation of liberty.[217] However, if, as suggested above, the underlying reason for discussion of deprivation of liberty is as a way of ensuring protection of the rights and interests of adults with incapacity, it seems difficult to see why location should make a difference.[218] Objectively, if the adult is under continuous supervision and unable to leave, it is not clear why where this takes place should make any difference.[219] Where an adult is in their own home it may, however, be more difficult to argue that the element of attribution to the state, identified above, exists.

213 This is what happened in *JE v DE* [2006] EWHC 3459 (Fam). Other examples are a case in which it was held that placement of a 19-year-old man in a residential unit without proper authority amounted to a deprivation of liberty (*G v E, A Local Authority, F* [2010] EWHC 621 (Fam)) and a case where it seems to have been regarded as self-evident that placement of a woman with Alzheimer's disease in a residential home involved deprivation of her liberty (*A County Council v MB, JB, A Residential Home* [2010] EWHC 2508 (COP), see also *Dorset CC v EH* [2009] EWHC 784 (Fam)).

214 *Muldoon, Applicant* 2005 SCLR 611, *JE v DE* [2006] EWHC 3459 (Fam) and *PJ v A Local Health Board* [2015] UKUT 480 (AAC).

215 For example, *Tower Hamlets LBC v TB* [2014] EWCOP 53.

216 *Rochdale Metropolitan Borough Council v KW* [2014] EWCOP 45, *W City Council v Mrs L* [2015] EWCOP 20.

217 *Rochdale Metropolitan Borough Council v KW* [2015] EWCA Civ 1054.

218 Leaving aside the question of whether the decisions referred to in footnote 216 above are actually consistent with the decision in *P v Cheshire West and Chester Council* [2014] UKSC 19.

219 At least one of the judges in *P v Cheshire West and Chester Council* [2014] UKSC 19 contemplated the possibility that deprivation of liberty might exist at home, Lord Neuberger at [72].

What does it mean to say that a deprivation of liberty is attributable to the state? Two possibilities are relevant here.[220] First, a public authority, most likely the local authority in this context, could have been directly involved in the deprivation. This would clearly happen in the case where a placement followed on from a local authority assessment and subsequent decision to place the adult.[221] Second, the local authority may have failed to carry out its positive obligation to protect the adult from interference with their liberty. The European Court of Human Rights has said that:[222]

> The State is … obliged to take measures providing effective protection of vulnerable persons, including reasonable steps to prevent a deprivation of liberty of which the authorities have or ought to have knowledge.

It follows from this positive obligation that there may be a deprivation of liberty even where arrangements for the care of an adult were made entirely privately and without the involvement of the local authority[223] and, indeed, where the adult is living in their own home.[224]

It was concluded in one case[225] that there was no deprivation of liberty where the adult was living at home and that, in any case, any deprivation of liberty was not attributable to the state. It was not possible to attribute deprivation of liberty to the state because of the strong role that the adult's family played in setting up the arrangements and because of the view that Article 5 was concerned with limiting state interference in the life of individuals. As we have seen, this is not an accurate view of Article 5 and it is not clear why the involvement of a caring family is particularly relevant. Underlying Article 5 is a concern with the protection of vulnerable or extremely vulnerable people who 'need a periodic independent check on whether arrangements for them are in

220 See the discussion in *Secretary of State for Justice v Staffordshire County Council* [2016] EWCA Civ 1317, referring to *Storck v Germany* (2006) 43 EHRR 6. See also *Re A & C* [2010] EWHC 978 (Fam) and *Birmingham City Council v D* [2016] EWCOP 8.

221 The Scottish Law Commission concluded that 'it is very unlikely that there could be a deprivation of liberty in any residential establishment in Scotland which could not be imputable to the State' (*Discussion Paper 156, Adults with Incapacity* (2012), para. 6.14).

222 *Storck v Germany* (2006) 43 EHRR 6, para 102.

223 As was the case in *Secretary of State for Justice v Staffordshire County Council* [2016] EWCA Civ 1317.

224 See, the Law Society, Identifying a deprivation of liberty: a practical guide (18 March 2024), ch 9. See *W City Council v Mrs L* [2015] EWCOP 20.

225 *W City Council v Mrs L* [2015] EWCOP 20, the later decision in *Secretary of State for Justice v Staffordshire County Council* [2016] EWCA Civ 1317 reached the opposite conclusion without discussing this case.

their best interests'[226] and consistent with adequate respect for their rights.

If a deprivation of liberty does exist, what does this mean? Following on from the terms of Article 5, it will be necessary that the deprivation of liberty has a lawful basis, subject to review by a court. In practice this means (subject to what is said below about proxies) that, if there is no one who already has the power to determine the adult's residence, an application will need to be made for appointment of a welfare guardian with that power.

(2) Can a proxy consent to deprivation of liberty?

7.21 The view that this is possible is implicit in the Scottish court decisions referred to above and also seems to be contemplated by the European Court of Human Rights.[227] However, it has been suggested that there is some doubt about whether a guardian or attorney can give such consent. In relation to guardians this is based on the absence of consideration of this specific power in either the 2000 Act or in the Code of Practice.[228] However, it should be borne in mind that the powers over the life of the adult which the 2000 Act contemplates conferring on guardians are extensive and without any specific limitation which would prevent guardians giving such consent. In addition, it is likely that the power given to guardians to determine the place of residence of the adult will involve deprivation of liberty in a substantial proportion of cases. Since this is the case, the Act would be failing to promote the welfare of adults if consent could not be given. If such (appropriate) placements could not be made there is no other means for making such placements other than detention under the Mental Health (Care and Treatment) (Scotland) Act 2003 or an application to the inherent jurisdiction of the Court of Session.

(3) The adequacy of review

7.22 The requirement set out in Article 5 is for a person deprived of their liberty to be able to bring the matter before a court for review. In the case of an adult with incapacity who is placed in a setting which involves deprivation of liberty by a guardian or attorney, the only methods of doing this are to take action in one of the ways set out in **7.10**

226 *P v Cheshire West and Chester Council* [2014] UKSC 19 at [57].
227 *Shtukaturov v Russia* [2008] MHLR 238.
228 Ward, A, *Adult Incapacity* (2003), para 10–21. See also Scottish Law Commission *Discussion Paper 156, Adults with Incapacity* (2012), paras 6.4–6.11.

above, for example, by seeking recall of the guardianship or removal of the guardian. Such action, of course, depends on the initiative being taken by a person with incapacity, and there is no automatic process for review of deprivation of liberty which does not rely on the adult or another interested party taking the initiative. In the circumstances, it might be asked how realistic is this possibility and therefore how real is the right to bring the matter before the court. Despite this, a similar procedure has been held to be compliant with Article 5 and that remains the current position.[229]

(4) Conclusion

7.23 The current state of the law on deprivation of liberty is rather unsatisfactory. As discussed in **7.1** above, the Scottish Government is currently considering reform of the Adults with Incapacity (Scotland) Act 2000, this will form part of the Scottish Governments' wider response to the recommendations of the SMHLR (Scott Review) on Scottish mental health provision.[230]

229 *R (on the application of H) v Secretary of State for Health* [2005] UKHL 60; see also *Lothian Health Board v M* 2007 SCLR 478.

230 Scottish Government, *Mental Health and Capacity Reform: Delivery plan October 2023 to April 2025 (June 2024).*

Chapter 8

Mental health

INTRODUCTION

8.1 The principal source of law on mental health in Scotland is the Mental Health (Care and Treatment) (Scotland) Act 2003 (the 2003 Act). The 2003 Act was amended by the Mental Health (Scotland) Act 2015. Some aspects of the treatment of persons who have offended but are suffering from a mental disorder are addressed in the Criminal Procedure (Scotland) Act 1995. The 2003 Act is supplemented by a Code of Practice[1] and by good practice guidance issued by the Mental Welfare Commission (MWC).[2] This chapter will address two areas; local authority duties under the 2003 Act, and the procedures for compulsory treatment of those with a mental disorder.[3] Before going on to consider these it is necessary to explain the roles of those involved in implementing the legislation and to define some of the terms used. Implementation takes place in the context that mental health services must form part of the integration scheme under the Public Bodies (Joint Working) (Scotland) Act 2014 involving joint working between the health service and the local authority.[4]

(1) Mental health officers

8.2 Mental health officers (MHOs) play an essential role in the administration of the 2003 Act. To become an MHO a social worker must have at least two years full-time post-qualification experience,[5] and must complete a Mental Health Officer Award or have an equivalent qualification.[6] Once appointed, MHOs must, every year, complete a

1 Scottish Government, *Mental Health (Care and Treatment) (Scotland) Act 2003: Code of Practice* (2005) (*Code of Practice 2005*).

2 Mental Welfare Commission for Scotland, Good Practice Guidelines. Available at: www.mwcscot.org.uk/good-practice (Accessed April 2026).

3 Persons who have offended and who have a mental disorder are considered in **chapter 10**.

4 See **1.73**.

5 Or an equivalent part-time length of experience.

6 Mental Health (Care and Treatment) (Scotland) Act 2003 (Requirements for appointment as mental health officers) Direction 2009.

number of reports under the 2003 Act and other legislation. In addition, MHOs must complete a minimum of two days continuing professional development events in order to retain that status.[7]

(2) Approved medical practitioner

8.3 An approved medical practitioner is a doctor who has special experience in the diagnosis and treatment of mental disorder.[8] Health Boards and the State Hospitals Board are required to compile and maintain a list of medical practitioners having the qualifications, experience and training to act as approved medical practitioners. [9] Some types of authorisation can only be given, and some reports must be made, by an approved medical practitioner.

(3) Responsible medical officer (RMO)

8.4 The responsible medical officer is the doctor who is responsible for the care and treatment of a patient who is subject to compulsory treatment measures. [10] The RMO must be an approved medical practitioner.[11] If a patient is made subject to any compulsory measures a RMO must be appointed to oversee their care and treatment. Appointment of the RMO must take place as soon as reasonably practicable following the making of an order under the 2003 Act. [12]

(4) Mental Welfare Commission for Scotland

8.5 The Mental Welfare Commission has a variety of functions under the 2003 Act and under the Adults with Incapacity (Scotland) Act 2000.[13] Under the 2003 Act these functions include carrying out investigations, giving advice, visiting patients, dealing with complaints from patients and publishing guidance. In addition, the commission has the power to revoke certain compulsory treatment measures.[14]

7 Mental Health (Care and Treatment) (Scotland) Act 2003 (Requirements for continuing appointment as mental health officers) Direction 2006.
8 The Mental Health (Care and Treatment) (Scotland) Act 2003 (Qualifications, experience and training of approved medical practitioners) Directions 2019.
9 Mental Health (Care and Treatment) (Scotland) Act 2003, s 22(1) (2003 Act).
10 2003 Act, s 77.
11 2003 Act, s 230(1).
12 2003 Act, s 230(1).
13 Incapacity (Scotland) Act 2000, Part 1, s 9.
14 2003 Act, s 81.

(5) Named person[15]

8.6 The named person has an important role to play in relation to compulsory treatment. For example the named person must be sent a copy of an application for a compulsory treatment order and are entitled to take part in the proceedings following application for such an order.[16] Until 2017, the 2003 Act provided for the automatic appointment of a named person, but this automatic appointment will now only happen if the patient is aged under 16. [17]A patient aged 16 or over can nominate someone as their named person,[18] though this will only be effective if the person nominated agrees in writing to take on this role. A nomination can be revoked.[19] Unless such a nomination has been made, a patient aged 16 or over will not have a named person. If the patient is aged under 16 the named person will be either someone having parental responsibilities and rights in respect of a child (this can include a local authority)[20] or the child's primary carer.[21] An application can be made for a declaration that it is inappropriate for a named person to continue to act and, where the patient is aged under 16, for the appointment of a substitute.[22] The MHO is the person responsible for making an application to the Mental Health Tribunal Scotland (MHTS) when they believe it inappropriate for a named person to continue in the role.[23]

(6) Listed initiators[24]

8.7 The removal of the automatic appointment of a named person meant that there would be some cases where there would be no one who could make applications, appeal or receive notices on behalf of an adult patient if they had no capacity to do this themselves. A new category

15 2003 Act, ss 250, 252, 256 and 257. See also Scottish Government, *Interim Guidance on Named Persons* (2017).
16 2003 Act, s 60(1)(b).
17 2003 Act, s 252.
18 The nomination must be witnessed by a 'prescribed person' who must also certify that in their opinion the nominator understands the effect of nominating a person to be the nominator's named person and has not been subjected to any undue influence in making the nomination, 2003 Act, s 250. See Mental Health (Patient Representation) (Prescribed Persons) (Scotland) Regulations 2017, SSI 2017/175.
19 2003 Act, s 250(4).
20 Which may have parental responsibilities and rights by virtue of a permanence order, see **3.23**.
21 2003 Act, s 252.
22 2003 Act, s 255(7)
23 2003 Act, s 257.
24 Scottish Government, Mental Health Law in Scotland: Guide to Named Persons (2019).

of listed initiators has the power to do this.[25] This category includes the patient's guardian, welfare attorney, primary carer or nearest relative.[26] Listed initiators have, for example, the power to seek revocation of short-term detention certificates and compulsory treatment orders[27] and to appeal decisions of the Mental Health Tribunal for Scotland. They also have the authority to receive a variety of notices, for example notice of an application for a compulsory treatment order or a determination to extend such an order.[28] The Guide to Named Persons explains to patients the role of listed initiators if there is no named person.[29]

The patient can make a written declaration precluding a person from acting in this capacity.[30]

(7) Nearest relative[31]

8.8 The patient's nearest relative will be the person who comes highest up the following list of those related to the patient. The list is set out in the 2003 Act:[32]

- Spouse or civil partner, though not if legally separated or the patient or the spouse/civil partner has left the other.
- Someone who has been living with the patient as spouse/civil partner for at least six months.
- Child.
- Parent.
- Sibling.
- Grandparent.
- Grandchild.
- Uncle/Aunt.
- Niece/Nephew.
- Someone who has been living with the patient for at least five years.

25 2003 Act, s 257A.
26 2003 Act, s 257A(9).
27 Mental Health Tribunal for Scotland (Practice and Procedure) (No 2) Rules 2005, SSI 2005/519, rr 2(1A) and 55.
28 2003 Act, s 257A(4).
29 Scottish Government, Mental Health Law in Scotland: *Guide to Named Persons* (2019) para 3. pp 7–8.
30 2003 Act, s 257A(7).
31 2003 Act, s 254.
32 2003 Act, s 254(2) (a)–(j)

(8) Mental disorder

8.9 A mental disorder is defined as any mental illness, personality disorder or learning disability, however this is caused or manifested.[33] None of these terms are further defined in the 2003 Act, though it does specifically provide that someone is not mentally disordered only because of:

(a) sexual orientation;
(b) sexual deviancy;
(c) transsexualism;
(d) transvestism;
(e) dependence on, or use of, alcohol or drugs;
(f) behaviour that causes, or is likely to cause, harassment, alarm or distress to any other person;
(g) acting as no prudent person would act.[34]

(9) Medical treatment

8.10 Medical treatment is defined widely in the 2003 Act. It is restricted to treatment for mental disorder, but includes nursing, care, psychological intervention, 'habilitation' (this includes education and training in work, social and independent living skills) and rehabilitation.[35] We will see below that there are some restrictions on the type of treatment that can be provided to a patient without their consent.[36] Although treatment is restricted to treatment of the mental disorder, it can include treatment for the symptoms or physical consequences of a mental disorder, for example naso-gastric tube feeding of a patient who is severely malnourished as a consequence of an eating disorder[37] or specialised nursing care to alleviate the symptoms and effects of dementia.[38]

(10) The principles

8.11 The 2003 Act sets out a number of principles, and professionals discharging functions under the Act must have regard to these principles.[39]

33 2003 Act, s 328(1).
34 Mental Health (Care and Treatment) Act 2003, s 328(2).
35 2003 Act, s 329(1).
36 See **8.26** below.
37 *B v Croydon HA* [1995] 2 WLR 294.
38 *BG v Mental Health Tribunal for Scotland* [2015] CSIH 18.
39 2003 Act, s 1.

Discharge of functions includes taking decisions and actions in relation to the patient, but also extends to taking no action when there is power to act. Certain categories of actor are not required to have regard to the principles; these include the patient and their named person and primary carer, the patient's solicitor or advocate, a curator *ad litem* appointed by the Mental Health Tribunal, and any guardian or welfare attorney of the patient.[40] For those aged 18 or over the principles are:

(a) Regard is to be had (as far as relevant) to the following:[41]
 (i) the present and past wishes of the patient; these can be set out in the form of an advance statement, though if this is done the patient's wishes as set out there can still be overridden by the Mental Health Tribunal and by those providing treatment;[42]
 (ii) the views of the named person, carer and any guardian or welfare attorney;[43]
 (iii) the importance of the patient participating as fully as possible and the importance of providing the patient with information and support to enable this participation;[44]
 (iv) the range of options available in the patient's case;[45]
 (v) the importance of providing maximum benefit to the patient;[46]
 (vi) the need to ensure that the patient is not treated less favourably than someone who is not a patient would be treated in comparable circumstances, unless any less favourable treatment is justified by the circumstances;[47]
 (vii) the abilities, background and characteristics of the patient, including religious background, cultural and linguistic background, sexual orientation, age, sex, racial origin and membership of any ethnic group.[48]

(b) Functions are to be discharged in the way which 'appears', to the person discharging the function, to involve the minimum restriction on the patient's freedom that is necessary in the circumstances.[49]

40 2003 Act, s 1(7), though they will apply to a listed initiator who is the patient's nearest relative.
41 2003 Act, s 1(3)
42 2003 Act, ss 275 and 276. See **8.26** below.
43 2003 Act, s 1(3)(b).
44 2003 Act, ss 1(3)(c) and 1(3)(d).
45 2003 Act, s 1(3)(e).
46 2003 Act, s 1(3)(f).
47 2003 Act, s 1(3)(g).
48 2003 Act, s 1(3)(h).
49 2003 Act, s 1(4).

(c) As far as reasonable and practicable, regard is to be had to the importance of providing information to anyone who is carer to the patient which will help them to care for the patient and to the needs and circumstance of any carer, at least to the extent that the person discharging the function is aware of these and they are relevant to the discharge of the function. This principle does not apply to decisions about medical treatment.[50]

(d) The importance of providing appropriate services to a patient who is or has been the subject of compulsory treatment[51] must be considered. This includes consideration of the provision of continuing care once the compulsory order is at an end.[52]

For patients under the age of 18 there is an overall requirement to discharge any function[53] or exercise any power under the 2003 Act in the way which appears to the person carrying out the function or exercising the power to best secure the welfare of the patient.[54] In deciding what course of action best secures the welfare of the patient regard is to be had to factors (a) to (d) above.[55]

(11) Advocacy

8.12 Under the 2003 Act everyone with a mental disorder has a right of access to independent advocacy.[56] Advocacy services are defined as services of support and representation made available for the purpose of enabling someone to have as much control of, or capacity to influence, their care and welfare as is appropriate in the circumstances.[57] Local authorities and health boards have a duty to ensure that independent advocacy services are available and that people with a mental disorder have an opportunity to make use of them. This right of access is broad and extends not only to processes involving the 2003 Act, but to any other aspects of the person's life, for example, dealing with self-directed support.

50 2003 Act, s 1(5).
51 2003 Act, s 1(6)
52 2003 Act, s 1(6).
53 Unless there is only one way in which the function can be discharged.
54 2003 Act, s 2(4).
55 2003 Act, s 2(5)
56 2003 Act, s 259(1) See also Scottish Government, *Interim Guidance: Right of access to independent advocacy* (2017).
57 2003 Act, s 259(4).

(12) Links to other areas

8.13 There is a close relationship between the legislation on adults with incapacity and the mental health legislation. In some cases there may be an issue about which of these pieces of legislation is the most appropriate to take action under – for example an adult with Alzheimer's Disease may be at a stage where this qualifies as a mental disorder under section 328 of the 2003 Act.[58] The question may then be whether to proceed by seeking compulsory treatment, bearing in mind that 'treatment' includes nursing care, or by establishing an alternative decision maker to take decisions about the adult's welfare by seeking welfare guardianship.[59] There is also a link to the legislation on vulnerable adults; some adults with a mental disorder will, by virtue of that disorder, be vulnerable and may be at risk. A further link is with community care through the local authority obligation to provide services to people with mental disorders discussed below. All of these are services for adults, however there is also a link to the provision of services for children as there is no lower age limit for the application of the 2003 Act. It is therefore quite possible for children under 16 to be the subject of compulsory treatment under the 2003 Act. It may also be the case that the mental disorder of adults gives rise to concerns about their children. Even if the children are not at risk they may very well be children affected by disability. Children with disabilities will be the subject of local authority duties which can include the provision of services and assistance to other members of the child's family.

LOCAL AUTHORITY DUTIES

(1) Provision of services and support

8.14 Local authorities have a duty to appoint a 'sufficient number' of MHOs to carry out the functions reserved to MHOs under the 2003 Act, the Adults with Incapacity (Scotland) Act 2000 and the Criminal Procedure (Scotland) Act 1995.[60] It is not entirely clear what number is sufficient and there are considerable variations between local authorities in the number of MHOs per head of population and in the proportions of MHOs within qualified social work staff.[61]

58 2003 Act, s 328(1)(a).
59 2003 Act, s 329(1).
60 2003 Act, s 32(1).
61 See Scottish Social Services Council, *Mental Health Officers (Scotland) Report 2022*, Table 8.

Duties to provide various services are also imposed on local authorities. These services may be provided by the local authority or contracted to third-party providers. These duties are without prejudice to the duty to provide services under certain other legislation.[62] The services covered by the 2003 Act, which are explicitly defined as community care services,[63] are services for people who have, or who have had, a mental disorder and which:

(a) provide care and support, this includes providing residential accommodation, personal care and personal support,[64] but excludes nursing care;[65]
(b) are designed to promote the well-being and social development of the service users, this includes social, cultural and recreational activities, training for service users over school age and assistance in finding employment;[66]
(c) assist with travel to access the services described in (a) and (b).[67]

As these are community care services, decisions on provision will be made following an assessment in the same way as for other community care services. An assessment would need to be carried out when it came to the attention of a local authority that an individual for whom it was under a duty or had a power to provide, or to secure the provision of, community care services may be in need of any such services.[68] Despite this, the 2003 Act provides for two triggers of a community care assessment for the services described above:

(a) Notification of the local authority by an MHO that an individual may be in need of such services, this must follow on from the MHOs assessment that the patient should be assessed for such services.[69]
(b) A request from a mentally disordered person, or their primary carer or named person, for an assessment. [70]The local authority receiving such a request must respond within fourteen days to say whether it intends to carry out an assessment or not.[71] It is not clear what the basis for refusing to carry out an assessment

62 Specifically, services under Social Work (Scotland) Act 1968, ss 12(1), 13A, 13B and 14 and Children (Scotland) Act 1995, s 22(1).
63 Social Work (Scotland) Act 1968, s 12A(8). In addition, because there is no lower age limit for 2003 Act these duties are also owed to children, see **4.4**.
64 As these are defined in Public Services Reform (Scotland) Act 2010, Sch 12, para 20.
65 2003 Act, s 25.
66 2003 Act, s 26.
67 2003 Act, s 27.
68 Social Work (Scotland) Act 1968, s 12A(1).
69 2003 Act, s 227(1)(b).
70 2003 Act, s 228.
71 2003 Act, s 228(3).

would be, as the scope for an authority to refuse to carry out a community care assessment is very limited.[72]

Local authorities can seek assistance from health boards and NHS trusts in providing services,[73] and these bodies, together with voluntary organisations, are required to cooperate in the provision of services.[74] An assessment of the client's financial means may be carried out and charges can be made for these services in the same way as for other community care services.[75]

(2) Duty to inquire

8.15 A duty to make inquiries can arise in respect of someone aged 16 or over who appears to have a mental disorder where one of the following also applies:[76]

(a) the person may be, or may have been, subject or exposed to ill-treatment, neglect, or some other deficiency of care or treatment, though only if this has not happened in a hospital;[77]

(b) loss or damage may be or have been caused to the person's property, or there is a risk of this, though the loss or damage or the risk must arise because of the person's mental disorder. An example might be that a person is unable to care for their property or are likely to have it taken from them because of their disorder;[78]

(c) the person may be living alone or without care and unable to look after themselves or their property or financial affairs;[79]

(d) there is a risk to the safety of some other person because of the disorder and the person with the disorder is not in hospital.[80]

In order to complete these inquiries, the local authority can ask for assistance from a variety of other bodies, including the Mental Welfare Commission, the Public Guardian, Social Care and Social Work

72 See **6.5**.

73 2003 Act, s 31, bearing in mind that mental health services are covered by the joint working provisions of the Public Bodies (Joint Working) (Scotland) Act 2014, see **1.73**.

74 2003 Act, s 30.

75 Confederation of Scottish Local Authorities (COSLA) National Strategy & Guidance, Charges Applying to Social Care Support for People at Home, 2022/2023 Available at: www.cosla.gov.uk/__data/assets/pdf_file/0011/32033/COSLA-Social-Care- Charging-Guidance-2022-23.pdf.

76 2003 Act, s 33. See **Chapter 9**.

77 2003 Act, s 33(2)(a).

78 2003 Act, s 33(2)(b).

79 2003 Act, s 33(2)(c).

80 2003 Act, s 33(2)(d).

Improvement Scotland (the Care Inspectorate), NHS trusts and health boards.[81] Various warrants can also be obtained from a sheriff or a justice of the peace to help the authority to carry out its inquiries.[82] A warrant may be sought allowing entry to premises, authorising detention of the person who is the subject of the inquiries for a medical examination, and requiring the production of medical records.[83] The sheriff or justice of the peace must be satisfied, on the basis of evidence on oath from an MHO, that granting the warrant is necessary.[84] The MHO seeking the warrant will normally work for the authority carrying out the investigation. However, where the premises to which entry is sought are outside that local authority's area, the application must be made by an MHO working for the local authority for the area where the premises are situated.[85]

Once the inquiries are complete, a decision will need to be taken about what happens next. It may be that nothing further need be done because the concerns which prompted the investigation are unfounded. Where action is needed the sort of action which can be taken at the initiative of the local authority includes seeking appointment of a guardian (either financial or welfare or both) and the provision of community care services, as well as limited powers under the Adult Support and Protection (Scotland) Act 2007.[86]

(3) Removal order

8.16 A removal order authorises entry to premises and the removal of a person aged over 16 who has a mental disorder to a place of safety for up to seven days.[87] The order must usually be obtained from a sheriff, though where any delay in applying to a sheriff would be likely to be prejudicial to the person who is to be removed, an application can be made to a justice of the peace.[88] Before making the order, the sheriff (or JP) must be satisfied that one of the first three grounds ((a)–(c)) set out in **8.15** above applies and that the person is likely to suffer significant harm if not removed to a place of safety. [89] The sheriff must also give the person who is the subject of the order and a number of others, including

81 2003 Act, s 34.
82 2003 Act, s 35.
83 2003 Act, s 35(8).
84 2003 Act, s 35(1).
85 2003 Act, s 35(12).
86 See **chapter 9**.
87 2003 Act, s 293. See chapter 9: Adult Support and Protection (Scotland) Act 2007.
88 2003 Act, s 294.
89 2003 Act, s 293(2).

their nearest relative and any welfare attorney, guardian or primary carer, the opportunity to make representations before an order is granted. This requirement can be dispensed with if the sheriff considers that the delay which it would cause would be likely to be prejudicial to the person.[90]

If an order is granted, it must be executed within 72 hours.[91] If the person will have to remain in alternative accommodation for more than the seven days authorised by the order, alternative arrangements will have to be made. The alternative arrangements may be either compulsory treatment measures or securing the person's consent to staying in alternative accommodation.[92] An application can be made for variation or recall of the order.[93] The Mental Welfare Commission must be notified by the MHO of an application for a removal order, or for variation or recall of an order.[94]

COMPULSORY TREATMENT

8.17 The measures considered here, together with compulsion orders for mentally disordered offenders, are the only ways in which legal authority can be provided for the detention or for the detention and treatment of patients who do not (or cannot) consent.[95]

(1) Emergency detention certificates and short-term detention certificates

8.18 Both of these measures provide for detention of an individual for a short period of time and are granted by a medical practitioner.[96] The main characteristics of emergency detention certificates (EDCs)[97] and short-term detention certificates (STDCs)[98] are set out in Table 8.1 below. Both require that, if practicable, an MHO should be consulted

90 2003 Act, ss 293(5) and 293(6).
91 2003 Act, s 293(3)(iiia).
92 2003 Act, s 293(3)(c)(ii).
93 2003 Act, s 295.
94 2003 Act, s 295A.
95 2003 Act, s 291. See also *LM v Mental Health Tribunal for Scotland* [2010] Scot SC 150, Available at: www.mhtscotland.gov.uk/mhts/files/Judgements/M_v_MHTS_2010.pdf (Accessed April 2026)
96 2003 Act, s 36 (Emergency Detention) and s 44 (Short Term Detention).
97 2003 Act, Pt 5.
98 2003 Act, Pt 6.

before either of these certificates is granted.[99] The Code of Practice makes it clear that, if the MHO who is consulted does not consent to the granting of the certificate, the doctor should only in exceptional circumstances approach a second MHO. If this happens the second MHO should be told that the MHO initially involved had not consented.[100]

The Code of Practice indicates that the STDC is the preferred gateway order to compulsory treatment because of the involvement of the MHO and the greater rights conferred on the patient and on the named person.[101] This preference seems to be reflected in practice, since 2012 it has been more common for patient contacts to commence with a STDC than with an EDC or CTO. [102]

In relation to STDCs the duties of the MHO include interviewing the patient,[103] informing the patient about the availability of independent advocacy and taking steps to ensure that the patient has the opportunity to use this service.[104] The duty explained in Table 8.1 below – to produce a social circumstances report[105] when there is an STDC in place, or to notify the Mental Welfare Commission of the reasons for not completing a report – is complied with in less than half of cases.[106]

99 The Mental Welfare Commission expressed concern about EDCs granted without MHO consent and, in some cases, without contact with an 'MHO. See Mental Welfare Commission for Scotland, Mental Health Act monitoring report 2021–2022, Figure 9, p 17, showing that MHO consent to detention under an EDC is at its lowest as of 2021–22 at 40.5%.

100 *Code of Practice 2005,* vol 2, both ch 2, para 30 and ch 7, para 36, note that: 'it would be expected that a medical practitioner would not "shop around" for an MHO who will consent'.

101 See *Code of Practice 2005*, vol 2, ch 1, para 16.

102 Mental Welfare Commission for Scotland, Mental Health Act monitoring report 2021–2022, Appendix, Table A1, In 2021–2022 49% of all episodes began with a STDC, 48% with an EDC, and 2% with a CTO.

103 Reasonable steps must be taken to enable the patient to communicate during this interview, 2003 Act, s 261A. This requirement also applies to interviews before making an application for a CTO, see **8.19** below.

104 2003 Act, ss 45(1)(c) and 45(1)(d). See also Scottish Government, *Interim Guidance: Right of access to independent advocacy* (2017).

105 See **8.27** below.

106 Mental Welfare Commission, *Mental Health Act monitoring report 2021–2022*.at pp 5–6, For 43.3% of STDCs in 2021–2022 the Commission received notification that an SCR had been prepared or that an SCR would serve no purpose (and therefore had not been prepared). In 56.7% of cases we received no notification.'

Table 8.1

	EDC	*STDC*
Who makes?	*a* medical practitioner	an *approved* medical practitioner
Basis for certificate	• mental disorder • ability to make treatment decisions significantly impaired[1] • urgently necessary to detain to determine need for treatment • risk to patient or third party if not detained • STDC would involve undesirable delay	• mental disorder • ability to make treatment decisions significantly impaired • urgently necessary to detain to determine what medical treatment should be given or to give treatment • risk to patient or third party if not detained • granting STDC is necessary
MHO involved?	Yes, if practicable MHO must be consulted and, if consulted, consent	• Yes, if practicable MHO must be consulted and, if consulted, consent • Specific provision requiring that patient be interviewed by MHO if practicable and for recording of any reasons why this was not practicable
Duration	72 hours (starts from admission to hospital if not already in-patient)	28 days (starts from admission to hospital if not already in-patient)
Can application for revocation be made?	No, but can be/must be (if conditions no longer satisfied) revoked by RMO.	• Yes, to Mental Health Tribunal (MHT)[2] • Can also be revoked by MWC and RMO

Can it be extended/ renewed?	No, an STDC is required to continue detention	• Yes, by extension certificate for 3 days to allow application for CTO
		• If application made detention continued for further 5 working days.
MHO responsibility after certificate granted	Nil	Must prepare social circumstances report (SCR) unless this would serve little or no practical purpose.
Restrictions on making (ie certificate cannot be made if one of these circumstances applies)[3]	• Existing EDC	• Existing STDC or extension certificate
	• Existing STDC or extension certificate	
	• Detention pending review by, or further procedure before, MHT	• Detention pending review by, or further procedure before, MHT
	• During 5-day extension after application for CTO	• During 5-day extension after application for CTO
	• Detention of patient for failing to comply with community-based CTO or interim CTO	• Detention of patient for failing to comply with community-based CTO or interim CTO

1 See Shek, E, *et al*, 'Understanding "significant impaired decision-making ability" with regard to treatment for mental disorder: an empirical analysis' (2010) 34 *The Psychiatrist* 239.

2 There is no appeal against the decision of the Tribunal to revoke the STDC, The 2003 Act, ss 50 and 320.

3 See *M v Mental Health Tribunal for Scotland* 2010 SLT (Sh Ct) 235.

(2) Compulsory treatment orders

(a) Applying for and making the order

8.19

Table 8.2

<table>
<tr><td rowspan="6">BOX A</td><td rowspan="6">FIVE DAYS</td><td>Examination leading to Mental Health Report 1
By approved medical practitioner</td><td>Reports based on examination, doctors must be satisfied of:</td><td rowspan="6">Both reports must agree on at least one type of mental disorder and on the same measures of treatment. One report must state views on notification of patient and patient's capacity to arrange representation</td></tr>
<tr><td rowspan="5">Examination leading to Mental Health Report 2
By approved medical practitioner or patient's GP</td><td>• Existence of disorder</td></tr>
<tr><td>• Availability of treatment</td></tr>
<tr><td>• Risk to patient or some other person if patient not treated</td></tr>
<tr><td>• Incapacity of patient to decide on treatment</td></tr>
<tr><td>• Need for compulsory treatment</td></tr>
<tr><td rowspan="7">BOX B</td><td rowspan="7">FOURTEEN DAYS</td><td rowspan="6">MHO to prepare application for CTO</td><td colspan="2">MHO must:</td></tr>
<tr><td colspan="2">• Identify named person</td></tr>
<tr><td colspan="2">• Notify: named person (listed initiator); patient; MWC</td></tr>
<tr><td colspan="2">• Interview patient, inform of rights and about advocacy services</td></tr>
<tr><td colspan="2">• Prepare report and proposed care plan</td></tr>
<tr><td colspan="2">• Advise MHT if patient likely to need curator</td></tr>
<tr><td>Apply to MHT for CTO</td><td colspan="2">Standard form completed</td></tr>
</table>

BOX C	NO STATUTORY NOTICE PERIOD, MAY BE INFLUENCED BY DURATION OF AUTHORISATION FOR DETENTION, EG EXTENSION OF PERIOD AUTHORISED BY STDC FOR 5 DAYS	Tribunal Hearing	POSSIBLE OUTCOMES
		• No notice period	Application refused
			Interim order
			• Eg for further medical report, to allow legal representative time to prepare
			• Maximum 56 days
			Order made

Table 8.2 sets out the key requirements and processes involved in applying for a compulsory treatment order, which are discussed in more detail below. The time limits set out in the second column are the maximum periods permitted by the 2003 Act, for example, the second medical examination must take place within five days of the first.[107] (These reports are submitted to the MHO.) As discussed below, however, the period of time which may be available in practice for the MHO to carry out their various duties and prepare an application for a CTO are likely to be considerably less than the statutory maximum of 14 days.[108] A CTO can be either hospital based, where the patient is detained in hospital (but see **8.24** below), or community based, where treatment takes place in the community.

107 2003 Act, s 58(3).
108 2003 Act, s 57(7).

BOX A

The process of applying for a compulsory treatment order (CTO) is triggered by the completion of two reports based on examination of the patient by two doctors. Unless the patient agrees to being examined by both doctors at the same time, the examinations must be separate and there must be no conflict of interest in respect of the examinations.[109] If more than one type of mental disorder is identified it is enough that the reports agree on one as well as on the measures which should be authorised by a CTO.[110] A decision must be made whether or not to notify the patient of the intention to seek a CTO. A judgement must be made as to whether notification of the proposal to apply for a CTO would be likely to cause significant harm to the patient or to someone else.[111] There is a non-statutory form which is used in practice for these reports,[112] which need not be completed faultlessly, providing, on a fair reading, it contains the required information.[113]

BOX B

If the reports comply with the requirements set out in the final column of Box A, the MHO has a duty to make an application for a CTO to the Mental Health Tribunal (MHT). The terms of the 2003 Act suggest that tasks to be carried out by the MHO, for example the identification of the named person,[114] should be carried out after this duty arises.[115] The MHT may refuse to grant a CTO on the procedural grounds that the named person has been identified and contacted by the MHO before the second of the Mental Health Reports has been received. This conclusion is based on the wording of the 2003 Act which is that identification and notification should take place 'as soon as practicable after the duty to make the application arises'.[116] The duty to make an application only arises, of course, after the second report is received. The time which an MHO has to make application is often very short and, in practice, the MHO will know that a second examination has taken place, even

109 On examinations, see 2003 Act, ss 57 and 58. Conflict of Interest is dealt with in s 291A and the Mental Health (Conflict of Interest) (Scotland) Regulations 2017, SSI 2017/174.

110 See below for the measures which can be authorised by a CTO.

111 2003 Act, s 57(6).

112 See www.gov.scot/publications/mental-health-law-forms/ (Accessed April 2026).

113 *Beattie v Dunbar* 2006 SCLR 777.

114 2003 Act, ss 59 and 255 address the MHOs duty to identify a named person. If the MHO considers that the named person is inappropriate, an application *must* be made to the Tribunal for a declaration that this person is not the named person, s 255(6)(b).

115 2003 Act, ss 57, 59–61.

116 2003 Act, ss 59, 60(1).

though the report has not actually been received. Despite the criticism of named persons in the past,[117] they represent an important safeguard in the process. Early identification of named persons is necessary, not only because of the need to notify them of the application, but also because the guidance suggests that they should be notified of, and if possible attend, the interview which the MHO has with the patient.[118] This suggests that a CTO should not be refused purely on the basis that the MHO seems to have approached the nearest relative before the second report has been received. Support for this conclusion can be derived from the position taken in relation to another obligation which is imposed on MHOs after a duty to apply for a CTO arises, that is the duty to notify the patient that application for a CTO is to be made. Where the MHO had notified the patient before receiving the second report this was held[119] not to have prejudiced the patient and not to amount to a substantial deviation from the procedure set out in the 2003 Act. It was noted that there was nothing in the 2003 Act to prevent an MHO making early notification. It was further noted that early notification would assist in complying with the principle of providing the patient with information to allow them to participate as fully as possible.[120] Early notification also complies with the Code of Practice which emphasises the need to give the patient as much time as possible to prepare for the Tribunal hearing.[121] In light of this early notification seems to be entirely consistent with the 2003 Act.

Despite any recommendation expressed in one of the medical reports about whether the patient should be notified of the application, the MHO has the final decision on whether notification is made.[122] In the event that the MHO recommendation is overridden this should be discussed with the medical practitioner making the recommendation.[123]

The information on rights and advocacy services needs to be communicated effectively to the patient in order to ensure that they have as full an understanding as possible about these. The patient must not only be given information about advocacy services, but the MHO must

117 See Scottish Government, Limited Review of the Mental Health (Care and Treatment) (Scotland) Act 2003 Report (2010), ch 4.

118 Scottish Government, *Mental Health (Care and Treatment) (Scotland) Act 2003: Code of Practice*, vol 2, ch 3, para 55 (*Code of Practice 2003*). See also para 50 noting the desirability of allowing the named person as much time as possible to prepare for the tribunal hearing.

119 *JG v Mental Health Tribunal for Scotland* [2010] 10 WLUK 315

120 2003 Act, s 1(3)(d).

121 *Code of Practice 2005,* vol 2, ch 3, para 50.

122 2003 Act, s 60(2)(b) – the MHO 'may, if the mental health officer considers it appropriate to do so, give … notice'.

123 *Code of Practice 2003*, vol 2, ch 3, para 49.

also take steps to ensure that they have the opportunity to make use of the services.[124]

The patient must be interviewed, the Code of Practice notes that, '[i]t is unlikely to ever be completely impracticable for an MHO to comply with the duty to interview the patient'.[125]

The matters to be covered in the report[126] and the proposed care plan[127] are set out in Boxes 8.1 and 8.2. In the report the MHO should express a view on the medical reports. If the MHO disagrees with the content of the report, for example about the need for compulsory measures or the measures specified in the reports, this should be discussed with the medical practitioners. The MHO should also consider whether the measures proposed are the least restrictive possible.[128] In practice the report and the proposed care plan will not be separate documents, but will be incorporated into the *pro forma* CTO Application pack which prompts the MHO to address the necessary topics.[129]

Box 8.1

Required contents of MHO Report [130]

(a) the name and address of the patient;
(b) if known by the mental health officer, the name and address of:
  (i) the patient's named person; and
  (ii) the patient's primary carer;
(c) the steps that the mental health officer has taken to interview the patient and inform them about their rights and about advocacy services;
(d) if it was impracticable for the mental health officer to comply with the requirement to interview the patient, the reason for that being the case;
(e) in so far as relevant for the purposes of the application, details of the personal circumstances of the patient;
(f) the mental health officer's views on the mental health reports relating to the patient;

124 2003 Act, s 61(2)(d).
125 *Code of Practice 2003*, vol 2, ch 3, para 56, see also para 57 for practice points related to the interview.
126 2003 Act, s 61(4).
127 2003 Act, s 62.
128 *Code of Practice 2003*, vol 2, ch 3, paras 61–63.
129 See: www.gov.scot/publications/mental-health-law-forms/ (Accessed April 2026).
130 2003 Act, s 61(4)(a)–(h).

(g) if known by the mental health officer, details of any advance statement that the patient has made (and not withdrawn); and
(h) any other information that the mental health officer considers relevant to the determination by the Tribunal of the application.

Box 8.2

Required contents of Proposed Care Plan [131]

(a) the type (or types) of mental disorder which the patient has;
(b) the needs of the patient for medical treatment that have been assessed by the medical practitioners who submitted the mental health reports relating to the patient;
(c) in so far as relevant for the purposes of the application:
  (i) where the patient is a child, the needs of the patient that have been assessed under the provisions of the Children (Scotland) Act 1995 applying to children affected by disability;
  (ii) where the patient is not a child, a community care assessment has been carried out;
(d) the medical treatment which it is proposed to give to the patient (including the names of the persons who would give the treatment and the addresses at which the treatment would be given);
(e) any community care services or relevant services which it is proposed to provide to the patient in relation to each of the needs specified by virtue of paragraph (c) above (including the names of the persons who would provide such services and the addresses at which such services would be provided);
(f) in so far as relevant for the purposes of the application:
  (i) any treatment or care (other than treatment or care already specified in the proposed care plan); or
  (ii) any service (other than a service already specified in the proposed care plan),

  which it is proposed to provide to the patient (including the names of the persons who would provide such treatment, care or service and the addresses at which such treatment, care or service would be provided);

131 2003 Act, s 62(5)(a)–(l).

(g) which measures it is proposed that the compulsory treatment order should authorise;
(h) where it is proposed that the compulsory treatment order should authorise the detention of the patient in hospital or specific unit within a hospital, the name and address of the hospital or unit;
(i) where it is proposed that the compulsory treatment order should authorise measures other than detention and the giving of treatment, details of the measure (or measures);
(j) where it is proposed that the compulsory treatment order should specify:
    (i) any medical treatment specified, by virtue of paragraph (d) above, in the proposed care plan;
    (ii) any community care services, or relevant services, specified, by virtue of paragraph (e) above, in the proposed care plan; or
    (iii) any treatment, care or service specified, by virtue of paragraph (f) above, in the proposed care plan, that medical treatment, those services or that treatment, care, or service, as the case may be;
(k) where it is proposed that the compulsory treatment order should authorise measures other than the detention of the patient in hospital, the name of the hospital the managers of which should have responsibility for appointing the patient's responsible medical officer; and
(l) the objectives of:
    (i) the medical treatment which it is proposed, by virtue of paragraph (d) above, to give to the patient;
    (ii) any community care services or relevant services which it is proposed, by virtue of paragraph (e) above, to provide to the patient;
    (iii) any treatment, care or service which, by virtue of paragraph (f) above, it is proposed to provide to the patient; and
    (iv) the measures (other than detention of the patient in hospital) that it is proposed that the compulsory treatment order should authorise.

The MHO should inform the MHT as to whether the patient is likely to need to have a curator (whose function is to protect and safeguard the interests of the patient) appointed for the purposes of the Tribunal proceedings.[132] This will arise if the view is stated in one of the medical reports that the patient does not have capacity to represent themselves at the Tribunal. The need for appointment of a curator should be identified in a form accompanying the CTO Application, but may, in practice, be the subject of informal discussion with the MHT before the application is lodged.

Early notification of the patient and named person has been discussed above. One practical reason for this, and for the MHO starting to complete their report and the CTO application form before receipt of the second medical report, is the time constraint which arises in practice. Although there is a statutory maximum of 14 days, MHOs are unlikely to have anything like this time to prepare the application and to fulfil their other duties.[133] The reason for this is that most CTOs follow on from a short-term detention certificate[134] and, in many cases, a decision that a CTO is necessary is not made until late in the period of authorised detention under the STDC.[135] This sequence leaves limited time for the application to be lodged before authority to detain lapses (and also leaves limited time for a hearing to be convened to deal with the application).

BOX C

Once the application for a CTO is lodged by the MHO, a date for the Tribunal hearing will be set.[136] Because of the tight timescales the amount of notice received by the patient may be short. Legal representation is available to the patient through the Assistance by Way of Representation Scheme.[137] The Tribunal is composed of three members, a legally qualified chair, a member who is qualified as a psychiatrist, and a member with experience of mental disorder or of caring for people with such a disorder.[138] Since the application is in the name of the MHO it will be for them to introduce the application and set out the grounds for the application and the measures which are sought. After this, contributions will be sought from others, for example the RMO, the patient and named

132 *Code of Practice 2003*, vol 2, ch 3, para 79.

133 2003 Act, s 57(7).

134 In 2021–22 6,569 were recorded, 2.3% fewer than in 2020–21. Of those recorded episodes, 2.4% began with a CTO or an interim CTO, Source: Mental Welfare Commission, Mental Health Act monitoring report 2021–2022, p 5.

135 See, for example, Mental Welfare Commission, *Short Term Detention* (2010).

136 2003 Act, s 63(1).

137 Advice and Assistance (Assistance by Way of Representation) (Scotland) Regulations, SSI 2003/179, reg 3.

138 2003 Act, Sch 2, part 1, 'Members'.

person, and the patient's legal representative may ask questions.[139] The Tribunal members will also ask questions and the members have a much more active role in proceedings than a judge would normally have in court proceedings. Tribunal proceedings have been described as semi-inquisitorial.[140] Tribunal proceedings are intended to be conducted in a more informal setting and manner than court proceedings, the intention being to make it easier for individuals to participate in the proceedings. In practice, however, different Tribunals operate in different ways and there have been complaints that some operate in a way which is too formal and legalistic.[141]

After the hearing the Tribunal has a number of options. It can refuse the application.[142] It can make an interim order, initially for up to 28 days, although the interim order can be renewed as long as the renewal does not extend the total length of the interim order beyond 56 days.[143] The interim order might be renewed more than once, as long as the total period is not exceeded.[144] Interim orders can authorise any measures which can be authorised on a full order. Such an order might be used, for example, to allow time to obtain an independent medical report. Finally, the MHT might make a full CTO, which will last initially for a period of six months. [145]

Before the MHT makes a CTO or an interim CTO it must be satisfied that a number of criteria are satisfied, though even if the MHT concludes that all the criteria are satisfied it still has discretion about whether to make an order and the terms of any order. The criteria are:[146]

(a) the patient has a mental disorder;

139 2003 Act, ss 64(2) and 64(3), MHT duty to facilitate questions and submission of evidence.

140 *Laurie v Mental Health Tribunal for Scotland* [2007] 8 WLUK 253, Paisley Sheriff Court, 30 August 2007.

141 Jill Stavert, et al, 'The Mental Health Tribunal for Scotland: the views and experiences of Patients, Named Persons, Practitioners and Mental Health Tribunal for Scotland members', (2022), pp 40, 41 and 47.

142 2003 Act, s 64(4)(b).

143 2003 Act, s 65. NB Amendment to s 65 pending: '(7) If the patient has been detained in hospital by virtue of section 47(4)(a) or 68(2)(a) of this Act in connection with the application by virtue of which this section applies, the 56 days referred to in subsection (3) above is to be regarded as reduced by the period during which the patient has been so detained under that section.' Added by Mental Health (Scotland) Act 2015 asp 9 (Scottish Act) Pt 1, s 1(3) (date to be appointed).

144 2003 Act, s 65.

145 2003 Act, s 64(4)(a)(i).

146 2003 Act, s 64(5)(a)–(f).

(b) medical treatment is available for the patient and this treatment would be likely to prevent the disorder from getting worse or would alleviate the symptoms or effects of the disorder;
(c) there would be a significant risk to the health or safety of the patient or to the safety of some other person if the treatment was not provided;
(d) the ability of the patient to take decisions about the medical treatment is significantly impaired by their disorder;
(e) making the order is necessary, for example because the patient will not voluntarily accept treatment.
(f) where the Tribunal does not consider it necessary for the patient to be detained in hospital, such other conditions as may be specified in regulations.

If a full order is made after a hearing this will usually authorise the measures set out in the application. These measures, which will reference the initial medical reports and the application for a CTO, may be added to by the MHT, modifying them or removing particular measures.[147] If the MHT does intend to specify measures not set out in the application[148] it must give notice of this and allow representations to be made and evidence to be produced before a decision is made.[149] In considering whether to make a CTO and what measures to authorise, the Tribunal must take account of the principles set out in **8.12** above. The measures which can be authorised in a CTO are set out in Box 8.3 below.

Box 8.3

The following measures can be authorised in a CTO:[150]
(a) detention of the patient in the specified hospital (which may be the State Hospital), a specific unit within the hospital may be specified;

147 2003 Act, ss 64(6) and 64(7).
148 As it did, for example, in *Di Mascio v MHTS* [2008] 8 WLUK 26, where the Tribunal made a community CTO when the application specified a hospital-based CTO.
149 2003 Act, ss 64(7) and 64(8). NB The following amendments to s 64 are pending – '(8A) If the patient has been detained in hospital by virtue of section 47(4)(a) or 68(2)(a) of this Act in connection with the application by virtue of which this section applies, the 6 months referred to in subsection (4)(a)(i) above is to be regarded as reduced by the period during which the patient has been so detained under that section. (8B) Subsection (8A) above is of no effect if the patient has been detained in hospital in accordance with an interim compulsory treatment order made in connection with the application by virtue of which this section applies.' Added by Mental Health (Scotland) Act 2015 asp 9 (Scottish Act) Pt 1, s1(2). (At the time of writing, April 2026, a date of commencement is still to be appointed.)
150 2003 Act, s 66(1)(a)–(h).

(b) giving medical treatment to the patient;
(c) a requirement to attend for medical treatment at a place and times, these may be set out in the CTO or the requirement may be to attend for treatment as directed;
(d) a requirement on the patient to attend to receive community care services, relevant services or any treatment, care or service; as in (c), these can be set out in the CTO or be as directed;
(e) a requirement on the patient to reside at a specified place;
(f) a requirement on the patient to allow the MHO, the RMO, or anyone responsible for providing medical treatment, community care services, relevant services or any treatment, care or service to the patient who is authorised by the RMO to visit her/him in the place where she/he resides;
(g) a requirement on the patient to obtain the approval of the MHO to any proposed change of address; and
(h) a requirement on the patient to inform the MHO of any proposed change of address before the change takes effect.

In addition to the measures requested in the application and selected from the list above, the MHT will also set out the treatment to be provided and any other services which it considers appropriate, the treatment and other services are defined as 'recorded matters'.[151] The full list of matters which can be recorded leaves considerable scope for the Tribunal and includes 'such medical treatment, community care services, relevant services, other treatment, care or service as the Tribunal considers appropriate'.[152] The matter might also be referred to the MHT by the MWC under section 98 of the 2003 Act, which gives the MWC the power to make a reference where it appears to the MWC appropriate to do so. The CTO must also identify the types of mental disorder affecting the patient, and if the order is a Community CTO (i.e., the patient is not to be detained in hospital) it must identify the hospital whose managers are responsible for appointing the patient's RMO.[153]

The Tribunal must set out the facts found by it, the decision reached and the reasons for reaching that decision and notice of the decision must be given to those involved in the application. It has been said that:

151 2003 Act, s 64(4)(a)(ii). This definition was held not to be broad enough to include a requirement to consider an application for welfare guardianship, *AB v Rodriguez* [2012] Airdrie Sheriff Court 26/09/2012-Unreported.
152 2003 Act, s 96.
153 2003 Act, s 63.

> The reasons for a decision must be intelligible and they must be adequate. They must enable the reader to understand why the matter was decided as it was and what conclusions were reached on the 'principal, important controversial issues' … reasons need refer only to the main issues in the dispute, not every material consideration … decision letters must be read in a straightforward manner, recognising they are addressed to parties well aware of the issues involved and the arguments advanced. A reasons challenge will only succeed if the parties aggrieved can satisfy the court that he has genuinely been substantially prejudiced by the failure to provide an adequately reasoned decision.[154]

(b) After the order is made

8.20 After a CTO is made, the hospital managers identified in the order will have to identify an RMO for the patient and the local authority will have to designate an MHO who will be responsible for the patient. The 2003 Act specifies those persons who will have the opportunity to make representations before the Tribunal, these include; the patient, the patient's named person, welfare attorney, MHO, and the medical practitioners who made the reports concerning the patient.[155] The MHO must then, within 21 days of the making of the CTO (or the making of an interim CTO), prepare a social circumstances report (SCR) in respect of the patient.[156] The RMO must prepare a care plan for the patient.

(c) Review of the order

8.21 The RMO has a duty to keep the CTO under review and to revoke the order if the conditions for making a CTO have ceased to exist. The RMO may also make an application to the MHT to vary the terms of the order if this is appropriate. There is a formal duty to consult the MHO in cases where the RMO decides that the terms of a CTO need to be varied. In the absence of such a formal requirement in relation to

154 *Koca v Secretary of State for the Home Department* 2005 SC 487, per Lord Carloway at 499, cited in *Robbins v Mitchell* [2007] Scot SC 19 Unreported. (Available at: www.mhtscotland.gov.uk/mhts/files/Judgements/Robbins_v_Mitchell.pdf. (Accessed April 2026). See also *Scottish Ministers v MHTS* [2009] CSIH 9, referring to the need to give clear and intelligible reasons for rejecting expert evidence (at para [52]) and *AB v Mental Health Tribunal for Scotland* [2011] Scot SC 179, indicating that the Tribunal's decision should set out clearly why it considers that the criteria for making an order are met.

155 2003 Act, s 64(2) and 64(3).

156 2003 Act, s 231. See also **8.27** below.

determinations to revoke a CTO, the Code of Practice makes it clear that it is best practice for there to be continuing close consultation both with the MHO and with the patient's carers.[157]

A more specific duty to carry out a mandatory review arises in the period before the CTO, as initially made, or as subsequently extended, is due to expire.[158] As we have seen, a CTO will initially expire in six months. Within two months of the expiry date the RMO must review the order and this review will include consulting the MHO. The outcome of this review can be that the order is revoked if the grounds for making a CTO no longer exist.[159] Alternatively, the order can be continued unchanged, and this is done simply by a determination made by the RMO[160] which extends the order initially for a further six months, at the end of which period it can be extended for further periods of 12 months.[161] If the RMO proposes to extend the order, the MHO must be notified and then must then carry out the various actions set out in Box 8.4.[162] In light of the views of the MHO and of others consulted, the RMO must decide whether to make a determination extending the CTO; this is then recorded and submitted to the MHT.[163] The extension will only come before the Tribunal for a hearing if:[164]

(a) the mental disorder which is the basis for the extension is different from that set out in the original CTO;
(b) the MHO disagrees with the decision to extend;
(c) no determination of an application to review the order has been made by the Tribunal in the preceding two years; and
(d) the patient, the patient's named person or a listed initiator applies for revocation of the extended order.

157 *Code of Practice 2003*, vol 2, p 123, para 13.
158 2003 Act, ss 77 and 78.
159 2003 Act, s 79.
160 The form used can be found here: www.gov.scot/binaries/content/documents/govscot/publications/form/2019/01/mental-health-law-forms/documents/compulsory-treatment-orders-forms/extend-and-vary-cto-or-co---mhts---cto4b-v7.0-26-jun-2017/extend-and-vary-cto-or-co---mhts---cto4b-v7.0-26-jun-2017/govscot%3Adocument/CTO%2B4%2BPart%2BB%2Bv7.1.pdf (Accessed April 2026).
161 2003 Act, ss 84 and 86(2).
162 *Code of Practice 2005*, vol 2, ch 5, paras 33 and 55 and 2003 Act, s 85.
163 2003 Act, s 87.
164 2003 Act, ss 86 and 101.

Box 8.4

MHO tasks on notification by RMO[165]

(a) interview the patient (if practicable);

(b) tell the patient that the RMO is intending to extend the order (or extend and vary the order) and what the patient's rights are in connection with this extension (and variation);

(c) make the patient aware of the availability of advocacy services and do anything necessary to ensure the patient has an opportunity to use these;

(d) inform the RMO whether she/he agrees with the proposed extension and, if the MHO disagrees, what the reasons for this are and pass on any other information the MHO considers relevant. In the process of reaching their conclusions, the MHO should evaluate the effectiveness of the patient's care plan and the extent to which its objectives are being fulfilled as well as assessing the continued effectiveness of the order and the extent to which the patient would accept voluntary treatment.

A final outcome of a mandatory review may be that the RMO considers that the CTO should be both extended and varied. Variation may be in respect of the measures authorised by the CTO (e.g. varying from a hospital-based CTO to a community CTO), the treatment offered or other recorded matters.[166] If this conclusion is reached, the RMO will need to apply to the MHT. The RMO must notify the MHO of the intention to apply for extension and variation, and the MHO then must carry out the tasks set out in Box 8.4. [167]After consultation the RMO then has to decide whether or not to apply to the MHT. Unlike the initial application for a CTO which is made by the MHO, it is the RMO who is responsible for applying for an extension and variation of the order (or for a variation following a time-to-time review). [168]

Where a Tribunal is considering a case where the CTO is being extended and/or varied, a report must be provided by the MHO:

(a) where the case is being considered because the MHO disagrees with the proposed extension or,

165 2003 Act, 85(2)(a)–(d).
166 2003 Act, s 89.
167 2003 Act, s 85(2).
168 2003 Act, s 92.

(b) where the mental disorder which is the basis for the extension is different from that set out in the original CTO.[169]

In other cases, the Tribunal can request a report from the MHO. This report should include:[170]
(a) the steps taken by the MHO to fulfil their obligations after being notified by the RMO;
(b) the views of the MHO on the extension and/or variation and the reasons for these views;
(c) any relevant details of the patient's personal circumstances;
(d) details of any advance statements made by the patient; and
(e) any other information which the MHO thinks will assist the Tribunal.

(d) Appeals and revocation

8.22 As we have seen, a CTO can be revoked by the RMO following a review of the order. The Mental Welfare Commission (MWC) also has the power to revoke a CTO.[171] In addition the patient, the patient's named person or a listed initiator, can apply to the MHT for revocation of a CTO or of a determination extending a CTO, or for variation of any measures or recorded matters contained in the order.[172] Applications by the patient or the patient's named person can only be made after three months have passed since the last consideration of the order by the MHT.[173]

A patient who is detained in the State Hospital, or who considers that they are detained in another hospital or unit under conditions of excessive security, can apply to the MHT for review. The MHT can determine that the patient does not need to be detained under the security conditions which can only be provided in that hospital, and order transfer to another hospital.[174]

Finally, there is a right of appeal against final decisions and orders of the MHT.[175] Appeal is, in the first instance, to the Sheriff Principal, with

169 2003 Act, s 87A.
170 2003 Act, s 87A.
171 2003 Act, s 81.
172 2003 Act, ss 99 and 100.
173 2003 Act, s 100(4).
174 2003 Act, Pt 17, ch 3, Mental Health (Detention in Conditions of Excessive Security (Scotland) Regulations 2015, SSI 2015/364. See also Scottish Government, *Mental Health Legislation: Detention in Conditions of Excessive Security* (2015).
175 Subject to very limited exceptions, see 2003 Act, s 320.

further appeal to the Inner House of the Court of Session.[176] The right to appeal is conferred on the patient, the patient's named person, the patient's guardian or welfare attorney (if there is one), the MHO, the RMO and the listed initiator.[177] Any curator appointed for the purposes of proceedings before the MHT cannot appeal a Tribunal decision.[178] The grounds of appeal are that:[179]

(a) the Tribunal's decision was based on an error of law;
(b) there was a procedural impropriety in the conduct of the Tribunal hearing;
(c) the Tribunal has acted unreasonably in the exercise of its discretion; and
(d) that the Tribunal's decision was not supported by the facts found to be established by the Tribunal.

(e) Non-compliance with a CTO[180]

8.23 The 2003 Act provides procedures which allow the RMO to take action if a patient fails to comply with a CTO or an interim CTO. If the patient fails to attend for treatment or to comply with any other measure set out in the CTO the RMO can give authority for the patient to be taken into custody. [181] Where the non-compliance relates to attendance for treatment, the patient can be taken to the place where they are supposed to receive treatment or to a hospital. If the latter, the patient can only be kept there for up to six hours unless the CTO authorises detention in the hospital.[182] If the non-compliance relates to other measures the patient can be taken to a hospital where they can initially be detained for up to 72 hours.[183] Once in hospital the patient must be examined by a RMO. If the RMO is considering whether to apply to the MHT for variation of the CTO or has decided that the CTO should be varied, requiring an application to the MHT, the period of detention can be extended by 28 days.[184] This period will run from the time when the RMO grants a certificate authorising the further detention. Before an extension is authorised the MHO must be consulted and must consent.[185] Where the

176 2003 Act, ss 320 and 321.
177 2003 Act, ss 320 and 321 define these named as, 'relevant parties'. See also 8.7 above.
178 *Black v Mental Health Tribunal for Scotland* [2011] CSIH 83.
179 2003 Act, s 324(2)(a)–(d).
180 *Code of Practice 2003*, vol 2, ch 6.
181 2003 Act, s 112(3).
182 2003 Act, s 112(3)–(5).
183 2003 Act, s 113(5).
184 2003 Act, s 114(2).
185 2003 Act, s 114(3).

patient is subject to an interim CTO the RMO can, with the consent of the MHO, grant a certificate authorising detention for the remainder of the interim CTO.[186] The conditions applying to continued detention are that the RMO considers it, 'reasonably likely' that there will be a significant deterioration in the patient's mental health.[187] The patient or the patient's named person or listed initiator can apply to the MHT for revocation of the certificate authorising the extended detention.[188]

SUSPENSION OF DETENTION

8.24 Where a patient is detained by virtue of an EDC[189] or an STDC,[190] the RMO may grant a certificate specifying that detention of the patient is not to be authorised for a specific period. This power may be used to allow the patient to leave the hospital for specific event or for a longer period and may be subject to conditions, for example that the patient remains in the charge of a specific person. The certificate may be revoked by the RMO if they are satisfied that this is necessary in the interests of the patient or to protect another person.[191]

In the case of a patient subject to a CTO it is possible for the RMO both to suspend the authorisation for detention[192] and to suspend other measures authorised by the CTO.[193] A certificate suspending the authorisation of detention can, at any one time, be for a period of up to 200 days,[194] and combined periods cannot exceed 200 days in a period of 12 months.[195] Any suspension can be made subject to conditions. A certificate authorising suspension of other measures can last for up to 90 days. Other measures can be suspended for a number of shorter periods, subject to the sum of all periods not exceeding 90 days. Suspensions of other measures and suspensions of detention for a period exceeding 28 days must be notified to the MWC. Either type of certificate can be

186 2003 Act, s 115.
187 2003 Act, s 115(1)(c).
188 2003 Act, s 120.
189 2003 Act, s 41.
190 2003 Act, s 53.
191 2003 Act, ss 42 and 54.
192 2003 Act, s 127.
193 2003 Act, s 128.
194 Periods of suspension of up to 8 hours in any 24 hours do not count towards this; 2003 Act, s 127(2A).
195 2003 Act, s 127(2).

revoked by the RMO[196] where they are satisfied that this is necessary in the interests of the patient or to protect another person.[197]

It is not clear what the effect of exceeding these limits is. It has been held[198] that the consequence of a suspension of an authorisation of detention exceeding the statutory limits is that patient is to be treated as having absconded[199] and, if this continues for three months, the CTO ceases to have effect.[200]

NURSE'S POWER TO DETAIN

8.25 A patient who is not detained under any order under the 2003 Act but is in hospital and receiving medical treatment may be detained for up to three hours by a nurse.[201] The three-hour detention is to allow for a medical examination of the patient to be conducted by a medical practitioner and the following conditions must be met:[202]

(a) the patient has a mental disorder;

(b) it is necessary to restrain the patient from leaving the hospital either to protect their health safety and welfare or to protect the safety of another person; and

(c) it is necessary for a medical practitioner to carry out a medical examination of the patient for the purpose of determining whether the granting of (i) an emergency detention certificate; or (ii) a short-term detention certificate is warranted.

MEDICAL TREATMENT

8.26 As we have seen, the medical treatment which can be given to a patient is widely defined. It is possible that the patient may have made an advance statement setting out either the form of treatment which they wish to receive for mental disorder, or setting out the ways

196 2003 Act, s 129.

197 2003 Act, s 129(2).

198 *DC, Application for Judicial Review* 2012 SLT 521. In this case a preference was expressed for taking the three-month period mentioned below as starting on the first day of the unauthorised suspension.

199 2003 Act, s 304.

200 2003 Act, s 304(3).

201 2003 Act, s 299. The nurse must be a mental health or learning disabilities nurse registered in Sub part 1 of the register maintained by the Nursing and Midwifery Council, Mental Health (Class of Nurse) (Scotland) Regulations 2005, SSI 2005/446, reg 2.

202 2003 Act, s 299(3)(a)–(c).

in which they do not want to be treated.[203] The advance statement must be in writing and must be witnessed by someone who is a member of a class prescribed for the purpose of witnessing advance statements, these include solicitors, social workers, registered nurses, medical practitioners and people who provide, or who work in, care services.[204] As well as witnessing the signature the witness must also certify that, in their opinion, the person making the statement had capacity to do this. If an advance statement is received by a Health Board it must place this with the patient's medical records and notify the Mental Welfare Commission, which must, in turn, enter it into a register of advance statements.[205]

Once an advance statement has been made, regard must be had to it by anyone providing treatment to the patient and by a Tribunal in considering measures to be authorised by a CTO.[206] The advance statement can, however, be overridden, but if this is done the reasons for this must be recorded in writing and notified to: the patient making the statement, the named person, the patient's proxy (if any), and the Mental Welfare Commission.[207]

There are certain types of treatment which are subject to additional procedures and or authorisations before they can be given, though some of these are rare in practice. The first group involves brain surgery involving destruction of part of the brain or its functions, as well as deep brain stimulation. These procedures may only be carried out if the patient consents or if the patient is incapable of consent and does not resist or object to the treatment (i.e., there is no power to treat a patient with capacity who refuses consent[208]). Where the patient consents, a designated medical practitioner (DMP) appointed by the MWC must certify that the treatment is in the best interests of the patient.[209] In addition, the DMP and two others also appointed by the MWC (and who are not medical practitioners) must certify both that the patient has capacity to consent and that they consent to the treatment.[210] If the patient cannot consent, this type of treatment can only be given with the consent

203 2003 Act, s 275(1); Scottish Government, *Interim Guidance on Advance Statements* (2017).

204 2003 Act, s 275(2); Mental Health (Advance Statements) (Prescribed Class of Persons) (Scotland) (No 2) Regulations 2004, SSI 2004/429.

205 2003 Act, ss 276A–276B.

206 2003 Act, s 276.

207 2003 Act, s 276(7), (8). Such overrides are rare in practice. There were 55 in total in 2016–17, Mental Welfare Commission, *Mental Health Act Monitoring Report 2016–2017*, p 40.

208 2003 Act, ss 235 and 236.

209 2003 Act, s 235(2).

210 2003 Act, s 235(2) and 235(3).

of the Court of Session.[211] A second set of treatments involves Electro Convulsive Therapy (ECT) and some rare treatments.[212] These can only be given to a patient who cannot consent if a certificate is issued by a DMP which indicates, *inter alia*, that the treatment is in the patient's best interests, or, if the patient resists or objects to the treatment, that the treatment is necessary to save the patient's life, to prevent serious deterioration in their condition or to alleviate serious suffering.[213] Where the patient consents to this type of treatment and this is certified by the RMO or by a DMP it can be given.[214] The same certification requirement applies to giving certain other types of treatment to consenting patients. These are; medication for reducing sex drive, the giving of any medication for a period in excess of two months, and artificial feeding (for example by way of a nasogastric tube).[215] If the patient is incapable of consenting to such treatments, or is capable but refuses consent, it can only be given if a certificate is issued by a DMP, which indicates, amongst other things, that it is in the patient's best interests to give the treatment.[216] In assessing whether the treatment is in the patient's best interests, the DMP must have regard to the likelihood of the treatment alleviating, or preventing a deterioration in, the patient's condition.[217] If the patient refuses treatment, then the DMP must have regard to the reasons for that refusal and must state the reason(s) for being of the opinion that the treatment should be given.[218]

Aside from these special cases, treatment can be given where the patient, if capable of consent, consents in writing to the treatment.[219] If the patient is incapable of consenting or, being capable, refuses consent, the designated medical practitioner (DMP) must determine that giving treatment is in the best interests of the patient. In doing this the DMP must consider the reason for not consenting, the views of the patient and their named person; any advance statement made by the patient and the

211 2003 Act, s 234, Mental Health (Medical Treatment Subject to Safeguards) (Section 234) (Scotland) Regulations 2005, SSI 2005/291.

212 Transcranial magnetic stimulation and vagus nerve stimulation, 2003 Act, s 237, Mental Health (Medical Treatment Subject to Safeguards) (Section 237) (Scotland) Regulations 2005.

213 2003 Act, ss 237 and 239.

214 2003 Act, ss 237 and 238.

215 2003 Act, ss 240 and 238; there is provision for regulations to be made adding other types of treatment to this list, but no such regulations have been made.

216 2003 Act, s 241.

217 2003 Act, s 241.

218 2003 Act, s 241(2)

219 2003 Act, s 238. The UK Supreme Court held in *Montgomery v Lanarkshire Health Board* [2025] UKSC 11, that consent to any medical treatment must be 'informed consent', doctors must ensure the patient is aware of any risks of, and reasonable alternatives to, the proposed treatment.

likelihood of the treatment alleviating, or preventing deterioration in, the patient's condition. If the patient is in hospital, but not otherwise, treatment can be given by force.[220]

Urgent treatment can be given to detained patients in hospital regardless of consent.[221] Urgent treatment is treatment necessary to save the patient's life, to prevent serious deterioration in their condition, to alleviate serious suffering, or to prevent the patient either behaving violently or being a danger to themselves or others.[222] There are limits on the treatment that can be given – ECT cannot be given if the patient can consent but refuses. Treatment for purposes other than saving the patient's life must not be likely to entail unfavourable and irreversible consequences; and treatment to alleviate suffering or to prevent violent behaviour or danger must not entail significant physical hazard to the patient.[223]

SOCIAL CIRCUMSTANCES REPORTS

8.27 A social circumstances report (SCR)[224] must be prepared by an MHO in certain circumstances. The three events which trigger the duty to complete a SCR are the making of an STDC, the making of an interim CTO or the making of a CTO.[225] No report is required if the MHO is of the view that preparing such a report would serve little or no practical purpose. The SCR is distinct from the report which the MHO must prepare in connection with an application for a compulsory treatment order.[226]

The MHO's report for the CTO application should focus on the assessed needs of the individual and whether the MHO believes the criteria for compulsory powers are satisfied. A proposed care plan, while commenting on assessed needs, focuses almost exclusively on future care arrangements. Together these documents will contain much, but not all, the information included in an SCR. It should be possible to use much of the information from an SCR to help complete a MHO's report and a proposed care plan. There should not be any wasted effort if the decision is taken to proceed with a CTO application well after an MHO

220 2003 Act, s 242(6).
221 2003 Act, s 243.
222 2003 Act, s 243(3).
223 2003 Act, ss 243(3)(c), 243(3)(d), and 243(4).
224 *Code of Practice 2005* vol 1, ch 11; Mental Welfare Commission, *Social Circumstances Reports* (2022).
225 2003 Act, s 231 – details the responsibilities of MHOs in relation to SCRs.
226 2003 Act Code of Practice (Scottish Executive, 2005) vol 1, ch 11, para 16.

has begun the process of completing an SCR. The main added value of the SCR is that it summarises information on the personal and social circumstances of the individual, as well as the care and treatment history of the patient, and places this in the context of the current admission and future care planning.

If no social circumstances report is prepared, the reasons for this must be recorded and sent to the responsible medical officer and the Mental Welfare Commission.[227] Examples of situations where preparation would serve little or no practical purpose are given in the Code of Practice. These situations involve cases where the obligation to prepare a report arises because one event has taken place (for example short-term detention), following which a report has been prepared. The first event is followed shortly afterwards by another event triggering the obligation to compile a report (for example, making a compulsory treatment order). Where no social circumstances report is prepared the Commission has indicated that, unless there are compelling reasons not to do so, the patient should be informed of the reason for this.[228]

The report is to contain, as far as it is relevant to their care, the following information about the patient:[229]

(a) state of physical and mental health and mental health history;
(b) personal history, including details of employment, finances and accommodation prior to the use of compulsory powers;
(c) family situation, including information about children and dependents;
(d) regular social contacts;
(e) ability to care for themselves; and
(f) any history of offending (including consideration of victims and those affected) and any history of substance misuse.

227 2003 Act, s 231(2). The Commission has consistently noted that this actually happens in a very small proportion of cases in which the duty to inform it arises: Mental Welfare Commission for Scotland, Mental Health Act monitoring report 2021–2022, 'For 43.3% of STDCs in 2021-22, the Commission received notification that an SCR had been prepared or that an SCR would serve no purpose (and therefore had not been prepared). In 56.7% of cases, we received no notification' pp 5–6. See also the concerns noted by the Commission about the reasons which it receives: Mental Welfare Commission for Scotland, Social Circumstances Reports (April 2022). On p 11 it is noted that the fact that the patient is 'well-known to services' is not an acceptable reason for not producing a report.

228 Mental Welfare Commission, *Social Circumstances Reports* (April 2022) p 12.

229 Mental Health (Social Circumstances Reports) (Scotland) Regulations 2005, SSI 2005/310, reg 2. There is also a non-statutory pro forma (SCR 1) which should be used for the report. Available at: www.gov.scot/Resource/0052/00521695.pdf (Accessed April 2026).

In addition, the report must set out, again as far as is relevant to the care of the patient:

(a) Why compulsory powers were used and the views of the patient regarding their use. If the patient is unable to give a view, then, if these are available to the mental health officer the views of the patient's named person, carer, guardian and welfare attorney regarding the use of compulsory powers should be included.
(b) An assessment of the risk of harm to the patient and to others.
(c) The care being provided to the patient prior to the use of compulsory powers.
(d) Any matters which would trigger the local authority's duty to inquire.
(e) Any alternatives to the use of compulsory powers which were considered and ruled out.
(f) Ethnic, cultural and religious factors.
(g) Whether the patient has difficulty in communicating.
(h) Any plan which has been put in place to deal with any of the matters referred to in the report.

Chapter 9

Adult support and protection

INTRODUCTION

9.1 Much of the law considered in the last three chapters is concerned with the protection and provision of support to adults who might be described as vulnerable. In addition there are duties to investigate, and some powers to assist with such investigations, conferred by the Mental Health (Care and Treatment) (Scotland) Act 2003[1] and the Adults with Incapacity (Scotland) Act 2000.[2] In addition to these there is specific provision in the Adult Support and Protection (Scotland) Act 2007 (the 2007 Act).[3] The 2007 Act does a number of things. First, it establishes a duty of cooperation between agencies. Second, it creates multi-disciplinary Adult Protection Committees and sets out certain principles to be followed. Third, it imposes on local authorities a duty to investigate and it confers on them certain powers which can be used in carrying out these functions.[4] The 2007 Act does not provide for any long-term support or provision for an adult, so this will have to be undertaken under other legislation, e.g., appointment of a welfare guardian.

Adult Protection Committees[5] involve the local authority, the health board, the police, Social Care and Social Work Improvement Scotland, Health Improvement Scotland and others. The main functions of the Committee are to keep policies and procedures relating to safeguarding adults at risk under review and to provide information and advice. The bodies represented on the Adult Protection Committee, and others, have an obligation to cooperate with investigations and inquiries relating to adults at risk which are being carried out by a local authority.[6] Each of

1 See **8.15 and 8.16**.
2 See **7.2**.
3 Which followed on rather belatedly from the Scottish Law Commission Report on Vulnerable Adults (published in 1997). Functions under ss 4, 5, 6, 11, 14, 18, 22, 40, 42 and 43 of the 2007 Act must be delegated under the integration scheme required by the Public Bodies (Joint Working) (Scotland) Act 2014, see **1.73**.
4 2007 Act, s 4 and ss 7–10 (the 2007 Act).
5 2007 Act, ss 42 and 43. See Scottish Government, *Adult Support and Protection (Scotland) Act 2007: Code of Practice* (July 2022).
6 2007 Act, s 5.

these organisations also has a duty to report to the local authority any cases in which it believes that an adult is at risk and that action needs to be taken to protect the adult from harm.[7]

THE PRINCIPLES

9.2 The principles in the 2007 Act include a number of principles and factors which should be taken into consideration when carrying out any functions under the Act. As a general principle, any intervention must provide a benefit to the adult which could not reasonably be provided without that intervention.[8] In addition, where there is a range of options for action, the option which is least restrictive of the freedom of the adult must be chosen.[9]

Factors which must be considered in carrying out functions are:[10]

(a) the wishes of the adult, past and present;[11]

(b) the views of the adult's nearest relative, primary carer, proxy,[12] and any other person with an interest in the welfare of the adult. In practice active steps should be taken to get the views of these people;[13]

(c) the importance of the adult participating, and being enabled to participate (for example by the provision of appropriate support), as fully as possible in decisions and actions;[14]

(d) the importance of ensuring that the adult does not receive less favourable treatment than someone who is not an adult at risk would receive in the same circumstances;[15]

(e) the ability, background and characteristics of the adult.[16]

7 2007 Act, s 5(3)

8 2007 Act, s 1(a)

9 2007 Act, s 1(b).

10 2007 Act, s 2. See also *ASP Code of Practice* (July 2022), pp 13–14.

11 2007 Act, s 2(a)

12 Eg, an attorney or guardian.

13 2007 Act, s 2(c)

14 2007 Act, s 2(d); *ASP Code of Practice*, ch 4.

15 2007 Act, s 2(e).

16 2007 Act, s 2(f).

THE DUTY TO INVESTIGATE[17]

9.3 A duty on the local authority will arise where two conditions are met.[18] The first is that an adult is at risk.[19] The second is that the local authority may need to intervene to protect the adult's well-being, property or financial affairs.[20] Thcsc conditions raise the question of when an adult is at risk; this will be the case if three requirements are *all* met:[21]

(a) the adult is unable to safeguard their own welfare, rights or other interests; *and*

(b) the adult is at risk of harm (harm is defined below), all that is required is that there is a risk of harm, it is not essential that the adult is being, or has been, harmed; *and*

(c) the adult is more likely to be harmed because they are affected by disability, mental disorder, illness or physical or mental infirmity; the harm may be caused by the conduct of others or may involve self-harm.

Harm includes all harmful conduct and, in particular, includes:[22]

(a) conduct which causes physical harm;

(b) conduct which causes psychological harm (for example: by causing fear, alarm or distress);

(c) unlawful conduct which appropriates or adversely affects property, rights or interests (for example: theft, fraud, embezzlement or extortion);

(d) conduct which causes self-harm.

Once the investigation has been completed the local authority will need to decide what action to take. If it decides that no action is required a report on the enquiries undertaken, and the reasons for reaching the conclusion that no action is needed, should be added to the adult's case file.[23] Alternatively, the decision may be that some action needs to be taken. This may involve use of a removal order or a banning order,[24] or it may involve use of other legislation. Examples include provision of community care services or an application for guardianship under the Adults with Incapacity (Scotland) Act 2000.[25] Where the local authority

17 2007 Act, *ASP Code of Practice*, ch 6.
18 2007 Act, s 4, *ASP Code of Practice*, ch 2.
19 2007 Act, s 4(a)
20 2007 Act, s 4(a)
21 2007 Act, s 3; *ASP Code of Practice*, ch 1, paras 10–22.
22 2007 Act, s 53(1).
23 2007 Act, s 3; *ASP Code of Practice*, p 50.
24 2007 Act, ss 14 and 19.
25 Adults with Incapacity (Scotland) Act 2000, s 57 – Application for guardianship order.

decides that it needs to intervene it must have regard to the importance of providing appropriate services to the adult, including independent advocacy services.[26] A report must be made to the police if the enquiries indicate that a criminal offence has been committed against the adult.[27]

LOCAL AUTHORITY POWERS

9.4 Local authorities have a number of powers under the 2007 Act, some of which can only be exercised after application to court, and these orders granted by a court are generally described as 'protection orders'. The powers granted address identifying, assessing and managing adults at risk and must be exercised by someone authorised by the local authority. There are restrictions on the council officers who can be authorised – they must have at least 12 months' post-qualifying experience and be either:[28]

(a) registered as a social worker;
(b) registered as a social service worker;[29]
(c) registered as an occupational therapist; or
(d) registered as a nurse.

(1) Visits[30]

9.5 The local authority has the right of entry to premises to enable it to carry out enquiries or to assist it with those enquiries. There are no limits on the places that can be entered. The right of entry extends not just to where the adult lives, but to other locations. For example, somewhere the adult spends time during the day or the home of a person who is involved with the adult.[31] Any visit must take place at a reasonable time. There is a right to examine the place entered and to use any equipment required to fulfil the purpose of the visit, but there is no right to force entry to premises or to any part of them.[32] In order to force entry, for example to have a locked door opened, a warrant will be

26 2007 Act, s 6; *ASP Code of Practice*, ch 4, pp 41–42.
27 2007 Act, *ASP Code of Practice*, p 47.
28 2007 Act (Restriction on the Authorisation of Council Officers) Order 2008, SSI 2008/306.
29 Though such workers cannot exercise powers to apply for and implement protection orders.
30 2007 Act, ss 7–9, *ASP Code of Practice*, ch 6.
31 2007 Act, *ASP Code of Practice* pp 53–54,
32 2007 Act, s 36(4),

required.[33] This is usually obtained by application to the sheriff, though in cases of urgency a warrant can be issued by a JP. In implementing the warrant, the council officer must be accompanied by a police officer, who has the power to use reasonable force to fulfil the objectives of the visit.[34]

During a visit any adult can be interviewed. Anyone interviewed must be informed prior to the interview that they are not obliged to answer any questions.[35] The council officer is empowered to interview not only the adult, but also any other adults, for example a relative or carer. The aim in interviewing the adult is to establish whether they have been subjected to harm, whether they feel that their safety is at risk, and to discuss what action the adult wishes to take. In securing the consent of the adult to the interview, the adult's rights should be carefully explained rather than simply informing them that they are not obliged to reply to any questions.[36]

A medical examination can be carried out if the adult consents to it, and this will, unless the council officer carrying out the visit is a nurse, require that a health professional accompanies the council officer on the visit. Consent of the adult is required for such an examination.[37]

(2) Access to documents[38]

9.6 A council officer can require production of health, financial or other records relating to the adult, and it is an offence to refuse to comply with such a request, or to fail to comply with it unless there is a reasonable excuse for this.[39] Records can be required during a visit or at any other time. Any health records that are accessed can only be inspected by a health professional (aside from initial scrutiny to identify them as health records).[40] The purpose of looking at the records about the adult is restricted to enabling or assisting the local authority to

33 2007 Act, ss 37 and 38(2). Any warrant obtained will expire in 72 hours, see, 2007 Act, s 37(2)(a).

34 2007 Act, s 37(1)(b),

35 2007 Act, s 8(2), *ASP Code of Practice*, ch 7.

36 2007 Act, *ASP Code of Practice*, ch 7, p 57 notes: 'Seeking the consent of the adult to be interviewed requires a more proactive approach than simply advising the adult that they are not obliged to answer questions. The point is to ensure that the adult is given reasonable opportunity and encouragement to answer questions whilst respecting their right not to.'

37 2007 Act, s 9 – medical examinations.

38 2007 Act, s 10, *ASP Code of Practice*, ch 10.

39 2007 Act, s 49, *ASP Code of Practice*, ch 15, Obstruction of officers is an offence.

40 2007 Act, s 10.

decide whether it needs to take any action to protect the adult.[41] The adult's consent is not required before access to documents is sought, though the Code of Practice suggests that consent should be obtained whenever practicable and that the right of the adult to confidentiality should be considered before information is requested.[42]

(3) Protection orders

9.7 Three types of order, collectively described as 'protection orders', can be sought by a local authority. Before deciding to apply for any of these the authority must consider the principles set out in **9.2** above. The ASP Code of Practice also suggests that consideration be given as to whether the adult should be referred to an independent advocacy service or provided with other services.[43]

The first of the three types of order is an assessment order[44] which allows the authority to take the adult away from any place which is being visited. The authority may take the adult to another place to interview or carry out a medical examination of the individual. There is no need for the authority to have sought to interview or examine the adult before applying for the order. Before the order can be granted the adult must have consented to the order being made, unless any refusal of consent can be ignored.[45] The sheriff must consider the principles set out in **9.2** above and must be satisfied that:[46]

(a) the local authority has reasonable cause to suspect that adult in respect of whom the order is sought is an adult at risk who is being, or is likely to be, seriously harmed;
(b) the assessment is needed to establish whether the adult in fact falls into this category; and
(c) the place where the adult is to be interviewed or examined is both available and suitable.

The order is valid for seven days, and only authorises removal of the adult from the place being visited if it is impracticable to interview or examine them there, for example because of a lack of privacy.[47] The

41 2007 Act, s 10(4).
42 2007 Act, *ASP Code of Practice,* ch 10, p 71.
43 2007 Act, *ASP Code of Practice,* ch 3 and ch 4.
44 2007 Act, ss 11–13; *ASP Code of Practice,* ch 12.
45 See **9.8** below.
46 2007 Act, s 12.
47 2007 Act, ss 11(3) and s 13.

adult must, in spite of the order, consent to any interview or examination unless their refusal of consent can be ignored.[48]

As well as granting the assessment order the sheriff must also grant a warrant for entry to the place where the adult is to be visited.[49]

The second type of order is a removal order[50] which authorises removal of the adult for up to seven days and authorises the local authority to take steps to protect the adult who has been removed. The order is normally granted by the sheriff, though in urgent cases it can be granted by a JP (though this will only authorise removal for 24 hours). Before making an order, the sheriff must consider the principles set out in **9.2** above and can only grant the order:[51]

(a) if the adult consents, unless the refusal of consent can be ignored;[52]
(b) if they are satisfied that that adult in respect of whom the order is sought is an adult at risk who is likely to be seriously harmed if not moved to another place; and
(c) if the place where the adult is to be moved to is both available and suitable.

The order can regulate contact between the adult and another person and the sheriff must also grant a warrant for entry.[53] Implementation must take place within 72 hours (12 hours if the order is granted by a JP), and cannot take place unless the adult consents, unless any refusal of consent can be ignored. Where the order is made by a sheriff it is possible to apply for variation or recall of the order.[54]

The final type of protection order is a banning order.[55] This bans the person[56] who is the subject of the order from being in any place specified in the order and can have further conditions attached to it. Further conditions might include banning the person concerned from being in the vicinity of this place or authorising their ejection from the place.[57] The order will last for a specified period of up to six months, or, if no period is specified, for six months.[58] No provision is made for extension

48 2007 Act, s 13.
49 2007 Act, s 37. When an assessment order is granted, a warrant for entry under s 37 must be granted by the sheriff in relation to a visit under Section 7 of the Act.
50 2007 Act, ss 14–18; *ASP Code of Practice,* ch 13.
51 2007 Act, s 15.
52 See **9.8** below.
53 2007 Act, s 37.
54 2007 Act, s 17.
55 2007 Act, ss 19–29 and 32–34; *ASP Code of Practice,* ch 14.
56 Who need not be an adult.
57 2007 Act, s 19
58 2007 Act, s 19(5)

of a banning order so if it is still required a fresh application would have to be made for a new banning order.

The application for the banning order can be made either by the adult who would be protected by the order or anyone else who lives in the place[59] which will be covered by the order, or by the local authority. Indeed, the local authority has an obligation to apply for an order where it is satisfied that the criteria for granting an order exist. The authority must further be satisfied that nobody else is likely to apply for an order and that no other proceedings are before the courts which would have the effect of ejecting or banning the person who is the subject of the order from the place specified in the order.[60] Before making the application, however, the authority must consider the principles set out in **9.2** above. When an application is made for a banning order it can be accompanied by an application for a temporary banning order.[61] While a banning order cannot be made unless the affected person has been given an opportunity to be heard or represented in court, a temporary order can be granted before such a hearing has taken place.[62] The requirement to invite the affected person to participate in, or be represented at, a hearing can be disapplied by the sheriff where they are satisfied that doing so will protect an adult at risk from serious harm, or not prejudice any other person affected by this decision [63] The temporary banning expires on the earliest of the following dates:[64]

(a) the date on which the sheriff determines the related application for a banning order;
(b) the date by which subsection (3) requires the sheriff to determine the related application for a banning order;
(c) if a temporary banning order is recalled, the date on which it is recalled; and
(d) any specified expiry date.

An order can be made by the sheriff after considering the principles set out in **9.2** above, if the adult consents (or their failure to consent can be ignored)[65] and if the sheriff is satisfied that:[66]

(a) an adult at risk is being, or is likely to be, seriously harmed by another person;

59 For example, if the place covered by the banning order was the adult's home, anyone else who lived there.
60 For example, an action for interdict to keep the person away from a certain area.
61 2007 Act, s 22(3)
62 2007 Act, s 41(4).
63 2007 Act, s 42(2)
64 2007 Act, s 21(4)
65 See **9.8** below.
66 2007 Act, s 20.

(b) the adult's well-being or property would be better safeguarded by banning the person who is the subject of the order from a place occupied by the adult than it would be by removing the adult from that place; and

(c) either, the adult at risk is entitled[67] or permitted by a third party to occupy the place covered by the banning order, or, neither the adult at risk nor the subject of the order is entitled, or permitted by a third party to occupy the place covered by the order.[68]

Once an order has been made it is possible to apply for recall or variation of the order. An order (and a temporary order) can have a power of arrest attached to it which allows for the person who is the subject of the order to be arrested for breach of the order.[69]

(4) Consent[70]

9.8 The sheriff must not make a protection order if they know that the adult at risk has refused to consent to the granting of the order.[71] Similarly, a person must not, for the purposes of carrying out or enforcing a protection order, take any action if they know that the adult at risk has refused to consent to the action.[72] Refusal of consent implies that the adult has capacity to consent or to refuse consent to the action which is being taken. Where the adult has no capacity (or at least has no capacity in respect of the specific action) then there can be no refusal of consent for the purposes of the 2007 Act. In cases where the adult has no capacity there may be an attorney or guardian who can consent on behalf of the adult.[73] In this circumstance the sheriff will require evidence of a lack of capacity and best practice would be to consult the Office of the Public Guardian in order to ascertain whether an attorney or guardian may consent on behalf of the adult.[74] If not, then the Code of Practice suggests that the local authority should consider whether to make use of its powers under the Mental Health (Care and Treatment) (Scotland) Act 2003 or under the Adults with Incapacity (Scotland) Act

67 2007 Act, s 20(c)(i), eg, under a tenancy agreement or as a homeowner.

68 2007 Act, s 20(c)(ii), eg, if they are staying with a relative in the relative's home.

69 2007 Act, s 25(2)(a) and (b). Any such power of arrest is effective when it is served on the subject of the order.

70 2007 Act, s 35. Consent of adult at risk.

71 2007 Act, s 35(1)

72 2007 Act, s 35(2)

73 2007 Act, *ASP Code of Practice*, ch 11, p 76.

74 2007 Act, *ASP Code of Practice*, ch 11, p 76.

2000 (or, indeed, whether the authority may have a duty to apply for an order under the latter).[75]

In cases where there is a refusal of consent, this can be ignored where the person ignoring the refusal believes that the following two conditions apply:[76]

(a) The adult who has refused consent has been unduly pressurised to do so. One example of this given in the 2007 Act is the case where the action to which consent is refused is being taken to prevent harm being done to the adult by someone in whom they have confidence and trust. The undue pressure prevents consent, in that the adult would consent if they did not have confidence and trust in that person.[77] Other examples might be refusal of consent because the adult has been threatened.

(b) There are no steps which could reasonably be taken with the adult's consent which would protect the adult from the harm which the action or order is intended to prevent.[78]

75 2007 Act, *ASP Code of Practice,* ch 11, p 76

76 2007 Act, s 35(3), (4).

77 2007 Act, s 35(4).

78 2007 Act, s 35(3)(b).

Chapter 10

Law and crime

10.1 The management of the criminal law is the responsibility of the police, Crown Office, Procurator Fiscal Service and the courts. This chapter will look in more detail at the sentences available to courts and the roles that social workers play in the criminal justice system.

Traditionally, a link was made between crime and moral repugnance. Hume, for example, defined crime as 'a doleful or wilful offence against society in the matter of violence, dishonesty, falsehood, irreligion'.[1] With the passing of time and the growth in the number of offences this link has become weaker. It is difficult to imagine that a substantial level of moral outrage is generated by the behaviour of someone who is drunk and incapable or of someone convicted of a minor breach of the peace. This is even clearer in the case of a large number of statutory offences. It is common, for example, for motorists convicted of speeding not to regard themselves as 'real' criminals.

The majority of criminal offences in Scotland are the product of the common law: that is, their scope is determined by judicial decision rather than being defined in statute. This has important consequences. First, aside from the limits set on the sentencing powers of particular courts, there is no limit on the sentence that can be imposed for common law crimes and offences. This is in contrast to statutory offences where, usually, the statute creating the offence will set a maximum penalty. Secondly, following from this, all common law crimes are potentially punishable by imprisonment. Thirdly, these crimes are subject to redefinition and refinement by the courts, with possible extension to cover novel circumstances. Examples of this include the extension of breach of the peace to cover a man dressed as a woman walking about in a red-light district,[2] and the view of the High Court that selling what were effectively glue-sniffing kits amounted to 'a modern example of conduct which our law has for long regarded as criminal … [that is,] actions of any kind which cause or are a cause of real injury to the person'.[3]

1 Hume, *Commentaries* vol I, ch.i. 22, 1844 (3rd edn) Edinburgh, Bell & Bradfute, cited in *McLaughlan v Boyd* 1934 JC 19, Lord Clyde at 22.

2 Stewart v Lockhart 1991 SLT 835.

3 *Khaliq v HMA* 1984 SLT 137 at 142–43.

Furthermore, a distinction is sometimes drawn between crimes and offences (for example, in the presentation of criminal statistics) with the implication that crimes are more serious than offences. The term 'crime' is used to denote more serious criminal acts, whilst 'offences' is used for those acts considered less serious in nature. [4]

In 2022–23, of all recorded crimes, crimes of dishonesty were the largest group and accounted for 36%. Non-sexual crimes of violence accounted for 24%, crimes against society for 21%. Damage and reckless behaviour accounted for 15%. Sexual crimes made up 5% of recorded crime, an area where under reporting is thought to impact on statistics. Road traffic offences accounted for just under two thirds of offences (63%) in 2022–23, and antisocial offences for just under one third, 29%. Miscellaneous offences accounted for 7%. It should be noted that the number of offences recorded is affected by police activity and operational decisions as well as by the actual number of crimes.[5]

Social work functions

10.2 In Scotland, work specified by statute with persons who have offended is principally the responsibility of local authority social workers.

Criminal justice social work takes place within the context of guidance provided by the *National Outcomes and Standards for Social Work Services in the Criminal Justice System*[6], supplemented by some more detailed practice guidance covering particular areas. Examples are, Criminal Justice Social Work Reports Practice Guidance, Court based Services Practice Guidance, and Community payback Order Practice Guidance. These replaced the *National Objectives for Social Work Services in the Criminal Justice System* which were originally introduced in 1991. Services in the areas covered are 100% funded by central government. The overall aims suggested in the *National Outcomes* for criminal justice social work services are to:

(a) work to contribute to the protection of the public by seeking to reduce the risks of reoffending and serious harm;

(b) help individuals to change their behaviour and become contributing members of society;

4 Scottish Government, *Recorded Crime in Scotland, 2022–23*, p 8

5 *Recorded Crime in Scotland, 2022–23*, p 8

6 National Outcomes and Standards for Social Work Services in the Criminal Justice System, Scottish Government (2010)

(c) deliver effective supervision that is seen as credible by the courts and the public.[7]

These are seen as contributing to three key outcomes for social work services in this context:
(a) Community safety and public protection.
(b) The reduction of re-offending.
(c) Social inclusion to support desistance from offending.[8]

Services are now primarily provided by specialist staff, some of whom will work full-time in this area. In practice, working with those who have offended has proved a relatively attractive prospect to social workers who welcome the opportunity to work in a fairly prescribed and planned manner. The use of social workers' legally defined powers is an especially prominent feature of the work.

The social worker performing any of the functions noted above is accountable not only to the court but also to their own employer. Involvement with the criminal justice system is likely to be stressful for everyone, but especially so for the accused. A person who has offended may be at risk of losing liberty, family, employment and social status. The structures and procedures of the criminal justice system are complex and can be difficult to navigate for a person who is possibly in a state of crisis. In this situation, the social worker may contribute toward the alleviation of excessive anxiety and an absence of clear thinking on the part of the client. The social worker may take on both a supportive and an educative role. The legal environment is one not defined by social work values and knowledge. The role of the social worker in this environment may be to help to broaden the perspective of all parties to include wider social factors.

Delivery of services in the criminal justice system also takes place within the context of the *National strategy for Community Justice*[9] and the local community justice outcomes improvement plans. These are produced by the local authority and its community justice partners (these include the police and health service).[10] These plans must refer to national outcomes for community justice.[11]

7 Scottish Government *National Outcomes and Standards for Social Work Services in the Criminal Justice System* (2010), p 14.
8 *National Outcomes and Standards* (2010), p 15.
9 Scottish Government, *National Strategy for Community Justice* (2016).
10 Community Justice (Scotland) Act 2016, ss 13, 19–30.
11 Scottish Government, *Community Justice Outcomes, Performance and Improvement Framework* (2023). Outcomes include, 'Enhance intervention at the earliest opportunity by ensuring greater consistency, confidence in and awareness of services which support the use of direct measures and diversion from prosecution' pp 7–10.

(1) Court-based social workers

10.3 There are social work staff permanently based in larger busier courts, while in other courts the provision may be part-time. The main functions of these court-based social workers are dealing with requests for social enquiry reports and ensuring that the reports are provided on time. Court social workers are also required to monitor the standard of reports, conduct stand-down interviews (in which the social worker interviews the accused person during a brief court recess), and provide oral reports to the court. They are also responsible for interviewing clients immediately following a request for a report, and following custodial remand or sentence. Finally, court social workers are required to liaise with the other professionals involved in the operation of the court.[12]

Court-based social workers not only perform a range of services for the court but may also be able to provide assistance to the families of those on trial or who have been sentenced. In particular assistance may be provided to those who have been sentenced to custody, to victims of crime and to witnesses.[13] This twin role creates the potential for social workers to experience conflicts in relation to the various demands being made of them and their professional orientation. The social worker may be in a position to support and provide clarification about what is happening for the families of those appearing in court. When a client who has been found guilty first hears their sentence in court they may well be anxious and suffering from situational deafness, unable properly to hear and process what is being said. Moreover, some non-custodial disposals are not very widely used or known. In these circumstances it may be necessary and appropriate for social workers to assume an educative and interpretative role with their client, clarifying what the meaning and implications of various disposals are likely to be.[14] In addition, the court-based social worker may be providing an intake and referral service for those at the court who are in need.

12 Scottish Government, *Justice Social Work Reports and Court-based Justice Social Work Services Practice Guidance* (2023), section 4.

13 *Justice Social Work Reports and Court-based Justice Social Work Services Practice Guidance* (2023), p 13.

14 *Justice Social Work Reports and Court-based Justice Social Work Services Practice Guidance* (2023), p 10.

(2) Reports

10.4 Reports are most often prepared following a plea of guilty, or a finding of guilt, following which there is a hiatus while the court adjourns the case[15] prior to the decision regarding sentence or disposal of the case. Section 27(1)(a) of the Social Work (Scotland) Act 1968 (the 1968 Act) imposes a duty on local authority social work departments to make 'available to any court such social background reports and other reports relating to persons appearing before the court which the court may require for the disposal of a case'.[16]

Although the 1968 Act refers to social background reports, this report is now referred to in practice as a Criminal Justice Social Work Report (CJSWR). A detailed discussion of the contents of such reports and the methodology for preparing them is beyond the scope of this text, and detailed guidelines and standards can be found in the Practice Guidance.[17]

Reports, prepared by a local authority social worker, must be obtained in certain circumstances:

(a) Before making a community payback order, *except* where a level 1 unpaid work order[18] is being made.[19]

(b) Before imposing a sentence of detention on a person who has offended and who is aged between 16 and 20,[20] the court is required to obtain (either from a local authority officer or otherwise) information about the person's circumstances, and to take into account any information before it concerning the person's character and physical and mental condition.[21]

(c) Before passing a sentence of imprisonment on someone aged 21 or over who has not previously served a sentence of imprisonment,[22] the court is required to obtain (either from a local authority officer

15 Criminal Procedure (Scotland) Act 1995, s 201 1995 Act, s 201 (1995 Act) provides for the power of a court to adjourn a case before sentencing the accused. Here, the court will defer sentence for 3–4 weeks for the purposes of obtaining a Criminal Justice Social Work Report. This will enable inquiries into what is the most suitable method of dealing with the case.

16 Social Work (Scotland) Act 1968, s 27(1)(a).

17 *Justice Social Work Reports and Court-based Justice Social Work Services Practice Guidance* (2023).

18 See **10.25** below.

19 1995 Act, ss 227A(3)–(4) and 227B(4).

20 1995 Act, s 207(4).

21 1995 Act, s 207(3). Note: the wording in this provision, 'not less than 16' will be substituted with 'not less than 18' by the Children (Care and Justice) (Scotland) Act 2024, Pt 2, s 17(4) Not yet in force.

22 1995 Act, s 204(2).

or otherwise) information about the person's circumstances, and to take into account any information before it concerning the character and physical and mental condition of the person.

(d) Before sentencing a person specified in section 27(1)(b)(i)–(vi) of the Social Work (Scotland) Act 1968 a court other than a JP court must obtain a report.[23] Those specified in the 1968 Act are:
  (i) those under supervision because of a court order (eg, subject to a community payback order);
  (ii) those on supervision following release from prison/ detention;
  (iii) those subject to a supervision and treatment order;
  (iv) 16- and 17-year-olds subject to a compulsory supervision order imposed by a children's hearing because of commission of an offence; and
  (v) people charged but not prosecuted and referred to the local authority by the procurator fiscal or Lord Advocate.

The report is to be on the character of the individual, including their behaviour while under supervision or subject to the order.[24]

(e) Before making a supervised release order.[25]
(f) Before passing an extended sentence.[26]
(g) Before making a drug treatment and testing order.[27]
(h) Before sentencing someone convicted of incest or intercourse with a step child.[28]
(i) Before a review of a community payback order.[29]

Normally, the period available for preparation of the report is four weeks or, on cause shown, eight weeks.[30] These periods are reduced by the time taken to process the request and the need to complete the report in time. The report must be submitted to the clerk of court by midday on the day preceding the court hearing at which it will be considered. If the report has not been completed or further inquiries must be made, then, when the case is called, an explanation must be made to the court and the case can be continued for a further period equal to the original one. Where the person who has offended is remanded on bail, it is a condition of the bail that the person makes themselves available for the purpose

23 1995 Act, s 203.
24 1995 Act, s 203.
25 1995 Act, s 209(2).
26 1995 Act, s 210A(4).
27 1995 Act, s 234B(3)(b).
28 Criminal Law (Consolidation) (Scotland) Act 1995, s 4(6).
29 1995 Act, s 227B(4).
30 1995 Act, s 201(3).

of preparation of any reports.[31] Failure to co-operate should be reported to the court and failure of the person to make themselves available is an offence.[32] Further offending on bail becomes an aggravation to the subsequent offence and increases the maximum sentence available. [33]

It is not clear what should happen when the offender is available to meet the social worker, but refuses to co-operate. Moore and Wood suggest that failure to co-operate may amount to contempt of court and, while this may be a possibility, there is no legal authority on the issue.[34]

A copy of the report is made available to the person who has offended, their solicitor and the prosecutor.[35] The report will also be seen by the judge, and some comment may be made on its contents in open court. Sensitive information may need to be noted in the report, with a request that it is not disclosed in court. The court should be made aware of the sensitive nature of the information which is included within the report. Information which should not be shared in open court should be highlighted to the court by a preceding statement in bold within the report, requesting non-disclosure.[36]

(3) Supervision

10.5 Social work departments are expected to provide supervision in a variety of situations. The main examples are community payback orders, fine supervision orders, and supervision after release from custody. These are all considered more fully below. Social workers may also be involved in diversion schemes, where persons who are alleged to have offended are diverted into some form of social work intervention rather than being prosecuted, also considered below.[37]

31 1995 Act, s 24(5)(d).
32 1995 Act, s 27(1).
33 1995 Act, s 27(3) and (5).
34 G Moore and B Whyte, *Moore and Wood's Social Work and Criminal Law in Scotland* (3rd edn, 1998), pp 66–67.
35 1995 Act, s 203(3).
36 Scottish Government, *Justice Social Work Reports and Court-based Justice Social Work Services Practice Guidance* (2023), section 5.5, p 16. In *X v BBC* [2005] CSOH 80, it was suggested (at para 44) that 'the contents of social enquiry reports ought to be publicly available to allow contemporaneous reporting to take place'. It was further suggested that any information contained in the SER which was not publicly reported at the time was later to be regarded as confidential.
37 Scottish Government, *Diversion from Prosecution: Joint Review* (2023). This review provides more information on diversion as an alternative to prosecution. It was carried out by HM Inspectorate of Prosecution in Scotland, HM Inspectorate of Constabulary in Scotland, HM Inspectorate of Prisons for Scotland and the Care Inspectorate.

(4) Appearing in court

10.6 Social workers are occasionally called as witnesses in civil or criminal proceedings where they may be seen as experts on social concerns. They may also be the applicant in situations where there has been a breach of an order. In each of these situations, social workers may be cross-examined and must take an oath or affirm. It is important that the social worker prepare thoroughly, bringing notes and copies of the relevant material to court. This last can be important, since witnesses are allowed to refer to contemporaneous notes, that is, notes made at the time of or shortly after the events to which they refer, while they are giving evidence.

Colin Fishwick provides advice for social workers on adjusting to the formalities of the court.[38] Fishwick advises that social workers should be prepared to have their practice scrutinised, and ensure remarks are 'authoritative statements rather than interpretative remarks'. [39] Social workers appearing in court are advised to communicate in a clear and direct manner and to adopt an appropriate style of dress. As this list suggests, court proceedings generally take place in a very formal atmosphere subject to detailed rules of procedure. The rules for the giving of evidence are particularly rigid, and such rules also address what counts as evidence.[40] This formality is reflected in the forms of address: Justices of the Peace are referred to as 'your honour', sheriffs and High Court judges as 'your lordship' or 'your ladyship'.

(5) Court reports concerning children

10.7 When a child is charged with an offence which requires a court appearance, there is a requirement for the local authority to be notified.[41] The social work department must then provide the court with a pre-conviction report detailing the home background and social circumstances of the child to facilitate disposal of the case.[42]

38 C Fishwick *Court Work* (2nd edn. 1989)
39 C Fishwick *Court Work* (2nd edn, 1989).
40 See **1.39–1.56**.
41 Criminal Justice (Scotland) Act 2016, s 24.
42 1995 Act, s 42(8)

SENTENCING: OBJECTIVES AND CRITERIA

10.8 The objectives of sentencing and punishment have produced a substantial literature. The main objectives canvassed in the past have included individual and general deterrence; rehabilitation; reform or, more recently, supporting desistance;[43] retribution; denunciation; and containment or protection of the public.

On a more practical level there are factors which clearly have an influence on the sentence imposed in particular cases. These include the severity of the offence; the age of the person who has offended; the previous record of the person; the attitude of the person towards the offence; the culpability of the individual in the offence; the existence of any provocation; and background information about the individual. Additional factors include any statutory aggravations to the offence, such as a racial aggravation, or the offence being committed whilst on bail. On the other hand, if the accused pleads guilty the court can take into account when and in what circumstances it was indicated that a guilty plea would be made in fixing the sentence.[44] On the basis of these factors experienced practitioners, on both sides of the law, can often predict the likely outcome of a particular case. The High Court also has the power when hearing appeals against sentence to give its opinion on appropriate sentences in similar cases.[45] The Scottish Sentencing Council, set up in 2015, has as part of its remit the preparation of sentencing guidelines to be approved by the High Court.[46] Sentencing guidelines may relate to; the principles and purposes of sentencing, sentencing levels, the particular types of sentence which are appropriate for a particular offence, and the circumstances in which it is possible to depart from the guidelines.[47]

Although these factors exist, and have to some extent been given judicial recognition, there is some evidence of disparities in sentencing between different courts and between different judges.[48] Between 2020–21 and

43 See, e.g., McNeill, F & Whyte, B, *Reducing Reoffending: Social Work and Community Justice in Scotland* (2007), ch 3.

44 1995 Act, s 196.

45 1995 Act, ss 118(7), 189(7) and 197.

46 Criminal Justice and Licensing (Scotland) Act 2010, s 3..

47 Scottish Sentencing Council, *Principles and Purposes of Sentencing* (2017) with Scottish Sentencing Council, *Principles and Purposes of Sentencing* (2018).

48 B Tamanaha, *Beyond the Formalist–Realist Divide: The Role of Politics in Judging* (2010).
At p.187 – Judges are: 'unique individuals with bents, biases, and various strengths and limitations, as well as differences in moral and political views, and differing views of judging'.

2021–22 the total number of convictions resulting in a custodial sentence increased by 13%: from 7,239 in 2020–21 to 8,169 in 2021–22. Of the sentences imposed in 2021–22, 14% were custodial, compared to 17% in 2020–21.[49]

NON-CUSTODIAL DISPOSALS

(1) Absolute discharge

10.9 An absolute discharge is appropriate where, in view of the circumstances, including the nature of the offence and the character of the person who has offended, the court decides that it is not necessary to impose punishment.[50]

(2) Admonition

10.10 A person who has offended may be admonished where it appears to meet the justice of the case.[51] Admonishment is in effect a warning. The court may simply announce that the individual is admonished and leave it at that, or the court may add some well-chosen words of warning. This disposal counts as a conviction.

(3) Caution[52]

10.11 Following conviction on an indictment, an individual may be required to find caution for good behaviour. This involves lodging a sum of money in court. The period of good behaviour may be up to 12 months. If the person who has offended is of good behaviour during this period, then the caution, the sum of money lodged with the court, is returned with interest. If the person who has offended is not of good behaviour during the period, in particular, if they commit a further offence, then the caution is forfeited. A requirement to find caution can be imposed in addition to a fine or custodial sentence.[53]

49 Scottish Government, *Criminal Proceedings in Scotland* (2021–22), p 7
50 1995 Act, s 246(2), (3).
51 1995 Act, s 246(1).
52 Pronounced 'kayshun'.
53 1995 Act, s 227.

(4) Fines

10.12 This disposal takes the form of a financial penalty paid by the convicted person. Fines are by far the most common form of disposal, though their use is declining.

(a) Levels of fine

10.13 In fixing the level of fine the court must take into account the means of the person who has offended; there is clearly little point in levying a fine which the person has no practical prospect of paying. If a fine is excessive in relation to the means of the offender this will be a ground for appeal.[54]

The Justice of the Peace Court can impose a fine not exceeding £2,500.[55] A fine of up to £5,000 can be imposed by the Sheriff Court under summary procedure[56] and, on indictment, a sheriff may impose an unlimited fine.[57] Offending whilst on bail increases the sentencing powers of a sheriff above the maximum, a fine can be increased by a sum up to Level 3 on the standard scale (£1,000).[58]

Level 1	£200
Level 2	£500
Level 3	£1,000
Level 4	£2,500
Level 5	£5,000

It should be noted that the maximum fine that can be levied in the JP court is stated to be level 4, and the money value will therefore change automatically when the levels change.

(b) Time for payment

10.14 A person who has been required by the court to pay a fine must be allowed at least seven days to pay or, if it is to be paid in instalments, pay the first instalment of the fine.[59] The only exceptions to this, when

54 *Hamilton v Scott* 1987 SCCR 188.
55 1995 Act, s 7.
56 1995 Act, s 5.
57 1995 Act, s 211(1).
58 1995 Act, s 27(5).
59 1995 Act, s 214(1).

the fine is payable immediately, are: where the person who has been required to pay fails to satisfy the court that they have a fixed abode; where the individual appears to have sufficient means to pay the fine forthwith; where the individual indicates that time to pay is not wanted; or where the court is satisfied that other special reasons exist for not allowing time to pay.[60] Where the court refuses time to pay the fine, and the offender fails to pay, the court may exercise its power to impose imprisonment. In these rare circumstances, the court must state the "special reason" for this decision.[61]

A summary court may order the fined person to be searched and any money found to be applied to payment of the fine, unless the court is satisfied that the money belongs to someone else or that the loss of the money would be more injurious to the offender's family than their imprisonment or detention.[62]

The fined person may, either when the fine is imposed or subsequently, apply for more time to pay or to be allowed to pay by instalments.[63] Further time to pay must be allowed following an application unless it appears that the offender's failure to pay is wilful or that there is no reasonable prospect of paying the fine.[64]

(c) Alternative of imprisonment[65]

10.15 An alternative sentence of imprisonment may be imposed at the same time as the fine and will become operational without the need for a means enquiry court (see (e) below) in the event of default in payment. Such an alternative is not to be imposed unless the court considers it expedient having regard to three factors; the gravity of the offence, the character of the person who has been fined, or other special circumstances. The person who has offended must be present in court before an alternative sentence of imprisonment can be imposed.[66]

(d) Fine supervision

10.16 Where time to pay a fine is allowed then an enforcement order must be made unless the court considers that such an order would not

60 1995 Act, s 214(2).
61 1995 Act, s 214(2).
62 1995 Act, s 212.
63 1995 Act, s 214(7) and 215.
64 1995 Act, s 215.
65 1995 Act, ss 214(4), 219(1)(b).
66 1995 Act, s 219.

be appropriate in the circumstances.[67] (This is additional to the power to make a supervision order or to impose an alternative of imprisonment.) Once such an order is made a fines enforcement officer[68] can vary the time for payment on application by the person who has been fined. Fines enforcement officers also have extensive enforcement powers. The enforcement order authorises them to arrest the fined person's income or other funds[69] and they can ask the court to make an application for deduction from benefits being paid to the person. In addition, they have the power to seize and dispose of a motor vehicle belonging to the fined person. Finally, the fines enforcement officer can refer the case back to the court if they believe that payment is unlikely or for other reasons (eg, failure to co-operate).

10.17 In addition to an enforcement order, a person who has offended and been subject to a fine, and who is given time to pay or make payment by instalments, may be made subject to a fine supervision order[70]. For this purpose, the person will be placed under the supervision of a social worker or other social work department employee. The individual subject to the order does not need to consent to such an order being made, and the order remains in force pending one of four possible outcomes. First, the fine is paid in full; second, the individual is imprisoned for fine default; third, another order is made concerning the fine; fourth the order is transferred to another court area. [71] A person who has offended and who is under 21 cannot be detained in the event of non-payment unless placed on supervision, or unless it was not reasonably practicable to do this.[72] In the event of non-payment the supervising social worker should provide a report to the court hearing called to enquire as to the reasons for non-payment (the means enquiry court: see below). [73]

(e) Enforcement: imprisonment on default

10.18

Generally speaking, fines are payable to the courts which imposed them.[74] Financial penalties are paid directly to the court, or the fined person is given time to pay (seven days for the first instalment). A Victim

67 1995 Act, s 226B.
68 Fines enforcement officers have the responsibility for collecting fines.
69 See **2.16** and **2.17**.
70 1995 Act, s 217.
71 1995 Act, s 217(2)–(6).
72 Criminal Procedure (Scotland) 1995 Act, s 217(4).
73 Criminal Procedure (Scotland) 1995 Act, s 217(8).
74 Though it is also possible to pay online.

Payment can be added on as a compensation order where loss has been sustained.

The exceptions to this are High Court fines, which are collected by the appropriate sheriff court, and cases where the fined person has moved. In the latter case the fine will normally be transferred to the appropriate court covering the fined person's new place of residence.[75]

If the fined person fails to pay the fine they may, provided that the amount outstanding on the fine is £500 or more,[76] be imprisoned or detained instead. A community payback order (CPO) may be imposed as an alternative to imprisonment.[77] A CPO imposes one or more of the following requirements: (a) an offender supervision requirement, (b) a compensation requirement, (c) an unpaid work or other activity requirement, (d) a programme requirement, (e) a residence requirement, (f) a mental health treatment requirement, (g) a drug treatment requirement, (h) an alcohol treatment requirement, (i) a conduct requirement, (j) a restricted movement requirement. The latter requirement, restricted movement, has recently been added to the list of CPO requirements. [78]

Where time to pay has been allowed and no alternative imposed at the time of the fine, imprisonment can take place only after enquiry by the court as to the reasons for non-payment. Application may be made for further time to pay and the court will allow further time for payment. The court will however not allow additional time if it is satisfied that the failure to pay the fine was wilful or that there is no reasonable prospect of the fined person being able to pay if further time is permitted.[79] The hearing at which this enquiry is made is usually referred to as a means enquiry court. At this hearing the fined person may be imprisoned or given further time to pay. There is statutory provision for the period of imprisonment in the event of non-payment. The relevant amount for the purpose of calculating the period of imprisonment is the amount of the fine which remains outstanding.[80]

Where no additional time to pay is allowed, and immediate payment is not made, the fined person may, subject to the age related exception noted below, be committed to prison. Where the fined person is under 21 there is a presumption against detention in a young offender's institution.

75 1995 Act, s 222.
76 Where the fine is £500 or less a community payback order must be imposed, 1995 Act, s 227M(2)(a), see **10.21** below.
77 1995 Act, s 227A(1).
78 1995 Act, s 227.
79 1995 Act, s 215.
80 1995 Act, s 219(4).

The court shall not impose detention on a person under 21 unless it is of the opinion that no other method of dealing with the individual is appropriate.[81]The exception arises in the case of an individual who has not previously served a term of imprisonment or detention and who is not legally represented. Such an individual cannot be immediately imprisoned unless legal aid has been refused on financial grounds or, knowing of the possibility of applying for legal aid, the offender has chosen not to apply for it.[82]

Imprisonment for non-payment of a fine means that a person can be imprisoned for an offence which did not originally carry imprisonment as a possible penalty.

(5) Community payback orders[83]

(a) Introduction

10.19 Community payback orders (CPO) were introduced for offences committed after 1 February 2011 by the Criminal Justice and Licensing (Scotland) Act 2010 and replaced the following measures:

- probation orders;
- community service orders;
- supervised attendance orders; and
- community reparation orders.

The CPO is an order made by the court which imposes one or more requirements. These are listed in Box 10.1 below, and the list also sets out the requirements which can be made in the Justice of the Peace Court and the requirements which must be accompanied by an offender supervision requirement. [84]

Box 10.1

CPO requirements:[85]
(a) Offender supervision ‡
(b) Compensation* ‡
(c) Unpaid work or other activity ‡
(d) Programme*
(e) Residence* ‡

81 1995 Act, s 207.
82 1995 Act, s 204.
83 Scottish Government, *Community Payback Order Practice Guidance* (2022).
84 1995 Act, s 227A.
85 1995 Act, s 227A(2).

(f) Mental health treatment*
(g) Drug treatment*
(h) Alcohol treatment*
(i) Conduct* ‡
(j) Restricted Movement

Notes: *If this requirement is made, an offender supervision requirement must also be made; supervision is also required if more than one requirement is made or the offender is aged under 18.
‡ These are the only types of requirement that can be imposed by a JP court.

Some of these requirements are explained more fully below. Unpaid work or other activity requirements are imposed in more than three quarters of orders, supervision requirements in more than half. Other requirements are imposed much less often and little use is made of mental health treatment and residence requirements.[86]

(b) Requirements for making an order as a sentence[87]

10.20 In most cases a CPO will be made as a sentence following conviction. A CPO will be combined with other penalties, eg, a fine or restriction of liberty order. Before an order can be made, a number of requirements must be fulfilled:

(a) The offence of which a person has been convicted must be either:
  (i) punishable by imprisonment and the CPO is imposed instead of imprisonment; or
  (ii) punishable by fine and the CPO is made instead of imposing a fine, though in such cases only requirements (a), (c) and (i) set out in Box 10.1 can be attached to the order.[88]

(b) The offence must be serious enough to warrant making a CPO.[89]

(c) A report from a local authority officer must be obtained and taken account of (this will normally be a Criminal Justice Social Work Report).[90]The requirement to obtain a report does not apply where

86 Scottish Government, *Justice Social Work Statistics in Scotland: 2022–23.*
87 1995 Act, s 227A.
88 1995 Act, s 227A(3)(a).
89 1995 Act, s 227 B(2).
90 1995 Act, s 227A(4).

a level 1 unpaid work requirement (see **10.25** below) is being made.[91]

(d) The effect of the order and the consequences of breaching the order must be explained to the person who has offended, and they must indicate that they understand this and are willing to comply with each of thc requirements to be imposed. [92]

(e) The court must ensure that, so far as is practicable, there is no conflict between any requirement imposed and the religious beliefs, work or education commitments of the person who has offended.[93]

(f) Where more than one requirement is attached to an order, the requirements must be compatible.[94]

On making the order, the court must explain its reasons for so doing.[95]

(c) Making an order on non-payment of a fine[96]

10.21 A CPO can be imposed on a fine defaulter as an alternative to imposing a sentence of imprisonment for non-payment of a fine. Imposing a CPO is mandatory where the fine is £500 or below, otherwise it is at the discretion of the court. If an order is made, there is no need for a report on the fine defaulter to be obtained or considered, or for the defaulter to indicate a willingness to comply with the order. It is sufficient that the defaulter indicates understanding of the terms of the order and the consequences of breach. Only a level 1 unpaid work requirement can be attached to the order, though, if the offender is aged 16 or 17, an offender supervision requirement must also be made. If the fine is paid after the CPO is made, the order must be discharged.

(d) After the order is made

10.22 After an order is made there should be, preferably on the same day, a post-sentence interview.[97] The local authority will also have to nominate a responsible officer. The officer is responsible for making arrangements needed to enable the person who has offended to comply

91 1995 Act, s 227B (6).
92 1995 Act, 227B(9).
93 1995 Act, 227E.
94 1995 Act, 227B(3).
95 1995 Act, 227D(2).
96 1995 Act, s 227M.
97 Scottish Government, *Community Payback Order Practice Guidance Annexes* (2022), Annex 1.

with the requirements set out in the order. This entails promoting compliance by the person who is the subject of the order and taking steps necessary to enforce the order, or to vary, revoke or discharge the order.[98] Where an offender supervision requirement is made, the *CPO Guidance* refers to the responsible officer as a 'case manager'.[99]

(e) Offender supervision requirement[100]

10.23 This requires that the person who has offended is supervised for a period of between six months and three years, with the purpose of 'promoting the offender's rehabilitation'.[101]

(f) Compensation requirement[102]

10.24 This is a requirement for the person who has offended to pay compensation, either in a lump sum or by instalments. Payment has to be made by the earlier of either 18 months from the making of the requirement or two months before the end of the offender supervision requirement which has to be made along with the compensation requirement.

(g) Unpaid work requirement[103]

10.25 The requirement can relate either to unpaid work or to the performance of unpaid work and the completion of, or attendance at, other activities. Examples of other activities given in the guidance include specific training which addresses issues of literacy, numeracy and/or problem solving, improving interview skills, and anger management training.[104] It is for the person supervising the person who has offended (the responsible officer) to allocate time between unpaid work and other activity, but time spent on other activity must not exceed the lower of 30 hours or 30% of the hours specified in the requirement. The number of hours which may be specified is between 20 and 300. A requirement to

98 1995 Act, s 227C(3).
99 Scottish Government, *Community Payback Order Practice Guidance*, p 12.
100 1995 Act, s 227G; *CPO Practice Guidance*, section 11.2.
101 1995 Act, s 227G(1).
102 1995 Act, s 227H; *CPO Practice Guidance*, section 11.1.
103 1995 Act, ss 227I–227L, 227N and 227O; *CPO Practice Guidance*, sections 11.3 and 21.
104 *CPO Practice Guidance*, section 21.12.

undertake 100 hours or less is described as a level 1 requirement, with a requirement for more than 100 hours being a level 2 requirement. [105]

This type of requirement cannot be made in respect of a person under the age of 16 who has offended. Before making the order, the court must be satisfied that the person who has offended is a suitable person to undertake unpaid work. To this end the court must consider a report from an officer of a local authority which contains information regarding the person who has offended and their circumstances. [106]

The hours set out in the requirement must be completed within three months for a level 1 requirement and six months for a level 2 requirement, though the court can specify a longer period in the requirement. If the work is not completed within this time limit, an application can be made to the court to extend the time limit for completion of the work, even after it has expired.[107]

The placement to satisfy the unpaid work requirement should start within seven days of the CPO being made.[108]

(h) Programme requirements[109]

10.26 A programme requirement can only be made if the programme specified has been recommended in the Criminal Justice Social Work Report as one suitable for the person who has offended.

A programme is:

> … a course or other planned set of activities, taking place over a period of time, and provided to individuals or groups of individuals for the purpose of addressing offending behavioural needs.[110]

The programme requirement cannot extend beyond the end of the offender supervision requirement imposed as part of the same community payback order.[111] If compliance with the requirement would involve the co-operation of someone other than the person who has offended (e.g., the manager or provider of the programme), that person must consent before the requirement can be imposed. [112]

105 1995 Act, s 227I(6).
106 1995 Act, s 227B(4).
107 *Stewart v Dunn* [2015] HCJAC 93.
108 *CPO Practice Guidance,* section 21.4, p 78.
109 1995 Act, s 227P; *CPO Practice Guidance*, section 11.4.
110 1995 Act, s 227P(2).
111 1995 Act, s 227P(5).
112 1995 Act, s 227P(4).

(i) Residence requirement[113]

10.27 A requirement that the person who has offended resides at a specified place can be imposed. Such a requirement can last only as long as the offender supervision requirement which must be made at the same time. The specified place can be a hostel or other institution only if it has been recommended in the Criminal Justice Social Work Report as suitable for the person who has offended. [114]

(j) Mental health treatment requirement[115]

10.28 Treatment for mental disorder can be made a condition of a probation order. The court must be satisfied that the person who has offended suffers from a mental disorder which requires and may be susceptible to treatment, but that the mental condition is not such as to justify the detention of the person. The court can make this decision on the basis of the evidence in the form of a report from a registered medical practitioner. [116] The requirement will specify either in-patient treatment, out-patient treatment at a particular place, or treatment by a particular doctor or chartered psychologist. [117] Where a change in the method or location of treatment from that specified in the order is necessary it can normally be achieved without resort to court. The initiative for the change comes from the doctor or psychologist treating the patient concerned. If the change is agreed by the patient and their supervising officer, then it can be carried into effect. It is then the responsibility of the responsible officer to notify the court as to these changes, which are then regarded as having been incorporated into the order. Where agreement cannot be obtained to a change of treatment, or where the doctor/psychologist considers that treatment for a period longer than that contained in the order is necessary, they will report to the responsible officer who will then apply to court for variation of the order. The treatment cannot last for longer than the offender supervision requirement which must be made at the same time. [118]

113 1995 Act, s 227Q; *CPO Practice Guidance*, section 11.5.
114 1995 Act, s 227Q(2).
115 1995 Act, ss 227R–227T; *CPO Practice Guidance*, section 11.6.
116 1995 Act, s 227S(1).
117 1995 Act, s 227R(3).
118 1995 Act, s 227R(8)

(k) Drug treatment requirement[119]

10.29 This type of requirement can be made if the person who has offended is dependent on, or has a propensity to misuse, controlled drugs. [120] Additional requirements are that the dependency or propensity must require, and may be susceptible to, treatment and that arrangements have been, or can be, made for treatment to be provided. The requirement will require the person to undergo treatment, though it cannot last for longer than the offender supervision requirement which must be made at the same time. [121]

(l) Alcohol treatment requirement[122]

10.30 This type of requirement can be made when the person who has offended is dependent on alcohol. The Practice Guidance lists factors which, if a number of them are present over a period of time, suggest dependency.[123] These include a desire or sense of compulsion to consume alcohol, impaired capacity to control drinking, symptoms of physiological withdrawal when alcohol use is reduced or terminated, and preoccupation with alcohol. Additional requirements are that the dependency requires and may be susceptible to treatment and that arrangements have been, or can be, made for treatment.[124] The alcohol treatment requirement means the person subject to the requirement must undergo treatment, though it cannot last for longer than the offender supervision requirement which must be made at the same time.[125]

(m) Conduct requirement[126]

10.31 A conduct requirement is a requirement to do or to refrain from doing certain things. The requirement must be necessary with a view to securing or promoting good behaviour, or preventing further offending.[127] The conduct requirement must therefore specify particular types of conduct which, in the view of the court, will help to achieve the end of promoting good behaviour or preventing further offending. This

119 1995 Act, s 227U; *CPO Practice Guidance*, section 11.7.
120 1995 Act, s 227U(1).
121 1995 Act, s 227U.
122 1995 Act, s 227V; *CPO Practice Guidance*, section 11.8.
123 *CPO Practice Guidance*, section 11.8, pp. 45–46.
124 1995 Act, s 227V(6).
125 1995 Act, s 227V(5)
126 1995 Act, s 227W; *CPO Practice Guidance,* section 11.9.
127 1995 Act, ss 227W (1) and (2).

means that it is not competent to impose a requirement that the person who has offended 'refrain from committing any criminal offence'. Such a requirement would constitute the desired outcome, rather than setting out steps to be taken to achieve this end.[128] There is no provision for electronic monitoring as part of a conduct requirement, though, as noted above, a restriction of liberty order can be made at the same time as a CPO. A Conduct Requirement will be imposed only where there is an existing supervision order.[129]

(n) Review[130]

10.32 The court imposing an order may add a requirement for periodical (progress) review(s).[131] A report is to be prepared for each review hearing by the responsible officer.[132] Good practice requires that there should also be internal social work reviews where the person who is the subject of the order is subject to a supervision requirement. Such a review might consider, for example, whether to seek variation or discharge of the CPO.

(o) Variation and discharge of the order[133]

10.33 The person who is the subject of the order, or the responsible officer, can apply for variation, discharge or revocation of the order.[134] Before granting the application, the court must be satisfied that it is in the interests of justice to do so. The court must have regard for the circumstances which have arisen since the imposition of the order.[135]

(p) Variation of the order

10.34 Application can be made to the court for variation of the order. A variation can add to requirements, revoke or discharge them, or vary

128 *Kirk v Brown* [2012] HCJAC 96. See *Ross (Alistair George) v HM Advocate* [2015] HCJAC 80. In this case, the conduct requirement specified that R be restricted from accessing the internet or owning specific electronic equipment…
129 Scottish Government, *Community Payback Order Practice Guidance* (2022), section 11.9, p 47.
130 1995 Act, s 227X; *CPO Practice Guidance,* section 15.
131 1995 Act, s 227X(1).
132 1995 Act, s 227X(5).
133 1995 Act, ss 227Y–227ZB; *CPO Practice Guidance,* section 15.1.
134 1995 Act, s 227Y(2).
135 1995 Act, s 227Z(2).

them.[136] Before making any decision about variation, the court must obtain and take account of a report from the responsible officer with information about the person who is the subject of the order and their circumstances. The most common grounds for variation are stated in the Scottish Government, *Community Payback Order Practice Guidance.*

(a) Medically certified illness over a lengthy period of time which prevents the individual from performing the CPO in a satisfactory manner including where an individual is subject to a Compulsory Treatment Order under the Mental Health (Care & Treatment) (Scotland) Act 2003.
(b) Insufficient progress towards completion of the CPO even where absences have been for acceptable reasons.
(c) The individual's conviction for further offences resulting in a significant period of custody.
(d) The individual's employment circumstances over a significant period of time are such that there are no available and reliable times to fulfil the requirement. [137]

(q) Breach[138]

10.35 Commission of a further offence during the currency of the order is not in itself a breach of the order. Any new offence will be treated separately be subject to a separate judicial process.

The responsible officer has a duty to monitor compliance with the requirements in the CPO and to consider whether failures in compliance can be justified, e.g., because of ill-health. In the event that failures to comply cannot be justified, action for breach may need to be taken. The court must:

(a) provide the person who has offended with written details of the alleged failure;
(b) inform the person that they are entitled to legal representation; and
(c) inform the person that no answer needs to be given to the allegation.

All the above must take place prior to the court considering the alleged failure.[139]

136 1995 Act, s 227Z(4).
137 Scottish Government, *Community Payback Order Practice Guidance* (2022), section 21.15.1.
138 1995 Act, ss 227ZC–227ZD; *CPO Practice Guidance*, 21.14.
139 1995 Act, s 227ZC(5); *CPO Practice Guidance*, section 21.14.

The evidence of one witness is sufficient for establishing whether or not an offender has failed, without reasonable excuse, to comply with a requirement imposed by a community payback order.

(r) Options if breach established

10.36 For a CPO imposed as a sentence the options available to the court if breach is established are:

(a) to impose a fine, not exceeding level 3 on the standard scale, and leave the CPO in place;[140]

(b) where the CPO was imposed instead of a custodial sentence, the court may revoke the order and sentence the person who has offended for the offence in respect of which the CPO was made.[141] It is not permissible to add an additional period of detention/imprisonment for breach of the order;[142]

(c) where the CPO was imposed instead of or as well as a fine, to revoke the order and sentence the person to a custodial sentence of up to 60 days (JP court) or up to three months (other courts);[143]

(d) to vary the order to impose a new requirement, vary any requirement imposed by the order or revoke or discharge any requirement imposed by the order;[144] or

(e) both impose a fine under (a) and vary the order under (d).[145]

Where the order also imposes an offender supervision requirement, a restricted movement requirement can be added to the order. This can require the person who has offended:

(a) to be in a specified place at a specified time or during specified periods, or,

(b) not to be in a specified place, or a specified class of place, at a specified time or during specified periods. [146]

Where the CPO was imposed for fine default, the options are:

(a) to revoke the order and impose on the offender a period of imprisonment for up to 60 days (JP court) or up to three months (other courts); or

140 1995 Act, s 227ZC(7)(a).

141 1995 Act, s 227ZC(7)(b) Since the CPO was made as an alternative to custody this will be a custodial sentence.

142 *Russell (William) v Procurator Fiscal, Falkirk* [2018] SAC (Crim) 7.

143 1995 Act, s 227ZC(7)(c); See *Russell (William) v Procurator Fiscal, Falkirk* [2018] SAC (Crim) 7, In such cases the offender is being punished for breach of the order as the original offence only merited a fine.

144 1995 Act, s 227ZC(7)(d).

145 1995 Act, s 227ZC(7)(e).

146 1995 Act, s 227ZF.

(b) to vary:
  (i) the number of hours specified in the level 1 unpaid work or other activity requirement imposed by the order, and
  (ii) where the order also imposes an offender supervision requirement, the period of supervision.[147]

(6) Compensation order[148]

10.37 A compensation order is designed to provide compensation to the victim of an offence for the loss caused. It can be imposed in addition to or in place of any other penalty. The exception is that no order can be made in conjunction with a community payback order or an absolute discharge, and no order can be made when sentence is deferred.[149] In assessing the amount of compensation to order the court must consider not only the victim's loss but also the means of the person who has offended. In particular the court must consider whether it would be appropriate to impose a fine and a compensation order. Where it is found that the person who has offended has sufficient means only for the latter, a compensation order alone should be imposed.[150] The sheriff summary court can award compensation up to the amount of the fine that would have been payable.[151] The JP Court may impose a fine up to £2,500 (level 4) and solemn courts an unlimited amount.

Payments made by a person who has offended and who is both fined and ordered to pay compensation will be applied first to the compensation order. The provisions as to enforcement and application for time to pay etc., applying to fines are applied to compensation orders. [152] In addition, the person subject to the order can seek a review of the order if the compensation order included a sum for loss of property and the property is recovered.[153]

The award of a compensation order does not prevent the victim raising a civil action for damages against the offender. Any award in the civil case will however be reduced by the amount paid under the compensation

147 1995 Act, s 227ZC(8)(b).
148 1995 Act, ss 249–253.Note: Victims and Witnesses (Scotland) Act 2014 asp 1 (Scottish Act) s 24, amends these provisions (date to be appointed).
149 1995 Act, s 249(1).
150 1995 Act, ss 249 and 250.
151 1995 Act, s 249(8A).
152 1995 Act, s 252.
153 1995 Act, s 251.

order.[154] Payment of the sum ordered is made to the clerk of the court who passes it on to the victim.

(7) Deferred sentence[155]

10.38 Deferred sentence is not strictly a disposal, but amounts to the court deferring sentence for a period of time. The court adjourns the case and if the behaviour of the accused person is subsequently positive no further action will be taken. Adjournments to obtain reports are not deferments of sentence and the deferred sentence provisions cannot be used to avoid the time limits on such adjournments. Sentence is usually deferred for a longer period of three, six or 12 months. A court may defer sentence, subject to such conditions as it may determine. For example, the court may require a person who has offended to be of good behaviour during the period of deferment, or allow them to make reparation to the victim. In such cases the expectation is that if the condition attached to the deferment is fulfilled a lesser sentence will be imposed than otherwise. In addition, in some areas of Scotland, structured deferred sentence schemes are available which involve a programme to be completed during the period of deferment. Where sentence is deferred in a case where a report has been prepared, the court will often ask for a supplementary report to be prepared for the deferred hearing, and such a report will be required if the person concerned has participated in a structured deferred sentence scheme.[156]

If the person who has offended commits another offence during the period of deferment they may be brought before the court for sentence without waiting for the deferred date. The court may issue a warrant for the arrest of the accused, or a citation requiring the accused to appear before the court.[157]

There is no provision in Scotland for suspended sentences such as exists in England and Wales. A suspended sentence involves the imposition of a sentence of detention, the effect of which is suspended for a fixed period and will be served only if the person concerned commits a further offence punishable by imprisonment during that period.

154 1995 Act, s 253.
155 1995 Act, s 202. Amendments to this legislation are pending: Criminal Justice (EU Exit) (Scotland) (Amendment etc.) Regulations 2020/339 (Scottish SI) Pt 4 reg 13(10).
156 See Scottish Government, *Justice Social Work Guidance, Structured deferred sentences: Guidance* (2021).
157 1995 Act, s 202(2).

(8) Restriction of liberty orders[158]

10.39 Restriction of liberty orders can be imposed on anyone convicted of an offence punishable by imprisonment. The order can require them either to be at a particular place at a particular time, or not to be at a particular place at a particular time. This type of order is to be imposed as an alternative to a custodial sentence.[159]

Orders cannot impose requirements covering more than 12 hours per day and can last for up to 12 months.[160] There are provisions allowing application to court for variation or amendment of the order. On breach of the order the court has the power to impose a fine up to level 3, amend the order, or revoke the order and sentence for the original offence.[161] It is clear from the background to this provision that there will be little or no social work involvement unless the person concerned is, concurrently with the order, subject to a CPO with an offender supervision requirement. The exception to this is where the order is made in respect of someone under the age of 16. In this case the order cannot be made unless the court is satisfied as to the support and rehabilitation services the child will receive from the local authority for the duration of the order.[162]

(9) Drug treatment and testing orders[163]

10.40 This order can be made if the person who has offended is dependent on, or has a propensity to misuse, drugs. Consideration will be given to whether the dependency is treatable, and if the individual concerned is a suitable person to be made subject to this type of order.[164]

The drug treatment order requires the individual concerned to submit to treatment for their drug addiction and to testing for a period between six months and three years.[165] The court will appoint both a treatment provider and a supervising officer, the latter being a local authority social worker.[166] The role of the supervisor is to keep track of the person who is the subject of the order, provide court reports for the periodic

158 1995 Act, s 245A, as amended by Criminal Justice (Scotland) Act 2003, s 50.
159 1995 Act, s 245A, as amended by Criminal Justice (Scotland) Act 2003, s 50.
160 1995 Act, s 245A(2A) and (3).
161 1995 Act, s 245F (2).
162 1995 Act, s 245A(11A).
163 1995 Act, ss 234B–234K.
164 1995 Act, s 234B(3)(c).
165 1995 Act, s 234B (2).
166 1995 Act, s 234C.

reviews of the order, to liaise with the treatment provider and to take decisions on breaching or applying for revocation of the order.[167] The person who is the subject of the order must be tested at periods set by the court (though this cannot be more than once every month). The order must also be reviewed periodically by the court and, at least initially, the attendance of the person at these reviews is necessary. If the court finds that satisfactory progress is being made then the person's attendance can be dispensed with. Reviews have the power to vary or revoke the order. The order can be revoked on application of the supervisor or of the person who is the subject of the order, and can be used in combination with a community payback order and/or a restriction of liberty order. In addition, movements of the subject of the order can be restricted for up to 12 months and an electronic tag used to monitor this.[168]

If progress is not satisfactory, the order can be continued with a fine, varied or revoked. If the order is revoked the court has the same options as it had in sentencing for the offence.[169]

(10) Non-harassment order[170]

10.41 The prosecutor may apply to the court to make a non-harassment order against a person who has offended where that person was convicted of an offence involving misconduct, which includes conduct causing alarm and distress. [171] The order will require the person subject to the order to refrain from such conduct in relation to the victim as may be specified in the order for such period (which includes an indeterminate period) as may be so specified. This order will be concurrent with any other disposal which may be made in relation to the offence.[172] In deciding whether or not it is appropriate to make a non-harassment order, the court can take account of previous convictions, or fixed penalties accepted, for misconduct involving the victim.[173]

167 1995 Act, s 234C (7) and (8).
168 1995 Act, s 234CA (1).
169 1995 Act, s 234H (1).
170 1995 Act, s 234A.
171 1995 Act, s 234A (1) and (7). Note: s 234A (7) defines 'misconduct' as conduct that causes alarm or distress.
172 1995 Act, s 234A(1B).
173 1995 Act, s 234A(2A).

(11) Antisocial behaviour order[174]

10.42 Criminal courts have the power to make an antisocial behaviour order, either instead of or in addition to any other sentence imposed on conviction.[175] The offence must have involved an individual engaging in antisocial behaviour and the order must be necessary to protect others from antisocial behaviour. [176] The standard of proof to be satisfied in establishing the necessity for the order is the balance of probabilities. Once an order has been made it can be varied or discharged on the application of the person who is the subject of the order, applying to the court which made the order.[177]The only restriction on the powers of variation is that the order cannot be extended, though in the case of indefinite orders this will not be an issue. Notification of the order has to be made not only to the person who is the subject of the order, but also to the local authority which the court considers most relevant. This need not be the local authority where the person subject to the order is resident, but may be the authority for the area where it is likely that future antisocial behaviour will take place. The court will send a copy of the order to the named authority. [178]

ALTERNATIVES TO PROSECUTION

(1) Procurator Fiscal warnings

10.43 A Procurator Fiscal warning (FW) can only be given when there is enough evidence to prosecute the recipient but where prosecution is not considered to be in the public interest. If an FW is issued the person subject to the warning may not be prosecuted for the offence in respect of which the FW is issued. The warning may take the form of an in-person meeting or be delivered by letter. [179]

174 1995 Act, s 234AA–234AB.
175 1995 Act, s 234AA (1).
176 1995 Act, s 234AA (2).
177 1995 Act, s 234AA (8).
178 1995 Act, s 234AB(1)(b).
179 Scottish Government *Statistics – Criminal Proceedings in Scotland, 2021–22* Updated, 16. Crown Office and Procurator Fiscal Service, disposals. See also Crown Office & Procurator Fiscal Service, Prosecution Code, 2023, Options, Alternatives to Prosecution.

(2) Fiscal fines

10.44 These allow a procurator fiscal to make an offer of a fixed penalty in any case triable in the JP Court, subject to the exclusion in general of motoring offences. [180] The fixed penalties which can be offered are £50, £75, £100, £150, £200, £250 or £500. A report on the use of these fines showed that they were used for a wide variety of offences, for example, assault, theft, breach of the peace, vandalism, drinking in public and possession of class B or class C drugs.[181] If the offer is accepted no conviction will be recorded against the individual. If the offer is not accepted, the individual will be prosecuted in respect of the offence, though acceptance of an offer within the previous two years will be disclosed if the individual later appears in court charged with an offence.[182] Once accepted, a fiscal fine is similar to a fine imposed by a court as regards enforcement in the case of non-payment.

(3) Compensation offer

10.45 The procurator fiscal can offer the person who has offended the option of paying the victim compensation of up to £5,000.[183] If the offer is accepted within 28 days, then liability to conviction is discharged. The offences where such an offer can be made are all offences which are triable summarily and where a court could make a compensation order.

(4) Work offers[184]

10.46 A person who has offended may be offered the opportunity to complete a period of unpaid work of 10 to 50 hours. This work will be supervised by the local authority. If the offer is accepted the procurator fiscal will then make a work order.[185]

180 1995 Act, s 302.

181 Scottish Parliament, *Criminal Justice Committee, Fiscal Fines, Letter from the Lord Advocate, 9 June, 2021.*

182 1995 Act, ss 69(6)–(7), 101(9)–(11).

183 1995 Act, s 302A; Criminal Procedure (Scotland) Act 1995 Compensation Offer (Maximum Amount) Order 2008, SSI 2008/7.

184 1995 Act, s 303ZA.

185 1995 Act, s 303ZA(6).

(5) Setting aside of fiscal fine offers, compensation offers and work offers and orders

10.47 The procurator fiscal can set these aside, even if the offer has been accepted. This can be done where new information comes to the attention of the procurator fiscal and the procurator fiscal considers that in light of this the offer should not have been made.[186]

(6) Conditional offers of fixed penalty [187]

10.48 These relate to certain motoring offences, and operate in the same way as fiscal fines.

(7) Social work diversion

10.49 There are a large number of diversion schemes operating in Scotland which involve social work input, but may also engage a range of other professionals, for example, psychiatrists and psychologists. Diversion schemes generally involve diversion before prosecution. In other words, the person involved accepts some appropriate form of social work intervention, for example, to tackle an alcohol problem, as an alternative to prosecution. In some schemes the acceptance of social work intervention means that no prosecution will take place, while in others the decision not to prosecute is taken after assessing the outcome of the diversion.

COMPENSATION FOR CRIMINAL INJURIES

10.50 People who suffer personal injury as a result of violent crimes and are considered to be 'blameless' victims are entitled to claim compensation under the criminal injuries compensation scheme, which is administered by the Criminal Injuries Compensation Authority (CICA).[188] In considering applications the character of the applicant and any previous convictions are taken into account and this may result in a reduced award or no award being made.[189] The crime which forms the

186 1995 Act, s 303ZB.

187 1995 Act, s 302.

188 The rules are set out in the Criminal Injuries Compensation Act 1995 and the Criminal Injuries Compensation Scheme (2012) (amended). See www.cica.gov.uk (Accessed April 2026).

189 Criminal Injuries Compensation Scheme (2012) (amended), s 27.

basis for the claim need not have been established in a criminal court by a prior conviction but should have been reported to the police.[190] Awards are made on the basis of a tariff which sets a value against particular types of injury, the maximum award is £500,000, and claims which would result in an award of less than £1,000 will not be entertained.[191] Claims must normally be made within two years of the event causing the injury, though claims outside the time limit may be permitted where it is still possible to investigate the claim and where it was not reasonable to expect an application to be made within the two-year period, for example where the application relates to child abuse and the child could not report it until they became an adult.[192]

One specific area is the possibility of claiming compensation for child abuse. In such cases no award will be made in two circumstances. First, in cases where the injury happened before 2 October 1979 and the victim and person responsible for the injury were living in the same household. Second, if the guilty party would benefit from the award (as might happen if victim and perpetrator were once again in the same household).[193]

CUSTODIAL DISPOSALS

(1) Imprisonment

10.51 Imprisonment is a disposal available only for those aged twenty-one or over.[194] In the case of persons under twenty-one a distinction is made between imprisonment and detention. There is a presumption against the detention of persons under twenty-one, unless the court is of the opinion that there is no other appropriate method of disposal available.[195] Where a person who has offended has not previously been sentenced to imprisonment or detention the court cannot impose a sentence of imprisonment (except the mandatory life sentence for murder) without first considering information regarding the person's character, circumstances and physical and mental condition (usually provided in a Criminal Justice Social Work Report).[196] In addition, the

190 Criminal Injuries Compensation Scheme. Available at: www.gov.uk/claim-compensation-criminal-injury/eligibility. (Accessed April 2026).
191 Criminal Injuries Compensation Scheme (2012) (amended), ss 31 and 32.
192 Criminal Injuries Compensation Scheme. Available at: www.gov.uk/claim-compensation-criminal-injury/eligibility. (Accessed April 2026).
193 Criminal Injuries Compensation Scheme (2012) (amended) s 88A.
194 1995 Act, s 207(1).
195 1995 Act, s 207(3).
196 1995 Act, ss 204(2) and 204(2A).

court must consider that no other disposal is appropriate and, if it is a summary court, must state and record the reason for this opinion.[197] Someone who has not previously been imprisoned must have had legal representation, unless legal aid was refused on financial grounds or, having been informed of the right to legal aid, the individual has not applied for it.[198]

The maximum length of sentence may be restricted in the case of a statutory offence by the statute creating it. In other cases, the limit will be the maximum sentence the court can impose. In the case of Justices of the Peace this is sixty days.[199] In the sheriff summary court and where a summary sheriff is sitting in the JP court the limit is 12 months.[200] The sheriff solemn court can imprison for up to five years, and has the power, rarely used, to remit a case to the High Court for sentence where its powers are inadequate.[201] There is no limit on the period of imprisonment that can be imposed by the High Court.

Where an individual is convicted of two or more offences, sentences of imprisonment may be imposed which are concurrent or consecutive; if the latter, the terms of imprisonment follow on from each other. Courts' powers to impose consecutive sentences may be limited by their maximum sentencing powers: for example, a sheriff sitting in a summary court could not normally impose consecutive sentences which, when added together, exceeded 12 months.[202] This limitation will not apply where the convictions are on separate complaints or indictments and arise from distinct incidents. When imposing a sentence of imprisonment or detention, the court must take into account any period of time which the person who has offended has already spent in custody or on remand awaiting trial or sentence.[203]

There are restrictions on the minimum length of a custodial sentence. Summary courts cannot impose a sentence of imprisonment of less than 15 days[204] and there is a presumption against sentences of less than twelve months unless the court considers that no other method of dealing with the person is appropriate.[205]

197 1995 Act, s 204(3).
198 1995 Act, s 204(1).
199 1995 Act, s 7(6).
200 1995 Act, s 5(2).
201 1995 Act, s 195.
202 1995 Act, s 5.
203 1995 Act, s 210(1)(a).
204 1995 Act, s 206.
205 1995 Act, s 204(3A) as amended by Presumption Against Short Periods of Imprisonment (Scotland) Order SSI 2019/236 art 2 (4 July 2019).

The law relating to release is dealt with below.

(2) Detention of young offenders

10.52 Young persons aged between 16 and 20 and who have offended may be sentenced to detention in a young offenders institution.[206] Before sentencing a young person to detention, the court must consider the same information as is appropriate in the case of a person who has offended, is aged 21 and over, and who is sentenced to a first term of imprisonment. The court must also be of the opinion, based on this information, that no other way of dealing with the young person is appropriate and, except for the High Court, must record the reason for this opinion.[207] Young persons who are convicted of murder when aged between eighteen and twenty-one will be sentenced to detention without limit of time rather than a period of imprisonment.[208] Transfer from a young offenders institution to a prison will take place at some time between the person's twenty-first and twenty-third birthdays.[209] Other young offenders will also be transferred in the same way. Release is subject to the same rules as release from prison.

(3) Detention of children

10.53 Custody may be used by the court either before trial or after a finding of guilt. Before trial or sentence a child under the age of sixteen will generally be remanded to a local authority and the court has the power to require detention in secure accommodation.[210] For children aged sixteen or over the options are a young offenders institution or, where the child is still subject to a compulsory supervision order made by a children's hearing, committal to a local authority.[211]

A child under the age of eighteen who is convicted of murder is to be detained without limit of time in a place and on conditions specified by the Scottish Ministers,[212] with transfer to prison at the age of twenty-one. Children under the age of sixteen convicted in a solemn court may be sentenced to detention, again in a place and on conditions determined

206 1995 Act, s 207.
207 1995 Act, s 207(3).
208 1995 Act, s 205(2).
209 1995 Act, s 205.
210 1995 Act, s 51.
211 1995 Act, s 51.
212 1995 Act, s 205(2).

by the Scottish Ministers.[213] Initially this is likely to be local authority accommodation, transfer to a young offenders institution and then to adult prison will follow as the individual reaches the required age. The sheriff summary court may impose sentences of detention in residential care for up to 12 months on children who have offended and are under the age of sixteen. In this case the care is provided by the relevant local authority, and it is up to it, not the court, to select the appropriate accommodation.[214] Children sentenced in this way are looked after children. There is guidance on custody of children, particularly focusing on those sentenced (or to be sentenced) by a solemn court.[215]

The rules for release of children sentenced to a determinate sentence are similar to those applying to adult determinate sentence prisoners. Where a child is sentenced to detention at His Majesty's pleasure, release provisions are similar to those for life sentence prisoners.

Where a person under the age of seventeen-and-a-half and not subject to a compulsory supervision order is found or pleads guilty, the court may refer their case to the reporter for advice.[216] On receipt of this advice the court can then either dispose of the case itself or refer it back to the reporter for disposal.[217] Where a child under the age of sixteen is subject to a compulsory supervision order and is appearing in the sheriff court, their case must be referred to the reporter for advice.[218] The same requirement does not apply to the High Court, though this court has the power to make such a referral. Referral to the reporter will not be appropriate where the sentence for the crime of which the child has been found guilty is fixed by law, this would include murder and certain penalties for road traffic offences.[219]

213 1995 Act, s 208.

214 1995 Act, s 44; *B(EPC), Petitioner (A Child)* 1992 SCCR 596.

215 Scottish Government, *Practice Guidance: Custody of Children and Young People Convicted on Indictment under Section 205(2) or Section 208 of the Criminal Procedure (Scotland) Act 1995* (2018).

216 1995 Act, s 49(6)(c).

217 The court cannot partly dispose of the case itself, for example by imposing a disqualification from driving, and also remit the case back to the hearing for disposal, *McCulloch v Murray* 2005 SCCR 775.

218 1995 Act, s 49(3).

219 1995 Act, s 49(5).

(4) Social work in prison[220]

10.54 There are local authority social workers based in the prisons in Scotland with the general remit of providing a social work service to prisoners in need. The overwhelming fact of life for social workers engaged in this work is that security is the primary objective of the host institution and all other considerations are shaped by the security imperative. This manifests itself in practical challenges for social workers. These challenges include arranging to interview prisoners; arranging for 'welfare visits' for prisoners with their families; communicating information to prisoners and receiving information from prisoners; and, prison regimes restricting the time, timing and place for interviews. Other challenges include working with what might be the very different attitudes and assumptions of prison staff; working within the rigid hierarchy of the prison environment; and, possibly, working with one member of a family system which has been fragmented. Social workers should be familiar with the rules governing life in prison. These include rules about the reception of prisoners, health and welfare, communications and visits, work, education, recreation, discipline, requests and complaints, female prisoners, discharge and temporary release.

Integrated case management will apply to clients who have offended and are serving a custodial sentence.[221] This will involve prison-based social workers and, in cases where the individual will be subject to supervision after release, a community-based criminal justice social worker. Processes will include the exchange of relevant information between prison and community-based social workers, as well as joint involvement in planning for release.

RELEASE FROM PRISON AND DETENTION

10.55 Treatment depends on whether the prisoner is a short-term prisoner (serving up to four years), a long-term prisoner (serving four years or more) or a life prisoner.

220 See McNeill, F & Whyte, B, *Reducing Reoffending: Social Work and Community Justice in Scotland* (2007), ch 6.

221 Scottish Executive/SPS/ADSW, *ICM Practice Guidance Manual* 2007.

(1) Short-term prisoners

10.56 Short-term prisoners are to be released automatically on serving half of their sentence.[222] For sentences over four years the individual will serve the maximum period of the sentence, minus six months.[223] Release may be subject to a supervised release order[224] but, even if it is not, the individual may be returned to prison if they commit an offence before the term of imprisonment has expired. An individual released early from sentence, and who offends again before the expiry of the original sentence, can be returned to prison by a sheriff.[225] This can happen if the individual appears before a court which has at least the same level of sentencing power as the one which levied the original sentence and is convicted of an offence which is punishable by imprisonment. The court can order the balance of the sentence[226] still outstanding to be served, in addition to whatever other sentence is imposed.[227] Special provisions apply in the case of prisoners who are sentenced to six months or more and who will be subject to the notification requirements of the Sexual Offences Act 2003. Such prisoners will not be released unconditionally but will be released on licence after serving half of their sentence.[228] The licence will last until the end of the sentence. Despite the lack, in most cases, of a licence requiring social work involvement, the released person may, for the period of 12 months after release, request that the local authority provide advice, guidance and support and the local authority has a duty to do this.[229] In practice, this supervision would be provided by a social worker.

(2) Long-term prisoners

10.57 Persons sentenced to imprisonment in Scotland before 1 February 2016 are to be released automatically on a non-parole licence after completion of two-thirds of their sentence.[230] Persons sentenced after that date will only be eligible for this automatic release

222 Prisoners and Criminal Proceedings (Scotland) Act 1993, s 1 (1993 Act).
223 1993 Act, s 1.
224 1995 Act, s 209.
225 1993 Act, s 16.
226 Calculated as the period between the commission of the offence and the date on which the original sentence would have been completed. In most cases it will only be appropriate to return the offender to prison for part of this period.
227 1993 Act, s 16.
228 1993 Act, s 1AA.
229 Social Work (Scotland) Act 1968, s 27(1)(c).
230 1993 Act, s 1(1B)(2).

for the last six months of their sentence.[231] In all cases, once half of the sentence has been served the individual is eligible to be considered for release on parole. Before the halfway point the cases of persons eligible for parole are automatically referred to the Parole Board for Scotland, though prisoners can opt out of having their cases considered. The individual will be interviewed and a dossier prepared by the Scottish Prison Service. This dossier will include a home background report prepared by a social worker in the area where the individual intends to live on release, and a report from a prison-based social worker which will include an action plan for work with the individual in the period leading up to and immediately after release.

Ideally, the report is compiled by the social worker who wrote the original report for the court, if such a report was required. Alternatively, the report might be written by a social worker who has been working with the family of the person imprisoned, and who has maintained a through-care contact with the individual during sentence. Such a social worker would now complete the home circumstances report. Difficulties typically arise when there has been a break in the contact between the imprisoned person and the person(s) with whom they propose to live after release. Families who have adjusted to living without the imprisoned family member may appreciate the contribution of a social worker in helping them to clarify their thoughts and feelings about the prisoner's impending return to the community.

Most of the information in the parole dossier is disclosed to the individual who is the subject of the report and they may comment on it. Information classified as 'damaging information' may be excluded, but the individual must be told if information is not disclosed and must be given an account of the substance of this information.[232] Examples of 'damaging information' are information which is likely to adversely affect someone's health, welfare or safety, or to facilitate the commission of an offence. The dossier goes to the Parole Board which makes a recommendation to the Scottish Ministers as to whether the prisoner should be released on parole.[233] A prisoner must be released if the Board recommends this. A prisoner released on parole is subject to a licence lasting until the end of the sentence.

Social work with a person released on licence should always be based on a comprehensive systemic assessment of the individual and situation. There are, however, several special areas which must be considered.

231 Prisoners (Control of Release) (Scotland) Act 2015, s 1.
232 Parole Board (Scotland) Rules SSI 2022/385, r 9.
233 See Parole Board (Scotland) Rules 2022/385 schedule for information included within the dossier.

These include helping the individual to make sense of the new living environment which may have altered considerably during their absence. Practical problems usually take centre stage initially, such as arranging for the payment of benefits and finding accommodation. Relationships with others may have been strained beyond reparation while others may require much effort and understanding to rejuvenate. Finding work may be especially difficult. Former prisoners are generally very vulnerable to the problems associated with unemployment and deprivation and unless some of the problems which resulted in offending behaviour have been outgrown or resolved, they are likely to resurface relatively quickly. Here the support and guidance of a social worker can be invaluable.

(3) Life prisoners

10.58 All persons serving a life sentence must have a period of time specified as the 'punishment period' when they are sentenced.[234] Only after serving this period will the person be eligible to be considered for release on licence, and this consideration (by the Parole Board) must take place as soon as possible after the expiry of the punishment period. Where the Parole Board recommends release the person must be released.

(4) Compassionate release[235]

10.59 This provision is as it sounds and allows the Scottish Ministers to release, on compassionate grounds, any person serving a prison sentence. These grounds are not defined in the relevant legislation but would include a serious long-term or terminal illness. Any person released on compassionate grounds will be subject to licence conditions.

(5) Release on licence

10.60 Where a person is released on licence, the licence lasts until the expiry of the sentence imposed by the court (for life prisoners, until death). The licence will include the standard conditions to the effect that the licensee must:

(a) report forthwith to the officer in charge of the office at the address of the relevant supervising council;

234 Scottish Sentencing Council, 'Prison Sentences. Available at: www.scottishsentencingcouncil.org.uk/about-sentencing/prison-sentences/.

235 1993 Act, s 3.

(b) be under the supervision of such officer to be nominated for this purpose from time to time by the head of service with responsibility for criminal justice social work at the relevant council;
(c) comply with such requirements as that officer may specify for the purposes of risk management supervision;
(d) inform the supervising officer immediately if he/she is arrested or questioned by the police;
(e) keep in touch with the supervising officer in accordance with that officer's instructions;
(f) inform the supervising officer of any change in residence or employment;
(g) be of good behaviour and keep the peace; and
(h) not travel outside Great Britain without the prior permission of the supervising officer.

Further conditions[236] may be added to the licence on the recommendation of, or following consultation with, the Parole Board. The terms of the licence may be varied on application to the Criminal Justice and Parole Division of the Scottish Government.[237] A person sentenced to life terms remains on licence for life (though eventually all of the conditions attaching to the licence may have been cancelled). Those on determinate sentences are on licence until the date on which their determinate sentence would have been served in full, though the licence can be cancelled early.[238] If a person released on licence breaches their licence conditions, the licence can be revoked and they are returned to prison/detention.[239] Revocation of the licence and recall to prison is initiated by the supervisor making a report to the Criminal Justice and Parole Division. Once a report has been made, a decision will then be taken about whether or not to revoke the licence. In some cases, a decision can be made by the Scottish Ministers to revoke the licence without consulting the Parole Board,[240] but normally the Parole Board must be consulted and must recommend revocation before the licence can be revoked.[241] Where a licence has been revoked prior to consultation with the Board the case must be referred to the Board which has the power to order release.

236 1993 Act, s 12.
237 1993 Act, s 12A.
238 1993 Act, s 11.
239 1993 Act, s 17.
240 Where it is considered expedient in the public interest, and it is not practicable to await a recommendation from the Parole Board.
241 1993 Act, s 17.

(6) Home detention curfew[242]

10.61 Home detention curfew allows an imprisoned person to be released home early on a number of conditions,[243] the most important of which is that they are subject to a curfew for at least nine hours per day.[244]

In order to qualify for release on home detention curfew the imprisoned person must be either, serving a short-term sentence of three months or more, or, serving a long-term sentence and be a person whom the Parole Board has recommended be released on licence after serving half of their sentence. [245]In both cases the imprisoned person must have served at least one quarter of their sentence before they can be released. In addition, release cannot take place more than 166 days[246] before the day which is 14 days before the halfway point of the sentence, meaning that the effective maximum period on home detention curfew is 180 days, with a minimum period of 14 days (as release cannot be in the 14 days before the halfway stage of the sentence is reached). In addition, certain categories of imprisoned persons are excluded, e.g., those subject to a supervised release order or sex offender notification requirement.

Before release on home detention curfew a risk assessment will be carried out, which will involve the social work department. The final decision on release will be taken by a Prison Governor on the basis of this risk assessment and taking account of the following factors:

(a) protecting the public at large;[247]

(b) preventing re-offending by the prisoner;[248] and

(c) securing the successful re-integration of the released person into the community.[249]

242 1993 Act, s 3AA.

243 See Home Detention Curfew Licence (Prescribed Standard Conditions) (Scotland) (No 2) Order 2008, SSI 2008/125, different conditions apply to the different categories of prisoner released on HDC.

244 1993 Act, s 12AB.

245 1993 Act, s 3AA.

246 Home Detention Curfew (Amendment of Specified Days) (Scotland) Order 2008, SSI 2008/126.

247 1993 Act, s 3AA(4)(a). Note: Amendments pending, the Bail and Release from Custody (Scotland) Act 2023 asp 4 (Scottish Act) Pt 2 s.9(4)(b)(i) (date to be appointed), will add the words 'including any identifiable group of people' to s 3AA(4)(a) and the words 'protecting a victim or any member of a victim's family' to s 3AA(4)(aa).

248 1993 Act, s 3AA(4)(b).

249 1993 Act, s 3AA(4)(c).

(7) Commission of a further offence by a released person

10.62 A released person who re-offends can be returned to prison. A released person who pleads guilty to, or is found guilty of committing an offence, before the date on which their original sentence, if served in full, would have expired, may be returned to detention for a period not exceeding the length of time between the date of commission of the offence and the date on which the sentence would have been served in full.[250] Note that this applies whether or not the released person is on licence. Thus, a person released from a short-term sentence could be returned to serve the rest of the sentence under this provision.

(8) Supervised release orders

10.63 This is available to courts in respect of persons who are sentenced to less than four years' imprisonment.[251] In other words, it provides for supervision on release of those persons on short term sentences who would normally be released unconditionally. Before an order can be made the court must be satisfied that the person being released presents a threat of serious harm to the public and therefore requires supervision. A report must be obtained from the local authority, and the effect and consequences of any breach of the order must be explained to the released person by the court.[252] The order requires local authority supervision and compliance with the requirements set out in the order, and those reasonably specified by the supervising officer. The object of these requirements is to secure the good conduct of the released person, or to prevent or lessen the possibility of further offending. The order can be for up to 12 months, provided that it cannot extend beyond the expiry of the period of imprisonment fixed by the court. [253]

On breach of a supervised release order, the court can order return to prison for a period equal to the period between the date of the breach and the end of the order, or it can vary the order. The initiative for starting breach proceedings comes from the supervising officer and the evidence of an appropriate officer is sufficient to prove the breach.[254]

250 1993 Act, s 16, see also **10.56** above.
251 1995 Act, s 209.
252 1995 Act, s 209(2).
253 1995 Act, s 209(7).
254 1993 Act, s 18.

(9) Orders for lifelong restriction[255]

10.64 Orders for lifelong restriction are indeterminate sentences. They can be made only if specified risk criteria are considered to be met after a risk assessment report has been produced in respect of the person who has offended.[256] The risk criteria are that the nature of, or the circumstances of the commission of, the offence of which the convicted person has been found guilty, either in themselves or as part of a pattern of behaviour, are such as to demonstrate that there is a likelihood that they, if at liberty, will seriously endanger the lives, or physical or psychological well-being, of members of the public at large.[257] Once such an order has been made a risk management plan must be designed for the person which will apply to work with them, both in prison and following release.[258] The Risk Management Authority[259] was set up to provide accreditation for those who have to produce the risk assessment reports and to participate in the formulation of the plans. This type of order can only be made where a sexual offence, a violent offence or an offence endangering life has been committed or where the person who has offended committed an offence the nature of which, or circumstances of the commission of which, are such that it appears to the court that the person has a propensity to commit one of these offences.[260]

(10) Extended sentences [261]

10.65 Extended sentences[262] can be passed if a number of conditions are fulfilled:

(a) the person who has offended has been convicted on indictment of a sexual offence and the court intends to impose a determinate custodial sentence;[263] or

(b) the person who has offended has been convicted on indictment of a crime of violence and the court intends to impose a sentence of more than four years' imprisonment;[264] and

255 1995 Act, s 210.
256 1995 Act, s 210F(1).
257 1995 Act, s 210E.
258 Risk Management Authority, Standards and Guidelines: Risk Assessment Report Writing (2018), p 6, para 13.
259 See www.rma.scot/ (Accessed April 2026).
260 1995 Act, s 210B.
261 1995 Act, ss 210A and 210B.
262 1995 Act, ss 210A and 210B.
263 1995 Act, s 210A(1)(a)(i).
264 1995 Act, s 210A(1)(a)(ii).

(c) the court is of the opinion, after considering a report from a local authority officer, that an extended sentence is necessary to protect the public from serious harm.[265]

An extended sentence is designed to provide for an extended period of supervision after release, and consists of two components. The first of these is the custodial term, that is a period of imprisonment or detention.[266] The length of this will determine the date of release from this part of the sentence. Once the imprisoned person is released, the further period of supervision (the 'extension period') begins. The beginning of this extension period depends on whether the imprisoned person was on a short-term or long-term sentence. For those on short-term sentences the extension period begins on release, though it should be noted that they remain liable to be returned to prison until the date on which the whole of the original custody plus the extension period expires. For those on long-term sentences the extension period will begin at the end of the custodial term.

The maximum extension period for both crimes of violence and sexual offences on conviction in the High Court is 10 years, and in a Sheriff Court is five years.[267]

(11) Home leave

10.66 Imprisoned persons can be permitted periods of home leave, either in the course of their sentence or in the period running up to their release from prison.[268]

(12) Early release of children

(a) Children detained after sentence on indictment[269]

10.67 Detained children can be released on licence at any time on the recommendation of the Parole Board.[270] A child sentenced to less than four years' detention must be released on licence after serving half of the

265 1995 Act, s 210A(1)9(b).
266 1995 Act, s 210A(2)(a).
267 1995 Act, ss 210A(3)(a) and 210A(6).
268 See Scottish Executive Circular JD 1/2010, Integrated Practice Guidance for Staff Involved in the Home Leave Process.
269 1993 Act, s 7. See also Scottish Government, Practice Guidance: Custody of Children and Young People Convicted on Indictment under Section 205(2) or Section 208 of the Criminal Procedure (Scotland) Act 1995 (2018), pp 10–12.
270 1993 Act, s 7(2).

sentence; those serving four years or more must be released on licence after serving two-thirds of the sentence.[271] A child released on licence may be returned to detention on the commission of a further offence or have the licence revoked for breach of the licence conditions. Children sentenced to be detained without limit of time can be released on the recommendation of the Parole Board. The number of children involved is small.[272]

(b) Children detained after sentence on complaint[273]

10.68 Children detained after sentence on complaint are kept at a place determined by the local authority.[274] The local authority has the same powers and duties in respect of the child as it does towards a child subject to a compulsory supervision order.[275] The detained child may be released at any time, either conditionally or unconditionally, provided that a review has been carried out. The review must consider the best interests of the child and the need to protect members of the public. The child is entitled to be released after serving half of the period of detention, but the local authority may require the child to submit to supervision for the outstanding period of the sentence.[276] Once released, the child may be returned to detention if a further offence is committed before the end of the originally imposed period of detention. The arrangements for release are likely to be stressful for adults and young adults, but that pressure is likely to be considerably worse for the child and family going through similar processes. Social workers will already be involved in most of these situations and may be able to build upon established relationships to use this period constructively. The developmental stage and tasks, and the particular influence of the child's peer group, are liable to be relevant in the social worker's involvement as well as the re-establishment of viable familial relationships.

271 1993 Act, s 7(1).

272 Scottish Government, *Scottish Prison Population Statistics 2022–23*. Available at: www.gov.scot/publications/scottish-prison-population-statistics-2022-23/pages/young-people-in-custody/ (Accessed April 2026).

273 1995 Act, s 44.

274 1995 Act, s 44(1).

275 1995 Act, s 44(3) See also **4.14** onwards.

276 1995 Act, s 44(6)(a).

MANAGEMENT OF OFFENDERS

(1) Sex offender notification[277]

10.69 The Sexual Offences Act 2003 requires certain persons who have committed sexual offences to register with their local police force. There is a three day time limit for this registration.[278] The duration of the requirement for registration will depend on the sentence imposed by the court for the offence. Persons who have committed sexual offences, and who are required to notify, are subject to the multi-agency public protection arrangements described in **10.70** below.

(2) Multi-agency public protection arrangements

10.70 Multi-agency public protection arrangements (MAPPA) currently apply to a limited range of individuals, in particular:[279]

(a) those subject to notification requirements as a sex offender;[280]

(b) those who have been convicted of an offence inferring personal violence and made subject to a community payback order with an offender supervision requirement or imprisoned or detained and subject to supervision on release;[281]

(c) those who were prosecuted on indictment for an offence inferring violence, have been acquitted on the grounds of mental disorder and have been made subject to a hospital order with a restriction order;[282]

(d) those who have been prosecuted for an offence inferring violence but have been found to have a mental disorder in bar of trial;[283] and

(e) those convicted of any offence who, by reason of that conviction, are considered to be a person who may cause serious harm to the public at large.[284]

In respect of these categories, what are described as the 'responsible authorities' in an area have the duty to establish arrangements for the assessment and management of the risks posed by someone who falls into one of these categories. The 'responsible authorities' are the police, the local authorities, and Scottish Ministers acting through the Scottish

277 Sexual Offences Act 2003, Part 2 (Notification and Orders).
278 Sexual Offences Act 2003, Part 2, s 83(1).
279 Management of Offenders etc (Scotland) Act 2005, s 10(1)(a)–(e) (2005 Act).
280 2005 Act, s 10(1)(a).
281 2005 Act s 10(1)(b).
282 2005 Act s 10(1)(c).
283 2005 Act s 10(1)(d).
284 2005 Act s 10(1)(e).

Prison Service.[285] In establishing and implementing such arrangements, duties of co-operation are placed on these authorities and on others, including social landlords, the Principal Reporter and remote monitoring providers.[286] These statutory provisions are supplemented by extensive guidance.[287]

A first stage in respect of any individual is to carry out an assessment to determine the level of risk which they present, and to determine the level of management required. There are three levels of risk management envisaged under the guidance.

- *Level 1* At this level those assessed are likely to be of low to medium risk and be managed by one of the responsible authorities without significantly or actively involving others. Most persons who have offended will fall into this category. Those who are assessed as presenting a risk of serious harm to the public, i.e., category (e) above, cannot be assessed at this level because, by definition, they pose a significant risk to the public.
- *Level 2* Individuals assessed as requiring management at level 2 will require active involvement from a number of different agencies.
- *Level 3* Individuals who have offended and are considered high-risk will be managed at level 3 through a multi-agency public protection partnership. Individuals will fall into this category if they either present a high or very high risk of serious harm. In these circumstances there is a need for close co-operation between agencies at a senior level in order to manage this risk. The risks might include the likelihood that there will be a high level of media scrutiny of, and public interest in, the management of a particular case. Level 3 is distinguished from level 2 largely by the seniority of the representatives of the various agencies involved.

Persons who have offended will be subject to these arrangements for a period determined by their reason for qualifying for such arrangements. This means that when qualification derives from being subject to sex offender notification requirements, the arrangements will cease to apply when the offender is no longer subject to these requirements. Where the individual is subject to the arrangements because of a restriction order, or because they are subject to local authority supervision, the

285 2005 Act esp s 14 (Scottish Act), s 10 Statutory Annotations.

286 Scottish Government, *Multi-Agency Public Protection Arrangements (MAPPA): National Guidance* (2022). Registered social landlords, p 15 at para 3.8 and p 50 at para 7.7.The Principal Reporter, p 16 at paras 3.12 and 3.24. Electronic monitoring service providers, p 16, paras 3.9–3.11.

287 Scottish Government, *MAPPA*: *National Guidance* (2022).

arrangements will cease to apply when the order or supervision comes to an end. Those individuals who fall into the last category, i.e., category (e) above, will continue to be subject to these management arrangements for as long as they are assessed to meet the qualifying conditions.[288]

MENTALLY DISORDERED OFFENDERS

(1) Assessment and treatment orders

10.71 An assessment order[289] can be made in respect of an individual who has offended and who appears to have a mental disorder.[290] Such an order can only be made once an accused person has been charged and before the case has been disposed of (e.g., by conviction or acquittal).[291] The order may be applied for by the prosecution or can be made on the court's own initiative. The order must be supported by the evidence of one doctor and authorises detention and treatment for a period of 28 days from the day on which the order is made.[292] After an order is made a mental health officer (MHO) must be designated for the patient. The MHO must produce a social circumstances report unless this would serve little or no practical purpose.[293]

An individual who has offended and who appears to have a mental disorder may, in addition to an assessment order, be subject to a treatment order.[294] A treatment order requires two medical reports and authorises detention and treatment of the patient. The treatment order will end for a variety of reasons; for example, should the accused person be sentenced; or should a compulsion or interim compulsion order be made in respect of the accused person.[295] After an order is made an MHO must be designated for the patient and the MHO must produce a social circumstances report unless this would serve little or no practical purpose.[296]

288 Scottish Government, *MAPPA: National Guidance* (2022), chapter 4, The Assessment and Management of Risk, Level 1 at pp 27–29, Level 2 at pp 32–33, Level 3 at pp 33–35.
289 1995 Act, ss 52B–52J.
290 See **8.9**.
291 1995 Act, s 52D(4)(a).
292 1995 Act, s 52D(2) and 52D(6A).
293 Mental Health (Care and Treatment) (Scotland) Act 2003, ss 231(1), 231 (2) and 232(b)(iii).
294 1995 Act, ss 52K–52S.
295 1995 Act, s 52R(2).
296 Mental Health (Care and Treatment) (Scotland) Act 2003, ss 231(1) and 232(b)(iii).

(2) Post-conviction powers

(a) Compulsion and interim compulsion orders[297]

10.72 A compulsion order can be made following conviction of an offence other than murder which is punishable by imprisonment. The grounds for making an order are similar to those for making a compulsory treatment order,[298] except that there is no requirement that the ability of the patient to take decisions is significantly impaired. Before making the order, the court must consider a report from an MHO.[299] The compulsion order can authorise the same type of measure as a compulsory treatment order. Initially the order will last for six months, but it can be renewed for a further six months and then for further periods of 12 months.[300] The processes involved in extension are similar to those which apply in the case of compulsory treatment orders, except that the first continuation requires an application to be made to the Mental Health Tribunal.[301] A compulsion order cannot be combined with an interim compulsion order, a guardianship order, a sentence of imprisonment, a community payback order, a drug treatment and testing order; or a restriction of liberty order. [302]

Where, following conviction, a compulsion order with a restriction order or a hospital direction would be an appropriate disposal for the convicted person, the court may make an interim compulsion order. This order can be made if an assessment is needed to establish the availability of medical treatment for the patient and the likelihood of risk to them or to others without treatment.[303]

(b) Restriction order

10.73 A restriction order can be combined with a compulsion order where the court considers that this is necessary to protect the public from serious harm.[304] In deciding on the imposition of a restriction

297 1995 Act, ss 57A–57D.

298 See **8.19**.

299 Scottish Executive, Mental Health (Care and Treatment) (Scotland) Act 2003: Code of Practice (2005), vol 3, pt 1, ch 5, paras 32–44.

300 1995 Act, ss 57A(2A) and 53B(5)(b).

301 Mental Health (Care and Treatment) (Scotland) Act 2003, Explanatory Notes, Commentary on Sections, Part 9, Ch. 2, 286

302 1995 Act, s 57A(15).

303 1995 Act, ss 53–53D.

304 1995 Act, s 59, see also Scottish Government, *Memorandum of Procedure on Restricted Patients* (2010).

order the court must have regard to the following; the nature of the offence with which the individual is charged; the antecedents of the person; and the risk that as a result of a mental disorder the individual would commit offences if at large.[305] If a restriction order is made the detention authorised continues indefinitely, with special procedures for review. When a review takes place, the MHO must be consulted, the report following the review is sent to the Scottish Ministers and will be considered by the Mental Health Tribunal, which in such cases will normally be chaired by a sheriff.[306]

(c) Hospital directions

10.74 A hospital direction[307] is combined with a sentence of imprisonment where a person who has offended is convicted on indictment. The hospital direction means that the person who is the subject of the direction will initially be treated in hospital and, when discharged from hospital, transferred to prison. Before a direction can be made the court must consider a report from an MHO.[308] The hospital direction is reviewed annually and making a direction triggers an obligation to produce a social circumstances report, unless this would serve little or no practical purpose. If the person who is the subject of the direction is still in hospital at the end of the sentence of imprisonment they will be discharged, unless other measures are taken to authorise continued detention.[309]

(d) Guardianship or intervention order

10.75 In cases other than those involving a conviction for murder, a criminal court can make a guardianship[310] or intervention order.[311] The grounds for making such an order are the same as those set out in chapter 7.

305 1995 Act, s 59(1).
306 Mental Health (Care and Treatment) (Scotland) Act 2003, ss 182 and 185.
307 1995 Act, s 59A (as amended) 'Hospital directions'.
308 1995 Act, s 59A(5).
309 1995 Act, s 59, see also Scottish Government, *Memorandum of Procedure on Restricted Patients* (2010), Chapter 14, The Mental Health Tribunal.
310 1995 Act, s 58.
311 1995 Act, s 59A (as amended) 'Hospital directions'.

(e) Remand for medical examination

10.76 Where a court requires further information regarding the physical or mental health of a person who has offended, it has the power to order a remand for up to three weeks for medical examination. A condition of a remand for inquiry into the mental condition of the person concerned will be that the person must be examined by two doctors. If the remand is not in custody a condition as to residence may be imposed.[312]

(3) Mental disorder in bar of trial or as a ground for acquittal[313]

10.77 If a court is satisfied that a person appearing before it charged with a crime or offence is suffering from a mental disorder[314] so that the trial of that person cannot proceed or continue, then it must make a finding that this is the case; order an 'examination of facts', and remand the accused to appear at that examination. The remand may be to a hospital (by way of a temporary compulsion order) if the accused is suffering from a disorder, there is treatment available that would prevent the disorder from worsening, or alleviate the symptoms or effect of the disorder, and there would be a significant risk to health and safety if treatment was not provided.[315] Evidence both of the disorder and the degree of disorder must be provided by two doctors.[316]

The 'examination of facts' is a further court hearing at which the court has to decide two things.[317] First, it must decide if it is satisfied, beyond a reasonable doubt, that the accused committed the offence. Secondly it must be satisfied, on the balance of probabilities, that there are no grounds for acquitting the accused. If the court decides that it is satisfied on both of these then it must make a finding to that effect; if it is not so satisfied the accused is to be acquitted.[318]

Where a finding is made in these terms or where the accused is acquitted by reason of mental disorder at the time of the offence, the court has four options for disposal: a compulsion order with or without a restriction

312 1995 Act, s 200.
313 1995 Act, ss 53F–57.
314 Mental Health (Care and Treatment) Act 2003, s 328 defines mental disorder for the purposes of the Act.
315 1995 Act, s 54(2A).
316 1995 Act, s 54(1)(c)(i).
317 1995 Act, ss 55 and 56.
318 1995 Act, ss 55(2) and 55(3).

order; a guardianship order; a supervision and treatment order, or no order.[319]

(4) Supervision and treatment order[320]

10.78 This order places the individual under social work supervision for a period of up to three years. The order requires the individual to comply with the instructions of the supervisor and to submit to treatment for the improvement of their mental condition. Before an order can be made the court must be satisfied that four conditions are met. First, that the order is the most suitable way of dealing with the individual; second, that the person's mental condition is treatable and not such as to warrant the equivalent of a hospital or guardianship order; third, that the supervisor is willing to supervise; fourth, that arrangements have been made for the treatment specified in the order.[321] Before the order is made the effect of the order and the powers of the courts to review the order must be explained to the individual in ordinary language.[322] There are provisions for amending and revoking the order, but no specific provision for alternative action in the case of breach of its terms.[323]

(5) Detention of those acquitted[324]

10.79 Where someone charged with an offence is acquitted (other than on the grounds of mental disorder at the time of the offence) the court can order their detention in a place of safety for up to six hours.[325] Before this can happen the court must be satisfied, on the evidence of two doctors, that the person is suffering from a mental disorder, there is treatment available that would prevent the disorder from worsening or alleviate the symptoms or effect of the disorder, and there would be a significant risk to health and safety if treatment was not provided. Such an order ceases to authorise detention of a person where, following the medical examination of that person, an emergency detention certificate or a short-term detention certificate is granted by a medical practitioner.[326]

319 1995 Act, s 57.
320 1995 Act, Sch 4.
321 1995 Act, Sch 4, para 2.
322 1995 Act, Sch 4, para 3.
323 1995 Act, Sch 4, Pt III.
324 1995 Act, s 60C.
325 1995 Act, s 60C(4)(b).
326 1995 Act, s 60C(6).

REHABILITATION OF OFFENDERS

10.80 All persons who have offended, including parolees, are subject to the stipulations of the Rehabilitation of Offenders Act 1974, legislation designed to assist in the rehabilitation of individuals who have offended.[327] The main exceptions to the law are life imprisonment and sentences of more than 30 months. Once the period of rehabilitation is over, generally a period of three, five, seven or ten years which is halved if the offender was under the age of 17 at the time of the offence, then the person is to be treated as if the offence had not been committed. 'Spent' convictions need not be disclosed in applying for jobs, making agreements for credit or insurance, or giving evidence in civil proceedings. There are certain exceptions to this, offences relating to children or of violence must be disclosed when applying to work for a social work department. Individuals must also disclose that a fine for the conviction is outstanding, and when a prohibition or disqualification (as in driving) is in effect for a period longer than the period during which the conviction is spent. Finally, in the circumstances where there has been a royal intervention, (i.e., a pardon) this must be disclosed.

VICTIMS

(1) Victim statements[328]

10.81 These give victims of certain crimes the right to submit a statement to the High Court or a sheriff solemn court[329] setting out the impact of the crime on them. The crimes involved include crimes of violence, sexual offences, crimes of indecency, housebreaking and racially motivated crimes.[330] The court will have to take the statement into account in sentencing. The statement must be disclosed to the accused and the victim may be questioned about it. The opportunity to make such statements is available in all solemn courts.[331]

327 Rehabilitation of Offenders Act 1974.
328 Criminal Justice (Scotland) Act 2003, s 14.
329 Victim Statements (Prescribed Courts) (Scotland) Order 2009, SSI 2009/134.
330 Victim Statements (Prescribed Offences) (No 2) (Scotland) Order 2009, SSI 2009/71.
331 Criminal Justice (Scotland) Act 2003, s 14(5).

(2) Victim notification[332]

10.82 Victims of certain crimes,[333] particularly those involving violence or racial hatred and sexual offences, are entitled to be notified of certain events involving the person found guilty of the offence. The effect of an order is that where a person is convicted of an offence prescribed in the order and sentenced to a period of four years or more, the victim of that offence must be given the option of receiving certain information concerning the convicted person. That information may include the release, temporary release, transfer, death in custody or escape of the convicted person. The victim must also be given the opportunity, before any decision is taken to release the convicted person on licence, to make written representations to the Scottish Ministers in respect of such release and concerning the licence conditions applicable to the person on release. The victim must have intimated a wish to receive the information and to be given the opportunity to make representations.[334]

In addition, the victim must be given the opportunity to make representations before a decision is taken to release on licence the person who has offended, and if release is recommended the victim must be notified of this.[335]

332 Criminal Justice (Scotland) Act 2003, ss 16–17.
333 Victim Notification (Prescribed Offences) (Scotland) Order 2004, SSI 2004/411.
334 Victim Notification (Prescribed Offences) (Scotland) Order 2004, Explanatory Note, para 1.
335 Victim Notification (Prescribed Offences) (Scotland) Order 2004.

Chapter 11

Professional regulation, responsibility and accountability

INTRODUCTION

11.1 There is a recognition that social workers are unique in the extent to which they are expected to be legally, organisationally and ethically responsible and accountable. These expectations do not sit neatly together, are often confusing or vague and may even be contradictory. Social workers also have a special set of responsibilities arising from the nature of the work undertaken and by virtue of the vulnerability of many service users. Legal responsibilities are generally concerned with minimum acceptable standards and will be dealt with below. Organisational responsibilities are context-dependent but often relate to the managerial requirements of large bureaucratic structures which are reliant upon conformity to policy and regulations. Ethical responsibilities complicate this picture further. Social workers have a commitment to service user empowerment and all that entails and yet remain accountable to both service user and employer while continuing to fulfil legal responsibilities.[1]

The Scottish Social Services Council was established in 2001 to accredit and register qualified workers as well as impose sanctions for unacceptable practice.[2] Most social workers are employed by local authorities. Such authorities are bureaucratic hierarchies with command structures which can be less than amenable to the requirements of relatively autonomous professional workers. Within such a system individual workers must be provided with appropriate support and supervision to encourage and ensure good practice.

Few social workers embark on their career motivated by the prospect of financial gain. Most would argue that social work salaries are no

1 See BASW, *Code of Ethics for Social Work* (2021); Scottish Social Services Council, *Code of Practice for Social Service Workers (2024)*. The latter, at para 5, requires that: 'As a social service worker you must be accountable for the quality of your work and take responsibility for maintaining and improving your knowledge and skills'.

2 Regulation of Care (Scotland) Act 2001.

reflection of the level of responsibility inherent in the work, and the disparity is even more striking in residential social work. In spite of all of these factors, it has been suggested that social workers are unique in accepting a professional responsibility which is more in tune with their sense of moral responsibility than with the responsibility imposed on them by the law. We look below at the legal position regarding registration, accountability and liability.

REGISTRATION AND REGULATION

(1) Professional regulation

11.2 All social workers,[3] as well as most others employed in social work and in the provision of care services, including those who work in (adult) care homes and residential child care workers, must be registered with the Scottish Social Services Council.[4] In order to register, an applicant must satisfy requirements as to competence and qualifications, as well as fitness to practise.[5] Once granted, registration lasts for a fixed period at the end of which it must be renewed. The fixed period is three years for social workers. For most other categories of registered worker it is five years. During this period of registration anyone who is registered must comply with the *Code of Practice for Social Service Workers* and must comply with requirements for continuing professional development.[6]

Complaints about registered workers can be made to the Scottish Social Services Council. The Council has the power, ultimately, to remove a worker from the register if the worker's fitness to practise is impaired. A worker will be fit to practise:[7]

> if they meet the standards of character, conduct and competence necessary for them to do their job safely and effectively with particular regard to the Codes.

Complaints will be investigated by a Fitness to Practise Committee. If a worker is found to be unfit to practise the possible penalties include removal from the register, suspension from the register for a period

3 And student social workers.
4 Which also accredits educational provision leading to qualification as a social worker.
5 Scottish Social Services Council, Registration Rules 2025.
6 For established social workers this requires completion of 15 days of continuing professional development in every registration period.
7 Scottish Social Services Council, Combined Fitness to Practice Rules 2021, r 2(1).

of time, imposing conditions which must be fulfilled for the person's registration to continue,[8] and issuing a warning.

(2) Registration of care services

11.3 Before certain types of care services can be provided, the provider must register with Social Care and Social Work Improvement Scotland (SCSWIS, the Care Inspectorate).[9] Services which must be registered include child minders, support services, care homes, housing support services and adoption and fostering services.[10] It is also possible for a service provider which provides accommodation, but would not otherwise need to be registered, to apply for limited registration in order to allow the provider to make use of the provisions of the Adults with Incapacity (Scotland) Act 2000 relating to management of residents finances.[11] The requirement to register adoption and fostering services, and other services aside from field social work services, extends to local authorities as well as to other providers. There are, however, some slight differences in procedure applying to local authority adoption and fostering services and to other services which authorities have a statutory duty to provide. These differences cover both the process of application and enforcement action.[12] There are some exceptions to the requirement to register specific services, these apply where the service is provided informally (for example care within a family) or by the National Health Service.

Applicants to register a service must satisfy SCSWIS as to their fitness to run the service and as to the fitness of the premises from which the service is to be provided. In considering the application, SCSWIS will take into account the Health and Social Care Standards[13] and any other regulations relevant to the provision of the service. An application may be granted as applied for, it may be refused or it may be granted subject to conditions. In the last two cases the applicant must be notified of the proposed decision and given an opportunity to make representations before a final decision is made.

8 For example, a requirement to undertake further training.
9 Public Services Reform (Scotland) Act 2010, s 59 (2010 Act).
10 2020 Act, s 59, s 47 and Sch 12.
11 See **7.13**.
12 2010 Act, Pt 5, ch 4.
13 Scottish Government, *Health and Social Care Standards: My Support, My Life* (2017, as updated, 31/03/2022).

If an application for registration is granted the registered service provider must comply with a variety of regulations.[14] These cover matters such as a requirement to make appropriate provision for the health, safety and welfare of service users and to prepare personal plans for service users. Further regulations cover the fitness, qualifications and registration of staff employed to provide the service, and standards on staffing levels and record keeping. Services must also be provided in accordance with the Health and Social Care Standards.[15] Registered services are subject to periodic inspection.[16] Some services, including care homes and secure accommodation services, must be inspected annually. These inspections must be unannounced, and SCSWIS can also make additional unannounced visits.[17] After an inspection a report will be prepared which will also contain a grading for the service. The report may impose requirements on the service provider, which can lead to the imposition by SCSWIS of conditions (or additional conditions) on the service provider.

Deficiencies in service can be addressed in a variety of ways. If deficiencies come to light during an inspection it is possible to impose conditions on the service provider. A similar possibility exists, as will be noted below, if investigation of a complaint brings deficiencies to light. A further step which can be taken is the serving of an improvement notice on the provider. An improvement notice requires the provider to make a significant improvement in the service, the nature of this improvement is set out in the notice. The consequences of failure to comply with an improvement notice depend on the type of service involved. Where a notice is served on a local authority in respect of an adoption or fostering service, or another statutory service,[18] and the authority fails to make the required improvements, a report can be sent to the Scottish Ministers who have the power to require the authority to take corrective action. Failure to make improvements can lead to a proposal being made to cancel the registration of the service. There is, however no clear alignment between the grounds for serving an improvement notice, failure to comply with a notice, and the grounds for cancellation of registration.[19] A proposal to cancel registration

14 Social Care and Social Work Improvement Scotland (Requirements for Care Services) Regulations 2011, SSI 2011/210.

15 *Health and Social Care Standards: My Support, My Life*.

16 Public Services Reform (Social Services Inspections) (Scotland) Regulations 2011, SSI 2011/185, reg 3A.

17 *Alt-Na-Craig Ltd v SCSWIS* [2015] CSOH 59.

18 This applies only to those services which the authority has a statutory duty to provide, not to other services which the authority may provide.

19 *Hastie v SCRC* 2006 SLT (Sh Ct) 14.

can be made in two circumstances.[20] First, where someone has been convicted of one of a number of offences in relation to the service.[21] Second, the service is being or has been carried out in a way which is not in accordance with any requirements made by SCSWIS, or with a condition of the registration or the requirements of any regulations applying to the registered service. After a proposal to cancel registration has been made, the service provider must be given an opportunity to make representations in writing before SCSWIS decides whether or not to implement the proposal. Where no representations are made the registration must be cancelled unless SCSWIS considers that it is not appropriate to do so.

In emergencies, SCSWIS can apply to the sheriff for cancellation of the registration of a service.[22] Such an application may only be granted if it appears to the sheriff that there is a serious risk to life, health or well-being unless the order is made.

Registration may also be cancelled by the service provider applying for such cancellation, but any application for cancellation must set out what arrangements are being made to ensure that services continue to be provided to current users of the registered service.

Finally, it is a condition of registration that a registered service provider has in place a complaints procedure for dealing with complaints about its services.[23] Complaints about registered services can also be made directly to SCSWIS, and SCSWIS has a complaints procedure for dealing with complaints about its own operation. Complaints about care services may be dealt with through front line resolution. Such complaints are referred to the care service for investigation and reporting back to SCSWIS, or by investigation by SCSWIS in high-risk cases.[24] A number of options are available if the complaint is upheld by SCSWIS after investigation. Recommendations can be made for improving the service, conditions can be imposed on the provider (or existing conditions varied), the provider can be required to prepare an action plan for improvement, or an improvement notice can be served. If a complaint about a service not provided by a local authority is upheld there is no statutory requirement that the authority is notified of this.

20 2010 Act, s 64.

21 That is, any offence under the legislation governing registration or any other offence which SCSWIS considers makes it appropriate to cancel registration.

22 2010 Act, s 65.

23 2010 Act, s 79.

24 Care Inspectorate, *How we deal with concerns and complaints about care* (2017). Available at: www.careinspectorate.com/index.php/complaints. (Accessed April 2026).

(3) Inspection of social work services

11.4 SCSWIS has the power to inspect social services and must prepare a plan for carrying out such inspections. It currently carries out joint inspections of services for children and young people and services for older people with partners such as Education Scotland and Healthcare Improvement Scotland. If required by Scottish Ministers it must carry out an investigation of a specific social service or of the organisation or co-ordination of social services. Responsibility for reviewing strategic plans, delivery of services and compliance with the principles underlying integration of health and social care services[25] also lies with SCSWIS.

(4) Protection of vulnerable groups

11.5 There is a statutory framework which is designed to protect particular groups from those who are not suitable to work with them.[26] Anyone who is employed to undertake what is described as 'regulated work' with children or with protected adults must be a member of the Protection of Vulnerable Groups (PVG) Scheme which is administered by Disclosure Scotland.[27] This requirement will only apply when the normal duties of the person involve this type of work (see Box 11.1 below).[28] 'Work' includes unpaid work, but excludes work done for an individual in a family setting or in the course of a personal relationship.[29] 'Regulated' work is defined separately for children and adults[30] by reference to activities (eg, caring for adults or children), establishments (eg, a children's home or a care home for adults) and positions (eg, being a foster carer or the chief social work officer). A child is anyone under the age of 18[31] and protected adults are individuals over the age of 16[32] who are being provided with a range of services, including community care services and welfare services (ie, services which provide support, assistance, advice or counselling to individuals with particular needs)

25 See **1.73**.
26 Disclosure (Scotland) Act 2020.
27 These requirements do not mean that disclosure or enhanced disclosure may not be required for other types of work.
28 Derived from Disclosure Scotland, PVG scheme: Regulated roles guidance (updated June 2025).
29 Disclosure (Scotland) Act 2020, Sch 3, para 2.
30 Protection of Vulnerable Groups (Scotland) Act 2007, Schs 2 and 3 (2007 Act).
31 2007 Act, s 97(1).
32 So that a 17-year-old may be both a child and a protected adult.

which fulfil a number of additional requirements. The effect of this is that almost all social work with adults will be with protected adults.[33]

Box 11.1

Normal duties

The concept of normal duties is extremely important in limiting the scope of regulated work. For an activity or work in an establishment to be regulated work, the carrying out of the activity or the work in the establishment must be part of the individual's normal duties.

Normal duties can be considered as something the individual might be expected to do as part of their post on an ongoing basis, for example appearing in a job description. Normal duties exclude one-off occurrences and unforeseeable events.

No particular frequency for undertaking the work or duration of work are specified in the Act as these will depend on the context.

An activity or work is likely to be 'normal duties' when:

- it appears in an individual's job description, task description or contract (but these should not be manipulated to stretch the boundary of the PVG Scheme);
- it can reasonably be anticipated; *or*
- it occurs regularly.

An activity or work is unlikely to be 'normal duties' when:

- it is done in response to an emergency (unless by an emergency worker);
- it is arranged at the last minute to stand in for sickness or other unexpected absence of another worker; *or*
- it is done as a one-off activity of short duration which is not part of the individual's normal routine or occupation.

The statutory framework also provides for the keeping of two lists, one for adults and one for children, of people who are unsuitable to work with that group.[34] People who appear on these lists will be barred from undertaking regulated work with children (if they are on the children's list) or protected adults (if they are on the adults list) or both (if they are on both lists). Listing will take place after a referral to Disclosure

33 Protection of Vulnerable Groups (Prescribed Services and Activities (Protected Adult) (Scotland) Regulations SSI 2025/4.

34 2007 Act, s 1.

Scotland by a court following either a conviction for a relevant offence[35] or a conviction for another offence where the court considers that it would be appropriate for the person to be listed.[36] Referrals must also be made by employers where disciplinary action is taken against an individual (or would have been taken if the person had not left employment) on the basis of causing harm to a child or protected adult, putting such a person at risk of harm or engaging in inappropriate sexual conduct with such a person.[37] In addition, referrals can also be made by professional bodies including the Scottish Social Services Council.[38] Where a referral is made to Disclosure Scotland it must consider whether to list the individual concerned if the referral is from a court following conviction of a relevant offence.[39] In other cases it must consider whether to list in cases where the referral was not made for vexatious or frivolous purposes and where the information in the referral indicates that listing may be appropriate.[40] Information obtained as a result of routine vetting of a Scheme member may also suggest that listing should be considered. Where listing is being considered, the individual involved has a right to make representations (and consideration for listing does not in itself prevent them continuing to work). There is a right of appeal against a decision to list and a right to seek removal from the list.[41]

(5) Organisational duty of candour

11.6 A large number of organisations and bodies, including registered care services, health boards and local authorities providing social work services, are bound by an organisational duty of candour.[42] This requires the organisation to take steps following an unintended or unexpected incident in the provision of a health, care or social work service. However, it will only apply if, in the opinion of a registered health professional, the incident has caused death or harm, including impairment of intellectual functions or psychological harm. Once

35 These are set out in Sch 1 to the 2007 Act and are all offences involving children, including sexual offences, cruelty and neglect.
36 2007 Act, s 7.
37 2007 Act, ss 2 and 3.
38 2007 Act, s 8.
39 2007 Act, s 10.
40 2007 Act, s 10.
41 2007 Act, ss 21–24.
42 Health (Tobacco, Nicotine etc and Care) (Scotland) Act 2016, Pt 2; Duty of Candour Procedure (Scotland) Regulations 2018, SSI 2018/57; Scottish Government, *Organisational Duty of Candour: Non-statutory guidance* (2025). (Accessed April 2026).

triggered the duty requires the offering of an apology[43] to the person affected (or someone acting on their behalf if the incident caused death), the offer of a meeting where explanations can be given and questions asked, and carrying out a review of the circumstances leading or contributing to the event. After the review a report is to be produced and an offer must be made to share this with the person affected.[44]

THE LEGAL FRAMEWORK FOR LIABILITY AND ACCOUNTABILITY

11.7 People who are unhappy about social work decisions or actions may seek either to claim compensation for any harm they claim to have suffered as a result[45] or to challenge the decision or course of action. If they are seeking compensation, the normal way of doing this is by claiming breach of a legal duty. If they are seeking to challenge the decision, there are two avenues open to them: complaints procedures;[46] or judicial review.[47]

BREACH OF DUTY

(1) Introduction

11.8 The breach claimed may be breach of a statutory duty by an authority. Success in such a claim is difficult. The claimant has to establish that the statute was designed to protect a limited group of people of which the claimant is a member. The claimant must also establish that the terms of the Act in question indicate a clear intention to create a right to claim compensation for breach of a duty. The existence of other forms of redress and the wide discretion usually conferred on authorities make proving this second element difficult. In the context of child care there is a particular reluctance to interfere with the performance of authorities' statutory duties.

Breach of a common law duty of care may also be claimed. It may be argued that the authority itself owes a duty of care to the affected

43 Defined as 'a statement of sorrow or regret' in respect of the incident, Health (Tobacco, Nicotine etc and Care) (Scotland) Act 2016, s 23(1). Any apology des not amount to an admission of negligence, s 23(2).

44 Health (Tobacco, Nicotine etc and Care) (Scotland) Act 2016, s 22.

45 The harm may involve physical harm, damage to property or psychological harm.

46 Which have already been discussed. For local authority complaints procedures, see **1.60**; and see **11.3** above for complaints about other services.

47 See below and **1.59**.

individual or it may be argued that the individual worker owes the duty. Where the worker owes a duty and is doing what they are employed to do,[48] the doctrine of vicarious liability makes the employer liable for any damage caused by an employee's breach of duty. In some cases, local authorities will be vicariously liable for actions of foster carers.[49]

In general terms, you will owe a common law duty of care if:

(i) loss to the injured person is a foreseeable consequence of your actions (this may include inaction or giving advice);
(ii) the relationship between you and the person suffering the loss is close enough to give rise to a duty of care; and
(iii) it is just and reasonable to impose a duty of care in all the circumstances of the case.[50]

Once the existence of a duty of care is established, it is fulfilled by taking reasonable care in the circumstances. Liability is restricted to those harmful consequences which are foreseeable if the standard of reasonable care is not achieved, and which can be clearly said to follow from the breach of duty.[51] For professionals, the standard will be the standard of a reasonably competent member of the profession.[52] Following common practice will usually be enough to meet the standard of care required, but it should not be assumed that it will automatically do so, nor should it be assumed that departing from common practice will, in itself, amount to negligence. Departures will be acceptable where they are reasonable in the circumstances. Breach of this common law duty has formed the basis of a number of cases that we will consider below.

One potential difficulty is that claims for personal injury (physical or psychiatric) must in general be brought within three years of the injury occurring, though in the case of children this period does not start until

48 Though the vicarious liability of the employer can extend beyond any reasonable description of what the employee's role might involve, particularly in cases involving abuse in residential care, *Lister v Hesley Hall Ltd* [2001] UKHL 22, *Gorrie v Marist Brothers* 2002 SCLR 436, *J v Fife Council* 2009 SLT 160.

49 *Armes v Nottinghamshire CC* [2017] UKSC 60.

50 *Caparo Industries plc v Dickman* [1990] 1 All ER 568. See also *Mitchell v Glasgow City Council* [2009] UKHL 11.

51 See, eg, *Lambert v Cardiff City Council* [2007] EWHC 869 (QB). Various breaches of duty were established but were held not to have caused the loss suffered.

52 Though various inquiries into cases of child abuse reveal recurring failures of the same, or a similar, type, see eg, Laming, *The Protection of Children in England: A Progress Report* (2009), 2008–9 HC 330, ch 1 and Munro, *Munro review of child protection: final report – a child-centred system*, Cm 8063 (2011), para 1.5. Another way of looking at this requirement is to say that practice must be evidence-based and must learn from research, experience and the findings and proposals of various inquiries.

after the child reaches the age of 16.[53] There is special provision for cases involving historic child abuse, which may have occurred years, if not decades, before any legal action is raised. Such cases can proceed even though the three-year period has passed and, in limited cases, actions which have previously failed because too much time has passed can be re-started.[54]

There is almost no Scottish case law in this area; most of the cases referred to are therefore English. It is likely, however, that Scottish courts would reach similar conclusions.

Finally, a claim may be made that a local authority has failed in its duty to act compatibly with those rights set out in the European Convention on Human Rights which were incorporated into UK law by the Human Rights Act 1998.[55] Fulfilment of this duty is unlikely to require a standard of performance different to that required by the common law duty of care. Claims under the Human Rights Act must be made within one year of the date on which the act of the local authority which is complained about took place, though the court has the power to allow a claim made outwith the one-year period to proceed if it would be equitable to do so.[56]

(2) Child care and child protection

11.9 It is clear that local authorities have certain statutory duties in respect of child protection and certain duties towards children who are being looked after by them. If they fail in these duties, what remedy does the injured party have?

In the context of child protection there are two possible types of failure. First, the authority may have failed to intervene appropriately with the result that a child was harmed. Second, the authority may have intervened inappropriately, also causing harm to a child and to their parents. Both of these possibilities came before the House of Lords when they dealt at the same time with the cases of *X (minors) v Bedfordshire County Council*

53 Prescription and Limitation (Scotland) Act 1973, s 17 (1973 Act).

54 1973 Act, ss 17A–17D. Note: The Scottish Child Abuse Inquiry is an ongoing public inquiry into historical cases of child abuse in Scotland. The inquiry was established by Scottish Ministers in 2015 with the intention that it report in 2019. This deadline was subsequently extended and at the time of writing (March 2026) there is no date by which the inquiry is expected to deliver a final report. The inquiry website is available at: www.childabuseinquiry.scot/ (Accessed April 2026).

55 Human Rights Act 1998, s 6(1).

56 Human Rights Act 1998, s 7(5). The court has a wide discretion in taking this decision, *Rabone v Pennine Care NHS Foundation Trust* [2012] UKSC 2.

(the *X* case) and *M (a minor) v Newham London Borough Council* (the *M* case).[57] In these cases, children who claimed to have been harmed respectively by under and over intervention sought to claim damages from the authorities responsible. They set out three grounds for their claim.

First, they argued that there had been a breach of the duties imposed by statute on the authorities. This argument was rejected on the grounds that the statute involved did not confer a clear right on children to claim damages if duties were not complied with. All the statutory provisions concerned were in general terms and conferred considerable discretion on local authorities.

Secondly, they claimed that the local authority owed them a common law duty of care. Although it was accepted that the first two requirements for such a duty which were noted in **11.8** above applied, the claimed duty was rejected on the grounds that it was not just and reasonable to impose a duty on the authority. A variety of policy reasons were put forward for this, most of them, it must be said, highly contentious and speculative.[58] Amongst these were the arguments that allowing liability would give rise to defensive practice;[59] that resources would be diverted from child care to fighting compensation claims; that the decisions involved were very difficult and delicate (since they involved interfering between parent and child) and the courts should not intrude; that there were other remedies available by way of judicial review and the complaints process; and that imposing liability only on the local authority (and not in other agencies) would be unfair because of the multidisciplinary approach taken to children at risk.

Finally, it was argued that the authorities were vicariously liable for the actions of their employees. For this to be the case it would have to be established that the workers owed the children a duty of care. It was held that they did not because the children were not clients of the workers and the workers' job was to provide a report for the local authority. The position of the worker was likened to that of a doctor who carries out an examination to provide a report for an insurance company. Such a doctor owed a duty of care to the company, but not to the person examined.

57 [1995] 2 AC 633.

58 Guthrie, T, 'Legal Liability and Accountability for Child-care Decisions' (1998) 28 BJSW 403.

59 Though this seems to exist regardless of decisions imposing legal liability, see Whittaker, A and Havard, T, 'Defensive Practice as "Fear-Based" Practice: Social Work's Open Secret?' (2016) 46 BJSW 1158, also noting disagreement between workers about what amounts to 'defensive practice'.

The outcome of this case was quite clear: social workers and local authorities could not be liable for decisions they take in child protection; they could not be liable because they owe children no common law duty of care. This position appeared to have been changed by later decisions,[60] but the most recent decision makes it clear that there is no duty owed to children in respect of decisions about removing children from home,[61] the position as regards parents and others is considered below.

However, it is now recognised that there is a common law duty of care owed to children in respect of decisions taken or harm caused while a child is being looked after by the local authority. This would cover, for example, decisions about placement and about return to the child's family[62] and abuse suffered at the hands of foster carers.[63] This common law duty runs alongside the possibility of a claim being made that a local authority has not acted consistently with the child's human rights.

Following the decision of the House of Lords in the *X* case described above, the children who had claimed that the local authority had a duty to remove them from home applied to the European Commission on Human Rights claiming that their human rights as set out in the European Convention on Human Rights (ECHR) had been infringed by the failure to remove them. In conjoined cases the outcome was a finding that the conditions in which the children were living amounted to inhuman and degrading treatment and that the local authority was in breach of its duty under Article 3 of ECHR in failing to remove them.[64] The court also held that the failure promptly to allow an opportunity to respond to allegations of abuse amounted to a breach of Article 8.[65] The ECtHR upheld the decision of the UK House of Lords to reject the action alleging breach of statutory duty and negligence on the part of the local authority.[66]

There is no duty of care owed to the parents of a child (or anyone else) who is suspected of child abuse. This issue has arisen in cases where a

60 For example, *JD v East Berkshire Community NHS Trust* [2003] EWCA Civ 1151.

61 *CN v Poole Borough Council* [2017] EWCA Civ 2185, later upheld by the Supreme Court; *Poole BC v GN* [2019] UKSC 25. As discussed shortly, local authorities may, by their actions, have infringed the human rights of the child and/or parents. The *CN* case was slightly odd in that, although it was based on an alleged breach of a duty to remove children, it was really about the local authority's refusal to rehouse the family.

62 *Barrett v Enfield London Borough Council* [2001] 2 AC 550; *Pierce v Doncaster Metropolitan Council* [2008] EWCA Civ 1416.

63 *Armes v Nottinghamshire CC* [2017] UKSC 60.

64 *Z v United Kingdom* (2001) EHRR 97.

65 *TP v United Kingdom* (2001) ECHR 332.

66 *TP v United Kingdom* (2001) ECHR 332

local authority (often acting on medical advice) has taken action on the basis that a child has been abused only for it to be found subsequently that there has been no such abuse.[67] In such cases it has been held that no duty is owed by the local authority to the parent or other alleged abuser on policy grounds.[68] These are said to arise from a conflict of interest between the child and the suspected parent (or other abuser). Based on this it is considered that imposing a duty to the suspected parent, for example a duty to avoid causing psychiatric harm by concluding that he or she had abused the child, would have an impact on the duty owed to the child:

> If the doctor[69] is to be held liable in law for any injury to the parent occasioned by the taking of his child into care, that can only be because the doctor, in fulfilling his primary duty to safeguard the child against abuse, also owed the parent a separate duty to take account of his, the parent's interest, in not being unreasonably suspected of child abuse. I find it impossible to see how such a duty could fail to impact upon the doctor's approach to his task and create a conflict of interest. Of course, if he acts within the bounds of proper professional skill and care he is liable to no one. But if he were to act negligently he would know that whereas a negligent non-diagnosis of child abuse would expose him to liability only to the child, a negligent diagnosis based on suspicions unreasonably held would render him liable also to the parent.[70]

It has also, however, been noted (though without altering the application of the rule) that:

> The fact that there is such a conflict in this context does not mean that social workers cannot have regard to both conflicting interests and yet behave professionally. But it does not follow that, in acting professionally they owe a duty of care to each interest. …[71]

The lack of a remedy by way of a common law duty of care does not, however, mean that parents (in particular) may not have a claim against

67 For example, where broken bones appear initially to be the result of a non-accidental injury but subsequently it is established that they result from brittle bone disease.

68 *JD v East Berkshire Community Health NHS Trust* [2005] UKHL 23, *Fairlie v Perth and Kinross Healthcare NHS Trust* 2004 SLT 1200, *AD & OH v Bury Metropolitan Borough Council* [2006] EWCA Civ 1, *Lawrence v Pembrokeshire County Council* [2007] EWCA Civ 446, and *B v Reading Borough Council & Ors* [2007] EWCA Civ 1313.

69 It is accepted by the courts that the same principles apply to social workers.

70 *JD v East Berkshire Community Health NHS Trust* [2005] UKHL 23, *per* Lord Brown at para 129.

71 *Lawrence v Pembrokeshire County Council* [2007] EWCA Civ 446, *per* Auld LJ at para 52.

the local authority under either Article 6 or Article 8 of the ECHR, based either on defective procedures or on an unwarranted interference with the enjoyment of family life.[72] In two cases the European Court of Human Rights has upheld claims that parents' Article 8 rights were infringed, though it has noted that:[73]

> The Court would reiterate that mistaken judgments or assessments by professionals do not per se render child-care measures incompatible with the requirements of art. 8. The authorities, medical and social, have duties to protect children and cannot be held liable every time genuine and reasonably-held concerns about the safety of children vis-à-vis members of their families are proved, retrospectively, to have been misguided.

In one case the infringement resulted from a failure to carry out a fuller investigation recommended by a review of the case[74] and in the second from a failure to carry out a proper assessment and to intervene in a less intrusive way.[75] Both cases also involved a finding by the Court that there was a breach of a Convention right because the parents had no effective remedy as a result of the policy exclusion of such claims. This is no longer likely to be the case since, as noted, the parents will have a claim under, most commonly, Article 8.[76]

The duties under Article 8 do not require any higher standard of care than would be required by a common law duty of care, nor do they require that no harm or distress should be caused to the parents of the child. A recent judgment on a claim for breach of Article 8 in connection with a child protection investigation noted that:[77]

> Sadly the experiences of the appellant simply illustrate the truth that viable child protection procedures in any society will sometimes inflict what turns out to have been unnecessary distress on families. That does not make them or the exercise of them thereby unlawful.

72 The potential for this was recognised in *RK & AK v United Kingdom* (2009) 48 EHRR 29, though the claim that Article 8 had been breached was not upheld. The applicants in this case were the claimants in *J D v East Berkshire Community Health NHS Trust*. The claim arises because if Article 8 has been infringed the local authority will be in breach of its duty under Human Rights Act 1998, s 6 not to act in a way which is incompatible with a Convention right. See also *Re H (A child: Breach of Convention Rights: Damages)* [2014] EWFC 38.

73 *RK & AK v United Kingdom* (2009) 48 EHRR 29, para 36.

74 *MAK & RK v United Kingdom* (2010) 51 EHRR 14.

75 *AD & OD v United Kingdom* (2010) 51 EHRR 8 following on from *AD & OH v Bury Metropolitan Borough Council* [2006] EWCA Civ 1.

76 See also the cases discussed in **5.46**.

77 *A v East Sussex County Council* [2010] EWCA Civ 743.

(3) Liability in other cases

11.10 Outwith the area of child protection, there is no reason why individual social workers and social work departments should not owe a duty of care to service users and to members of the public. In the one case, for example, the point was made in the Court of Appeal 'that the social worker owes some duty to the person in his care; for example, he should not advise or encourage a child to engage in some activity which has a hidden danger, such as taking drugs or running across the road'.[78] Equally, a social worker having the care or supervision of a child, or indeed anyone else, will be under a duty to take reasonable care for their safety, for example, by ensuring adequate supervision or ensuring that they are not avoidably placed in a position where they risk coming to harm. In this respect the social worker is in the same position as everyone else.[79]

It is clear, however, that the duty may extend beyond this to cases where those under a social worker's charge cause damage to the property of another person. The best-known instance of this is a case where the Home Office was held liable for inadequate supervision of a group of borstal trainees which resulted in damage to property.[80] There are illustrations of this in the context of social work. A court social worker did not inform those responsible for placing a child remanded into the care of a social services department of the child's suspected involvement in arson. He was placed in a community home under light supervision, left the home, and set a fire in a church causing considerable damage.[81] It was held that the authority was in breach of its duty of supervision of the child, though this case also involved negligence by the court social worker in failing to pass on all the relevant information.[82]

Aside from cases where the person causing damage is under the control of the local authority or where the authority has assumed responsibility for the protection of an individual, a local authority will not be liable for damage caused by third parties. In *X v Hounslow London Borough Council*[83] the local authority was providing services to two adults with learning difficulties, as well as providing services to their children. The

78 *M (a minor) v Newham London Borough Council* [1994] 4 All ER 602 at 629i, per Staughton LJ.
79 See *Kirkham v Chief Constable of the Greater Manchester Police* [1990] 3 All ER 246 for an example of duties owed by the police to people in their care suffering from mental illness.
80 *Dorset Yacht Co Ltd v Home Office* [1970] AC 1004.
81 *Vicar of Writtle v Essex County Council* (1979) 77 LGR 656.
82 *Vicar of Writtle v Essex County Council* (1979) 77 LGR 656.
83 [2009] EWCA Civ 286.

local authority was aware of the threat posed to the couple by a number of younger people living in the area and was seeking to arrange a change of accommodation for the couple and their children. Before this could happen, they were seriously injured and harmed by the young people. It was held that the council was not liable for failing to protect the couple. It had no duty to do so and the provision of services to the couple under statutory powers was not enough to create a duty of care or to amount to an assumption of a duty of care.

Liability can arise not only for damage caused by an action on the part of a social worker, or indeed inaction on their part, but also for negligent advice. Where advice is offered in the knowledge that the person receiving the advice is likely to rely on it in deciding what to do, the person giving the advice will usually, provided the advice is given in a professional capacity, be regarded as undertaking a duty of care towards the person advised. Most reported cases of this concern other professions, but there is one case illustrating this in the context of social work.[84] A mother wanted to place her son, T, with a child minder. She identified one possibility and phoned the social worker who co-ordinated child minding for the local authority to check on her suitability. The advice given was that there was no reason why the child should not be placed with the particular child minder. This advice was given despite the fact that the worker giving it knew that a child had previously suffered a non-accidental injury while in the care of the child minder and that the minder had voluntarily agreed not to accept any young children into her care. T suffered a non-accidental injury while in the care of the minder and sued the authority. He was successful in a claim based on negligent advice given by the worker. The worker had undertaken to give advice to T's mother and in doing so had undertaken a duty not to give negligent advice.[85] Potential liability for negligent advice could cover a wide range of advice given by social workers, but it should be stressed again that the worker's duty, in law, is to take reasonable care, not to guarantee the accuracy of the advice.

Another example of potential liability is a case where a child is placed for adoption but is then discovered to have a serious medical condition. This question arose in *M and M v Glasgow Corporation*[86] where a child placed with the pursuers was later diagnosed as having a severe mental disorder and would consequently always be dependent on them. They sued, arguing that the local authority (acting as adoption agency) had a duty of care to ensure that a child medically unfit in this way was not

84 *T (a minor) v Surrey County Council* [1994] 4 All ER 577.
85 *T (a minor) v Surrey County Council* [1994] 4 All ER 577.
86 1976 SLT (Sh Ct) 45. See also *P v Tayside Regional Council* 1989 SCLR 165.

placed for adoption. They were unsuccessful as the adoption agency did not have, and could not be expected to have, the medical skill needed to foresee the problems that arose in this case. The sheriff did, however, canvas the possibility of action if the agency had failed to carry through the correct procedures, for example, by failing to obtain a medical report and concluded that:

> If a local authority negligently ignored some medical warning in the statutory medical report that a child was medically unsuitable for placing for adoption they might well be required to answer for it ...[87]

Subsequent to this decision the duty of local authorities in respect of provision of information to adopters (and foster carers) has been considered in the English courts. In relation to adopters, it has been held that the authority has a duty to make sure that it does, in fact, pass on any information which it has decided is to be communicated to the adopter (either as an explicit decision about information to be communicated in an individual case or as a matter of policy). Beyond this there is no duty to pass on other information about the child unless the decision not to communicate any specific information was one which no reasonable authority would have taken.[88] The same approach has been taken to duties towards foster carers,[89] though there is authority to the effect that there is a potentially broader duty towards foster carers.[90] That case involved a placement with foster carers of a child who had previously sexually abused another child. The parents had made it clear that they did not want to have a sexual abuser placed with them, and after the placement was made the placed child abused the children of the foster carers. At an earlier stage in the court proceedings, it was held that the authority owed a duty of care to the children of the foster carers.[91]

JUDICIAL REVIEW[92]

11.11 As we have already seen, judicial review offers a means of challenging decisions made by local authorities. Sometimes the consequence of a successful application for review will be that a local authority is directed to act in a particular way. On other occasions the decision of the authority will be set aside and will have to be taken again, often with a strong hint from the court about what the new

87 *M and M v Glasgow Corporation* 1976 SLT (Sh Ct) 45 at 49.
88 *A v Essex County Council* [2003] EWCA Civ 1848.
89 *Lambert v Cardiff City Council* [2007] EWHC 869 (QB).
90 *W v Essex County Council* [2001] 2 AC 592.
91 *W v Essex County Council* [1999] Fam 90.
92 See **1.59**.

decision should be. It is not, in general, possible to claim compensation in judicial review proceedings and applications may be refused where there are other remedies available, most notably, in this context, the complaints and representations procedure.[93]

An applicant for judicial review must argue that there has been a defect in the decision-making process rather than simply arguing that the decision is wrong, and the grounds for such arguments are relatively restricted. They can be categorised in a variety of ways. One approach sets out three categories:

(i) The authority has acted *ultra vires*; it has, in other words, done something which it has no power to do. This may involve exercising a power which it is not entitled to or reaching a decision in a way in which it is not entitled to.

(ii) There has been a breach of the requirements of natural justice. Briefly, these require decision-makers to be impartial and to give people likely to be affected by a decision the right to put their point of view before the decision is taken.

(iii) The authority has acted unreasonably. Examples of this might include taking into account things which were irrelevant to the decision or failing to take into account something which they were required by law or by guidance to take account of.

Following the implementation of the Human Rights Act 1998, the court may take into account human rights considerations in determining an application for judicial review and an application for judicial review may be based on a claimed human rights infringement.[94]

It has been suggested that applicants for judicial review bear a heavy burden of establishing that a local authority has acted unlawfully,[95] making it difficult (though not impossible) to succeed in a claim.

The following paragraphs give some further examples, beyond those already given in previous chapters, of areas where judicial review has been used (or the attempt has been made to use it) to obtain a remedy.

(1) Fostering cases

11.12 Under this broad heading are cases dealing with decisions to remove a child from a foster placement; decisions to remove a person

93 See *R v Birmingham City Council, ex parte A* [1997] 2 FLR 841 and the discussion at **1.59**.

94 Human Rights Act 1998, s 7.

95 *R (on the application of Ireneschild) v Lambeth LBC* [2007] EWCA Civ 234, para 44.

from a list of approved foster carers; and decisions to inform other foster carers of allegations of sexual abuse against a foster parent.

In the last category is *R v Lewisham London Borough Council, ex parte P.*[96] The applicant had been a foster carer. Allegations of sexual abuse had been made against him by one former foster child and the authority decided, following its policy, to advise people having care of children who had previously been fostered by P of the allegations of abuse and the identity of the alleged abuser. P successfully challenged the decision to identify him. The court took the view that the authority had simply carried out its policy without properly weighing up all the relevant factors in the case, for example, the reliability of the accusations, and had therefore acted unreasonably.

Where removal from the list of foster carers takes place, the prospects of success in an action for judicial review will depend on the reasons behind the removal. If they relate to the character or temperament of the foster carer, they will not be reviewable. On the other hand, if they arise from allegations about the conduct of the foster carer that individual has a right to be informed of the allegations and to be heard in reply. Where a foster carer was not told the substance of the case against her and given the chance to make a case to challenge them, her removal from the list was quashed on review.[97] The ground for this decision was that the requirements of natural justice had not been complied with. This case also makes the point that the decisions that have to be made about reputation, character, etc in approving a foster carer are not open to challenge.

If foster carers are closely involved in the decision as to placement of a child, especially when the placement is to be a long-term one, they have a legitimate expectation that they will be consulted before the child is taken out of their care. Failure to consult and to allow them to make representations will be a breach of natural justice.[98] This requirement to consult would not arise in cases where serious allegations were made about the foster carers which required urgent action on the part of the local authority to protect the interests of a child. In such cases the local authority would have a statutory obligation to take action.[99] Removal of a child from foster carers may also give rise to arguments about breach

96 [1991] 3 All ER 529.

97 *R v London Borough of Wandsworth, ex parte P* [1989] 1 FLR 387. Contrast *R v Avon County Council, ex parte Crabtree* (22 March 1994, unreported) QB, where a foster carer was given the opportunity to be heard and their removal from the list could not be challenged by judicial review.

98 *R v Hereford and Worcester County Council, ex parte D* [1992] 1 FLR 448.

99 See eg, Looked After Children (Scotland) Regulations 2009, SI 2009/210, reg 47.

of rights under Article 8 of the European Convention on Human Rights as part of the judicial review claim.[100]

(2) Child protection cases

11.13 In *R v Harrow London Borough Council, ex parte D*[101] the applicant for judicial review was a woman whose children had been placed on the child protection register after a case conference which the applicant was not allowed to attend, though she was allowed to make written submissions. The decision of the authority was not regarded as unreasonable. There was medical and other evidence suggesting that the applicant was responsible for injuries to the children. The court held there to be no breach of the requirements of natural justice because the mother had been given the opportunity to put her version of events before the case conference.[102]

One notable point to come out of the *Harrow* case is that it will be very difficult in cases involving child protection to succeed in a case based on judicial review.[103] The Court of Appeal took the view that review would succeed only in an exceptional case raising an important point of principle, and that the decision of the local authority would have to be utterly unreasonable.[104] The reason for this is that in the child protection system the interests of the adults involved come second to those of the children. The point was made as follows by Butler-Sloss LJ:

> In balancing adequate protection for the child and fairness to the adult, the interests of an adult may have to be placed second to the needs of a child. All concerned in this difficult and delicate area should be allowed to perform their task without looking over their shoulder all the time for possible intervention of the court. The important power of the court to intervene should be kept very much in reserve, perhaps confined to the exceptional case which involves a point of principle which needs to be resolved, not only for the individual case but in general, so as to establish that registration is not being conducted in an unsatisfactory manner … In this area unbridled resort to judicial

100 See **5.46**.

101 [1990] 3 All ER 12. See also *R (on the application of A) v Enfield LBC* [2008] EWHC 1886 (Admin).

102 *R v Harrow London Borough Council, ex parte D* [1990] 3 All ER 12.

103 *R v Harrow London Borough Council, ex parte D* [1990] 3 All ER 12.

104 *R v Harrow London Borough Council, ex parte D* [1990] 3 All ER 12.

review could frustrate the ability of those involved in their effort to protect the victim of abuse.[105]

(3) Removal from parents while on home placement

11.14 Social work departments have a statutory duty to seek to have the care of a child who is being looked after by them taken over by that child's parent(s). Where the authority has parental rights or responsibilities and placement with the parents is not working, can the parents seek review of a decision to remove the children from their care, and in what circumstances is such a review likely to succeed? The only reported cases on this issue suggest that a parent will succeed in an application for review only if the reason for removal was an unsubstantiated allegation and the parent was not given an opportunity to respond to it before the decision to remove was made.[106] On the other hand, where a decision is based on a number of factors, such as the knowledge of social workers, assessments of the parent(s), reports from school and the views of doctors, the decision will not be challengeable. Such a decision is well within the scope of parental discretion allowed to an authority which has parental rights or responsibilities.[107]

What all these cases indicate is that, as suggested in *Harrow*,[108] the courts will be prepared to intervene only where a decision is based on an allegation which the complainer has not had the opportunity to challenge: in other words, where there has been a failure to comply with the requirements of natural justice. In the absence of a case based on natural justice, the courts are reluctant to overturn a local authority decision on the grounds that it is unreasonable. Courts often refer to the words of Lord Diplock in defining what criteria have to be met before a decision can be regarded as unreasonable. He said of unreasonableness that:

> It applies to a decision which is so outrageous in its defiance of logic or of accepted moral standards that no sensible person who had applied his mind to the question to be decided could have arrived at it.[109]

105 *R v Harrow London Borough Council, ex parte D* [1990] 3 All ER 12 at 17b–e. This point is reflected in one of the policy reasons given in the *X* and *M* cases for refusing to recognise the existence of a duty of care.

106 *R v Bedfordshire County Council, ex parte C* [1987] 1 FLR 239.

107 *R v Hertfordshire County Council, ex parte B* [1987] 1 FLR 239.

108 *R v Harrow London Borough Council ex parte D* [1990] 3 All ER 12.

109 *Council of Civil Service Unions v Minister for the Civil Service* [1985] AC 374 at 410D.

This standard is so exacting that it is very difficult to meet.

It would also be possible to argue that removal of the child had infringed rights under Article 8 of the European Convention on Human Rights.[110]

(4) Other cases

11.15 Although judicial review may be difficult to use in the context of child protection, there is no reason why it should not be used successfully in other areas of social work provision. For example, in *R v London Borough of Ealing, ex parte Leaman*,[111] Mr Leaman applied for assistance towards the cost of a holiday under the Chronically Sick and Disabled Persons Act 1970. The council, without considering the merits of the application, responded that because of financial constraints no grants were available for private holidays. It was held that they had acted improperly in declining to consider the application and simply applying a blanket policy without consideration of the merits of the application.

In *R v Avon County Council, ex parte M*,[112] the placement of M, an adult with Down's Syndrome, was the subject of a dispute between the local authority and M's parents. It was agreed that M's needs would be assessed by the review panel set up under the council's complaints procedure. This panel heard evidence and reported, recommending a placement at an establishment called Milton Heights. The recommendation went to the social services committee who overturned it and substituted an alternative placement. That decision was overturned on application to the court, partly because the committee had failed to take M's psychological needs into account as required by the relevant legislation, and partly because the committee had failed to give proper weight to the panel's recommendation.[113]

EMPLOYERS' LIABILITY TO SOCIAL WORKERS

11.16 The contracts of employment which affect most social workers imply the acceptance of some degree of liability by the employer for the social worker. There are obligations for the social worker to be accountable to the employer and abide by the employer's policies and procedures. The employer agrees to accept responsibility for the actions of the social worker undertaken on its behalf. Most of the major

110 See **5.46**.
111 [1984] 1 WLUK 552.
112 [1993] 7 WLUK 42.
113 *R v Avon County Council ex parte M* [1993] 7 WLUK 42.

employers are covered by insurance for these areas and with respect to their employees suffering accidental injury or death. It must be noted, however, that most employers require social workers to take out their own insurance coverage for personal effects and for using their cars for business purposes. In practice, when there is public scrutiny of the actions of a social worker and the implication that malpractice may have occurred a moral panic may ensue. Such a situation occasionally results in the employer jettisoning responsibility for the social worker and the direct line manager either in the short term or the long term. In light of the frequency of this experience, the major professional association, the British Association of Social Workers, has an advice and representation service and provides liability insurance coverage for members.[114]

The nature of social work is such that sometimes it requires close contact by isolated workers with very vulnerable and needy people in situations which can be extremely stressful. An almost inevitable consequence is that occasionally a service user will resort to the use of violence directed at the social worker. Whether a social worker uses self-defence or retreats will depend on the particular circumstances and what is reasonably necessary to stop the violence. A social worker choosing self-defence is as liable as any other individual to prosecution if the worker's actions are considered unreasonable by the procurator fiscal.

Anecdotal and research evidence[115] suggests that assaults on social workers are relatively frequent and reported to senior managers usually when there is no alternative. It is very important to report any assault to senior managers and many organisations have instituted policies which require the reporting of any incident which is beneficial in relieving the possibly traumatised worker from the decision.

Like any other employer, the employer of a social worker owes employees certain duties of care. Some of these will be under the Health and Safety at Work etc Act 1974, but the employer also owes common law duties to the employee. One of these is the duty to provide a safe system of work. Breach of this obligation was the basis for a successful action by a social worker who claimed that stress at work

114 See, the website of the British Association of Social Workers (BASW) website. Available at: https://basw.co.uk/support/advice-representation (Accessed April 2026).

115 Balloch, S 'Working in the social services: How staff cope with violence and stress' *Research, Policy and Planning* (1996) 14(1), pp 74–76. See also Turner, A 'Over 40% of social work staff have faced abuse from public this year' Community Care 14 June 2022 and Shraer, R, '85% of social workers were assaulted, harassed or verbally abused in the past year', *Community Care* 16 September 2014.

had caused him a nervous breakdown.[116] The social worker had suffered one nervous breakdown, for which the authority was not liable because it was not reasonably foreseeable. He then returned to work. He raised concerns about his workload with his employers and they knew of his previous breakdown. In the circumstances it was foreseeable that he might suffer another breakdown if overworked. The employers' failure to take steps to reduce his workload was held to be in breach of their duty to provide a safe system of work. The duty they owed him was formulated as follows:

> It is clear law that the employer has a duty to provide his employee with a reasonably safe system of work and to take reasonable steps to protect him from risks which are reasonably foreseeable. Whereas the law on the extent of this duty has developed almost exclusively in cases involving physical injury to the employee as distinct from injury to his mental health, there is no logical reason why risk of psychiatric damage should be excluded from the scope of an employer's duty of care ...[117]

The broad scope of this duty should be noted. It is arguable that it extends to circumstances where a social worker is being sent into a situation that is known to be dangerous. For example, a worker being sent to interview someone who is known to be violent, has a history of attacking workers or has a history of sexual assault. In such cases it would appear likely that the employer owes the worker a duty to guard against such risks and that an injured worker could sue the employer.

Later reported claims by social workers have been less successful. In these cases the worker was unable to establish foreseeability because the effect of their workload on their health was not drawn specifically to the attention of their employer.[118] It is clear that if a worker has concerns about the impact of workload on their health this should be drawn clearly to the attention of their employer, for example through supervision sessions, and supported by appropriate evidence. It has been suggested that:[119]

116 *Walker v Northumberland County Council* [1995] 1 All ER 737. See also *Selwood v Durham County Council* [2012] EWCA Civ 979 where Health Boards were held to have a duty of care to a local authority social worker who worked in close proximity and co-operation with the Boards' employees.

117 At 749c–e, per Colman J.

118 *Green v Argyll & Bute Council*, [2002] 2 WLUK 764, 28 February 2002, *Patley v Surrey County Council* [2003] EWCA Civ 1067.

119 *Barber v Somerset CC* [2002] EWCA Civ 76, para 29.

Unless he knows of some particular problem or vulnerability, an employer is usually entitled to assume that his employee is up to the normal pressures of the job.

CONCLUSION

11.17 This survey indicates that there are a number of areas where social workers and their employers will clearly be legally liable for what is done in the course of their work. The precise contours of this liability are not always entirely clear. The law is subject to development and in recent years this has been particularly under the influence of the European Convention on Human Rights. There has been some discussion in the case law about the impact of imposing liability on the creation of defensive practice and, in relation to the possible existence of a duty to suspected abusers, of trying to manage inconsistent interests. There are also pressures from the media (and the public) which often seems to assume that there is clear evidence available to social workers and that it is possible to minimise risk (for example, to children) to a vanishingly low level, although this is not the approach adopted in the courts. The focus of competent social work practice should be on what the law requires, whether in a negligence claim or in a claim under the Human Rights Act 1998. Such an approach will be at one with the ethics and standards of the profession, emphasising the fundamental importance of good, accountable practice. Employers have a part to play in this process in ensuring that the structures, resources and supervision are in place to encourage and support good practice.

Index

References are to paragraph number.

L